Irving Stone is one of America's foremost literary figures and its greatest story teller. From the initial success of Lust for Life, *his biographical novel of Vincent Van Gogh, he has gone on to write numerous bestsellers about the men and women who shaped America— Eugene V. Debs, Mary Todd Lincoln, Clarence Darrow, to name just a few—as well as many magnificent works about the world's greatest and sometimes most tragic figures.*

Born in San Francisco in 1903, Stone grew up surrounded by the aura of the glory days of the Old West. With this as his inspiration, he has been collecting material for MEN TO MATCH MY MOUNTAINS all his life.

Books by Irving Stone

BIOGRAPHICAL NOVELS

LUST FOR LIFE
(Vincent Van Gogh)

IMMORTAL WIFE
(Jessie Benton Fremont)

ADVERSARY IN THE HOUSE
(Eugene V. Debs)

THE PASSIONATE JOURNEY
(John Noble)

THE PRESIDENT'S LADY
(Rachel Jackson)

LOVE IS ETERNAL
(Mary Todd Lincoln)

THE AGONY AND THE ECSTASY
(Michelangelo)

THOSE WHO LOVE
(Abigail Adams)

THE PASSIONS OF THE MIND
(Sigmund Freud)

THE GREEK TREASURE
(Henry and Sophia Schliemann)

BIOGRAPHIES

SAILOR ON HORSEBACK
(Jack London)

THEY ALSO RAN
(Defeated Presidential Candidates)

CLARENCE DARROW FOR THE
DEFENSE

EARL WARREN

HISTORY

MEN TO MATCH MY MOUNTAINS

NOVELS

PAGEANT OF YOUTH

FALSE WITNESS

BELLES-LETTRES

WE SPEAK FOR OURSELVES
(A Self-Portrait of America)

THE STORY OF MICHELANGELO'S
PIETA

WITH JEAN STONE

DEAR THEO
(Vincent Van Gogh)

I, MICHELANGELO, SCULPTOR
(Autobiographies through letters)

COLLECTED

THE IRVING STONE READER

IRVING STONE'S JACK LONDON

EDITOR

THERE WAS LIGHT
Autobiography of a University
Berkeley: 1888–1968

LINCOLN: A CONTEMPORARY
PORTRAIT
(with Allan Nevins)

BOOKS FOR YOUNG READERS
THE GREAT ADVENTURE OF MICHELANGELO

IRVING STONE

MEN TO MATCH MY MOUNTAINS

THE OPENING OF THE FAR WEST, 1840–1900

BERKLEY BOOKS, NEW YORK

This Berkley book contains the complete text of the original hardcover edition.
It has been completely reset in a typeface designed for easy reading, and was
printed from new film.

MEN TO MATCH MY MOUNTAINS

A Berkley Book / published by arrangement with
Doubleday & Company, Inc.

PRINTING HISTORY
Doubleday edition / September 1956
Berkley trade paperback edition / May 1982
Seventh printing / August 1986

ISBN: 0-425-09351-4

A BERKLEY BOOK ® TM 757,375
Berkley Books are published by The Berkley Publishing Group,
200 Madison Avenue, New York, New York 10016.
The name "BERKLEY" and the stylized "B" with design are trademarks belonging to
Berkley Publishing Corporation.
PRINTED IN THE UNITED STATES OF AMERICA

To JEAN, my wife

who never gives less than her best

June 6, 1956

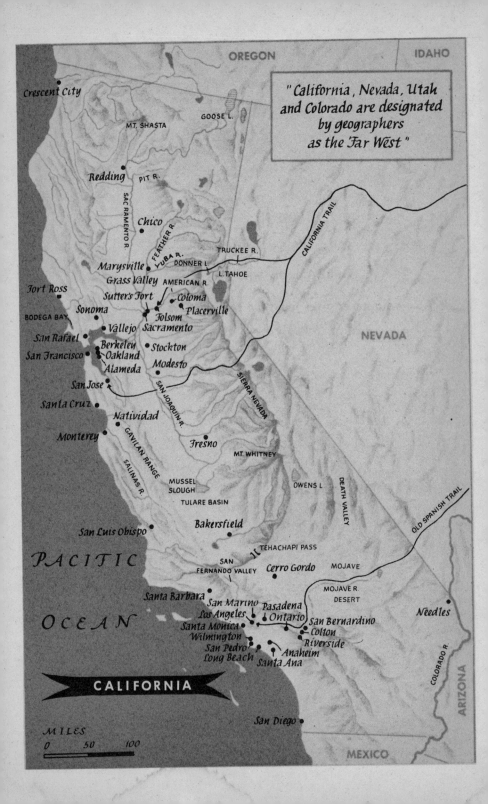

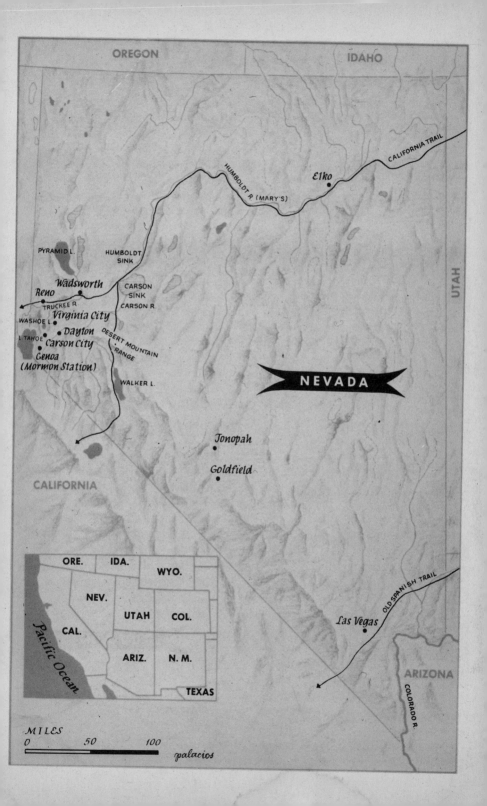

OREGON

IDAHO

CALIFORNIA TRAIL

HUMBOLDT R. (MARY'S)

Elko

UTAH

PYRAMID L.

HUMBOLDT
SINK

Wadsworth

Reno

CARSON
SINK

TRUCKEE R.

CARSON R.

WASHOE L.

Virginia City

L. TAHOE

Dayton

DESERT MOUNTAIN RANGE

Carson City

Genoa
(Mormon Station)

WALKER L.

NEVADA

Tonopah

Goldfield

CALIFORNIA

ORE.   IDA.

WYO.

NEV.

UTAH   COL.

Pacific Ocean

CAL.

ARIZ.   N. M.

Las Vegas

OLD SPANISH TRAIL

ARIZONA

TEXAS

COLORADO R.

MILES
0   50   100

palacios

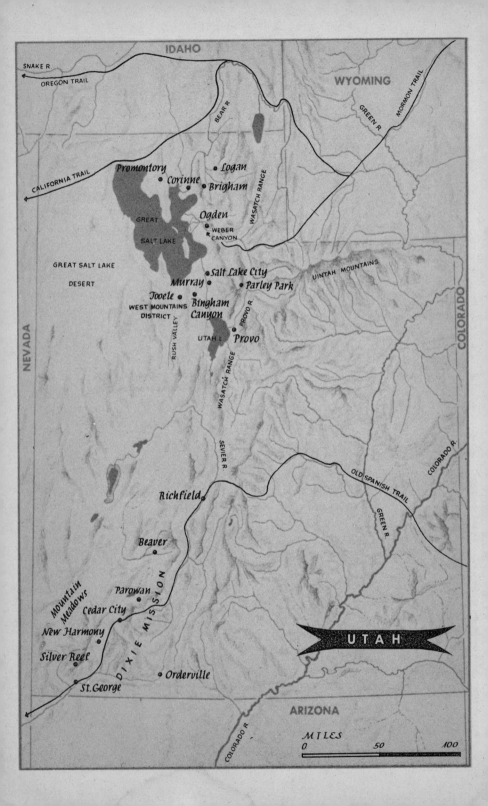

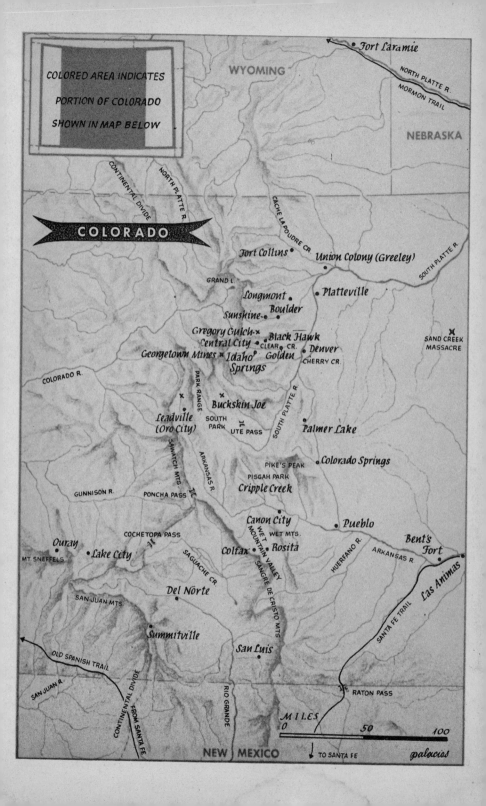

Contents

BOOK THREE: *COLOR IN A COUNTRY*

BOOK FOUR: *THE BUILDING OF A CIVILIZATION*

Book One

REVOLT IN PARADISE

CHAPTER I

The Time, the Place, the Cast

THIS IS THE STORY of the opening of a land and the building of a civilization.

It is told in terms of the people who opened that land and built that civilization, each life story an integral part of the mosaic. The Far West is the hero.

The land consists of the present-day states of California, Nevada, Utah and Colorado, the area designated by geographers as the Far West. This was the vast empire inherited by Mexico when it won its independence from Spain in 1821.

Except for a handful of hunters and trappers in the Colorado Rockies, scattered Indian tribes, and a few hundred settlers on the California coast, the region is totally unsettled and uninhabited.

The land has a common cast of characters. What happens in any one region is of tremendous consequence to the others. Their biographies, their resources and destinies are so closely bound together that each is ineradicably woven into the fabric of the whole. For in the beginning they were one.

Now, in 1840, there was trouble in the land.

CHAPTER II

One Man Wants a Wilderness...

CAPTAIN JOHN AUGUSTUS SUTTER had cause to be concerned.

Had he fled the imminence of a Swiss debtors' prison only to end in a political prison in California? And just at the moment when his colony here in the Sacramento Valley, launched in the teeth of harrowing hardships, was about to be realized?

Though the foreigners who had already been arrested for conspiring to overthrow the Mexican government were hangers-on at the distillery of their leader, the American Isaac Graham, and Sutter had had nothing whatever to do with their loud, sometimes drunken threats to turn California into a republic, still Sutter had only a temporary permit to remain in California. The eleven leagues in the Sacramento Valley, something over seventy-six square miles of land which he had staked out as his empire, would not be legally his until he became a Mexican citizen at the end of his year of residence, in July 1840.

When Sutter had presented himself at the capital in Monterey, just arrived by ship from Honolulu and Sitka, Alaska, with letters of introduction, Juan Bautista Alvarado, California's first native-born governor, had been friendly. Yet from the beginning he had warned Sutter to stay away from the northern frontier because that part of California was "commanded over by Colonel Mariano Vallejo, who could not agree with an adventurous nature coming to the country to live independently."

There was no other way Sutter would have consented to live in California; nor would he have settled for anything less than total wilderness. Captain John Wilson, a Scotsman, who had first sailed into San Francisco Bay in 1833, had thought Sutter out of his mind when he refused to buy at a modest price Wilson's magnificent,

4

stocked ranch in Sonoma Valley, near Mariano Vallejo's settlement thirty miles north.

"Well, my God," Wilson cried angrily, "I should like to know what you really want!"

John Sutter, for the first time in his thirty-six years, knew exactly what he wanted.

"I noticed the hat must come off before the military guard, the flagstaff and the church," he commented, "and I preferred a country where I could keep mine on, where I should be absolute master."

John Sutter's settling of the Sacramento Valley was the result of neither blind accident nor fumbling exploration. Long before his ship came through a narrow unnamed strait into San Francisco Bay and anchored in a mud-flat cove called Yerba Buena, Sutter knew where he was going to found his empire. Before he set foot on California soil he already knew more about the arterial Sacramento Valley than any man living in the Far West. He went to it with the swift, uneering instinct of his colonizing genius.

"I intended to settle in the valley because a captain who had sailed up the Sacramento River for a short distance had told me about the beauty and fertility of that district."

The dozen Americans, Englishmen and Europeans living around Yerba Buena cove had given John Sutter a robustious all-night party on board the *Monsoon*, out of Boston, the only ship in the bay. They were fond of handsome Sutter, the dering-do flare of his semi-military uniform, the flowing hair, and welcomed him heartily to this lonesome frontier where settlers were scarce, cultivated men even scarcer. They wanted him to succeed in his plan. But Dr. John Marsh, whose ranch was on the east side of Mount Diablo, described Sutter's choice as "a settlement in the worst place he could find." Yerba Buena called it "a simpleton's journey" on which there was little chance of success, and in all likelihood would end in disaster and death.

They did not know their man.

John Sutter bought a light ship's boat from Captain Wilson; he also rented the schooners *Isabel* and *Nicolas* from Nathan Spear and William Hinckley, two Americans who owned the Yerba Buena trading post. With credit earned from his sale of merchandise he had brought from Honolulu to Yerba Buena, Sutter loaded his three boats with equipment to start his colony: guns for hunting; ammunition for the cannons he had brought from the islands; seed and farm equipment; blacksmith and carpenter tools.

The little flotilla then set out across the uncharted San Francisco Bay: Sutter, with his title of captain which he had invented in the same manner that he had conjured up his role of empire builder, the eight Kanaka men and two Kanaka women who had contracted to stay with him for three years and help build his settlement; a fourteen-year-old Indian boy whom he had bought for $100 in the Wind River Rendezvous; a German cabinet-maker; three recruits from Yerba Buena; and several sailors on the beach.

Sutter set out in the lead, four Kanakas rowing the small ship's boat northeast across the wide, choppy bay lying within its frame of soft, sensually shaped hills, haycock tan in the August sun. By dusk they had covered thirty miles, camping where Carquinez Strait emptied into Suisun Bay. The next morning Sutter mistook the San Joaquin River for the Sacramento, and lost two hard days of upstream rowing before he realized that this was not the valley that had been described to him. Several days later he found the mouth of the Sacramento and, leaving messages for his two straggler boats to follow (he placed his messages alongside the Indian tokens of white feathers hanging from bushes to propitiate their gods), made his way up the broad quiet river which flowed between dark jungles of tule and towering trees.

Suddenly he came in sight of a clearing. Several hundred Indians, dressed in full war paint and little else, shrieked their battle cries. But John Sutter understood the Indians; he had lived among the Delawares. Restraining his men who wanted to open fire, he went ashore, unarmed.

"*Adios, amigos,*" he said, with his warm, charming smile.

What saved Sutter from a real *adios* at this point was the same quality that was to save him time and again in recurrent tight spots: his lovable, disarming personality. He was a broad-framed, medium-height man with a fascinating big-eyed face which managed the miracle of being bland and strong at the same time; a long bony nose, a powerfully rounded chin under which his dark side whiskers met, slashing dark eyebrows, mustaches trimmed neatly and romantically over a fleshy mouth.

The Indian chief, Anashe, liked Sutter's friendly manner; he gave him time to explain that he had come to settle, to be their friend, to show his agricultural implements and samples of the presents he would give to each of the Indians if they would visit him at his settlement.

Sutter had won his first battle of the wilderness by his adroit handling of the natives; but the following day his tired and apprehensive crew threatened to mutiny if he did not turn back. He promptly selected a site just beyond the confluence of the Sacramento and American rivers, put his supplies ashore and announced to the men that all who had no further desire to explore the wilderness could return to Yerba Buena on the two larger boats. He was staying.

Six of the white men decided to return. Sutter gave them a nine-gun farewell salute. William Heath Davis, captain of the returning *Isabel*, reported in *Seventy-five Years in California*:

"A large number of deer, elk and other animals of the plains were startled, running to and fro, stopping to listen, their heads raised, full of curiosity and wonder, while from the interior of the adjacent woods the howls of wolves and coyotes filled the air, and immense flocks of water fowl flew wildly about the camp."

Left alone with his loyal Kanakas, the Indian boy and Wetler, the German cabinetmaker, Sutter quickly found an elevation about a mile from the river, cut a road to his landing place, began work on a forty-foot adobe brick building divided into a kitchen, bedroom-office and blacksmith shop, then named his little settlement New Helvetia or New Switzerland.

The settlement was a success from the instant of its inception. Sutter organized whole Indian tribes, called "bad Indians" by Governor Alvarado, to hunt and trap for him; wandering French-Canadian trappers joined his settlement; sailors, coming into Yerba Buena after two-year scurvy-laden voyages, heard of Sutter's colony and jumped ship to make their way up the river; Octave Custot, a Frenchman who had worked for Vallejo, joined Sutter as his secretary. His merchant friends gave him credit in supplies and tools with which to make furniture and additional plows.

The land was rich with a plenitude of game for fresh meat. Wild grapes grew in profusion. Although his beaver trappings had not been too successful he had collected some skins to send down to Yerba Buena against his debts. He was passionately in love with the Sacramento Valley, writing to his wife and children in Switzerland, whom he had not seen for almost six years:

"Man can fashion this place into a paradise."

Now paradise was about to be lost.

Now, in the spring of 1840, when he was laying plans to construct a fort which would make his position invulnerable, having sent a group of men some twenty miles up the American River to cut pine trees to serve as giant beams; when he had his Indians making adobe bricks to enclose a rectangular space one hundred fifty by five hundred feet, the walls to be eighteen feet high and three feet thick, with bastions at the corners to house his cannon, with living quarters inside the fort, along with forges, shops, granaries: now Colonel Mariano Vallejo had been ordered by Governor Alvarado to arrest all foreigners and bring them by ship to Monterey, whence they would be sent to Mexico as political prisoners.

He had failed so many times before; all of his life up to this point had been a failure. On July 1, 1839, after five years of continuous wandering he had reached what for him was the Promised Land. It had been a circuitous route: Kandern, Burgdorf, Basle, New York, Cincinnati, St. Louis, Santa Fe, Vancouver, Honolulu, Sitka, and now the Sacramento Valley. His succession of mediocre jobs, the bankruptcy of his shop and humiliating eviction from his home by his wealthy mother-in-law, his business failures in America, all had been wiped out by his bold approach to the unmapped West, his successful organization and sale of the cargo of the *Clementine* in Yerba Buena. There was no longer any doubt in his mind; he knew that he possessed the talent to carve a culture out of the chrysalis of the Far West.

If he were arrested now, and deported, where could he go?

CHAPTER III

A Good Soldier Is Embarrassed

COLONEL MARIANO VALLEJO was as disturbed as John Sutter. He sensed that the arrest of foreigners would reveal the weakness of Mexico's Californio government to the outside world. He knew that the deportation of a group of Americans, Englishmen and Europeans could have serious repercussions; the governments of these men could consider it a breach of international law. California, ignored, neglected, hardly wanted by the Republic of Mexico, had not the strength to resist the feeblest invader.

Vallejo knew Governor Juan Bautista Alvarado very well

indeed; they had been raised together in Monterey, and though he was only a year or two older, he was Alvarado's uncle; he had seen how his nephew's ascent to power had made Juan nervous and insecure.

"I was insulted at every turn by the drunken followers of Isaac Graham," complained Governor Alvarado. "When walking in the garden they would come to its wall and call to me in terms of the greatest familiarity. 'Ho! Bautista, come here, I want to speak to you. Bautista here, Bautista there, and Bautista everywhere!'"

No one had ever insulted Mariano Vallejo. Now thirty-one, commander general of the Mexican forces in the north, he had single-handedly founded and built one of the busiest communities in California: Sonoma, in what the Indians called the Valley of the Moon; for, like John Sutter, Vallejo was above all a colonizer. Having been sent north at the age of twenty-three, when he was commandant of the San Francisco Presidio, to learn the reason for the Indian unrest and to investigate the visit of the Russian governor of Sitka to Fort Ross, the Russian settlement on the coast some fifty miles north of the Presidio, the young lieutenant had mounted the crest of a hill and seen spread out before him an undulant valley covered with oaks, manzanita, golden poppies, with superb pasture lands and shining streams. Mariano fell in love at first sight, even as Sutter had with the Sacramento Valley; a year or two later, when he was appointed director of colonization for the north, Vallejo remembered his Valley of the Moon, returning to lay out a square, build barracks for his troops, a two-story *Casa Grande* for himself and his family, break the fields to raise corn and grain: all of this without one *real* of help from either Mexico City or Monterey.

"I could not bring myself to lead the lazy, carefree life so common of the general population," said Vallejo.

He was broadly handsome of face, powerfully built, a grim fighter when aroused, a talented executive with a first-rate intellect, in his own person the bridge between two ages in California. His mother, who came from one of the best Spanish families of California, the Lugos of San Luis Obispo, was described as having "a Puritanic strength of character, imparting to her children a resolute will and an ambitious spirit." Mariano was trained in the tanning of hides, the making of bricks, shoes, cigars; and given a love for books and learning which lasted all his life. At the age of seven he revolted against being forced to learn Ripalda's *Christian Doctrine* at the end of a cat-of-nine-tails, an uprising which he completed at the age of twenty-three when he bought several boxes

of books off a ship in Yerba Buena even though he knew they were
banned by the clergy who, he said:

"Kept guard over all the ports and bays of California like St.
Peter at the gates of heaven, to prevent the entrance of books of a
liberal tendency."

Vallejo paid four hundred hides and ten kegs of tallow for his
find, worth $1000, thus establishing the best library in California.
He had ordered thousands of bricks made of clay and straw,
doorways cut from live oaks, stones shaped for archways, red tiles
baked to make waterproof roofs, logs hand-hewn to make
hardwood floors when even the most prosperous of his countrymen
lived contentedly on earthen floors, unleashing a tornado of
activity in "pastoral California" where it had been charged that men
would do nothing that could not be done on a horse.

Though he had received short shrift from the Mexican
government and had been obliged to raise his own army, clothe,
feed, arm and pay it, he was passionately devoted to that army, to
its rules and appearances as well as its preservation. His father, who
had come up from Mexico as a foot soldier in the guard of mission-
building Father Junipero Serra in 1774, had been a fractious
soldier, constantly in trouble. That was why Mariano had resolved
to be a good soldier. Deeply in love with fifteen-year-old Francisca
Carrillo, he had waited two full years for marriage because army
regulations said that an army officer could not marry without
permission from the War Department, and the emissaries he had
dispatched over the two-thousand-mile journey to Mexico City
were not in as burning a hurry as the young bridegroom. That was
why he was stiff-necked and demanding of his ragged and half-
starved troops, why outsiders sometimes thought him pompous,
pretentious: he stood for the dignity, the integrity, the strength of
the Mexican army in California.

Mariano Vallejo had never seen Mexico. His entire devotion
was to California, his birthplace, his home, the land he loved. He
felt by now that California could never grow nor prosper under
Mexican rule, that it was too far away, of no conceivable value or
interest to Mexico. He knew also that several foreign governments
were keeping a sharp eye on the land: the United States, Great
Britain, Russia, France, any one of whom, sending a solitary
warship into Monterey, could take the country.

Vallejo liked the foreigners and felt closer to them in mind and
temperament than he did to his own countrymen; oh, not Isaac
Graham and his cronies, but men like Jacob Leese, born in Ohio,
John Cooper, born in England, both men married to his sisters, and

owners of ranches in the Sonoma Valley; William Hartnell, the Scotsman who had been his teacher in Monterey.

When John Sutter had come to Sonoma eight or nine months before, bringing messages from his Russian friends in Sitka to their Russian comrades at Fort Ross, Vallejo the soldier had been suspicious of the purpose of a Swiss going to a Russian fort just a few miles from Sonoma; but Vallejo the Californio had liked this dashing, educated foreigner, had extended the bounteous hospitality of a land where there were no inns and every family fed, entertained and bedded strangers who came riding up or down the road, then provided Sutter with fresh mounts and a guide for his journey to Fort Ross.

An astute student of history, Mariano Vallejo sensed that the Far West was rapidly approaching a crisis. He was convinced, after years of total frustration with the Mexican government, that California could only be developed into a great empire if it became American. He was the first and nearly the only native-born Californio to think so.

He was bitterly disillusioned in Governor Alvarado, who had promised to institute all the reforms needed to convert California to a modern province, and had instead taken to drink, become bloated, ill. And now Alvarado had ordered him to engage a vessel in Yerba Buena, arrest all foreigners and transport them to the Monterey jail.

He would obey the order from his commander-in-chief. But it was not a task to his liking.

CHAPTER IV

Heroic Frauds, or None at All

NO AMERICAN IN CALIFORNIA had less to fear from these arrests than Dr. John Marsh; and none was more surprised when he landed in Monterey's flea-infested jail. He had come to Los Angeles in 1836 from Santa Fe, taking the westward trail along the Gila River and crossing the Colorado into southern California, had become a naturalized citizen and, when he wanted to buy the cattle ranch at the eastern base of Mount Diablo, had been baptized a Catholic as the law said he must in order to own property in California.

True, he was practicing medicine illegally, having presented his Harvard Bachelor of Arts degree as a medical degree. Since no one in southern California could read Latin, the authorities had granted him a license to practice, thus fulfilling his lifetime ambition. Apparently he had been practicing good medicine, for few of his patients died prematurely. The Californios had little basis for comparison since he was the only doctor in the Far West, and the climate was salubrious. What the Californios knew for sure was that Dr. Marsh practiced expensive medicine: twenty-five cows on the hoof for a professional visit, fifty take-home cows if he had to remain overnight. One outraged housewife deducted twenty-five cows from his bill for washing a couple of his shirts.

John Marsh and John Sutter, now close neighbors in central California, since their settlements were only fifty miles apart, had met in Santa Fe in 1836. Marsh knew that Sutter had as little right to call himself a military captain as Marsh had to call himself a doctor of medicine. Yet on the frontier one perpetrated heroic frauds or none at all. The Far West was little concerned with a man's past: he could become anything he could prove himself to be.

John Marsh, born in Danvers, Massachusetts, weighed two hundred eighteen pounds, stood six feet two in his stockings, was bronzed and powerfully built in spite of his nervous disposition. He was a fierce-looking, ugly man, with the right lid drooping down to cover part of a piercing eye, and two large unabashed warts decorating the crease line from the right side of his nose to the corner of his mouth. The first college graduate to settle in the Far West, he was, characteristically, first to bring a good working library of medical and agricultural books in his saddlebags, these books being his only material possessions. He was thirty-six when he reached Los Angeles, having already lived half a dozen lives. He had hated the grinding poverty of his family's farm, which was barely able to feed the seven Marsh children. Endowed with a vigorous intellect, he was graduated from Phillips Academy at Andover, and worked his way through Harvard by teaching school at Danvers during the winter.

While still an undergraduate John Marsh did extracurricular work in anatomy and worked as an assistant to a Boston doctor.

There simply were no funds for medical school, and so he took a tutoring job in the Michigan Territory with a salary which would enable him to save enough money in two years to return to Harvard. He walked off the scene of New England and onto the pages of history: organizer of the first school in Minnesota, Indian agent and friend of the Tribes, compiler of the first dictionary of the Sioux language, a judge in the territory, organizer of Prairie du Chien's defense which averted a massacre.

He fell in love with Marguerite Decouteaux, daughter of a Sioux mother and a French-Canadian father; slender as a reed, with flashing white teeth and a lovely slender face. Marsh took Marguerite into his home as his wife, though no formal ceremony seems to have been performed. Marguerite guided him on his journeys through the wilderness, helped him to write *Rudiments of the Grammar of the Sioux*, bore him a son.

Marsh studied under the army surgeon at Fort St. Anthony for two years, until the medical man died. The tragic break in his life came in 1831 or 1832 when, having been responsible for a retaliatory Sioux massacre of the Fox tribe, he felt obliged to move his wife and six-year-old son southward to the safety of New Salem, Illinois, to protect them from avenging Fox warriors. Marguerite, about to bear a second child, and finding life insupportable without her husband, made her way back, alone and on foot, to Prairie du Chien where she and her infant died in childbirth, both too feeble to survive.

Obsessed with guilt over Marguerite's death, Marsh nearly lost his reason, becoming a wanderer and an outcast. Captured by Indians on the Santa Fe Trail, he saved his skin by extracting an arrowhead from an ailing chief. In Santa Fe he heard of the wonders of California, decided to make his way to Los Angeles and present himself as a practitioner of medicine.

On February 25, 1836, in a one-room mud hut on a sun-baked, sleepy and dusty plaza, thirty-six-year-old John Marsh became Dr. John Marsh. He was busy from the outset, treating smallpox, fevers, hydrophobia, and achieving quite a success as an *accoucheur*. Since he was paid in dried cowhides or tallow, his adobe looked and smelled more like a warehouse than a doctor's office.

Though there was no life for him in the few unpainted adobes around the square, he stayed in Los Angeles for a year, leaving because so few Boston sailing ships stopped in southern California that he could find no market for his hides, piled all the way to the ceiling, and because he thought the country too desert-like for the

kind of cattle ranch he envisaged for himself. Making his way north
on horseback, he explored the country around Monterey and
Yerba Buena, which then consisted of three houses at the foot of a
cove so small that it seemed more like the end of a lake than part of
the world's largest bay. The biggest of the houses was owned by
William A. Richardson, an English sailor who had jumped ship and
settled in 1822, now serving as captain of the port for the
Californios. Jacob Leese, who later married Vallejo's sister, owned
the most popular grocery store in California, for his empty boxes
and kegs, set around a stove which kept out the penetrating fogs,
became the gathering point for all Americans and foreigners.
Marsh moved in with Leese, the two men living on tortillas, frijoles,
chile con carne and salt fish. In 1837 Marsh bought the Los
Meganos ranch, saying of it:

"I have at last found the Far West, and intend to end my
ramblings here."

The boundaries of the ranch were described in the informal
manner of a country with millions of available acres:

"... from a round-topped hill standing in the range southwest,
known as Brushy Peak, to the river, thence following the river to
Antioch..."

Here John Marsh built himself a three-room adobe hut with an
earthen floor, with bulrushes for a roof, furnished with a table,
bench and a bed, took an Indian squaw for a housekeeper-wife,
made trips of fifty to one hundred miles to attend sick patients. He
remained essentially a hermit, taking pleasure mainly from his
books, which he read under a huge oak in the yard, building his
ranch to fifty thousand acres, five thousand head of cattle, five
thousand sheep, still treasuring as his most valuable possession the
Harvard Bachelor of Arts degree which he kept locked in a little
trunk.

But over the years he was developing a second passion, as great
as his love for medicine: a dedication to California and a desire to
see it settled by hundreds of Americans who would turn it into a
part of the United States. It was a letter he wrote to friends in
Missouri which became responsible for the first train to cross the
plains to California, precursor of the flash flood of emigrants which
would, in one short decade, turn the somnolent and unknown Far
West into one of the most talked-about and romantic portions of
the earth's globe.

In April of 1840 Marsh went on business to Mission San Jose,
some miles to the south. He knew that all the foreigners around San
Jose and Monterey were being arrested for the purpose of

deportation, but he was a legal citizen, and so he set off undisturbed. Here he was seized by the military and taken as prisoner to Monterey.

There were some who thought he had been arrested for his fees rather than his fealty.

CHAPTER V

An Honest Scoundrel Thickens the Plot

UNLIKE "DOCTOR" MARSH and "Captain" Sutter, Isaac Graham presented an honest face to the Far West: he was a scoundrel, he had never been anything but a scoundrel, and he made no effort to dissemble. Leader of the *aguardiente* or saloon set of northern California, he had gathered about him a group of deserters and adventurers who helped him drink up the profits of his still at Natividad, near Monterey. Hubert Howe Bancroft, gargantuan source historian of the Far West, says:

"Graham was the worst of the foreigners, and the cause of all the troubles by his boastful, quarrelsome spirit. He thought he could play hell and turn up jack." An American who had known Graham in New Mexico described him as "noted for being a bummer, a blowhard, a notorious liar." He had come to California over the Old Spanish Trail.

He was a picturesque figure, his face a forest of wild beard and mustache with eyes and nose peering out from the thicket. He wore a wide-brimmed hat at a bravo angle, with a horseman's tie around the collar of his long hunting jacket exquisitely accoutered for the brawl, with a savage hunting knife decorating his belt close to his left hand, a powder horn slung from his shoulder, quickly available to the omnipresent rifle in his right hand.

Yet there was a time when he had almost become respectable: four years before, when Alvarado overthrew the governor sent from Mexico City. Alvarado had enlisted Graham and his rifle-toting friends in his ranks by promising them a bounty of rich lands. Once in power, Governor Alvarado had not kept his promises, and so he had failed to reform Graham, just as he had failed to reform the antiquated government of California.

Isaac Graham's feelings had been hurt. For the past year he had been heard making threats against Alvarado's government. Had not a group of daring Americans taken Texas away from Mexico and set it up as a Republic?

Graham was not saying anything that was not being said more quietly by other Americans in California, but Graham was not always discreet. Tom the Trapper, thinking he was dying, confessed to a priest that Graham was brewing a revolution as well as *aguardiente* in the still behind his hut. In his anxiety Alvarado professed to see a conspiracy. Graham writes quaintly:

"About three o'clock in the morning, I was awakened by the discharge of a pistol, the ball of which passed through my neckcloth. I sprang out of my bed, when they discharged six pistols at me. I had not run four or five yards when they overhauled me with drawn swords, and leveled most deadly and heavy blows at me—which I had the good fortune to evade. Jose Castro then ordered four balls to be shot through me, but was prevented from doing so by an Indian, who continually placed himself as a barrier before me."

Graham was put in chains and carried to Monterey. The only jail in the Far West consisted of a single adobe cell, eighteen by thirty feet, with one small tightly barred window and an earthen floor, damp in the April weather. Alvarado was now embarrassed by finding about forty prisoners crowded into a cell which had previously held only an occasional Indian who had borrowed a horse.

Monterey had been discovered two hundred thirty-eight years before. Cabrillo, exploring the coast in 1542, caught a glimpse of the bay, but did not put in; Sebastian Vizcaino, described as a merchant-explorer, sailed into the bay in 1602, and under one of California's giant oaks gave thanks to God and planted the Spanish flag, naming the spot Monte-Rey, after Spain's viceroy to Mexico. He then made an indigenous error which has come down as inviolable precedent to all California writers: he praised the country in such sonorous superlatives that for the next hundred sixty-seven years all voyagers failed to recognize Monterey from his description.

The name California is the invention of another Spanish fiction writer: one Ardonez de Montalvo, who wrote around 1510:

"At the right hand of the Indies there is an island called California, very near to the Terrestrial Paradise. This island is inhabited by robust dark women of great strength and great warm hearts; when children are born the females are preserved but the males are killed at once, saving only those required to guard against depopulation...."

Portola, in charge of the Spanish soldiers marching north from Mexico in 1769 to protect Father Junipero Serra while he built a chain of missions: San Diego, San Juan Capistrano, San Gabriel, Santa Barbara, Monterey, Carmel, San Jose, San Francisco, Sonoma, passed Monterey twice without recognizing Vizcaino's description. He pushed so far west that he accidentally discovered San Francisco Bay.

Not until the spring of 1770 did Portola find that the adjectives matched the landscape. In 1775 the King of Spain recognized Monterey as the capital of California. By 1803 the first presidio or fort in the Far West had been completed, with barracks, a chapel and homes for the officers. The soldiers as well as the arms were good; no nation made sheep's eyes at the Far West while Spain was acknowledged to be its owner.

As the capital and the only port where foreign ships could declare their cargo, Monterey grew rapidly. As late as 1840, when San Diego was described by visitors as "wretched," Yerba Buena as "squalid," Los Angeles as "the noted abode of the lowest drunkards and gamblers of the country," Monterey had a population of three hundred, some thirty of them Americans and British.

It was the center of the Far West's governmental, social and business world, with the charming whitewashed adobe houses with their red tile roofs built in a semicircle just beyond the white, sandy beach, standing on brilliantly green lawns, the houses covered with flowering vines, pine-covered hills as a background and overhead an Italian-blue sky. There were bullfights on the plaza, dances and fiestas; although there was a law against selling liquor there does not appear to have been any edict against drinking it.

The jail had not been built with an eye to affording a beautiful vista; all the charms of Monterey were momentarily lost on its inmates.

The cell soon became untenable, with the air quite vile, and so crowded that only a few men could stretch out for sleep while the rest stood their turn. Governor Alvarado either had no public money or saw no reason to spend his scarce funds on feeding prisoners who would soon be on the ship chartered by Vallejo to haul them away. As a consequence no food was brought to the prison cell for forty-eight hours.

Since John Marsh had been the most illegally arrested, and was coincidentally the most persuasive talker in the jail, he managed to get himself released by the end of the second day, promising his fellow inmates that he would bring them help. Once out he knew precisely where to go for help: to his old friend Thomas O. Larkin, known as the Yankee from Boston as well as California's first millionaire, the best-liked, or at least the most respected, American in the region.

CHAPTER VI

The Time of Action Begins

THOMAS OLIVER LARKIN was thirty years old when he arrived in Monterey. In the eight years that had elapsed he had acquired the first American wife in the Far West, his son was the first American born there, and he pioneered the technique of remaining a Yankee in California while absorbing the privileges of the native Californio. He did a great deal to change the Far West, but the Far West was able to change little in him: the years of living in the warm sun of Monterey surrounded by easygoing, pleasure-loving Californios had imperceptibly slowed his pace, but his New England character had remained impregnable. In the polyandrous marriage of a number of ardent gentlemen to near-virginal California, Thomas O. Larkin was one of the fathers of westward migration.

He was born in Charlestown, Massachusetts, in September 1802, his father's forebears having come over on the *Mayflower* to become freemen of Charlestown in 1638, his grandfather having fought at Bunker Hill in 1775. Losing both parents when he was sixteen, Larkin moved to Boston where he went to work at the noble profession of making books. By the age of twenty he had decided that Boston and New England were too crowded, that he wanted to pioneer. He moved to North Carolina, fitting in so well that within three years he had graduated from stranger and business clerk to merchant, postmaster and justice of the peace.

Larkin had a half brother, Captain John Cooper, former master of the S.S. *Rover* out of Boston, who had settled in Monterey in 1826, married a lovely dark-eyed sister of Vallejo, been baptized into the Church, acquired Mexican citizenship, vast tracts of land and a mill.

Envisaging a similar fate for Thomas, the Larkin collaterals tried to dissuade him from sailing around Cape Horn. They had reckoned without his rocky-coast character: he refused to court the luscious, land-rich but husband-starved Californio girls, refused to take Mexican citizenship or join the Church, though he could have had a land grant of twenty thousand acres almost anywhere in California had he been willing to do so.

Thomas Larkin was not physically robust, nor what one would call a handsome man: his hair was already growing scarce on the frontal dome of his head, he was thin-lipped and thin-nosed, yet his light shrewd eyes were likable. He was a meticulous dresser, wearing his black stock and boiled shirt to business as though he were still in Boston.

Having worked as clerk and bookkeeper in Yerba Buena to get the feel of the new country, he then moved to Monterey and opened his first store on a borrowed $500. He had found the Californios to resemble the North Carolinians; he enjoyed the rare talent for liking strange people and getting along with them. Soon he was not only selling supplies brought in by Boston ships, but had built a flour mill, was contracting to erect buildings with his own lumber and shingles, and had started a vigorous trade in flour, soap, potatoes and sea otter skins.

On the long voyage from Boston to California by the usual route to Hawaii, Thomas Larkin had become friends with twenty-five-year-old Rachel Holmes, born a few miles from him, who was trying to join her husband, a sea captain whom she had married in Massachusetts five years before but had not seen for two years. In Hilo Mrs. Holmes learned that her husband was dead. Larkin, already in love, resolved that Rachel would come to California and marry him. By correspondence he won her acceptance, arranged for her passage to California. He boarded Rachel's ship as it lay outside of Santa Barbara, was married by the American owner of the vessel, who was also United States consul at Honolulu, thus, in a sense, being married on American soil and in a ceremony of their own faith since no ordained Protestant minister had yet set foot on Far Western soil. The new Larkin family remained American, and their progeny would be American too.

Never one to be cavalier with a coin, Thomas Larkin set out to build the first truly American home in the Far West, two-storied, multiwindowed, with wide verandas. He left one set of figures which will wring the heart of every home builder:

	Estimated Cost	Actual Cost
Harry's work	$ 4.00	$ 8.00
3500 adobes	20.00	70.00
7 pr. sashes	50.00	70.00
putting up walls	136.00	203.00
2100 shingles	126.00	210.00

The Larkin home became the focal center of newly arrived Americans, Englishmen and Europeans, an unofficial American capital.

From the moment he set foot in Monterey Larkin wanted California for the United States. He pursued California with a combination of efficiency and ardor, as a smart trader who knew that both partners profit from a fair deal. He planned to attach the land, from its Pacific coast to the crest of the Rockies, peaceably, by legal treaty and purchase. Since California was a dead loss to Mexico, and had been ever since Mexican independence in 1821, why should it not negotiate and sell the unwanted territory to the United States for a fair price?

He also knew that few people in the United States yet wanted the country, which had been represented as reachable only by a rough, dangerous seven months journey around Cape Horn or by an equally long, rough and dangerous traversing of thousands of miles of barren, trackless plains, death-dealing deserts and immense mountains.

Larkin had full faith in his own ability and that of men like Marsh and Sutter to persuade people of the beauty and opulence of California despite the hardships of reaching this last outpost, of which he wrote home, "... me and my countrymen are living in the farthest West, for we are far beyond what is known by the 'Far West' in the States."

All that was required for this commercial *coup d'état* was that everyone behave with propriety. But alcohol rather than propriety had been distilled by Isaac Graham, and now Larkin's plan had received a severe setback. Respectable people did not steal millions of acres of land, any more than they stole flour or candles out of a shop.

Helping the prisoners would bring down on him, for the first time in his eight years among them, the disfavor of the native Californios. Yet Thomas Larkin could not abandon his countrymen. He went to Alvarado, secured permission to send food to the men. David Spence, a Scotsman who had come to California from Peru in 1824 to superintend a meat-packing establishment, got permission at the same time to bring in sufficient hides to cover the damp floor. They also secured the release of the non-Grahamites and brought a halt to the arrests. Sutter escaped because Governor Alvarado decided to keep him in the north as a counterforce to Colonel Vallejo.

The one thing that neither Larkin nor Spence could provide was a legal system which would afford the prisoners a trial, witnesses, a jury and a judge. According to Mexican law Governor Alvarado was all of these things rolled into his one badly frightened person.

After thirteen days forty-odd prisoners were taken out of jail and marched between two files of soldiers to the nearby shore, then rowed out to the ship which Vallejo had engaged for the purpose. Graham, in irons, was carried to the boat on the shoulders of several Indians. The entire population of Monterey and inhabitants of the ranches for miles inland were on hand to watch; nothing so exciting had happened since 1818 when the French pirate Bouchard had sacked the town.

No man is such a wretch but that he cannot find a defender. A lawyer from Maine who had gone overland to Oregon, and from there by ship to Monterey, carrying the portentous name of Thomas Jefferson Farnham, arrived the day before the deportation. He wrote in white heat:

"The doors of the prison were opened; its emaciated tenants came out, some of them with no clothing except a ragged pair of pantaloons. The Spaniards had robbed them not only of their cattle, horses, mules, but also of their freedom. Poor old Graham seemed utterly heartbroken."

Farnham cried to Graham as he went by, "Be brave! Let no Tennessean ever think of yielding in this way!"

From his vantage point on the Indians' shoulders, Graham looked down and moaned:

"I can never be a man again. To be chained and exported like a tub of lard, by these here scabs of mankind, is mighty bad."

When Thomas Jefferson Farnham wrote of the deportation in his perfervid style, accusing Governor Alvarado of wanting to get

Graham out of the way because he owed him $2235, and published his account in an eastern newspaper, all loyal, red-blooded Americans who read it were outraged. The "bummer, blowhard and liar" who "thought he could play hell and turn up jack" was converted into a national hero.

Soon the small boats plying back and forth had transported the last of their cargo; sail was raised and filled with wind; slowly the *Joven Guipuzcoana* moved out of the bay. Governor Alvarado and the Californios thought that all would now be serene in California.

Captain John Sutter, Dr. John Marsh, Colonel Mariano Vallejo, Thomas O. Larkin, good students all, knew better. This was not an end but a beginning. The white sails dropping gracefully over the horizon were a curtain descending on a prologue known as the pastoral age in California.

Book Two

THE OPENING OF A LAND

CHAPTER I

John Sutter Takes the Big Plunge

CHIEF FACTOR JAMES DOUGLAS, resourceful head of the Hudson's Bay Company in Canada, raised the curtain on 1841 by appearing on New Year's Day in Monterey Bay with a party of thirty-six trained hunters and trappers which would prove a formidable force in the event the Hudson's Bay company, advance arm of the British government, were in an expansionist mood.

It might well have been; for foolhardy John Sutter had just given the lion's tail a pain-fraught twist. If England were not careful, this stocky blue-eyed Swiss refugee with his camp of Kanakas, Indian allies and a few mechanics might more effectively rid the Far West of the British than the United States Senate had succeeded in doing after years of negotiation over Oregon.

Each spring since 1832 the mountain men of the Hudson's Bay Company had made their way south through Oregon over unmapped trails to trap in the Sacramento Valley; each fall they had illegally portaged back to Canada a small fortune in beaver skins and hides. But the preceding fall John Sutter had informed Douglas that he might never again send his men into the valley, since all of its hunting and trapping rights belonged to him. Nor had Captain Sutter left any doubt but that the next appearance of the Hudson's Bay hunters would bring about a shooting war.

It was a gesture which for nerve had few equals. But it worked. Instead of sending his trappers overland, Douglas brought them down by ship, and applied for official permission to send them into the Sacramento. Governor Alvarado replied diplomatically that Sutter should perhaps have issued a request rather than an order, but now that there was an accredited Californio settlement in the Sacramento Valley, for John Sutter had received his citizenship papers and had been made a minor official of the government, the Hudson's Bay parties must withdrew to more distant fields.

Douglas, who wrote in his journal, "California is a country in many respects unrivaled by any of the globe," was an able maneuverer.

He now requested of Governor Alvarado that the company be allowed to purchase a lot in Yerba Buena, where no one but Mexican citizens could legally own land; to erect a building to house their trading post; to put several of their ships under the Mexican flag, and to naturalize their British captains; thus giving them a "most favored nation" position. Alvarado was amenable.

"I told Governor Alvarado," said Douglas, "that the wishes of the government would be attended to in every particular." To his own people he confided, "We have also other objects of a political nature in view, which may or may not succeed according to circumstances, but in the event of success the results will be important."

He could only have meant: When Mexico loses California we want to be in a position to take the country for Great Britain.

In the wrestling match of history each exertion of force brings forth a counterdisplay: Douglas's securing of special privileges aroused in the Americans in California the fear that they might once again become subjects of England. Not that Great Britain would be so indecorous as to steal the Far West out of the international till, but Mexico owed England $50,000,000 in cash. Why not pay the debt with an unproductive colony? It was to become an omnipresent fear.

Having beaten the British, John Sutter moved on to his second *coup*. The Russian American Fur Company at Fort Ross, fifty miles up the coast from Yerba Buena, had exhausted after nearly thirty years of too assiduous hunting the sea's supply of otters, those beautiful silver skins which brought up to $200 apiece in Canton. It was ordered to abandon its California experiment and bring the community back home to Sitka, Siberia and Mother Russia. The more valuable personal possessions, rare volumes, costly draperies, art works and piano could be loaded on a ship and taken home; but what about the several cannon, the meticulously built homes, granary, church, the twenty-two-ton launch, four small boats, forty-nine plows, ten carts, harnesses, bridles, seventeen hundred oxen, cows and calves, nine hundred forty horses and mules, two hundred sheep, not to mention the loading facilities of Bodega Bay, close by the fort?

The land itself the Russians could not sell, for they never had

had a legal right to settle. They had not recognized Spanish authority north of San Francisco Bay and, knowing that the Mexicans had no army, they had remained, hospitable and friendly neighbors, a bright cultural center with Old World music, beautifully gowned women, brilliant conversation and fine wines. They had even paid the Indians for the lands they occupied; the price was small: three blankets, three pairs of breeches, two axes, three hoes and some beads.

At all times between their arrival in 1812 and their decision to sell in 1840, the Russians were a threat to the possession of California. Provisioning for conquest could have come quickly and amply from Sitka. But the Russians had behaved circumspectly. Now they were preparing to depart, leaving behind formidable resources which could help any nation to become the next owner of California.

Though the Russian American Fur Company had taken out millions in otter skins, it quite humanly wanted to sell its immovable assets at the best possible price. The Russian commander properly offered Mexico the first opportunity to buy. Mexico City assumed that the Russians were moving away in defeat, and ordered Governor Alvarado to occupy the fort, an attitude in which they were encouraged by Alvarado, who informed Mexico City that the Russians would find no purchaser.

The Russian commander next offered the assets to Colonel Mariano Vallejo, his nearest neighbor. Vallejo offered to buy the livestock only. The property was next offered to the Hudson's Bay Company for $30,000. Sir George Simpson, overseas governor of the company, refused to buy on the grounds that they "could not hold the soil, but merely the improvements."

John Sutter now stepped up and offered to pay the full asking price. The Russians liked Sutter: he had been a welcome guest at Sitka. They thought him charming, intelligent, forceful. What if he did not have the $30,000? What if he could barely scrape together $2000 as a down payment? Was he not building a vast empire? Did he not have fields sown with wheat and corn, hunting parties out gathering a wealth of skins; forges, shops turning out goods?

And so they sold to Sutter all the property at Fort Ross and Bodega Bay. The terms were liberal, four yearly installments, beginning September 1, 1842, two of $5000 each, the third and fourth of $10,000; the first three payable in wheat, peas, beans, tallow, soap, the fourth in cash.

Had the Russians remained another seven years, until the discovery of gold in 1848, they would have been in position to reach the richest lodes first. Had Mexico bought the cannons and livestock it could have armed and fed its army and put down the Bear Flag Revolt in 1846 at Sonoma, only a day's march from Fort Ross. Had the Hudson's Bay Company bought Fort Ross and Bodega Bay the British could have been so solidly entrenched by the time the Californio government dissolved that California might have fallen quite easily into their hands.

The prize went to John Augustus Sutter, precursor of generations of American plungers, the only man in the Far West with the vision to realize the importance of Fort Ross's assets. Though already deeply in debt to Sir George Simpson of the Hudson's Bay Company, to Thomas O. Larkin of Monterey, to Nathan Spear of Yerba Buena, to his neighboring ranchers, Martinez, Marsh, Sunol, he was possessed of the true gambler's courage which would lead him to treble his debts and put himself in hock for years to come. Yet under the premise of his own planning he was profoundly right; up to this point New Helvetia was a chancy affair. Did he have enough weapons to stave off massed Indian attacks? Did he have sufficient plows, carts, mules to practice large-scale agriculture? Did he have sufficient tools and shop equipment to sustain a colony? Did he have the requisite standing to uphold the grants of land he was making freely to newcomers whom he wanted to settle nearby?

Having arranged to move the boats, cannons and cattle to his fort, John Sutter, son of the foreman of a paper mill and a pastor's daughter, failure as a clerk in a printing house, drapery shop and grocery, who revealed his character by paying twenty-five *livres* for the complete works of Sir Walter Scott while heavily in debt, this same John Sutter had in little more than two years become the most powerful individual in the Far West. Whichever government he threw in with, always providing he did not set up his own empire, would have the inside track for the possession of California.

The move cost him Alvarado's friendship. Jose Castro, military commandant of San Jose, threatened to wipe out New Helvetia. Sutter's naturally red cheeks flamed with anger. He wrote an excited letter to Jacob Leese, the American brother-in-law of Colonel Vallejo.

"It is too late now to drive me out of the country. I will make a declaration of Independence and proclaim California for a Republique."

It was a blustering message, telling of his ten guns and five field pieces, of "50 faithful Indians which shot their musquet very quick."

Yet Sutter would have fought and would probably have defeated Castro's ill-equipped soldiers.

Or at least Castro thought so.

Having forced the Hudson's Bay trappers out of California, kept the Mexican government from absorbing without cost the Russian possessions, John Sutter proved himself stronger than the Mexican army and justified his claim to a military title. Captain John Sutter had succeeded in fulfilling what Governor Alvarado described as "the idea of making the Californios believe that he was fate and providence to them."

He was.

CHAPTER II

"The state of society is exceedingly loose"

RUSSIA HAD SCRATCHED HER entry in the Far West sweepstakes. England, France and the United States were fishing skillfully in troubled waters.

In early May of 1841 France made her entry in the form of an elegant and delightful young attaché of the French legation at Mexico City. Eugene Duflot de Mofras, who spoke Spanish, English and German as well as his native French, arrived on the bark *Ninfa* at Monterey with a concealed but challenging assignment: to cover all of California, draw charts of its coastline, rivers and harbors, investigate its soil, climate, resources, make studies of the life and the people; and report everything back to Paris. William Heath Davis describes de Mofras as "a close observer of everything." Just how closely he was observing and for what purpose was revealed only to his government.

"The presidio of Monterey is now entirely demolished, few traces remaining. A small battery stands on the west side of the anchorage. On the sea approach its sole support is a small earthen embankment, four feet high. The battery has neither moat nor counterguard and can readily be approached on all sides. . . . California will belong to the nation that has the courage to send there a corvette and two hundred men. . . . It is the lot of this province to be conquered, and we do not see why France should not collect her part of this magnificent heritage."

The entry of the United States on the scene was late, October 19, 1841, but formidable, taking the form of a flotilla of four armed naval vessels, the U.S.S. *Vincennes, Porpoise, Flying Fish* and *Oregon*, under the command of the Commodore Charles Wilkes. This charting expedition had mapped the hitherto unexplored arctic and antarctic ice fields, as well as the islands of the Pacific. Wilkes had been ordered by his government to put into San Francisco Bay for a sufficient stay to chart the area. Washington had not bothered to secure permission for this survey from Mexico City, nor when Wilkes anchored in the bay did he ask, "By your leave?" a situation somewhat analogous to an auctioneer walking uninvited into a private home while the owner is out, and drawing up an itemized list of valuables which he calculates will one day come under his hammer.

Charles Wilkes was born in New York City in 1798. He had an intensely puritan nature to which all pleasure except that of the intellect was immoral. Interested in ships from his earliest childhood, he studied navigation and nautical science, shipped out while awaiting an appointment from the navy, at the age of twenty was summoned for his training, sailed the Mediterranean and the Pacific on warships, and in 1838 received command of the exploring expedition.

Wilkes was dedicated to the interests of science and exploring; dedicated men, be they artists or scientists, are rarely social-minded. Unlike the charming de Mofras, Wilkes refused to mix with the Californios, to leave his ship to attend their dinners or balls. He disliked the natives, those of Spanish derivation, with whom he had no contact, apparently watching them from his poop deck with a high-powered telescope.

"The state of society here is exceedingly loose; envy, hatred, and malice, predominate in almost every breast, and the people are wretched under their present rulers; female virtue, I regret to say is also at a low ebb; and the coarse and lascivious dances which meet the plaudits of the lookers-on, show the degraded tone of manners that exists."

His shivering officers "compared the climate to that of Cape Horn with the cold, blustering winds and cloudy skies," but exclaimed over San Francisco Bay:

"This is ours!"

Wilkes was unimpressed.

"The country has by no means an inviting aspect. There are no symptoms of cultivation, nor is the land on either side [of the bay] fit for it. The first view of California was not calculated to make a favorable impression either of its beauty or fertility."

One sentence of Wilkes's report matched that of de Mofras:

"I was surprised when I found a total absence of all government in California, and even its forms and ceremonies thrown aside."

The Wilkes report was discouraging, but one of his orders, issued while still in the northwest, designated young fun-loving Lieutenant George F. Emmons to head a party including a navy geologist and artist to make the overland journey southward from the Willamette Valley of Oregon through the mountain country in which the Sacramento River had its course. He also gave permission to a party of twenty-four American civilians, who had come over the Oregon Trail from the east and were awaiting an opportunity to head south for Sutter's Fort, to accompany the navy expedition.

It took the Emmons Party a month to reach Mount Shasta in northern California. They arrived at Sutter's Fort on October 19, 1841. They had suffered hunger and exhaustion, but when it was learned in the East that the entire party, including at least three women and a seven-month-old child, had entered California by the Oregon route in safety, it gave impetus to a pattern of family migration.

The arrival of the Emmons Party also marked the beginning of Sutter's role of *paterfamilias* to all emigrants coming over the mountains. Lieutenant Emmons reported:

"In his brilliant uniform of a Mexican officer and his magnificent presence, he looks as I have in fancy pictured Cortez in his palmiest days. Everything the heart could wish was supplied from the bountiful storehouse of this large-hearted man. Fresh provisions were sent to the camp daily, including fresh-baked bread, milk, fish, groceries and the delicacies our sick and feeble men so much required."

Commodore Wilkes remained in San Francisco Bay only two weeks, then the fleet raised anchor and sailed for Honolulu preparatory to returning home. He remains unique in the story of the Far West for publishing in 1844 the most dismal account of California to be found in the records.

If three nations were staking out Mexico's western lands, in the last analysis it was no one of these government-sponsored expeditions which was to decide the outcome. It was instead a twenty-two-year-old former schoolteacher from Chautauqua County, New York, John Bidwell, who organized and led the first group of emigrants across what had been described as burning deserts, arid plains, impassable mountains and brought them down safely to the ranch of Dr. John Marsh. They had neither map nor guide beyond Marsh's breezy:

"The difficulty of coming here is imaginary. The route I would recommend is from Independence to the frontier rendezvous on Green River, then to Soda Spring on Bear River above the Big Salt Lake, thence to Mary's River until you come in sight of the gap in the great mountain, through that gap by a good road and you arrive in the plain of Joaquin, and down that river on a level plain through thousands of elk and horse. Three or four days journey and you come to my house."

If it sounded easy this can perhaps be ascribed to the fact that Marsh had never come over this route, having entered California by the Old Spanish Trail near the southern border.

The Californios were none too happy over the fact that their coast had suddenly become an international spa.

CHAPTER III

"The difficulty of coming here is imaginary"

THE FORMATION OF THE Bidwell Party resulted from the juncture of two streams on the topography of time, neither of which, flowing alone, might have been strong enough to work its way through solid rock.

Dr. John Marsh after his imprisonment in Monterey was confirmed in his earlier opinion that the Californios were incapable of governing their country. To remedy this situation he began writing to friends in Missouri urging them to come to California. One letter was published in the St. Louis *Daily Argus*: "This is beyond all comparison the finest country and the finest climate. What we want here is more people. If we had fifty families from Missouri, we could do exactly as we please without any fear of being troubled. The difficulty of coming here is imaginary...."

Within a matter of days of the publication of the letter, on October 31, 1840, a French trapper by the name of Antoine Robidoux appeared in the same Missouri county where Marsh's communication was being avidly read and discussed. John Bidwell, big-built, with the powerful patrician head of a Roman senator, listened to Robidoux talk about the Far West.

Bidwell was born August 5, 1819, of English parentage. His biographer describes the Bidwell stock as having "a genius for invention, invincible determination to perseverance, sometimes carried to the point of obstinacy." The boy moved westward with his parents to Erie, Pennsylvania, when he was ten, to western Ohio when he was fourteen. He was principal of a small academy at eighteen, having memorized all of Kirkham's *Latin Grammar* to confound the examining board. Having saved $75 he decided to see something of the western prairies. The $75 and a strong pair of legs carried him through Iowa and Missouri to the Kansas Territory where he taught school for a while, then staked out a claim of a hundred sixty acres. The following summer, 1840, he made a trip down the Missouri River to St. Louis to buy supplies, only to find upon his return that his claim had been jumped. It was at this ripe moment in his life that he encountered the inflammatory words of Marsh and Robidoux. His normally cool nature was set on fire.

"Robidoux's description of California was in the superlative degree favorable, so much so that I resolved to see that wonderful land, and with others helped to get up a meeting at Weston. Robidoux described it as one of perennial spring and boundless fertility.... He said that the Spanish authorities were most friendly, and that the people were the most hospitable on the globe: that you could travel all over California and it would cost you nothing for horses or food. His description of the country made it seem like a Paradise."

Bidwell helped form the Western Emigration Society, pledging along with five hundred other enthusiasts to "purchase a suitable outfit, and to rendezvous on the ninth of the following May, armed and equipped to cross the Rocky Mountains to California." No one knew how to get there, nor yet where California was, except that it

was at the extreme west of the Far West, and that one had come to
the end when he found himself wading in the Pacific Ocean. The
only map Bidwell could find showed two or three rivers as big as the
Mississippi River which flowed from Salt Lake into the Pacific. The
owner of the map advised young Bidwell to take the tools for
building boats!

Then in March of 1841 Thomas Jefferson Farnham, panting
defender of Isaac Graham, published a lachrymose letter in a
newspaper, his tears washing out the entire Western Emigration
Society... except John Bidwell.

"Our committee fell to pieces notwithstanding our pledge was as
binding as language could make it. When May came I was the only
man that was ready to go of all who signed the pledge; and there I
was with my wagon!"

As with so many lost causes and lost days, one heroic figure
larger than life size can turn a rout into a hard-won victory. In a
short time George Hinshaw, an invalid, joined Bidwell on a fine
black horse; then Robert H. Thomas and Michael Nye agreed to go;
in Weston a wagon with four or five persons joined; at Sapling
Grove, the place of the agreed rendezvous, another wagon was
waiting for them; then a group of eight men under John Bartleson
came in from Independence. Within a matter of five days some
sixty-nine men, women and children has assembled, some from as
far away as Arkansas. The party was a series of "private messes,"
held together by the officers they elected: Bartleson as captain,
because he refused to join the party unless he was named leader,
Bidwell as secretary.

No member of the party had ever been west. No one had a map,
an account of the nature of the terrain or the availability of water,
food or forage for the animals, for the good reason that none had
ever been written. They would have to go it blind.

Then there arrived a group of Catholic missionaries headed for
Oregon. They were led by Father Pierre Jean de Smet, who had
traveled in the wilderness of the Northwest, guided by "Broken
Hand" Fitzpatrick, one of the immortal mountain men of the
1830s. For the next three months, while they crossed the prairie and
followed the Platte River through what is now Nebraska and
Wyoming, Bidwell and his group learned hour by hour the prairie
lore of preservation. At Soda Springs, just north of present-day
Utah, the party split, thirty-two of the original Bartleson-Bidwell
train deciding to accompany Father de Smet and Fitzpatrick to
Oregon. John Bidwell and thirty-one others, including Benjamin
Kelsey, his wife and small daughter, resolved to make their way to

California. The only advice Fitzpatrick was able to give them was: "Find the Mary's, follow it to its end, then push west, ever west."

Under the captainship of John Bartleson the party entered on or about August 13, 1841 what is now the state of Utah at a point a few miles north of Ogden's Hole and Great Salt Lake, and began a voyage of inestimable courage. Historians Charles and Mary Beard say:

"Compared to the trials and sufferings endured by this party, the hardships of the voyagers in the *Mayflower* seem positively slight. Certainly the events of this path-breaking expedition, though not as celebrated in annals of history as the doings of the Pilgrims, deserve their vivid chapter in the great American epic."

Bidwell, who had promised a publisher in Missouri he would keep a detailed journal of his travels for the guidance of future parties, wrote as they came in full view of Salt Lake:

"Started early, hoping soon to find fresh water, where we could refresh ourselves and animals, but alas! The sun beamed heavy on our heads as the day advanced, and we could see nothing before us but extensive arid plains, glimmering with heat and salt; at length the plains became so impregnated with salt that vegetation entirely ceased; the ground was in many places white as snow with salt and perfectly smooth—the midday sun made us fancy we could see timber upon the plains. We marched forward with unremitted pace till we discovered it was an illusion."

They killed their oxen for food, abandoned their wagons and equipment, pushed ahead sometimes until midnight, sending out scouts to search for water, grass, game, rivers. On September 7 the party was abandoned by its captain, Bartleson, and his original group, who found the progress too slow, depriving the rest of the company of eight riflemen for protection.

John Bidwell took over, led the party on foot through "valleys between peaks. Having ascended about half a mile, a frightful prospect opened before us: naked mountains whose summits still retained the snows perhaps of a thousand years. The winds roared—but in the deep dank gulfs which yawned on every side, profound solitude seemed to reign."

Reduced to killing their horses for food, then their mules, followed now by hostile Indians, winter began closing in. Bidwell kept alive by eating the "lights" of a wolf, led his people across more mountains, more valleys, more steep, rocky gorges, their shoes in tatters, their clothes in rags, wondering how many more days, more mountain ranges and more deserts away this chimera of California could be.

Only two white parties had made the overland crossing before them: Joseph Walker, in 1833, with a party of thirty-five to forty mountain men; Jedediah Smith, who had entered southern California in 1826 through the Old Spanish Trail, and had crossed the Sierra coming east. The chances of John Bidwell bringing the party through were lessening by the hour.

They had come into Utah by the Bear River, had circled the north end of the Great Salt Lake and struck southwest across the salt desert toward what is today Nevada, seeking the Mary's River. They stumbled into the Mary's in what is now called the Humboldt Valley, made their way down the river to a shallow swamp later called the Humboldt Sink, crossed the Desert Mountains which precede the Sierra Nevada range, then passaged a way up the savage eastern slope of the Sierra Nevada. They were lost for a week in a near delirium of staggering mountain canyons, peaks, unending summits, trying to find their way down the western range.

Bidwell brought his party in, starved, ragged, hollow-eyed but intact. He had been indefatigable, riding through the night to recover lost oxen, struggling down perpendicular cliffs with Indians to purchase their meager supply of acorns, even having the charity to welcome Bartleson back into camp when their former leader cried:

"If I ever get back to Missouri, I would gladly eat out of the trough with my pigs."

On November 1, something over seventy days from their first entrance into Utah and the Far West, Bidwell and his party saw two of their men, Jones and Kelsey, who had gone ahead a week before, come riding up the mountainside. Down in the valley they had come upon an Indian who had spoken one word of English, the one word for which they were thirsting:

"Marsh!"

Three days later, on November 4, 1841, Bidwell led his party onto the ranch of John Marsh, completing successfully the first overland journey of an emigrant party to California.

CHAPTER IV

Schoolteacher Bidwell Lands in Jail

BIOGRAPHY IS NOT ALWAYS a sweet tune, even when played by master musicians.

Dr. John Marsh received the Bidwell Party with great joy: they were old neighbors from Missouri and he was proud, as he wrote his parents in Massachusetts, that "they arrived here directly at my house with no other guide but a letter of mine.... It is an object I much desire, and have long labored for, to have this country inhabited by Americans."

For his welcoming dinner Marsh killed two pigs. He liberally used part of his small supply of seed wheat to provide each of the party with a hot baked tortilla. Grateful for the warmth of their reception, Marsh's guests proffered him gifts from their equally scanty possessions: a few cartridges, a butcher knife, an inexpensive set of surgical instruments. Marsh gave his bedroom to the Kelsey family, spread cowhides over the earthen floor to bed down as many as the adobe would hold. Before bidding his friends good night, he invited them to kill a beef to roast over their breakfast fire.

The next morning Marsh went out into the yard to find that Bidwell and his friends had mistakenly slaughtered and largely devoured his best-trained work ox. The affable host of the previous evening was replaced by an angry and acidulous stranger who cried:

"The company has already been over a hundred dollars expense to me, and God knows whether I will ever get a *real* of it or not."

Bidwell took his people into conference. They decided to leave Marsh's at once, half of them to hunt and trap in the San Joaquin Valley, the rest to seek out the town of San Jose to find work.

When fifteen of the party reached Mission San Jose they were arrested by subprefect Antonio Sunol and put in jail for entering

37

Mexican territory without a passport. Colonel Mariano Vallejo
was staying at the mission. As an admirer of Americans he was
delighted to learn that they had forced the Sierra Nevada and
intended to settle in California. As the commanding general of the
northern territory he had to take official alarm at this band of
armed men, constituting a military force as large as his effective
army! Informed that they had made the trek at Marsh's
importuning, Vallejo dispatched one of the party to bring Marsh on
the double.

Marsh went bond for fifteen members, Vallejo himself
graciously went bond for another five, whom he invited to go to his
hacienda in Sonoma, there to be housed as his guests until they
could find work or buy land. Apparently Marsh did not ask for a
passport for John Bidwell. When Bidwell found that there was no
passport for him, he quarreled with Marsh, then made his way to
the Mission San Jose. Here Sunol arrested him.

"I was marched into the calaboose and kept there three days
with nothing to eat. There were four or five Indians in the prison,
they were ironed, and they kept tolling a bell, as punishment, for
they were said to have stolen horses."

While in jail Bidwell learned that the Emmons Party which had
reached Sutter's Fort just sixteen days before had suffered no such
flea-bitten reception on the part of the authorities. They had put
themselves under the protection of Captain John Sutter who, as a
Mexican official with loosely defined powers, regally assumed that
he had the right not only to issue passports to all new arrivals, but to
make them grants of land in the Sacramento Valley as well.

Bidwell finally attracted the attention of Thomas Bowen, an
American living in San Jose, who went bond for him and secured
his passport from Vallejo. His three days in the calaboose had
embittered him. When he left for Sutter's Fort, where he was told he
could find work, he carried with him a lifetime hatred for John
Marsh; the first of a legion of quarrels between settlers which was to
turn the tranquil, gracious Far West into a land of brawling
violence.

The men of the Bidwell Party, the first caravan to make the
direct overland crossing to California, settled in the Sacramento
and San Joaquin valleys and the rich lands between Yerba Buena
and San Jose, to dig their heels resolutely into the native earth and
play, each in character, his part in the uprising, the war, the
formation of a new state and a new culture.

As 1841 drew to a close a third emigrant train reached

California. John Rowland, William Workman, Benjamin Wilson and a group of Americans living in Taos and Santa Fe under Mexican rule had been making a living as traders and trappers for some ten years, Wilson having moved down the Santa Fe Trail for purposes of his health. Some of them had been in correspondence with the leaders of the Texas uprising; there was talk of a Texas expedition coming in to take New Mexico and join it to Texas. In the summer of 1841 the government of New Mexico got wind of the conspiracy and, says Wilson:

"Under the circumstances Rowland and Workman and myself, together with about twenty other Americans, concluded it was not safe for us to remain longer."

The Workman-Rowland Party made up at Abiquiu, high in the north central part of New Mexico, a few miles from Taos. In it were two men, Isaac Given and Albert Toomes, who had arrived at Sapling Grove, Missouri, too late to join the Bidwell Party, a number of New Mexico traders as well as a group of scientists whose purpose was to study the terrain, and several Mexican women. A flock of sheep were driven along the trail to supply food.

The party left in the first week of September to avoid the worst of the desert heat, their route being sharply northwest. Within a few days they were cutting across the southwest corner of present-day Colorado. Continuing northwest, they crossed the Colorado River, then the Green and the Sevier, separated by only twenty days and two hundred miles from the suffering Bidwell train.

The Old Spanish Trail turned sharply south, following the Sevier and then the Virgin rivers through the overpowering, brilliantly hued cathedral spires of what are now Bryce and Zion National Parks, across the Mojave Desert, over Cajon Pass and down into the milk and honey and orange groves of the San Gabriel Mission, the trail constituting roughly what is now the main highway from Salt Lake City to Los Angeles.

In contrast to the harrowed diary of John Bidwell, Benjamin Wilson, who was going to California only because he wanted to catch a ship for China, confined his total description of their voyage to one sentence:

"We met with no accidents on the journey; drove sheep with us, which served us as food, and arrived in Los Angeles early in November."

Rowland took a list of his company into Los Angeles, where the authorities issued permits for the party to stay. Workman and Rowland, because they had Mexican wives and had become Mexican citizens in Taos, were permitted to buy the Puente ranch in the San Bernardino Valley; Benjamin Wilson, refusing to give up his American citizenship, still felt free to buy the Jerupa ranch, even though he was on his way to China.

In 1841 three separate emigrant trains had made their way to California. But Sir George Simpson, head of the Hudson's Bay Company, managed to get in the closing word for Great Britain. On December 20 Simpson, arriving on a round-the-world tour, observed:

"English, in some sense or other of the word, the richest portions of California must become. Either Great Britain will introduce her well-regulated freedom of all classes and colors, or the people of the United States will inundate the country with their own peculiar mixture of helpless bondage and lawless insubordination."

Sir George may not have been the most tactful visitor in California, but one must admire him for his forthrightness.

CHAPTER V

A Fort Plays Host

WHEN JOHN SUTTER LEARNED that the Bidwell Party was floundering its way down the Sierra Nevada he had loaded two mules with provisions and sent two of his men to guide the emigrants to safety at the fort. No contact had been established. Now it took a week of hard slogging for John Bidwell to make the hundred-mile journey to Sutter's, for it was the height of the rainy season.

"Streams were out of their banks, plains were inundated. Game was plentiful but hard to shoot in the rain; it was impossible to keep our old flintlock guns dry, and especially the powder dry in the pans."

The hardships of the journey were forgotten in the warmth of Sutter's welcome, with hot food, strong brandy, companionship and offer of employment. John Bidwell, who went to work for Sutter, reported, "As long as he had anything he trusted everybody with it, friends and strangers alike. Always liberal and affable, his establishment was a home to all Americans, where they could live as long as it suited them without charge. Everybody was welcome— one man or a hundred."

One of Sutter's biographers comments:

"He was one of those Falstaffian creatures that live for the sensation and tickle of being alive. His entire physique was a radiating mass in which the joy of life became contagious. Therein rested the fascination of his personality which, in its best moments was a marvel of nature, a lusty phenomenon like an enchanting cataract, a geyser or a magnificent thunderstorm."

It was an important part of Sutter's concept that he must get his fort completed and impregnable before somebody decided he had grown too strong and had better be driven out. He had sent supplies to the Bidwell Party not only to afford succor but to bring the party into New Helvetia where the men could enter his employ as trappers, mechanics, farmers, soldiers. He had no money to pay them, but he could offer them the more important compensations of food, shelter, protection and ultimately a grant of land, not altogether legally, but who in the Californio government would be strong enough to take it away?

When Bidwell reached Sutter's on January 28, 1842, he found the fort pretty well finished, with bastions above the walls to command the gateways, its Honolulu and Fort Ross cannons sitting before the entrance. Inside the fort, utilizing the back of the main wall, were a number of rooms used for sleeping, cooking and eating, a blacksmith shop, tannery, storehouse and still. At the center of the fort were corrals and dwelling houses. Sutter now had in his employ about thirty foreigners, among them Robert Ridley, a cockney who ran the boat on the river. Ridley, known as "the most facile, artistic, bare-faced liar in California," was liked by Sutter because he played a good game of whist. Perry McCoon was the overseer of the stock; William Daylor, a former sailor, was the cook; Frenchman Custot still acted as Sutter's secretary. There were two Germans, Nicolaus Allgeier and Sebastian Keyser, Pablo Gutierez, who had been with Sutter on the Santa Fe Trail, and Joel Walker, who had come from Oregon with the Emmons Party. Sutter still had his eight loyal Kanakas and the two Kanaka women. Former mission Indians made adobes; several hundred untamed braves were herded in by their chiefs to till the ground with crude pointed sticks. The Indians were fed in the open court, out of wooden V-shaped troughs which were filled with a hot gravy-mush made of bran with scraps of meat and vegetables. The Indians kneeling on either side of the troughs scooped the oozing mixture into their mouths with their hands.

Sutter sent John Bidwell to Bodega Bay to help ship the supplies from Fort Ross. Joseph Chiles of the Bidwell Party returned to Missouri to get his family, carrying Bidwell's chronicle of the journey west. Once published it spread widely the news of the women and children who had gone through safely to California.

But Chiles departed a little too soon to carry another interesting bit of news: in March of 1842 a Mexican laborer, pulling wild onions on the land of Ignacio del Valle in the northern section of the San Fernando Valley, found a pebble that contained a metal which looked like copper but proved to be gold. A number of Mexicans from Sonora explored the land. They found that by washing out the gravel of the Santa Clara River as well as the sand and earth of the land drained by the river they could placer about $2.00 worth of gold a day. Thinking there might be a rush, the prefect of Los Angeles appointed owner del Valle as justice, with the right to charge a rental fee on the land being washed.

The $2.00 a day dwindled to a few cents; few Mexicans continued with the unrewarding chore.

CHAPTER VI

The Scene Shifts to Colorado, "a Legal Fiction"

A COLORADO HISTORIAN MAINTAINS that "Colorado is a legal fiction because it has no natural boundaries." It was assembled from portions of four existing Territories: Kansas to the east, Utah to the west, Wyoming to the north, and New Mexico to the south.

Claimed by Spain through Columbus's discovery of the New World, a corner of the land was possibly touched by Coronado in 1541-42 in his futile search for the Seven Golden Cities of Cibola.

The first documented expeditions of white men into Colorado were led by Juan Archuleta in 1664 and Juan Uribarri in 1706, with Spanish soldiers and Indian allies pursuing runaway Indians from New Mexico. The Spanish called the area Santo Domingo, but it was the title they gave to the *color*ful river on the western slope of the Rockies: Colorado: Spanish for red, which emerged as its name.

When France claimed Colorado because of the explorations of Joliet in 1673 and La Salle in 1682, a group of twenty French Canadians trying to reach Santa Fe made its way in 1706 to the foothills of the Colorado Rockies. Tragedy struck a Spanish military force under Pedro Villasur in 1720 when almost the entire expedition of forty-two Spaniards and sixty Indians was wiped out by a surprise Pawnee and French attack.

The French began a search for the treasure of gold, silver and furs which Coronado had failed to find: in 1724 Bourgmont traveled from the Illinois country to the eastern border; in 1739 the Mallet brothers came up from Santa Fe to eastern Colorado. In 1763 the French, defeated in the Indian Wars, withdrew from the sea, leaving it in Spanish possession. In July of 1776, while a group of intrepid political explorers in Philadelphia, Pennsylvania, were signing papers which outlined a hazardous voyage into an unmapped socio-economic wilderness, the first real exploring party left Santa Fe under Padres Dominguez and Escalante, assigned by the Spanish government to establish a land route to the California missions.

Escalante set out to penetrate the wilderness north and west of Santa Fe, camping along the San Juan River. This spot he called Our Lady of the Snows, the first-named site in Colorado of which the date is known. The party crossed the Grand Mesa and the Colorado River, then made its way into Utah, and got as far as Utah Lake before being turned back by the cold and the mountains: thus establishing, in 1776, the first half of the Spanish Trail.

In 1803 the United States made the Louisiana Purchase and three years later Captain Zebulon Pike was sent into Colorado by the army with twenty-three men to establish peaceful relations with the Indians, map the southwest boundary of the Louisiana Purchase, which seemed to cut through the middle of the Colorado Rockies, but more importantly to make a scientific survey of the new land: its geography, botany, population, mineral resources, navigation, routes: instructions similar to those the army would issue to Lieutenant John Charles Fremont in 1842. Pike came in view of the Rockies on November 15, the first American to see the majestic mountains, and on November 23 he built the first

American structure on Colorado soil, a breastwork close to the present site of Pueblo. He sighted what he called "Grand Peak," spent a week trying to scale it, failed, but later had it named after him. His expedition toured the Royal Gorge, South Park, followed the Arkansas River northwest, and suffered a frozen, crippling experience in crossing the Sangre de Cristo Mountains. The well-written account of his journey was published in 1810 and aroused interest in Colorado not only in the eastern United States and Great Britain, but Europe as well.

The second army expedition sent out by the United States Topographical Engineers was headed by Major Long and Lieutenant Swift, both experienced map makers, accompanied by a zoologist, a botanist, a naturalist and a landscape painter. This party of twenty entered Colorado at its northeast corner, paralleled the South Platte, sighted Long's Peak and followed a trail southward through what is now Denver and Colorado Springs. When Long designated the eastern part of Colorado, right up to the foothills, as "The Great American Desert," and declared it "almost wholly unfit for cultivation," he discouraged migration westward for almost three decades.

The period between Major Long's expedition of 1820 and Lieutenant Fremont's of 1842 is dominated by the epochal story of the hunters and trappers who, in search of ever fresh sources of beaver skins, explored and created trails through Colorado that would have taken twenty or more army expeditions to duplicate. The story of early Colorado *is* the story of these mountain men: Jedediah Smith, Jim Bridger, Thomas "Broken Hand" Fitzpatrick, Kit Carson, William Ashley, the Sublettes, Joseph Reddeford Walker, James Ohio Pattie, the Bent brothers, Antoine Robidoux, Caleb Greenwood, Vasquez, St. Vrain, Peter Skene Ogden were the greatest woodsmen since Daniel Boone and his confreres opened the Kentucky wilderness. Either working for themselves or attached to the big fur companies, squaw men, they spent most of the year in the wilderness, emerging in summer with their bundles of valuable pelts at one of their trading posts or open-air rendezvous, to "barter for food, liquor, trinkets for their wives, and enjoy a week of wild carousal" before returning to the solitude of mountain lakes and streams for another year of danger, adventure and, of necessity, exploration. At these summer fairs there were sometimes as many as two hundred whites and two thousand Indians.

The posts, serving as forts against hostile Indian attack, were always built by commercial traders who brought in goods from the East: flour, sugar, coffee, cloth, guns, knives, whiskey, tobacco, which they traded for furs. In the early years beaver skins, worth $6.00 to $8.00 apiece, buffalo robes $3.00 to $4.00 apiece, were bartered for one pint of whiskey, particularly to the Indians who, as the Arapaho told Colonel Dodge in 1835, listed the desirable things in life as:

"First, whiskey; second, tobacco; third, horses; fourth, guns; fifth, women."

Between 1826 and 1840 there were eight important trading posts: Bent's, El Pueblo along the Arkansas River, on a fairly straight line in the southeast section; a couple of hundred miles north, on the South Platte were Vasquez's, Sarpy's, Lupton's and St. Vrain's; in the extreme northwest corner Davy Crockett's, close to the Utah border; and Uncompahgre on the Gunnison. Out of these eight forts were sent many millions of dollars worth of furs and skins, to New York, Boston, Paris, Berlin; so many, in fact, that the beaver and buffalo were depleted and the era of the mountain man, the trading post, the rendezvous was on its way to extinction.

This chain of trading posts was roughly equivalent to the chain of Spanish padre-built missions of California; though they did not last, the adobe walls crumbling to ruins, the posts were Colorado's first settlements. Around them, as around the missions, towns sometimes grew. If the mountain men were through as hunters there was an equally important role awaiting them: the only whites who knew every mile of the mountains and streams of this most easterly portion of the Far West, they would become the indispensable guides to the army expeditions and emigrant trains headed for California.

Colorado was one of the wildest, most awe-inspiring and savagely beautiful geographical areas on the face of the earth; in 1842 its mountains, as staggering as the Swiss Alps, would finally be breasted and settled.

CHAPTER VII

"There is no man to whom I owe as much as Fremont"

ON JULY, 9, 1842, there arrived in northeastern Colorado the most controversial character ever to fight his way into the Far West: a small, lean, handsome, wiry, indefatigable, melancholy-eyed, near genius who, a full century after his part had been played, was still raising dust storms of printed partisanship among biographers.

Lieutenant John Charles Fremont, of the United States Topographical Corps, twenty-nine years old, married to the most brilliant girl in Washington City, Jessie Benton, daughter of the western-expansionist senator from Missouri, Thomas Hart Benton, was now leading a third government expedition into the West. Unlike Captain Zebulon Pike and Major Long, who carried trained soldiers with them, Lieutenant Fremont was the only army man in his expedition. The balance of his party, assembled in St. Louis and on the Mississippi River, consisted of civilians paid by the army: a topographer, a hunter, nineteen French voyageurs, all experienced fur trappers; and most important, a medium-height, broad-shouldered, clear-eyed mountain man, the contemporary and equal of Jim Bridger and Broken Hand Fitzpatrick: Kit Carson, who served as guide. Between Fremont and Carson there sprang up a deep and abiding friendship.

Fremont said, "Carson and Truth are one."

Carson said, "There is no man to whom I owe as much as Fremont."

Together, during three expeditions filled with discovery, danger and violent death, they did more to explore, map and publicize the routes to the Far West than any combination in the expansionist years.

John Charles Fremont was the illegitimate son of a Royalist

French émigré teacher and a high-born Richmond, Virginia, woman married to an aged Revolutionary War hero named Pryor. Fremont was born in Savannah, Georgia, and grew up in poverty. A brilliant student in scientific subjects, he became an assistant with the U.S. Topographical Corps on a railroad mapping expedition, and another to the Indian frontiers of the Cherokees. Through a friendship with Secretary of War Poinsett he became a second lieutenant in the Corps in Washington City where he was trained by Joseph Nicollet, the country's ablest cartographer, who took him as an assistant on an expedition into the Indian country of the upper Missouri.

By the time he was twenty-seven, he and sixteen-year-old Jessie Benton were deeply in love. Separated by an order, arranged for by Senator Benton, to explore and map the Des Moines River in Iowa Territory, Fremont returned six months later to marry Jessie without her parents' consent. Senator Benton stormed, then welcomed his son-in-law into the Benton home, westward-expansion center of Washington City. Most of the Congress was indifferent to acquiring such distant territories as Texas, Oregon and California. Senator Benton pushed through a bill to map the route to Oregon, and John Fremont was named to head the expedition.

What the Congress and President Tyler did not know was that neither Benton nor his dynamic young son-in-law had the slightest intention of stopping at a map for Oregon. They would not be content until they had discovered and established new routes along which thousands of American families could travel to settle the Far West and claim it for the United States.

Fremont spent less than a week in Colorado on his first expedition. He wanted to explore the Rockies for a shorter, quicker pass into California, but his orders obliged him to turn sharply north in order to map South Pass, above the present Colorado-Utah state lines. He determined to return the following year. Upon that iron-willed determination much would hinge, including the heroic Mormon trek to Great Salt Lake: for when Brigham Young, ill with mountain fever, rose up on one elbow in the lead wagon, in the hills above the Salt Desert, and said to the driver:

"This is the place!" he meant, in part:

"This is the place described by Lieutenant Fremont."

CHAPTER VIII

Commodore Jones Goes out on a Yardarm

A MONTH AFTER John Fremont left the northern border of Colorado there appeared in San Diego Harbor the last of the Mexico City governors for a remote and increasingly troublesome colony: handsome General Micheltorena, who had fought under General Santa Anna, now President of Mexico, against the Texans. Micheltorena arrived with an army of some three hundred fifty men on three ships, largely in reply to the realistic reports of Colonel Mariano Vallejo to the effect that he had had no military force large enough to repel the Emmons or Bidwell parties, or the larger expeditions reported on their way. California, insisted Colonel Vallejo, could no longer be held for Mexico without trained, armed and well-financed troops. But when the *Chato* unloaded its soldiers and their families, one of the Americans watching the operation gasped:

"They presented a state of wretchedness and misery unequaled. Not one individual among them possessed a jacket or pantaloon, but naked and like the savage Indians, they concealed their nudity with dirty miserable blankets. The greater portion of them had been charged with the crime of either murder or theft."

Aside from having no arms with which to soldier, a trade for which they had no stomach, the troops had no commissary and Micheltorena no funds with which to feed them. Soon the hungry legion had spread over southern California like a plague of locusts, stripping the countryside bare of food, a task for which the anguished Angelenos claimed they had plenty of stomach, indeed.

The Mexicans were not the only ones making a show of military strength in the fall of 1842; the Pacific Ocean was awash with warships: the United States was represented by five ships with one hundred sixteen guns; the English by four ships with one hundred four guns; the French by eight ships with two hundred two guns.

Commodore Thomas Ap Catesby Jones of the U.S.S. *United States*, in charge of the American flotilla, had orders from the Secretary of the Navy:

"The unsettled state of the nations bordering on the coast included in your command, renders it necessary to protect the interests of the United States in that quarter." However, "Nothing but the necessity of prompt and effectual protection to the honor and interests of the United States will justify you in committing any act of hostility."

Commodore Jones was out on a yardarm: if he let the prize of California fall into British or French hands he could be court-martialed for the treason of inaction; if he moved boldly in to seize California he would even more quickly be fed to the sharks.

In the beginning of September, returning with his flotilla from a cruise, Commodore Jones was faced with three decisive pieces of evidence: the British fleet was sailing under sealed orders; a letter from the United States consul at Mazatlan informed Commodore Jones that a war with Mexico over the annexation of Texas was about to break; a Boston paper carried the story that Mexico had ceded California to England to cover a $7,000,000 debt. Commodore Jones conferred with the United States consul at Lima, then with the commanders of his three ships. All agreed:

"Strike! Strike swiftly!"

On October 19, 1842 Commodore Jones reached Monterey. He was intensely relieved to find that the British had not preceded him. Believing that Micheltorena's army marching by the overland route was within close range, the commodore sent one of his captains ashore to demand the surrender of the government.

The Californios had no armed troops in their capital. The two most astonished and hurt people on shore were Governor Alvarado and Thomas O. Larkin: Alvarado because he was being stripped of office; Larkin because he believed his countrymen were behaving in a highhanded fashion.

At midnight Larkin accompanied two Californio commissioners to Commodore Jones's ship. The articles of capitulation were drawn up, Larkin serving as interpreter. At nine the next morning they were signed; at eleven, Commodore Jones sent one hundred fifty sailors and marines ashore. The Mexican flag was lowered at the fort. The American flag was raised, the first to fly in the Far West.

Commodore Jones was happy that the conquest had been

bloodless. His happiness was short-lived. Thomas Larkin showed the commodore recent newspapers and commercial letters from Mexico, proving that Mexico and the United States were waging a cold war rather than a hot war.

"This change in the aspect of international affairs called for prompt action on my part," cried Commodore Jones. To the Californios he said, in effect:

"Ooops, sorry!"

He issued orders to haul down the American flag. The Mexican flag was raised in its place. To show there were no hard feelings, Jones had his guns fire a salute of honor.

Thus, in October of 1842, the United States was in possession of California for about thirty hours. Larkin, who believed with all the passion of his neat and orderly business soul that California could be purchased peaceably from Mexico, returned to his sumptuous home, relieved. Commodore Jones wrote:

"I may forfeit my commission and all that I have acquired in seven and thirty years' devotion to my country's service."

According to eyewitness accounts, the Californios appeared more surprised and pained by the return than by the capture; Alvarado's treasury was empty, all salaries seriously in arrears. When the natives of southern California heard of the conquest they asked only two questions:

"Will they meddle with our ranches? Will they interfere with our religion?"

The high-spirited Californio women were far more resentful than their men, the female of the species frequently being more touchy and violent than the male when it comes to causes and loyalties.

As the military commandant of the northern section, Colonel Vallejo should have been outraged at Commodore Jones. Officially he was. But when the commodore made a trip to Sonoma with a group of his officers, Vallejo found that he liked the American naval commander enormously, entertaining him with a full day of rodeo and Indian dances, and forever after spoke highly of the first American officer to claim California for the United States.

It was Governor Micheltorena in Los Angeles who had the final word: after keeping Commodore Jones dangling for three months in anterooms in Monterey and Yerba Buena, the governor decided to open the New Year of 1843 by permitting the commodore to submit his official apology. On January 19 the Mexican government gave the American officers a formal ball of forgiveness.

Governor Micheltorena asked as reparations for the grievous

insult $10,000 in cash, eighty new military uniforms, and a set of instruments from the band on board the U.S.S. *United States*, thus ending the untimely incident on a note of musical comedy.

CHAPTER IX

£1,000,000 to Drive out the Americans

ABOUT JUNE 20, 1843, a twenty-four-year-old lawyer by the name of Lansford W. Hastings, from Mount Vernon, Ohio, a bright, handsome, strong-jawed, fast-talking opportunist, reached the northern California border, where the Shasta River crosses into Oregon. The previous spring Hastings had turned up at Elm Grove, Kansas, twenty miles west of Independence and joined the Reverend Elijah White's party of approximately one hundred sixty people starting for Oregon. Within a few days brash, aggressive Hastings, a tenderfoot with little or no frontier experience, had managed to replace the veteran Dr. White as head of the expedition! However, a few miles out of Fort Laramie, Dr. White hired Broken Hand Fitzpatrick to lead them to the Willamette Valley in Oregon.

The following spring Hastings was moving energetically about Oregon, successfully selling a California he had never seen to a group of fifty-three settlers, twenty-nine of them armed men, the rest women and children.

"Myself again having been honored with command," he wrote, the party set out on June 1 with a guide for Sutter's Fort. Somewhere on the Rogue River, two or three days distance from the border, they were met by a party from California driving a herd of cattle north to sell. Their stories of life in California were so discouraging that Hastings lost his guide and almost half his party. Not at all abashed, he followed the route used by Emmons in 1841 through the present Grant's pass, down a tributary of the Rogue

River, skirted Shasta Lake, followed the Sacramento River flowing south out of the lake until he reached Sutter's.

The journey had taken forty traveling days. Where Emmons had managed to avoid fights with the Indians, Hastings had several battles, one on the Shasta, another in the Sacramento Valley, one of his men emerging with an arrow in his back. Nonetheless he made a safe crossing. With nine hundred people migrating from the Missouri border to Oregon in the year of 1843, the Hastings passage not only meant that many more emigrants to Oregon would essay the southern journey to a warmer, drier California; it also established Lansford W. Hastings as a leader and guide...at a future cost of human suffering unequaled in the annals of man's anguish.

When the party reached the bank of the Sacramento River opposite Sutter's on July 10, a young couple impetuously crossed the river to have Sutter marry them instanter; the balance of the party made the crossing the next day, to be heartily received by Sutter who:

"Rendered every one of the party every assistance in his power."

Captain John Sutter was by now an outsized figure on the landscape. His fort was complete, a marvel in the wilderness, he was governing a self-sustaining community with blacksmiths, gunsmiths, carpenters, shoemakers, a gristmill, weaving shops. He was known in the East not only as host and helper of Americans coming into California, the growth in his power indicated by the belief that he had the right to marry people, but as overlord of an empire.

Yet Sutter, with all his military prowess, imagined and real, had been able to conquer neither the mosquitoes, the fleas, nor that most formidable of all bloodsucking insects, debt: like most visionaries he had overextended himself. The money he owed to Larkin in Monterey or Nathan Spear in Yerba Buena, or Vallejo, he was not being pressed for: these men liked him, believed in the importance of his empire in the wilderness. But Sutter had suffered an intense year of drought and had no grain to pay the Russians; his tannery was not yet working successfully, the brandy of his distillery was still raw. He had accomplished a miracle of building in three years, creating the beginnings of modern-day Sacramento in the midst of an unexplored virgin forest; but the larger he grew, the more he fell in arrears.

Perhaps Sutter used these debts as an excuse for not sending for his wife and children in Switzerland; an untoward accident had forced the Sutters into a marriage neither of them had wanted or enjoyed. A journal written in German by Heinrich Lienhard, Sutter's major-domo during this time, insinuates that both of the Kanaka women whom Sutter had brought from Honolulu had served as substitute wives, while one of them, Manaiki, was said to have borne him several children. Lienhard also suggests that Sutter had several children by a number of the squaws at the fort. In contrast to John Chamberlain, the Irish blacksmith of the fort, however, Sutter seems abstemious: Chamberlain apparently married nineteen Indian women in swift succession.

If John Sutter did not meet his payments, the Russians could move into the Sacramento Valley and take over the fort, establishing a new base in the Far West; this time they would have rich agricultural lands behind them and the strategic position to repel all American migration coming south from Oregon or west from Missouri.

Sutter also had William Rae, representative of the Hudson's Bay Company, on his mind. Rae was being a bit stuffy about the money Sutter owed his company and had started legal action against him in an effort to attach either his boats or produce, a step which the residents considered most unfriendly and considerably less than cricket. Rae had been heard to say, while in his cups, that it had "cost the Hudson's Bay Company £75,000 to drive the Yankee traders from the Columbia" and that they would "drive them from California if it cost a million."

The international situation now seemed to depend on how much wheat John Sutter would reap and harvest before his next payment to the Russians came due; and how successfully he could keep the Hudson's Bay Company from possessing his fort.

CHAPTER X

Wagons? Impossible!

ON MARCH 1, 1843, John Charles Fremont submitted the report of his expedition along the South Platte River in Colorado to Colonel Abert of the Topographical Corps, and to the Congress. The House not only ordered the report published but authorized a second expedition, this time to go all the way to Oregon on its combined map-making, exploring voyage.

Fremont now stepped forth with considerably increased confidence and power: this time Congress had authorized him "to connect the reconnaissance of 1842 with the surveys of Commander Wilkes on the coast, so as to give a connected survey of the interior of our continent." Commander Wilkes had mapped San Francisco Bay and the Sacramento River as far as Sutter's Fort.

Fremont, without the knowledge or consent of the Topographical Corps, took along a twelve-pound howitzer. Senator Benton believed war with Mexico would in all likelihood begin by the time Fremont reached California; and Fremont had every intention of leading his group of thirty-nine armed, hard-bitten frontiersmen into action.

But at the moment there was exploratory work to be done: to find and chart a route through the Rockies of central Colorado which would save the emigrant trains many hard days of travel. On July 4 he and his men set out almost due south, along the comparatively easy route which now connects Greeley, Denver, Colorado Springs and Pueblo, remaining in American territory, but carefully studying the mountains to the west which led to the Mexican holdings that extended one thousand miles to the Pacific.

Colorado was beginning to make its transition from an outpost country to that of settled communities: Fort Lupton, ten miles down the river from St. Vrain's, was a well-stocked farm, growing vegetables, raising cattle, hogs, turkeys and chickens; at the other end of Fremont's trek south, where Boiling Spring River enters the Arkansas, Fremont found a fair-sized community of former hunters and trappers who were farming and ranching, having successfully albeit reluctantly made the transition from mountain men of the thirties to settlers of the forties.

Here Fremont was joined by Kit Carson. He had also hired Broken Hand Fitzpatrick. Neither Carson nor Fitzpatrick had heard of a pass through the Rockies. Fremont sent Fitzpatrick with the wagons and howitzer along the northern route to Fort Hall, while he, Carson and twelve men turned west. For five days they struggled through "scenery very wild and beautiful. Towering mountains rose round about, their sides sometimes dark with forests of pine, and sometimes with lofty precipices. The green river bottom was covered with a wilderness of flowers."

On August 1 they crossed into what is present-day Wyoming.

A month after Fremont withdrew his expedition northward, the most important emigrant party of 1843 came southward from Fort Hall, in present Idaho, into the extreme northeast corner of Nevada, headed for the Mary's River. The party was led by one of the greatest mountain men of his era, Joseph Walker, who ten years earlier had explored the region west of Salt Lake forcing a passage through the mountains to the coast. Walker was now assaying the task of leading a caravan of heavy, slow-moving wagons across the salt desert trail and wall of mountains that had been traversed by the Bidwell Party on foot.

The daring idea was conceived by Joseph B. Chiles, who had crossed with Bidwell in 1841, returned over the Sierra Nevada in 1842. He bought an entire mill, boxed the separate parts to be loaded into a wagon, and then assembled a party of about fifty to accompany him on his return to California. Chiles's wife had died, a misfortune which had sent him wandering to find a new land and a new life just as ill-health, business failure, lack of opportunity, boredom or sheer hunger for travel and adventure, as well as free lands, would send so many thousands.

When the Chiles Party reached Fort Hall it was late in the season, August 27. Chiles, resolving to lighten the expedition, decided to take nine men with him on horseback, go northwest to Fort Boise, then cut southwest through a route suggested by the hunters, coming into California at its northeast corner. He entrusted his wagon, with everything he owned in the world invested in the disassembled mill, to Walker's care, to be brought

into Central California over the route which Walker had pioneered
a decade before, a journey of a thousand miles in country through
which nothing larger than a horse or slower than a man had ever
been taken.

Joseph Reddeford Walker was now forty-four. He had been
born in Virginia just before his family moved west to Tennessee. In
1832 he had gone to work for Captain Bonneville as his chief
lieutenant in an effort to compete with the American, Hudson's Bay
and Rocky Mountain Fur companies. Bonneville sent Walker from
the Green River rendezvous to explore the Great Salt Lake and
country beyond, country never before seen by a white man, and
instructed him to try to make his way to California to find new
sources of fur. The clerk of the expedition said of Joseph Walker
that:

"To explore unknown regions was his chief delight."

Now, in 1843, Walker led his caravan around the north side of
the Great Salt Lake to the Mary's River, westward to the Sink, then
due south to Walker Lake, after which he cut west into California
and followed the barren, terror-striking eastern slope of the Sierra
Nevada where it is said even of the Indians that in order to survive a
man must be able to sleep in the shadow of his arrow. After
traveling the base of the mountains for days, and hauling his party
up the rocky slopes to Owens Lake, Walker now feared for the very
existence of the people under his care. He ordered the first
immigrant wagons to enter California to be abandoned, burying
the parts of Joseph B. Chiles's mill in the sands of the Owens Valley
desert, not to be found again until some miners accidentally
unearthed them twenty-five years later.

At last on Christmas Day the party found what they described as
"a little paradise" at the headwaters of a tributary of the Salinas
River, with grass and game and water. They descended into the
Salinas Valley, found their way to the Gilroy rancho, delegated
Walker to secure their passports, then scattered throughout central
and northern California.

About October 20 Chiles and his party of nine men had reached
Goose Lake in the northeast corner of California, moved rapidly
down the Pit River to the Sacramento River and by November 10
were in Sutter's Fort, having pioneered a new and relatively safe
route to California . . . but not for wagons, any more than Walker
had found his eastern slope of the Sierra Nevada navigable for the
big slow, heavy, clumsy land schooners.

That stupendous drama was still a few years in the future.

CHAPTER XI

The Men Match the Mountains

Two mornings after Christmas, Lieutenant John C. Fremont stood on the southern border of Oregon. To the east lay the Oregon Trail and a quick, safe journey homeward; to the south lay the unexplored deserts and mountains of what is now western Nevada. His party of twenty-five men had been away from home for nine months, they were hungry, many of their pack animals had died or been stolen by Indians; all of their topographical orders had been carried out. If he turned homeward, his job as cartographer would be brilliantly completed.

But New Year's Day of 1844 found him slogging southward through harsh, cutting, black volcanic rock. He was a man of savage insistence, as well as a sensitive poet.

"We continued down the valley, between a dry-looking black ridge on the left and a more snowy and high one on the right. Our road was bad along the bottom, being broken by gullies and impeded by sage. The soil in many places consists of a fine powdery sand, covered with a saline efflorescence, and the general character of the country's desert."

The next two weeks were spent in this frightening deathlike country until the party reached a thirty-five-mile-long lake which Fremont called Pyramid Lake, and from which his men gorged themselves on salmon trout. On this newly garnered strength they pushed through to the present site of Reno, and south of that to Carson River, once again suffering from empty innards and rock-torn feet: probably the lowest point of their morale.

Fremont, who had the gift for histrionics as well as heroics, chose this moment to tell his tattered troop that they were going to force a crossing of the Sierra Nevada westward to the Sacramento

Valley. The men had only to raise their eyes to see what Allan Nevins, Fremont's biographer, so graphically describes as:

"This mighty range, in places fourteen thousand feet high, rising precipitously from the east, steep on steep, to the point where, in January, all is silent frozen waste of snow and rock, as bleak, empty and bitter as the Himalayas themselves."

No white man and probably no Indian had ever crossed the Sierra Nevada in the depth of its winter, a fact which Fremont very well knew.

Not a man demurred; Kit Carson would have guided Fremont to hell and back, had his friend said it must be done. On January 19 they plunged boldly into the mountains. As they came into Antelope Valley, beyond which the ice barrier of the main range shot upward through the sky, friendly Indians warned them not to attempt the crossing. The snow was impassable.

Impassable and impossible, these were fighting words in the lexicon of John Fremont. On February 2 he gave the order to start upward. As though he did not have trouble enough, he was still dragging the army howitzer! His instruments told him that only seventy miles directly west lay Sutter's Fort.

It was to prove one of the longest seventy miles in the history of exploration: within two days the trail that the men were hacking out was strewn with packs and personal possessions. Even the animals could go no farther. An old Indian warned them:

"Rock upon rock, snow upon snow; even if you get over the snow, you will not be able to get down the mountains."

Their last Indian guide deserted. It became clear to Fremont that he could not take his train through until he had found a trail and a pass. The next morning, leaving behind all of the party except Kit Carson and Broken Hand Fitzpatrick, these three indestructible ones went reconnoitering on snowshoes, crossed an open basin in subfreezing cold, moved relentlessly upward for about ten miles against icy barricades.

The men matched the mountains.

Through sheer will power they forced their way. Finally:

"Far below us, dimmed by the distance, was a large snowless valley, bounded on the western side, at a distance of about a hundred miles, by a low range of mountains which Carson recognized with delight as the mountains bordering on the coast."

In the lesser distance was Marsh's Mount Diablo. When Carson saw it he exclaimed:

"There is the little mountain. It is fifteen years since I saw it; but I am just as sure as if I had seen it yesterday."

It took twenty days to bring the animals and supplies up to the peak. The men suffered from snow blindness, from the exhaustion of carving a road out of icy mountains, from such starvation that, inured to a lifetime of hardship as they were, they were reduced to eating their pet dog, Klamath.

One month from the day of the first attack on the salient, Fremont and Carson led the emaciated expedition through to the Sacramento Valley and Sutter's Fort, "two human skeletons wearing Scotch caps."

He had made the first winter crossing of the Sierra Nevada. His only loss was the cannon, which not even the army had been able to get him to abandon; it had had to be left behind in the snows.

John Fremont's forcing of the Sierra Nevada was more than an act of individual heroism; it was a kinetic moment in history, moving the young lieutenant and his country toward what they both thought of as their "manifest destiny." What Fremont could do with an exhausted, unprovisioned band of volunteer voyageurs, the United States Army could do any time it wished! The mountains were no longer insuperable. The last barrier had been breached.

And, for the first time since Commodore Jones had come ashore at Monterey in October of 1842 to accept the premature surrender of the Far West, the United States armed forces were represented on California soil.

Captain John Sutter immediately set about provisioning the twenty-five men, supplying them not only with food but with cattle and fresh mounts, horseshoes, bridles, pack saddles. He made a present to Fremont of a beautiful white horse called Sacramento.

Fremont could allow himself and his men only two weeks of rest; he was in California without passport or permit, and word had been brought that Governor Micheltorena was sending his military commander, Jose Castro, to the fort to investigate Fremont's reason for being there.

John Fremont was only three hundred miles more illegal at this point than he had been when he stepped across the Oregon border into Nevada: according to the maps of the time, California extended eastward at least halfway through present Colorado. In fact, as three California historians have pointed out, Underhill, Goodwin and Scherer, *California and the entire Far West were one and the same*.

"This 'island' of California had no eastern boundary until the California government set it up in 1849. Though California was roughly thought of as extending to or through the Sierra Nevada, actually that natural boundary was not a legal, mapped, or designated boundary. The Fremont-Preuss map of '48 includes most of the Far West in the California area, and at the Constitutional Convention at Monterey in 1849 there was a strong movement, almost successful, to include all of Nevada and a sufficient portion of Utah to include Salt Lake and the twenty thousand Mormons living in the Salt Lake Valley. Actually California extended to the very foothills of the Rocky Mountains. ..."

Fremont's official instructions were to map and explore. The western-expansionist group had urged him to learn how large an American force would be needed to capture the country. He discreetly stayed away from the California coastline, about which the Mexican authorities were sensitive, and made his way south along the western base of the Sierra Nevada. An Indian guide told him of an unused pass, the Tehachapi. On approximately April 1, 1844, he and his troop once again crossed the mountains, this time heading eastward.

The next time he would move into California with a well-armed band of sixty-five to seventy trained men, to play a stormy, disputed, decisive role in its conquest.

CHAPTER XII

Larkin Becomes Consul with a Gold-headed Cane

WITHIN A MATTER OF hours after Fremont's party raised its last cloud as it left the eastern Sierra and moved out into the sand and sage flats of Nevada there arrived in Monterey an official document naming Thomas O. Larkin as United States consul in California. This was the first acknowledgment on the part of the United States that there was a government existing in California; and more important, that anything going on in that aboriginal region could conceivably require the presence of an American official, though

the British had named James Forbes to be their consul at San Jose
in 1844, and a little later the French instructed one of their officials
to proceed to Monterey and open an office of the French
government there.

April 2, 1844, was the proudest day of Thomas O. Larkin's life;
he was convinced that now, with the government in his hands, he
could in time effect a peaceable transition to American ownership.
He so deeply loved his job that, although the spending of money
was to him an exquisite mixture of pleasure and pain, he
nonetheless wrote to his friend Alfred Robinson, in New York,
asking Robinson to order him a resplendent uniform with gold
epaulets. Apparently he did not stipulate what kind of uniform,
there being none for a consul; just any handsome uniform would
do. The symbol of authority in California had always been a cane,
and Robinson, who dearly loved a practical joke, ordered Consul
Larkin two canes with solid gold heads, the bill for which elicited
screams of mortal agony that could be heard all the way from
Monterey to New York.

Consul Larkin's duty was to represent the United States in all
the land between the Pacific coast and the Rocky Mountains, the
southern border of Oregon and San Diego. While his chief task was
to facilitate trade he soon found himself officiating at marriages
and funerals of the Protestant residents, sitting as judge over
quarrels between Americans on ships on the high seas. His
immediate duty became the caring for sick sailors off American
vessels, many of whom he took into his own home, literally feeding
them out of his own pocket. When their number grew too large he
built the first hospital in California. His major difficulty was that
there were no doctors available.

Dr. John Marsh's informal entry into the profession without
benefit of the Hippocratic Oath had been followed by two more
practitioners: Joe Meek, a colorful Rocky Mountain character,
said to his companions while coming down from Oregon with an
emigrant train in 1843:

"Boys, when I get down among the greasers, I'm going to be a
doctor."

Though Meek could neither read nor write, his friends promptly
called him "Doctor" Meek, and when he reached Monterey he
found a following: for in one of his first cases, that of a Mexican boy
who had cut off his toe with an ax, Meek stuck the boy's toe back on
with mud, and it grew.

The second to enter the field was G.M. de Sandels Waseurtz,
who wrote a colorful description of his journey through California

in 1842 and 1843. Waseurtz was a mining engineer who visited with John Sutter in 1843, studied the countryside, and informed his totally disbelieving host, who had long ago heard the Indian's tale of Coloma's Lake of Gold ruled over by a carnivorous monster, that there was unquestionably gold in the region of the Sacramento. He then went on to Monterey, which he described as "not yet grown out of its quilts, though the inhabitants, both Creole and foreigners, are a very kind, hospitable, and merry sort." Here, because of his botanizing and mineralizing, the rumor got around that Waseurtz was a "medico."

"I had studied the *Materia Medica*, I could look grave and wanted business, so I became a doctor. I laid down some broad principles, one was to charge well, the other, never to prescribe anything that was not disagreeable to take."

The California Medical Association now consisted of "Doctor" John Marsh, "Doctor" Joe Meek, and "Doctor" G.M. Waseurtz, all of them charging high prices and apparently only mildly impeding nature in its cures.

By one of the ironic coincidences which turns history into fascinating melodrama, at the same moment that Thomas O. Larkin became United States consul for California, Governor Micheltorena issued the most forward-looking set of ordinances the long-neglected territory had known since the progressive regime of the Spanish Governor Borica in 1800. He ordered the establishment of the first public school system in the Far West, with schools at San Diego, Los Angeles, Santa Barbara, San Jose, Yerba Buena and Sonoma. Attendance was compulsory for both sexes between the ages of six and eleven, the parents to be fined in case of absence; the teachers' salaries were set at $480 a year. He passed laws regulating excessive medical fees, declared Yerba Buena an official port of entry, where foreign ships could pay fair landing fees and duties, and tried to put an end to smuggling and the bribery of Mexican officials. He also returned the missions to the padres, though for exclusively religious purposes, in an effort to stop the beautiful buildings from falling into utter ruin.

Micheltorena is the last of the Mexican governors to play an important part in the pageant of the Far West. He was probably the handsomest man to enter California, tall, slender, with a warm personality in spite of a military bearing, gray kindly eyes, light complexion and brown hair; wealthy, well read, well disposed to all the people under him. Had the Mexican government been seriously interested in retaining California, had it provided Micheltorena with an army of one hundred well-armed, trained soldiers instead of convicts and marauders, the conquest of the Far West might have changed radically in character.

In honor of becoming an official port, and Governor Micheltorena's appropriating the sum of $800 for the building of a customs house, the fifty residents clustered along the little cove of Yerba Buena petitioned to become a *pueblo* or town. By 1844 Yerba Buena had only a dozen houses. It was not merely the cold fog, nor was it the lack of vessels coming through the strait; more and more whaling vessels were anchoring in the bay though they preferred the north side of the strait where there was good water, abundant wood, proximity to the ranchos and fresh food. Nor was it that the inhabitants were too somber, for Marsh in an irascible moment described their chief activity as:

"Getting drunk and running up and down hills."

Richard Henry Dana, in a book called *Two Years Before the Mast*, recently published in Boston, was saying:

"The Californians are an idle, thriftless people, and can make nothing for themselves. The country abounds in grapes, yet they buy bad wine made in Boston, and buy shoes made of their own hides and carried twice around the Horn."

Somehow the town had not caught on: it had become mainly a trading outpost for the Hudson's Bay Company, which American and European settlers did not enjoy. The Mission Dolores, four to five miles out from the cove, was falling into ruins, the presidio overlooking the strait, built by the Spaniards in 1776, had been pilfered almost down to its foundation by people wanting free adobe brick and lumber for their own buildings.

It was not a bad place in which to settle; there were wild strawberry patches on the hills out toward the ocean, and each spring when the berries ripened families would come in from as far south as San Jose, and Sonoma to the north, and the entire town of Yerba Buena would pack its blankets and cooking apparatus and move out onto the dunes for a week of picnicking and dancing and whatever entertainment could be provided by the officers of the ships in port. Down the peninsula there was good horseback riding and hunting for deer and bear. On the same block in which William Rae had his headquarters for the Hudson's Bay Company (he and his wife and daughter lived behind the store), there was a public house with a billiard room and bar owned by Jean Vioget, a Swiss, where the single men of the town gathered in the evenings to be

joined by captains and supercargoes for heated political arguments
on the relative merits of James K. Polk and Henry Clay for the
presidency.

A trading ship fitted up below deck with counters full of
merchandise, as though it were a shop in Boston, would sell
between $15,000 and $20,000 worth of goods in a three- to four-
week stay, receiving in payment hides, tallow, sea and land otter
skins, beaver skins, some few Spanish or Mexican doubloons, the
residents of Yerba Buena and the ranchos taking home with them
the highly prized sugar, tea, coffee, clothing, blankets, jewelry and
rich cloths for the making of beautiful gowns.

Yet nobody wanted to settle in Yerba Buena, no one from the
Emmons Party from Oregon, the Bidwell Party from Missouri, the
Workman-Rowland Party from Santa Fe, the Joseph Chiles and
Joseph Walker Party. The tiny mud and adobe hamlet was the ugly
duckling of the Far West.

CHAPTER XIII

Seed Wheat of the Western Migration

TOWARD THE END OF August there moved majestically into the
northeast corner of Nevada, coming southwest from Fort Hall, the
only overland party of 1844 headed for California. The Stevens
Party proved to be the archetype of all emigrant parties, seed wheat
of the westward migration.

Each emigrant train has an indiviudality and life cycle
comparable to that of a human being: conception, birth, youth,
maturity, death, dissolution and immortality...bestowed by
biographers.

The conception of the Stevens Party was similar to other
emigrant trains, accidental and consisting of strange elements. The
leader was probably the ugliest man to cross the plains: Elisha
Stevens, about forty years old, born in South Carolina of a French

Huguenot family, was raised in Georgia, became a blacksmith by trade but spent most of his adult years as a hunter and trapper in the Northwest. He is described by the members of the party as courteous but silent to the point of taciturnity, a lean turkey-necked man with a long, narrow, misshapen head and a huge beaked nose which looked like a caricature of an eagle. He came alone to the meeting place on the Missouri River (later called Council Bluffs) in the early spring of 1844 with a well-built wagon and animals fitted for the trail, without knowing whether there would be a group heading west, and bumped into a party of fifty men, women and children who, although total strangers to Stevens, concluded after a few days that:

"He was born to command."

The largest individual segment of the Stevens Party was the twenty-member Murphy clan led by Martin Murphy, who had been born in Ireland, emigrated to Canada looking for more political freedom, and from there to Missouri. In Missouri the family had been plagued by malaria; there were no schools or churches. After the death of his wife, Martin Murphy met a Catholic missionary who told him about California, where good health and religion were abundant. As to the location of this wonderful land, the missionary knew only that it was on the shore of the Pacific Ocean, that it lay in a westerly direction from fever-stricken Missouri; as to the distance or route or character of the country, he had no knowledge. Yet every member of the Murphy family agreed wholeheartedly that, come spring, they should move out for California.

The second largest segment of the party was the Townsend and Montgomery group, who were friends and neighbors in Missouri, numbering seven.

Though the coming together of the leader and the two major groups of the party was accidental, there was nothing of chance about the fastidious preparation that preceded their departure from Council Bluffs on May 18. There were eleven wagons in the train, all good farm wagons, some built for the specific purpose of crossing the continent, drawn by good oxen and accompanied by many horses and a large herd of cattle. The success or failure, the amount of suffering and tragedy to be encountered is dependent upon the organic structure of each party: the ratio of old men and young children to those in the prime decades of life; the trades and skills that are represented; the ability of the members not only to choose wisely in their leader, but to submerge differences of racial origin, religion, economic and cultural backgrounds in the interests of the whole train. The Stevens Party had an authentic medical man along, a Dr. Townsend; it had a blacksmith and a gunsmith; there were three men with mountain experience, in addition to Caleb Greenwood, who had been picked up as a guide, his two half-breed sons and three French Canadians who had had backwoods experience.

Four of the twenty-six men could be considered old, there were three youths of seventeen and eight boys ranging in age from three to thirteen. The other twenty men of the party ranged from John Sullivan at twenty up to Stevens at forty, all at the height of their physical powers. The women too were of a favorable age for such a long and dangerous journey: of the eight, five were wives under thirty-six. There were one widow and two unmarried girls. The main body of the party was composed of successful families who had been able to purchase the best equipment and put in supplies to last for eight months.

The Murphys, Townsends and Montgomerys, though they had the votes to elect anyone of their choice, indulged in no such prideful egoism; they fixed upon Elisha Stevens and gave him their confidence. Therein lies their genius as a party; in this lack was born the tragedy of the Donner Party: between their extremes of total fulfillment and total tragedy fall all the hundreds of emigrant trains that filled the prairies and mountains in the second migration decade from 1849 to 1859 in the most fabulous westward trek the world has ever known.

The first third of the Stevens journey was uneventful; from Fort Hall the party followed the Walker wagon trail of the previous year down the Mary's River to the Sink, which it reached on October 1. On this date the Stevens Party sat around its campfire to make a fateful decision: to follow the Walker tracks which led south even though there was no way to know whether the Walker Party had been successful; or to push directly west into the mountains, for which a majority voted. At that moment an old Indian, talking to Caleb Greenwood by means of signs and diagrams drawn on the dusty floor of the Nevada desert, told of a river some fifty miles directly west across the desert in the mountains, which flowed down the east side of the Sierra Nevada; by following this river to the crest, he claimed, they could descend into California.

Captain Elisha Stevens with Dr. Townsend, Joseph Foster and Truckee the Indian set out to determine whether the river was there, and whether it could be ascended. They returned three days later to report that they had found the river, with good trees and grass, and that there probably was a pass somewhere beyond it in the mountains.

The Stevens Party took time to cook two days rations, to fill all available receptacles with water and to prepare its wagons, then made a forced march of thirty-six hours to Boiling Springs on the desert, and another twelve-hour march which brought it to the river. Resting for two days to refresh the cattle, the party began the ascent of the river, named it Truckee after the Indian guide, flourished on the plenitude of food, water, grass and game.

After a few days the ranges began to pack closer, the country became rough, wagons and animals had to be led up the bed of the stream, which was so crooked that in one day it had to be crossed ten separate times. The first snowfall buried all grass.

"The poor footsore oxen, after toiling all day, would stand and bawl for food all night in so piteous a manner that the emigrants would forget their own misery in their pity for the cattle."

After weeks of winding up canyons the party reached the fertile grasslands of a meadow surrounded by pine-covered mountains, then moved through the heavily forested country to an icy lake. Ahead stood a great wall of granite domes.

Here again Stevens went out with the best of his men to scout the towering peaks, finding a narrow, winding trail which he believed was a break in the range, and which could take them over the summit.

The tremendous mountains discouraged Dr. Townsend, who was bringing in a wagonload of merchandise to be offered for sale in California. Moses Schallenberger, Dr. Townsend's seventeen-year-old adopted son, agreed to remain on the lake and build a cabin for comfort, hunting and passing an adventuresome winter. In the spring Dr. Townsend would come back with oxen and they could take in the salable merchandise without risk. Two other young men, Joseph Foster and Allen Montgomery, offered to stay with the lad.

On the face of the great mountain two feet of snow had already fallen. The wagons had to be unloaded, the contents carried on the backs of the men, the teams doubled or trebled to haul the empty wagons. Halfway up the mountain the Stevens Party met a vertical cliff, solidly blocking the trail. Inch-by-inch searching revealed a narrow crevice by means of which a man could painstakingly lead the oxen one at a time up through the face of the rock.

Then, at the bottom, chains were fastened to the tongue of a wagon, the cattle at the top hitched to the chains, the men at the bottom pushing and straining and shoving the wagons, the animals hauling from above. Every last wagon was successfully brought up the face of the formidable rock. Once again the men had matched the mountains.

A twenty-five-mile push westward brought them to the headwaters of the Yuba River. Here a number of the families settled down with their wagons to wait for the end of the hard snows. Many of the able-bodied men started down the side of the mountain, reaching Sutter's Fort between the tenth and thirteenth of December 1844.

Back at the lake the three young men protecting Dr. Townsend's wagon faced a winter of starvation, the heavy snows making hunting impossible. Fashioning crude snowshoes, they set out to cross the mountains. Foster and Montgomery made it, Moses Schallenberger became ill, turned back to a winter alone in the desolate cabin.

The remainder of the Stevens Party descended the mountains into the California valley in good health and good spirits, their wagons and equipment intact. John Bidwell and Chiles-Walker, who had attempted to bring wagons through, had lost their possessions en route. The Stevens Party not only opened the last third of the California Trail but proved to be the forerunner of the colorful covered-wagon era just ahead.

CHAPTER XIV

A Democratic Army, Out for No Good

THERE WAS LITTLE OF cruelty in the nature of the Californios; in their internecine quarrels they dueled with pointed proclamations rather than swords. Aside from hunting grizzly bears and wild horses, their sport was largely confined to incredible feats of horsemanship; they were reputed to be the greatest since Genghis

Khan, so skillful that they could pick up a kernel of corn from the earth, coming at full speed.

When in July 1844 word was received in Monterey from the Minister of War in Mexico City that war would be declared as soon as the United States Senate ratified the treaty annexing Texas, and that a citizens' army must be rallied for the defense of Mexico, the longsuffering Californios decided not to recruit, but rather to get rid of Micheltorena's convict troops, who had been despoiling their fair country. Alvarado and his military commander, Castro, warned Micheltorena to ship his soldiers back to Mexico; when Micheltorena refused on the ground that bad troops were better than none, Alvarado and Castro rounded up a force of forty to fifty followers. Not a shot was fired nor a blow struck, despite the fact that the opposing men rode and maneuvered for two weeks. Nor is it likely that anything more untoward would have happened had it not been for John Sutter, who came riding onto the scene on his white charger.

On July 21, 1844, Governor Micheltorena had appointed Sutter captain of all the troops of the Sacramento Valley; and at long last Sutter's fiction of having been a captain was turned into a resplendent truth. It was a heady realization for the man; no accomplishment of his life gave him more prideful pleasure. It also came close to being the death of him.

The appointment did not catch Sutter unprepared. His fort had been organized on a military basis from the beginning, with drill every evening after supper, his Indians wearing the uniforms with red trimmings which came with the purchase of Fort Ross, goose-stepping to barked German or Swiss commands of one of Sutter's drill sergeants, carrying on their shoulders the Fort Ross flintlocks which Napoleon had reputedly left behind in his retreat from Moscow.

In October Sutter learned of the impending revolt of Alvarado and Castro against Micheltorena. Sutter brought the warning to Governor Micheltorena who, delighted at this unexpected support, gave Sutter a formal dinner, sent up a balloon for entertainment, promised Sutter not only more leagues of land for himself in northern California but the legal right to make land grants to all men who would fight under Sutter's command.

Even as Sutter returned to his fort to organize a brigade, Alvarado and Castro captured Micheltorena's few artillery pieces at San Juan, where Micheltorena had moved his troops. Micheltorena signed a treaty agreeing to send his soldiers back to Mexico, which satisfied Alvarado, Castro and even Vallejo, who had remained neutral but urgently wanted the convict army out of the country.

But Captain John Sutter was not giving up so easily what might be the only war of his lifetime. He sent out calls to every man in the valley to join his troop, drilled the entire population of his fort; even ordered John Marsh, on pain of military arrest, to join his army as a foot soldier.

Without Sutter's support, Micheltorena would have been obliged to send his cholos back to Mexico as he had agreed to do; with Sutter ready to put almost a hundred armed men into the field, Micheltorena reasoned that he had the strongest army in California. He ordered Sutter to capture Alvarado and Castro. Sutter tried to get a hundred horses from Vallejo for the campaign, but received instead as brilliant and passionate a series of letters as have been written on California soil, in which Mariano Vallejo, the wisest and ablest of all the Californios, made a number of trenchant points which should have put an end to Sutter's folly. Vallejo had discharged his garrison at the end of 1844 on the grounds that he could no longer support the troop of thirty soldiers, thus removing himself, as he had in Alvarado's uprising in 1836, and in the arrest and deportation of Graham and his followers in 1840, from the internecine wars.

It was at this point that twenty men of the Stevens Party dropped into Sutter's Fort, looking for a chance to get a good start in California. Sutter showed them his official document from Governor Micheltorena promising free and legal land, perhaps a league in length, to each man who fought against what Sutter claimed was a group of upstart rebels. The opportunity was too good to miss; every man, including Elisha Stevens and Dr. Townsend, agreed to go to the wars.

At dawn of New Year's Day, 1845, the now Colonel John Sutter rode forth to glory wearing "a tilted cap, a blue frock coat, immaculate trousers, polished boots, a moustache and a marked military air." Behind him was his Army of the Sacramento, approximately two hundred twenty men, the Sacramento settlers, the fresh recruits from the Stevens Party, a hundred Indians. About half the men were mounted; at the rear came Sutter's artillery and his supply wagons pulled by oxen.

It was a thoroughly democratic army, out for no good.

The fort was left in charge of Pierson B. Reading, fifteen whites and thirty Indians, a dangerous procedure, but Sutter seemed more concerned about his favorite common-law wife than his fort, for he wrote to Reading:

"In case I should be killed, you will see that Manaiki receives her wages coming to her until the last day of her being at the establishment."

It was dashing red-cheeked Colonel Sutter's plan to meet the ninety-man army of Alvarado and Castro at San Jose and overcome them in a decisive battle. By January 9 he had joined Micheltorena's forces at the Salinas River. But Alvarado and Castro had no intention of accommodating Sutter's quick plan for conquest; they began moving southward. The heavy rains of the central California valley began making mud baths of the roads. Micheltorena fell ill and had to travel in a carriage. The army moved only four miles a day, provisions gave out, the men were cold and drenched. At this point Marsh, enjoying his revenge, began to ask the Americans why they were getting involved in somebody else's family argument. No one had an answer.

Yet Sutter managed to hold them together, slogging their way southward to Santa Barbara, living off the cattle they could find along the way, foraging at the missions, then down the coast for several more weeks, until on February 19, after seven weeks away from home, Sutter's army made its way to the oak-studded desert plain of the San Fernando Valley and saw the rebel army.

Alvarado and Castro had gone to Los Angeles and convinced that somnolent community that Sutter and his foreigners were going to burn Los Angeles to the ground. They enlisted the help of most of the local Americans, including such old residents as Abel Stearns, the men who had come across with the Workman-Rowland Party and forty recently arrived American mountaineers.

On the morning of February 20 Colonel Sutter ordered his three artillery pieces to begin firing. He was answered by Alvarado's and Castro's two cannons in a barrage which lasted for a couple of hours, after which Castro withdrew his troops westward through Cahuenga Pass. The next morning Colonel Sutter's troops found to their astonishment that the opposing troops were not Californios but Americans, among them old friends from Missouri and Santa Fe.

Private John Marsh took over command from John Sutter, signaling for a truce. The two groups of Americans came together with exclamations of joy and demands for news of friends and relatives back home. Marsh made a speech convincing both sides that they had no place in this war but should rather save themselves for the real contest which would make California American. The Americans left the field of battle arm in arm.

That was the end of the war. Historians cannot agree on the

casualties; they range from one horse to four. All authorities agree
on the loss of one of Castro's cannon wheels.

Colonel John Augustus Sutter, of the Sacramento Army,
Retired, was captured, stripped of his uniform, jailed. The irate
Angelenos who blamed him for the foolish fracas disagreed on only
one point: should he be shot or hanged for his crime?

Sutter wrote an abject letter to the new governor, Pio Pico,
putting the blame on former Governor Micheltorena: Was he not
simply following inescapable orders? Pio Pico and the amiable
Alvarado not only pardoned Sutter, allowing him to keep his fort
and his empire, but confirmed the grant of three additional leagues
of land nine miles wide by a hundred miles long promised him by
Micheltorena if he would fight. They also confirmed the land grants
he had promised to the Americans and Europeans who had joined
his army. Everyone was happy, even Micheltorena, who was tired
of California and wanted to get back to Mexico City.

Meanwhile William Rae, head of the Hudson's Bay Company in
Yerba Buena, earned for himself the dubious distinction of
becoming California's first suicide, an act which his contemporaries
agreed was due to a combination of business difficulties and getting
caught with his inamorata. Because of this tragedy the Hudson's
Bay Company decided to shut up shop in Yerba Buena. John Sutter
had one less creditor on his neck, but the future of the town of
Yerba Buena looked gloomier than ever.

When, two years later, the British lost California partly because
they had no representation there, they could console themselves by
blaming the loss on a woman.

John Sutter returned to find his fort and affairs badly neglected.
Nevertheless he immediately dispatched Caleb Greenwood to Fort
Hall to divert any Oregon-bound caravan to California and Sutter's
Fort by means of his pledge to give them free land!

In July of 1845 he welcomed with his usual hospitality the
Clyman-McMahon Party of thirty-nine men, a widow, and her
three children, down from Oregon. Green McMahon, who had first
come into California in 1841 with the Bidwell Party, had led them
on a thirty-one-day voyage down a chain of rivers: the Klamath,
Shasta and Sacramento. The international flavor of the Far West
settlement was in evidence, for the party included a Frenchman, a
Canadian, two Germans, the others being British and American.
Equally varied were its crafts: there were a soapmaker and a
chandler, a saddler and a tailor, a blacksmith, a shoemaker, five
carpenters, a sailor, twenty-four farmers; James Clyman, who kept
a diary of the journey and hence got his name attached to the party,
James W. Marshall, a coachmaker and a number of mountain men.

CHAPTER XV

The Rugged Individualist Train

IN COLORADO FIVE COMPANIES of United States Dragoons, two hundred fifty to three hundred strong, led by Colonel Stephen Watts Kearny, were the first troops to enter any part of the Far West since Captain Zebulon Pike in 1806 and Colonel Stephen Long in 1820. About July 10 Kearny brought his mounted infantrymen into Colorado from Wyoming where he had supposedly been protecting the emigrants on the Oregon Trail from Indian attack. Since the Oregon trains had been going through in safety for several years now, the Kearny expedition obviously had another purpose. Kearny swung down sharply to Bent's Fort, immediately across the line from Mexico's southwest territory, where he enjoyed what the Bent's Fort's biographer described as "a lavish dinner spread in the big apartment," while he discussed Mexico's military strength with Charles Bent, as a prelude to his commanding, the following year, the Army of the West.

Stephen Watts Kearny was descended on his mother's side from such wealthy and socially elite Dutch families as the Van Cortlandts and Schuylers. His paternal great-grandfather came from Ireland in 1704; his father became a prosperous wine merchant in Perth Amboy, New Jersey, then lost everything because he supported the British cause in the War of the Revolution. No one ever doubted Stephen's loyalty. He entered Columbia College in 1811 at the age of seventeen, but left to join the army at the beginning of the War of 1812, and in the course of one year had distinguished himself for bravery, been wounded, captured, exchanged and made a captain. Army life was to his liking. At the close of the war he was sent on expeditions to the frontier to build outposts and forts, to command Fort Crawford at Prairie du Chien in 1828, where John Marsh had

73

had him arrested for illegal use of stolen lumber, and for resisting civil authority.

Now fifty years old, Colonel Kearny was an experienced frontiersman, but a plodding, routine commanding officer who had seen no warfare for thirty-three years.

Kearny and his dragoons stayed in Colorado three weeks before heading east again about August 1, probably passing on the trail Captain John C. Fremont's Third Expedition, consisting of sixty mountain men, which reached Bent's Fort on August 2. Fremont's party included Joseph Walker, Basil Lajeunesse, the experienced hunter Lucien Maxwell, Edward M. Kern of Philadelphia, an artist, and a dozen Delaware scouts who were fanatically loyal to Fremont. Fremont sent a message to his friend Kit Carson, who was ranching on the Cimarron. When Carson learned that Fremont had been ordered to explore a route through the central Rockies of Colorado, as well as to map the Great Salt Lake, he promptly sold his ranch and joined the expedition.

Fremont spent two weeks at Bent's Fort, then with twelve new carbines which he would give as prizes for marksmanship set out for Pueblo where they camped on August 20, continuing up the Arkansas Valley in fine, late summer weather, enjoying the pine woods and the Rocky Mountain streams of southern Colorado and following an old Indian trail which Pike had used in 1804 but which no one had evaluated for the possibility of emigrant trains.

At this same time there came into Nevada four emigrant groups variously known as the Snyder-Blackburn, the Swasey-Todd, the Sublette and the Grigsby-Ide, all part of the same train of a hundred wagons which had assembled in Missouri over a period of several weeks. Only fifteen wagons were going to California; the rest were headed for Oregon.

They were, that is, until they got to Fort Hall where Caleb Greenwood and his sons were waiting for them with Sutter's promise of free land in California. The leader of the party made a passionate speech to hold his train together; he forbade any wagons that had agreed to go to Oregon to turn off on the California Trail under the threat of being held mutinous.

The threat did no good. Greenwood convinced as many as sixty wagons with over a hundred people to turn south at the beginning of the California Trail.

The first party to strike off was led by one of Greenwood's sons, and consisted of twelve young men on horseback with pack animals. They traveled quickly across Nevada to the Mary's River, down to its Sink and then over the trail blazed by Stevens the year before, dropping into Sutter's Fort at the end of September, the fastest crossing in the history of western expansion, with no untoward incident except that young John Greenwood, the half-breed, managed to shoot and kill an Indian.

The Grigsby-Ide Party was the largest to hold together as a unit, consisting of fifty men, besides the women and children. William B. Ide had been a teacher when he was not well enough to practice his trade of carpenter. He is best known as the leader of this party, not because he made the most important contribution but because he was a good writer who left a vivid account for ravenous biographers to absorb. Ide, who was born in Rutland, Massachusetts, in 1796, very early fell victim to western fever and moved first to Kentucky, then to Ohio, then to Illinois. He could not resist the call of this ultimate West, and so over the winter of 1844-45 he carefully selected the timbers for two of his three wagons, had them made to order with the canvas covers sewed by Mrs. Ide and their seventeen-year-old daughter Sarah. Ide painted the bed of the wagon and the canvas a slate gray, installed cooking utensils and provisions to last six months, in addition to a circular saw and some mill-irons with which to begin life in the Far West; he also rounded up a hundred sixty-five cattle and twenty-eight work oxen. On the back curtain of his hindmost wagon he painted in bold black letters, OREGON. Caleb Greenwood changed his mind.

Once the Ide Party was in Nevada their guide, "Doctor" Joe Meek, whose medical practice in Monterey apparently had fallen off, told them there was no longer any danger from the Indians. The party abandoned the central discipline which had character-ized all trains up to this time, each family camping separately at night.

Facing Nevada Mountain, Ide found several level spaces between the cliff ascents where teams, if led up one by one, could stand and haul up the wagons by pulley and tackle. He persuaded the group to work together, to empty their wagons while the men carved out a road six or seven feet wide, cutting down trees and hauling rocks out of the way. When the road was ready, each ox was led up the cliff by ropes; when five or six oxen had been assembled at the first level, each wagon was hauled up the side of the cliff: each wagon up one hitch, block the wheels, beak the teams, take another hitch, move forward a few feet, block the wheels. Within forty-eight hours the entire train had reached the summit, the men exhausted and the oxen bleeding. But they were ready to begin their descent.

With the conquest of Nevada Mountain all remaining cohesion vanished, every wagon dashing ahead to be the first to arrive, and to get the best free land, by its actions earning the title of The Rugged Individualist Train of 1845.

John Sutter wrote in high glee to Thomas Larkin at the beginning of October, enclosing a list of the emigrants:

"It will no doubt be gratifying to you to learn that they are in better condition than any other emigrants who have ever come to this country. They are generally well provided with all the necessary articles useful in keeping house, farming, and also in a number of mechanical branches. The majority of them are also provided with money to a greater or lesser extent."

Apparently California was attracting a better class of emigrant.

By October 10, 1845, when the first of the Grigsby-Ide Party had already pulled its wagons inside the main gate of Sutter's Fort, Fremont's expedition reached fresh-water Utah Lake. They fed well on deer, elk and a stray herd of buffalo which they were surprised to find so far west, and on buffalo fish named from the hump on its back. Traveling northward, Fremont learned that he had made an error in connecting Utah Lake with the Great Salt Lake; he spent two full weeks on the shores of the Salt Lake sketching and making maps. Now a couple of hundred miles south of the regular Mary's River trail, Fremont wanted to head directly west.

"The route I wished to take lay over a flat plain covered with sagebrush. The country looked dry and of my own men none knew anything of it. The Indians declared to us that no one had ever been known to cross the plain."

Carson says of this desert in his autobiography:

"It had never before been crossed by white men. I was often here. Old trappers would speak of the impossibility of crossing, that water could not be found, grass for the animals, there was none. Fremont was bound to cross. Nothing was impossible for him to perform if required in his explorations."

Fortunately, Fremont had ingenuity to match his courage.

"Nearly upon the line of our intended travel, apparently fifty to sixty miles away, was a peak-shaped mountain. This looked to me to be fertile. I arranged that Carson, Archambeau and Maxwell should set out at night, taking with them a pack-mule with water and provisions, and make for the mountain, I to follow with the party the next day and make one camp out into the desert. They to make a signal by smoke in case water should be found."

Fremont and the main body of men set out late the next afternoon and traveled all night. Before morning Archambeau came riding back with the happy news that he and Carson had found water, grass and wood at the foot of the mountain. Another stretch of westering desert had been conquered.

Fremont's Third Expedition had come straight across Utah and Nevada from the Great Salt Lake and proved that all the maps up to this point, which had shown this basin to be "a sandy, barren plain without water or grass," were wrong; it was not one vast desert, but was "traversed by parallel ranges of mountains, their summits white with snow while below, the valleys had none. Instead of a barren country, the mountains were covered with grasses of the best quality, wooded with several varieties of trees, and containing more deer and mountain sheep than we had seen in any previous part of our voyage."

Fremont elatedly renamed the three-hundred-mile-long Mary's River, which became known as the "Highroad of the West," the Humboldt River, after his idol, the German naturalist geographer Alexander Humboldt.

On December 10 he made an easy descent into Sutter's Fort by way of Walker's Lake. This time he did not leave California; he remained, indirectly causing the seizure of the Far West, the war in California, and the setting up of the first American government. He thereby earned for himself either fame or infamy, depending on which book you read: for biography is a disputatious art.

Among the rugged individualists of the Grigsby-Ide train Fremont would find many kindred spirits who, the following year, would be at the heart of the Bear Flag Revolt.

CHAPTER XVI

"Why is Captain Fremont here?"

EIGHTEEN FORTY-SIX WAS the year of resolution for California. Mariano Vallejo of Sonoma had written to Mexico City on November 22, 1845:

"The emigration of North Americans to California today forms an unbroken line of wagons from the United States clear to this Department, and how can they be turned back without forces and resources? It is necessary, sir, it is indispensable that the Supreme Government should send us both. This has been for some years my incessant supplication. Troops and money! Only by uniting both can they save us from the imminent danger that surrounds us. It would be very desirable to close that door of communication between the United States and this country, even at some sacrifice. Castro having made propositions to Sutter for the purchase of his establishment, he said that he would cede it to the government for one hundred thousand dollars. I grant that this is a very high price to pay for a few pieces of cannon, a not very scientifically constructed bastion, some moats, ten or twelve adobe houses, and corrals of the same material; but the security of the country is what is to be paid for, and that is priceless."

The question of the security of Mariano Vallejo's country was eliciting a good many other letters.

Merchant Thomas O. Larkin, who at the beginning of 1846 would transfer the management of his mercantile business in Monterey to a young associate, Talbot H. Green, so that Consul Thomas O. Larkin could devote full time to the acquisition of California for the United States, had written to Secretary of State James Buchanan:

"The Mexican troops about to invade the province have been sent for this purpose at the instigation of the British government."

Secretary of State Buchanan's reply, written in Washington on October 17, 1845, is imperative to the understanding of Captain Fremont's uprising in California and of the misbegotten war with Mexico:

"The future destiny of that Country is a subject of anxious solicitude for the Government and people of the United States. The interests of our Commerce and our Whale fisheries on the Pacific Ocean, demand that you should exert the greatest vigilance in discovering and defeating any attempts which may be made by Foreign Governments to acquire control over that Country. In the contest between Mexico and California we can take no part, unless the former should commence hostilities against the United States; but should California assert and maintain her independence, we shall render her all the kind offices in our power as a Sister Republic. Great Britain by the acquisition of California would sow the seeds of future war and disaster for herself; because there is no political truth more certain that that this fine Province could not long be held in vassalage by any European Power. The emigration to it of people from the United States would soon render this impossible."

By the end of January 1846 Fremont arrived in Monterey with eight of his men for a visit with Consul Larkin. Colonel Alvarado and Prefect Manuel Castro at Monterey, alarmed at this conjoining of officials of the United States Departments of State and War, sent a polite but firm inquiry to Consul Larkin:

"Why is an American army officer in California with a body of troops, and why is Captain Fremont in Monterey?"

Captain Fremont, a man of charm, appeared before the officials and with the utmost tact replied that his followers were not soldiers, but mountain men helping him to survey and map a tenable route to the Pacific; that he had left the main body of his men "on the frontier," that as soon as his group had recouped its strength, and he had laid in supplies he would leave California for Oregon, and then home. The meeting was friendly.

Then there occurred one of those fateful accidents which etch the external pattern of events. When Fremont told Alvarado and Castro that he was in California on an exploring expedition, and that he had left the main body of his men "on the frontier," he was telling a half-truth. Even so he was doing better than Secretary of State Buchanan, whose letter was filled with quarter-truths. The main body of Fremont's men were in the mountains, but he had not left them there: they were lost. While still in the Nevada desert, he had sent forty-four of his voyageurs southward under Joseph Walker to enter California by the pass discovered by Walker in 1832, then to make their way down the San Joaquin Valley to the Kings River. Walker had waited instead at the fork of the Kern River. Scouting to find out where his commander was, Walker located him near San Jose, and by mid-February brought his men to join him.

Captain Fremont now had with him a band of sixty armed, devoted and disciplined riflemen, the most effective military force California had ever seen. Had Walker taken his men north to Sutter's as planned, Fremont, accompanied by only eight men, would have returned to Sutter's. But with his entire troop assembled, waiting for advice that the United States was at war with Mexico over the annexation of Texas, Captain Fremont was reluctant to take his force far from Monterey where he expected to raise the American flag.

He reached the coast near Santa Cruz, and the same kind of weather that had bogged down Sutter's army the year before gave him his excuse to stay. By March 1 he headed south along the coast toward Monterey, encamping at the Alisal ranch of the Englishman William Hartnell in the Salinas Valley. He could no longer effectively claim that he was exploring. Fremont wrote Larkin that he was going to remain in the Salinas Valley until spring when, he was certain from everything that had been told him in Washington, the war would have commenced.

The Mexican officials had to confront Fremont or lose face. On March 5, 1846, the near-shooting war over California began.

"In the afternoon the quiet of the camp was disturbed by the sudden appearance of a cavalry officer," wrote Fremont. "Lieutenant Chavez seemed disposed to be somewhat rude and abrupt. This one brought me peremptory letters from the general and prefect, ordering me forthwith out of the department, and threatening force in the event that I should not instantly comply with the order. I expressed to the envoy my astonishment.... And I desired him to say in reply to General Castro that I peremptorily refused compliance to an order insulting to my government and myself."

The intensity of Fremont's explosion was probably sparked by his sense of guilt; an opportunist himself, he was the perfect selection to carry out the opportunistic policy of his government. The next morning he "moved up the mountain and encamped on a small wooded flat at the top of a neighboring eminence, Hawk's Peak in the Gavilan Mountains," built a log fort and raised the American flag.

It was now three and a half years since Commodore Thomas Ap Jones had raised the American flag at Monterey in his thirty-hour acquisition of California; both outbursts were indicative of the trigger-happy frame of mind to which the United States Departments of State and War had fanned their officers.

Fremont, from the top of his mountain, could see Mexican troops assembling at San Juan with artillery. He wrote as charming a gasconade as ever came from the gifted Mexican authorities:

"If we are attacked we will fight to extremity, and refuse quarter, trusting to our country to avenge our death. If we are hemmed in and assaulted here [he had established his camp with a perfect escape hatch down the rear of the mountains!], we will die, every man of us, under the flag of our country."

On the second evening a troop of Mexican cavalry came part way up the mountain. Fremont took forty men down the mountain to a concealed thicket to meet them. Happily, no one fired a shot, and both parties returned to their camps; Colonel Castro to issue a proclamation charging that "a band of robbers commanded by a captain of the United States army... sallies forth making scandalous skirmishes."

The word "robbers" was occasioned by the accusation that Fremont's men had stolen some horses; the phrase "scandalous skirmishes" by the charge that a couple of Fremont's mountain men had burst into a ranch house and frightened three young Californio girls.

The next day when the sapling holding aloft the American flag fell down, Fremont issued a proclamation that the falling of the pole was an omen that their stay in the fort on Hawk's Peak should be concluded.

Thus the army was no more successful than the navy in making the conquest stick. In the contest of international good manners, the Mexican officials won an indisputable victory.

While Captain Fremont took his men slowly, reluctantly northward to Sutter's Fort and then up the American River toward Oregon, a meeting took place in Consul Larkin's drawing room that is perhaps the most illuminating in the Mexican ownership of California. The subject under discussion was:

To whom should California and the lands of the Far West belong?

General Castro declared for annexation to France for religious reasons. David Spence and William Hartnell spoke in favor of their native England. Thomas O. Larkin and Victor Proudon favored the United States. Colonel Mariano Vallejo made a scholarly speech explaining the Constitution of the United States, "and how under it California would have representation in Congress as well as any other state of the republic."

Rafael Gonzales provided the fireworks, springing to his feet from the Larkin sofa with the ringing words:

"*California libre, soberance, y independiente!* California free, sovereign and independent!"

No one went on record as favoring, or believing remotely possible, any continued allegiance to Mexico!

CHAPTER XVII

Confidential Agent

ON APRIL 17, 1846, six months to the day after he had received his secret orders from Secretary of State Buchanan, there appeared in Monterey a lieutenant of the United States Marines who had made his way across Mexico from Vera Cruz to Mazatlan, then by the U.S.S. *Cyane* to Honolulu and to Monterey. His name was Archibald Gillespie; he purported to be either a merchant in pursuit of business or a semi-invalid in pursuit of health. A more explosively healthy marine officer has never lived; sending him in disguise to California with dispatches for Consul Larkin and Captain Fremont was as subtle as it would have been to send the U.S.S. *Cyane* into Monterey Harbor with its forward guns firing. On the previous October 30, President Polk had written in his diary:

"I held a confidential conversation with Gillespie of the Marine Corps about eight o'clock P.M. on the subject of the secret mission on which he was about to go to California. His secret instructions and the letter to Mr. Larkin, United States consul at Monterey, in the Department of State, will explain the object of his mission."

Polk discreetly refrained from confiding to his diary the content of the secret orders; Gillespie with equal discretion never set them down in writing. Before reaching Vera Cruz, Gillespie committed to memory all dispatches from Buchanan intended for Consul Larkin, carrying across Mexico only his letter of introduction to Larkin and family letters to Captain Fremont.

Lieutenant Gillespie was warmly received by Larkin, who had been advised of his coming in a letter from Secretary of State Buchanan which set forth the plan as hatched in Washington:

"In addition to your Consular functions, the President has

thought proper to appoint you a Confidential Agent in California. You will take care not to awaken the jealousy of the French and English Agents there by assuming any other than your consular character. Lieutenant Archibald H. Gillespie of the Marine Corps is a Gentleman in whom the President reposes entire confidence. He has seen these instructions and will co-operate as a confidential agent with you, in carrying them into execution."

Lieutenant Gillespie apparently brought news of an April war with Mexico, for Larkin, after hearing Gillespie's secret instructions, had the temerity to tell Vallejo that the United States flag would be flying over California by the Fourth of July!

Consul Larkin now entered the conspiracy by writing a double-talk letter to Vice-Consul Leidesdorff of Yerba Buena in which he said that Gillespie:

"Has not enjoyed good health and wishes to travel through your part of California to enjoy the climate."

He told Leidesdorff to provide Gillespie with boat, horses, men, to be charged to Larkin, then added that Gillespie "is a Gentleman of much information, and well acquainted with the countries he has passed through."

He also provided Gillespie with letters of introduction to Americans and Europeans whom he believed were anxiously awaiting conquest: Nathan Spear, important merchant of Yerba Buena, Jacob Leese, Dr. John Marsh, William Richardson, captain of the Yerba Buena port, and John C. Sutter. This last proved a mistake, for peripatetic Sutter reported to General Castro, when Gillespie came up the Sacramento River looking for Fremont, that he was sure Gillespie lied when he told the people he was traveling for his health:

"I have seen his name in a list of officers. It is my opinion that Gillespie is a courier for Captain Fremont... with important dispatches from his government... and it may be that Fremont will return from the frontier."

Important naval officers on the Pacific had apparently also been advised that war would start in April. When Commodore Sloat, a cautious commander, heard of Captain Fremont's stand at Hawk's Peak he sent Commander Montgomery of the U.S.S. *Portsmouth* from Mazatlan to Monterey with orders to break all records in getting there. Commander Montgomery told Consul Larkin that in his opinion, "Commodore Sloat may by the next mail have a declaration on the part of the United States against Mexico."

Up the Sacramento, Sutter quite plainly told Gillespie that he knew he was an active officer for the United States; but that did not prevent him from providing Gillespie with his best mule and guide. With the help of experienced settlers Lassen, Stepp and Neal, Gillespie again set off. It took him eleven hard pushing days during which his group suffered near starvation and threats from hostile Indians before he met with Fremont at Klamath Lake just north of the California border. Gillespie delivered to Captain Fremont letters from his wife, from his father-in-law, Senator Thomas Hart Benton; and oral accounting of the confidential letter of Secretary Buchanan to Consul Larkin; President Polk's secret instructions; and the immediate news that the U.S. warship *Portsmouth* was in San Francisco Bay.

Gillespie may also have communicated to Fremont the message from Secretary of the Navy Bancroft which Bancroft later testified he had sent to Fremont:

"Being absolved from any duty as an explorer, Captain Fremont was left to his duty as an officer in the service of the United States, with the further authoritative knowledge that the government intended to take possession of California."

Fremont's letters from his wife and Senator Benton, couched in the cryptic language peculiar to intimates who have discussed a subject thoroughly over a period of years, appeared to Fremont to urge him to play the leader's role in acquiring the Far West for the United States.

"I saw the way opening clear before me," said Fremont. "War with Mexico was inevitable; and a grand opportunity now presented itself to realize in their fullest extent the far-sighted views of Senator Benton, and make the Pacific Ocean the western boundary of the United States. I resolved to return forthwith to the Sacramento Valley in order to bring to bear all the influences I could command."

By the end of May Fremont and Gillespie had made their way down the Sacramento Valley, camping at Lessen's rancho, and the farm of Neal and Dutton on Deer Creek. Both men were exhausted by the forced march and diet of horse meat, but they were prepared for immediate action. Gillespie left on Sutter's launch for San Francisco Bay and the U.S.S. *Portsmouth* with a requisition from Fremont for guns, ammunition, money, food, medical supplies. As an army officer Fremont had no right to requisition navy supplies; if Commander Montgomery honored the order it would appear that he had orders to do so.

The Americans in central California were excited by the return of Fremont: it could only mean that Gillespie had brought him instructions to take California. Despite the fact that the sorely tried

Californios had behaved with exemplary kindness to the Americans, a cold war of propaganda was flashed from rancho to rancho with the speed of the swiftest horses: General Castro had been to Sonoma to secure horses and men and was about to attack in force.... Mexican troops would arrest all Americans, take away their lands, deport them eastward over the Sierra Nevada.... Mexico had sold California to England.... British warships were en route to San Francisco Bay.... Mexico was granting three thousand square leagues of land to Father Eugene McNamara, an Irish colonizer, for which he was bringing over three thousand families to settle in California and vote California into the British Empire....

Believing that delay might mean the loss of California to England, that if they did not strike fast and hard, Mexican troops would attack and capture them, the Americans in the Sacramento, Napa and Sonoma valleys decided to rise in armed rebellion.

To their astonishment Fremont refused to ride out at their head as their commanding officer: it had been made clear to him that the United States did not wish to appear predatory. However he left no doubt that although he must remain in the background he would support and sustain them in their uprising. He chose for what he called his "field lieutenant" a tall, spare, rawboned trapper named Ezekiel Merritt, whom Fremont called "fearless and simple." In the forenoon of June 9 Merritt set forth from Fremont's camp with eleven or twelve emigrants and hunters, of a class which Fremont describes as "having nothing to risk." The next morning Merritt surprised Arce, General Castro's secretary and militia lieutenant. Arce was properly indignant at having been surprised, and hence cheated of the opportunity to fight. Lieutenant Merritt offered to repeat the maneuver, *sans surprise*. A more amiable solution was reached when Merritt gave Arce and his men back their guns and their private horses, keeping the military supplies.

Merritt returned to Fremont's camp, increased his band to thirty-three men and, on Fremont's orders, headed southwest through the Napa and Santa Rosa valleys, picking up American volunteers on the way. Their instructions were to capture Colonel Vallejo's garrison, seize all the arms and take command of Sonoma.

At dawn on June 14 Mariano Vallejo was awakened from sleep by the sound of gun butts rapping the big front door. He had reason to sleep soundly, for he was the single most successful rancher in all of central California: he owned leagues of land, his herds were increasing and he was building a library he loved deeply. In order to stay out of the intra-governmental quarrels between General Jose

Castro and Governor Pio Pico he had dismissed the last of his remaining troops; the barracks on the north corner of the plaza were deserted. Vallejo was so disinterested in the mounting tempers between the Californios and the Americans that when he went to sleep he left on guard two aged Indians and an old dog, all of them sleeping as soundly as their master when Ezekiel Merritt's men came down from the hills and through the plaza.

Vallejo, still in his nightgown and nightcap, went to the window and saw standing in the square a group of men "armed, mounted, fierce-looking," wearing flat coonskin or coyote-skin caps, and others with red bandana handkerchiefs. Dr. Robert Semple, who was one of the leaders, wrote:

"Almost the whole party was dressed in leather hunting-shirts, many of them were greasy; taking the whole party together they were about as rough a looking set of men as one could well imagine. It is not to be wondered at that anyone would feel some dread in falling into their hands."

It is doubtful if Mariano Vallejo had ever felt the emotion of dread; he donned his uniform, went down to the ground floor and ordered the doors opened. Captain Merritt, Robert Semple, William Fallon and Samuel Kelsey came into the big hall. Vallejo asked:

"Gentlemen, what is it you would have of me, and who is the leader among you?"

He was told, "We are all leaders here."

Merritt was designated as the spokesman, explaining to Vallejo that the Americans were determined to make California independent, adding:

"Towards you and your family we have no other feeling than regard, though we find ourselves under the necessity of taking you and your family prisoners."

For Vallejo this was by no means a surprising or unhappy moment; it had been his conviction since 1840 that California would one day become part of the United States. It was also his conviction that becoming part of the United States was the best thing that could happen for the development of California. If the group of hunters and ranchers standing before him in their buckskin pants and greasy shirts were neither an imposing nor an edifying sight, Mariano Vallejo had read widely enough to know that history is not always made by the washed or the genteel.

By this time Jacob Leese, who was married to Vallejo's sister, had come into the great hall along with Victor Proudon, Vallejo's secretary, and Salvador Vallejo, Mariano's brother. When Merritt demanded immediate surrender of the guns, cannon and powder connected with the former garrison, Colonel Vallejo turned them over and then suggested that they sit down at his table in the *sala* and draw up the articles of capitulation, asking only that life and property be carefully guarded. Vallejo assumed that the group was acting under the orders and supervision of United States Army Captain John C. Fremont; although he had never met Fremont, this fact gave him assurance that everything would be done in an official and decorous manner.

Vallejo's excellent *aguardiente* proved a trifle strong for the empty stomachs of the negotiators, who had not the slightest idea of what should go into the treaty. After being joined by John Grigsby, and then William B. Ide, of the Grigsby-Ide Party, Vallejo completed the drawing up of his paper of capitulation, which apparently he did without intervention from the Americans around the table; for in this, his last official paper, Colonel Vallejo was still trying to play the part of the conscientious Mexican officer who had been overwhelmed by a superior force.

When the paper was read aloud to the men outside, dissension broke out among the Americans. Grigsby, who had understood he was working under Captain Fremont, stepped down from leadership when he realized that this was a freebooting movement. Loquacious, excitable, spluttering Ide took over command. There was strong dissent against releasing the Vallejo family, Leese, Proudon and the other Sonomans on their word of honor not to take up arms.

Vallejo, who had expressed the hope that Captain Fremont would come immediately to Sonoma and set up American headquarters there, was not disturbed when informed that he and his brother, and Proudon, were to be taken to Fremont's camp under arrest. Since his friendship for all Americans in California was of such long standing, he assumed that he and Captain John C. Fremont would shake hands, then Vallejo would express his pleasure that California was at last to become part of the United States; that he would thereupon be paroled or invited to join the American forces. He assured his wife, Benicia, that he would be back in a few days.

It had been a peaceable revolution. No one had been hurt, no property had been disturbed. The only breach of decorum was that the *aguardiente* Vallejo had sent out to the men in the plaza made them a little noisy.

With the departure of Vallejo from Sonoma, the California Republic was formally born. The Americans decided that they must have a flag and William Todd, nephew of Mary Todd Lincoln, set out to design one. Mrs. Elliott cut a piece of white cloth from a bolt of cotton she had in her home, a red stripe for the bottom was provided by Mrs. Josefa Mathews, while paint was secured from the Vallejo home. The Americans wanted a star on their flag to tie them into the tradition of Texas; this was put in the upper left-hand corner, then to the right young Todd tried to draw a California grizzly bear. He was not a very good artist, and the bear came out looking like what the amused natives of Sonoma called a pig. Underneath the star and the bear there was printed in crude lettering:

CALIFORNIA REPUBLIC

Probably at dawn of June 15, 1846, the day following the seizure of Sonoma, the Bear Flag was raised.

CHAPTER XVIII

Paradise Grows a Trifle Ugly

WHILE WAITING FOR news of Merritt's band, John Fremont moved down to Sutter's landing with a few picked men, leaving his main body up on the American fork. Here he learned that Gillespie had returned from the *Portsmouth* and that three officers from the *Portsmouth* had been sent to assist him: the purser with some bags of American coin to help finance operations, Lieutenant Hunter in charge of the launch, and a Dr. Duvan "to arrange my medicine chest and to render any assistance in his power," suggesting that Commander Montgomery anticipated a certain amount of fighting.

The arrival of cash, supplies and officers from the United States warship Fremont interpreted to mean that the navy was under orders to render him full co-operation, that from this point forward the conquest would be a joint army and navy operation. If any further corroboration was needed by Fremont it was contained in Commander Montgomery's letter:

"I am also informed by Lieutenant G. of your having expressed to him a desire for the presence of a vessel of war at Santa Barbara; if you shall still think that the presence of a ship of war at Santa Barbara may prove serviceable to you in carrying out the views of our Government, and will do me the favor to communicate your wishes with information as to the time you will probably reach that part of the coast, I shall not fail (Providence permitting) to meet you there with the *Portsmouth*."

Captain Fremont next sent Kit Carson and a small group of men to Sutter's Fort to demand its surrender. Captain John Sutter was an army officer as well as a civil official of the Mexican government, but his need for military heroics had been satisfied in the civil war the year before. In one vast renunciatory gesture he stripped himself of his captaincy in the Mexican army and control over his fort by throwing open the gates and welcoming Kit Carson as Fremont's emissary. His reign as monarch of the Sacramento Valley, which had begun with his arrival in the wilderness in the fall of 1839, was ended.

Now John Fremont, who knew nothing about Mariano Vallejo except that he was the military commandant of the Mexican forces in the north, sent Vallejo and his party to Sutter's Fort as prisoners. Sutter received them with open-armed hospitality; over the years he and Vallejo had sometimes disagreed, but the two men respected each other. Sutter installed the group in his parlor. Bidwell, who was working as Sutter's secretary, brought them their meals and sat chatting with them while they ate.

Fremont was fighting a war under equivocal conditions; if he played a major role in capturing California for the United States, anything that might be interpreted as an irregular action would be forgiven him; but if he failed ... He therefore sent his map drawer and artist, Edward Kern (who had been sadly needed in Sonoma two days before to make the California bear look like a grizzly instead of a pig), into Sutter's Fort to take command, and to institute a stricter regime over the prisoners. Vallejo and his group were locked in inadequate quarters, they were allowed no visitors, the food was poor. The days passed, the four or five which Vallejo thought would bring him home, and the weeks passed, and still they were locked in their rooms in the fort.

The harsh treatment of Colonel Vallejo and his family was a breach of etiquette which all too soon gave way to gunshot wounds.

By June 17, when Sonoma had been under the Bear Flag for three days, an alarm was spread throughout the bay area that General Castro of Monterey was advancing on the Sacramento Valley to recapture the seized garrison.

William Ide, still in command at Sonoma, sent two Americans, Fowler and Cowie, northward toward the Russian River to pick up a keg of powder at the Fitch ranch. Since there were in the neighborhood some twenty armed Californios under the command of Juan Padilla waiting to join forces with Castro, the two men were urged not to travel by the main road. Fowler and Cowie were not worried about their opponents; they stayed on the road, were captured by Padilla and executed near Santa Rosa.

Ide sent out a small party to search for Fowler and Cowie; they had a skirmish with Padilla, wounding one of the Californios and capturing another who informed the Sonoma garrison of the shooting of the two men.

With this news the entire tone of the conflict changed; Americans and other foreigners who had wanted no part of the conflict came into Sonoma as volunteers, Grigsby returning to take charge of the rifle company. Families from the surrounding valleys were brought into the garrison for protection. Fremont left Sutter's Fort at the head of his troops, publicly acknowledging leadership of the conquest.

He reached Sonoma on June 25, a hundred sixty men under him. Finding no danger there he headed toward the bay, and in his first service as a military captain was outmaneuvered by de la Torre, a Californio who, needing time to get his men across the rough San Francisco waters, planted a false message to fall into Fremont's hands. Fremont wheeled his force; by the time he learned of the ruse and had returned to San Rafael, de la Torre had moved his troops across the bay. As a retaliatory measure Kit Carson, when he saw three Californio civilians land in a small boat nearby, shot them.

Paradise was growing a trifle ugly.

The poetic Californio officer, Arce, said:

"California is like a pretty girl, everybody wants her."

The courtship was getting rough.

From San Rafael Fremont crossed the bay with his troops, went to Fort Point, the presidio founded by the Spanish. The ancient guns were harmless but he went through the ceremony of spiking them, assisted by Captain William D. Phelps and his crew off the

Yankee trading vessel, the *Moscow*, thus getting the merchant marine involved in the uprising.

The Sacramento Valley and all lands north of San Francisco Bay were now in American hands. Captain John C. Fremont, conquerer of central California, sat for his portrait to Captain Phelps:

"Captain Fremont, a slender and well-porportioned man of sedate but pleasing appearance...dressed in a blue flannel shirt open at the collar, over a deerskin hunting shirt, blue cloth pantaloons and neat moccasins, all of which had evidently seen hard service: a light color handkerchief bound tightly around his head. A few minutes conversation convinced me that I stood in the presence of the King of the Rocky Mountains."

It was a sentiment the Californios, somewhat naturally, did not share.

Commodore Sloat, aging, conservative officer in charge of the Pacific flotilla, had his orders to help capture California once war with Mexico was declared. Unwilling to repeat the premature flag-raising *faux pas* of Commodore Jones in 1842, Sloat took the halfway measure of sending the U.S.S. *Levant* and the *Cyane* to California, but remained himself in the Mexican port of Mazatlan hoping that each hour would bring him the declaration. At last, without it, he sailed north to Monterey, arriving there on July 2 on the *Savannah*. There had been no Mexican flag flying in Monterey for two months, nor were there any soldiers in the garrison. Governor Pio Pico had established his capital in Los Angeles.

On July 4 Fremont stepped into the plaza of Sonoma, addressed the people and declared martial law. A committee consisting of John Bidwell, William Ide and Pierson B. Reading was directed to draw up a plan of government for Sonoma and northern California. In typical frontier fashion the three could not agree, each writing his own organizational report. Bidwell's was selected as the official one, probably because of its brevity.

Although Commodore Sloat took Fremont's action in stepping forth as the head of the Bear Flag insurgents as meaning that Fremont had specific orders from Washington, it still required strong language from one of his own officers, Captain Mervine of the *Savannah*, to get him to move:

"It is more than your commission is worth to hesitate in this matter!" cried Captain Mervine.

Commodore Sloat and Consul Larkin spent July 6 on board the *Savannah* drawing up proclamations, copies of which were sent to

Commander Montgomery on the *Portsmouth* in Yerba Buena.

"I have determined to hoist the flag of the United States at this place tomorrow," wrote Commodore Sloat, "as I would prefer being sacrificed for doing too much than too little. If you consider you have sufficient force, or if Fremont will join you, you will hoist the flag at Yerba Buena, or at any other place, and take possession of the fort and that portion of the country."

At ten o'clock in the morning of July 7 forceful Captain Mervine went ashore at the head of two hundred fifty marines. As there were no Mexican officers to surrender the Monterey garrison, the captain led his men up to the customs house and read aloud the declaration saying that California now belonged to the United States. For the third time an American flag was hoisted in the Far West. The marines gave three cheers, the ships multiplied this with a twenty-one-gun salute. After several thousand years of belonging to the Indians, two hundred seventy-nine years as a province of Spain, twenty-five years as a Mexican province, and twenty-four days as a Bear Flag Republic, California had now become American.

And just in time. When the English warship H.M.S. *Collingwood*, which had been playing hide-and-seek in Mexican waters, came around the point and Admiral Seymour saw the United States warships in the harbor, with the American flag flying over the town:

"The British admiral stamped his foot in rage and flung his hat upon the deck."

Two days later, July 9, 1846, Commander Montgomery took seventy men ashore at Yerba Buena, marched them to the public square, read the proclamation and raised a second American flag. Lieutenant Revere of the *Portsmouth* had left his ship at two that morning with a third flag and copy of the proclamation, riding at top speed to Sonoma where the flag was raised in the plaza sometime after noon.

To oppose the Americans there were, between Yerba Buena and San Diego, two potential forces: General Castro and Governor Pico in Los Angeles. If these two ranking Californio officers were to combine forces they could give Fremont a fight, but under no consideration could they have waged a serious contest with the marines and four United States ships of war in the harbors: the U.S.S. *Savannah*, of fifty-four guns, the sloops of war *Cyane* and *Levant*, of twenty-four guns each, the frigate *Congress* with sixty thirty-two-pounder long guns.

On July 19, no word having yet been received of a declaration of war, Commodore Sloat met with John Fremont in Sloat's cabin aboard the *Savannah*. The scene was volatile and angry. Commodore Sloat expressed himself as horrified that Fremont should have acted without official U. S. Army orders. At that moment the U.S.S. *Congress* came into Monterey Harbor, Commodore Stockton commanding. Stockton not only approved what Fremont had done, but greatly admired his course of action.

Feeling put upon, Commodore Sloat learned with profound relief that Commodore Stockton, young, vigorous, adventuresome, was willing to accept full responsibility for everything that had happened. Sloat gratefully turned over his command to Stockton and sailed out of the Far West waters, relieved to get out of the unresolved mess with no greater opprobrium than "indecisive."

Commodore R.F. Stockton and John C. Fremont liked each other on sight, forming a friendship based on identity of temperament. Stockton raised Fremont's rank to major, Gillespie's to captain, and officially took the California Battalion of volunteers into the navy.

Hoping to end the conflict quickly, Major Fremont moved his battalion to San Diego on ships of war and, on August 1, even as General Kearny was leaving Bent's Fort on his way west with his army, Commodore Stockton sailed with three hundred sixty marines and seamen in his flagship *Congress* for San Pedro to effect a meeting with Fremont and subdue southern California, including the new capital at Los Angeles. Consul Thomas O. Larkin sailed with Stockton. Fremont and Stockton believed they would have to defeat General Castro's troops in a major battle in order to put an end to the hostilities, but Consul Larkin, who had been living happily with the Californios for fourteen years, believed that an honorable peace could be negotiated which would enable the Mexican officers to save face and become a willing part of the new American regime.

Larkin nearly succeeded. He wrote to Abel Stearns, who had lived in southern California since 1829, asking him to urge General Castro to send envoys to Commodore Stockton. General Castro assumed that Larkin spoke for the commodore and did so, telling Commodore Stockton:

"Wishing then, with the governor, to avoid all the disasters that follow a war like that which your lordship prepares, it has appeared convenient to the undersigned to send to your lordship a commission . . . to know the wishes of your lordship. . . ."

All that was required was the kind of gesture that Commander Montgomery was at this time making to Mariano Vallejo, who had been confined in Sutter's Fort for almost a month. Captain Montgomery issued an order for Vallejo's release and, learning that Vallejo was ill, sent Dr. Henderson from the *Portsmouth* to Sonoma to care for him. Although Vallejo had returned home, in his own words to Larkin "half dead," and found that he had lost a thousand cows and horses during his absence, Commander Montgomery's graciousness healed the wounds. Vallejo became an enthusiastic citizen of the new order.

However Commodore Stockton refused to negotiate with General Castro's commissioners; the tone of his reply to Castro offended every Californio. Castro, unable to wage war, and Pico, unable to maintain his government, had little choice but to flee to Mexico.

Two days later, on August 12, official word reached California that the United States and Mexico were at war.

The Californios were to rise, in anger and in pride.

CHAPTER XIX

"There's that damned flag again!"

IF THE SIDE OF Commodore Stockton that went to war was undemocratic, he made up in part for his unseemly conduct by ordering the first popular elections to be held in the Far West; by asking that California's first newspaper be created for the dissemination of news; by appointing as the first American alcalde or chief magistrate of Monterey and its surrounding territory the Reverend Walter Colton, United States Navy, born in Vermont in 1797, son of a devout father who had served for fifty years as deacon of the Congregational Church. At the age of twenty-one Walter Colton had entered Yale, was ordained at twenty-eight, taught at an academy in Connecticut for four years and then moved to Washington, D.C., as editor and chief writer for the *American*

Spectator and Washington City Chronicle. For purposes of improving his health he became a chaplain in the navy, toured the Mediterranean for three years and published two volumes of his observations.

Colton had bushy eyebrows and black sideburns that framed normally unattractive features, the nose too bony, the mouth line ragged, but the long, big-domed face was dominated by a pair of burning scholar's eyes.

On Thursday, July 16, 1846, nine days after the American flag had been raised in Monterey, the Reverend Mr. Colton, then forty-nine, came into the thick fog of Monterey Harbor on board the *Congress*, and for the next three years worked wisely and wittily to dispel the fogs obscuring the transition of California to an American possession. Together with Robert Semple, the dentist-printer who had come into California in 1845 with the Hastings Party, a man whom Colton in *Three Years in California* describes as "wearing a buckskin dress, a foxskin cap; is true with his rifle, ready with his pen, and quick at his type-case," he created the *Californian,* finding a small press that had been used by a monk for printing religious tracts, using the wrappers of cigars for paper.

Colton could turn a sentence: "Our bay is full of the finest fish, and yet it is rare to meet one on the table. Put a fish on land, and give him the speed of a buck, and he would have a dozen Californians on his trail...." He put out the first edition of his weekly paper on Saturday, August 15, printed in English and Spanish.

As chief magistrate, judging personal quarrels as well as crimes and business disputes, the Reverend Walter Colton gave Monterey its first democratic decisions. Previously, for identical offenses, "The custom had been to fine Spaniards and whip Indians. This discrimination is unjust: I have substituted labor; and now have eight Indians, three Californians and one Englishman at work making adobes."

Colton also introduced modern penology by feeding the prisoners well, paying them one cent an adobe over the required fifty per day, and using no guards. No one ever ran away; if the Indians, given three months for taking another's horse when their own tired, or the Mexicans, given a similar sentence for slaughtering a convenient cow when they got hungry, were puzzled by this sudden change in the concept of private property, they were no more puzzled than was Magistrate Colton when the tangled love affairs of the territory were brought to him for settlement: the case of a Californio girl who, having run away with her lover, but still "as chaste and pure as the driven snow," changed her mind and refused to marry the man. How was bachelor Colton, still remembering the painful time when he had been jilted, to persuade the girl to let him perform the marriage ceremony?

When an important and wealthy Mexican who owed a humble Californio $800 was insulted by the fact that he could be hauled into court by a former servant who could neither read nor write, Magistrate Colton quickly made it clear that the only issue to be discussed was whether or not the don owed the money:

"Law which fails to protect the humble, disgraces the name which it bears."

He confounded two Californios quarreling over a gambling settlement by fining them both; impaneled the first jury ever to sit in California, making it one third Mexican-born, one third California-born, and one third American-born, using English-born William Hartnell as interpreter. The people of Monterey were delighted with this newfangled idea, and came to understand what Magistrate Colton meant when he observed:

"If there is anything on earth besides religion for which I would die, it is the right of trial by jury."

If the Reverend Mr. Colton had no competition as a magistrate, it did not take long, only two months, for a competitive newspaper to emerge in Yerba Buena, published by Samuel Brannan, who on July 31 had sailed into San Francisco Bay on the *Brooklyn* out of New York and around the Cape, at the head of some two hundred thirty-eight Latter-day Saints seeking a new home in the Far West. Their purpose in coming to California was to join the main body of their Chruch, which was moving westward, perhaps to California, no one could be sure. Brannan is said to have exclaimed in disappointment when he sailed into the bay:

"There's that damned flag again!"

Sam Brannan did not possess the self-discipline required of a dedicated Saint; his career in the Church as well as in California was a stormy one. He had been excommunicated a few years before, only to be reprieved by one of the Prophet Joseph Smith's brothers. On his arrival in Yerba Buena he was brought up on charges by his fellow Mormons for misconduct during the voyage. Commander Montgomery presided over the jury trial.

At the beginning of August 1846 there were upwards of two hundred residents in Yerba Buena; when two hundred thirty-eight Saints disembarked, Yerba Buena became, as Bancroft commented, "largely a Mormon town."

Their arrival helped to secure the permanence of Yerba Buena, still being threatened by the possibility of other communities being started on the bay where the ships would be closer to fresh water, food and good anchorage. The hundred-odd Mormon families consisted of able farmers and mechanics who had brought their tools and skills and immediately set to work, some as lumbermen across the strait, which had been named by John Fremont the Golden Gate Strait, others to start a colony called New Hope on the Stanislaus River where they built a barn and mill and cultivated eighty acres in order to have a food supply against the arrival of Brigham Young, who was leading his people out of the bloody battlefield of Nauvoo, Illinois, their sacred city, and across the plains.

There was some fear and suspicion of the Mormons among the Americans in California, yet the people of Yerba Buena made many of the families comfortable in the old mission buildings, while the rest set up a tent colony.

Sam Brannan and his party were not the first Mormons to come into the mountain-banked amphitheatre of the Far West. A few months earlier, in the spring of 1846, a party of forty-three Saints traveling in nineteen wagons had left the Mississippi, missed the main body of Mormons moving west, and had struck southward along the eastern foothills of the Rockies with a trader as a guide, finding their way to present-day Pueblo. Welcomed by the small group of Americans and Mexicans living around the adobe post, this vanguard had gratefully built cabins and put in crops while waiting for news of their people. It was the first group since Father Junipero Serra and the mission padres in 1769 to come into the Far West inspired by their religion to seek new frontiers for the purpose of colonizing.

During the winter the colony increased to two hundred seventy-five by the moving in of the sick soldiers of the Mormon Battalion with their families; seven children were born, thought by historians to be the first all-white children to be born in what is present-day Colorado. Yet the colony proved to be temporary, as were the Mormon colonies in Yerba Buena and on the Stanislaus River. The heroic trek and settlement of the main body of the Latter-day Saints in the Far West was still in the future.

CHAPTER XX

Armed Conflict

MOST OF SOUTHERN CALIFORNIA was up in arms. A full-scale revolt had been mounted by the Californios, who had become fighting mad. Their good and sufficient cause was Captain Archibald Gillespie, enjoying his first real taste of power, a man of fertile talent who has been inadequately recognized by history: wherever he passed he dropped the seed of discord, and soon the spot would be blessed by a goodly crop of confusion. Having been made military commander of the southern department and instructed to order martial law in a territory that was largely Mexican, Captain Gillespie became a tyrant over a people who were friendly and, for the most part, persuaded that the Americans would give them a stable government and, since property values in Monterey had increased forty per cent in a few weeks, prosperity as well.

Captain Gillespie knew little about the Californios and liked them even less. With a garrison of fifty men behind him, he became a dictator: no two persons could walk on the streets together; there could be no gatherings in homes, no provision shops open after sundown, no liquor sold without his permission. He shut down their amusements, arrested the leading Californios on frivolous grounds...all of which the perplexed but patient people might have withstood had not Gillespie made it all too plain that:

"He looked down on Californios and Mexicans as an inferior race and a cowardly foe."

Four hundred men took up whatever scattered arms were available and, under the leadership of former army officers Captain Jose Flores as *comandante general*, Jose Carrillo as second and Captain Andres Pico third in command, warmed up for their campaign by besieging and capturing the Chino rancho of Isaac

98

Williams, where twenty Americans and foreigners were under the command of Benjamin Wilson. On September 30 they captured Captain Gillespie and his garrison, Gillespie not even attempting to put up a fight.

The Californios might have been justified in rolling the bumptious Captain Gillespie over a barrel in the plaza; instead they permitted him an honorable surrender, and let him march his men to San Pedro. On October 2 another force of Californios marched on Santa Barbara, but Captain Theodore Talbot, instead of surrendering his small garrison, led it in an escape to the hills while the Californios retook the town.

When word reached Yerba Buena of the uprising in the south, Captain Mervine and the *Savannah* were sent to San Pedro where Captain Gillespie, on parole not to fight any more, joined Captain Mervine, adding his fifty men to Mervine's three hundred forty. The Californios had dug up an old four-pounder celebration cannon from the plaza in Los Angeles, manufactured some gunpowder at San Gabriel and marched out to meet the Americans, killing six and wounding six others with their cannon fire before the American forces retreated to the harbor and re-embarked on the *Savannah*.

The success of the Mexican victories in the south started guerrilla warfare throughout the state, with bands of Californios capturing Consul Larkin on his way to Yerba Buena, and five sailors at San Mateo; a Californio force under Manuel Castro fought a battle with American troops under Captain Thompson at Natividad, the scene of Isaac Graham's early distillery, with each side losing five or six dead and a like number wounded. Word spread that, aside from the ports which the American warships and their big guns could control, all of California would soon be back in the hands of its former owners.

On October 19 Commodore Stockton sailed from Yerba Buena on the *Congress* for San Pedro to take command, after ordering Major Fremont to recruit in the Sacramento Valley and raise a hundred seventy experienced riflemen. Fremont embarked his men on the U.S.S. *Sterling* for Santa Barbara, whence he was to march south to join Commodore Stockton and recapture Los Angeles. When Fremont reached Santa Barbara he learned of Captain Mervine's defeat, and the fact that the Californios had denuded the intervening country of horses, cattle and supplies. He returned on the same ship with his hundred seventy sharpshooters to Monterey. It was one of the rare instances in his life when Fremont had acted too cautiously, or so Commodore Stockton thought in castigating his friend in a report to the Navy Department. It was another substantial victory for the Californios.

Heading almost straight south along the Rio Grande River was an American armed force under Stephen Watta Kearny. Kearny, who had been made a general for his quick, albeit unopposed subjugation of Santa Fe, had with him a force of three hundred dragoons, about the same force he had brought briefly to Colorado the previous spring. On October 6 General Kearny encountered Kit Carson, who was on his way to Washington with dispatches. Reading Commodore Stockton's proclamation to the effect that California was subdued, General Kearny ordered two hundred of his dragoons back to Santa Fe. He then insisted that Carson give the dispatches to Broken Hand Fitzpatrick for delivery in Washington, and himself guide Kearny to California.

Carson guided Kearny's force further southward, then struck west along the Gila River across present-day Arizona to where the Gila and Colorado rivers join. By crossing the Colorado river, Kearny entered the extreme southeast corner of California. Carson then led him northward to avoid the terrifying desert lying between the mountain range and San Diego. At San Pasqual Kearny was reinforced by Gillespie, sixty mounted riflemen and a third howitzer to join the two cannons the dragoons had dragged all the way from Santa Fe.

On December 6 Kearny's troops came into contact with a smaller force of Andres Pico's mounted guerrillas. Suffering from Gillespie's malady of contempt for the Californios, and failing to obey the elementals of military tactics, Kearny sent an advance guard down a steep hill to charge the Californios, who stood firm, killing Captain Johnson, the commanding officer, and another dragoon. Without order or organization, Kearny's troops now dashed into battle, strung out according to the speed of their horses and mules. Pico, surveying the situation from a knoll, led his eighty men into a charge against the Americans, who were mounted on tired or unbroken horses and intractable mules, much of their flint and powder wet from the rain. The Californios, among the greatest horsemen in the world, had their most effective weapon, their lances, ready.

The result was one of the worst military defeats for an American force since the War of 1812: twenty-one killed, including a number of officers, nineteen wounded, including General Kearny and Captain Gillespie, the loss of a howitzer. The Californios suffered minor injuries.

A relief party sent through the lines to San Diego was captured by the Californios, who again outmaneuvered General Kearny at the San Bernardino ranch. A second rescue party consisting of Kit Carson, Edward Beale and an Indian boy managed by magnificent woodcraft and endurance to get through the lines to San Diego. On December 11 a large force of marines and sailors rescued General Kearny. The next day, December 12, Kearny marched his force into San Diego to combine with Commodore Stockton's men.

If the combined American forces meant big trouble for the Californios, and the war was just about over, trouble for the American commanders was just beginning.

John C. Fremont, who had learned before leaving Monterey with his enlarged battalion, now numbering over four hundred armed and mounted riflemen, that President Polk had appointed him a lieutenant colonel, spent Christmas Day of 1846 in the roughest terrain of the Santa Inez mountain, suffering from cold, wet and exhaustion, with a hundred fifty to two hundred of the horses dying, the men forced to drag their cannons by hand over the steepest stretches. In San Diego the weather was warm, bright, sunny and dry, but General Kearny was none the happier for it. Though his rank as a general was in every way equal to that of Commodore Stockton, and though in any land push such as they were now planning to put down the remaining fragments of the Californio rebellion, an army general should rightly have been in charge, Commodore Stockton had assumed command of the combined forces.

Kearny, rankling over his defeat, the loss of his men and his howitzer, was profoundly resentful. He was determined to take the command away from Commodore Stockton as soon as the Californio forces had been defeated, not merely the military command which he felt his orders entitled him to, but the civil command as well. Therein lay the makings of a monumental quarrel, all of it played on California soil, but magnified by a Washington court-martial until it became a permanent part of the heritage of the Far West: for the civilization of a country is made up not only of its mountains and deserts, fertile valleys, coastline and mineral resources; the character of a country is formed as much by the character of the men who come onto its terrain.

On January 1, 1847, the Californios, realizing that the Americans now had a well-armed force of some five hundred men marching north from San Diego, and that Lieutenant Colonel Fremont was marching south with another four hundred, sent a letter signed by Jose Flores, under the title of governor, suggesting that since the unpleasantries between Mexico and the United States were probably over by now a truce be declared and negotiations begun for peace.

Commodore Stockton again refused. General Kearny asked for and was granted actual command of the troops under Stockton. This time he sent a strong party of skirmishers ahead to protect his two nine-pounders and four field pieces. The Californios charged in force on the American left flank. The troops held. The Californios retreated. This was the Battle of San Gabriel, the first victory for General Kearny.

The next day, halfway between San Gabriel and Los Angeles, the Californio cavalry dashed out of a concealed ravine and attacked the Americans on both flanks. Using Indian warfare techniques, General Kearny formed his troops into a square with the wagons at the center and the guns at the corners. The Californio attacks failed to push the Americans back and, having a limited amount of powder, they retreated northward.

The following day Captain Gillespie raised the American flag in the plaza at Los Angeles where he had been obliged to haul it down some three months before. Two days later, on January 12, Lieutenant Colonel Fremont, who was near the mission of San Fernando, received a message from General Andres Pico, who apparently had no stomach for surrendering to either Commodore Stockton or General Kearny. Fremont granted Pico a friendly and generous peace in which the Californio officers and men could return to their homes with honor and dignity. He also took back General Kearny's howitzer.

John C. Fremont had created much good will: he had kept his California Battalion rigidly in control on its march down from Monterey, for which the Californios respected him; when he had been obliged to take horses and cattle for his men, he had paid for them with government scrip; he had saved the life of Jesus Pico, one of the most influential men in central California; and he had granted the surrendering Californios all the rights enjoyed by Americans.

The next day he marched into Los Angeles in a heavy rain.

"A more ragged, ill-provided, unprepossessing battalion it would have been difficult to imagine, they might have been taken, as one of them remarked, for a tribe of Tartar nomads... only their military order and arms made them seem soldiers."

Commodore Stockton so heartily approved the Fremont treaty that he named Fremont governor of California and commander-in-chief of all the forces.

This was the insult supreme to General Kearny, culminating his weeks of frustration since the defeat at San Pasqual. He promptly wrote to Commodore Stockton and Lieutenant Colonel Fremont announcing that he was commander-in-chief in California, that Commodore Stockton was to cease attempting to set up a civil government, and ordering Fremont to perform no act in government without the specific approval of General Kearny. Commodore Stockton replied angrily that the civil government had already been operating for a number of months, that General Kearny had no power here, and that he would send the insolent letter to President Polk and ask for Kearny's recall.

The next morning, January 17, was the fateful day for young Fremont: being summoned to General Kearny's tent, Fremont gave the general his written reply in which he said that he had been mustered into the navy with his battalion under Stockton and felt that he owed his allegiance to Stockton:

"I feel myself, therefore, with great deference to your professional and personal character, constrained to say that, until you and Commodore Stockton adjust between yourselves the question of rank, where I respectfully think the difficulty belongs, I shall have to report and receive orders, as heretofore, from the Commodore."

This was an error in judgment on Fremont's part, though he had something of reason on his side: Stockton's orders from Washington to set up civil government were dated later and were more decisive than Kearny's; Kearny had acknowledged Stockton as commander-in-chief on the march up from San Diego. But Fremont was an army man, he had been an army officer for nine years; he was responsible to the army.

Grim, hard-bitten Kearny, who had spent most of his life on the Indian frontiers, now showed considerable patience and tenderness for young Fremont, whom he had known from the home of Fremont's wife's family in St. Louis and Washington. Kearny quietly advised Fremont to tear up the letter and to put himself under Kearny's orders or he would end his career in the army.

Fremont remained adamant. Kearny sailed for Monterey with his dragoons, where he set himself up as governor of California, a post Fremont was holding in the south. Commodore Shubrick arrived in Monterey, commanding the frigates U.S.S. *Independence* and *Lexington*. Stockton's command was terminated, and with it Fremont's legal right to serve as governor. Commodore Shubrick, seeing General Kearny's orders, declared him to be "head and commander of the troops in California." From this moment the army and navy worked closely together. Fremont made a wild ride to Monterey, quarreled further with Kearny, was refused permission to take his battalion to Mexico for action or to move his original exploring party back to Washington at his own expense.

There was talk in California military circles that Lieutenant Colonel Fremont would be shot for refusing to obey orders. What actually happened was more degrading to a man of Fremont's high spirit and high pride: he was ordered to follow in the dust of General Kearny's dragoons back to Washington as a military prisoner, there to stand court-martial.

CHAPTER XXI

The Furies Pour Their Pent-up Vengeance

ONE GROUP OF MEN, not strictly an emigrant train, had come over the mountains in 1845. Into the gates of Sutter's Fort had ridden Lansford Hastings, who had returned east from California the year before promising that he would lead back a large emigrant party. Hastings had spent the previous winter lecturing in Missouri on the evils of intemperance in order to raise enough money to publish his book, *The Emigrant's Guide to Oregon and California*; fittingly enough the book was full of intemperate judgment and autointoxication. Hastings was an opportunist whom Bidwell, after considerable association, described as a political adventurer. He had hoped to bring so many people into California who would owe him a personal debt of gratitude that through them he would seize California, either to be joined to Texas or to be part of the United States, with himself as governor of the new territory.

Hastings was handsome, strong-faced, quick and intelligent of speech. In Missouri he had assured everyone that he had been over the California Trail, which was a total fiction. He had been able to assemble only twenty-two men by mid-August, twelve of them soon dropping out. Despite the fact that he was several months too late to risk the journey, Hastings had led the horseback party in over the Walker-Stevens, Fremont Trail. It was the only party ever received by genial John Sutter with a severe reprimand: Sutter looked up toward the Sierra Nevada and the December snows and told them that had they been delayed by even one day they would have been cut off and perished in the mountains.

During the last week of April 1846 Lansford Hastings had again left Sutter's Fort to return east, his purpose being to find a faster, more direct route between Sutter's and Fort Bridger in northeastern Utah, and to persuade emigrant trains to accept his leadership and use his route west . . . at ten dollars a head. With him was a man named Hudspeth, who had been his companion on every trip since the initial one in 1842, Caleb Greenwood and twenty-three others.

During the first week of May a number of emigrant wagons arriving in Missouri at the same time banded together to form trains: the Bryant-Russell Party, the Young and Harlan parties, the Boggs and Aram parties, the Reed-Donner Party. These groups were no longer as compact or distinct as they had been in the days of the Bidwell, Grigsby-Ide or Stevens parties. With two thousand emigrants on the march, and five hundred teams of oxen, mules and horses, the trail from Independence to Fort Bridger had become an almost continuous stream of men, families and wagons.

Pushing ahead rapidly to reach Fort Bridger before the first emigrant trains arrived from the East, Hastings crossed the Sierra Nevada, descended by way of the Truckee River, followed the Humboldt River. At Bishop's Creek he saw the hoofprints of the Fremont Party of 1844, when Carson and Fremont had crossed the salt desert south of the Great Salt Lake. Hastings wanted his party to take this new, shorter route east; Greenwood refused, taking most of the party northeast to Fort Hall. Hastings, Hudspeth and five men mounted on good horses made the crossing in twenty hours.

On July 20 the first party of 1846 emigrants came into the Far West, the Bryant-Russell Party composed of men who had sold their wagons and oxen for mules, guided by Hudspeth. Lansford Hastings led the Young-Harlan Party of a hundred sixty people. Instead of taking them over the route he had just traversed, he guided them through the unknown, precipice-walled Weber Canyon, barely getting the wagons out onto the salt plain. He then rode up to the top of the canyon, stuck a note on top of a bush warning any oncoming parties not to essay the canyon, but to take the cut-off he had used coming east. He then rejoined his party, followed the Bryant-Russell tracks just ahead, circled Great Salt

Lake on the south, and crossed the salt desert on Fremont's trail. The party almost perished because of his serious underestimate of the distance to water, the stock dying, the wagons abandoned, the women and children making their way on foot.

At the south end of the Great Salt Lake, Hudspeth had told the Bryant-Russell Party, because of the scarcity of water:

"Put spurs to your mules and ride like hell!"

They rode like hell, making Sutter's by September 1, in time to join Fremont's California Battalion on its way to San Diego.

By October 10 Lansford Hastings brought in the Young-Harlan group. His timing was dangerously close. Once again he was fortunate, his people safe. The Donner Party coming behind them would have no such luck.

Hastings had been able to persuade only three groups that they should abandon the longer but safer Fort Hall-California trail for his own cut-off: the Bryant-Russell group of nine men, the Young-Harlan Party and the Donner Party of twenty wagons and seventy-three people. Jessy Quinn Thornton recorded in his diary at the Little Sandy River, where the Oregon section of the train separated from the Donners:

"The Californians were much elated and in fine spirits, with the prospect of a better and nearer road to the country of their destination. Mrs. George Donner was, however, an exception. She was gloomy, sad, and dispirited in view of the fact that her husband and others could think for a moment of leaving the old road, and confide in the statement of a man of whom they knew nothing, but who was probably some selfish adventurer."

Tamsen Donner, forty-five, former schoolmistress who was carrying books, school supplies and art materials with which to educate her five young daughters in California, was a woman of considerable prescience.

James Clyman, mountain man, who had just come over the salt desert cut-off and up the Wasatch Mountains, talked his heroic heart out trying to dissuade them from taking any part of Lansford Hastings's advice. As Bernard DeVoto recreates the scene in *The Year of Decision: 1846*, Clyman warned this slow-moving train, already late, already depleted by illness, quarrels, blinding sun and dust, to take the well-established trail:

"It is barely possible to get through [before the snows] if you follow it—and it may be impossible if you don't."

The Donner Party's trek to the new frontier was to become "the greatest catastrophe in the opening of the Far West."

*　　　*　　　*

The party made up in Springfield, Illinois, not far from the home of Abraham and Mary Lincoln on Eighth Street. They carried a copy of Hastings's *Emigrant's Guide* in their wagon, along with Fremont's *Reports*. There were nine in the Jacob Donner family, seven in the George Donner family and seven in the James F. Reed family, plus eight hired men and one hired girl, neighbors of the Donners and Reeds working their way across the country to start a new life. There were young William Eddy, his wife and two children, the McCutchen family of three, the Widow Murphy, leading five unmarried children, her two married daughters and their families, Irish Patrick Breen, with his wife and seven children, German Lewis Keseberg, with his wife and two small children, the wealthy German Wolfinger family, Charles T. Stanton, and the assorted single men typical of every emigrant train.

Gentle, amiable, wealthy sixty-two-year-old George Donner was perhaps the first of the secure but tired Midwest farmers to head for California and retirement. James F. Reed, forty-six, a dynamic and wealthy furniture manufacturer, had had considerable success as an executive and handler of men. On the morning of August 3 when the party crossed the Bear River into present-day Utah they were led by George Donner, who had been elected captain on July 20, 1846, but it was James Reed who led the thinking when the party received a letter from Lansford Hastings urging them to use his cut-off, and made the decision to take advantage of the four hundred miles shorter route. At the rate the caravan was moving, ten to twelve miles a day, this cut-off could save them a month of hard travel.

It was Reed who replied to Jim Clyman from the vast abyss of his ignorance of the Far West:

"There is a nigher route, and it is no use to take so much of a roundabout course."

As was the universal practice of emigrant trains, the party took a vote. There is no evidence that the women were permitted to participate; responsible for thirty young children, they probably would have agreed with Tamsen Donner and voted not to gamble with the lives of their young. The men declared for Hastings's cut-off. Hastings in his letter had promised to wait for them at Fort Bridger and guide them safely "to the Salt Lake, and then continuing down to the Bay of San Francisco."

A day or two before they reached Fort Bridger they met Joseph Walker, one of the ablest mountain men in North American history, opener of the great paths to the Far West. He urged them vehemently not to take the Hastings cut-off, but to turn north to Fort Hall.

When the party reached Fort Bridger they found that Lansford Hastings had not waited for them. Without a guide, with not one experienced mountain man or plains traveler among them and, with one exception, not even an experienced hunter, they were still determined to save that four hundred miles.

Now three days into the Far West, on August 6, they arrived at the top of Weber Canyon and found the note Hastings had left on a bush, rejecting his own recommended route down the unexplored canyon. The Donner Party settled into camp and sent Reed, Stanton and McCutchen on horseback down the Weber Canyon after Hastings. They needed the time for neither rest nor repairs, they had just taken four days for this purpose at Fort Bridger. Clyman and Walker had warned them that they were already late, yet for five days they waited until James Reed returned, without Hastings, who had refused to leave the party he was with. Reed had come up the Wasatch Mountains from the west, in the general direction indicated by Hastings's hand-pointed directions.

Once again James Reed was the deciding factor, for he had now traveled down the Weber Canyon and up the Wasatch Mountains. He advised the party that the Wasatch was the better, a decision in which his *Palace Car* with its side steps, top deck for beds, built-in stove, private inner compartment, basement floor for storing food, wider and heavier than any covered wagon yet to set forth on the trail, was of crucial importance. For Reed had seen the steep, twisting Weber Canyon in which the walls finally narrowed to precipices on either side of the river, where the wagons of a previous party had had to be lowered by ropes and tackle, one of them smashing to splinters on the rocks below.

And so in mid-August they began their crossing of the mountains, forced to build their own road every desperate mile of the way, cutting through underbrush, through forests of twenty-foot alder and aspen, crossing a creek twice to a mile, filling ravines with tree stumps, drying out swamps. The party was poorly composed for such work, with only twenty able-bodied men in the group. Blisters and tempers rose, quarrels and recriminations. Range after range of unmapped mountains extended ahead. The journey to Great Salt Lake which they had been told would take a week consumed twenty-one days for the distance of thirty-six miles.

By now the party was split into hostile factions. By now it was

September 1. They faced the dread-inspiring vast, hot, crystalline, waterless white salt desert . . . without guide or leader.

Just before entering the "dry drive" the party came upon a board with a written message, parts of which had been torn and scattered. The pieces were brought to Tamsen Donner, who laboriously put them together. It had been written by Lansford Hastings about twenty-one days earlier. It read:

"Two days and two nights of hard driving to reach the next grass and water."

They spent two days resting the animals, cutting grass, cooking, then followed Hastings's trail toward a range of mountains and made the top by late afternoon. Below, as far as the eye could see, lay desert.

The next day their wheels sank into the light salt sand, the merciless sun beat upon them, the oxen faltered. The train spread out, every man for himself, with the heavily laden Reeds and Donners falling behind because their wagons were filled with a fortune in laces and silks and other merchandise to be traded in California. George Donner had $10,000 in bills stitched inside a quilt.

By the end of the third day the entire train faced death, their water gone, oxen dying under their yokes. James Reed left his wagons at noon, on horseback, and by nightfall reached the base of Pilot Peak and the spring Fremont's advance party had located the year before, just inside the border of present-day Nevada. When he rode back to his family, passing the emigrants struggling forward like ghost-white salt figures in the darkness, he found that his cattle had stampeded into the desert and were lost. Reed now had to bury his *Palace Car* with its fortune in goods in the desert and get his family on foot to the spring.

The "dry drive" had been eighty miles instead of forty, had taken six days instead of two; four wagons were abandoned, one of Keseberg's, one of Jacob Donner's, two of Reed's. The wealth of merchandise owned by the Donners and Reeds, which even as a cold business decision should have kept them on the safe California Trail, was totally lost. The desert trail was strewn with mahogany beds, bureaus, rockers, musical instruments, all the tokens of continuity between the old life and the new. The party faced a sheer and doubtful struggle merely to stay alive. But the common suffering of this ordeal by thirst did not draw the exhausted, frightened fragments of the Donner-Reed train together. Instead, it led to further disintegration.

They spent the next full week resting, searching the desert for their lost animals, bringing in food from the abandoned wagons, sending Stanton, a bachelor, and William McCutchen, a family man, ahead to Sutter's in the hope they could bring back relief. Having no choice, they continued to follow Hastings's tracks, only to find that Hastings, still improvising, had declined to take the route over the Ruby Mountains and instead had driven south for three days looking for an easier pass, only to double back. Since he did not warn those to follow, the Donner Party spent another week following the futile trail south and then north.

On September 30 they reached the Humboldt River and joined the California Trail. The last of their companions from Independence, who had gone by the Fort Hall road, had passed this point from thirty-five to forty-five days before, and the Joseph Aram Party of twelve wagons and fifty people were in sight of Johnson's ranch in the Sacramento Valley. Reed's "nigher route" had proved to be desperately longer in time.

Five days later they were again in serious trouble. In a row precipitated by frayed and anxious nerves, James Reed, trying to quiet the popular but hot-tempered John Snyder from quarreling with Milt Elliott over whose team should have precedence in pulling up a hill, was so severely beaten over the head by Snyder's bull whip that he drew his hunting knife and sank it in Synder's chest. Synder died immediately.

The party was totally shattered. One segment wanted Reed executed. Instead he was banished, without gun or food, leaving his sick wife and children unprotected. Split now into warring factions, the train floundered to the Humboldt Sink. They had no knowledge of how to defend themselves against the Indians, who killed or ran off most of the remaining oxen and cattle.

On October 20 they reached the meadows of the eastern base of the Sierra Nevada. Here Stanton, having returned from Sutter's with two Indian guides and seven mules, found them. Sutter's mules were laden with flour and dried beef. There were now only five hard days driving up the Truckee River to the pass. There had been snow, but Stanton, who had risked his life in the return, urged them to "rest, recoup their animals in this meadow." Even heroes can be guilty of bad judgment.

The party rested for five days, then began the ascent of the Sierra Nevada. The vanguard, the Breens, Eddys and Kesebergs, pushed ahead, passed the cabin built by Schallenberger of the Stevens Party in 1844, and made for the pass. On November 1, when they were only three miles from the summit, they lost the trail in five feet of snow. They turned back to the Schallenberger cabin near the lake, where they dug in. The rest of the party, except the slow-moving Donners, came up and camped. The next day the weather was better and the party started once again for the pass, the children being carried by the adults, Stanton making the summit with his Indians to force a new trail through the snow. He returned to find the half-frozen party camped around a fire, urged them to continue upward the last two or three miles that led to the top of the ridge and safety.

They refused. They were cold, tired, they wanted to rest overnight. They did; but the snow began falling. By morning the drifts were ten feet deep. The pass was closed. They fought their way back to the cabin on the lake. As George R. Stewart observes in *Ordeal by Hunger*:

"The trap which closed behind them at Fort Bridger had closed in front."

Any one day would have saved them: one of the four spent resting at Fort Bridger, one of the five spent waiting for Reed to return from his trip to overtake Hastings, one of the seven spent pursuing Hastings's trail south and then north again, one of the five in the Truckee meadows, the last day's refusal to push the final three miles behind Stanton; one day that the devastating snowstorms might have held off. Or any one of the innumerable days spent in quarreling, refusing to help each other, to share food, water, oxen, friendship, leadership.

In the pioneering of a new land not all the emigrants will come equipped with the moral or physical skills to create an Eden. As diverse as were the impulses to pull up roots and possessions to cross deserts and mountains to a new country, equally diverse were the talents and abilities to cope with it.

There were signs of unselfishness and strength: Reed had divided his food when abandoning his wagon; Eddy had lost his wagon and coupled his team to Reed's when Reed had lost his animals; Stanton had returned from Sutter's with help. There was also the cruelest selfishness and violence: the refusal of the camp to lend Eddy a horse to go back and look for the lost and alone Hardkoop, who consequently perished in the desert; Breen's refusal of water to the suffering Eddy children, and Eddy's getting it only by swearing that he would kill anyone who tried to stop him . . . but not taking any for himself; Walter Herron and James Smith, wanting to buy oxen from the Breens, who had the largest supply of food, had to pledge two animals for one when they reached California. There was the uncontrolled temper of Snyder, quarreling over who should cross a mountain first; Reed's flashing knife; Graves's insistence that Reed be shot for his crime, the pitiful plight of Reed's wife and five children when he was banished.

All this they took into camp with them on the fourth day of November 1846 at the base of the towering snow-covered implacable western Sierra Nevada.

It was not merely the cold, for there was plenty of firewood and, at first, men to cut in; nor was it the hunger and malnutrition, for at first there were a few beeves, oxen, then the remaining few horses, mules and finally dogs. Their inability to accept discipline or leadership, the inter-family hatreds that pursued them right down to their deaths, so that there never was any sharing of food or hope or comfort . . . these caused their slow destruction; these deprived them of their strongest psychological weapon for survival.

If they suffered from bad judgment, they also had bad luck.

Charles Stanton led a party of sixteen men, six women and two Indian guides across the pass, then refused to continue on because he wished to protect Sutter's property, and the mules were exhausted. Eddy offered to reimburse Sutter, crying out that twenty-two human beings were worth more than seven mules, but Stanton remained adamant. Most of the men and women who forced the pass that night later perished; the mules wandered off in the snow and were lost.

A "snowshoe party," consisting of ten men who were physically able to travel, five younger women and two half-grown boys, forced the pass and for six days fought their way against twelve-foot snowdrifts, subzero weather, snow blindness, totally without food. A new storm descended upon them. Stanton, too weak to continue, saved his companions the problem of abandoning him by saying that he would be along later, then died by the side of the trail in lonely dignity.

The rest knew they must perish unless they had something to eat. They discussed drawing lots to see which one should be killed and eaten, but in the end decided to struggle on until someone died.

The first to go was Antonio, the Mexican herdsman, then Uncle Billy Graves, then Patrick Dolan, the bachelor, then thirteen-year-old Lemuel Murphy. Lying at the bottom of a twelve-foot hole of snow, ice water seeping in at the bottom, "they stripped the flesh from the bodies, roasted what they needed to eat and dried the rest for carrying with them."

No one would eat the flesh of a member of his own family.

Lost and kept going only by the unconquerable courage of Eddy, they made their tortured way westward mile by mile. Mrs. Foster had to watch her younger brother Lemuel's heart broiled over the coals and eaten. Later it was Mrs. Fosdick's turn to watch Mrs. Foster cut the heart and liver out of Fosdick's body and broil them over a fire.

"It was the necessity, not the act, that was deplorable."

But for the killing of the two defenseless Indians there was no moral justification, as Eddy and three women, now so close to death they could barely drag their feet over the trail, testified by refusing to touch the flesh.

Of the ten men who started out with the "snowshoe party," five died on the trail, two were killed, and one boy died before the two remaining men, Eddy and Foster, one boy and all five of the women (the female of the species has greater endurance than the male, as countless stories of the opening of the Far West prove) stumbled into Johnson's camp thirty-three days after leaving the lake; a grisly saga that has no counterpart for suffering or for unquenchable courage.

The slow-moving Donners had never caught up with the main body of the train, but stopped five miles east of the lake at Alder Creek, cut off from all contact or co-operation with the main camp. At the lake the cabins were now buried in nine feet of snow so that they were "cold and damp caves." The men had grown too weak to cut firewood, the last of the animals had died, the main food was the hides which had been used as roofing, boiled to a gelatin-like pulp, and bones of animals long since devoured. Mrs. Reed had been in the gravest danger from the loss of her husband and animals, and had five children to feed as well as several dependents. At the Reed cabins the two drivers turned their faces to the wall and died: Baylis Williams, the family protector, later Milt Elliott. Old Mrs. Murphy cut him up and ate him, all except his face.

One of the Keseberg children died, the baby Catherine Pike died, the first Eddy boy died, then Mrs. Eddy, who had put her last piece of bear meat in her husband's pack when he left with the "snowshoe party." The Breens took in Mrs. Reed and her five children, giving them hides and thrice-boiled bones to eat, or they too would have perished. Mrs. Breen secretly gave some of her remaining food to fifteen-year-old Virginia Reed, who had been on the verge of falling into the coma preceding death, thus saving the girl; yet at this point Breen forced Mrs. Reed to pay him the money they owed for cattle he had given the Reeds earlier.

Human character is unendingly contradictory; and interesting.

Relief was at last on its way; a party organized at Sutter's set forth early in February: seven men, all strangers to the Donners, none of them mountain men, forced a crossing in fourteen days of incredible stamina. The "canyons raced with wild rivers"; it was subfreezing cold; every man, on foot, carried on his back a pack of fifty to seventy-five pounds of food. They scaled range after range of the Sierra Nevada, at night huddled around a fire, unable to lie down. Obliged to make a final trailless crossing of the highest peak, had they become lost they would have died in the ice and snow.

But they were great in heart. They triumphed: Ned Coffeemeyer and Joseph Sels, former sailors; Aquilla Glover and Sept Moultry, farmer-emigrants to California in 1846; John and Daniel Rhoads, brothers who had come into California with the Mormons; Reasin "Dan" Tucker, also an emigrant.

The rescuers rested a couple of days, then started back over the wall of snow with three men, four women and seventeen children. John Rhoads offered to carry little Naomi Pike on his back. They could leave no food behind with the fifteen who remained in the camp, or the twelve at Alder Creek: the Donners, the Breens, the Graveses, the sick and the very young children.

The trek began to be a repetition of the "snowshoe party": Mrs. Reed had to send back two of her children who were too weak to travel; Denton, the Englishman, failed, quietly died wrapped in the quilt left with him by the freezing Dan Tucker; then little Ada Keseberg died. Moultry and Coffeemeyer were supermen, they forged ahead, located packs of beef from a cache and returned as the majority of the children were weakening.

Then into their camp arrived a second rescue mission led by James Reed, who had been banished more than four months before on the desert. He brought word that all of northern California had risen on hearing of the tragedy, and that a strong, well-supplied rescue party was on its way.

The children's party with Moultry and Coffeemeyer made Sutter's safely, while Reed pushed eastward with nine experienced mountain men to the lake. Here they found conditions of indescribable filth, the small children too weak to walk. Those who died had been eaten.

Reed and his men started for the pass with three Donner children, the Reed children, the Breens and the Graveses. Again men carried small children, again they ran into violent storms.

On the mountains they met Eddy and Foster, returning from Sutter's with supplies to save their families. When the two men reached the lake they received bad news. Keseberg confessed to having eaten the last of the Eddy boys after he had died. Old Mrs. Murphy, who had done a heroic job of keeping the young Foster boy alive, cried out in bitterness that one night Keseberg had taken George Foster to bed with him and the next morning the boy was dead. Keseberg had hung the body "in sight, inside the cabin, on the wall," and then had eaten it. Eddy very nearly killed the demented Keseberg.

Eddy now wanted to lead the rest of the party over the mountain, but Tamsen Donner, here at the lake with her three children, had a sick husband five miles back at Alder Creek whom she had promised to "love, honor and obey until death do us part." She refused to leave her dying husband, though he had only a short time to live, kissed her three girls good-by, knowing they would be safe with Eddy, and walked through the trees, back five miles to the east, thinking perhaps of how she had known all this would happen from the very first hour they had set foot on this Far West. She returned to their tent to be with her husband when he died the next day ... and to die herself before the next rescue party would get in.

They say of you now, Tamsen Donner, more than a hundred years later, that as you walked through the woods to your duty and to your death, leaving behind three young daughters, you never looked back.

The Donner Party has a mystical meaning in the settlement of the Far West: it is Greek tragedy, moving one to pity and terror, the bloodletting *par excellence*; the ultimate cup of grief into which all of the tears avoided by former parties are shed. All of the bad judgment and bad luck somehow skirted by the others is heaped upon the hapless heads of the one party on which the furies pour their pent-up vengeance at having been cheated of their victims these five long years during which dumb, stumbling men had overcome the unscalable mountains, unendurable salt and sand deserts. It is the ultimate tragedy without which no distant frontier can be conquered; and which gives a structural base of blood and bone and suffering and sacrifice and, in a sense, of redemption, to a new people creating a new life in a new world.

CHAPTER XXII

"It is enough. This is the right place."

IN THE LATE AFTERNOON of July 10, 1847, there arrived on a small tributary of the Bear River, at the northeast corner of present-day Utah, the pioneer party of the Latter-day Saints, led by their forty-six-year-old president, Brigham Young. Every man rode into the camp by the side of his own wagon, his gun slung across his back, no man left his wagon without permission. Scouts who had gone ahead had selected the best camp sites, not only for comfort but for protection; at night the wagons were drawn into a tight military formation, a guard was posted. Shoemakers set up their benches, blacksmiths their anvils; small cave ovens were dug out of the side of the hill and the dough which had been made while traveling was baked and spread with the butter that the Mormon women had learned could be churned by the constant bumping movement of the wagons. Within a half hour supper was ready to be served; then, after brief prayers and the singing of a few hymns and folk songs, at eight o'clock the bugle ordered the party to retire. On Saturday night, the night given to joy and celebration, musical instruments were brought out and the camp had its festivities: dancing, a hoedown, a humorous mock trial. Alone among the parties to cross the continent the Mormons did not travel on Sunday, but gave the day to meditation, prayer and preaching, in short, to God. For the Latter-day Saints considered themselves children of God: Neff says in his *History of Utah*:

"The Mormons believed as implicitly that they were under the inspiration of the Almighty as the Hebrews are credited with being under Moses."

The figure is not too far strained. Beginning on February 11, 1846, the Mormons had been driven out of the city of Nauvoo which they had built from a wilderness into a prosperous community, given the choice of fleeing their homes or being massacred, much as had happened when their leader and the founder of their religion, the Prophet Joseph Smith and his brother Hyrum, were murdered in the jail in Carthage, Illinois, on June 27, 1844.

The Saints had special reason to celebrate this Saturday night, and to offer their thanks to God on Sunday morning: they had been on the road from their Winter Quarters on the Missouri River in Iowa and Nebraska since April 16; though they had suffered constantly from mud, heat, dust and lack of water, there had been no casualties, and they knew by the computation of their *odometer*, which had been invented on the journey by Orson Pratt, and built by a carpenter "fixing a set of wooden cog wheels to the hub of a waggon wheel," that they stood on the threshold of what Brigham Young called "Eastern California." By the following Sunday, according to their maps and calculations, they should be worshiping on the site of their new temple and their new and final home.

Brigham Young was born on June 1, 1801, in Whitingham, Vermont, one more New Englander to figure importantly in the settling of the Far West; the ninth child of a stern moralist father who had fought under General Washington but never thereafter could find a proper or prosperous place for himself. The family became wandering farmers through New York and into Vermont, apparently living at a subsistence level, with Brigham helping with farm chores, skilled with his hands at making a chair, repairing a clock; becoming a house painter, glazier and joiner for "six bits a day."

Raised in a fertile field and time for revivalist religions, Brigham, whose family was Methodist, sampled them all.

"I saw them get religion all around me. Men were rolling and bawling and thumping but it had no effect on me. I felt that if I could see the face of a Prophet, a man that had revelations, to whom the Heavens were opened, who knew God and his character, I would freely circumscribe the earth on my hands and knees."

At the age of twenty-nine Brigham Young found his Prophet, Joseph Smith, founder of the "Church of Jesus Christ of Latter-day Saints." Brigham Young's sister, wife of a clergyman, was converted first, then his brother Phineas. Brigham studied *The Book of Mormon* for two years before he was convinced; when he was, he and his closest friend, Heber Kimball, were baptized on April 15, 1832. Upon the death of Joseph Smith, Brigham Young, through brains, force of personality and organizational talent, took command of the hard-pressed Saints to become their president and lead them onto the terrain of the Far West.

He was not a large man, but he was compactly, powerfully built, with small, all-encompassing eyes under tremendous brows; a rugged, enigmatic male face with a thrusting, bone-ridged nose, a monumental chin, the most formidable to be found in American portraiture.

When he had been asked where he was taking the Saints, he had replied, "I am getting them away from Christians!" He said also, "The business of the Saints is to journey west." One of his gentile biographers, M.R. Werner, says:

"Without Brigham Young the Mormons would never have been important after the first few years of their institutional life, but without the Mormons, Brigham Young might have been a great man."

A close study of the life and work of Brigham Young proves him to be one of the most brilliantly resourceful executives to rise in the United States.

The Mormons, in spite of the fact that they had been driven out of Nauvoo with an almost total loss of their homes, farms, businesses, in spite of the fact that they had spent months in open tents in twenty-below-zero freezing weather with few resources except their own integrity and devotion to their religion, prepared their train on a completely scientific basis. All available reports of expeditions to the West were studied, printed maps sent for, including Fremont's *Reports*, Mitchell's new map of Texas, Oregon and California; a complete set of astronomical instruments was brought from Europe by one of the Mormon missionaries to England.

Brigham Young said, "I will recognize the site of our new home when I see it, and we will continue as the Lord directs us."

But Brigham Young also believed that the Lord helps those who help themselves, and so he had made a thorough survey of all the lands available for settlement. He had rejected Oregon, Vancouver and Texas and had pretty well decided that the place for the Mormons to built their new civilization was in the Great Basin, shown on the early maps as Bonneville's Lake, bounded on all sides by towering mountains: once a great sea, now evaporated and mostly desert, with Great Salt Lake to the north and fresh-water Utah Lake to the south.

The vast bowl of the Basin was a natural fort and could be defended against any mob such as had formed in Missouri and

Illinois to drive the Saints out of their homes. No one lived there
except a few nomadic Utes, Paiutes and Shoshoni Indians, and
nobody else wanted it. There was no settlement within hundreds of
miles, and hence there would be no outside influences or pressures.
If the Mormons were to build a life here they could be secure in the
practice of their religion. But they would have to build it with
monumental labor and dedication.

President Brigham Young and the Twelve Apostles had been
warned by Moses Harris and also by Miles Goodyear, who had a
little farm up at verdant Ogden's Hole and was the sole white man
living in Utah, that the Salt Lake Valley "had frosts, cold climate,
that it was difficult to produce grain or vegetables in any of this
mountain region." Jim Bridger considered it "imprudent to bring a
large population into the Great Basin until it was ascertained that
grain could be raised," though he showed Brigham Young how best
to take the Mormons there. Energetic Sam Brannan, who had come
from Yerba Buena to urge the Saints to go to the Pacific coast, and
who had just come through the Great Basin, warned that it was
God-forsaken.

But Brigham Young remembered an extremely important line
from the Fremont *Report*. Fremont wrote that he had tested the
soil around the rim of the Basin and that he had found it excellent in
its ingredients. Brigham Young believed that in this soil he could
plant and grow crops. His people were skilled farmers and
craftsmen, they were unquestioningly obedient (the head of the
Church spoke for God, and so they were obeying God), by their co-
operative effort they could create a tenable world where other men
and other families working alone might perish.

The Mormon congregation was a mixture of rugged individualism combined with private capital on the one hand, and an
economic co-operative church society on the other. No family had
been allowed to join the trek across the continent unless he had a
good wagon, good teams and eighteen months supplies, including
three to five hundred pounds of flour per soul. The Elders had
inspected each family's supplies to make sure that their computa-
tions were accurate.

Yet on the march, which was under strict military organization,
divided into companies of a hundred with a captain, and squads of
ten with their officer or sergeant, many aspects of the train were
communal. Nine men were assigned by Brigham Young as hunters,
and the meat they brought him was apportioned equally. When
wolves were killed for the protection of the train, the grease from

the animals was distributed to all the wagon wheels. Each day ten or twelve men were sent in advance of the company to work on the road.

When some of the families complained of the slowness of travel they were invited to co-operate or leave. A few did leave. Ammunition was controlled for the good of the entire party, the rifles were repaired communally, the heavy guard posted at night was shared by every man. When the Mormon Battalion was formed at President Polk's request to help General Kearny conquer California, the several thousand dollars paid in advance as expenses for the five hundred volunteers was used by Brigham Young for communal purposes.

They broke a "Mormon Trail" on the north bank of the Platte, set up the first "prairie post office." A company clerk kept a journal of each day's events, for the Mormons believed that whatever is recorded on earth is recorded in heaven, and conversely, what is not recorded on earth is not recorded in heaven. A Mormon historian comments:

"The Mormon exodus was predominantly the movement of a church congregation. Therefore its entire moral, ethical, and behavior tones were controlled by its president. When, after a few days on the march, President Young saw that there was gambling going on, and some profanity, or coarse jokes, he had the entire party assemble at bugle call the next morning and preached a scathing sermon.

"'The brethren will play cards, they will play checkers, they will play dominoes, and if they were where they could get whiskey, they would be drunk half the time, and in one week they would quarrel, get to high words and draw their knives to kill each other. Joking, nonsense, profane language, trifling conversation and loud laughter do not belong to us.'"

The erring Saints had their choice of conforming to the high behavior standards of the Mormons or of pulling their wagons out of the encirclement.

When Brigham Young and the Twelve had decided to form a pioneer party to find a permanent home for the several thousand Saints living in Winter Quarters, Young selected one hundred forty-four vigorous, tested men, mostly from the high priesthood of Mormonism. There were seventy-three wagons, ninety-three horses, fifty-two mules, nineteen cows. Later, Winter Quarters would slowly be emptied out according to the direction of the Church leaders.

But now mountain fever had hit the train. Brigham Young was

so ill that he could not make the last step of the journey. When Orson Pratt came to President Young's wagon for his instructions, early on Monday morning, July 12, 1847, Brigham Young said:

"My impressions are, that when you emerge from the mountains into the open country, you bear to the northward and stop at the first convenient place to put in your seed."

Orson Pratt had the best formal education and intellect of the Mormons, with a strong scientific talent, so good that his observations and map making on this trip, published as *The Latter-Day Saints Emigrant's Guide*, were the most accurate yet recorded. He had a dimple in his chin, a nose that swept at an angle toward the right corner of his mouth, thick lobes of hair almost concealing his ears; the eyes of a student and a leader. It took Pratt's advance party precisely a week to find the Donner-Reed wagon road over the Wasatch Mountains. They worked forward and backward on the road to get it in better condition for the Mormon wagons to follow.

On July 19 they climbed a mountain and got a view of the Great Basin and of Salt Lake Valley. It was an awe-inspiring sight: a natural, oblong amphitheatre, big enough to house an empire, surrounded totally by mountains, some of them snow-capped; others of the same dry, brown desert aridity as the floor of the great plain.

On July 21 Orson Pratt and Erastus Snow descended into the valley to explore, turning north toward the Salt Lake as Brigham Young had instructed them. Erastus Snow had a piquant face, his eyes wondering, perhaps a little sad. Orson Pratt wrote in his diary:

"For three or four miles north we found the soil of a most excellent quality . . . yet the grass had nearly dried up for want of moisture."

Apostle Pratt pushed on to a little stream where there was a growth of cottonwood trees and underbrush. Two days later the wagons came down out of Emigrant Gap, turned northward and made camp among the willows. Within two hours of their arrival they were plowing and within four hours, having found the soil so hard it broke two plows, they had dug irrigation ditches and were bringing water to the earth in which tomorrow they would plant their communal potatoes and corn.

It took Brigham Young twelve days to reach the spot on Little Mountain where he could get a view of the Great Salt Lake Valley. On Saturday, July 24, lying in a bed in Wilford Woodruff's carriage, he leaned up on one elbow, looked out of the carriage to the west, seemed enrapt in a vision for several moments. Then, as he recorded it:

"The Sprit of light rested upon me, and hovered over the valley, and I felt that there the Saints would find protection." A number of years later Woodruff reported that Brigham Young said:

"It is enough. This is the right place."

Three women were included in this advance party, one of Brigham Young's wives, Clarissa Decker Young, one of his brother's wives, Harriet Page Young, and one of Heber Kimball's wives, Ellen Saunders Kimball. No shout of joy was wrung involuntarily from their lips. They broke down and wept: for this seemed a place beyond the end of the earth: parched, barren, hard-crusted, desolated, forsaken. But that moment, at five in the afternoon, the first of many Mormon miracles took place: a shower of beneficent rain fell. . . .

The following day, Sunday, the pioneers gathered for thanksgiving and prayer and the reading of scripture from *The Book of Mormon*.

Zion was born. The Saints had come home.

On July 28, four days after his arrival, President Brigham Young, with Heber Kimball, Willard Richards, Orson Pratt, Wilford Woodruff, Amasa Lyman, George A. Smith and Thomas Bullock went to a spot between two forks of City Creek and here Young stuck his cane into the ground, indicating the spot where the Temple was to be built:

The Temple, which was the center of the Mormon religion, would be the center of the new city built in the desert.

In his wisdom as a political governor as well as a religious leader, Brigham Young pronounced a series of long-range policies: all water available for irrigation would be owned communally and no one might make a profit from it; every man was to own privately the same size piece of land, but "no man will be suffered to cut up his lot and sell a part to speculate out his brethren; each man must keep his lot whole, for the Lord has given it to us without price. The Temple lot will be forty acres, and adorned with trees, ponds." Following Joseph Smith's original design Young, the city planner, decreed that the streets were to be laid out enormously wide, each house set back so many feet, the fronts to be beautified with fruit trees and gardens; and four public squares of ten acres laid out in various parts of the city for public grounds. Young, the engineer, ordered that water be routed through the streets to carry off all filth; then Young, man of action, set his Saints to building a bower for Sunday services, a road to the canyon to bring out timber, a timber and adobe fort to protect them against Indian raids, a boat to explore Salt Lake. So galvanic was the conduct of the Saints that eight days after the first plow had been turned, Stephen Markham reported:

"Thirty-five acres of land had been broken up and planted in corn, oats, buckwheat, potatoes and garden seeds. About three acres of corn was up two inches above the ground, and beans and potatoes were up and looking well." It was true, as Brigham Young had divined from Fremont's *Report* that there was rich, virgin soil here, hungry to produce for those hungry to till.

By August 23 twenty-nine log cabins and adobes had been built. The community was named Great Salt Lake city.

No infant city ever grew so fast: in August a group of two hundred ten arrived from the Mormon Battalion which had wintered at Pueblo, Colorado; next a party of forty-seven came in from Missouri; then a continuing flow from Winter Quarters, led by Parley P. Pratt, brother of Orson Pratt. By early October almost two thousand Mormons had poured into the Great Basin, bringing horses, cattle, sheep, pigs, chickens. The Saints bought out Miles Goodyear at Ogden's Hole; they wanted no antithetical colony of gentiles to form there. Goodyear was equally eager to sell, for the Saints had settled only forty miles from his farm, and that was too close for a genuine western man to have neighbors.

There were in 1847 no whites living in present-day Nevada, and only a few wretched Digger Indians: the population of what the Saints called Western California, the land lying between the Sierra Nevada and the Pacific Ocean was far, far away.

Zion was safe.

CHAPTER XXIII

A Curse Is Removed, San Francisco Is Born

AT THE OPENING OF 1847 Yerba Buena was still a reluctant lady, unable or unwilling to grow. Perched on a sheltered cove of the bay which sailors for a hundred years had agreed was the greatest harbor on the face of the earth, capable of housing comfortably all of the assembled navies of all the nations, it rarely harbored more than one whaler or trader at a time. There was little reason for merchants to settle here, since there were few ships and fewer people to trade with. The land itself consisted of sand dunes, unfitted for agriculture. There were no ranches. On January 1, 1847, Yerba Buena had about three hundred white residents; of whom two hundred were Mormons, most of whom would depart when the main Mormon Church settled elsewhere. Viewed from a rowboat in the bay, the hamlet showed about fifty houses, wood and adobe dwellings, half a dozen of them two-storied, starting from the sands of the cove and straggling backward up the bleak surrounding hills.

Then, on January 30, Alcalde Washington Bartlett, otherwise known as Lieutenant Bartlett of the U.S.S. *Portsmouth*, decided that there was too much confusion in the fact that the town was known as Yerba Buena by those inside its small environs, but to the rest of California was known as San Francisco because of its mission. Bartlett issued a pronouncement that Yerba Buena would in the future be known as San Francisco, and had the news published in the first newspaper of the town, the *California Star* which Sam Brannan had begun publishing with a press he had brought out to establish a newspaper for the Mormons. Bartlett also named Jasper O'Farrell to survey the city proper, to draw up an official map, to lay out streets, all of them to intersect at right angles and to be seventy-five to eighty feet wide.

Instantly, as though some medieval curse had been removed, San Francisco sprang to life. Within a few days news arrived from Washington that the cargoes of American vessels would be admitted duty-free into the harbor; word of this promptly spread through the maritime world. Then General Kearny released to San Francisco from United States Government ownership a large block of land consisting of the beach and water lots on the eastern front of the town facing the bay. On March 6 another decisive event took place: the first of four army transports dropped anchor in the bay and began discharging a thousand volunteers who had joined up on the condition that when their term of service was over they would be allowed to remain in California. Many of these men were skilled mechanics; they brought not only an incomparable source of manpower to the newly rebaptized city, but army tools, army supplies and army pay, all of them needed in the building of the town.

On March 16 Edwin Bryant, whose *What I Saw in California* was published the following year, and who had succeeded Bartlett as alcalde of San Francisco, offered up lots in the new tract for sale, particularly those on the waterfront and extending out into the bay so that wharves and jetties might be built to receive incoming ships, and warehouses to store the arriving merchandise.

In May the *Californian*, the newspaper started in Monterey by the Reverend Walter Colton and Robert Semple, transferred its press and operations to San Francisco. The arrival of the newspaper was a tacit admission that in a few short months San Francisco had become the most important settlement in central California. Monterey, which was struggling to maintain its position as the capital of California, received another severe blow, administered to a group of entrepreneurs who were trying to bring in fresh industry: fifty gamblers had moved into Monterey and opened a monte game. The cards had hardly gotten warm before Alcalde Colton surrounded their hotel with a troop of soldiers, arrested the gambling ring and sent them scattering. Most of them took their talents to the growing metropolis of San Francisco, where they would be appreciated.

By June of 1847 the population of San Francisco had risen to three hundred seventy-five whites; four fifths of the population was under forty years of age, making the city one of the world's youngest populations. From its inception San Francisco was international, with men from the United States, Mexico, Canada, England, France, Germany, Ireland, Scotland, Switzerland, Denmark, New Zealand, Peru, Poland, Russia, the Sandwich Islands, Sweden and the West Indies. Most of the professions and occupations were also represented: twenty-six carpenters, twenty laborers, thirteen clerks, eleven farmers and eleven merchants, seven bakers and seven butchers, six blacksmiths and six brickmakers, five grocers, four each of masons, shoemakers, tailors, three each of lawyers, doctors, coopers, hotel keepers; two tanners; two gunsmiths; a schoolteacher, brewer, cigar maker, gardener, miner, Morocco-case maker, navigator, painter, saddler and watchmaker. By now there were eight general stores, seven groceries, three butcher shops and bakeries, two hotels and two printing offices.

In September the first City Council was elected by popular ballot. Democratic government took over in San Francisco.

Once the army, with Kearny riding at its head and Fremont bringing up the rear, had departed from the Sacramento Valley a new wave of enterprise swept over Sutter's Fort as well. Sutter was building new granaries, a new threshing floor and outbuildings, sending exploring parties to find fresh sources of the lumber which he needed for "barrels, shingles, rafts and boats, for wagons, spinning-wheels and weaving-looms, for pumps to irrigate his vegetable gardens, for fences, for the making of charcoal needed in the smithy, and the bark of the oak for the tannery."

John Sutter was now forty-four years of age and at the height of his powers. Sometimes he sat at his desk until four o'clock in the morning writing letters and messages which his couriers carried on swift horses. He was delivering grain and cattle, hides, hats, a dozen other products produced in his shops. Still described by people visiting the fort as being in looks and manner "an old school gentleman," he was growing stout, his good-looking face a little florid, his clear blue eyes still twinkling, his manner totally charming. He had a well-tended mustache and side whiskers, never left his office without his silver-topped cane, the mace of authority in California: the Patriarch of the Sacramento Valley.

The war had hurt John Sutter by stopping many of the activities at the fort; the supplies and animals he had unstintingly provided John Fremont, taking government scrip in return, now seemed lost because Kearny had declared Fremont's scrip worthless. The possessions he had sent out to help rescue the Donners and other emigrant parties would almost surely be unreturned. He had not been able to supply enough wheat to wipe out any notable part of the $30,000 price he had paid the Russians for Fort Ross. Sutter calculated his debts to be somewhere between $80,000 and $100,000, all of it used to open and develop the country, to start new ranches and industries.

In late August 1847 he was in process of building a large flour mill five miles up the American River, a mill which he believed could pay off all of his debt, but he was held up for lack of lumber. What he needed was a sawmill high in the mountains, where there were magnificent stands of timber.

On August 25 there arrived at the fort the first contingent of the Mormon Battalion, which had been disbanded in southern California and was making its way back east to rejoin family and friends. The men settled two miles from the fort on the American River awaiting news from Brigham Young. Within a day or two Captain John Brown came into the Sacramento Valley from Great Salt Lake to buy cattle and feed for the Saints, and to bring instructions to the young Mormons: Brigham Young and the Elders urged them to remain where they were over the winter, to work and earn what money they could.

The Mormons were young, vigorous, good workers and many of

them skilled mechanics, the one commodity for which Sutter had hungered from the day of his arrival. They now offered to go to work for Sutter. Because of this unexpected windfall, on August 27 Sutter entered into a contract with his carpenter, James Wilson Marshall, to build a sawmill on a spot recommended by Marshall, fifty miles up the south fork of the American River.

John Bidwell, Sutter's most devoted friend and adviser, was aghast at the foolhardiness of the project. He did everything he could to dissuade Sutter from pouring into the mountain wilderness the stream of wagons, provisions, tools and raw materials necessary to build a sawmill. But Sutter was visioning visions: the sawmill would bring him the finest lumber ever known in California; the Mormons would be able to complete construction of his flour mill. Bidwell said:

"It is hard to conceive how any sane man could have selected such a sight for a sawmill. Surely no other man than Marshall ever entertained so wild a scheme as that of rafting sawed lumber down the canyons of the American River, and no other man than Sutter would have been so confiding and credulous as to patronize him."

As far as Sutter's future was concerned, Bidwell proved to be right, but for the wrong reasons. Since Sutter had on hand his fine supply of earnest laborers and mechanics, all of whom he would lose in the spring when they made their way over the mountains to Great Salt Lake, he decided that this was a God-given opportunity. He heartily joined Marshall's wild gamble.

Thus it was that in the year 1847 the Mormons not only settled Bonneville's Lake, bringing a whole new people and new culture to the Far West, but the presence of members of the Mormon Battalion, poising at Sutter's for the winter, was also instrumental in bringing to California, traversing Colorado, Utah and Nevada en route, the greatest rush of humanity ever to pour into a country from every radius of the earth's circumference.

CHAPTER XXIV

"It's GOLD!"

JAMES W. MARSHALL WAS a westering wanderer, a solitary, silent, sometimes cantankerous and almost totally friendless master carpenter who was born in Hunterdon County, New Jersey, on October 8, 1810, given some moderate book and schoolroom education, but mostly trained by his father who was a coach and wagon builder. He had earned his living as an itinerant carpenter first in Crawfordsville, Indiana, then in Warsaw, Illinois, then continued his wandering until he located a homestead near Fort Leavenworth, on the frontier, built a fairly prosperous farm, and might have been content to remain there had he not suffered from the Missouri fever and ague.

At the end of six years he gave up the struggle and, having heard of California, joined a caravan of a hundred wagons leaving Missouri on May 1, 1844. Marshall had no wagon, he was on horseback, traveling alone and carrying his kit of carpenter's tools. He wintered in Oregon, then came south to California in June of 1845 with the Clyman-McMahon Party. By July he was at Sutter's Fort and most gratefully employed by Sutter as a mechanic, building spinning wheels for blanket weavers, mending the fort wagons, putting up outbuildings. Within a period of a year Marshall had accumulated enough money to buy a ranch. He also put in a small herd of cattle, and appeared content to settle down as a rancher when he became involved with the California Battalion and spent a number of months as a soldier.

When Marshall returned at the end of the war, *sans* pay, he found that his cattle had either been stolen or wandered off. Having no funds with which to begin again, he sold his land and went back to work for Sutter. But in the spring of 1847 Marshall, not yet thirty-seven, ambitious, and unwilling to work out the rest of his life as an employed carpenter, went to his boss and proposed that Sutter lend him an Indian guide so that he could explore the mountain river country, find a good spot for a sawmill in the midst of the lumber supply of the Sierra Nevada, and float the lumber down the river to Sutter's Fort. At first Sutter thought this a harebrained idea; however Marshall had his heart set on the sawmill project. Why he chose the particular spot of Culloomah, as Coloma was known by the Indians, is best told in Marshall's own words:

"The river here flowed through the centre of a narrow valley, hemmed in on both sides by steep, and in some parts almost precipitous hills...the river makes several bends in its course through this valley, and on the south side a point of land formed by one of these curves in the stream presented the explorer with the mill site he was in search of. The water power was abundant, and the surrounding hills furnished timber in apparently inexhaustible quantities."

James Marshall was a taciturn, phlegmatic man with considerable driving power. His securing of a contract, money, supplies and men from Sutter was the first step in his determination to become a man of substance.

With the turn of the New Year, 1848, the mill was completed, but there was a structural defect which Marshall had to correct: the tailrace was too shallow at its end, so that the dammed-up water rushed back and prevented the flutter wheel from turning. The channel had to be deepened by blasting.

On the morning of January 24 Marshall closed the gate which shut off the water from the river, then walked down the forebay or tailrace, to see whether the flow of water had removed the sand and gravel during the night. What happened was set down later by Marshall's biographer:

"Having strolled to the lower end of the race, he stood for a moment examining the mass of debris that had been washed down, and his eye caught the glitter of something that lay, lodged in a crevice, on a riffle of soft granite, some six inches under the water. He picked up the substance. It was heavy, of a peculiar color, and unlike anything he had seen in the stream before. For a few minutes he stood with it in his hand, endeavoring to recall all that he had heard or read concerning the various minerals. The weight assured him that it could not be mica. Could it be sulphurets of copper? He remembered that that mineral is brittle; he turned about, placed the specimen under a flat stone and proceeded to test it by striking it with another. The substance did not crack or flake off; it simply bent under the blow."

Marshall returned to the mill, his usually crusty face beaming, and cried:

"Boys, by God, I believe I have found a gold mine!"

He showed his nuggets as proof. His workers were not impressed. They continued about their tasks. On the morning of the fifth day, after having in the course of his inspection of the tailrace and of the shallow side of the river selected several more yellow nuggets, enough to make three ounces tied in his kerchief, Marshall started out on horseback to cover the fifty mountain miles down to the fort, sleeping that night under an oak tree. He was ostensibly searching for a wagonload of supplies which Sutter had promised.

At nine o'clock on the morning of January 28, 1848, sopping wet from a cloudburst which had enveloped him in the last eight miles, Marshall arrived at the fort. He asked Sutter where they could talk with privacy. Puzzled, Sutter took him to his bedroom, sitting room in the main building, locking the door. Marshall asked for two bowls of water, a stick of redwood and some twine and sheet copper to make a scales. Sutter told him that he had scales in the apothecary shop and went for them himself, failing to lock the bedroom door when he returned. A clerk walked in with some papers just as Marshall was about to dump the yellow nuggets onto the table. Marshall cried in consternation:

"There! Didn't I tell you we had listeners!"

Sutter quieted his overwrought partner, then gazed down at the yellow nuggets which James Marshall poured out of his kerchief onto the table. Sutter examined the specimens, pulled down a volume of his *Encyclopedia Americana*, studied it for a time, tested the nuggest with *aquafortis*, which had no effect on them, balanced them on the scales with a like amount of silver, then dipped the scales into water, the yellow nuggets quickly outweighing the silver.

Sutter turned his now wide and flashing eyes up into the face of the wildly excited Marshall.

"It's gold," Sutter said. "At least twenty-three-carat gold!"

Book Three

COLOR IN A COUNTRY

CHAPTER I

"A frenzy seized my soul"

THE FORTY-EIGHTER, in pursuit of gold, was a reluctant bridegroom. His portrait bears little relation to his highly publicized cousin, the Forty-Niner, yet in many ways he is the more interesting, or at least purer, personality. Sutter, Marsh, Vallejo, Larkin, Bidwell, Hartnell, Robinson made their hesitant way into the hills, but they did not stay long, and few took out any appreciable sum. The early settlers had not come to California for gold, yet how could a man justify his not stooping to pick up the essence of wealth when all he had to do was scratch it out with his pocket knife?

John Sutter and James Marshall tried to keep their discovery secret, Sutter extracting a promise from the workmen at Coloma to remain for the six weeks necessary to get the sawmill into operation. He also urged his employees at the mill to say nothing of the nuggets. But for a surprising length of time there was no secret to leak: the workmen thought these few gold nuggets to be in the American River by chance. They continued with their tasks. All, that is, except young Henry Bigler, one of the Mormon Battalion working for Sutter; on Sunday young Bigler picked up his gun as though he were going hunting, crossed the stream out of sight of his comrades and searched for gold. He found a few particles. The next day after work he scratched up a little more. The following Sunday he found a full ounce, and on Washington's Birthday he went out in a snowstorm, still ostensibly to hunt game, unearthing a nugget. When he returned to the mill, wet and frozen, his companions demanded an explanation. Bigler untied his shirt tail, scattering $22.50 worth of gold onto their crude table. He also confessed that he had written of his findings to their fellow Mormons at Sutter's flour mill.

Bigler did considerably better than his employer in keeping the secret, for on February 10, only thirteen days after Marshall's arrival at the fort with the packet of gold, the ebullient Sutter wrote to Vallejo:

"I have made a discovery of a gold mine which, according to experiments we have made, is extraordinarily rich."

Mariano Vallejo kept the secret without being asked to; like most Californios he knew from the outset that gold was the ultimate gamble.

Sutter, as had the Russians at Fort Ross before him, bought a three-year lease from the Indians around Coloma, the only two such instances on the record books of the Far West. If Sutter gave false reasons for acquiring his lease, it was not because he hoped to keep all the gold for himself, but rather because he needed a few more weeks to complete the work on his flour and sawmills.

By now the dozen employees at Sutter's sawmill, earning about a dollar a day and their keep, saw from Bigler's find that they could mine the American River with their pocket knives for ten to twenty times their wage. Yet not one man ran out on his promise to Sutter to work the six weeks necessary to complete the mill; they simply used their spare hours to go fishing for gold.

Henry Bigler, when he wrote to his Mormon companions at the flour mill, urged them to keep the matter secret but to come up for a short visit. Levi Fifield, Wilford Hudson and Sidney Willis accepted the invitation, came to Coloma and worked over the tailrace where Marshall had seen the first golden glints. Picking through the accumulated sand and gravel they found nuggets weighing in at $6.00 These three members of the Mormon Battalion, by traveling forty-six miles to look for gold, became the first Forty-Eighters.

On their return journey they stopped long enough to prospect on a sand bar about halfway down to Sutter's; here they found gold lying very close to the sand surface. By their stop of perhaps an hour they became the discoverers of Mormon Island, from which a fortune was subsequently taken by other prospectors.

Two things now happened simultaneously to break the news: one of Sutter's haulers, Jacob Wittmer, arriving at Coloma with a wagonful of materials and provisions, was told by one of the young Weimar boys:

"We have found gold up here."

When Wittmer ridiculed the idea, Mrs. Weimar gave the teamster a good-sized nugget as a gift to prove her son spoke the truth.

At the same moment John Sutter sent a Mormon in his employ, Charles Bennett, to the governor of California, Colonel R.B. Mason at Monterey, to secure a confirmation of his Indian lease. Bennett was ordered to say nothing about the discovery of gold, but when he met a group of prospectors searching for a coal mine near Dr. Marsh's rancho on Mount Diablo, this was too rare a joke to keep to himself: men grubbing for coal when there was gold lying all along the American River!

Bennett took out his pouch of gold dust and nuggets to convince the unbelieving coal prospectors.

Jacob Wittmer, arriving back at Sutter's fort, went into a general supply store that had been opened in one of Sutter's outbuildings by Samuel Brannan, ordered a bottle of brandy and put down Mrs. Weimar's gift on the counter to pay for it. Brannan's partner, George Smith, sent for Brannan; they refused to believe this nugget was gold, even as the coal-mining prospectors had refused to believe Bennett's evidence. Jacob Wittmer had no recourse but to send for Captain John Sutter.

Sutter could not lie with the nugget staring back at him from the counter. He confirmed the discovery. The date was February 15, 1848. On the same day Charles Bennett reached San Francisco and showed the gold dust to everyone who would look. With the exception of one man, Isaac Humphrey, a former gold miner from Georgia, nobody believed it was gold. Isaac Humphrey bought a pick, shovel, basin and materials to build a rocker, and left all alone for the hundred-fifty-mile journey to Coloma, the first man of the Exodus.

There was no valid reason for San Francisco to grow excited about a rumor of gold in the distant Sierra Nevada; since that day in 1846 when Fremont had spiked the rusty guns of the presidio the forsaken hamlet of half a dozen mud huts on the cove had grown to a community of two hundred buildings. Two fair-sized hotels had been built, two wharves, warehouses, twelve stores, some of them representing long-established firms in the East and Honolulu. There were billiard and tenpin alleys, an advertisement in the *Star* on March 1, 1848 for a schoolteacher, and on March 5 a public sale of town lots found fifty-two buyers at an average and gratifying price of $22.50. San Francisco might soon become the great city of the Pacific coast, center of trade from the East and Europe and the Orient. The *Californian* reported the discovery of gold on March 15, and the *Star* on the eighteenth, but in a quiet, back-page line.

Now, almost two months after the discovery, Marshall's sawmill was completed; about the twentieth of March the first logs were sawed into planks. Having proved that the sawmill they built could work, the entire crew quit and went prospecting. As John Caughey says in *Gold Is the Cornerstone*:

"The instrument of discovery thus fell victim to the overpowering force that it unloosed."

John Sutter suddenly had the roof over his empire fall in on him: the staff of his just completed $30,000 flour mill also resigned and struck out for the mountains. The tanners in their shop at the fort caught the fever and walked out on two thousand fresh hides which rotted away. His long-time crew of Indians showed admirable restraint in remaining long enough to harvest the forty-thousand-bushel wheat crop, then vanished silently in the night, leaving Sutter's wheat to spoil in the sun because there was no one to thresh, any more than there was anyone to complete the shoes, hats, barrels, blankets or any of the dozen other articles that Sutter had been manufacturing.

Thus Sutter, who had caused the gold to be discovered, also provided the manpower for the official start of the gold rush.

It was Sam Brannan who acted as the catalyst for the outside world. Having milked Mormonism of its last procurable tithe from the Battalion boys in the gold fields, Sam now abandoned the Latter-day Saints, who returned the compliment by excommunicating him for a second time. Clever opportunist, high-powered adventurer, shrewd trader and manipulator, Brannan burst into San Francisco on May 12, riding horseback through the streets, waving his hat over his head and crying at the top of his lungs:

"Gold! Gold! Gold from the American River!"

His histrionics galvanized a city which two months before had gazed indifferently at Bennett's pouch.

Sailors in the harbor deserted their ships, their captains right behind them. Doctors walked out on their patients, judges on their supplicants, the mayor and his city council on their citizens . . . most of whom were already gone. The little school, after its brave start, had to close, the two newspapers shut down for lack of printers, as did the stores because there were neither clerks to sell nor customers to buy. Soldiers walked off their posts and never returned; hotels had neither managers nor guests; farmers made for the hills, leaving their grains and vegetables to die. Property which had been valuable a few days before was hawked for half price with no takers. Within a matter of days the city looked as though a plague had struck it, with only one fourth of its male population left.

In Monterey, when the first gold was shown on the streets, the town emptied out so completely that the Reverend Walter Colton ruefully reported: "A general of the United States Army, the commander of a man-of-war and the Alcalde of Monterey, in a smoking kitchen, grinding coffee, toasting a herring and peeling onions!"

Commodore Thomas Ap Catesby Jones, who had inadvertently seized Monterey in 1842, now found that as commander of the Pacific Squadron he did not have enough sailors left to capture Catalina Island.

Sailors who, by jumping ship to get to the mines, sacrificed four years pay, must have felt the way another goldrusher did when he gazed upon the well-filled pouch of a digger:

"A frenzy seized my soul; houses were too small for me to stay in; I was soon in the street in search of necessary outfits; piles of gold rose up before me at every step; castles of marble, dazzling the eye with their rich appliances; thousands of slaves bowing to my beck and call; myriads of fair virgins contending with each other for my love . . . were among the fancies of my favored imagination. The Rothschilds and Astors appeared to me but poor people; in short I had a very violent attack of the gold fever."

As actual bags of gold began to come down from the mountains, town after town emptied out in dramatic fashion. Sonoma, which had just been laid out as a city and subdivided into lots, "lost two-thirds of its inhabitants. Most of its houses are empty, all work has stopped and here, as every where else, there is not a single carpenter left nor a joiner nor a blacksmith nor any laborer to do the least work."

Thomas O. Larkin wrote from San Jose that "everyone had gold or yellow fever. Nine-tenths of every storekeeper, mechanic and day laborer leave for the Sacramento."

Luis Peralta, an aging Californio gentleman who had been given a vast grant comprising the present cities of Berkeley, Oakland and Alameda, refused to be stampeded. He said:

"My sons, God has given this gold to the Americans. Had he desired us to have it, He would have given it to us ere now. Therefore, go not after it, but let others go. Plant your lands, and reap; these be your best gold fields, for all must eat while they live."

Mariano Vallejo rode up to Coloma, watched other men successfully mining gold, picked up a few flakes as a matter of scientific interest, then rode back to his home in Sonoma, never again bothering to go into the gold fields. Nor did the Californio families from San Luis Obispo south join the rush; they remained on their land and within a year, as Luis Peralta had predicted to his sons, found that their herds of cattle were richer gold fields than Coloma or Mormon Island.

CHAPTER II

It's as Easy to Find Gold as Steal It

THE GOLD THAT HAD been freed from its deposit in the mountains had been carried by the rivers of the Sierra Nevada. The streams naturally found their way down canyons and declivities; the sun circled over the cool, heavily timbered areas for perhaps a couple of hours a day, hardly enough to warm or dry the ravines.

The prospectors were getting their feet wet in some of the coldest melted-snow water to tumble down a mountainside.

Aside from Marshall's settlement in the fairly wide valley at Coloma there were no towns, no houses, no food and no roads on which to get in. The first prospectors from Sutter's went into the mountains on horseback or on foot, carrying a blanket roll inside of which they cached such provisions as were available: flour, bacon, coffee. Dangling from the straps of the blanket roll was the triumvirate of the tenderfoot: a pick, a shovel and a frying pan, all a man allegedly needed to found his fortune.

Reaching the mines from San Francisco was an involved process; prospectors either had to cross the wide bay or make the forty-mile journey down the peninsula almost to San Jose, and then double back northward. Rowboats that had been worth $50 now sold at $500. Wagon trains drawn by oxen or mules made the circling land movement around the bay but the largest number of the prospectors went on foot, rifle in hand. One man crossed alone on Robert Semple's ferry at Martinez late in April 1848; two weeks later he found a hundred wagons waiting for the ferry with a small army of men inside a wide ring of campfires, each name written on a waiting list.

John Bidwell, who had been told immediately by Sutter of Marshall's discovery, made a careful examination of the terrain

138

around Coloma and decided that it was similar to the country on the Feather River where he had bought a large ranch. He returned north, found light particles of gold far down the Feather River and reasoned that the heavier particles would remain near the hills. At Chico he organized his friends and neighbors. Bidwell says that in nearly all the places they prospected they found the color, but his companions felt the gold they were panning was too light, and lit out for the American River.

Bidwell and two friends continued up the Feather River, soon striking a rich deposit which became known as Bidwell's Bar. By discovering the color thirty miles to the north of Coloma, Bidwell opened the entire area as possible gold country.

Pierson B. Reading, who had come in with the Chiles group in 1843 and was ranching at the extreme north of the central California valley, followed Bidwell's example, studied the terrain at Coloma and returned home to find gold on Clear Creek near his own land. Men now fanned out in all directions looking for geographical situations similar to Coloma. By May prospectors were taking out the metal some ten miles west of Coloma toward Sutter's, and ten miles east, deep into the heart of the Sierra Nevada.

Men on foot, searching for new and promising diggings on all the forks and tributaries, laid their blanket rolls under the trees, then built campfires. Those who had come on horseback or with wagons sometimes had tents; a few of the more experienced had brought axes with which to cut timber and build a lean-to. Some anchored their wagons with rocks and slept in them. Thus were the first mining towns born. Few of those who came in on foot could remain more than a week; that was as long as their provisions lasted. There was no way to buy a morsel of food. Most of the prospectors had been skeptical, but what they found or saw others finding sent them back to Sutter's and sometimes all the way back to San Francisco to settle their affairs, buy all the food and tools their money would provide and strike out again, this time to stay.

By July some two thousand Americans were in the mining regions, with another two thousand Californios and Indians working alongside them. With the passing of the months four thousand more Americans, including deserting sailors and soldiers, came to prospect, crawling over the foothills of the Sierra Nevada picking up all the gold in sight.

The first miners to reach the diggings did not bother to stake out claims. They skimmed over the waterways scooping up the surface gold, quickly moving on. As their number increased and knowledge spread as to the gold-bearing potential of each camp or gulch, the men came together at the new general store and held a meeting to decide the size of the claim that each man could call his own, varying from ten feet square in the early camps to ten feet from the center of the stream all the way back to the base of the hills. The setting down of a man's pick or shovel on the spot was enough to make his claim legal.

These first informal meetings were the beginnings of self-government in the mountain mines; Colonel Mason was the military governor of the state, stationed in Monterey, but no other government existed. As Charles H. Shinn says in *Mining Camps*:

"The miners needed no criminal code. It is simply and literally true that there was a short time in California, in 1848, when crime was almost absolutely unknown, when pounds and pints of gold were left unguarded in tents and cabins, or thrown down on the hillside, or handed about through a crowd for inspection. An old pioneer writes me that, 'In 1848 a man could go into a miner's cabin, cut a slice of bacon, cook a meal, roll up in a blanket, and go to sleep, certain to be welcomed kindly when the owner returned.' Men have told me that they have known as much as a washbasinful of gold-dust to be left on the table in an open tent while the owners were at work in their claim a mile distant."

It was as easy to find gold as steal it. Anybody taking his neighbor's gold would be stealing more for fun than profit. One or two tried it toward the end of the year and were hanged without trial or tears.

The mountains were arcadia during 1848; the miners were young, there were no social distinctions, and if one man found a considerable lay of gold today, tomorrow would be his neighbor's turn. Friends or neighbors made a common pot of their food, each man cooking in turn. The result was frequently poor but "no man shall grumble at the cook's failures, under penalty of cooking for twice the usual period." Everyone was open-handed to new arrivals. Shinn reports the story of a ten-year-old boy who arrived in camp alone, starved and without the essential tools for even the simplest mining. The men at the diggings agreed to work one hour for the boy, at the end of that time turning over to him enough gold dust to buy a complete outfit, and the stricture that he would now have to "paddle for himself."

There was no social life in 1848. Few camps had even one woman, though later in the year a few arrived with their husbands to open restaurants or boardinghouses. At night, after work, the men gathered around campfires, spinning yarns, speaking nostalgically of home or their journey to California while they sat in the blackness surrounded by strange giant trees and mountains. Friendship was their greatest pleasure; in this all-male society partnerships were formed that have been described by participants as "indissoluble as marriage." The only family life was that of the Californios, who brought their wives, children and Indian servants, the families dancing in the evenings "on the green, before the tents." The young Americans found it "quite a treat, after a hard day's work, to go at nightfall to one of these fandangoes."

This sylvan aspect lasted almost to the end of 1848, though by late fall the outside influx had begun: Californios up from southern California; the first out-of-state goldrushers from Oregon; four thousand native Mexicans from Sonora; the first gold-rush arrivals by sea, an early contingent from Hawaii and another from Chile.

By October winter descended upon the mountains, with rain, snow and intense cold. A few of the more hardy decided to remain and built rude log cabins. Eight hundred men stayed on at Dry Diggings, later called Hangtown, then Placerville, taking out about five ounces a day. The vast majority, with the waters in the river unendurably icy, made their way out of the hills and into the warmer plains. Some had made their pile, many were disappointed and sick, ragged, grim and bespotted:

"Cursing the country and their hard fate."

By the beginning of September San Francisco had ceased to be a ghost town. Men had begun to return from the mines, some feverish to spend their pouches of gold, others just feverish. By October enough of the City Council had returned to hold a meeting, and one hundred fifty-eight returnees cast their ballots in the alcalde election. At this encouraging sign real estate went up fifty per cent, one courageous soul erecting the first brick house ever built in San Francisco; stores and merchandise that had been hawked for any price they would bring went back to their pre-gold values, and by December land and buildings were selling for double what they had cost.

Enough printers as well as subscribers had returned from the mines for the earliest California papers, the *Star* and the *Californian* to combine and resume publishing; and by December 12 the public school, which had opened for a few weeks in the spring, resumed classes with tuition set at $8.00 a term, probably the best buy in a city where it now took $100 in gold dust to buy a blanket, a pair of boots or a gallon of whiskey.

San Francisco appointed the Reverend T.D. Hunt, a Presbyterian, as town chaplain and the Reverend Mr. Hunt officiated at the first Protestant services, aside from the Mormons', to be held in San Francisco. In San Jose there was a first meeting of Americans looking toward the formation of a government for California, which now had only an alcalde and council in San Francisco, the Reverend Mr. Colton as alcalde in Monterey, alcaldes in Santa Barbara and Los Angeles. Colonel Mason, military governor of the "possession," had so little power that his plan to establish license fees where gold was being dug, in order to collect taxes with which to run the country, was never attempted, most of his army having deserted. However he did assure the people that the United States Congress would soon:

"Confer on them the constitutional rights of citizens of the United States."

Emigration across the plains from Missouri in the spring months of 1848 had been modest. Captain Chiles, who had led a small horseback party through Nevada in 1843, had brought in forty-eight wagons with perhaps one hundred fifty people. Bancroft's *Register* shows only five hundred twenty names of incoming pioneers.

But few phenomena inflame the mind of man so universally as the discovery of gold. For word had to get out: ships leaving San Francisco Harbor plowing the seas to Honolulu, Victoria, Vancouver; members of the Mormon Battalion traveling to Salt Lake; a letter from L.W. Boggs to his brother in Oregon, other letters written by young men wanting to tell their families and friends all over the country about their adventures.

The Baltimore *Sun* had run the first newspaper story about the gold discovery in September, quickly followed by articles in the New York *Herald* and the New York *Journal of Commerce*. But they were too exaggerated to be believed:

"People are running over the country and picking it out of the earth here and there just as 1,000 hogs let loose in a forest would root up ground nuts."

The official reports were more important: Thomas Larkin's report to Secretary of State Buchanan sent east by the flagship *Ohio*; Colonel Mason's report to the Adjutant General, accompanied by either a tea caddy or an oyster can full of gold for visual and tactile proof, sent to Buchanan.

President Polk incorporated Colonel Mason's report in his message to Congress on December 9, 1848, publicly displaying the gold at the War Office, and crying:

"The accounts of the abundance of gold are of such an

extraordinary character, as would scarcely command belief were they not corroborated by the authentic reports of officers in the public service."

That would do it.

CHAPTER III

What Gambler Ever Refused to Play?

HOW MUCH DID THE Forty-Eighters take out of the river beds, sand bars and loose rock? It varied according to a man's strength, ambition and luck. At first nearly everyone could pan from $10 to $15 of gold dust if he worked from dawn to dark. Considering the fact that in San Francisco prior to the discovery a cook received $25 to $30 a month and a clerk $50 to $60, these were considered good findings.

As in all such strikes there were the fortunate ones: John Sullivan, an Irish teamster who had been earning $5.00 a day, took out $26,000 from the diggings named after him on the Stanislaus River. A man named Hudson obtained some $20,000 in six weeks from a canyon between Coloma and the American middle fork. A boy called Davenport found seventy-seven ounces of pure gold one day and ninety ounces the next. At Dry Diggings a Mr. Wilson took $2000 from under his doorstep. Three Frenchmen discovered gold in removing a stump which obstructed the road from Dry Diggings to Coloma and within a week dug up $5000. On the Yuba River middle fork one man picked up nearly thirty pounds of gold from a piece of ground less than four feet square. Amador relates that he saw diggings which yielded $8.00 to every spadeful of earth. He and a companion, with twenty native laborers, took out from seven to nine pounds of gold a day. Robert Birnie, an employee of British Consul Forbes, saw miners at Dry Diggings mining from fifty to a hundred ounces daily.

Soule, who was the closest of the California historians to the gold rush, tells in his *Annals of San Francisco*:

"Well authenticated accounts described many known persons as averaging from one to two hundred a day for a long period. Numerous others were said to be earning from five to eight hundred dollars a day. If, indeed, a man with a pick and pan did not easily gather some thirty or forty dollars worth of dust in a single day, he just moved off to some other place which he supposed might be richer."

A correspondent of the *Californian* wrote from Dry Diggings in the middle of August 1848 that "the earth is taken out of the ravines and is carried in wagons and packed on horses from one to three miles to the water, where it is washed; $400 has been an average for a cart load. Instances have occurred here where men have carried the earth on their backs, and collected from $800 to $1500 in a day."

But there were complications in the golden paradise. Men unaccustomed to hard physical labor found that working knee-deep in the icy water all day, filling a pan or an Indian basket with dirt, lowering it into the water, then shaking the pan vigorously to wash out the sand and clay; sleeping at night in the cold and dampness; eating little more than bacon, sourdough bread and coffee brought them down with colds, fevers, pneumonia, dysentery. With their rudimentary equipment they could mine but shallowly, and the surface gold was quickly exhausted. Though they might earn well for a few weeks they would then have to go scurrying over the mountains looking for fresh deposits.

The supplies which now began to come in over the Indian trails took their prices not merely from the costs of hauling: freighters charged $300 to transport three barrels of flour, one of pork and two hundred pounds of small stores the fifty miles from Sutter's to the diggings; but also from the belief that the men who pick up wealth from the ground should share it with those self-sacrificing enough to deny themselves this great opportunity. Pans worth twenty cents now cost from $8.00 to $16. A fifty-cent box of Seidlitz powders cost $24. Every pill, regardless of its value, cost $1.00. Forty drops of laudanum cost $40. Shirts sold at $16 apiece. The Reverend Mr. Colton, touring the mining area in October, wrote:

"We pay at the rate of $400 a barrel for flour; $4.00 a pound for poor brown sugar, and $4.00 a pound for indifferent coffee. And as for meat, there is none to be got except jerked-beef, which is the flesh of the bullock cut into strings and hung up in the sun to dry."

As entrepreneurs came into the camps to build little hotels and restaurants, prices went even higher. A breakfast at Coloma consisting of a box of sardines, bread, butter, cheese and two bottles of ale cost $43.

By the fall of 1848 those prospectors who were mining an ounce a day, about half of the mining population, were spending their ounce for the basic necessities and consequently were working for their keep. Another quarter, dogged by bad luck or just slower, found that they could not average the ounce a day necessary to live on, and had to go to work for someone who could guarantee their food. The remaining quarter took out a profit ranging from a few hundred dollars to sizable fortunes, the latter accumulated by perhaps five per cent of the prospectors.

What gambler ever refused to play because the odds were heavily against him? No attention was paid to the exhausted, the sick and emaciated who returned, though some of them lay ill for months and many died. The ones who caused the great excitement were those who returned to the towns flashing a pouch full of gold; then another wave of humanity started for the mines.

Even Thomas O. Larkin, who had said, "We cannot imagine the bad results to California if this fever continues," finally could not resist forming a company with the foreman of his Sacramento Valley rancho and a clerk in his office at Monterey to round up all the Indians they could find and go into the mines on shares. He also sent in a supply of goods with which to open a general store.

Dr. John Marsh organized a company among his neighbors. They loaded pack animals with food and mining equipment, donned the red shirts and boots which were becoming standard equipment for prospectors, and made their way north to the Yuba River. Here Dr. Marsh struck a rich bar, taking out $50 of gold an hour from the very beginning.

Larkin was satisfied with a modest three hundred per cent profit on his goods, but Marsh sold beads and sugar to the Indians at the rate of a cup of beads for a cup of gold! When he ran out of supplies he ended by selling the red shirt off his back to an enchanted Indian for $300. But Marsh, now forty-nine, was too old for this rugged existence. He became ill and had to return home, carrying with him $40,000 in gold for something under six months of work; a bonanza, if you don't mind getting sick, and selling the shirt off your back. Nor did John Bidwell stay with mining after his Indians went off to seek gold for themselves; he too opened a store.

Until his discovery of gold James W. Marshall had had little luck or success, partly because he was an irascible wanderer. His tenacity in finding a logical site for a sawmill and getting Sutter to stake him to it should have established him, but no one would work his mill. Throngs of incoming miners squatted on his land surrounding the mill and he could not get them off. His oxen, worth $400 per yoke, "went down into the canyon and thence down hungry men's throats." When he went prospecting he returned to find that migratory miners had taken his mill apart to use for their own purposes. Nor did he have any greater success as a miner; Sutter twice provided him with a prospector's outfit, but the spirits he believed were directing his search were apparently out prospecting on their own:

"Should I get to new localities and commence to open a new mine, numbers flocked in and commenced seeking all around me, and, as numbers tell, someone would find the lead before me, and the ground was claimed. Then I would travel again."

John Sutter, who had no help to run his sawmill, flour mill, tannery, or to thresh his grain, compensated for his losses by opening a store at the fort, which was on the main line to the mines, renting out space to merchants. He also grubstaked several prospectors on a share-and-share basis. He declared optimistically:

"There is no need for me to go into the mountains to make my pile of gold, the gold will flow to me."

The arrival of his twenty-two-year-old son August seemed a more discouraging prospect. It was the imminence of this son in Burgdorf which had obliged Sutter to marry August's mother and endure years of marital unhappiness. Sutter had never intended to see any member of his Swiss family again. When he heard that August was in San Francisco, John Sutter fled to Coloma where he prospected in the bottle, keeping himself drunk to wipe out the gnawing question of, Once the son had arrived, could the mother be far behind?

August Sutter proved to be a loyal and level-headed young man who might have saved his father from the utter ruin that now began to engulf him. August comments:

"Indians, Negroes, Kanakas, and white men of any nation indiscriminately by applying to my father, easily obtained letters of credit from him to any amount for any stores then existing in or about the fort.... From the books I received I never could obtain any knowledge of the state of affairs on account of their dreadful confusion."

The widespread rumor that Sutter had been made a millionaire by the discovery of gold brought the rest of his past down upon him. Colonel Steward, new Russian consul in San Francisco arrived at the fort to collect about $31,000 still owed for Fort Ross. James Douglas, head of the Hudson's Bay Company, paid a personal visit to the fort to collect $7000 he claimed Sutter owed them. Antonio Sunol, a Californio neighbor, came to present a bill for $3000 for cattle and supplies. As the unkindest cut of all there arrived a Mr. French who claimed that Sutter owed him $3000 for the loan of the ship on which Sutter had sailed his cargo from Honolulu to Yerba Buena in 1839. Dozens of other creditors presented themselves. Captain John Sutter, who had given away a large part of his patrimony to exhausted emigrants, had only the vaguest notion of what he owed whom.

Half mad with the pressure and confusion, Sutter made his son the legal owner of his holdings and once again fled to the mountains. August faithfully set about the Herculean task of putting his father's accounts in order; the only way he found to do so was to agree to Sam Brannan's proposal that they create a town, to be called Sacramento City, between Sutter's Fort and the Embarcadero on the river, all of which land Sutter owned.

John Sutter had already laid out a town in 1846 which he had proudly named Sutterville. It was three miles down the river and safe from the yearly floods. A few buildings had been put up but the town was off the route to the gold mines and hence got no trade. Sacramento City was a hit from the moment August put the land on the market, enough cash coming in for him to pay off Douglas, Sunol, French and to give Consul Steward $10,000 in cash and $21,000 in lot values in Sacramento. Steward then absconded with the money, the Russians never getting a penny out of Fort Ross.

In a matter of months Sacramento City, a tent and lean-to town, sprang into existence. Sutter's Fort found itself out in the country, abandoned. August sold it for $40,000.

All this money could have paid Sutter's debts many times over, except that Sutter was gone, wandering aimlessly, and the overconscientious son paid all claims presented to him, whether fabricated or real.

Sam Brannan next hatched a conspiracy to cheat the Sutters out of the best of the remaining land of Sacramento City, succeeding so brilliantly that August went down with a fever . . . though not before arranging to have his mother, two sisters and brother brought from Switzerland. In his illness August returned to his father the legal ownership of his estate; but what had been a vast property only two years before was now gone. Nothing remained but the Hock Farm, the first one that Sutter had cultivated outside his fort.

Here Sutter moved with his personal possessions. Onto the Hock Farm came the family from whom he had fled fourteen years before. Here Sutter lived without money, his family doing the house and farm work, but remaining the patriarchal figure of California, visited by hordes of people all of whom he tried to feed and entertain in the grand manner, even as he had at Sutter's Fort.

The discovery of gold had undone him.

By the end of 1848 there were some eight to ten thousand miners in the Sierra Nevada. By the end of the year $10,000,000 worth of gold had been dug out of the golden rectangle, of which $2,000,000 was shipped east to establish credit; $2,000,000 was consumed by the miners in food, clothing and utensils, animals, medications and drink; another $1,000,000 was spent in building the hundred-odd mining communities, a few of which became permanent towns, the majority vanishing when the gold was exhausted. Of the remaining $5,000,000 about half would have been taken by successful miners to their home towns: Sonoma, San Francisco, San Jose, Santa Cruz, Monterey, to be invested in ranches, business and residential property, and to buy or build stores, shops, hotels, homes.

Some of the balance would be saved by thrifty individuals like Dr. John Marsh, but most of it would be spent on luxuries by the comfort-starved miners returning after months of isolation in the mountains, or transferred from excitement-hungry miners to the black pockets of the early gamblers.

The $10,000,000 taken out in gold represented two thirds of the price paid by the United States to Mexico for the Far West, Texas, parts of New Mexico, Arizona and Wyoming, an area of over half a million square miles, between fifteen and twenty per cent of the contemporary United States.

CHAPTER IV

Dedicated Saints

NO MORE STARTLING CONTRAST to the life of the Forty-Eighter can be conceived than the 1848 community being built on the Great Salt Lake. There were about eighteen hundred Saints living on the desert. They had been blessed with a mild winter, so that their rye and wheat were up by February to what Parley P. Pratt described in his *Autobiography* as "a beautiful green that contrasts with the gray, wild wormwood of the countryside." By March three to four thousand acres were under cultivation.

Brigham Young believed that for a people to remain happy they must be kept in constant labor: the symbol of the Mormon community was the beehive. Over the winter the men worked co-operatively to build roads, irrigation ditches, bridges, a twelve-mile stone fence around the jointly owned fields. For private living and capitalistic business enterprise the Saints had also built over four hundred houses, a number of stores, three sawmills, two gristmills, a water-power threshing machine on City Creek. Crude furniture was manufactured, pots made from native clay, shoes, breeches, harnesses by tanners. Expeditions were formed by the Council to send men along the emigrant trail to bring back abandoned metal which the Mormon artisans made into plowshares.

But God was not yet through testing His children. He now sent such visitations that Apostle Rich, preaching out of doors from his open wagon, warned the Saints not to part with their wagons and teams, intimating that they might once again have to go searching for the Promised Land.

Late in March came the rains. The houses which had been plastered with salt desert clay as well as built with clay bricks began to melt. The roofs poured water. Bedbugs came out of the exposed logs and tormented the families. Mice were so multitudinous that in their burrowings under the houses they weakened the structures; the houses shook at the slightest tremble, and no family would dare to go to bed at night without catching two dozen of them. Wolf packs hunted through the city at night; poisons left on a front porch would kill several.

The rain had been as good for the fields as it had been devastating for the houses. By May the crops were green and thriving. Then came an unexpected frost; all crops were damaged, particularly the corn and wheat. Isaac Haight, inspecting his vegetable garden, saw that the beans, cucumbers, melons, pumpkins and squash had all been killed.

Next came the crickets: big, black, voracious. The Saints had noted them when they first entered the valley the year before but they had not known that they would advance in a solid phalanx, devouring every living thing in their inexorable march for food. They had already eaten a good portion of what had not been destroyed by the frost when, in the words of Priddy Meeks:

"I heard the voice of fowls flying overhead that I was not acquainted with. I looked up and saw a flock of seven gulls. In a few minutes there was another larger flock passed over. They came faster and more of them until the heavens were darkened with them and lit down in the valley till the earth was black with them and they would eat crickets. A little before sundown they left. . . . In the morning they came back again and continued until they had devoured the crickets. . . ."

Without the gulls the crickets would have scorched the earth. With almost two thousand of their fellows due from Winter Quarters and Missouri the Saints considered this deliverance their greatest miracle; ever since, sea gulls have been spared in Salt Lake.

The August harvest of wheat and corn was good enough to send relief parties east with food for the incoming pilgrims. By the end of September five thousand Saints were in the salt desert. Brigham Young and the Council extended the limits of the city so that all new arrivals could share the land equally with the original settlers. They also disbanded the communal fort.

On September 28 the members of the Mormon Battalion who had mined gold at Mormon Island reached Salt Lake, having been separated from their families a total of twenty-six months. A natural gold fever shook the pulse of Salt Lake but it was quickly checked by Brigham Young, who knew the corrosive value of quick and easy wealth, not only on individual character but on a homogeneous church community. He forbade the Saints to mine for gold:

"If we were to go to San Francisco and dig up chunks of gold or find it in the valley it would ruin us."

Should the Saints find any gold in their own front yard in Utah they might not mine that, either.

At a meeting before his congregation on November 26 Brigham Young created a new excitement instead: every Saint when "called," either to preach the gospel in a foreign land or to colonize part of the vast desert between the Rockies and the Sierra Nevada, must sell his possessions and move at once to his assignment.

He laid out the country he thought should belong to and be settled by the Saints: from the Oregon line south to the Mexican border, from the Rockies west to the Sierra Nevada, with a stretch of southern California to give the Saints a seaport. The Mormon state, to be called Deseret, would consist of present-day Utah, Nevada, Arizona, half of Colorado, pieces of Wyoming, Oregon, Idaho, New Mexico and California. This vast empire Brigham Young would settle with skilled dedicated Saints who would make the desert bloom, create cities even as they had Salt Lake where Saints could live in the sweat of work and the sweet of peace, worshiping God according to the dictates of their consciences.

CHAPTER V

Give Colorado Back to the Indians

WHILE CALIFORNIA WAS ROCKING with the discovery of gold and Brigham Young was solidifying the structure of Deseret, the staggeringly beautiful area of what is modern Colorado, just come into possession of the United States through the treaty with Mexico, had reached its lowest level of settlement in the fifteen years since the Bent brothers built their fort in 1833. The fort itself, after serving as unofficial headquarters for the Santa Fe Trail traders and the United States Army, was about to be sold or abandoned because the fur trade was exhausted. No one lived here now except William Bent and his Indian family, with his partner Ceran St. Vrain, and occasionally old trappers like Broken Hand Fitzpatrick and Old Bill Williams. Pueblo, which had had a start when the sick of the Mormon Battalion and their families stopped there temporarily in 1846, was now falling into ruins, with only a half dozen of the old trappers with their wives and children still remaining in the adobe huts.

The small forts on the North Platte had already been abandoned. Two or three trappers kept a cabin at Hardscrabble, a few miles west of Pueblo, where they planted corn in the spring; four or five families were trying to eke out a subsistence by farming in the San Luis Valley, southwest of Pueblo. In 1847 a man named Hatcher had his horses and mules stolen by the Indians, who then killed all the cattle except three. Hatcher hitched his lone remaining team of oxen to a two-wheeled cart and moved... the last white man to attempt a settlement on the Purgatory River for many years.

It looked as though Colorado would be given back to the Indians; which was precisely what the Indians intended. Colonel Gilpin and his dragoons had been sent in from St. Louis to wipe out the tribes warring on the white settlers; nothing could have made the Indians more determined that no white man should be allowed to remain in Colorado.

There were only three men to hold out hope that Colorado could ever become a settled part of the United States: Dogged William Bent, who had already buried his two brothers outside the fort, was grimly determined to hang onto the settlement he had created. Old Bill Williams, with William Bent, had found traces of gold, though they paid no attention to their improbable find. Irish-born, well-educated, white-haired, three-fingers-missing Thomas "Broken Hand" Fitzpatrick had begun work as United States Indian agent, attempting to locate a permanent agency in Colorado either at Cherry Creek or at Big Timbers, an Indian wintering place where the Arkansas River left Colorado. Fitzpatrick hoped to hold conclaves between the warring Arapahos, Sioux and Utes, provide them with grants of good agricultural land as well as seed, tools and provisions to get started, and convert them from hunting and warring nomadic tribes to settled peaceable farm families. Broken Hand was known and respected by the tribes; he alone had a chance to end the wars in Colorado and open the region to settlers.

On November 16, 1848, John C. Fremont once again reached Bent's Fort with an expedition, promoted this time by his father-in-law and financed by southern interests seeking the shortest pass through the southern Rockies for the first railroad line to California.

CHAPTER VI

The Men Do Not Match the Mountains

JOHN FREMONT'S FOURTH EXPEDITION into the Far West was superbly organized. Carrying with him $10,000 worth of equipment and scientific instruments, a portion of which represented his own savings, it included Charles Preuss, the topographer who had been with Fremont since his First Expedition; Antoine Morin and Vincent Tabeau, French voyageurs who had been on the Second Expedition; Charles Taplin, a frontiersman; Thomas E. Breckenridge, an experienced westerner; John Scott, a hunter; a man named Long; and three California Indians. There were twelve greenhorns along but most of them were scientists, like Frederick Creutzfeldt, a botanist, whose stamina was equal to their dedication.

Fremont reached Bent's Fort in the midst of one of the earliest and severest winters Colorado had known; or so he was told by the Indians. His friend Kit Carson, who had given up his ranch and left his wife for the Third Expedition, could not see his way clear to leaving his family and farm again. Broken Hand Fitzpatrick maintained that as a federal Indian agent he could not leave his post. For a guide Fremont was obliged to settle on Old Bill Williams, wintering in Pueblo to nurse a bullet-shattered arm which he had received fighting against the Utes. Past sixty now, cantankerous Old Bill was an expert mountain man who knew the southern Rockies. To Fremont's question of whether he could get the party through, Old Bill replied:

"Sure, but there'll be trouble."

Now, at Hardscrabble, Fremont's party enjoyed the warmth of adobe cabins for a couple of days while they shucked the corn to be loaded into the packs of their train of more than a hundred first-rate mules. There would be enough food to enable the mules to survive for twenty-five days from Hardscrabble over the three ranges of mountains: the Wet, the Sangre de Cristo and the San Juans, the central bastions of the Rockies, and down into what later came to be known as Gunnison Valley, where there would be grass.

Old Bill Williams rode in the lead, "his body bent over his saddlehorn, across which rested a long heavy rifle, his keen grey eyes peering from under the slouched brim of a flexible felt hat, black and shining with grease."

The Wet Mountains had been accurately named: snows clogged the canyons, which were also choked by thick stands of aspen. The mules fell against the trees and rocks, ripping off their packs and losing corn. At nine thousand feet there was no water. In the Wet Mountain Valley there was no game. Though the journey was in its first days Dr. Ben Kern wrote in his diary, "After wading through the slush of melting snow...all very tired."

Old Bill decreed that they take the Robidoux Pass over the

Sangre de Cristo Mountains. They struck heavy snows and a screaming gale. Campfires were impossible to sustain. "The winds were caught in the valley and never got out, and then blew wildly in all directions at once." By December 2 when they started up Robidoux Pass the mules were shaking from cold. The saddlebags of corn were vanishing rapidly. Fremont, who had always insisted on a full day's march, had to call a halt early in the afternoon for the sake of the shivering animals.

On December 3, in the language of the Colorado trappers, "They took the mountain." They descended the Sangre de Cristo and came onto the floor of the San Luis Valley; it took the party four days to cross the snow-covered dunes and to reach the Rio Grande River, from where they moved to the mouth of Wagon Wheel Gap. Here in an evening conference at the base of the San Juan Mountains, facing straight up into the main assault of the Rockies, a serious dispute arose between Old Bill Williams and Fremont; and a decision was made which proved to be a death warrant not only for eleven men of the Fourth Expedition but subsequently for Old Bill himself.

Fremont was dissatisfied with Old Bill's choice, his instincts telling him that they were headed wrong, that they should turn at this point for Cochetopa Pass, which was less difficult of access. Old Bill swore that "he knew every inch of the country better than the Colonel knew his own garden." Alexis Godey, Fremont's second-in-command, writes:

"Williams was so strenuous in his efforts to carry his point, that I was completely in his favor, and told the Colonel that I myself was perfectly willing to trust Williams and follow him."

Fremont had no choice; what he did not know was the the route Williams proposed taking up to the Continental Divide, the Wagon Wheel Trail, had been his own discovery and was his favorite child.

From the first moment of their assault on the boulder-strewn, snow-packed Alder Canyon the Fourth Expedition's difficulties began: on this day the first mule died, others sinking down in the snow, their packs needing to be reset by men whose fingers were already frostbitten. At night the camping spot was so precipitous that it was impossible for the men to stay on their feet while unpacking the mules. They traveled through three to four feet of snow at the beginning, then snow up to the mules' bellies. Seven or eight miles of pushing upward was a tremendous distance to accomplish from sunrise to sunset, and after a fierce snowstorm struck, two hundred yards an hour was the maximum that could be achieved.

The third day the men and mules were obliged to stumble onward after dark to find any kind of tenable camp. Fremont and his mountain men began to suspect that Old Bill was lost. Already twenty days out of Hardscrabble, most of the corn was gone; the snow was twelve to fourteen feet in height through which the men had to beat a path by flailing ahead with their bodies and clubs. The weather was twenty below zero. The intense cold and high altitude made it painful to breathe. The men were bleeding at the nose.

The suffering of the mules was even greater. They cried all night in the bitter cold. Brandon describes them in *The Men and the Mountain*:

"By now they were skeletal creatures made of heavy flanks and yellow teeth, with mucus frozen at their eyes and nostrils and frozen scabs of sores hanging from their coats."

The men worked all day and much of the night to keep the mules alive. But they were dying slowly, their faces turned away from the storm, their heads sinking lower and lower until they fell.

For the men the passage of time was a continuous nightmare, unable to sleep for the thunder of the snow slides, the roaring gale and above it the pathetic crying of the mules. Yet no man faltered, their loyalty and dedication to Fremont holding firm in the midst of the death-dealing hell. On December 15 as they tried to force a ridge in the teeth of a howling gale and were thrust back, Old Bill lost consciousness while riding his mule.

On December 17 the party camped on the Continental Divide at 12,287 feet, the highest point they would come. They had one more valley to traverse, then up through the narrow Carnero Pass and down the west slope of the Rockies toward warmer climate and grass.

The next morning Fremont broke camp early. They were no sooner started than the worst storm of the journey struck, so fierce that no man could make a yard of progress against it. They were physically blown back into their camp on the crest of Wannamaker Creek.

Here for four days they dug into deep holes in the snow to fend off the howling storm. They spent their time butchering the mules who were dying. Here, on December 20, John Fremont at last admitted defeat, and gave the order for the party to turn back. Had they been able to leave the crest before this ultimate storm struck they could have made their way to Carnero Pass, and the final push would have taken them only a day or two past their twenty-five-day allotted span. Like the Donners, the Fourth Expedition was a matter of hours late.

John Fremont had to turn back, but he would attempt to save all of his equipment and scientific instruments for a future assault.

On December 22 he sent a relief party to make its way down out of the mountains to Taos to bring back supplies and fresh mounts. Three of the most experienced men volunteered, Old Bill, Creutzfeldt and Henry King, who had been with Fremont's former expeditions. Fremont asked Breckenridge to go along. He gave the party sixteen days to make Taos and to get back, while the rest of the expedition would be working its way down the mountains with the equipment, which they would have to carry on their backs.

A subtle form of disintegration now began to break up what had been a cohesive party. John Fremont had lost or abandoned his gift of leadership; he allowed the men to travel down the mountain in separate messes, spread over the trail by as much as seven to nine miles, with three hundred man-loads of equipment, each man carrying sixty to seventy pounds of weight. Fremont sometimes lost contact with the body of his men trailing behind him, the weakest and oldest bringing up the rear, all still living in the bitter cold with little to eat but frozen mule meat.

The first casualty came on January 9. Raphael Proue, trying to carry a pack across the open flats in what was described as perfectly unbearable cold, collapsed because his legs froze under him. Vincenthaler wrapped a blanket around him, but when he returned from having taken his pack to the river Proue had died. Micajah McGehee said:

"We passed and repassed his lifeless body, not daring to stop long enough in the intense cold to perform the useless ritual of burial."

Two days later, since the sixteen days which had been allotted for the relief party to return had passed, Fremont himself set out, not only to find his men, but to reach Taos and send back supplies. He took with him Godey, Preuss, Godey's nephew Theodore and Saunders Jackson, an ex-slave from the Benton household in Washington. He also took some food, a little sugar and tallow candles, leaving the same amount for the remaining twenty-five men.

Two days later he came upon his relief party. They had already eaten their footgear, their belts and knife scabbards, and could no longer travel on their frostbitten feet. Weak and almost unable to see from show blindness, the experienced Henry King had said, "I can go no further, I am sorry, but I am tired out, will sit here until I am rested. I will follow." When the others stumbled back later to see what had happened to him, he was dead, sitting where they had left him.

With the men left behind, despair set in rapidly. Fremont had appointed as their captain Vincenthaler, a man who was incapable of holding the group together for a last-ditch stand against their common enemy, death.

The men started down the Rio Grande River, their supplies consumed, and no game within sight. Teeth fell out of their mouths, their faces became black from the fires over which they crouched for warmth. Every small scratch became a running sore. They could make only two miles a day, even in the flat country. Henry J. Wise staggered a few feet and fell. Two of the Indian boys dug a shallow grave for him. A third of the Indian boys, Manuel, after having the rotted soles of his frozen feet fall off, laid down and died by the river. Next Rohrer died, insane, then Midshipman Elijah T. Andrews, a young and inexperienced traveler from St. Louis. On the twenty-sixth Benjamin Beadle, one of the veterans, died; then Carver from Illinois, then young George Hubbard from the Iowa border; then John Scott, all perishing of exhaustion and starvation. Every last shred of equipment was left behind on the mountains and the plain.

By the twenty-eighth of January eleven men, more than a third of the Fourth Expedition, were dead. The following day Alexis Godey came in with fresh mounts and Indian guides secured by Fremont in Taos. The remaining men were saved.

John Fremont borrowed money from old friends in Taos and offered to mount and take with him any members of the expedition who still wanted to go on to California, where he had planned to meet his wife Jessie and daughter Lily. While he had been struggling to conquer the icy Rockies they had been making their way to California, the first white women to cross the tropical jungle of Panama. Two years before, even as Fremont was starting on his return to Washington, riding in disgrace behind General Kearny, he had turned over to Thomas O. Larkin a sum of three thousand dollars with which to buy a fine piece of land called the Santa Cruz ranch, originally cultivated by the mission padres, with vines and orchards already bearing. Fremont had walked over this land with Larkin, and it was to this Santa Cruz ranch that the Fremonts were heading on their separate ways, to build a hearth and a home in California.

Several of the survivors of the expedition decided to accompany

Fremont as he set out over the Old Spanish Trail.

Old Bill Williams and Dr. Kern went back into the mountains to retrieve some of the treasure lost there, and were never seen again.

The men had not matched the mountains.

The first of many human sacrifices had been made to the building of a transcontinental railroad to California.

CHAPTER VII

"How do we get to the gold?"

THE FORTY-NINER WAS an out-of-stater who gave up his home, his job and his girl to "see the elephant," that is, experience the ultimate in adventure and hardship. Few knew anything about California. Few cared, for they were going to return home as soon as they had made their pile.

Forty thousand prospectors poured into California by the end of 1849. A handful returned home; the great body remained . . . with or without gold. About two fifths came by sea: the seventeen-thousand-mile journey around Cape Horn, or by sea to Chagres, across Panama on foot or muleback, and then up the Pacific coast, arriving in San Francisco after a seven months journey in good health though bored, in the same outfits that had so startled the people in the streets of New York: red flannel shirts, broad felt hats of a reddish-brown hue, loose coats reaching to their knees, high boots, revolvers and knives at their belts: veteran Californians even as they sailed into the bay.

Their first question as they waded across the shallow waters of the cove was:

"How do we get to the gold?"

Their initial view of San Francisco was disenchanting. The lone brick building had encouraged few followers, tents and shacks still overwhelmed the solid structures, the streets were a funnel of dust in the heat and a swamp of mud in the rain. The city itself was in the throes of a political scandal, Alcalde Leavenworth having been suspended for misappropriation of funds, the sheriff raiding his office to seize the records. Prices were so high that a man could be shorn of his capital before he could get proper directions to the mines. One passenger caustically wrote home:

"Just arrived. San Francisco be damned!"

In 1848 seven hundred ships had sailed into San Francisco Bay, most of them being abandoned by crews that had signed on merely to get a free ride to the gold fields. The bay had become a stick-forest of masts as the ships rotted and sank slowly into the cove mud.

The greater portion of the Forty-Niners came overland, following the California trail blazed by the Bidwell-Bartleson, Chiles-Walker, Kelsey, Bryant, Stevens, Grigsby-Ide, Clyman parties, twenty-five thousand men and over a hundred thousand animals working their way westward.

They were equally disenchanted.

By the time the parties reached Utah their supplies were low, their stock lean and tired, with the hardest part of the journey ahead. A portion of the Forty-Niners followed the Mormon Trail into Salt Lake, though many other trains avoided the Mormon city, depriving themselves of important help. Both sides were suspicious and frightened, the Mormons because the emigrant parties originated in Missouri where the Saints had suffered violence; the Forty-Niners because, though they had never laid eyes on a Mormon, they had been taught to believe that the Saints were the incarnation of evil.

Immediately the Mormons found the gentiles (Mormon word for everyone outside their religion) to be friendly, they offered the hospitality of Salt Lake, and there was trading of considerable advantage to both sides. The Saints bought the emigrants' extra solid rations and surplus tools, metals, mechanical equipment; the emigrants received fresh stock and repair services for their wagons. The Mormons asked high prices for their milk, butter and fresh vegetables, but also nursed the emigrant sick, sharing their homes with the trail-weary families and putting up quite a few for the winter, Brigham Young setting the example by offering the hospitality of his own home to incoming strangers.

It was not until the trains started across the desert that real suffering began, not only from thirst but from Asiatic cholera. The trains came into the valley of the Humboldt, which Fremont and Bryant had described as "a valley rich and beautifully clothed in blue grass and clover," and found that the stock of the increasing hordes had consumed all the blue grass and clover. Man and beast alike drank the sparse water. By autumn they were renaming the Humboldt the Humbug and the Hellboldt, one rhymster complaining of:

> Scribbling asses
> Describing nutritious grasses.

The ordeal of the desert, to be played to a climax a few months later by the Jayhawker and Manly parties on the scorching sands of Death Valley, was marked in the summer of 1849 by a trail of shallow graves, the bleaching skeletons of twelve hundred animals, of abandoned household goods, beds and bureaus, stoves and trunks, and finally of the wagons themselves, their canvas and staves bleaching like the white bones of played-out animals.

"The Humboldt was filled with what the Lord had left over when he made the world, and what the devil wouldn't take to fix up hell."

Water sold for $15 a glass, but only vinegar could cure a man's mouth of scurvy. One thousand wagons were abandoned within a distance of forty-two miles. The weaker folk went insane, one woman setting fire to their camp when her husband refused to turn around and go home. There were heroic marches, men who pushed ahead in the burning heat to find water and bring it back to dying men and animals. Every group except the very early and the very young left part of its family or some of its friends behind forever in the wastes.

When they did reach water and the eastern slope of the mountains, exhausted, rations gone, there was the formidable Sierra Nevada to be crossed, wagons to be hauled up the sides of cliffs, before they could enter the gold mines by following the rivers and canyons down from the seven-thousand-foot height to the mining camps. Little wonder that so few were willing to return home, with such an investment of suffering and fortitude. Their tears and blood had watered the mountains and the plains. California was to be theirs forever. Hulbert says in his *Forty-Niners:*

"The finding of gold is luck; you will not be held blamable if you are unlucky. But making the journey, overcoming obstacles, fighting your way through, that is a matter of grit, not luck. Do that, get there, and you are absolved, you have mastered the part of the game that depended on you."

*　　　*　　　*

Most of the Forty-Niners spent most of 1849 in travel; not until August and September did the overlanders begin to reach the mines. By the end of the year there were a hundred thousand people in California, of whom eighty thousand were gold-fever arrivals: eight thousand along the Old Spanish Trail into southern California and then north to the mines; nine thousand Mexicans, mostly from the border province of Sonora; forty-two thousand overland, almost entirely Americans, and thirty-nine thousand by sea, of whom twenty-three thousand were Americans.

The Forty-Niners who had come by ship were largely city men, described as "editors, ministers, traders, the briefless lawyer, starving student, the quack, the idler, the harlot, the gambler, the hen-pecked husband, the disgraced..." Then, as a sobering aside, Bancroft adds, "with many enterprising honest men and devoted women."

Those who set out from Missouri for the two-thousand-mile trek across plains, mountains and deserts were by contrast mostly farmers and mechanics who were accustomed to handling wagons and stock and living with the frontier.

Of the eighty thousand arrivals only forty thousand went into the mines, the others staying in the towns and settling the farms; exactly half the gold-fever arrivals making the long hard journey not to mine but to begin a new life in a new country which, they reasoned, must become rich and provide magnificent opportunities for all because of the millions in gold being pumped into the economy.

By fall the Forty-Eighter camp had been converted into the Forty-Niner town, five times as large as its antecedent, with the tents and lean-tos on the hillside giving way to cabins, stores, saloons and hotels on either side of a one-block street. The simple "pan" had given way to the larger and slightly more complex "cradle" or rocker. The Forty-Niner did not find gold paving on top of river streets; he had to use his pick and shovel in order to dig below the sand, raising a bumper crop of blisters. He found gold, over $20,000,000 worth of it in 1849, but with five times as many men digging, the ratio fell off to such an extent that one ounce a day was considered an average take, and many of the emigrants were forced to "mine for beans."

Spectacular finds were less common. The Forty-Eighters believed that the gold was inexhaustible; the Forty-Niners said the gold was there but that it would take hard work and luck to get it.

The atmosphere remained colorful. Vigorous young men in red shirts, pants stuffed in their boots, wearing beards and swathes of hair like sheep dogs constituted an all-male society: hard-working, -drinking, -swearing, -playing; the weaker ones coming down with everything from homesickness through scurvy and dysentery to rheumatism, typhoid, tuberculosis and smallpox. They were buried in their blankets. Doctors tiring of the unaccustomed physical labor of the mines had gone back to their practice, charging one ounce of gold per consultation and one dollar for a drop of medicine. There were still few women: at the dances the men matched to see which should be the ladies. On Sunday the men went down to the river to soap and pound their clothes.

"Have two shirts. Wear one until it is dirty. Hang on a limb exposed to wind, rain and sun. Put on second shirt. Wear until dirty. Then change to clean one."

The first laundresses to reach the mining towns made more money than their prospecting husbands.

Though some of the miners brought their violins or guitars, though they played cards to pass the time, though all holidays were riotously celebrated and elaborate practical jokes played, the Forty-Niners were lonely men isolated from the civilized world. A few had copies of Dickens, Homer or the Bible, but books were scarce and newspapers cost a dollar each. Their being away from home, family, friends and traditions accounted for the rapid success of the saloon and gambling hall, which garnered at least as much of the miner's gold as went into the rapidly developing general stores, grown from packs on mules and supplies sold from open wagons to wooden structures with proper counters where a man, for a price, could now buy anything.

"Preserved oysters, corn and peas at $6.00 a canister; onions and potatoes, whenever such articles made their appearance; Chinese sweetmeats and dried fruits; champagne, ale and brandy, sardines, lobster salad."

Life in the mining region in 1849 changed quickly from the Garden of Eden of 1848. Crime, of which the Forty-Eighter saw little, began to mount. The age of chivalry had lasted only one short season. Though the English, Irish, Australians and Germans were quickly assimilated, and the Californios were liked, the Chileans and Sonorans respected for their mining skills, racial antagonism began to spring up among the thousands of strangers thrown together into a political vacuum. The Indians were run out of their mountains, the Chinese and Mexicans pushed out of the better claims, the French, called Keskydees from their omnipresent question, *"Qu'est-ce que se dit?"* ("What did you say?") remained clannish.

San Francisco became as colorful as any mining camp when the early rains poured down from the skies and the miners poured down from the freezing mountains. The clay streets became quagmires into which the city threw "loads of brush wood and limbs of trees; as a result mules stumbled in the streets and drowned in the liquid mud, and the possibility of being thrown because the horse's legs were entangled in the brush, was a constant dread." Sometimes horse and wagon were swallowed up, the owner barely escaping.

At the corner of Clay and Kearny a sign was posted:

> This street is impassable;
> Not even jackassable.

A whole cargo of stoves, worthless because so many had arrived at one time, was thrown into the sea of mud and served as excellent steppingstones . . . unless you happened to land on one of the lids and have it come off!

From San Francisco too the brotherly atmosphere of 1848 had vanished. Among the thousands attracted by gold were men who had been problems back home in settled communities with working governments. This rough element ganged together under the name of The Hounds, and one night descended upon the defenseless colony of Chileans to beat them up, kill a few, and wreck their easily wreckable quarters. The city rose in its wrath to kick The Hounds out of town, reimbursing the Chileans for their losses.

It was a prologue to one of the most violent decades ever experienced by an American city.

CHAPTER VIII

New States for the Union

THE AMERICANS WHO CAME into the Far West had been born into self-government, absorbing its nutritious milk from their mothers' breasts and from the town pump as well. They knew how to set up their own government as surely as they knew how to practice their profession or craft. The twenty-five thousand Americans who came overland to California in 1849 voted their laws and traveled under their elected officials to such an extent that the migration has been called "a marching laboratory of political experiment." To these adepts at democracy the idea of living under a military government was unacceptable, even though amiable Colonel Mason issued few decrees and had even fewer troops with which to enforce them.

As early as December 11, 1848, a meeting had been held in San Jose expressing the need for a constitutional convention representing all of California. This meeting sparked others; in San Francisco, Sacramento, Monterey, Sonoma. On April 15, 1849, Brigadier General Bennett Riley, a sixty-one-year-old Marylander who had fought in the War of 1812, the Black Hawk and the Mexican wars, described by his contemporaries as "A grim old fellow and a fine, free swearer," with no experience whatever in governing, arrived to take over the civil governorship from Colonel Mason. When he learned that Congress, immersed in its near-bloody discussion of whether these new lands acquired from Mexico were to be admitted as slave or free, had adjourned without providing either statutes or government for California, he issued a call for a constitutional convention to take place in Monterey, asking that delegates be elected in August from every district.

California would set itself up as a state, even if Congress did not want it!

In Utah the Mormons were having similar difficulties in being recognized by the federal government. The Great Basin, which they had named Deseret, a *Book of Mormon* word meaning honey bee, had complete civil government. As Franklin D. Richards, one of the Twelve Apostles said:

"Theoretically state and church are one. If there were no gentiles, and no other government (federal), there would be no civil law."

What the Mormons called their "kingdom" was originally meant in a spiritual sense. Now the Saints spread out geographically and politically: to the south, Fort Utah was built near the present town of Provo, on Utah Lake; to the north, on the road to Ogden, were Bountiful and Farmington. Brigham Young proclaimed that it was not enough to claim a land; his Saints must also occupy it, cultivate it, populate it. Then, when the gentiles came in, the Mormons would predominate and control.

The law of the Church was the total law of the people, a body of law handed down directly from God, through His own selected High Council, and every part of it was for the total good of the Mormons. The High Council, none of whom received a salary (the Mormons have rarely paid a salary to any of its priests or officials), had passed laws controlling prices, divorce, idleness, stealing, profanity and fornication. But the Saints were highly moral and highly obedient, probably the most obedient group in the entire history of the United States, for to have disobeyed would have been to lose their place in the Kingdom of Heaven. The president and Twelve Apostles put paper money into circulation, appointed a clerk, a historian, a meteorologist, a postmaster, a marshal and a military commander over the Nauvoo Legion, in which all Mormons from eighteen to forty-five had to train. The Council disapproved of litigation between Saints, yet there were courts of arbitration. Tithes were set at ten per cent of a man's *gross* earnings; a splinter group which had broken off from Nauvoo after Joseph Smith's murder would fail, among other reasons, because they tithed ten per cent of the *net*.

The Mormons realized they could never get into the Union with a purely ecclesiastical government, and so on March 4, 1849, while Zachary Taylor was being inaugurated President in Washington, D.C., the High Council instructed the marshal to call a public meeting at the Old Fort:

"For the purpose of electing and appointing officers for the government of the people in the Great Salt Lake and vicinity."

When the Saints gathered in the Old Fort it was not to nominate

their political officers but to confirm an already named slate headed
by Brigham Young for president, Richards for secretary of state,
Kimball for chief justice and the bishops or lay leaders of the
nineteen wards magistrates for their districts. All political officers
except President Young were to serve without pay. Thus the
Mormons chose their church government to serve as a political
government.

The committee writing the state constitution completed its task
so quickly it is logical to assume that Brigham Young had brought
to Deseret copies of the New York and Illinois state constitutions it
so strongly resembled. There was to be a two-house legislature, a
judiciary rising to a supreme court, all free white males over twenty-
one were eligible to vote. On April 30, 1849, some two thousand
signatures were affixed to a petition asking for a:

"Territorial Government of the most liberal construction
authorized by our excellent federal constitution, with the least
possible delay."

On July 2 the First Deseret General Assembly met, and Almond
W. Babbitt was elected Mormon delegate to Congress. But the
petition he was taking to Washington, despite the fact that the
Mormons had only one sixth of the population required for
statehood, now asked that Deseret be admitted as a state rather
than a territory.

The Mormons adopted a firm tone with the United States
Congress, reminding it of its sins of omission: failure to provide
civil government for any part of the Far West, failure to supersede
the rifle, the revolver and the bowie knife by the law of the land.
However the Congress need not worry over any lawlessness in
Deseret: the Mormons had created a provisional government under
which the laws of the land were obeyed. They had also built a
legislative hall at their own expense, as fine as any in the East.

But a half century of conflict would pass before Utah and the
Saints would take their peaceable place at the Union board.

The California convention opened in Monterey on September 3,
1849, six months after the Mormon meeting, in a solid two-story,
native yellow sandstone edifice which the Reverend Mr. Colton had
built for a schoolhouse and assembly hall with funds raised from
"town lots and gamblers' banks." Forty-eight delegates had been
elected, from San Diego on the southern border to the most
northerly mining camps on the Trinity River, toward the Oregon
line.

Six of the delegates were Californios, representing the finest tradition of the Mexican period: Mariano Vallejo from Sonoma, Andres Pico from San Jose, Jose Carrillo from Los Angeles, Jose Covarrubias from Santa Barbara, Miguel de Pedrorena from San Diego and Pablo de la Guerra of Monterey, whose beautiful and cultured wife made their home a gathering place for the delegates. Mrs. Thomas O. Larkin also extended hospitality, as did Mrs. Jessie Benton Fremont in her charming Spanish house with enclosed patio.

Jessie, waiting in the Parker House in San Francisco, where she and John had planned to meet when they separated on the Missouri border, had been informed that her husband had perished in the snows of the Rockies. She was ill and despondent, yet certain within herself that this man was indestructible. He joined her more than a year after their parting.

To their stupefaction the Fremonts learned that Thomas O. Larkin had not bought the Santa Cruz ranch with the money John had given him, as he had agreed to do, but instead had bought for them a wild tract of land somewhere high in the Sierra Nevada called the Mariposa ranch. It was inaccessible, a hundred miles from the ocean or nearest settlement, several hundred miles from San Francisco, with no farming land, too wild and cold in winter even to graze cattle, and overrun with hostile Indians. Larkin explained that as Fremont's appointed agent he felt he had the right to use his own best judgment, that he did not believe Fremont would ever make a farmer, and that he had learned the soil on the Santa Cruz ranch was no good anyway. The Fremonts were further confounded to learn that Larkin had bought the Santa Cruz ranch for himself: a rare, unexplained and equivocal act in the life of Thomas O. Larkin.

Having found themselves without farm or home, the Fremonts had made their way down to Monterey in the hot July sunshine, where they rented a beautiful Spanish home, and where Jessie prepared to hold open house for the delegates who would soon be assembling for the constitutional convention. It was the Fremonts' ambition that John should be the first senator from California. This would wipe out the disgrace of a court martial!

Of the thirty-seven American delegates at the convention, twenty-two came from free states, fifteen from slave; there were four, including John Sutter, who were born out of the country. It was a young man's convention, nine being under thirty, twenty-three under forty. Almost all of the early settlers were there: Thomas O. Larkin representing San Francisco; Joel Walker, Sonoma; Lansford W. Hastings, of the Hastings cut-off, represented

Sacramento, rancheros from southern California such as Abel Stearns and Hugo Reid, the Scotsman who had married an Indian girl and planted excellent vineyards. Robert Semple of Benicia, who ran the ferry across the Carquinez Strait, was elected chairman; William Hartnell was named interpreter. There were fourteen lawyers, twelve farmers, seven merchants, a scattering of printers, engineers, bankers, doctors.

The outstanding personality of the convention was William Gwin of Tennessee, newly come to California with the express purpose of being elected one of California's first senators. He was described by a reporter as having "grandeur of exterior, magnificence of person, of herculean figure." He had something of greater importance, copies of the constitutions of New York and Iowa, having gone to the personal expense of having the newest state constitution, that of Iowa, printed in San Francisco so that each delegate might have a copy before him.

The most difficult problem of the convention was where California's eastern boundary should extend. The Gwin-Halleck proposal, which had considerable backing, suggested that California should consist of all the land acquired from Mexico by the Treaty of Guadalupe Hidalgo, that is, the entire Far West. When the actual maps were drawn, the group modestly contented itself with Nevada, the near half of Utah, which included all the Mormon settlements as well as that portion of Arizona embracing present-day Phoenix. The opposition claimed the area was too large to be manageable, and that it included thousands of Mormons who were not represented. The boundaries as sketched on one of Preuss's maps from Fremont's expedition led the delegates to set the eastern border in the Sierra Nevada, which traverses the greater part of the state.

The question of slavery in California never got started, the bill to forbid slavery passing unanimously. There were heated debates on whether dueling should be allowed (it was not); whether women should be allowed to control all property in their possession before marriage (they were). When it was proposed that all persons charged with criminal offenses be tried by a jury of their peers, one delegate shouted:

"What do we want with peers? This ain't no monarchy!"

The convention of near strangers went peaceably through the weeks, evolving a liberal constitution which provided for equitable taxation and a good educational system. Through Gwin's persuasive politicking, as well as the copies he had provided, the constitution of Iowa was largely followed. The Californians, like the Mormons, quickly waved aside the unworthy idea that they should ask for mere territorial status, informing the United States Congress that they were, and would be, a full-blown state.

On October 13, when the last of the delegates had signed the constitution, General Riley fired a thirty-one-gun salute because California expected to be the thirty-first state of the Union. John Sutter sprang to his feet and cried with tears streaming down his face:

"Gentlemen, this is the happiest day of my life . . . a great day for California!"

The delegates, aware of the millions in gold coming out of the mines, paid prodigally for all services. Each member received $16 a day plus $16 per mile traveled; $10,000 was appropriated for J. Ross Browne, clerk of the convention, to print the convention's report in English and Spanish; Governor Riley was to be paid at the rate of $10,000 a year as governor, Captain Halleck $6000 as secretary of state until the popular election.

The delegates then assessed themselves $25 each for a gala costume ball, held in the convention hall that evening to celebrate their creation of the new state, the delegates and Monterey society dancing most of the night unrepressed by the chill thought that Congress wanted no part of them.

The canvass for the approval of the constitution and for the election of the state officers was short; there had been so little time for electioneering that one miner exclaimed:

"When I left home I was determined to go it blind. I voted for the constitution, and I've never seen the constitution. I've voted for all the candidates, and I don't know a damned one of them."

All-seeing or blind, the constitution was approved, 12,061 to 811; Peter H. Burnett, one of Sutter's former assistants, was elected governor. General Riley proclaimed that military rule in California was ended.

When the legislature met on December 20, John C. Freemont was elected United States senator on the first ballot, and William M. Gwin on the third.

The character of John C. Fremont was beyond permanent defeat, as it was beyond permanent victory. Having ridden into the Sierra Nevada to inspect his seventy-square-mile totally useless ranch, he discovered gold; not merely "the color" or gold dust, not merely small nuggets that had been eroded by the weather and washed down by the rain and the streams to the valleys below. Here on the Mariposa John Fremont discovered a mother lode, a body of gold that had been cast up by the vast volcanic action which formed the mountains, veins of gold bedded in the rock of the mountainside.

Within a matter of a year after Fremont had acknowledged defeat on the summit of the Great Divide he became the single largest owner of gold in California, a millionaire, setting forth for Washington as the first elected senator from the fabulously rich and romantic California. He could not be seated until Congress admitted California as a state, but to the Fremonts as to all Californians this was an unimportant detail.

Thus, at the end of 1849, though Nevada was still a totally unoccupied terror-laden desert and Colorado a mountain wilderness occupied by warring Indian tribes, two governments, Deseret and California, had been created, with representatives on their way to Washington to achieve statehood for the folks back home.

By the forced movement of an entire church community of over eleven thousand Mormons to Deseret, and the discovery of gold which cascaded a hundred thousand people into California in a little more than year, there had been created a totally new phenomenon on the American political scene where territories had been settled slowly and painfully over a long period of years.

CHAPTER IX

Death Valley Earns Its Name

IN OCTOBER OF 1849, there assembled at Provo on Utah Lake, some sixty miles south of Salt Lake, a number of traveling groups, families and young men on horseback, unknown to each other prior to this meeting, which would make up the Death Valley Party. The majority of the party had come south to Provo instead of north around Salt Lake to join the California Trail because they had heard the grisly details of the Donner Party. Judging that it was too late to risk the winter snows of the Sierra Nevada, they decided to take the longer but safer route into southern California, then north to the mines. Word had been spread that there would be a rendezvous at Provo for all wishing to travel the Old Spanish Trail.

In the party when it started for Los Angeles on October 9 there were eighty wagons, two hundred fifty people, and one thousand head of horses and cattle. For their guide they hired Captain Jefferson Hunt, a member of the Mormon Battalion who was being sent to California to buy cattle and seed for the community in Salt Lake. Hunt imposed Mormon military discipline on the train: it moved like an army, divided into seven divisions, each under its captain. The train named itself the Sand Walking Company.

No crueler nor more accurate title could be divined.

Captain Hunt made an early error: he took a wrong turning. Though he was soon back on the main trail this undermined confidence in him, and when a Captain Smith with a party of nine Mormons heading for the California mines rode up with a map or waybill which claimed that there was a cut-off, what James Reed of the Donner Party had called "a nigher way," over Walker's Pass from which they could descend into the Tulare Valley close to the mines, and save themselves four hundred wearisome miles, the Sand Walking Company went into a Committee of the Whole around a campfire to debate the desirability of taking Smith's cut-off. When Captain Hunt was asked his opinion, he said he doubted if any white man had ever traveled it; that young men alone might make it but families with wagons would have serious trouble:

"If you all wish to go and follow Smith I will go also. But if even one wagon decides to go the original route, I shall feel bound by my promise to go with that lone wagon."

The Reverend John W. Brier, described in the journal of one of the listeners as a "man who always liked to give his opinion on every subject," declared forcibly for the cut-off, despite the fact he was traveling with a delicate wife and three young sons. So did a number of others.

The next morning, as the wagons and men came to the fork in the road, Smith and the Reverend Mr. Brier prevailed, even as Lansford Hastings and James Reed had helped make the decision for the Donners over the advice of experienced mountain men. Only seven wagons continued on the known trail with Captain Hunt. A hundred wagons seceded, including the Briers, Bennetts and Arcanes, the Wade and Dale families, all of whom had children; and the entire Jayhawker party of single men.

For two days Smith's party crossed green valleys with plenty of water. But that was as far as the anonymous map maker had traveled. Caught in an impassable canyon, with evidence of worse terrain ahead, seventy-two wagons turned back to the Old Spanish Trail. Though they never caught up with Hunt, they followed him into southern California, arriving in Los Angeles before the seceders had even reached the heart of their inferno.

Smith had also thought better of his decision; he cut back with his mounted Mormons to the Old Spanish Trail and safety without informing the remaining eighty-five emigrants that he had changed his mind. Meeting about their campfire at Misery Mountain, guideless, they too seemed to have little choice but to turn back, when scouts rode into the camp with the message that they had seen a good pass which would carry them into California.

They decided to plunge ahead, but not as a unifed train with a leader; instead they split into three separate groups. The Jayhawkers, young, unencumbered, started out first and fast; the Reverend Mr. Brier's party came next with his three children and two young men who were part of their mess; third, and bringing up the rear, the Bennett, Arcane and Wade families, the two Earhart brothers with two sons, several unattached men, and twenty-one-year-old William Manly, who was to be their guide. It was Manly's first trip west.

Juliet Brier was born in Bennington, Vermont, September 26, 1813, and educated at a seminary. She was a wisp of a woman, nervous by nature, the mother of three sons, aged eight, seven and four. The first white woman to enter Death Valley, the sight that greeted her eyes from the ridge of the eastern range was one to strike terror into the stoutest heart: utter, hopeless, unalleviated desolation: eight to fourteen miles wide, one hundred thirty miles long, with the lower-lying, aptly named Funeral Range in the center. There was nothing living as far as the eye could sweep, only wind-blown and rippled Sahara wastes of sun-baked sand and crusted slat-mud flats, with barren mountains surrounding on all sides and bearing not a tree, bush or blade of grass; what Bancroft calls:

"The region of mirage, accursed to all living things, its atmosphere destructive even to the passing bird."

When the Reverend Mr. Brier went ahead looking for water, says Mrs. Brier, "I was left with our three little boys to help bring up the cattle. Poor little Kirke gave out and I carried him on my back, barely seeing where I was going."

She stumbled on, hour after hour, in the hot choking dust, the cattle bellowing for water. When darkness fell she lost the two men of her group and had to get on her knees to search out the ox tracks in the starlight. Not until three in the morning did she reach camp, where the men had found hot and cold springs.

It was Christmas morning. At the springs, which they named Furnace Creek, one of the men asked, "Don't you think you and the children better remain here?"

"I have never kept the company waiting," replied Mrs. Brier. "Neither have my children. *Every step I take will be towards California*."

The next morning when they reached the Jayhawker camp the Briers found the young men burning their wagons in order to travel faster: for it needed only one surveying look about them to know that they all faced imminent death.

The Briers also abandoned their wagons, packing their rapidly vanishing foodstuffs on the failing oxen. The Reverend Mr. Brier asked the Jayhawkers for permission to travel with them; the Jayhawkers did not want to be encumbered by a woman and small children, and objected. Then they looked at Mrs. Brier, all skin and bones, and relented. William Manly, leading the Bennett Party, also arrived at the springs. He reports:

"She was the one who put the packs on the oxen in the morning. She it was who took them off at night, built the fires, cooked the food, helped the children, and did all sorts of work when the father of the family was too tired, which was almost all of the time."

The combined train struggled through mile after mile of salt marsh, sinking in sand to their shoe tops. One of the Brier boys remembers:

"Twenty miles across naked dunes, the wind driving the sand like shot into the faces and eyes."

Their tongues grew swollen, their lips cracked, the oxen laid down in the sand never to rise again. That night the men climbed up the rock-strewn mountain to the snow line, bringing back snow in their shirts, some eating it hard, others melting it for the cattle.

They went for the next forty-eight hours without water, unable to eat the meat of their slaughtered oxen because they could get nothing down their parched throats. A Dr. Carr suggested that they return to Furnace Creek where there was water; he broke down and cried when Mrs. Brier repeated, "Every step we take will be towards California."

By New Year's Day they camped at the head of the Panamint Valley, totally lost. The stronger of the Jayhawkers pushed ahead, leaving in Mrs. Brier's care the older and weaker men.

The first to die of thirst was the fifty-year-old Reverend Mr.

Fish, who was traveling to California in hopes of finding the money to pay off his church's debt in Indiana.

On January 6 the two single men who had been in the Brier mess, and who had the only flour in the party, decided they would strike out alone in the hopes of saving themselves. They baked up all their dough except for a small piece they gave to Mrs. Brier, then shook hands good-by. Mrs. Brier baked her dough into twenty-two crackers, all they would have for twenty-two days of nightmare and terror.

Next to die was middle-aged William Isham, who crawled four miles on his hands and knees searching for water, then dropped on his face.

"Give up?" cried Juliet Brier. "Oh! I knew what that meant—a shallow grave in the sand."

Their tongues became black and hung out of their mouths. Ahead there was a cruel mirage of the desert: water, an oasis, trees, greenery. When water came it was a muddy pool at what is now Borax Lake; the few remaining cattle stamped into it first, then the humans scooped up the mud-laden water, forcing it down their parched throats.

The next waterless stretch lasted nearly five days. In camp the men, with burnt faces and skeletal frames, lay down and waited for death. Mrs. Brier went behind a rock, prayed to God for strength, then gave them a combined sermon and tongue-lashing that shocked them back onto their feet. At that moment the Reverend Mr. Richards came running into camp, crying:

"Water! Water! I have found water!"

Four miles away he had come upon a group of Indians, had made friendly signs, then gestures of thirst. The Indians guided him to a brook at the base of the mountains, hidden by shrubs, which ran clear and cold before disappearing into the sands of the desert.

When the party finally struggled to the top of the range and looked back at the valley behind them, they named it Death Valley. But the Mojave Desert into which they descended in the middle of January 1850 was little better; a desert of alkali, with no known trails or springs. Emaciated from dysentery and exhaustion, they faced days of heat, dust, thirst, rocks that cut their feet. One man said, "I will just take a little nap," and never woke up. Another said, "I have a presentiment I shall never reach California," fell off his pony and died. At a spring, another drank too copiously; he was the seventh to perish.

The Reverend Mr. Brier, who had been hobbling along with the aid of crutches, lay down in camp, bade his wife farewell and closed his eyes. Juliet Brier pleaded with her husband to hold on, gathered some acorns, ground and cooked them and fed them to him from a spoon. He survived: to sire three daughters, and campaign for Lincoln.

The Bennett-Manley Party had equally bad luck in trying a southerly trail: they got trapped in the hopeless waste bordered by a black range of mountains through which there could be no conceivable pass. Finding a spring at Tule, near the southern end of the valley, they decided not to dissipate their failing strength, but to remain encamped. Bennett asked young Manly and Rogers, a burly butcher, if they would push on alone, find civilization and bring back relief. There was neither map nor food the men could take with them, nor knowledge of what lay ahead except days of purgatory.

But they went . . . passing the dead bodies of Jayhawkers who had given out. Their trek, as told by Manly in *Death Valley in '49*, is one of the West's great sagas of man's will against the implacable elements:

"Black and desolate ranges and buttes to the south, great dry plains, salt lakes and slippery alkali water to which we walked, only to turn away in disappointment, little sheets of ice that saved our lives, hawk and crow diet, lameness . . ."

They got out in fourteen days, sustaining life by sucking on rocks or single blades of grass, breaking trail over trailless mountains, deserts and valleys until, more dead than alive, they cleared one more range and saw below them the green cattle ranch of San Francisquito.

Settling in for a long wait, the Bennetts took off their wagon covers to make protecting tents for the cattle and themselves against the heat and sandstorms, rationed their food, watched it vanish. Mrs. Arcane, knowing she must abandon her clothing, but not wanting it to be too good for the Indians who would inherit it, dressed herself in her finest garments every day. Captain Richard Culverwell, who had gone exploring, died trying to get back to camp. After three weeks the men agreed:

"If those boys ever get out of this hole they are damned fools if they ever come back to help anybody."

Manly and Rogers waited only four days to regain their strength, then borrowed horses to load with oranges and other foodstuffs, and spent the next week retracing their steps, exploring for better passes and water holes. When they got their first view of the camp not a soul was in sight; they concluded they had made the journey for nothing.

Manly fired a shot. From under a wagon a man emerged. He threw his arms high over his head and shouted:

"The boys have come! The boys have come!"

They were saved.

The Brier party also emerged, as images of death, onto the opulent hospitality of the Californios who owned San Francisquito ranch. Mrs. Brier came down out of the San Gabriel Mountains, leading her three sons, in rags, the last of the moccasins she had made of the hides of dead oxen worn through; seventy pounds of bone, grit and indestructibility.

Thirteen men had lost their lives in the Sand Walking Company. The women were tougher; they endured. Juliet Brier's inner strength saved not only her own family but several of the Jayhawkers as well.

CHAPTER X

Nevada and Colorado Show Their Color

ON MAY 1, 1850, a complete American city government was installed in San Francisco. Through the sale of city-owned lots the Council had $635,000 with which to buy a city hall, build a hospital and extend its wharves, to grade and plank its important business streets. Houses and stores rolled unfalteringly up the hillsides from the beach until the original cove was settled, neighboring valleys were bought and subdivided, with a toll road of planks built out to the Mission Dolores.

This mid-century moment San Francisco ceased to be a mining town. Red flannel shirts were replaced by white linen, slouch hats by beavers, high boots, tuck-in pants and round rough coats by frock coats, trousers and shoes taken from sea chests. Only the gamblers persevered in their colorful costume of diamond-studded shirt, sombrero and scarlet sash.

It was not easy to be a gentleman in San Francisco; laundry was $8.00 a dozen, regardless of whether the article was a handkerchief or long-drawers underwear. The service was so slow that men sent their linen by ship to Honolulu or Canton to be laundered. This unfair competition gave rise to Washerwoman's Lagoon, just over a sand dune, where washermen set up a large-scale industry with boiling kettles, fluted washboards and ironing tents.

"When one of these great, burly long-bearded fellows got a shirt on the board the suds flew and the buttons also."

Early 1850 saw the arrival of three of the Big Four who would build the Central Pacific Railroad and control California for a generation, the dramatis personae who would replace in importance Sutter, Vallejo, Larkin, Fremont. Only Charles Crocker came across the plains in the hope of making his fortune in the gold mines. The other three, Collis P. Huntington, Mark Hopkins and later Leland Stanford, came across Panama and into San Francisco Bay to make their fortunes by trading with the miners.

Charles Crocker was a burly two-hundred-fifty-pounder when at the age of twenty-six he left Indiana with a group of young fellows, including two of his brothers, for the trip over the California Trail to the gold fields. He had been born of poor people in Troy, New York, left school at the age of twelve to help support his family, moved to Indiana with his parents, helped clear the land and farm, then worked in a sawmill and an iron forge. Discovering a small deposit of ore, he built a combination blacksmith shop and forge, which he sold in order to provision himself for the westward journey.

"I grew up as a sort of leader," says Crocker, "I had always been the one to swim a river and carry a rope across."

His quality of leadership was of no help in the California mines where he spent two lean years as an unsuccessful prospector. He then opened a store with his brother in one of the Eldorado mining camps, for which he drove the team and did the hauling, expanded to Sacramento, and here the man who in a few years could boast, "I built the Central Pacific!" made his first success in dry goods.

The most important of his future partners, Collis P. Huntington, worked for one half day as a gold miner, then took the supply of goods he had bought in New York and Panama to Sacramento City. Born in Connecticut, son of a miserly tinker, raised in poverty and painful thrift, he had earned and saved over a hundred dollars by the time he was fourteen. He worked as a hired man on a neighbor's farm, opened a store with his brother in Oneonta, peddled jewelry through Ohio and Indiana, collected bills in the deep South, sold butter in New York City, and while held up on the Isthmus in 1849, rented a little schooner and brought foodstuffs into Panama for $1000 a month profit. By the time he opened his store in Sacramento in 1850 he was one of the shrewdest traders to reach California, so sharp that as financial head of the Central Pacific he would bargain Congress out of $100,000,000 and milk the Far West of billions.

Another partner did not waste even half a day in the mines, for Mark Hopkins was a conservative merchant. The lean man of the Big Four (his partners all weighed over two hundred pounds), he was called "thin as a fence post," was a vegetarian with a bird-like appetite, and refused to smoke, drink, curse, gamble or spend money. A perfect inside man for Huntington, who roamed California buying merchandise cheap and holding it in his warehouses until the supply was scarce, Hopkins was described as too cautious in business ever to become rich. When Charles Crocker said:

"One man works hard all his life and ends up a pauper. Another man, no smarter, makes $20,000,000. Luck has a hell of a lot to do with it," he was describing "Uncle" Mark Hopkins as much as he was himself, the main distinction being that the possession of more than $20,000,000 was "against Hopkins's better judgment," and he acted "as if he wanted to apologize for his millions."

By the end of 1850 San Francisco had a population of over thirty thousand. "This figure," reports Asbury in *The Barbary Coast*, "included two thousand women, most of whom were harlots from Europe and eastern and southern United States, principally New York and New Orleans."

Salt Lake was growing with equal vigor, with more than eleven thousand Saints in Deseret by the end of 1850. The Mormons had started their first newspaper, the *Deseret News*, chartered a university, the first in the Far West, and organized a Music and Dramatic Society.

And by 1849 Nevada had its first building.

In March of 1849 an expedition was formed in Salt Lake to go to California to mine and trade. The secretary of the expedition was a twenty-four-year-old Mormon by the name of H. S. Beatie, from Virginia, with some college training. Beatie took along a supply of goods to sell, but going through Carson Valley in the spring he fell in love with the country at the eastern base of the Sierra Nevada, a green paradise in the midst of pine and aspen, with clear mountain springs and "oceans of good feed for stock." The spot was about five thousand feet high, with a superb view of Carson Valley and the sagebrush desert extending forty miles east to the Washoe Mountains, while towering behind to the west was the majestic Sierra Nevada.

By building a corral and a double log cabin with rooms connected by a passage but without a roof or floors, Beatie became the father of the first Nevada settlement. His enthusiasm was so great that eight other men of the expedition, including the leader, apparently all Mormons, remained with him. By July, when emigrants started streaming down the Humboldt and Carson valleys on their way to California, and ran out of flour and meat, Beatie found his trade so brisk that he had to make two trips across the Sierra Nevada, the first time driving three yoke of cattle over Carson's Pass to trade for supplies, the next time going over with pack mules to buy goods on the American River.

Beatie had no interest in looking for gold, but Abner Blackburn, who accompanied him on the trading trips, is one of the three men credited by Nevada historians with finding the color. The first was one of the Henry W. Bigler group of Mormon Battalion members who had worked for John Sutter and discovered Mormon Island. Bigler told how his party, coming east across the Sierra Nevada in August of 1848, "discovered gold in western Utah" as Nevada was known.

The following May, 1849, Mormon John Orr stopped his wagon train at noon for a brief respite in the shadow of Sun Mountain. His companion, Prouse, began panning instead of resting, and found sufficient tracings of gold for John Orr to name the canyon in which they had halted "Gold Canyon." The Orr train started over the mountains but when the axle broke in one of the wagons they put back to Mormon Station, and while it was being repaired, Orr and Prouse returned the forty miles to Gold Canyon where Orr found the first piece of gold-bearing quartz.

Abner Blackburn reports in his diary that he went prospecting with his bread pan and butcher knife, scratched up some color in a gulch, and that when he showed it to the other men they "grabbed up pans, knives and kettles and started out. They scratched and paned [sic] until sundown, taking out $9.00 to $10.00 worth of dust." Having neither tools nor provisions, they continued on to California.

By now there was a little community of prospectors in western Utah: Mexicans who had not been kindly treated in the California mines, emigrants to California halting briefly, Mormons coming from California to Gold Canyon to prospect, other Mormons from

Salt Lake who had heard that Beatie's trading post had been a success. By late summer there were some twenty lean-to trading posts dotting the Carson Valley, the closest one to Beatie's being fourteen miles away. Spafford Hall, a non-Mormon from Indiana, built a station just a mile and a half from the mouth of Gold Canyon, on Carson River.

Before the snows fell Beatie sold his trading post to a man called Moore and returned to Salt Lake. Most of the other traders collapsed their lean-tos and went east to Salt Lake if they were Mormons, or west to California. In September the last of the twenty-odd prospectors left Gold Canyon, complaining:

"There is no water, no food, only buzzards."

Besides, the gold was mixed in with some unfortunate flaky blue stuff that made mining difficult and unprofitable.

Nevada's flurry proved premature. But soon the young Grosh brothers would come over the Sierra Nevada from Volcano, California, carrying with them books on mineralogy and chemistry, and as full a set of chemicals as they could assemble.

In the mid-century year of 1850 two brothers by the name of Ralston from the Cherokee lands of Georgia, where they had been gold mining, entered Colorado by way of the Arkansas River, leading a party of Cherokee Indians, to whom they were related by marriage, to the California gold fields. They passed Bent's Fort, the almost deserted village of Pueblo, then turned north along the front range and Pike's Peak. Being experienced miners, they did some experimental panning as they moved north. When they reached the mouth of Cherry Creek they camped for a few days to prospect. Smiley in his *History of Denver* reports:

"They found 'color,' but not enough to hold them from their original objective, California."

The Ralstons and their Cherokee party stayed in California for two years, mining with moderate luck. The memory of the "color" at Cherry Creek never left their minds. They did not return to the Colorado gold fields, but imparted their knowledge to relatives in the Cherokee Territory of Georgia, leading directly to the first real prospecting party and to the incredible Colorado strikes.

In this fashion did the Nevada and Colorado finds result from the original California strike which brought prospectors through the Far West, opening the land and weaving the three greatest American gold fileds into an integrated frontier pattern, all parts of a geographical and cultural whole.

CHAPTER XI

Gold and Mormonism Settle a Land

BY CONTRAST TO VIGOROUS San Francisco and Salt Lake, Los Angeles of 1850 was standing still, a sleepy village of mud huts surrounded by extensive ranchos, without a public school, newspaper or library. With its hot, waterless, dusty near-desert climate, its main activity was fighting Indians who were raiding the ranchos, the Paiutes driving off as many as five hundred head of cattle. Two thirds of the population was illiterate; the one third that could read and write was busy sending petitions to Congress asking that southern California be separated from northern California and called the state of Central California, a separatist movement which was due to the feeling of the southern Californians that they had nothing in common with northern California. At the moment they were right.

Northern California was a lean hard-bitten mountain man, a Jedediah Smith or Joseph Walker fighting his way across the snow-clad Sierra Nevada with a hunter's gun slung on his back; male, rugged, disciplined, carrying the seed of a new civilization. Southern California was a lush, red-lipped, sensual female who came up from Acapulco in the cabin of a well-rigged Spanish ship, sunning herself in a patio surrounded by bougainvillea, her gown cut sufficiently low to intimate how abundantly the coming generations might be nourished.

San Franciscans were beginning to take on the character of the perpendicular hills they had to climb, and the submerged grimness of the cold, foggy weather. They were a stony people, astonishingly like New Englanders: stubborn, proud, willful, self-contained, tenacious, fiercely independent, rooted in rocky tradition. The international flavor persisted, yet at the same time there was a curiously insular quality, almost like that of an island folk.

San Francisco's first theatrical season began on January 16, 1850, in Washington Hall, with the Eagle Theatre Company playing a farce and a drama. A few weeks later the National was opened, a proper theatre of brick, with a French company. The government was installed in its first City Hall, the former Graham House, a four-story wooden building on the corner of Kearny and Pacific, with four flights of continuous balconies overlooking the busy streets.

In May a fire broke out before dawn in a rickety gambling saloon; for seven hours the wind-driven flames raced up and down the hills, burning three hundred houses, including the City Hall, two sides of Portsmouth Square and the three important business blocks. The loss was over $4,000,000, accounting for nearly half the gold dug out of California in 1849, making Brigham Young sound like a prophet when he told his Saints:

"The true use of gold is for paving streets, covering houses and making culinary dishes."

Within ten days half of the burned city was rebuilt, the first volunteer fire department organized and every home owner warned to keep six buckets of water on hand for future emergencies. It would not be quite enough; not even the five fire companies with pretentious names like the Empire Engine Company, the Protection or the Eureka could keep San Francisco from becoming the most frequently burned-down city in the world. On June 12, forty days later, a fire started in a broken chimney in the Merchants Hotel and the business district from Kearny Street to the waterfront burned down, another $3,000,000 vanishing in smoke; in September one hundred fifty houses burned, in October another $250,000 worth of property, including the City Hospital; in December there was a $1,000,000 loss of wood and corrugated iron wall buildings. . . .

California was having an equally hard time becoming a state. On January 1, 1850, Senator John C. Fremont, his wife Jessie and their daughter Lily had boarded the S.S. *Oregon* in Monterey Harbor en route to Washington to have California admitted. They were rowed out to the ship by Indian boys in a torrential downpour of rain, but no greater than was the torrent of speeches which kept Fremont out of the Senate and California out of the Union through the spring and summer months until the South's unwillingness to admit another free state was compromised. Now on October 18, 1850, the S.S. *Oregon* sailed into San Francisco Harbor flying all its bunting and signaling that California had been admitted.

San Francisco promptly went wild. All business houses and courts were locked, guns began firing from the hills surrounding the city, bands and paraders stomped through the streets, the ships in the harbor broke out their flags, newspapers off the S.S. *Oregon* sold for $5.00 apiece. At night bonfires blazed from the peaks.

"Mounting his box behind six fiery mustangs lashed to the highest speed, the driver of Crandall's stage cried the glad tidings all the way to San Jose, 'California is admitted!', while a ringing cheer was returned by the people as the mail flew by."

On the twenty-ninth of October came the official celebration, with a procession led by marshals in crimson scarves, buglers sounding all the way to Portsmouth Square, the native Californios carrying a banner with thirty-one stars, the Chinese colony in their native costumes attesting their loyalty by carrying a blue silk banner reading *The China Boys*.

By contrast the Saints took their admission as Utah Territory quietly. It was not that the Mormons were against celebrations; on July 24, the anniversary of President Young's arrival in the valley with the first group of Saints, there had been the firing of a cannon, speeches, Captain Pitts's brass band, which had been converted as a unit in England, playing martial music, a feast to which all strangers were invited. It was just that the Mormons were disappointed in not being given their total freedom as a state as California had been. In their status as a territory they would be controlled from Washington, and gentiles would be appointed to be their territorial officers.

Nor was that all in California upon which Brigham Young had cast a covetous eye. He had always wanted the port of San Diego for his state of Deseret, so that newly converted Saints arriving from Europe could come to Salt Lake over a route controlled by Mormons. He also wanted "a settlement in the vicinity of the sea coast, a main route to the Pacific stations between the Iron County [Utah] and California; also to cultivate the olive and manufacture olive oil, grapes, sugar cane, cotton and other desirable fruits and products."

San Diego was now part of the state of California, and so were all the rich farming lands between southern Nevada and the Pacific Ocean. There could be no Mormon route for converts which traversed exclusively Mormon country. Nevertheless two Mormons traveling the San Bernardino Valley, east of Los Angeles, wrote to Brigham Young saying:

"The Williams Ranch contains advantages for a settlement of

our people. . . . Here is the soil and climate and water to raise crops of any kind. It is situated within 40 miles of the port of San Pedro and 112 miles of San Diego."

Brigham Young appointed Elders Lyman and Rich to head the expedition, asking for twenty volunteers. Five hundred showed up. Young's intuition told him that many had been lured by the love of gold.

"I was sick at the sight of so many of the Saints running to California after the gods of this world," said Young, "and I was unable to address them."

The Mormon expedition moved southward toward the spring at Las Vegas. Every stream, field of grass, stand of trees, potential stone quarry was noted for future Mormon stations. From Las Vegas through the Mojave Desert the expedition traveled a barren and destitute stretch, suffering from thirst and exhaustion, pushing across endless uphill wastes, and over a seven-thousand-foot mountain range.

The Los Angeles *Star* announced on May 31, 1851, that one hundred fifty Mormon families were at Cajon Pass, and assumed they were coming to Los Angeles.

"If it be true that the Mormons are coming in such numbers to settle among us we shall, as good and industrious citizens, extend to them a friendly welcome."

The Mormons were doubtless touched by this show of civic rectitude, but they had not the slightest intention of settling among the gentiles; they would carve out their own community. The Elders rejected the Williams rancho and continued their study of the valley. In the meanwhile temporary farming lands were bought and planted; they had brought with them a supply of livestock for milk, butter, cheese. For protection they built a split-log fort of which the west wall consisted of log houses, the other three walls of rightly compacted, twelve-foot willows to keep out raiding Indians. A ditch was dug from a nearby creek into the fort so that the Mormon wives would not have to leave the enclosure to get water. There was no government in the San Bernardino Valley; the Mormons brought their own: a ward and a stake were set up, with its bishop and president, and a high council to serve as a tribunal.

The second Protestant community in southern California was founded in the same valley six weeks later by a group of emigrants from the Oatman Party which had left Independence in 1850, heading for the northern gold fields. They had suffered such severe losses through Indian raids, starvation and thirst that they vowed they would make their home at the first place where there was an abundance of water. This proved to be El Monte, "a wooded spot," about five miles east of Los Angeles.

"Here a little stream trickled through a mass of watercress and rushes while wild grapes matted the willows and alders on the bank."

Here Ira Thompson made camp, persuading others of the exhausted families to settle permanently, "earning the distinction of being the first strictly American settlement in southern California."

Once again, gold and Mormonism were opening and settling a new land.

CHAPTER XII

Rise of the Vigilantes

THE YEARS OF VIOLENCE and Vigilance Committees started innocently enough at a special session of the Great Salt Lake County court where on January 3, 1851, the first jury impaneled in Utah tried what the Mormons called "winter Saints" (transients who had decided to spend a comfortable winter in the bosom of the Church) for stealing, a crime unknown in the semi-co-operative Mormon beehives. The miscreants were convicted and sentenced to hard labor, but since no one could be obliged to work harder than the Saints worked voluntarily this could not be considered harsh treatment. Brigham Young released them for deportation to California.

This was no favor to either San Francisco or Los Angeles, which had by now collected their own gallery of rogues. San Francisco's government had not only broken down in the eight months since it was installed but had in large measure been taken over by ruffians and former members of the Australian penal colony. Thousands of strangers were streaming into a town in no way prepared to assimilate them, where businessmen were so busy accumulating profits they refused to serve on juries or to vote. As a consequence the officials voted themselves handsome salaries, began tapping the coffers for cash, spending large sums with no accounting. The police force had become rife with criminals and their allies. Burglaries, holdups, shootings became every-night occurrences.

Then on February 19, 1851, two thieves entered the store of the popular C. J. Jansen, beat him unconscious and robbed his safe of $2000. Two Australians were promptly arrested and identified by Jansen: Robert Windred and James Stuart, the former suspected of a murder at Foster's Bar. An angry crowd tried to take the prisoners from the police, who succeeded in getting them safely into court. Here Stuart claimed he was Thomas Berdue, a respectable British subject.

Saturday when court adjourned, the crowd became convinced that the two culprits would get off, as had others before them. That night five thousand men jammed into Portsmouth Square led by the ubiquitous Sam Brannan.

"We are the mayor, the hangman and the laws!" cried Brannan. "The law and the courts never yet hung a man in California!"

There were a few less bloodthirsty voices, in particular that of William T. Coleman, a twenty-seven-year-old Kentuckian who had come to California in 1849 to open stores in Placerville, Sacramento and now San Francisco. Big, open-faced, tremendous-jawed Coleman stepped forward to address the near mob, managing to cool its blood lust by asking that a committee be formed to name a judge and jury and give the accused a fair trial.

"We're willing to give them a fair trial," cried one man, "so long as we can hang them right after!"

A committee of fourteen, the first Vigilance Committee, was appointed to handle the affair, most of whom were rewarded for their sterling efforts by becoming street names: Jones, Ellis, Howard, Folsom, Green. The next day a jury was appointed, heard the evidence and voted that it was insufficient for a conviction. The two men were then tried in court, and convicted. The hanging was temperately set a month ahead. A good thing, too, for Thomas Berdue was telling the truth: that was his proper name, and his only crime was that he closely resembled James Stuart. He was released.

The committee dissolved itself in a welter of activity, electing an honest mayor, city attorney and marshal.

But there seemed no way to stop what the businessmen were convinced were incendiary fires. On May 4 a fire again devastated the city, after which a volunteer night patrol was established; on June 2, when another fire started, the businessmen had Benjamin

Lewis arrested. When the judge quashed the indictment, Sam Brannan called a meeting in his office. Here the real Vigilance Committee was born, Brannan being elected president and spokesman. A constitution was drawn, parliamentary rules set up. Members hastened to enroll, even William T. Coleman, who signed as number 96 on the constitution. Williams in *Vigilance Committee of 1851* describes them as:

"A group of responsible citizens, bound together by a permanent organization, with the declared purpose of protecting lives and property in emergencies where lawful means prove ineffective."

The first official act of the group was to arrest John Jenkins, who had stolen a safe out of Long Wharf and dropped it into a boat. Tried in Brannan's office before a committee jury, Jenkins was declared guilty. When the committee seemed reluctant to execute Jenkins for stealing a safe, even though grand larceny was punishable by death under the 1851 statute, William D. M. Howard threw his cap disgustedly on the table and cried:

"Gentlemen, as I understand it, we came here to hang somebody."

Even the resourceful Coleman could not stop them by pleading a wait until morning. The whole town was in the streets, summoned by a tapping of the California Engine Company bell. Surrounded by a solid phalanx of armed committee members, Jenkins was marched to the old Plaza and hanged.

Within a day or two the coroner's jury publicly listed nine of the men implicated in the hanging, suggesting that they be tried by the courts. The complete list of a hundred eighty men who had signed the constitution was now published by the committee. The courts could not indict so many leading citizens, and did not try to; whereupon the membership rose to over seven hundred, the committee arresting ninety culprits charged with incendiarism, robbery and murder, trying them, hanging three, whipping one, deporting fifteen, turning fifteen over to the regular courts, releasing forty-one.

When Los Angeles heard about San Francisco's Vigilance Committee, the mayor and Council promptly organized one of their own, on July 13, 1851, one day after they had organized southern California's first police force. They needed a Vigilance Committee to protect themselves against San Francisco's committee, whose vigilance drove several thousand desperadoes into the summer vineyards of Los Angeles.

"The backwash of the gold rush, murderers, horse thieves and

highwaymen, escaping the nooses of the gold country, made Los
Angeles headquarters. The number of individual murders is not
known, but according to the records there were forty 'legal' hangings and thirty-seven impromptu lynchings."

Unified by violence, Los Angeles was now incorporated as a
city, and welcomed the first child of American parentage on both
sides. Doubtless as a direct result, the first public school was opened
by the Reverend Henry Weeks, the city helping him with $150 a
month. The new city also saw its first freight train, ten wagons
loaded with salable goods brought in from Salt Lake by Mormon
D. W. Alexander.

The lowest income and education strata of the Californios,
feeling unwanted and dispossessed by the transition to American
government, became outlaws, preying on life and property. On a
still lower social rung there were several thousand Indians living in
and around Los Angeles, all that was left of the mission experiment,
employed on the ranches during the week. On Saturday nights they
assembled in a back street near the Plaza, drank up their week's
wage of a dollar, brawled, and at dawn were rounded into a corral
for the Lord's Day. On Monday morning they were bailed out by
ranch owners who paid their dollar fine as their wage for the coming
week's labor.

"Their condition lasted," says Willard succinctly in his *History
of Los Angeles*, "until the Indians were all dead."

In Colorado their demise was accomplished more subtly: a
treaty was drawn between the United States Government and the
Arapaho and Cheyenne Indians as arranged by Broken Hand
Fitzpatrick, out of which the Indians got small gifts, pledges, and
fifteen days of games, dances and speechmaking.

"Within thirty years," comments Fritz in *Colorado*, "the
Indians were treatied out of a state."

CHAPTER XIII

The Glory of Polygamy

ONLY IN SAN BERNARDINO did there remain a vestige of the Terrestrial Paradise.

The Saints had purchased the San Bernardino ranch of thirty-five thousand acres from the three Lugo brothers for a little over $75,000. Though this was a group purchase and the Mormons worked together, sometimes with communal tools, to lay out a town on the same plan as Salt Lake, to build a bowery for their religious meetings, an adobe schoolroom, roads to the timberland and irrigation ditches, yet at the same time it was an individual and capitalist society. Each man secured a city lot and a proportion of the rich agricultural lands; he repaid the Church, which financed the original purchase, from his subsequent earnings. Orchards were laid out, vineyards planted, saw and flour mills built. Neighbors helped each other in planting and building, but beyond that each man kept, aside from his tithe, everything he earned. The community prospered from its inception. With a regularly scheduled wagon line established between San Bernardino and Salt Lake, San Bernardino was on its way to becoming an important city and the second strongest Mormon stronghold.

So it would have been had not the trouble with the "winter Saints" in Salt Lake faded into the larger canvas of a permanent, indigenous problem. That Deseret had needed to become a state was immediately apparent when the first three territorial officers, appointed in Washington, reached that city in July of 1851.

Only a few days after the arrival of Judges Perry E. Brocchus of Alabama, Lemuel G. Brandebury of Pennsylvania, and Secretary of the Territory B. D. Harris of Vermont, President Young spoke at a Founder's Day ceremony. He commented, according to his own recollection:

"I know Zachary Taylor, he is dead and damned and I cannot help it."

Associate Justice Brocchus claimed he said, "Zachary Taylor is dead, and in hell, and I am glad of it."

The difference may have been one of semantics, but Brocchus took umbrage. He asked permission to speak before the general Church conference, appropriately reproved those who had spoken disrespectfully of the federal government, and then addressed himself to the Mormon women, demanding that they return to lives of virtue. The judge, described as a "vain and ambitious man, full of self-importance, fond of intrigues, corrupt . . . ," was also guilty of a nonsequitur: no more virtuous women than the Mormon women ever lived. Those who accepted the tenet that polygamy had been divinely revealed to Prophet Joseph Smith made genuine sacrifices, having not more than one husband, as Judge Brocchus was implying, but considerably less.

The Saints were outraged. President Young cried:

"If I had but crooked my little finger the sisters alone felt indignant enough to have chopped him in pieces."

From that moment there was no peace between the Saints and the territorial officials: Secretary of the Territory Harris claimed that President Young's census taking had been improperly conducted and the legislature illegally elected, therefore it could not meet or pass laws. The Mormons ostracized the three officials, their only intercourse being the exchange of angry letters.

At the end of six weeks the three men departed, taking with them the territorial seal, files and federal funds. Brigham Young knew that their departure could cause serious problems in Washington, perhaps delay statehood; he got out an injunction against their going, but he did not attempt to keep either the men or the materials of office in Utah by force.

Three months later, in Washington, Judge Brocchus made his report, claiming that they:

"Had been compelled to withdraw in consequence of the lawless acts and seditious tendencies of Brigham Young and the majority of the residents; that the Mormon church controlled the opinions, actions, property and lives of its members . . . disposing of the public lands, coining and issuing money at will, openly sanctioning polygamy, exacting tithes from members and onerous taxes from non-members, and requiring implicit obedience to the council of the church as a duty paramount to all obligations of morality, society, allegiance, and law."

Now that the antagonism had begun, the Mormons decided to meet it head on. On Sunday, August 29, 1852, President Young and his Council assembled the Saints in the Salt Lake Tabernacle and announced to the world that plural marriage was an integral part of their religious doctrine, and henceforth would be practiced by faithful Mormons.

Competent observers have said that from the founding of Salt Lake in 1847 until the proclamation that polygamy was an ineradicable part of their Church, only two to three percent of the Mormons had more than one wife. The process of cultivating the desert would not in five short years have enabled many men to accumulate sufficient resources to support more than one family. In addition the doctrine of plural marriage which the Prophet Joseph Smith had announced as a divine revelation in 1843 had not yet totally convinced the Mormon people. Polygamy had been practiced in privacy in Salt Lake, though Forty-Niners passing through had noted evidence of it.

Brigham Young would have preferred Utah to become a state before announcing the doctrine, so that there would be no federal interference with what the Council considered a purely local religious matter, coming under the heading of the First Amendment to the federal Constitution which declared that the federal government could not legislate on the subject of religion in a state. Now, in August of 1852, Brigham Young apparently felt sufficiently secure in his mountain stronghold to dignify and proclaim officially what the American people were already gossiping about.

At this all-important meeting in the Tabernacle, which was to have nationwide consequences, President Young asked Apostle Orson Pratt to speak first. Pratt began with the basic Mormon premise that since all human souls are immortal, and marriage was a religious sacrament, husbands and wives were united in wedlock: "Not only for time, but for all eternity."

Since Father Abraham of the Old Testament had assured his descendants that they would be as numerous as sands of the sea, Apostle Pratt informed the congregation that "Multiplication of the species would provide necessary body tabernacles for the countless myriads of pre-existent spirits deserving of earth life, an intermediate stage in the scheme of eternal progression; and plural marriage would facilitate the sacred objectives in this infinity of planning."

He then went on to his most urgent plea:

"I think there is only about one-fifth of the population of the globe that believe in the one-wife system; the other four-fifths believe in the doctrine of a plurality of wives. They have had it handed down from time immemorial, and are not half so narrow and contracted in their minds as some of the nations of Europe and America, who have done away with the promises and deprived themselves of the blessings of Abraham, Isaac, and Jacob. Even those who have only one wife, cannot get rid of their covetousness, and get their little hearts large enough to share their property with a numerous family . . . they do not know what is in the future, nor what blessings they are depriving themselves of, because of the traditions of their fathers; they do not know that a man's posterity, in the eternal worlds, are what constitute his glory, his kingdom, and dominion."

Brigham Young, knowing how greatly his people wanted to avoid conflict, assured his congregation:

"There is not a single constitution of any single state much less the constitution of the federal government, that hinders a man from having two wives; and I defy all the lawyers of the United States to prove the contrary."

When pressed on all sides by almost unendurable pressures to rid Mormonism of plural marriage, Young struck back:

"If you tell them a 'Mormon' has two wives they are shocked . . . if you whisper such a thing into the ears of a gentile who takes a fresh woman every night, he is thunderstruck with the enormity of the crime. They are hired the same as you would hire a horse and chaise at a livery stable; you go out a few days for a ride, return again, put up your horse, pay down your money, and you are freed of all further responsibility.

"I would rather take my valise in my hand today, and never see a wife or a child again, and preach the Gospel until I go into the grave, than to live as I do, unless God commands it. I never entered into the order of plurality of wives to gratify passion. And were I now asked whether I desired and wanted another wife, my reply would be, It should be one by whom the Spirit will bring forth noble children."

When the news reached Washington that the Latter-day Saints had openly acknowledged and were urging all their members to participate in plural marriage, the Mormon delegate to Congress,

Dr. John N. Bernhisel, wrote to Brigham Young and his friend Heber Kimball:

"The cat is out of the bag!"

Brigham Young and Apostle Kimball replied:

"The cat has many kittens, which will always be the source of antagonism."

Then Apostle Kimball voiced the most intriguing comment in the whole controversy:

"For a man of God [Latter-day Saint] to be confined to one woman is small business; for it is as much as we can do now to keep up under the burdens we have to carry; I do not know what we should do if we only had one wife apiece."

To understand fully the attitude of the Mormons toward plural marriage after this portentous Tabernacle meeting of August 29, 1852, it is necessary to read the considered comment in the contemporary *Utah: A Guide to the State*, written by the W.P.A.:

"Church doctrine has been that plural marriage was divinely ordained, a high order of marriage, as much advanced over monogamy as monogamy over celibacy. A man's wives and his children added to his glory in heaven, and they shared in that glory. Acceptance of plural marriage was thus, for Church members, an act of faith and belief, an essential expression of religious conviction."

In the indigenous story of the Far West, plural marriage was a fascinating chapter. For the Mormons it invoked bitter strife, conflict that would build and magnify until President Buchanan would declare the Mormons to be in a state of rebellion, and order an army into Utah.

CHAPTER XIV

Enterprising and Excitable Young Men

IN NORTHERN CALIFORNIA 1852 was a peak year, with one hundred thousand miners digging over a Sierra Nevada rectangle twenty miles wide by sixty miles long, into which the volcanic age had erupted more than $2,000,000,000 worth of obtainable gold. In this year individual entrepreneurs, each his own capitalist by dint of a pick, shovel, rocker and a three-hundred-foot claim, took out $80,000,000. Dr. Fayette Clappe's wife, Dame Shirley, who accompanied her husband to the mines, wrote home to her sister from Rich Bar that they paid a rugged price:

"Imagine a company of enterprising and excitable young men, settled upon a sandy level, about as large as a poor widow's potato patch...with no books, churches, lectures, lyceums, theatres and pretty girls, most of them living in damp, gloomy cabins, the most remorseless, persevering rain which ever set itself to drive humanity mad, has been pouring doggedly down, sweeping away bridges, lying in puddles about nearly all the habitations."

Gold fever creates recklessness; with spring, and mining possible again, even those men with good claims from which they were taking more in a month than they had earned in a year at home, went searching for better diggings, tens of thousands of men wandering inside the golden rectangle, passing each other to take each other's claims. Dame Shirley observed:

"...if a person works his claim himself, is economical and industrious, keeps his health, and is satisfied with small gains he is bound to make money. And yet I cannot help remarking, that almost all with whom we are acquainted seem to have lost."

The isolation of the miner was so complete that there was no way of receiving the tons of mail that came into the tiny San Francisco post office from round Cape Horn, piling up as dead letters while the men languished for news from home. A young miner, Alexander Todd, homesick for mail, started what the miners called the "jackass express," forerunner of the romantic Pony Express.

Determined to go to San Francisco to find the mail he was certain was there, Todd first toured the neighboring camps and registered at a dollar a head those miners who wanted him to bring back their mail. At Stockton the merchants asked Todd if he would also carry their gold to San Francisco; when he agreed they put $150,000 of dust into a butter bag! He charged the merchants five percent of the gold he carried. Todd was sworn in as a postal clerk, paid the post office twenty-five cents for each letter he collected for a subscriber, then bought a whaleboat and offered passage across the bay for one ounce of gold per passenger, providing the men each pulled one oar. Across the bay, Todd loaded his mail in the saddlebags of his mule and took into the mountains hundreds of letters for which the lonesome miners paid him $4.00 apiece for delivery, and $8.00 for an eastern newspaper.

It was not long before every creek, camp or city had its pony express, carrying mail and gold. "The rider was always a bold, bright young fellow who owned the line, horses and all, and had his 'office' in some responsible store. He would die in the saddle rather than delay ten minutes over the expected time; always a dashing rider, he dressed gayly and blew a small bugle as he went up and down the creek at a plunging rate."

The moving in of supplies was more difficult. Since the mountain trails were narrow and steep, rising to nine thousand feet, all supplying had to be done by slow-moving mule pack, driven by the expert Californios. The trains were a welcome sight, bringing such luxuries as onions, butter and potatoes, which sold for forty cents a pound. The mules were so carefully handled that one miner described them as "sleek and fat as so many kittens."

There were no clergymen in the mines; the Sabbath was consecrated by broken heads. On the Fourth of July there was no Declaration of Independence to read from; the crowd got drunk on whiskey and patriotism and beat up a group of Mexican miners. An outgrowth of San Francisco's Vigilance Committee of the year before was a growing carelessness among the men about taking the law into their own hands. A young Mexican woman, having been intruded upon by a drunken miner, stabbed him and was hanged for her pains, without benefit of jury. At Rich Bar a Mexican who asked an American to return a small sum of money owed him got steel in the chest instead of gold for his pocket; no one paid the slightest attention.

"In the space of twenty-four days, we have had murders, fearful accidents, bloody deaths, whippings, a hanging, an attempt at suicide and a fatal duel."

By the summer of 1852 there were five hundred small mining communities scattered through the mountains, each setting up its own impromptu rules for juries, running from six men to the entire community. There were neither courts nor jails, the facts were heard hurriedly, the punishment inflicted instantly: an Iowan convicted of stealing money was given thirty-nine lashes on the bare back, and run out of town. Two New Englanders found with stolen horses were hanged where they were caught.

Anti-foreign sentiment also reached its peak in 1852; one out of every five miners was a recently arrived Chinese, another one out of five was either Mexican, Chilean or Indian. The Chinese were encouraged in their tong wars because they provided colorful spectacles; whole Indian tribes were massacred over a real or imagined offense by some unidentified Indian.

Retaliation was inevitable; a number of Mexicans who had been badly treated robbed travelers, stores and saloons, organizing into gangs as their success spread through the region. By an odd coincidence, as Joseph Henry Jackson pointed out in *Bad Company*, all the Mexican bandits were called Joaquin, and soon they were thought to be the same man even though Joaquin's crimes, committed on the same day, took place as much as two hundred miles apart.

California newspapers badgered the legislature into appropriating money for a company of mounted rangers, headed by a Texan named Harry Love. In July, Love's rangers came across a band of Mexicans around a fire, killed two of them, and brought back one head in alcohol in order to claim the governor's reward. No one knew what name the head had formerly possessed; they called it Joaquin and the press agreed:

"The famous bandit, Joaquin, whose name is associated with a hundred deeds of blood..."

Ranger Love collected his reward, the head traveled California's museum circuit and the matter was about to be interred when a part-Cherokee named "Yellow Bird" published a book in San Francisco called *The Life and Adventures of Joaquin Murieta, Celebrated California Bandit*. It was so completely a work of fiction as to verge on a fairy tale, but the book caught on, was translated into many languages, and is often accepted as a true story about California's Robin Hood.

This chaos in social relations, which had taken only four years to develop from the Elysian atmosphere of the Forty-Eighters, was reflected in the chaotic mining methods which in a few years would drive all of the prospectors out of the mountains and leave the balance of the gold, $1,500,000,000 worth, to big companies with heavy machinery.

"Disorganized enterprise" built ten separate dams within a ten-mile stretch of the Yuba River by ten separate groups. In Iowa Hill ninety different tunnels were dug. Hundreds of miners were each trying to divert a small portion of the Yuba River, spending $3,000,000 in their efforts; but individual capitalism in the winters of 1852 and 1853 began to run out because most of the gold that had been washed down in the streams had been garnered. There were left two major sources, difficult to get at: the solid gold-bearing quartz, buried in the original rock formations, and the layers of rock and sand high upon the hillsides that had been deposited there by rivers long since disappeared.

Hydraulic mining was originated by a man who attached a nozzle to the end of a hose and aimed a stream at a mountainside or cliff to wash down the gravel and gold-bearing sand. It quickly swept the Sierra Nevada clean of its wandering thousands of prospectors. The operation took a combination of men and money, and began the mining of gold as big business. It also began the devastation of the golden rectangle, spewing millions of tons of rock and debris over river and stream banks, and over miles of fields that have never since been cleared.

Nor was the mining of gold the only aspect of organized industry coming to the golden rectangle, to break up the isolation of the miner, the small mining communities and eventually the Far West.

The first stagecoach line for passengers was originated at Sacramento by a twenty-one-year-old Argonaut from Providence, Rhode Island, named James E. Birch, who bought a light emigrant wagon and a team of high-spirited mustangs and carried passengers on a regular schedule to Mormon Island, a distance of thirty miles over what could sometimes pass for a trail road, for a sum ranging from $16 to $30 a person, paid in the fluid form of one to two ounces of gold dust. Birch soon expanded his line so that he had coaches connecting all the towns of central California.

The greatest single need of the Americans in California was the getting of mail in the quickest manner. Letters coming across Panama could now reach California from New York in a month, if all conditions were right; it took additional weeks for the mail first to reach New York from such border areas as Wisconsin or Missouri. Californians tried hard to convince the federal government that mail could go over the Sierra, through the Carson Valley to Salt Lake, then east along the established route. The postal department declared the plan unworkable.

So it might have been if not for the pioneering of Major George Chorpenning, Jr., experienced trail blazer. He set out from San Francisco to determine where by-stations could be established, and how much time would be required for the San Francisco-Salt Lake journey of nine hundred miles over mountains, sand and salt desert. In January of 1851 the federal government asked for bids; Chorpenning was low man among thirty-seven bidders, and was given a four-year contract at $14,000 a year to maintain a monthly service from San Francisco to Salt Lake. Chorpenning contracted to deliver the mail with "certainty, celerity, and security," or thirty days for each leg of the route.

He carried his first consignment to Sacramento on a river

steamer, transferred it to muleback and left for Placerville with half a dozen hard-bitten drivers and armed guards. At Placerville, last stop before tackling the crest of the Sierra Nevada, the whole town turned out to scribble hasty notes to their families and cheer the departure of the first overland mail.

Chorpenning made it to Salt Lake in fine fashion; so did his partner, Absalom Woodward. All through the summer and fall they headed the alternate east-west parties. But with winter rose two enemies: marauding Indians, and the relentless mountain snows. The Indians struck first: Woodward left Sacramento with four men in November and was attacked within a hundred miles of Salt Lake City. He and his train were wiped out, the mail lost.

In February, with Woodward gone, Edison Cody and five new recruits left Placerville in the height of the winter storms; the government contract had to be fulfilled every month or it would be canceled. Cody's mules froze to death. The men carried the mail on their backs, living on frozen mule meat. For the last four days before they stumbled into Salt Lake they were totally without food. But they brought in the mail.

After this experience, and the finding of the skeletons of Woodward and his four men, Major Chorpenning could get no one in Salt Lake to accompany him back to San Francisco with the westbound mail. Chorpenning set out alone, making his way over a nine-hundred-mile trail controlled by marauding Diggers and Utes, voracious for plunder. He delivered the mail safely to Sacramento, an exhibition of man's courage and perseverance in a country where courage and perseverance were the coin of the realm.

Late in 1849 Adams and Company had opened an office in San Francisco, advertising in the *Alta California* that it was ready to provide express service to the mines. Owing to a stricture in the California constitution that no corporation could be set up for the purpose of banking, the express companies of necessity became the banking houses, not only in Sacramento and San Francisco but in every mining camp as well; for when the express company took a miner's gold for the purpose of shipment it first had to assay it, then weigh it, give the miner a receipt and guarantee the safety of his deposit. Thus the express company's iron safe became the local bank. Within a short time Adams and Company covered the entire state with its offices, express wagons and riders, earning $500,000 profit in its first year of business.

In Sacramento a group paid scant attention to the state's constitution, opening a bank in a stone house on the river front. The new bank took in one hundred fifty pounds of gold dust in a banking day which extended from six in the morning until ten at night, the three clerks armed with Colt revolving pistols and bowie knives.

Wells Fargo and Company, from which originated some of the most romantic tales of the Far West, was born appropriately enough in the back room of a bookstore in Syracuse, New York, in 1852. Henry Wells had operated an express service between Albany and Buffalo and from Buffalo west to St. Louis. On March 18, 1852, at the Astor House, he launched the Wells Fargo company with $300,000 capital subscribed in $100 shares.

By July two of its experienced men had arrived in California, one to run the express, the other the banking. In its first announcement in the *Alta California*, Wells Fargo explained that it was not only prepared to "forward packages, parcels and freights of all descriptions between the City of New York and City of San Francisco," but also to "purchase and sell Gold Dust, Bullion and Bills of Exchange, the payment and collection of notes, bills and accounts." The most interesting line of the advertisement spoke of "iron chests for the security of treasure and valuable packages," giving birth to the classic line:

"Throw down the box!"

But all this activity was petty cash compared to the $40,000,000 the recently arrived Leland Stanford would take out of transportation across the Far West. Son of a farmer-innkeeper, educated in a Methodist seminary and by three years of apprenticeship in an Albany law firm, Stanford married in 1850 and opened a law office in a small village in Wisconsin Territory, while his five brothers went to California in the gold rush. Two years later, when a fire wiped out his law library, his office and the businesses of most of his clients, Stanford returned his wife to her parents' home in Albany, took a ship for California and was set up in the grocery business by his brother, first in the worked-out mining camp of Cold Springs, then in the thriving camp of Michigan Bluff. When his brothers took over a larger business in San Francisco, Leland Stanford became manager of the Sacramento store. The mushrooming city of Sacramento had become the third largest in California, though its residents insisted that "the valley of the Sacramento was originally and is now during the greater part of the rainy season a part of the Pacific Ocean." When the Sacramento and American rivers overflowed their banks the town, caught between the two rising floods of water, became an American Venice where large quantities of merchandise floated out of the stores, the adobe buildings dissolved, and all traffic moved in whaleboats.

It was here Leland Stanford prospered; here he met three other successful Sacramento merchants: Huntington, Crocker, Hopkins. Here he went into politics with them, and then into the business of building a transcontinental railroad.

Here they became The Big Four.

CHAPTER XV

For Los Angeles, Neither Boom Nor Bust

SAN FRANCISCO HAD TRANSFORMED itself from a boom site into a world metropolis, developing a water company, horse-drawn omnibuses, a public library with three thousand volumes, twenty foreign consulates, eighteen churches, twelve daily newspapers and ten public schools, all in four frantic years. Where only two years before ships had sailed into the bay to be abandoned and sink into the mud, now more than a thousand ships sailed through the Golden Gate Strait bringing in $35,000,000 worth of goods for sale: a hundred million pounds of beef and pork, or rice, sugar, coffee, tea and particularly liquor, sold in more than five hundred different places, with a bartender for every sixty-eight inhabitants. Even so the lads were overworked.

Times were plush, not only with more than fifty thousand inhabitants but with millions of dollars in gold that was being fed into the construction of six hundred new brick and stone buildings, a hundred sixty hotels and boardinghouses, sixty-six restaurants and twenty bathing houses. The city's waterfront lots, twenty-five feet wide and sixty feet deep, now sold for $10,000 each. Everyone had money, businesses sprang up as fast as there were houses to hold them. The city completed its first telegraph line to the important mining centers of Sacramento, Stockton and Marysville, as well as a southern extension to San Jose. Agriculture was booming, with a hundred ten thousand acres under cultivation.

"There was still the same old energy and vigor among the people, the same rapid making and reckless spending of money, the same extravagance, gambling and vice. But the city had improved immensely in appearance. Its houses resembled palaces; its broad streets bustled with activity; its wharves were crowded; its banks, hotels, theatres, gambling houses, billiard rooms and drinking saloons were filled; its stores and shops contained and displayed the richest articles of taste and luxury; immense amounts of coin circulated; the finest horses and carriages, the most elegant dressing, the costliest delicacies for the table; everybody was young and wide awake...."

So many duels were advertised in the 1853 San Francisco newspapers and drew such large crowds that the year was described as "the most famous slaughter year when everyone who chose killed his man." Though San Franciscans were still importing their ice from Boston, they had a literary magazine, *The Pioneer*, as well as four theatres, the American, Adelphi, Union and Metropolitan, where they could take their choice of the Booths doing Shakespeare, English drama such as *The School for Scandal*, Lola Montez, near naked on a white horse, or little Lotta Crabtree, California's entertainment product from the mines.

The old-timers were becoming conscious of the swath they had cut across history; there was established the Society of California Pioneers with such members as Sutter, Larkin, Vallejo, Marsh, Leese, Hartnell, Semple, Bidwell. Larkin would die enormously wealthy in San Francisco of typhoid fever at the age of fifty-six; Vallejo remained the prosperous patriarch of Sonoma Valley into his eighty-first year; Bidwell became a key figure and large landowner in northern California; Marsh fell in love after a twenty-year hiatus following the death of his Marguerite.

Fifty, wealthy and lonely, John Marsh had written to his brother in New York asking if he could find him a good wife and send her out to California. Instead the good wife found him: Abigail Tuck from Massachusetts, who had come to California to clear up an annoying cough, and became principal of a girls' school just opening near San Jose. Her hosts at the Santa Clara hotel introduced her to many suitors. Abby refused them all. Captain Appleton exclaimed:

"I don't know who will suit you, unless it is John Marsh."

When Appleton had finished telling her about Marsh, Abby said, "He is the very man. I'll set my cap for him and marry him."

She thought Marsh good-looking, was fascinated by his vast

fields, vineyards, flocks. She married him quickly, and presented him with a daughter. For Abby, alone in all the world, Marsh opened his purse strings, buying her pearls set as a bunch of grapes, and building her the largest and most expensive stone house in all California.

Their happiness lasted but a short time: Abigail died of tuberculosis, Marsh was stabbed to death by three of his Mexican *vaqueros* with whom he had been ungenerous about pay.

There were new and colorful personalities to take the place of the old-timers. Because of the rapid increase of Chinese in San Francisco, rice was the most ardently sought staple. When ships failed to arrive from China the price soared to ridiculous heights, which caused Joshua Norton, son of British colonists, to build the first rice mill, cleaning and buffing the unhusked rice in from the paddies of China. Norton was already growing rich by buying up shiploads of rice for his mill when he decided to corner the rice market. He did. Then three unexpected ships came in through the strait in a matter of days. The bottom dropped out of the market and Joshua Norton went broke. He also went mad, reappearing some time later as Emperor Norton, wearing a blue military uniform with brass buttons, large gold epaulettes on his shoulders, a high beaver hat with an enormous plume, and in his hand a rough-hewn walking stick, symbol of authority.

Flourishing and graceful San Francisco fully accepted Emperor Norton. He occupied a place of honor in reviewing stands, was welcome in all restaurants and saloons to eat and drink without charge, rode the omnibuses and boats by royal ukase, published his decrees in the local newspapers at no space rates, taxed a citizen or business house for four bits on those rare occasions when he needed cash, and was greeted courteously on the street with:

"Good afternoon, Your Majesty."

Then, in the winter of 1853, came a dry spell: there was insufficient rain to wash out the gold. Production fell sharply. So did the influx of emigrants, warned by their friends and relatives in the mines that the streams of the Sierra Nevada were no longer flowing with gold. There were no buyers for the newly completed homes or business blocks or opened tracts. Real estate operators went broke. Imported goods found no consumers as hundreds of ships glutted San Francisco with more merchandise than could be used in a decade. Businesses that had mushroomed on a shoestring of experience and cash closed their doors.

The crash held off until the beginning of 1855 when a mail steamer brought the news that the banking house of Page Bacon and Company of St. Louis was in financial difficulties. Instantly a run began on the local Page Bacon and Company, forcing it to close. The next day, a Friday, Adams and Company, the oldest and best known express-banking house, failed to open its doors. Thus started the first of the country's Black Fridays, with almost two hundred firms going bankrupt to the red tune of over $8,000,000.

San Francisco had become an inseparable link in the nation's economic chain.

Los Angeles, in contrast to San Francisco, was achieving neither boom nor bust. There were fugitive signs of growth in 1852: the city had started a harbor at San Pedro, sixteen to twenty miles away, the closest body of water resembling a bay; the City Council passed an ordinance which instructed the residents to wash their linen in the little canals instead of the river which provided the town's drinking water; the manufacture of beer and vinegar was begun. The *Star* chronically complained that it took four to six weeks for mail to reach Los Angeles from San Francisco, longer than it took from New York to San Francisco; and an effort was made to collect from the streets, described as pitfalls of filth and mud during a rain, "all the heads and remains of cattle and other dead animals, that they might be set on fire to be thoroughly consumed and the air purified." The city staged a horse race during which the backers of the California horse, wagering $50,000 on their favorite, suffered the equivalent of the closing of Adams and Company in San Francisco, when the Australian horse came in first.

Los Angeles should have been prosperous, for the surrounding ranchers had made fortunes driving their beef to San Francisco and the gold mines, while the vineyardists were sending their wine north; but as late as 1854 the town could boast no more than a chapel facing the Plaza, and fifty buildings, with half a dozen of them two-storied, placed like cardboard boxes on a treeless, flowerless, shadeless, baking semi-desert plain. Apparently the ranchers and wine makers were spending their money elsewhere.

A reign of lawlessness engulfed Los Angeles at the beginning of 1855: David Brown, who had killed a fellow undesirable, and been sentenced to hang, won a stay of execution. The mayor resigned, joined with a group of vigilantes and lynched Brown. An account of the lynching appeared in the press a number of hours before the actual scene in order that the paper might make a ten o'clock ship leaving for San Francisco.

The lynching did not put an end to the murders; gangs or horse and cattle thieves roamed southern California, killed the sheriff of

Los Angeles and three of his posse before being hunted down by United States troops acting with several companies of volunteers.

However Los Angeles was no more lawless than San Francisco. The two cities were part of the wild frontier. In periods of prosperity the government was abandoned by the reputable business community and fell into the hands of those who were determined to use it as a means of getting rich. By 1855 the government of San Francisco, purged by the Vigilantes of 1851, was $1,000,000 in debt, on which it was paying thirty-six percent interest, and had so far deteriorated that one of its judges had been trained in penology by serving sentences in eastern penitentiaries. If the interlocking pattern of the country's high finance had reached the Pacific Ocean, so had the mechanical genius of the American people made its way west, in the form of a ballot box with false sides and bottom, pre-stuffed with conveniently marked ballots. In one election in San Mateo the political machine achieved the miracle of counting nineteen hundred marked ballots in a community of five hundred citizens.

CHAPTER XVI

"Don't shoot, I am unarmed!"

IT TOOK SEVERAL COLD-BLOODED public shootings to ring the fire bell of the California Engine Company, summoning the Vigilance Committee of 1856.

The opening shot was fired by handsome Charles Cora of San Francisco's underworld. Of dark melancholy eyes and black mustache, Cora was the lean, supple figure of the professional gambler, dressed in the gambler's uniform of richly decorated vest, a cape thrown carelessly about his shoulders, wearing light kid gloves, carrying himself with the nonchalant air of a gentleman. He had arrived in San Francisco with a pretty young girl, Annabelle

Ryan, known as Belle, whom he had taken out of a New Orleans house of prostitution. She was now living with him as his wife. The killing resulted from an outraged sense of the proprieties: Mrs. William H. Richardson, wife of the United States marshal, complained to her husband when Cora brought Belle to a performance at the American Theatre and boldly sat in an open box with his mistress instead of discreetly hiding in a curtained rear stall.

Richardson spoke sharply to Cora, with whom he had been feuding. The next day the two men met in the Blue Wing saloon, apparently settling their quarrel. Once out on the street, Cora seized Richardson by the collar and drew a pistol from his pocket. Richardson cried:

"Don't shoot, I am unarmed!"

Cora shot the marshal through the breast. Richardson died instantly. Sam Brannan made an impassioned speech in an effort to get Cora hanged, but was arrested for inciting to riot. San Francisco believed Cora could be convicted legally.

Before Cora could be brought to trial his employer, one of the town's most notorious gamblers, was made marshal. At the trial Cora was defended by Edward D. Baker of Springfield, Illinois, who received $10,000 from Belle for a spellbinding defense which accomplished what San Francisco considered impossible: a disagreement on the grounds of self-defense.

A second brutal murder crystallized the committee: the shooting of James King of William, editor of the *Evening Bulletin*, by James P. Casey, a former inmate of Sing Sing but now a county supervisor, a reward for having imported the ingeniously false ballot box. King, born in the District of Columbia, was thirty-four; his brother Henry had died on Fremont's relief party to Taos. He had come to California for his health in 1848, served on the Vigilante Committee of 1851, opened a bank, prospered and then lost $250,000 in the depression of 1854. Described as "honest, brave, terribly in earnest, but often rash," King borrowed a few dollars from friends and started the *Evening Bulletin* for the purpose of exposing the underworld control of San Francisco politics. His blistering editorials seared every crook in town.

That is, until he printed the fact that County Supervisor Casey had served a sentence in Sing Sing. As he came out of his printing office and crossed the street, Casey stepped from behind an express wagon and shot him. While King lay wounded, Casey rushed to the police station, which was controlled by his friends. People thronged the streets demanding that Casey be lynched. A brother of King made an impassioned plea that Casey be hanged. The crowds in front of the jail grew dense. Troops arrived to reinforce the jail guard. Mayor Van Ness pleaded:

"Let the law have its course. Justice will be done."

But the people had seen justice perverted in the Cora case. They refused to disperse.

That night William T. Coleman was asked to head a new Vigilance Committee. Coleman declined: he was just back from a two-year stay in the East, he did not approve of extra-legal government. He changed his mind when he was convinced that the mob would riot if the people were not organized and disciplined.

Level-headed, a brilliant organizer, he put a notice in the papers:

The members of the Vigilance Committee in good standing will please meet at No. 105 1/2 Sacramento Street, this day, Thursday, 15 inst. at nine o'clock A.M. By order of the Committee of Thirteen

That morning a crowd gathered in front of the Sacramento Street hall. Before noon fifteen hundred men acceptable to Coleman and the committee had signed. Coleman was elected president; every man took an oath of obedience and secrecy and was assigned a number. By evening two thousand citizens had signed. Coleman had them collect in companies of one hundred, elect their officers, plan for immediate drill. The Executive Committee was extended to thirty-seven members, rotating in groups of twelve, three top officers of each Hundred serving on the Board of Delegates. Members contributed money; muskets and shot were rented from George Law, who had bought them from the government.

By the seventeenth of May, three days after King was shot, the committee had eight thousand members. They leased a three-story building at 41 Sacramento Street and mounted cannon on the roof. Out from the building, extending to the middle of the street, they built an eight-foot-high enclosure of gunnybags filled with sand, placed cannon at the corners and left holes for riflemen inside the enclosure. At the rear there were stables with cavalry and artillery horses. The Vigilance Committee was now an army, organized, disciplined, with $75,000 of contributions available to purchase arms. Its headquarters was named "Fort Gunnybags."

The original 1851 bell which the committee had borrowed from the California Engine Company was sounded to assemble the members, and three quarters of the city's men came running, gun in arm, a piece of white ribbon in the buttonhole.

The committee adopted the same constitution as the Committee of 1851, then set about the business for which they had been formed. On a serene Sunday morning at ten, Coleman's captains gave their companies the command, "Forward, March!" Twenty-five hundred Vigilantes moved on the jail, with fifteen thousand spectators streaming along the route of march. The companies surrounded the jail, a troop of sixty men aimed a piece of field artillery at the jail door. The jailkeeper quickly surrendered Casey, who was taken by Coleman in a carriage to Fort Gunnybags. An hour later the carriage returned for Charles Cora.

On May 20 Casey and Cora were tried before a twelve-man jury selected from the Vigilante Executive Committee and sitting at Fort Gunnybags. Cora asked for a member of the committee to defend him. Witnesses were brought in from the outside to testify. Cora was convicted by a majority vote. He announced himself as satisfied with the trial.

During Cora's trial the grand marshal of the committee had come into the trial room to announce that James King of William had just died.

James Casey was brought in and convicted unanimously. The executions were set for May 22, the date of King's funeral.

Hinged platforms were built outside the second floor of Fort Gunnybags. Three thousand Vigilance troops stood at attention in the streets below. Cora and Casey were led out of tall windows, though not before Belle and Cora were united in marriage. As each man came out on his platform a noose was put around his neck, a white cap slipped over his head.

A church bell tolled. Every bell in San Francisco answered. As the funeral procession of James King of William left the Unitarian Church a block away, the executioner cut the ropes.

During the next weeks the Vigilance Committee called before it dozens of political malefactors, tried and deported them, paying their transportation when necessary. In June, Governor Johnson decided that San Francisco had been out of hand long enough and took steps to put an end to the Vigilantes. He declared a state of insurrection, issued a second call for the state militia, the first call issued by William T. Sherman having been ignored. When President Pierce refused his request for troops and guns, the governor wrote to U.S. Major General Wool at Benicia and to Navy Captain David Farragut at Mare Island.

Both refused.

When arms from the arsenal at Benicia were finally made

available to the state guard, the Vigilante Committee raided the boats bringing them to San Francisco, seizing the guns and ammunition.

Having run the rascals out, the Executive Committee decided that it had no further pressing business, and set July Fourth for the official breakup celebration. Then came the gratuitous stabbing of Sterling Hopkins, executioner of Cora and Casey, by Supreme Court Justice David S. Terry.

David Terry, a towering Texan, hot-headed and violent, with an ever ready bowie knife, was born in Kentucky, was a volunteer in the war for Texan independence, and a lieutenant of Texas Rangers in the Mexican War. A lethal fighter in the courts, he had ridden into the state Supreme Court on the tails of weak, Know-Nothing (anti-Catholic) Governor Johnson.

Vigilance President Coleman had issued an arrest order for a James Maloney. Maloney was with Justice Terry when writ-server Hopkins caught up with him. A brawl ensued, during which a revolver went off. Judge Terry drew out his bowie knife and buried it in Hopkins's neck.

The Vigilance Committee was of necessity in business again; but if Hopkins died, could an ex officio committee hang a justice of the state Supreme Court? Terry, a prisoner in Fort Gunnybags, sought help from the captain of the U.S.S. *John Adams*, who demanded that Judge Terry be surrendered or he would be obliged to "use the power at my command," that is, his naval guns.

The Vigilance Committee faced armed conflict with the federal government. However Captain David Farragut quieted the captain of the U.S.S. *John Adams*, Hopkins recovered, and the Vigilance Committee convicted Judge Terry only of assault.

Two more gruesome murders had to be dealt with: one Joseph Hetherington, to whom a Dr. Andrew Randall owed some money, shot the doctor to death in a hotel lobby. Philander Brace, who was serving a term for larceny, killed Captain West of the police force. The Vigilance Committee caught, tried and hanged Hetherington and Brace in the last of its judicial proceedings.

The committee finally disbanded itself on August 18, but retained an informal organization long enough to nominate candidates for all city offices under the heading of the People's Party, and to appoint responsible watchers for the November 4, 1856 election at which Democrat James Buchanan defeated Republican John C. Fremont for the presidency. Having hanged ten murderers, deported political swindlers (some eight hundred left town of their own volition), the People's Party swept the election. Those policemen who had joined the Vigilantes went back to their jobs, and San Francisco began a decade of clean government.

The Vigilance Committee put on a parade, with a band, the members marching in "long frock coats buttoned up to the neck, with glazed caps and white satin badges shining from their left coat lapels," the officers with "bouquets of flowers on their muskets."

William T. Coleman emerged as a hero and was offered every political nomination up to the presidency of the United States. He rejected them all. Under his stern hand judicial procedure had been followed to the letter; no member, having taken his oath, committed a depredation. Coleman, quoted by James B. Scherer in *Lion of the Vigilantes*, justified the committees of 1851 and 1856 by saying:

"Who made the laws and set agents over them? The people. Who saw these laws neglected, disregarded, abused, trampled on? The people. Who had the right to protect these laws, and administer them when their servants had failed? The people."

A measure of permanent government had come to San Francisco.

CHAPTER XVII

"You have struck it, boys!"

IT IS NOT EASY to settle a land, nor to strike a precious vein. Many years are spent, and many lives.

In the spring of 1851 two movements, one consisting of the Reese brothers wagon train out of Salt Lake City traveling west, the other of the Grosh brothers traveling east from Volcano, California, simultaneously began the settling of modern-day Nevada: John Reese, his brother and companions building the first permanent trading post; Allen and Hosea Grosh leading to the mines.

John Reese was a forty-three-year-old New Yorker who migrated to Utah in 1849, setting up a store in Salt Lake. Having heard that the Carson Valley was fertile and unsettled, the Reeses and fourteen companions loaded ten wagons with flour, butter, eggs, beef, tools, made the passage across the salt marshes and sand deserts, and at the western end of Carson Valley either took over Beatie's abandoned post or bought it for two sacks of flour. They built an L-shaped log house, store and fort, two-storied, thirty feet wide, fifty feet deep, with two sides forming a pentagon-shaped fort which became known as Mormon Station.

Sixty thousand gold seekers passed through the Humboldt and Carson valleys on their way to California. Reese said:

"The word came that 1852 was going to be a great immigration year. I mixed things around and plowed up to be ready."

Allen and Hosea Grosh, in their mid-twenties, abandoned the California gold fields where they had done only fairly well. They had heard things about the Nevada gold region which excited their studious young minds. They went farther up Gold Canyon in Nevada than anyone had ever ventured before, bringing down the so-called "blue stuff" which clogged their rocker and essayed some crude tests. They wrote to their father that they were convinced there was plenty of gold in Sun Mountain, and quantities of silver as well.

John Reese too had been confirmed in his particular form of prospecting. His turnips proved to be the "color," bringing one dollar a bunch.

"I never saw such things to make money on," exulted Reese. "I had seventeen men working for me, but not enough could be raised to supply the demand. There were a good many ranches took up. I put up a blacksmith shop."

Nevada, a western county of Utah, four to five hundred grueling miles from Salt Lake, had no government. Though a majority of the settlers were Mormons, and the Utah legislature had squared off Western Utah into three counties by drawing lines due west from the Utah border to California, it sent in no officials or money. Mormon discipline began to erode.

The settlers' first need was to legalize their land claims. On November 12, joined by four others from Eagle Station a few miles away, where a prospector named Frank Hall had shot an eagle and spread its skin before his cabin, Reese and the men of Mormon Station held a meeting and voted to petition Congress for a territorial government, independent of Utah; also to ask Washington for a survey of all their land claims as well as the appointment of one of their members as surveyor. They ended their meeting by appointing a committee of seven to govern. John Reese headed the committee on laws, which appointed a recording secretary and treasurer and decided that each settler, since land in these few fertile valleys was scarce, could claim only one quarter section. In two further meetings, a week later, they set up the framework of an entire government, not the slightest whit deterred by the fact that they had no right to set up such a government. Courts, a justice of the peace, a sheriff and a jury were provided for, all offices being promptly filled; a decree was passed that timbered lands should be held in common; settlers were given the right to sell their claims in order to take up new ones, though the new ones had to be improved $500 worth in six months.

Emigration from the East was so heavy that Reese and Isaac Mott, whose wife was the first woman to settle in Carson Valley, applied to the squatter government to put a toll bridge across the river, receiving permission to do so providing they would also improve the road over the mountain to California. The government set the toll: one dollar for a wagon, twenty-five cents for horses or mules, ten cents per head for horned cattle, two and a half cents per head for sheep. Isaac Mott, who had settled four miles south of Mormon Station, built himself a larger house, then opened his original log cabin as a school.

Thus in Nevada self-government was born almost whole in a small room of a log cabin trading station.

Thomas S. Williams, a merchant-lawyer driving a herd of cattle to California, sent a frantic report to Brigham Young:

"Citizens of Carson Valley declare that they will no longer be governed by nor tried by Mormon laws . . . declare they will pay no taxes what are levied on them from the Territory of Utah."

The Mormons wanted Nevada to remain one of their counties.

It would take ten years before President James Buchanan would sign the bill which made Nevada an independent territory.

Allen and Hosea Grosh went back over the mountains to California, but they were determined to continue their experiments. In the spring of 1853 they returned to Nevada, this time bringing with them a "considerable number of books of scientific works, chemical apparatus and assayers tools."

Though there were some one hundred eighty prospectors in Nevada the Grosh brothers were the only ones to think the country rich in silver; the only ones, that is, except the Mexicans who had gone from Sonora to California in 1850. Experienced silver miners, the Mexicans kept saying, *"Mucho plata"* ("Much silver"), but nobody listened. The prospectors were looking for gold. Neither did they want to be bothered with the Mexicans, to whom they felt superior. The Grosh brothers liked the Mexicans, and gave them friendship, in particular to Old Frank, who surveyed the country with them and showed them the best geological lays for silver veins.

The Groshes built a fieldstone cabin on American Flats, halfway between Six Mile Canyon and what would become Virginia City, with a $370,000,000 metal foundation. They also built two furnaces, one for smelting, the other for assaying, then prospected a vein resembling sheet lead, broken and very fine, a dark gray tarnished mass. They ground the blue stuff to a fine powder, baked it in a rock oven. When it cooled the brothers found a small dark, solid mass. They dropped it into a container of nitric acid, watched the metallic button slowly dissolve. That was all the embryo metallurgists needed to know!

Lyman, in *The Saga of the Comstock Lode*, writes, with a sense of the hyperbole which the Grosh brothers must have felt, sitting all alone on the top of a seemingly solid mountain of silver:

"On the result of that assay hung the fortunes of thousands, national welfare, the future of a race, the outcome of a great war. Out of that assay sprang dozens of millionaires! Blocks of San Francisco's marble buildings! A telegraph cable to girdle the earth! A state, legislation, a great mining school, a mining code! Engineering enterprises that were to make the mountain famous! Out of that assay sprang the pomp of kings, the power of principalities, the glitter of coronets!"

The Groshes decided to keep their find to themselves. They would need more capital, more prospecting, to know how best to proceed.

Non-Mormon emigrants coming over the trail fell in love with Carson Valley, with the land that dipped and rolled toward the mountain range, studded with squat juniper and nut pine, and settled there instead of continuing on. Others failing to find El Dorado in California remembered the sunbursts along the river, the wild peach trees with flame-colored flowers, and came back over the mountain to take up land on the eastern slope of the Sierra Nevada. Brigham Young had been sending in a few families to maintain a Mormon majority, but he hesitated to colonize in strength because of reports that there was gold in Nevada. His hand was forced in February 1853 when, not yet having received territorial status from Washington, a petition was signed by forty-three citizens of Carson Valley asking the legislature of California to annex them.

Edwin D. Woolley, a Mormon from Salt Lake, wrote home: "I have my doubts whether Mormonism can exist in the country as far as I have seen." He was distressed that the Mormons did not want to meet on Sundays and sing, "The Spirit of God Like a Fire Is Burning," preferring to sing with the gentiles:

> The Mormon girls are fat as hogs,
> The chief production cats and dogs.

On New Year's Eve, the first dance was held at Spafford Hall's station, "nine females attending, including little girls, this number constituting three-fourths of all the fair sex in Western Utah." Unfortunately for Nevada's burgeoning social life the Washoe Indians ran off all the stock while the men were dancing. Marital life in Nevada started out stormily too, the first bride, only fourteen, being taken away from her ardent husband by a returning father, bloodshed being averted by the bride's decision that she would rather continue on and see California.

Shortly after, Elder Orson Hyde arrived at Mormon Station from Salt Lake with a party of thirty-five men and families and quickly called for an election of county officers under the Utah Legislative Act. Since a number of the residents were insistent about being ruled from California, Elder Hyde requested that California run a survey line to determine whether the Carson Valley lay in California or Western Utah. The survey showed it to be in Utah. More and more Mormons poured into Carson Valley, soon numbering two hundred. They were now able to elect their candidates to every office except prosecuting attorney, and organized the area on the Mormon plan: new towns, wide streets, irrigation ditches on either side. They also organized Carson Valley's social life: there was to be no frivolous adornment, everything was for use, with hard work the greatest virtue.

Busy Orson Hyde also changed the name of Mormon Station to Genoa, laid out a second community called Franktown in Washoe Valley, began work on a $10,000 sawmill, prepared to house another sixty to seventy families being sent in by Brigham Young, and dedicated the Carson Valley Mission as a stake of Zion. The rebellious Mormons returned quietly to the fold.

But the Nevada gold fields were petering out. Whatever gold had been washed down the stream beds from the quartz in the mountains seemed to have been gathered up, prospectors rarely earning more than $5.00 a day. Even the frugal Chinese said disgustedly:

"Two pan, one color."

Then the Groshes, in the spring of 1855, "found a perfect monster of a vein." They organized the Utah Enterprise Mining Company, attempting through their father to bring in "kindred and friends from mid-Atlantic states." Throughout 1856 their father remained their sole subscriber. Early in 1857, with a Canadian friend, Richard M. Bucke, they determined to stake out their rich claims and commence mining operations. Only one man in Nevada believed they had anything: George Brown, who owned a trading post and mail station on the Humboldt River. He promised Allen and Hosea his savings of $600 plus all the cash he could raise from the sale of his merchandise and his store.

It would be enough. The monster claim the Groshes staked out as the Frank Mining Company, after their old Mexican friend; other promising stakes they claimed for their Utah Enterprise Company and, as they wrote to their father, "a smaller but richer vein, much more promising because more easily worked," they put in their own name. There still was no government agency with which to file their claims, so they drew accurate maps in their journal.

At this point they gained an admirer: "Pancake" Henry Comstock, mountain man, unsuccessful gold miner, lazy (he got his name because he was too lazy to make bread, just dropping his batter on a hot griddle), shiftless, illiterate. But smart enough to follow the Groshes around.

The Groshes no sooner set to work opening their monster vein than Hosea buried the edge of a pick in his foot. During the last week in August, Laura Ellis, who had come into the valley with her husband in June of 1853, taken up a land claim and built a log house, rode past the Grosh cabin, saw Hosea soaking his foot in a tub in front of their cabin and relayed some additional bad news: George Brown had been killed by the Indians. No money would be available to them.

The Groshes were downcast. Laura Ellis offered them $1500 with which to carry on their operation. Brightening, Hosea picked up a piece of sample ore, pointed at a nearby mountain peak and told Mrs. Ellis that their mine lay at its base. Hosea was pointing at the "monster vein."

On September 2, 1857 Hosea Grosh died of gangrene. His brother Allen was prostrated by grief; he would not continue the mining operation nor, as winter approached, could his friend Bucke get him to start over the mountains for the warmer climate of California. Finally, on November 15, the two men made their start. It was too late. They were caught in a tremendous snowstorm high in the crest of the Sierra Nevada, with all trails obliterated. Forced to kill their mule for meat, they plunged through the trackless snows carrying their supplies on their backs. Their powder and matches got wet, they went for four days without food or fire, their toes froze, then their feet. By the time they stumbled into a Mexican miner's camp their legs were frozen to the knees.

Bucke permitted the amputation of one leg and his second foot. Allen Grosh refused permission to amputate. On December 19 he died of gangrene of the leg, as had his brother Hosea.

The Groshes were not to enjoy any part of their discovery. The harvest of their seven years of study, prospecting, perseverance and faith was to be gathered by other men, strangers to them. Not even their father could collect the few dollars he had scraped together to send to his sons. Yet Allen and Hosea Grosh, like John Sutter and James Marshall in California, go down as the discoverers of the titanic wealth of Nevada.

A few weeks after the death of Allen Grosh, Pancake Comstock, who was now living in the Groshes' abandoned house, went prospecting with John Bishop and a man called "Old Virginia" just below the divide at Devil's Gate where the Groshes had made their strike. Surface-digging with a pick, shovel and rocker they found enough gold to stake out claims. The next morning, Friday, January 29, 1858, some prospectors from Johntown moved up to examine the diggings; others from Chinatown, down the canyon, reluctantly left their homes where they were panning about $5.00 a day.

Those who stayed found about $10 a day in gold dust, built shanties, then log cabins at what became Gold Hill, about a hundred men digging in the barren, rocky, sand and sagebrush desert. They had no idea they were working over vast veins of silver; that secret was buried with Allen and Hosea Grosh.

Then in June 1858 an illiterate prospector by the name of Peter O'Riley, who with his friend Patrick McLaughlin had staked out a claim at the base of Sun Mountain, began digging a ditch up the hillside toward a spring, hoping the extra water would enable them to raise the discouraging wage of $2.00 a day they had been earning. Digging down four feet at the spring in order to make a reservoir, they came upon a strange-looking strata, several feet wide, mixed with blue stuff. They began panning and found they were testing out gold by the pound instead of the ounce.

Pancake Comstock stumbled across the two prospectors, watched them work for a while, then exclaimed:

"You have struck it, boys!"

A fast talker, he also persuaded the two discoverers that he and Old Virginia had already staked out this particular claim. Rather than get involved in a quarrel, O'Riley and McLaughlin wrote the others into their claim, which became the Ophir Mine. Comstock also convinced the prospectors that he owned the spring from which the water was coming, securing another hundred feet for himself below the original three-hundred-foot claim. This became the Spanish or Mexican Mine.

The next morning, June 11, the first miners' meeting was held near Gold Hill, a hundred to a hundred fifty men participating. In protest against Comstock's acquisitions of the day before they voted to adopt the California mining code, which would restrict each man's claim to three hundred feet, with an extra three hundred for the original discoverer.

Within two days the rush was on: the last skeptical ones from Johntown and Chinatown, the farmers from the nearby Carson, Washoe and Eagle valleys, including the future Queen of the Comstock, Eilley Orrum, renegade Mormon. They were still mining for gold, still ignoring the excited cries of the Mexicans who kept saying:

"*Mucho plata! Mucho plata!*"

Only one man, a spectator, put any credence in the cry, B. A. Harrison, from the Truckee Meadows. He was not tempted to mine, being a confirmed rancher, but when he returned to the Truckee Meadows he tied onto his saddle a bag full of the black rock which everyone was ignoring. Back home, he showed it to a neighbor, J. F. Stone, who ran a trading post. Stone had to cross the mountains to California to buy supplies, and offered to take the stuff along.

Over the crest of the Sierra Nevada and down in Nevada City, California, Stone showed the samples to E. G. Waite, editor of the *Nevada Journal*. Waite split the bag in half, giving each half to an experienced assayer. That same day, even before the assay results could be determined, Judge James Walsh and Joseph Woodworth started over the mountain, reaching Gold Canyon in three days of forced march. They obtained an interest in a rich claim for their gamble.

On July 1, 1858 the *Nevada Journal* published the results of the two assays: the black rock was incredibly rich. It not only proved the Mexican cry of "*Mucho plata*" with its one-third assay of silver, but also contained high proportions of gold, antimony and copper.

Hundreds of miners walked out of the California mines and made their way over the Sierra Nevada on horseback, muleback and foot. The first legal claim office was set up in V. A. Houseworth's saloon. In Gold Canyon the old-timers were lost in a flood of newcomers.

By mid-July all roads and trails over the mountains were jammed with thousands of men pouring into the new fields.

CHAPTER XVIII

The Mountain Meadows Massacre

THE CONFLICT BORN WHEN the first federal officers walked out on Utah Territory continued to gather momentum, for Brigham Young was candid in announcing that he would govern Deseret.

The next appointees from Washington proved to be amiable men; Associate Justice Leonidas Shaver of Virginia and Chief Justice Lazarus Reid of New York held court only on those cases in which federal law was involved. They believed the Mormons' religion to be their own, the freedom to follow it guaranteed by the federal Constitution. But with the accession of Franklin Pierce to the presidency in March 1853 it was rumored that Brigham Young was going to be replaced as governor of Deseret by a non-Mormon.

"I am and will be governor," thundered Brigham Young, "and no power can hinder it, until the Lord Almighty says, 'Brigham, you need not be governor any longer.'"

The blast proved Brigham Young's courage, if not his tact. Published in the *Deseret News*, it was soon known in the East, not only deepening the latent antagonism against the Saints but putting President Pierce in an untenable position. To accede to Brigham Young's claim would be to lose face; to remove him would cause strife. Pierce found a workable compromise: Lieutenant Colonel E. J. Steptoe had been in Salt Lake and was liked by the Mormons. He was sent to Utah as combination civil governor and military head, bringing with him soldiers, artillery and dragoons. He also carried instructions from the War Department to build a military highway across the territory. Thus the troops had work to do which would keep them in Utah from September 1854 until spring of 1855, without the Mormons being made to feel that the army had been sent to enforce the edicts of the federal government.

Although Lieutenant Colonel Steptoe's commission gave him the power to take over the governorship, he remained tactfully in the background, removing his headquarters forty-five miles from Salt Lake so as not to come into competition with Brigham Young, engaging only in those simple military duties assigned by the War Department. The Mormons declared him "mild-mannered, moderate in his conceptions, and tolerant in his views."

At New Year's of 1855 Steptoe joined with the non-Mormon federal judges in a petition to President Pierce to retain Brigham Young as governor.

Pierce reappointed Young. Steptoe marched his troops out of the territory.

The first shot of the Utah War was fired in court. Associate Justice George P. Stiles, a former Mormon who had served as legal counsel for the Prophet Joseph Smith, found that although there was a federal marshal who had full power over court matters, the Utah legislature had appointed a territorial marshal and granted him the right to empanel jurors and enforce writs. The federal marshal could do nothing which President Young and the Twelve Apostles had decided against. When Justice Stiles ordered certain matters brought into his court for jurisdiction, the Mormon lawyers declined to obey.

Stiles appealed to Brigham Young, who informed the federal judge that if he could not enforce his own edicts he had best resign. Since Stiles had no troops to back him, the Mormons seized his papers and appeared to burn them in a huge bonfire. Stiles quit, went back to Washington and accused the Mormons of burning the court records. His companion on the Utah bench, William W. Drummond, also resigned, returning to Washington by way of California and filing a set of charges which horrified the nation:

"The Mormons look up to Brigham Young, and to him alone for the laws by which they are to be governed; therefore no law of Congress is by them considered binding in any manner."

Drummond accused the Mormons of having a secret organization to resist the laws of the country; of having a group of men set apart by special order of the Church to take the lives and property of persons who might question the authority of the Church; of insulting and harassing the federal officers of the territory; of traducing the American form of government...

The Mormons liked Drummond as little as he liked them, accusing him of being a "gambler and bully who had come to Utah solely to make money," and of having brought into Utah an inamorata who "sat on the bench beside him and wrote *billets doux* to the judge while he was supposed to be listening to the evidence."

Drummond's charges were added to Stiles's charges and to those of a non-Mormon mail carrier who, having lost his contract to Brigham Young, reported to President Buchanan that the "civil laws of the territory are overshadowed by a so-called ecclesiastical organization as despotic, dangerous and damnable as has ever been known to exist... and which in a brief space of time will reduce the country to a condition of a howling wilderness."

This was, of course, howling nonsense; the Mormons were building solid communities out of the red-sand desert, not only in Salt Lake, Provo and Ogden but newly settled areas in the south.

All President Buchanan could know was that the federal officials returned with violently adverse reports; that with the departure of the justices and the secretary of state there was no federal official in Utah except an Indian agent. Also there were Brigham Young's own angry words:

"My power will not be diminished. No man they can send here will have much influence with this community. If they play the same game again [sending in troops], so help me God, we will slay them."

Considering the fact that Steptoe's soldiers had played no worse game than getting drunk in Salt Lake and rowing with the Mormon militiamen, this seemed not merely harsh but near-treasonable language. In his message to Congress, President Buchanan said:

"The Mormons believing that he is governor of the Territory by Divine appointment, they obey his commands, as if these were direct revelations from Heaven. If, therefore, he chooses that his government shall come into collision with the government of the United States, the members of the Mormon Church will yield implicit obedience to his will."

He decided that the Mormons were in a state of insurrection and dispatched to Utah troops from Fort Leavenworth, Kansas.

The Mormons were celebrating the tenth anniversary of their arrival in the Salt Lake Basin when scouts came riding down from the mountains with the news. Anger and resentment was at white heat: the United States Army had been ordered into Utah to wipe out the Latter-day Saints, their church and homes, and after murdering their leaders would drive them again into the wilderness even as an earlier mob had murdered Prophet Joseph Smith and driven the Saints from their holy city of Nauvoo.

But this time the Saints were prepared! They would fight fire with fire! The Nauvoo Legion, commanded by its best officers, was dispatched eastward over the mountains to raid United States Army camps, stampede the animals, burn the forage, destroy the supply trains; in every way to block the advance of the troops...but, said the Mormon war council, without loss of life.

However, if the United States Army managed to reach Salt Lake in spite of all the Mormon troops could do to prevent it, they would find no rich prize: plans were made to evacuate all women and children and burn the city to the ground. The Saints would move on once again, looking for an even more remote desert.

It was a crisis much needed by Brigham Young. The Saints had been going through bad times: drought, crop failures; in the southern settlements of Parowan, Washington and Cedar City floods had swept away the dams and carried off the little arable land, reducing the pioneers of the southern trek to eating greens which gave them the "scours," turning their faces blue and their stout-hearted bodies to lean-boned skeletons. In the south too, there had been trouble with the Indians, settlers killed by a swift arrow while working the fields, herds of cattle driven off. The southern settlements had had to become a series of walled towns.

All over Utah the faint-hearted, the weak, the exhausted had begun to fall away, particularly in the light of letters arriving from the milk and honey land of southern California, and from the Carson Valley of Nevada where the Mormon settlements were prospering. The Saints were losing faith in their leaders and their religion, in the promises of their God that they were the Chosen People. Attendance at Sunday services had fallen off sharply; there was also a falling away from the rigid moral codes. When Brigham Young asked a revival meeting how many of the men had committed adultery, a large percentage of the men present rose. Astonished, Young cried, "No, I mean since you have become Mormons, came to Salt Lake." The men remained standing.

In Salt Lake the Mormons felt that their fall from grace was a result of their hardships. In the isolated southern settlements the Church leaders announced that it was the other way around: the loss of their land, crops, health came as a punishment from God for the evil of their ways. As a result the southern colonies became revivalist camps with entire communities assembled to pray on their knees, to be rebaptized and rededicated, to cry out their repentance, their faith. Emotion ran high; but emotion was all the sickly, hungry frontier settlements had to feed on.

Brigham Young and the Apostles tried to keep Salt Lake keyed up to a rebaptismal fervor; if the process of disintegration from within were not stopped their religion would decay at its roots. Brigham Young was no pacifist, he preached the violence of fire and sword against those who would destroy the Saints:

"There are sins that men commit for which they cannot receive forgiveness in this world, or in that which is to come, and if they had their eyes open to see their true condition, they would be perfectly willing to have their blood spilt upon the ground, that the smoke thereof might ascend to heaven as an offering for their sins. . . . You consider it is strong doctrine, but it is to save them, not to destroy them."

The Church's highest officials backed President Young with impassioned appeals. Apostle Heber Kimball exclaimed, "Send twenty-five hundred troops here, to make a desolation of this people: God Almighty helping me, I will fight until there is not a drop of blood in my veins."

Brigham Young knew how to whip up his people to whatever sticking point he thought necessary for their preservation. He began publishing in the *Deseret News* the story of the persecutions in Nauvoo, the murder of Prophet Joseph Smith and his brother Hyrum, the brutal driving out of the Mormons from the homes they had built, their sufferings in the bitter cold.

In the southern hamlets, where it was feared that United States armies were descending upon them, one over the mountains from the east, another from nearby California, where their physical health was undermined and logical reasoning suspended in the turmoil of the reformation and the bloodletting sermon of the worshiped leader, the state of frenzy induced hysteria. The Indians were stirred up to fight on the side of the Mormons or "The United States will kill us both."

Into this atmosphere rode the Fancher Party of about one hundred forty men, women and children, some seventy of them from Arkansas, connected by family or friendship ties, the balance a group of hard-headed Missouri frontiersmen who had joined the Fancher Party en route. Hundreds of emigrant trains had passed through Utah in the eight years between 1849 and 1857, but this summer of 1857 was different. In Salt Lake, Elder Rich advised the Fancher Party not to take the southern route, but to go north and join the regular California Trail over the Sierra Nevada.

The Fancher Party declined this advice for what they thought to be a valid reason: like the Sand Walking Party, they knew by heart every detail of the Donner Party tragedy, the starvation, the freezing, the cannibalism. It was already late August, the first snows might strike before they could get over the crest of the Sierra Nevada... Thus one tragedy became the progenitor of another.

The Fancher Party struck almost due south, through the alkaline desert, through the red-sand desert, over the volcanic jagged black-rock mountains. The southern Mormons were accused of refusing to sell them food, of locking the gates of their walled towns and making the party break time-consuming trails around them. The Fancher Party was accused of naming their oxen Brigham Young and Heber Kimball and shouting curses at them, of insulting the Mormons by bragging that they were the ones who had killed Prophet Smith, of poisoning the wells after using them, of abusing the Mormon women, destroying Mormon property.

The Fancher Party was the torch to the tinder-dry southern colonies.

Considering that the Mormons were already at war, President Isaac Haight called a meeting on Sunday, September 6, of his Stake High Council in Cedar City. He recited the list of charges against the Fancher Party, saying they were the right and proper ones to be attacked. Someone by the name of Philip Klingonsmith agreed with President Haight; the rest of the council advised caution and passed a resolution that a message be sent to Brigham Young asking for instruction. The messenger left immediately.

This same Sunday the Fancher Party remained in camp, holding services in Mountain Meadows, with a river running through it, and good grass for the cattle, at the narrow end a Mormon ranch. The following morning there was a surprise Indian attack in which several of the men were killed and wounded. The party dug defensive pits inside the wagon circle and drove off scattered attacks for three days. They made no attempt to break out of the meadows in which they were trapped. No Mormons entered the meadows to rescue them.

Deciding that they must have help, they sent William Aiden and two other men with an appeal to the Mormons at Cedar City, thirty miles away. Aiden was ambushed, shot and killed by a white man. His two companions were killed by Indians.

At this point there stepped forth from hiding, apparently with the Indians whom he appears to have incited to the initial attack, the evil genius, Major John D. Lee, Brigham Young's adopted son, possessor of nineteen wives, with a prosperous community which he had built at Harmony, fifty miles from Cedar City, and "farmer to the Indians" over whom he had considerable influence. On Wednesday evening after the killing of Aiden, Lee sent a scout to Cedar City for Mormon militiamen.

That night fifty Mormon volunteers arrived at Mountain Meadows. They had no idea why they had been sent for. The chain of command consisted of Colonel William Dame, head of all Mormon troops in the south, President Haight, thirty-year-old Major John M. Higbee, assistant to Haight, and Major Lee. After a series of messages and conferences, these men reached the decision that the Indians should be allowed to annihilate the Fancher train, the children to be spared if possible.

The plan did not prove feasible, possibly because the Indians refused to attack unless the Mormons fought with them. A new plan was hatched: Major Lee, carrying a white flag, went into the emigrant camp, promising Mormon protection against the Indians providing the emigrants gave up their arms, put their smallest children into one wagon, and came out of the meadows with the women and children ahead, the men at the rear, each emigrant walking with a Mormon militiaman at his side. The entire party was to be taken into Cedar City safely.

The emigrants accepted the terms. The party formed, began its movement out of the meadows. Suddenly there was a cry:

"Halt! Do your duty!"

The Mormon militiamen wheeled around, each shooting down the emigrant walking at his side. Those emigrants whose militiamen refused to kill rushed to protect their women and children. As described in Mormon Juanita Brooks's *The Mountain Meadows Massacre*, the Indians then:

"Leaped from the brush on both sides of the road at once . . . fell upon their victims with knives and hatchets, and soon quieted them."

Major Lee and Major Higbee saw to it that the wounded were killed so they could never give evidence. Seventeen children from two months to seven years old were spared on the grounds they would be too young to remember. One hundred twenty men, women and children were murdered. Most of the victims were scalped and dismembered by the Indians. None was buried. The Indians stripped the bodies of the clothing, taking also the wagon covers and bedding supplies. The Fancher Party had been worth from $60,000 to $70,000; the Mormons helped themselves to these riches. One tragic story is told of a small emigrant child later recognizing his dead mother's dress on a Mormon woman.

The wolves ate the bodies.

By the next day revulsion set in. The militiamen who had done the killing realized that they had committed planned murder. The leaders, going back to the scene of carnage, began quarreling over responsibility for the horrible act, ending by binding each other to secrecy and putting the full blame on the Indians. Major John D. Lee was sent to Salt Lake to report the incident to Brigham Young, whose message to Cedar City, which reached there two days later, had instructed President Haight not to meddle with the train; to let it go in peace.

Lee told President Young that the Indians alone had massacred the Fancher Party. The true story could not be suppressed. When the details of the treachery and mass murder reached the rest of the United States the country was confirmed in its worst opinions of the Mormons. The San Francisco *Bulletin* spoke for much of the nation on October 12, 1857:

"Virtue, Christianity and decency require that the blood of the incestuous miscreants who have perpetrated this atrocity be broken up and dispersed. Once the general detestation and hatred pervading the whole country is given legal countenance and direction, a crusade will start against Utah which will crush out this beastly heresy forever."

Brigham Young was as shocked and horrified as the rest of the nation. Apostle John Taylor spoke for the majority of his people when he said:

"There is no excuse for such a relentless, diabolical, sanguinary deed. That outrageous infamy is looked upon with as much abhorrence by our people as by other parties, in this section or in the world."

But it was too late for Brigham Young to explain that by his "blood spilt upon the ground" theory he had not meant mass murder of innocent people; too late to recall the war alarums, the inflaming articles on the Prophet's murder; too late to keep the Indians quiet: Brigham Young, the Apostles and all the members of the Latter-day Saints were blamed equally. Brigham Young knew too that President Buchanan would now have a legitimate excuse to wreak retribution upon all of Utah.

As president of the Church Brigham Young called home the Mormon communities of San Bernardino in southern California and Carson Valley in Nevada. The faithful gave up their homes, their farms, their businesses, obliged to sell out for a pittance; those who wanted to acquire the Mormon lands and buildings had only to wait a few days to take possession without any cost at all.

There had been some apostasy in San Bernardino, which the Church believed was the result of Saint and gentile living too close together; yet over ninety percent of the three thousand Mormons packed their personal belongings into wagons and made the long journey back to Salt Lake to fight, defend and perhaps die for the Kingdom. There was a handful of apostates in the Carson Valley as well: John Reese, who had broken away from Salt Lake at the very beginning; his nephew; Eilley Orrum; several others. The rest obediently gave up the fruit of their years of labor and returned empty-handed to Zion. President Young also called home the faithful from Las Vegas, and from the eastern Utah outposts of Fort Bridger and Fort Supply.

The war for which they were summoned did not materialize. Six months later Congress began to call the sending of troops into Utah "Buchanan's Blunder." The troops were pulled back to their Midwest bases; the new gentile governor sent from Washington was respected by the Mormons.

Conditions seemed to return to normal; but the Mountain Meadows massacre could not be undone. Nor could war with the United States be avoided permanently.

CHAPTER XIX

"There is gold in Colorado. We saw it ourselves!"

COLONEL WILLIAM GILPIN WAS a University of Pennsylvania graduate who, like Nevada's Groshes, had been trained in the natural and geological sciences. After having led troops through the San Luis Valley during the Mexican War and later through the mountain areas pursuing hostile Indians, he reported to Missourians at Independence in January of '49 that he had found evidence of gold in five separate places in Colorado: Cherry Creek, South Park,

Pike's Peak, Cache la Poudre, Clear Creek.

No one paid the slightest attention to Colonel Gilpin.

In the next four years a group of hunters from Georgia, being led across the eastern slope of the Rockies, found color at Cache la Poudre. In 1850 the Ralston brothers found traces on the South Platte. In 1852, Parks, a Cherokee dealing in cattle, prospected Ralston Creek and found corroboration of color. Finally in the summer of 1853 a man named Norton, bound for California, went north from Colorado to Fort Laramie and showed a quantity of gold dust. When the men at the fort asked where he had found it, Norton replied:

"Down near Pike's Peak."

That was the end of interest in Colorado's gold for another four years.

Not so the interest in Colorado as a formidable mountain range that had to be crossed in order to push a railroad through to California. Three expeditions came through that year, two of them sent out by Secretary of War Jefferson Davis and financed by the Railroad Survey Act of Congress: the Beale Expedition of twelve, all civilians; the Captain Gunnison Party of twenty-two soldiers and civilian scientists; and John C. Fremont's Fifth Expedition, again financed by Thomas Hart Benton.

The Beale Party, traveling light and in mid-July weather, took the route of Fremont's tragic Fourth Expedition and went across the Pase del Norte for which Fremont had been aiming. Captain Gunnison had with him from Fremont's Fourth Expedition Richard Kern and Creutzfeldt. His twenty wagons went over Cochetopa Pass while he explored unsuccessfully to the north for a lower and easier pass. In July he took his men over the mountains north of Cochetopa Pass, and was killed along with Kern, Creutzfeldt and four soldiers by rampaging Paiutes. On November 30 of a mild winter John Fremont took his expedition of twenty-two men from Hardscrabble through Williams Pass in the Sangre de Cristo and over the Cochetopa Pass.

But no transcontinental railroad was ever built through Colorado. The Rockies were too formidable.

Then in the spring of 1857 Mexican miners from Sonora panned out a good quantity of gold three miles above Cherry Creek.

It was the first spark in what was to prove a forest fire.

The second came through Major John Sedgwick, campaigning against warpath Indians, who reported he had seen some gold dust found near Cherry Creek by a group of Missouri prospectors.

Major Sedgwick's Delaware Indian guide, Fall Leaf, began prospecting, and when he returned to his reservation in eastern Kansas he proudly exhibited the gold he had found.

This was the first Colorado gold actually seen east of the Rockies. Fall Leaf's evidence led to the formation of the fifty-man Lawrence Party, so named because it made up at Lawrence, Kansas, the first party organized for the purpose of discovering gold in Colorado. The leader was John Easter, former town butcher of Independence.

Rumors and tales began to fly through the East. Traders, trappers, army men, Forty-Niners who had passed through Colorado substantiated the rumors:

"It's true. There is gold in Colorado. We saw it ourselves!"

The second important party was formed at the instigation of John Beck, a part-Cherokee preacher who had been to California with the Cherokee Party of 1850. He wrote to William Green Russell in Georgia, to whom he was related by marriage, urging Russell to organize a large prospecting party for the spring of 1858, and to be the first to make a strike in Colorado.

Russell and his two brothers, Oliver and Dr. Levi, began work to assemble members. Fifty-seven was a good year in which to recruit, for the panic which San Francisco had disenjoyed two years before had swept the entire country. Businesses were closing down, mortgages being foreclosed on home and farm, savings being wiped out, unemployment was high. To add to rumor and tall tale, the newspapers on the border picked up every yarn and magnified it; expeditions coming through meant business and prosperity. The eastern papers were skeptical, but the unemployed and dis- possessed were hungry for an opportunity to repatriate themselves. All one heard was excited talk about "Pike's Peak Gold Region."

The Russell Party of nineteen men from Georgia, plus forty-six Cherokees from their reservation in Indian Territory, reached Bent's Fort on June 12, 1858, with fourteen wagons and thirty-three yoke of cattle, taking the same route used by the Cherokee Party of 1850: past Pueblo and up the front range. With the arrival of the Russell Party, modern Colorado as a mining state can be said to have begun; yet ten days after their arrival John Beck quit in discouragement and took his Cherokees back to their reservation. Some of the Georgians also returned home; the Russells and a small group were left alone in the woods around Cherry Creek.

On July 9 and 10 they found a good site; each man began panning $10 a day. Thus the Russell Party became the first discoverers of gold in Colorado in paying quantities. John Cantrell, a trader on his way from Salt Lake to Missouri, joined the Russells, dug with a hatchet and washed out with a frying pan three ounces of gold, then gathered up a bag of the same silt and continued on his way. The gold he showed to the folks in Kansas, the pouch of gold-bearing earth he took to Kansas City where he had the gold assayed.

The assay ran high. On August 26, 1858 the Kansas City *Journal of Commerce* carried a headline:

THE NEW EL DORADO

The St. Louis *Republican* carried the story on August 29, the Boston *Daily Journal* on August 30. Other eastern newspapers published the story of the gold find. Parties formed on the Missouri border: merchants, mechanics, professional men, adventurers.

In early September the Lawrence Party reached Dry Diggings, laid out a town which they called Montana City and built about twenty cabins. But the pickings were lean. No one came to Montana City. The cabins were abandoned. The party disbanded. Those who were left moved to the head of Cherry Creek and originated the St. Charles Town Company on the east side of the creek, though the only sign of a town was a "four-log improvement," four logs laid in a square on the ground to make their claim legal.

Meanwhile Dr. Levi Russell, because of his medical knowledge, advised his brothers and Georgia friends to move to the head of the creek for the winter. He indicated the west side of the creek for a camp site, and with the Russells' work on a double cabin with a chimney began the characterful and amusing birth of Denver.

The Russells planned for a spring of 1859 attack, Dr. Levi to go south to the San Luis Valley to collect supplies, William and Oliver to return to Georgia to enlist further men and mining equipment.

They were sure the gold was there.

So were the multitudes from the Missouri Valley who arrived from October to the end of 1858 in parties ranging from ten members to seventy. By the end of October a caravan of parties had reached the creek with fifty-six men and the first woman settler. Two merchants arrived with merchandise in four wagons, hauled by oxen, setting up business in a tent until they could complete a double cabin. Jones's squaw wife made some whiskey, with the result that Smith and Jones emptied their Colts at each other.

Culture had caught up with Colorado.

On October 30 one hundred eighty men living on the west side of Cherry Creek held a meeting. The town of Auraria was founded.

Because the territory of Kansas extended to the crest of the Rockies, Auraria and St. Charles were in Kansas. St. Charles remained unoccupied until November when a group from Leavenworth and Lecompton headed by William Larimer and including a judge, sheriff and a commissioner appointed by Governor Denver jumped the town site and laid it out as Denver, in honor of the governor of the Kansas Territory.

Rivalry began at once: John Kinna arrived in Auraria with a stock of hardware, sheet iron and tools to make miners' equipment and stoves, but was seduced over the creek by Denver. At its second meeting Auraria voted itself the right to issue scrip at ten percent interest, and voted a lot to John D. Baker to build a house of entertainment. Then the Reverend G. W. Fisher, a Methodist, preached the first sermon in Denver, making the east bank of the creek the religious center.

Altogether, three hundred people had arrived at the mouth of Cherry Creek by December. The last weeks of 1858 were spent in frantic building on both sides of the creek to provide cabins against the imminent snows.

By New Year's Day 1859, fifty cabins had been completed in Auraria, twenty-five in Denver. "Two forlorn groups of squatty cabins," Smiley describes them in his *History of Denver*, "built of cottonwood logs, roofed with grass and earth, chinked with billets of earth, reinforced outside with plastered clay."

The fact that there still had been only a few gold discoveries did nothing to constrain the lonely miners from writing home glowing reports of the richness of these gold regions: an exaggeration that was to be exceeded only by the reality. The opening of the first saloon in Auraria, kmown as the Hote de Dunk until it was corrupted to the Hotel de Drunk, did not help to diminish the stream of golden fiction pouring out of Cherry Creek.

By the end of January the rival towns were prospering, with gun and carpenter shops and an express to Leavenworth which charged a dollar a letter. Yet unless there was a large strike, and soon, both towns would wither; gold had brought people there, there was no other product on which they could exist.

The find was in process in the persons of George A. Jackson, twenty-seven-year-old California miner, originally from Missouri, now broke except for the stock of goods that he wanted to trade with the Indians around Pike's Peak; and John Gregory, described as a "sandy-haired, ill-favored Georgian cracker, whose vocabulary consisted mainly of oaths," en route to the British Columbia gold mines from the Georgia gold mines. Gregory arrived in Fort

Laramie as a teamster and heard of gold in the Pike's Peak area.

Jackson struck first. An experienced Indian trader, he had sold all his goods and on December 30, 1858, with two friends, Thomas Golden and James Sanders, moved into the mountains directly west of Denver. On January 1 the trio sighted a herd of elk. Golden and Sanders went hunting; Jackson continued into the mountains to prospect. The three men agreed to meet a week later at their winter quarters some miles away.

Jackson moved resolutely up Mount Vernon Canyon into Clear Creek Valley over several feet of snow. On January 5 he made camp under a fir tree on Chicago Creek, a small tributary of the South Fork of Clear Creek. He had only two days' food left. The next morning, picking the most likely spot, he "built a big fire on the rimrock, or side sand bar to melt the snow and thaw out the gravel." He kept the fire burning all day. The next morning, as he records in his diary, he "removed the fire embers and dug into the rim on the bedrock, farmed out eighty treaty cups of dirt, and found nothing but fine colors. In the 9th cup I got 1 nugget of coarse gold."

On January 9, out of food, he built a new fire over the old one, filled it in with the diggings to conceal it and, marking his find on a pine tree, returned to winter camp. His friend Golden was already there, but Sanders had disappeared. When Jackson shared his news with his friend, they agreed to keep it quiet until the arrival of spring weather and the acquiring of a grubstake.

On March 17 a group of Chicagoans came through with food and mining equipment. Jackson liked the men and wanted to offer them a partnership. Golden disagreed, simply walking out on Jackson and his discovery. Jackson guided the new party to his site, where they staked out claims, formed the first mining district organized in Colorado, and began taking a tremendous amount of gold from the gravel and dirt of Clear Creek.

There was no way to keep the find a secret. At the beginning of May, Jackson had to return to Denver to get supplies. He also had to pay for them with gold dust. Hundreds of gold-starved prospectors followed him back to camp. The gulch was soon solid with miners crawling over the hills and "Chicago Creek."

News of the John Gregory strike reached the two towns within a matter of days. Gregory had worked his way south on the front range, along the Cache la Poudre River, and gone into the Rockies by way of Clear Creek, but a whole mountain away from the Jackson site. On the North Fork he panned the side of a gulch and found good color. Snow and the lack of provisions drove him back to the foothills, to the town of Arapahoe. Here Gregory found his grubstake in a group led by David K. Wall, a former California miner leading a party from Iowa and Missouri.

Wall and his party agreed to grubstake Gregory in return for claims at his find. They moved quickly to Gergory's site and laid out a mining district. In the sides of the gulch they found veins of gold quartz, the mother lode solidified in the Rocky Mountain rectangle, about the same size as the Sierra Nevada rectangle.

The news leaked out through Arapahoe, reaching Auraria and Denver by May 15, 1859. The Gregory rush, more tumultuous than the Jackson scramble, began. By the end of the summer fifteen thousand men were crawling over Gregory Gulch, which was only two hundred yards at its widest point, and two to three miles long! Tent and shack towns sprang up overnight, men breaking their wagons to build shanties.

At this moment Horace Greeley, editor of the New York *Tribune*, A. D. Richardson of the Boston *Journal*, and Henry Villard of the Cincinnati *Commercial* reached Denver and struck out at once for Gregory Gulch. Their vivid dispatches sent east by fast express brought more thousands of panting prospectors.

In color, drama and opulence, Colorado's Fifty-Niners were a match for California's Forty-Niners. "Pike's Peak or Bust" moved fifty thousand men into the region before the year was over, a veritable stampede across the plains in an almost continuous stream of ox teams, wagons, men on horseback and on foot, forcing up the prices of lumber and flour, with tobacco, coffee and sugar exchanged for their equivalent weight in gold dust. There was a percentage who discouraged easily: finding no gold they started east again, and were home in four to six weeks, one of the main differences between the Fifty-Niners and the Forty-Niners.

Fossett in *Colorado* says:

"Gold hunters of this year were the best the states could furnish, men of education, enterprise and energy."

A fourth new land was opened, taking its place alongside California, Utah and Nevada. A fourth rich, dramatic, flamboyant civilization started building.

Book Four

THE BUILDING OF A CIVILIZATION

CHAPTER I

Pike's Peak or Bust!

UNLIKE THE CALIFORNIA FORTY-EIGHTER who was an old-time settler, the Colorado Fifty-Eighter came for one purpose only: to find gold.

Colorado's Fifty-Niners were blood brothers of the California Forty-Niners, the whole hundred thousand of them who poured into Colorado in the period of five months between the Gregory and Jackson discoveries and the coming of the 32° below zero cold which froze them out of the mountains.

Aside from such mining camps as Gregory Gulch and Chicago Gulch, Denver and Auraria comprised the only towns. Denver was a settlement of log cabins with trails through the sand, its water carried in barrels from the river. There were hardly facilities to take care of a hundred newcomers, let alone a hundred thousand. The name "Colorado" had not yet officially emerged; eastern newspaper headlines read:

GOLD IN KANSAS TERRITORY!!! THE PIKE'S PEAK'S MINES!!!

The whole area became known as Pike's Peak. People wrote **PIKE'S PEAK OR BUST** on their prairie schooners, even though they were headed for the country west of Denver, a hundred miles away.

"The two little words 'Pike's Peak' are everywhere; only the latest from Pike's Peak interests them; Pike's Peak figures in a million dreams, it is the magnet of the mountains toward which everything and everybody is tending."

Onto the banks of the Missouri River they came from every state in the East and Midwest. They came by steamboat, on horseback and muleback and on foot, with knapsacks over one shoulder and rifles over the other; a young crowd, under thirty, as were the California Argonauts, described as having "light hearts and a thin pair of breeches," having left behind their jobs, homes, wives, children, many of them setting out across the Kansas prairies for the eight-hundred-mile trek with no more than a week's provisions.

Lines of prairie schooners wallowed through the deep spring mud of Missouri and Iowa. The Pike's Peak Transportation Company advertised that it would carry passengers from St. Louis, Missouri, to the Pike's Peak area for $125 a person, including fifty pounds of baggage; but when the wagon trains started across Kansas the passengers learned to their amazement that only their baggage was to be transported. They themselves had to walk the full eight hundred miles to the Rockies.

Unlike the California Argonauts, more than half of the Pike's Peak or Bust enthusiasts busted very early and walked back to the Missouri River. They had run out of food and faith.

Some forty thousand persisted, forcing open a new and shorter trail across central Kansas called the Smoky Hill Trail, reaching Denver by summer. The effect on Denver was instantaneous. Log cabins were faced with sidings, frame buildings were erected with board floors and glass in the windows. In July work was begun on the Apollo Hotel, which soon became the central gathering place. Shops opened along the main street; one outfit came out from a Boston mercantile house to catch the trade. Soon there were a meat market and a drugstore, a bakery and a barbershop, whose proprietor, Murat, claimed to be a descendant of Murat, brother-in-law of Napoleon, and consequently charged $1.00 a shave.

The prospectors who continued westward into the Rockies, twenty-five thousand of them, settled around the earlier mining camps. Each cluster of huts gave itself a town name, like Mountain City or Central City. A few miners built rude cabins but most slept on the ground. Each man cooked his food on an open fire before his tent or wagon; there were the proverbial bacon, beans, flapjacks and coffee. The frying pan, tin plate and coffeepot were recognized along with the pick, shovel and pan as the tools of the miner's trade.

The camps had no government; neither did they have any sanitation rules. Follwing the Far West pattern, the first legal organizations were the miners' courts and Claim Clubs, made up of groups of men who vowed to support the validity of each other's claims, at the end of a shotgun if necessary.

"Men from all parts of the nation and from many foreign countries came to Colorado: doctors, lawyers, preachers, farmers turned miners, unschooled lads and university graduates jostling each other in the narrow gulches and voting in mass meetings to make laws for their districts."

The Claim Clubs elected their own officers and juries, wrote their own constitutions. As in the Sierra Nevada camps, these spontaneous groups soon became the law.

"We never hanged on circumstantial evidence. But when they were found guilty they were always hanged. There were no writs, no appeals, no pardons."

In hangings, all the jurymen held the rope and pulled on it at a given signal. Perjury and theft were punishable by ten to twenty-five lashes on the bare back, banishment and confiscation of property.

Women are rarely among the first arrivals at frontier mining camps, yet they move into the remotest areas with astonishing celerity. There were four of them among the Fifty-Eighters in the mining area: an Indian squaw married to John Smith, a Kentucky trapper, living with their son Jack in a cabin where Cherry Creek flowed into the Platte. Mormon Mrs. S. M. Rooker came east at the end of August from Salt Lake with her husband, daughter and son, the first white women in the area. There were Katrina Murat, wife of the barber, and Uncle Dick Wootton and his wife, who arrived on Christmas Eve from New Mexico with a blessed wagonload of groceries and Taos Lightning.

Because she was the only one of the women to remain, Katrina Murat became known as "the mother of Colorado," the blue-eyed, rosy-cheeked, golden-haired "countess" earning this distinction by serving as cook and chambermaid when her husband built a log cabin hotel. When Katrina learned that the first express coach was to arrive in Denver from Leavenworth, Kansas, opening a transportation route between Colorado and the East, she took from her trunk a red merino skirt bought in Paris, cut strips from her undergarments and sewed an American flag, which was flying bravely from the hotel when the coach drew up at the end of its inaugural run.

Katrina had company early in 1859: Mrs. Mary A. Hall and Mrs. Augusta Tabor, wives of prospectors; Mrs. William N. Byers, wife of the founder of the *Rocky Mountain News*, and Mrs. Joseph Wolff, whose husband had been forcibly ejected from Wheeling for publishing an anti-slavery paper. The women settled close together in log cabins with dirt roofs, though the spirited Mrs. Wolff "refused to have her better things sent out until she really had a roof over her head."

Her husband quickly put on shingles.

The fall of 1859 saw the first all-white child born, a girl named Auraria, whose parents "were given several corner lots by the Town Company for helping to populate Auraria"; and the first wedding. When wives or sweethearts arrived, six months to a year behind their men, the entire community turned out to give them a welcoming dinner and dance. Those who had arrived by express coach needed the welcome, for the trip from Omaha took eight days and nights of continuous riding, with three stops in twenty-four hours, the identical menu on all stops: rabbit, buffalo or antelope steak, soda biscuits, black coffee.

A woman's duty was to learn how to shoot, for there were frequent Indian scares, and part of each day's routine was target practice with pistol and rifle. For single girls who had the courage to try frontier life it was particularly good hunting: the area was settled by celibates under thirty, and the girls were rushed from the instant of their arrival. All married very quickly.

By the end of 1860 Denver was no longer a male town. Stewart's Department Store imported across the plains the costliest silks, copies of the newest Parisian fashions, dainty bonnets and patent leather gaiters. Though the men crowded the street corners and stores and auction blocks dressed in buckskins, red shirts and luxuriant beards, well-groomed women promenaded the main street as though they were home in Albany or Richmond.

Education made its entrance into Denver through Cherry Creek in the colorful form of "Professor" O. J. Goldrick, cracking a bull whip over his ox team and arrayed in a glossy black hat, yellow kid gloves, a black broadcloth suit, "his pockets containing a B.A. from the University of Dublin, an M.A. from Columbia . . . and fifty cents." Professor Goldrick promptly opened school in a log cabin with two pupils. The community was so proud of their professor that the citizens met each new emigrant wagon train with the cry:

"We've got a school!"

The clergy had a rather more difficult time getting started. The earliest service held in the area was in June or July, with several hundred miners sitting in the open air on logs and stumps. The earliest church was thrown up in a single Sunday building bee. At the first funeral service one of the prospectors, Pat, standing with the mourners, leaned down to examine the dirt shoveled from the grave and instantly staked out a claim. The minister, watching him, ended his prayer:

"Stake me off a claim, Pat, this we ask for Christ's sake, amen."

The first Methodist minister in Denver, sans church, preached from behind the bar of a saloon. His sermon began, "Ho, everyone that thirsteth, come ye to the waters, come buy wine and milk without money..." while behind him were signs reading:

NO TRUST. PAY AS YOU GO.

An Episcopal clergyman, also went without a church, was given a room on the second floor of Edward Jumps's gambling hall, but the congregation could not hear the sermon for the noise of the gambling. The following Sunday Edward Jumps suspended the gambling for one solid hour, a sacrifice which he firmly believed would earn him entrance into heaven.

Realizing that this unholy alliance of saloon and church could come to no good end, the town directors of Denver donated four lots each to the Presbyterian and Methodist churches. Auraria countered with a free lot to the first four denominations that would build churches, regardless of their faith. Denver bounced back into the lead by donating, as a Christmas present, ten lots to the Hebrew congregation and then, a little later, eight lots to the Catholics, sixteen to the Episcopal church and six each to the Presbyterians and the Baptists. No one has suggested what this prodigal though uneven distribution of real estate was based on; but the grants were made on Denver's coldest day in history.

Denver had grown miraculously. The previous September a dance had dedicated the opening of Apollo Hall in the new Apollo Hotel, and two weeks later Colonel Charles R. Thorne's wagon train came into town with a full show troupe, building a temporary platform at the end of Apollo Hall. Admission was paid in gold dust which was weighed in the scale at the box office. An audience of about four hundred sat around on benches and watched *Richard III* played on the candle-illuminated stage.

The Elephant Corral, known as "the Astor House of the gold fields," offered a unique competition to the Apollo: when a guest was killed on the premises he was buried by courtesy of the management. The undertaker, who also owned the cemetery, was a thrifty soul who buried the corpse and brought the coffin back to the Elephant Corral for its next occupant.

A number of Denver homes were well furnished, the families'

furniture, rugs, linens and silver having been brought across the plains in covered wagons, but the life of the housewife, as reflected by a local advertisement, could not have been all beer and skittles:

Wanted: a girl to do housework. She will be permitted to receive company every day of the week, and a good substantial fence will be provided to lean against while courting.

Domestic law favored the husband. In Colorado's first divorce, the Court approved the husband's official quitclaim deed:

Know all men by these presents, that I, John Howard of Canyon City, do hereby give, grant, convey and quit-claim all my right, title and interest to the undivided whole of that ancient estate known as Mary Howard.

Like the gold-field humor of California and Nevada, Colorado's humor was broad. One merchant put a sign on his shop: "Gone to bury my wife; be back in half an hour." The sign on "Count" Murat's barbershop read: "Barber-ous. Come get your hair and beard mowed." A saloon advertised, "Free Drinks Three Times a Day—Ice Water!"

The early practical joke of firing gold dust into a hillside and then watching excited newcomers rush to file their claims gave way to more elaborate ones: a man by the name of Baker proclaimed that he had discovered gold in the wild southwest San Juan Mountains, a couple of hundred miles from Denver, bringing a thousand prospectors in the rush. It was a temporary joke: a decade later gold yielding $4000 to the ton was found in the area.

Another popular trick was counterfeit gold bricks, one corner of which was real gold. A chip was cut off this corner for assay purposes by the seller. One newly arrived banker bought $20,000 worth.

Other towns began building; Colorado City, on the road up from Pueblo on the front range, was organized in August of 1859. A group laid out a town site covering twelve thousand acres, consisting of two hundred houses in the fall and winter of 1859, and a hundred more the next spring on the assumption that there actually was gold around Pike's Peak. The gold was there, and silver as well, but they would keep their charms concealed for a number of years, forcing Colorado City into eclipse.

On July 6 Golden City, directly west of Cherry Creek, was

surveyed; fifty houses were built and almost two thousand men and seventy women settled there. Each miner carried a small buckskin bag containing his gold dust; one pinch, or as much as was held between the thumb and forefinger, bought twenty-five cents worth of merchandise.

A small group, known as the Provisional Government party, tried to set up the Pike's Peak area as Jefferson Territory. They held a mass meeting in Auraria and drafted a constitution, but the Fifty-Niners were too busy mining to bother about establishing a government. In late December 1859 the Provisional Government party levied an assessment of $1.00 per person on everybody living in the area in order to get funds with which to run Jefferson Territory. Six hundred miners signed a pledge to give the tax collectors bullets instead of dollars. The *Rocky Mountain News* ran a notice in its obituary column:

DIED. In Pike's Peak, of black vomit and convulsions, the Provisional Government party.

The equivalent of San Francisco's Hounds of a decade before were Denver's Bummers, an organized and heavily armed riffraff which was preying on the surrounding country. They precipitated what became known as the "Turkey War" by appropriating a wagonload of wild turkeys, then staging an armed parade through the main street of Denver. The Jefferson Rangers, organized only two weeks before, picked up their guns and came on the double. The Bummers fled.

In the absence of all government a Committee of Safety was formed, similar to the California Vigilance Committee. When a drunken bravo killed a popular young German the committee pursued him through the Kansas Territory, brought him back to Denver, tried and hanged him. Harassed by organized horse thieves, the committee caught one of them and hanged him, but not before he had confessed that the leaders of the ring were a local lawyer and a town director. A secret tribunal tried the two men, hanged one and shot the other, few knowing who the prosecutors or executioners were.

The Hurdy Gurdy girls, who sold a five-minute dance for fifty cents to one dollars worth of dust, were called "painted women who charged exorbitant sums to show their legs above the knees." Colorado folklore insists that the most popular of them, Silver Heels of South Park, became a devoted nurse during a smallpox plague and had a peak named in her honor. Every saloon had its orchestra of fiddle player, banjo, cornet, sometimes a piccolo, always an off-key piano, the musicians being described as the kind that took their wages at the bar. The chief product served was still Taos Lightning, the imported whiskey of which the settlers said:

"No one indulging in it ever lived long enough to become an addict."

Life in Denver was primitive. Most of the meat was brought in by hunters: deer, antelope, mountain sheep, bison, trout from the streams. A flour mill was built in the San Luis Valley, the only place in Colorado where agriculture had been carried on consistently for a decade; from here the flour was freighted in wagons up the front range northward to Denver. A few experimenters had turned to farming; the first turnip crop was eaten by grasshoppers; potatoes were so rare that one man who took two hundred pounds of them into town returned to his farm at the end of the day with three fine cows. A few members of the original Lawrence Company, seeing that corn was bringing fifteen cents a pound, decided that farming was less hazardous than mining and planted cornfields around a town they called Fountain City, site of present Pueblo, ninety miles south of Denver. Though a Mrs. Miller from Wisconsin was selling sewing machines to the housewives at $160 apiece, it was almost impossible to buy fresh fruit. One outraged innkeeper put a sign on his wall:

"Any man who won't eat prunes is a son-of-a-bitch."

The monte, chuck-a-luck, roulette and *rouge et noir* tables were full, night and day; but almost no one was rash enough to gamble on Colorado real estate. In Denver lots of twenty-five by a hundred twenty-five feet sold for a dollar or two; their equivalent in Auraria was worth even less. One owner of a hundred twenty-four lots in Auraria and eighty in Denver, who needed to get to Salt Lake, offered to swap all of his land for a horse, a saddle and a bridle. He was turned down. Part of the insecurity was due to the fact that many thousands of the miners came back from the mountains empty-handed, piled their few remaining possessions into their wagons and painted under the PIKE'S PEAK OR BUST their new legend:

BUSTED, BY GOD.

D. C. Oakes, who had been in Colorado the year before and had published a guide to Pike's Peak which had been accurate in its maps but extravagant in its claims, was buried in effigy all the way east through the Kansas Territory, usually with a verse written on a buffalo skull and placed at the head of the grave:

> Here lies the body of D. C. Oakes,
> Killed for aiding the Pike's Peak hoax.

CHAPTER II

"Crazy" Judah and the Big Four

THE DECADE OF 1859–1869 was forcibly pried open by that *rara avis*, an authentic genius, Theodore D. Judah, who was brought from New York in May of 1854 to build California's first railroad. Described in Oscar Lewis's *The Big Four* as "studious, industrious, resourceful, opinionated, humorless and extraordinarily competent," Judah was the fifth wheel without which the Big Four of Huntington, Stanford, Hopkins and Crocker would never have rolled . . . not all the way across the United States on a transcontinental railroad.

Theodore Judah was born in Bridgeport, Connecticut, in March 1826, son of an Episcopal clergyman. When the family moved to Troy, New York, Judah studied engineering at a local technical school, moving without a wasted day from his classroom to engineer on a railroad being built from Troy to Schenectady. Before he was twenty he had surveyed railroads in Massachusetts and Connecticut, built a section of the Erie Canal; at twenty-two he helped to plan and build the Niagara Gorge Railroad. He also built a cottage at the edge of the Niagara River for the pretty Anna Pierce, his bride. Judah told his wife admiringly:

"You always have the right gaiters on."

She needed them. Her peripatetic husband moved her twenty times in the first six years of their marriage.

When Judah was twenty-seven and building part of the Erie Railroad system, he received a telegram from the governor of New York, Horatio Seymour, summoning him to a conference with C. L. Wilson, president of a group of Californians who wanted to build a railroad from Sacramento to the Sierra Nevada mines.

Governor Seymour recommended Judah as the most competent young railroad builder in the East. But Judah did not want the job. There were too many railroads to be built in the East; his brother Charles, who had gone to California in the gold rush and was now practicing law in San Francisco, was one of the few pioneers who found the Far West "harsh" and uninviting.

Wilson held an ace. He must have played it at the right moment, for on the third day after Judah had left his wife to meet with the governor, Anna received a telegram:

"Be home tonight; we sail for California April second."

Wilson could only have asked Judah: Once you have built a railroad to the foothills of the Sierra Nevada, is not the next logical step to cross the Sierra Nevada? And with the mountains bridged, was not a transcontinental line inevitable? This dream was not new to Judah. His wife says:

"He had always read, talked and studied the problem."

Judah set up an office in Sacramento, then went into the field to survey and draw his maps for a Sacramento Valley railroad. Never a man for waste motion, he completed his report in a few weeks, ordered iron rails from New York and, in February of 1855, set a hundred men to grading a roadbed and laying the first rails in California. With an eighteen-ton locomotive and two small flatcars that came around Cape Horn, Judah took a San Francisco delegation for a ride northward through the valley; and in February of 1856 there was an excursion and ball to celebrate the successful completion of the line to Folsom, in the Sierra Nevada foothills, shortening by a full day the wagon and stage journey between the two towns.

His job completed, Judah was free to give himself to what had now become his dominating passion: a railroad which would link the Atlantic and Pacific oceans. When he was hired to survey a possible wagon road across the Sierra Nevada to Gold Canyon in Nevada, he returned enthusiastic about a railroad pass he had located over the mountains.

He was too early. No one would back him. Unemployed, short, punchy Theodore Judah, with the broad flat face and unswervable eyes of a sphinx, used up his savings and devoted full time to talking and writing about a transcontinental railroad. He stood alone, a brilliant monomaniac who worked his vision so hard that Sacramento people grew weary, turned away from him saying:

"Here comes Crazy Judah!"

Three years later, in September of 1859, in San Francisco's largest assembly hall, a meeting of the Pacific Railroad Convention provided the incubator where the highly improbable seed of a railroad to the Pacific was given the warmth of life. Theodore Judah had organized the meeting, masterminded it with charts, maps and reports, and probably paid all the expenses as well. In recognition of his one-man show the convention unanimously elected him their delegate to go to Washington, also at his own expense, to convince Congress that it should pass a bill appropriating money with which to start a transcontinental railroad to run through Colorado, Utah and Nevada to California.

Mrs. Judah again donned the proper gaiters. The Judahs set sail for New York. By a fortunate coincidence Congressman-elect John C. Burch was traveling on the same ship.

"No day passed on the voyage that we did not discuss the subject," reports Congressman Burch. "His knowledge was so thorough, his manners so gentle and insinuating, that few resisted his appeals."

Nor did Congress. He was given a room in the Capitol where he opened the Pacific Railroad Museum, assembled and dramatized railroad exhibits, educating congressmen, writing letters to the newspapers, publishing brochures, lecturing: a one-man lobby for a coast-to-coast railroad, liked and respected by everyone.

But it was the winter of 1860. Slavery was convulsing the nation and its lawmakers. The problem of whether the railroad should follow a northern or southern route created an impasse higher than the Colorado Rockies which had turned back John C. Fremont. And so, after a year of effort, Theodore Judah returned to California empty-handed.

Back at Sacramento he went again into the Sierra Nevada, determined to map a practical route across the mountains, and to establish an accurate cost survey. He stayed so long he was nearly trapped by the winter snows. He came down to Dutch Flat, focal point of his route through the foothills, assembled his drawings on the counter of Dr. Daniel W. Strong's drugstore, and then drew up the "Articles of Association of the Central Pacific Railroad of California." By his calculations it was one hundred fifteen railroad miles from Folsom across the crest of the Sierra Nevada and down to the Nevada line. Since California law decreed that $1000 of capital stock had to be subscribed for each railroad mile before work could begin, Judah would have to assemble $115,000 in stock pledges before he could begin a roadbed.

The "Articles of Association" were "passed from hand to hand around the village of Dutch Flat." Judah and his druggist friend Dr. Strong subscribed for more stock than either could afford, the little town and countryside subscribing the balance up to $45,000, a vote of confidence in Judah's engineering. Needing only another $70,000 to start work, Judah left for San Francisco and a meeting with the city's capitalists. He assured his wife, who spent most of her time waiting for him in strange hotel rooms, that their troubles were over.

He returned to the hotel, his lips trembling but his eyes snapping with anger, crying in the bitterness of his disappointment:

"Anna, remember what I say to you tonight: not two years will go over the heads of these gentlemen . . . but they will give up all they hope to have from their enterprises to have what they put away tonight!"

He was as sage a prophet as he was a railroad engineer.

Judah and Anna packed their bags, took the morning boat for Sacramento. Sacramento would benefit enormously from such a railroad, yet for five years the town had given him little but indifference and hostility. Lionhearted, he walked the streets, collared people, got groups into conference where he could lay out his charts, demonstrate the idea of California and the East being connected by an inexpensive daily means of travel. When he considered he had worked up enough interest, he called a meeting at the St. Charles Hotel.

Few came, only curiosity seekers. He resumed his efforts to stir up interest, called a second meeting in a room above a hardware store owned by Collis P. Huntington and Mark Hopkins, local merchants. About a dozen men attended, among them Dr. Strong, a surveyor by the name of Leete who seems to have helped Judah plot the route, two Rayburn brothers who aspired to be railroad promoters, James Bailey, a local jeweler, Lucius Booth and Cornelius Cole, Judah's two hosts who had loaned him the room, Huntington and Hopkins, a lawyer turned wholesale grocer by the name of Leland Stanford, and a dry goods merchant, Charles Crocker.

"A druggist, a jeweler, a lawyer, the owner of a dry goods store, two hardware merchants: this hardly seemed promising timber to carry out the vast scheme Judah had envisaged."

Judah knew better than to try to sell such hardheaded businessmen a transcontinental railroad. They would not have risked a dollar on so visionary a scheme. Instead he presented the idea of backing a survey across the Sierra Nevada for a good and shorter wagon road, if not a railroad, to the Comstock Lode, which Sacramento was supplying with hundreds of thousands of dollars worth of foodstuffs and heavy mining equipment. The men who could corner this traffic would make millions.

Since the investors had to put down only ten percent of the stock value, they would be risking less than $7000 among them. Huntington, Stanford, Hopkins and Crocker filled up the stock quota and voted themselves officers. Judah was content to remain chief engineer. In his hotel room he exulted to his wife:

"If you want to see the first work done on the Pacific Railroad, look out your bedroom window this afternoon. And I am going to have these men pay for it."

"It's about time somebody else helped," replied Anna Judah wistfully.

That afternoon Judah began his survey line in the street below his wife's window. He then moved eastward to tackle the towering Sierra Nevada whose western flank rises sharply to seven thousand feet, torn and lacerated by swift-flowing mountain streams descending through jagged canyons. It was a formidable task, made to order for an engineering genius.

By the end of the summer Judah emerged with an almost precise railroad route. He also brought news from Nevada which interested his associates: a railroad would be able to bring out the low-grade ores now being discarded at the top of the mine shafts, worth a fortune to those who owned it.

The Big Four were shrewd and successful traders; they were also pugnacious, acquisitive and largely conscienceless. They quickly pushed out of the picture Judah's druggist friend from Dutch Flat, the surveyor who had helped Judah, the two promoter brothers, the jeweler. They would provide the organization to build the railroad!

The Judahs once again sailed for the East in the hopes of persuading Congress to finance the railroad. Judah reached Washington in October 1861, three months after the Union defeat at Bull Run; Congress knew it was in for a long war. Judah revised his approach accordingly, rewriting the Pacific Railroad bill as a war measure urgently needed to keep California and Nevada, with their rich gold and silver deposits, in the Union. He then adroitly managed to have himself appointed secretary of the Senate Committee on Railroads and clerk of the House Subcommittee on Railroads. Even from this vantage point it took him a full year to maneuver the measure through both Houses. But what a bill it was: giving the builders, free and clear, ten alternate sections per mile of the public domain on either side of the line, and lending them millions of dollars of the public funds with which to build the railroad. Judah sent a message along the newly completed transcontinental telegraph:

"We have drawn the elephant. Now let us see if we can harness him up."

When Theodore Judah returned to Sacramento he was no longer "Crazy" Judah, but a man of remarkable accomplishment who had talked Congress out of millions of dollars and millions of acres of land. This man was no visionary, he was a financial wizard!

Judah's troubles began when he wanted to build his railroad, and the Big Four wanted to build their fortunes. Because the government was lending the railroad from $16,000 a mile in flat country to $48,000 a mile in mountain country to build their road, the Big Four organized their own construction company and gave this construction company a contract at the highest possible price. If the railroad never ran, the Big Four could not lose, they would take their millions out of their construction company profits.

Judah fought the combine heroically. He obliged them to abandon their scheme. By his victory he was doomed.

When Huntington, Hopkins, Crocker and Stanford tried the next maneuver on their cost maps, moving the foothills into the flat of the Sacramento Valley because the government gave them $32,000 per mile to build in the foothills against $16,000 per mile in the valley, Judah again protested.

The Big Four wanted him out. They took away his powers as chief engineer. He was obviously not the man to build their railroad.

Defeated by a you-buy-us-out or we'll-buy-you-out ultimatum, Judah finally accepted their offer of $100,000 to resign and turn over his stock. In October 1863 he and his wife took ship once again for New York. Judah came down with yellow fever at Panama, and died in New York before his thirty-eighth birthday.

The Big Four set out to obliterate his name. From then on the Central Pacific would be theirs, and theirs alone. Theodore D. Judah was one more man sacrificed to the concept of a transcontinental railroad.

CHAPTER III

The Civil War Makes Its Way West

THE CIVIL WAR PROVIDED the Far West with the start of its transcontinental railroad; it also opened California to years of conflict over the capture of the rich mineral areas for the Confederacy. It was the first time California politics erupted over a national issue.

The first shot was fired in September 1859, when Chief Justice David S. Terry challenged United States Senator David C. Broderick to a duel on the San Francisco sand dunes. Terry, a Texan, had southern slavery antecedents; Broderick was a northern free labor advocate. The Republican party had not established a strong position in California in the presidential election of 1856, Democrat James Buchanan defeating John C. Fremont by a better than two-to-one vote. But now the Democratic party was split internally.

Democrat David Broderick was the big man of California politics: big physically, bluff, incorruptible, dedicated to people who had to earn their living, "his large mouth filled with strong white teeth, his countenance sombre, his steel-blue eyes steadfast." His origins were modest, his father having been a stonecutter on the Capitol being built in Washington, D.C. The burly son made his living as a stonecutter in New York, fought his way up to the leadership of a Christopher Street boys' gang, a volunteer fire department, a Tammany Hall ward and a prosperous saloon.

He was twenty-nine years old when he set out for California, arriving in 1849, determined to return East as senator from California.

In San Francisco David Broderick worked in an assay office, saw the need for circulating coins to replace the gold dust as a medium of exchange, began to manufacture $5.00 and $10 gold "slugs" containing $4.00 and $8.00 worth of gold, his gold factory becoming an ex officio mint. He made a mint. Secure now, he went back to his first and only love (he never married, nor, apparently, loved a woman): politics, working his way up from a San Francisco delegate to the constitutional convention at Monterey to state senator, to lieutenant governor by 1851, painstakingly over the next five years becoming the leader of his party in California.

Few felt moderately about David Broderick. To his friends he was a statesman plodding hundreds of miles up mountain areas and down the farm valleys, speaking in his dry, ponderous, utterly sincere fashion, earning friends among the common folk. Certain of the well-born elements called him, because he had labored with his hands, a "mudsill," despised him, saw only his lack of tact.

When the California legislature met in January of 1857 to elect two United States senators, it was largely Democratic owing to Broderick's campaigning; it also looked to him for leadership. Broderick had himself nominated for the first senatorial post, then used his power to have William M. Gwin re-elected. This was a fatal error; Gwin was a pro-slavery man whose ambition was to split California. He spoke for the strong southern bloc in California when he told the United States Senate in December 1859:

"I say that a dissolution of the Union is not impossible, that it is not impracticable, and that the northern states are laboring under a delusion if they think that the southern states cannot separate from them either violently or peaceably; violently if necessary."

David Broderick returned from Washington to find himself stripped of his local power by the candidate he had pushed aside to get Gwin elected. The slavery forces also were out to eliminate the anti-slavery Broderick. Chief Justice David S. Terry, who had stabbed the deputy sent by the Vigilance Committee in 1856 to serve a warrant on one of Terry's followers, declared at a Democratic convention:

"Broderick's professed following of Douglas meant, not Stephen A. Douglas, the statesman, but Frederick Douglass, the mulatto."

This was intended, and recognized, as an insult. Broderick read Terry's speech in a San Francisco newspaper while breakfasting at the International Hotel. He told friends at his table that although he had thought of Terry as an honest man, he could no longer hold that opinion. The remark was heard at the adjoining table by one of Terry's cronies, D. W. Perley.

Perley challenged Broderick to a duel. Broderick refused the challenge, saying, "He was put forward by designing men who desired to get rid of me."

The San Francisco newspapers applauded Broderick for his refusal to participate in a duel; but Chief Justice Terry resigned his position (he had two months more to serve) and challenged Broderick in a series of letters which Broderick felt he could not ignore and still remain active in California politics.

Broderick was a good shot. Terry was a bowie knife expert. But the events of the next few days tipped the scales; the dueling pistols were made available to Terry, who learned that one of them had a hair trigger "so light and delicate that the pistol would be discharged on a sudden jar or motion, without touching the trigger."

Broderick spent the weekend putting his personal and political house in order and on Monday night drove out to Lake House, an inn on the Mission Road two miles from the sea. Here he spent a sleepless night, rose at dawn and drove to the sand dunes where Terry's party was waiting. Sixty men had left the city at midnight to watch the spectacle. Terry won the choice of weapons.

The pistols were loaded, the two men stood back to back, walked off ten paces. One of the seconds asked, "Gentlemen, are you ready?" The men raised their revolvers. Broderick's gun went off without his touching the trigger, the bullet going into the ground. Terry took careful aim, shot Broderick through the right breast.

Broderick died three days later, saying, "They have killed me because I was opposed to the extension of slavery."

Terry and Senator Gwin had won the first battle in a shooting war; but it was to prove a costly victory. When San Francisco learned that Senator David Broderick was dead a dense gloom spread over the city. Business houses closed, putting black crepe on their doors, thirty thousand people assembled in the plaza where his body rested on a catafalque, and Edward D. Baker, whose eloquence had earned Charles Cora a hung jury three years before, pronounced a deeply moving eulogy which made David Broderick a martyr in the cause of freedom, and united all pro-Union forces.

Kennedy in *The Contest for California* writes:

"California had always been a Democratic state, and men of southern birth and southern principles had controlled its affairs. Nearly all the leaders, elected or appointed, were southerners, subservient to southern interests."

With Broderick out of the way, California was now represented by two senators who favored secession, Gwin and Latham. Of the two congressmen, John C. Burch maintained that if the Union should be dissolved he favored California becoming an independent Pacific Republic; C. L. Scott said, "If this Union is divided, and two separate confederacies are formed, I will strenuously advocate the secession of California and establishment of a separate republic on the Pacific slope."

The Gwin element now organized to capture control of the state government, forming secret secessionist societies that could rise as a military force. The editor of the Marysville *Express* conducted a clearinghouse of all news and information for the secret Knights of the Golden Circle which boasted eighteen thousand members. After the election of Lincoln in November 1860, the Knights began flying palmetto flags and looking for a military commander.

Union Clubs were formed to oppose the Knights. In San Francisco a mass meeting of forty thousand listened to speakers and paraded behind bands, while Thomas Starr King, a clergyman from Boston, spoke passionately for freedom and union.

With secession and the firing on Fort Sumter, the Tulare *Post* called Union men "bloodhounds," changed its name to *Equal Rights Expositor* and so inflamed its readers that they killed two volunteers from a nearby military camp. Militia troops then wiped out the paper and its plant. Edmund Randolph spoke for Californians with southern antecedents when he said in Sacramento:

"Far to the east, in the homes from which we came, tyranny and usurpation is this night perhaps slaughtering our fathers, our brothers and sisters, and outraging our homes. If this be rebellion, then I am a rebel!"

The danger of California being taken out of the Union became more acute when, under Senator Gwin's influence, the commander of the military forces in the state was superseded by Albert Sidney Johnston. Johnston made no attempt to control the armed southern sympathizers. On April 24, 1861, through the influence of Edward D. Baker, he was relieved by Unionist General E. A. Sumner.

General Sumner immediately brought troops down from Oregon, moved other troops in from Fort Mojave to Los Angeles. Captain Winfield Scott Hancock reported secessionist incidents at El Monte; Jefferson Davis was cheered at San Bernardino; Santa Barbara asked for loyal troops because the secessionists were armed and active. General Sumner wrote to Washington:

"The disaffection in the southern part of the State is increasing and becoming dangerous, and it is indispensably necessary to throw reinforcements into that section immediately."

After the Union defeat at Bull Run the secessionists were confident they would elect their own governor. A petition was sent by the leading Unionist men of San Francisco to Secretary of War Cameron:

"About three-eights of our citizens are natives of slaveholding states and are almost a unit in this crisis."

Senator Gwin sailed out of San Francisco Bay on the same ship as General Sumner, who was reporting to Washington. When the general learned that Gwin had approached several of his Union officers with offers to join the Confederacy, he had Gwin arrested and imprisoned. After his release Gwin went to France. Upon returning to the United States in 1865 he was again arrested and imprisoned in Fort Jackson.

Like David Broderick, William M. Gwin had come to the Far West with the ambition to become California's senator to Washington. Both men had realized their ambition; and it had brought them disaster: Broderick's reward was a bullet at ten paces, Gwin's a traitor's prison.

A number of California's secessionists made their way south to join the Confederate army, among them David Terry and Albert Sidney Johnston. Unionists such as John C. Fremont and William Tecumseh Sherman left for Washington to be commissioned officers.

Congress, convinced of the conspiratorial plot in California, required easterners to secure passports before they could go to California.

The Civil War had made its way west.

CHAPTER IV

The Comstock Has as Many Troubles as It Has Prospectors

UNLIKE THEODORE JUDAH, who was forced out of the greatest gold mine the Far West was to produce, the unearthers of Nevada's silver and gold sold out voluntarily. They got little more from their discoveries than did their California predecessors, James Marshall and John Sutter. Because Pancake Comstock could talk more fluently about the lode than anyone else, it bore his name, yet he quickly sold his holdings for $11,000. He then ran away with an alleged Mormon's wife and, when the husband caught up with him, bought the woman for a horse, a revolver and $60 in cash, insisting on getting a bill of sale!

Alvah Gould, half owner of the Gould and Curry mine, sold his interest for $450, then rode his horse down Gold Canyon, crying for all to hear:

"I've taken the Californians!"

Peter O'Riley, who first dug up gold at the spring, sold well at $40,000, but Pat McLaughlin, Penrod and Osborne sold their interests in the Ophir mine for $3000 to $8500. They were all surface miners who imagined they had exhausted their claims; they understood nothing about veins that went thousands of feet deep into the mountains. Every last one of them was dogged by bad luck, even as Allen and Hosea Grosh had been: Comstock, penniless, killed himself; O'Riley died in an asylum; Gould ended up running a peanut stand in Reno; McLaughlin, after working as a cook, died broke.

In the fall of 1859 a single street was laid out on Sun Mountain, now named Mount Davidson after Donald Davidson, the first man to purchase its ore. On this street men hastily threw up a few board

254

shanties and tents. Old Virginia came home to his cabin one night hilariously drunk, fell at the door and broke his bottle of whiskey. Waving the neck of the broken bottle in the air, he cried:

"I baptize this ground Virginia Town."

The name stuck, though the residents changed it to the more formal Virginia City. Having, like Comstock, earned his immortality, Old Virginia once again got raving drunk, fell off his horse and was killed.

The Indians around Coloma were right: where there was gold, there was a carnivorous demon.

These mountains were the only spur the Sierra Nevada threw into Nevada. The area was named after the Washoe Indians, its original settlers. The prospectors who made it into Washoe Valley that fall before the snows fell bought out the old-time settlers, prospected and covered the hillsides with "location monuments" as the claim markers were called. Old Nevada settlers found themselves surrounded by outlanders, but most of the California prospectors were surface miners and when they learned that they could not work with a pick, shovel and pan out in the fresh air, but would have to dig tunnels into Mount Davidson and work like moles in the dark, they quit in disgust, and went back to California.

Winter came early in 1859, catching the mining camp unprepared. Five to six feet of snow fell, cutting off Virginia City from Gold Hill, a little settlement only a mile away. There were shelters to house but a small portion of the men, who spent their days and nights huddled around the blazing stoves of the saloons, playing poker and dreaming of rich strikes. Twenty-five feet of snow fell in the Sierra Nevada this winter, blocking the road up from Placerville, turning back the stouthearted mules with supplies in their saddlebags. On the bare hillsides and on the flat deserts of the Washoe the cattle, horses and donkeys died from cold and hunger. Men starved too, for the painfully scarce flour sold for $75 a hundred pounds, with bacon and coffee equally prohibitive.

But before the snows fell the permanent settlers of Carson Valley again held a convention in Carson City, drawing up a constitution based on that of California and electing a delegate to go to Washington to ask that Nevada be separated from Utah and made an independent territory. It was a demand the settlers had been making since John Reese, Frank Hall and the men of Eagle Station had come together at Mormon Station in November 1852. This time the delegate took with him visual proof of Nevada's wealth: a hundred-thirty-pound piece of rich Comstock ore.

A goodly quantity of the same ore had been sent to San

Francisco in the saddlebags of mules, there being only four primitive stamp mills in operation on the Comstock. The ore was smelted into several bars of gleaming silver and carried through the streets of San Francisco.

In Washington the ore, along with Congress' perennial quarrel with the Mormons, would earn Nevada its territorial status. The silver bars carried through the streets of San Francisco created the same excitement that Sam Brannan had evoked a decade before when he rode through the streets holding a quinine bottle aloft and crying, "Gold! Gold from the Sierras!"

By February 1, 1860 the sun came out and winter was over on the Nevada desert. By March a line of thousands of Californians were already trying to break trail in the snow. Few of the early ones got through; they died in the freezing cold, lost their feet and legs even as had the Groshes. The trail was littered with broken wagons, abandoned packs, carcasses of animals.

The first trader to reach Virginia City in March put up a tent, took in $200 over his bar in the first night and rented blankets plus sleeping space for $1.00 each to forty men.

Then the snows melted and the trail was opened. Suddenly there were thousands of prospectors making camp wherever there was water and wood to be cut, falling over each other's monuments, spread out for miles along the hills. But there was no shallow Mormon's Bar, no penknife mining, no easy scratching up of the day's keep. Nor was there any way for individual prospectors to remain independent, as they had in the early years in California. Since the gold and silver had to be followed deeper into the mountain, the mines had to be industrialized at once, with heavy machinery and steam hoists brought in from California. There were a few owners with the necessary capital; everyone else was immediately an employee. Those who had trades practiced them at the mines and in the newly built mills and smelters; the others became shaft miners or returned home.

With heavy supplies flowing into Virginia City, more streets were notched higher and lower on the hillside. Someone with a sharp eye painted a portrait of Virginia City in the spring of 1860:

"Frame shanties pitched together as if by accident; tents of canvas, of blankets, of brush, of potato sacks and old shirts, with empty whiskey barrels for chimneys; smoking hovels of mud and stone; coyote holes in the hillsides forcibly seized by men; pits and shanties with smoke issuing from every crevice; piles of goods and rubbish on craggy points, in the hollows, on the rocks, in the mud, on the snow, everywhere scattered broadcast in pellmell confusion."

Board and lodging cost $4.00 a day. Wages were $5.00 a day, which did not leave too wide a margin for the extravagances of life. There were still no proper streets, only trails used by pack mules and miners across the slope of Mount Davidson. As the traffic grew heavier in the summer the trails were widened so that wagons could pass each other, and then were designated A, B and C streets, there being no Pancake Comstock or Old Virginia around to provide more colorful names. The streets were unpaved and dust-laden until the rains came, when they were mud bogs, while the trails which went straight up and down the mountain were more like vertical leaning ladders.

By late spring the Comstock had as many troubles as it had prospectors. Indians, outraged at the whites mistreating two of their women at Williams Station, burned down the settlement and killed its occupants. The first avenging force of Nevadans, green in the ways of Indians, walked into an ambush in a narrow valley. All but twenty-five of over one hundred were massacred. Volunteer companies were formed in the California towns of Downieville, Nevada City and Sacramento in answer to pleas from Virginia City, where the few women and children were being protected in a quickly built stockade. The new force included two hundred soldiers and five hundred miners. It was not until they had gone back to the same valley and killed almost all of the Paiute warriors that it was learned that the Paiutes had not burned Williams Station; it had been burned by braves from the Bannock tribe.

On Mount Davidson there was chaos. V. A. Houseworth, blacksmith turned saloonkeeper and keeper of the books of mining claims, let everyone enter his own claim. The erasures outnumbered the original entries. Since even the most legitimate claims were vaguely marked in the unmapped desert, and because the valuable veins ran *sideways* through a mountain, while mining claims ran *straight down*, the untimbered Comstock became a jungle of lawsuits.

It was also becoming apparent as the mine owners drove deeper into the mountainside, slanting along with their veins, that instead of growing narrower the veins were growing wider: to forty feet, then to fifty, and finally to sixty feet, probably the widest veins the world had known. Twenty-four stamp mills, manufactured in San Francisco, were brought over the mountain to the Washoe; by the end of the year their owner had sixty-four in operation. Along with the greater potential of wealth went an equally great potential of danger, for there was constant water seepage into the shafts, and cave-ins due to the soft crumbling nature of the Nevada ore. California mining methods of putting logs across the top of other logs to support the roof would not work. As the men got a hundred feet in and then two hundred feet, the overhead pressures became so great that the logs splintered and the miners were buried where they stood.

The owner of the Ophir mine called in a German miner named Philip Diedesheimer, then working a quartz lode in California. Diedesheimer evolved a system of propping known as "square sets," made of short timbers cut from the Sierra Nevada, twenty miles away, from which were built self-supporting cells, as in a beehive, each so solid that other cells could be built upon them. Diedesheimer's engineering solved the problem of shoring in the mines of the Comstock. He became superintendent of the Ophir.

Among the first of the post-winter arrivals had been David Terry, fresh from the killing of David Broderick, allegedly carrying a commission as governor from Jefferson Davis . . . as soon as he could bring Nevada into the Confederacy. While waiting for secession he chose three vantage points near the Comstock and began building forts.

The first Pony Express rider came into Spafford Hall's Station on April 12, only nine days out of St. Joseph, Missouri, which made the miners feel as though they were next-door neighbors to the East. When another Pony Express rider came through in mid-June bringing the news from San Francisco of the Republican nominee for the presidency, the miners asked each other:

"Who in hell is Abraham Lincoln?"

Then on March 2, 1861 Congress officially created Nevada Territory out of western Utah. Though David Terry had not realized his ambition to become governor, he had organized southern sentiment so well that when a Confederate flag was raised over the Newman-Waterhouse saloon a crowd of armed sympathizers were able to patrol the boardwalk and keep it from being hauled down. A Union sympathizer rode to Fort Churchill for troops. Captain Moore brought twenty dragoons to lower the flag and make a house-to-house canvass, seizing all arms.

In July 1861 Nevada's first territorial governor arrived, James W. Nye, a forty-seven-year-old lawyer who had been commissioner of police in New York City, an experienced politician and amusing stump speaker who had campaigned for Lincoln. His party of

Nevada officials, all of whom he had appointed himself, consisted of old-time New York political friends.

Nevadans were so happy at the arrival of government that they fired a welcoming salute on the twelve-pound cannon John C. Fremont had been forced to abandon in the region fifteen years before.

Nevada was now a federal territory. Except for the fertile Carson Valley, it was a barren wasteland: tens of thousands of square miles of brown sand, sage, rock and mountain, awesome to look at, dwarfing man, unhospitable, without the resources with which a land, once opened, can build its civilization: an irreparable fact which would have a strong influence on its future.

Governor Nye established courts, appointed judges, made preparations for an election for the first Nevada territorial legislature. His first census showed that Virginia City, which had been the side of a mountain just two years before, now had almost thirteen thousand inhabitants, among them several wives who were angry and outraged: Julia Bulette, attractive young madam of one of the Comstock *maisons*, had been given the honor of riding in the Fourth of July celebration as the patron and mascot of a fire company!

By summer of 1861 the town which a year before had been "tents with empty whiskey barrels for chimneys" had built almost forty stores, twenty-five saloons, ten livery stables, nine restaurants, eight hotels and a hundred solid homes. The old California Emigrant Trail was widened and improved by the Pioneer Stage Company, which kept a constantly moving stream of wagons across the Sierra Nevada, carrying mahogany bars for saloons, lumber for the mills and mines and private homes, such heavy equipment as a fifteen-horsepower steam engine for the Ophir mine. The miners who the previous year had frozen and starved were now provided with all the luxuries that had reached the California mines by the summer of 1849: wines and liqueurs, tins of oysters and caviar.

The town did not yet boast a bank, though thirty-seven companies with a capital stock of $37,000,000 were working nineteen major mines, including the Savage, Gould and Curry, Yellow Jacket, Kentuck, Crown Point, Chollar-Potosi, Mexican, Best and Belcher, and some $7,000,000 of ore was being mined. Wells Fargo undertook to provide banking, paying in coin for bullion. More of this coin was needed now, for wages of carpenters, metalworkers and machine operators had risen to $6.00 a day, so much higher than the wage being paid in California that it started a migration of mechanics over the mountain.

It did have a rip-roaring newspaper, the *Territorial Enterprise*, with the tone and flavor of a wild-west mining camp. One of its reporters, Samuel Clemens, who had walked in from a neighboring but poor mining town, was rehearsing humor and elaborate practical jokes on a highly appreciative audience.

After a brawl of an election, with free swinging and ballot-box stuffing, agricultural Carson City was gerrymandered into being the territory's capital. The legislature moved into a two-story building which some earlier resident had had the foresight to build, the bottom floor a hotel, the top floor a legislative hall. The legislators covered themselves with glory by voting a library for Nevada; they also approved a petition from the Big Four's Central Pacific to grant a railroad license across the state of Nevada, an act they would live to regret.

By fall the Comstock population was up to twenty thousand, of whom a considerable number were a new kind of speculator. The mining laws were still wide open, any man could stake out a claim anywhere in the desert and sell shares in it for ten cents to $75 a linear foot, so long as he could find people to buy. With the nineteen big mines producing tens of thousands of dollars of bullion a month, and almost the entire population consisting of workers who would never have an opportunity to strike it rich through their own claims, a frenzy of share speculation overcame the Washoe. A large part of the inhabitants sank every dollar they owned into wildcat claims where never a shovel had been turned, the majority of them fraudulent in inception and purpose.

Because the telegraph line had been extended from Salt Lake to San Francisco via Virginia City, this speculative contagion was passed over the wires. San Franciscans invested their savings, buying blind into such new properties as the Bobtailed Nag or the Roote Hog or Die. Stocks were rising to hundreds of dollars per share in mines where not one dollar in gold or silver had been taken out.

With the coming of winter San Francisco suddenly woke up to the fact that it had been had. Mechanics, clerks, housewives lost every dollar they had invested . . . as did a number of the smarter businessmen of the city.

The bottom fell out of the Comstock market.

In Virginia City, where every saloon had been a twenty-four-hour stock exchange, the results were calamitous. The savings of the town were wiped out. Stocks of the best-producing mines fell to a negligible fraction of their value, some selling at a penny in cash for dollars worth of value. Panic hit the city, and the victims took the trail back to California. By the time winter closed in upon the Comstock the area was seriously depopulated, its joy largely spent.

In December came the worst storm since Fremont forced the mountains, six feet of snow, then a long, heavy rain. A torrent swept down Mount Davidson, carrying with it a number of houses and the winter's supply of hay and grain. The mining shafts were filled to the brim with water.

The wealth that had not been wiped out by the stock crash now vanished. William M. Stewart, able thirty-four-year-old lawyer who had practiced law and politics for ten years in California before setting up the first law office in the Comstock and cornering all the big mining suits, woke up on the morning of the flood to find his mine and mill property, valued at $1,500,000 the week before, worthless.

It looked as though the Washoe Valley would be given back to the few surviving Paiutes.

CHAPTER V

You Have to Get Up Early to Beat Brigham Young

HAVING LOST THE WESTERN three fifths of their territory to Nevada, the Mormons made a bold move to obtain statehood: they would be loyal to the federal government providing they were permitted to govern themselves. The Mormon delegate said in Congress:

"We show our loyalty by trying to get into the Union, while others are trying to get out."

Importuned by the South to secede and have its grievances redressed as a Confederate state, the Mormons replied:

"We have had our difficulties with the government, but we

calculate they will be righted in the government, or we will endure them."

Brigham Young settled the doubts of both the North and the South by suggesting a plague on both their houses. He did not object to slavery on moral grounds, having told Horace Greeley in Salt Lake:

"Utah will be a free state. Slavery here would prove useless and unprofitable." To his own people he said:

"The rank, rabid abolitionists have set the whole national fabric on fire. I am not an abolitionist, neither am I a pro-slavery man. The southerners make the Negroes and the northerners worship them: that is all the difference between slaveholders and abolitionists."

Abraham Lincoln agreed that the Mormons should remain neutral. He declared his administration policy in three simple words:

"Let them alone."

But Brigham Young wanted Utah let alone as a state, not as a territory. He said, "We must organize a government for ourselves, and take care of ourselves."

A convention was called to draft once again a state constitution and to nominate officers. At the election more than ten thousand votes were recorded for the constitution and the officers, without one dissenting vote. The Mormons announced this result as a triumph of their unity; the unanimity made certain eastern groups fear that there were no free elections in Utah.

The Utah legislature elected two United States senators and sent them to Washington. Here Senator Latham of California, wanting a strong and unified Far West, urged the admission of Utah's senators. But the Republican party controlling Congress had campaigned on an anti-slavery and anti-polygamy platform, bracketing the two institutions as "twin relics of barbarism." It had already passed a bill in 1862 to punish and prevent the practice of polygamy.

The expectant senators and the Mormons of Utah were turned away.

Utah sent no volunteers to the Civil War. The official history of the Church says:

"Under all these circumstances it is not surprising to find a feeling that the war between the states was a matter in which the Latter-day Saints need have no particular concern."

That did not prevent territorial Governor John W. Dawson, from castigating the Mormons over their lack of loyalty. He was obliged to resign, then was beaten up while leaving Utah, the Mormons claiming his assailants were a gang of ruffians, Governor Dawson claiming they were Mormons in good standing, among them a policeman.

Dawson's successor, Governor Stephen S. Harding, appointed because he had formerly been friendly with the Mormons, arrived to a warm welcome in March of 1862; but a year later the Mormons were incensed against him because he had joined with Utah's two federal judges in petitioning Washington for more power for the federal courts over the county probate courts, and for the federal government to have the right to commission militia officers. A mass indignation meeting was held in the Tabernacle in which the "governor and two judges were denounced as conspirators against the liberties of the people and the interests of the Territory." Brigham Young and Elder John Taylor made "strong speeches." Governor Harding was removed, but not before he had officially welcomed the newly arrived United States troops when they assembled before his headquarters.

The troops were California volunteers under the command of Irish-born Colonel Patrick Edward Connor, fiery-whiskered, a captain of the Texas Volunteers in the war with Mexico, a goldrusher to California, then postmaster and prosperous building contractor at Stockton, California. They had been sent into Utah because the mail and transportation route had been disrupted by Indian attacks, with sacks of mail and other valuables destroyed, the telegraph poles and stations burned down.

It would be the last welcome the troops would hear in their three long years of service in the Great Basin, the deserts and mountains of Utah. All federal troops in Utah had had trouble, even those under the friendly Colonel Steptoe. As the seven hundred fifty infantrymen and cavalrymen marched into Salt Lake behind their brass band they found the streets lined with spectators gazing at them in dead silence.

Colonel Connor's task of protecting the overland mail was a simple one for his well-armed soldiers, but like nearly every federal officer sent into Utah, civil or military, he was soon fighting bitterly with Brigham Young, the Elders and the Church. Neither was Colonel Connor conciliatory.

"It would be impossible for me to describe what I saw and heard in Salt Lake, so as to make you realize the enormity of Mormonism; suffice it that I found them a community of traitors, murderers, fanatics and whores. The people publicly rejoice at reverses to our arms, and thank God that the American government is gone, as they term it. The federal officers are entirely powerless, and talk in whispers for fear of being overheard by Brigham's spies. Brigham Young rules with despotic sway, and death by assassination is the penalty of disobedience to his commands."

He believed Mormonism, "as preached and practiced in this territory, is in conflict with civilization," maintaining that the federal government should come to the "relief of a people oppressed and downtrodden by a most galling church tyranny."

With the California Volunteers and their muskets poised above them, ill feeling mounted to the point where Salt Lake became convinced the troops were going to arrest Brigham Young and take him to Washington to stand trial for the crime of "being married to more than one woman." When cannon were fired at camp to celebrate Colonel Connor's promotion to general for having defeated the Indians in battle, a thousand Mormon men grabbed up their guns and rushed to the capitol to save Brigham Young from arrest!

Having been instructed by his superior officer to be "prudent and cautious" and by his President to "let them alone," General Connor remained in Utah for a year without finding any way to weaken Mormonism until one day toward the end of 1863, when he took a group of officers and their wives to Bingham Canyon for a picnic. One of the ladies picked up a loose piece of rock from the side of the hill. It looked interesting. Soldiers guarding the horses began prospecting. They found a gold vein. To General Connor this was a golden opportunity to flood the Great Basin with miners, even as California, Nevada and Colorado had been, and thus create a majority of gentiles who would be able to outvote the Mormons.

Through the general's efforts several mining companies were formed to exploit Utah's mineral wealth. Brigham Young did not try to stop them. He said to his Latter-day Saints:

"Work for these capitalists, and work honestly and faithfully. Haul their ores, build their furnaces, and take your pay for it, build houses, improve your farms, buy your stock, and make yourselves better off."

More than $500,000 was taken out of the Utah gold and silver mines, but costs were too high, particularly transportation; most of the mining companies lost their investment.

General Connor had failed to populate Utah with non-Mormons. The Mormons had earned much-needed cash from the outside.

You had to get up early in the morning to beat Brigham Young.

*   *   *

Utah was Brigham Young's community. He was absolute master of its every detail. He knew every Mormon in Salt Lake City, his name and family, his assets and problems. When he visited St. George, the Mormon settlement near the southern Nevada border, he entered every home, embraced every Saint. When he ordered a thing to be done, it was done: Tabernacle, temple, towns, schools, state buildings, walls, roads, irrigation ditches, theatre, library, a simplified language...which did not take hold.

The door of his office was always open. If a group wanted to give a ball, his permission had to be obtained, and later his approval of the guest list. Plays appearing in the theatre had to have his approval. Marriages required his consent, and courtships as well. If a man wanted to enter a business or trade, Brigham Young had to approve. When he asked a man to give up his home, his business and his life in Salt Lake to go on a foreign mission, or to any other of the desert communities, that man went on the mission. When he told a man to enter into plural marriage, that man took another wife. Whatever he said was the religion of the Mormons; when he said that a man or group was apostate that man or group was excommunicated.

Heber Kimball, Young's first in command, told the congregation:

"If Brother Brigham tells me to do a thing, it is the same as though the Lord told me to do it."

Brigham Young took the same tone with his congregation:

"No man need judge me. You know nothing about it, whether I am sent or not; furthermore, it is none of your business, only to listen with open ears to what is taught you, and serve God with an undivided heart."

His parishioners he advised to "Pay your debts, keep your bowels open, walk uprightly before God, and you will never have a care."

If it seemed that the Mormon was not overburdened with personal decisions, Sir Richard Burton, who visited them as a friend in Salt Lake in 1860, said that Brigham Young's policy was based upon:

"The fact that liberty is to mankind in mass, a burden far heavier than slavery."

When the power of the Church was not challenged, it was just and generous. Brigham Young would allow no Mormon to be without food and shelter; he made work for the indigent:

"I build walls, dig ditches, make bridges, and do a great amount and variety of labor that is of little consequence only to provide ways and means for sustaining the destitute. Why? I have potatoes, flour, beef, but it is better for them to labor for these articles, so far as they are able and have opportunity, than to have them given to them."

Because he was trying to build a totally independent civilization in a desert, he forced an implacable regime of hard labor and austerity; concepts of art, beauty, culture and leisure were not only wasteful but dangerous. Mormons who had been with him since Winter Quarters said:

"He slept with one eye open and one foot out of bed."

And all this he did without pay, for he never drew one dollar in salary from years of service to the Church. There never was a time when he did not operate his own stock-raising, agricultural, lumbering and other industries. He was prosperous in the latter years of his life, and when he died his estate was said to approximate $2,000,000. If this seems a lot of money to have made, it must be remembered that he turned the desert of the Great Basin into a community which at his death was worth many hundreds of millions to the Church and the Mormons who settled there.

A growing symbol of the Church of the Latter-day Saints was an eye, with the motto beneath it: "Holiness to the Lord." As the Mormon community grew, this eye was everywhere. A few of the less submissive Mormons were known to speak of it as Brother Brigham Young's all-seeing eye, or the eye of "the big boss."

Brigham Young was a powerfully built man with a tremendous face, awe-inspiring voice, flashing, commanding eyes and a deep-seated indestructible energy, vitality and inner authority which provided the structural backbone for the Church of the Latter-day Saints and the Mormon community.

That strength and leadership would be needed in the fight over polygamy. Utah's "neutrality," the mounting northern defeats and prolongation of the War Between the States would give Brigham Young a respite; but this one aspect of life in Utah was arousing millions of words throughout the country, hot, passionate, fighting words from men's vocal cords and type cases.

The clergy was the most vehement.

One clergyman cried, "The Asiatic institution was never meant to flourish on American soil, and has resulted here in a slaughter of the innocent which is saddening to contemplate."

Another, "Mormonism is not a religion. It is a crime, therefore it cannot be entitled to protection and tolerance under the laws and Constitution of the United States as a matter of conscience. It is not a religious superstition but a system of masked sensuality, and hence subversive to every principle of morality...."

De Witt Talmage, well-known Brooklyn clergyman, preached that polygamy was essentially prostitution.

Harriet Beecher Stowe, having helped whip up the fight to abolish slavery, now strove to do the same service for the second of the "twin relics of barbarism."

"May we not then hope that the hour is come to loose the bonds of cruel slavery whose chains have cut into the very hearts of thousands of our sisters—a slavery which debases and degrades womanhood, motherhood, and the family?"

Prophet Joseph Smith had started it all by disclosing his revelation:

"If any man espouse a virgin, and desires to espouse another, and the first give her consent; and if he espouse the second, and they are virgins, and have avowed to no other man, then is he justified; he cannot commit adultery with that that belongeth unto him, and to no one else."

Whatever may have been Prophet Joseph Smith's purpose in bringing his revelation to his followers, by the time the Mormon community was growing up in Utah it had become as much a sacred part of their religion as any other revelation.

Werner, in his biography *Brigham Young*, says, "It became the general opinion in the eastern states that polygamists were some species of beast, not at all resembling other forms of humanity, except in general, deceptive appearance. Those who opposed it could see in polygamy only a violent form of adultery, which was all the more reprehensible because it was practiced openly."

Plural marriage, according to the Mormon religion, had a single purpose: the providing of tabernacles on earth for those myriads of unborn souls waiting to come into this world, the bringing forth of children who would be raised in the image of the Latter-day Saint Church and consequently live for all eternity, an eternity into which Mormons could enter only if they had borne children. This conviction was so strong on the part of many Mormon women that if their marriages proved barren, the first wives went out themselves and sought other wives for the husband so that he might have children and hence be entitled to a place in eternity.

Two of the most important of the Mormon Council attempted to prove that Jesus Christ was not only married but that he had practiced plural marriage. Orson Pratt said:

"One thing is certain, that there were several holy women that greatly loved Jesus—such as Mary, and Martha, her sister, and Mary Magdalene; and Jesus greatly loved them, and associated with them much; and when He arose from the dead, instead of first showing Himself to His chosen witnesses, the Apostles, He appeared first to these women. Now it would be very natural for a husband in the Resurrection to appear first to his own dear wives, and afterwards show himself to his other friends. If all the acts of Jesus were written, we no doubt should learn that these beloved women were His wives."

Orson Hyde added:

"It will be discovered that no less a person than Jesus Christ was married on that occasion. If he was never married, his intimacy with Mary and Martha, and the other Mary whom Jesus loved, must have been highly unbecoming and improper to say the best of it."

But Brigham Young said:

"I want you to have more children. Children are our means of building up Zion and hastening the day when her enemies will be stamped out and their evil designs become as naught, when the blood of the prophets will be avenged and righteousness cover the earth as the waters the mighty deep."

In the matter of plural marriage, which he felt to be at the heart of Mormonism, Brigham Young set out to do his full duty.

His first wife having died young, he remained single a number of years before marrying Mary Ann Angel at Kirtland, Ohio, when he was thirty-three years old. He took his first plural wife at Nauvoo when he was forty-one years old. Her name was Lucy Ann Decker, she was twenty, and she bore him seven children. Some eighteen months later he married twice in one day, Harriet Cook, who was nineteen and bore him one son, and Augusta Adams, forty-one years old, who appears to have been a widow of Joseph Smith to whom he wanted to give protection. After another six months, on May 8, 1844, Brigham Young married sixteen-year-old Clara Decker, a younger sister of Lucy Ann, his first plural wife. Brigham Young was now forty-three; Clara Decker bore him five children, and was the wife he selected to accompany him to the Great Salt Lake in the first party of pioneers.

Four months later he took two more wives, thirty-year-old Clarissa Ross, who bore him four children, and Emily Partridge, twenty years old, who bore him seven children. The following year he married a second of the Prophet's widows, Olive Frost. In 1845 he again married twice, the first time Emmeline Free, who bore him ten children, and next Margaret Pierce, a twenty-two-year-old widow. He was now forty-four.

The climactic year for Brigham Young was 1846, when the Mormons were being driven out of Nauvoo. Not knowing where they would end or what his opportunities for marrying might be in the future, Brigham Young married eight times in this year: Louisa Beman, thirty-one-years old; Margaret Alley, twenty years old; on January 21, four wives: Susan Snively, thirty, Ellen Rockwood, seventeen, Martha Bowker and Maria Lawrence, another of Joseph Smith's widows. Twelve days later he married Zina Huntington and the next day Naamah Carter. En route to winter camp in March 1847 he married two sisters, Mary Jane and Lucy Bigelow.

After the Mormon community was settled in Utah he married Eliza Snow, a poetess, on June 20, 1849, then Eliza Burgess in October of 1852, then twenty-five-year-old Harriet Barney in 1856. Though Amelia Folsom, whom he married in 1865, at the age of sixty-one, because "he fell passionately in love," for whom he built "Amelia's Palace," buying her expensive jewelry and clothing and carriages, bore him no children, the other twenty-seven wives (he would marry twice again, Mary Cott in January 1865 and Ann Eliza Webb in April 1868) bore him a total of fifty-six children.

In plural marriages, where the family was in good economic circumstances, the plural wives were permitted to say whether they would live in the same house with the other wives or would have homes of their own. No wife until the beautiful, imperious, musically inclined Amelia Folsom ever lived out from under Brigham Young's patriarchal roof. He built two beautiful homes on the main street, a block up from the Tabernacle, the first of which was called the Lion House, the second the Bee Hive. The Lion House had large social rooms on one side of the hall, where all the wives and children congregated for a social or prayer hour before going to the communal dining room at the rear of the house, which was served by a communal kitchen. On the other side was a series of smaller identical social rooms. The upstairs was divided by a central hallway between a series of bedrooms, also identical in structure and furnishings, each occupied by a wife and her children. The second solidly constructed home, for Brigham Young was in the beginning a carpenter and furniture maker, used a similar plan but contained a private library-study and office for the master.

Some of the childless wives found their purpose in life in helping to raise the brood of Brigham Young children; one wife who had no liking for anything domestic became the keeper of accounts; those who liked to sew had the making of endless clothing, others who liked to clean and scrub or launder were given a free hand to clean and scrub or launder, while those who liked to cook had a full-time job at cooking. Certainly no one was ever lonely, without company, or without something to occupy her in Brigham Young's households.

Until the arrival of Amelia Folsom, Brigham Young played no favorites and was attached to all the children. With the exception of Ann Eliza, his twenty-seventh wife, who sued him for divorce, all of his wives seemed to live happily, or at last peaceably, together.

Ann Eliza not only divorced Brigham Young in the public prints, and wrote a scandalous book called *Wife No. 19*; she also charged him with cruelty, neglect and desertion, said he was worth $8,000,000, had an income of $40,000 a month and asked for $1000 a month for herself during the period of the trial, $14,000 on the granting of her final decree and $200,000 for her maintenance.

Brigham Young's defense was based on the fact that his marriage to Ann Eliza could not be considered legal by a United States court, which would not grant legal recognition to polygamists' wives. *If the court in which she was fighting her case would declare her marriage to him legal, thus legitimatizing all Mormon plural marriages, he would willingly pay the $200,000!*

The court was willing and able to do no such thing. Ann Eliza went out empty-handed.

CHAPTER VI

Inside the "Twin Relic of Barbarism"

FOR EVERY MORMON MAN who practiced polygamy, there were six Mormon men and families living in monogamy. The figures, based on an objective study of the records by Kimball Young, himself a grandson of Brigham Young, show that nearly fifty-three per cent of the plural marriages fell into the category of highly or reasonably successful; that one fourth were moderately successful, with some conflict, but on the whole fair adjustment; that less than one quarter came into the category of severe conflict, including some separation or divorce.

Part of the success of plural marriage was due to the Mormon women's dedication to the Principle, that is, plural marriage as part of their revealed religion.

One, Mrs. Gallagher, was so completely convinced that her own glory in heaven would be lessened because her husband refused to take another wife that she divorced him after only two years of marriage and promptly married another man who had plural wives.

Kimball Young reports that in one family the second wife, when asked about the first wife's consent, replied, "The first wife sanctioned it! She was more anxious about it than he was." The husband was forty-five years old at the time, the prospective bride seventeen.

The second Mrs. Joseph Wright maintained, "Nothing in my father's household made me dislike polygamy. I always believed ... it was a true Principle, and through it and it alone could we obtain the greatest blessings and live as fully as we should."

Helen Kimball Whitney in *Why We Practice Plural Marriage*, considered the most thoroughgoing defense of polygamy from the viewpoint of a wife, said:

"To live one's religion meant sacrifice. I did not try to conceal the fact of its having been a trial, but confessed that it had been one of the severest in my life; but that it had also proven one of the greatest blessings. I could truly say that it had done the most towards making me a Saint and a free women, in every sense of the word. . . . Most Mormon women have easier access to the throne of grace and any suffering here will but add greater laurels to their crown in the world to come."

The Mormon women were asked to conquer all possessiveness, all sexual jealousy, all desire for romantic love. If polygamy could be made to work at all, particularly with a people who came out of a tradition of monogamy, the Mormons would make it work well. Plural wives were enjoined by their religion, and preached at constantly from the pulpit, never to ask for or even yearn for more of the husband's time than was proportionately theirs; nor to carry to their husbands tales of other wives. They were never allowed to discipline or punish another wife's children, were taught that recriminations or quarreling with other wives were sins against their husband and their religion.

Orson Pratt enunciated one of the basic tenets of the plural marriage philosophy, one repeated by everyone high in the Mormon Church:

"A man can love more than one wife in the same manner that he can love more than one child. . . . If several women mutually agree to be the wives of the same man, we see no cause existing for jealousy. Loss of confidence in a husband by his infidelity might give rise to jealousy but not when each wife knows that the other wives are as much entitled to the attention of the husband as herself. What faithful, virtuous woman would not prefer to stand as the sixth or seventh wife of a good and faithful man, rather than to have no husband at all throughout the endless ages of eternity?"

Brigham Young pronounced his ultimatum in the Tabernacle:

"I am going to give you from this time to the sixth day of October next for the reflection that you may determine whether you wish to stay with your husbands or not, and then I am going to set every woman at liberty and say to them, Now go your way, my women, with the rest, go your way. And my wives have got to do one of two things: either round up their shoulders to endure the afflictions of this world, and live their religion, or they may leave, for I will not have them about me. . . ."

The ladies behaved.

Mormon women were taught from the moment they entered school and their stake houses that the man was master of the family and that woman's highest duty was obedience.

Plural marriage was most successful in Utah when the family was prosperous and there was enough money for all of the wives and children to fare well, to have homes of their own if they desired, or to live in the two-family dwellings which would be called "cohabs" by federal officers sent into the territory to hunt down all polygamists after another, more drastic federal law had been passed declaring them to be bigamists. In the cohabs the two halves of the house were identical, each having its own front door, its own tiny front room with its single window, and behind it a tiny bedroom and kitchen. When a man had more than two wives he frequently tried to get them all to live together under one spacious roof, each wife with an apartment for herself and her children, but with a common dining room, social room, kitchen and laundry. For the first few years the children were kept with their mother, then all the girls were put in one large room, all the boys in another. They had been taught from the cradle to make no distinctions between the children of a family; they were all brothers and sisters. Upon a married man's death each of his wives and each of his children received their proportionate share of the family property.

One Mormon wife, Sister Terry, did not object to the Principle of polygamy but said that her husband "had no business marrying another wife when he couldn't support one."

Another requirement for happiness was that the husband treat his wives with equal kindness. There was no set rule for the habits of husbands among their wives. In some cases a man spent one night with each wife in rotation, though, as one wife testified, her husband always came to visit the other families before he retired to make sure they were all right, kissing the wives and children good night.

A plural-marriage daughter of Allen Tiffin said:

"Father spent one week with each wife. When he got up in the morning, he made the fire, called the family and fed the cattle. Then he would go over to the other house, make their fire, call the family and feed the livestock there. After that he would go back to the place where he was staying to have his breakfast."

Other men spent two nights with each wife in rotation. Frederick James built a comfortable, attractive home for each of his three wives, spending one week with each in rotation; when he went out to dinners or to church or dances he always took "the wife of that week" with him.

Women who were sociable, who were lonely with their husbands away all day, who were obliged to do many kinds of housework for which they were unfitted or which they disliked, found plural marriage companionable. They liked having the other women around, and all the children as well. They also enjoyed, in large households such as those of Brigham Young, Heber Kimball, the Pratts and others of the wealthier important Church hierarchy, being permitted to concentrate on the one specialized job they liked best.

Opposition of Mormon women to plural marriage originated in part from young women who grew up in unhappy plural marriages, another portion from distaste for the idea and a disbelief in the divine revelation of the Principle. Though one first wife is reported as having told her husband, "Well, you may as well marry 'em as to want 'em!" others were by no means so resigned. When Brother Richard Gordon of St. George was asked why he never took another wife, Gordon pointed to his wife and said, "She wouldn't let me." Mrs. Gordon cried, "I told him that if he ever took another wife, when he brought her in the front door I would go out the back."

One Elder in Paragoonah, wanting a second wife but being afraid of his first, told her that he had a revelation to marry a second girl, and that she must give her consent. The next morning the first wife announced that she too had had a revelation:

"To shoot any woman who became his plural wife."

Several wives went on record as telling their husbands that they would divorce them instantly if they brought in second wives.

Mormon doctrine said that a first wife had to give her consent to a second marriage, and stand up with a second bride in the church wedding. Sometimes not only two wives but as many as half a dozen got along extremely well together; almost a fifth of the men entering polygamous marriages married sisters who not only gave their consent but frequently promoted the second marriage.

The sixth wife of George Mackay, nineteen-year-old Jennie, was brought home to the family house in Provo after the wedding, where the five other Mrs. George Mackays had co-operatively prepared a wedding feast for their husband and the new bride. Jennie, obliged to eat her first marital meal under what she called "the watchful eyes of her husband's five other wives," commented that she could "have sunk through the floor." She did not, and the picture of the first five wives preparing a wedding feast for the sixth indicated that Jennie had amiable company.

However if the first wife refused to give her consent to a second marriage and the Church authorities believed the man worthy, they could give him permission to go ahead without that consent. Others gave it grudgingly when told by the heads of the Church that the refusal of their husbands to take more wives would hurt them in the Church hierarchy and hence in the business world.

James Hunter's first wife agreed to accompany him to the endowment house and be present at the wedding ceremony, which she did with good grace, but that night she was reported as unable to sleep, "and walked the floor all night as she thought of her husband lying in the arms of his new bride."

Apparently the first Mrs. Hunter managed to reconcile herself to the new wife, but another first wife could not:

"There is one real tragedy in polygamy that I can remember. One evening a man brought home a second wife. It was in the winter and the first wife was very upset. That night she climbed onto the roof and froze to death."

In the family of Jonathan Baker, who had been married for over six years, it was the deception that hurt the first wife, for Baker came home one day, told his wife to lay out his Temple clothes. Baker's daughter reports, "Ma thought he was just going to do some (Church) work. She asked him what he intended to do and he said he was going to marry Eliza Bowen. It was a blow to Ma, and naturally she resented it and never got over it."

A third and urgent requirement for successful plural marriage was that the first wife be of amiable disposition; and a fourth, that there not be too many years in age separating the first wife from the latter ones. If the first wife was growing old it was difficult for her to have a young girl brought into the house as wife number two. Sexual jealousy, as well as jealousy over the amount of time spent with each wife or the amount of favors or goods conferred, could cause trouble.

In the Roger Knight family, when the first wife was pregnant Knight brought home a prospective bride.

"I felt so ungainly and awkward at the time that it was more than I could endure to see the attractive young girl sitting on my husband's lap, being kissed and fondled by him."

What some of the plural wives suffered in terms of old-fashioned jealousy is flashed into focus by a first wife pleading with her husband to spend the night with her, then wailing:

"All right, then, go to your darling."

If in some homes polygamy was a heavy burden, it was a burden the Mormon women carried in confidence; with the exception of a few apostates from the religion itself, no plural wife would complain to a gentile, or allow a gentile to live within her home and watch plural marriage function.

Male opposition to plural marriage came from men who did not like women in the first place: they refused Brigham Young's plea that the young female converts coming into Utah from all over the world be married quickly and given homes and children to raise; from those men who could afford but one family; and from a small segment of the more educated who did not believe in the Principle, and felt that with it Utah could not take its place in the family of American states.

Although there does not seem to have been any important disparity in the ratio of the sexes, and although the young unmarried men sometimes complained because the older and more prosperous Mormons who already had one or more wives came in and courted the available young girls of the community, the one advantage which many Mormon women spoke of highly was the every Mormon girl could find a husband and a home, in the words of Heber Kimball, "even if she had a head three feet long." Apparently there were no old maids among the Mormons, nor for that matter any bachelors.

One truth was demonstrable: the children of polygamy accepted plural marriage as natural and inevitable, entering into it with growing ease.

A young Mormon woman said: "I always thought of it (plural marriage) as a natural thing. Father was a polygamist and all his families lived together and we got along very well. . . . I fell in love with my husband and married him, just as a girl would today, only it was in polygamy."

The second wife of Benjamin Wolfe, who was born in a polygamous family, tells the story of how she married her brother-in-law:

"I was in love with him for years before we were married. Nowadays I guess the girl would try to take the man away from his wife, but not in polygamy. My sister agreed that I could have a share in her man but that I could not take him away from her. And so we lived in polygamy and I am proud of it."

Another made the curious observation, "I hadn't wanted to live in polygamy, but I believed in it and thought it was the right thing for me to do. I didn't mind his doing it. I suppose I'm not of a jealous disposition and I wasn't in love with him. . . ."

Within another generation multiple marriage would become as universally practiced among the Mormons as their economic prosperity would allow.

Practically all Mormons practicing polygamy, men and women alike, came from Puritan tradition, either in the United States, Great Britain or Europe, a background in which monogamy had been the cornerstone not only of the religion but of the entire social and ethical life; plural marriage had been practiced only a little by the leaders of the Church prior to reaching Salt Lake. Now, what had been the undisputed base of marriage in the Christian world for almost two thousand years was turned topsy-turvy in less than two decades.

It was said of the Mormons that their creed was singular and their wives plural. This was the nicest thing that was ever said on the subject of polygamy from the outside.

In *Isn't One Wife Enough?* Kimball Young writes:

"After the Civil War when the first relic of barbarism had been liquidated, Mormonism and polygamy rivaled with prostitution and prohibition as the main interest of American reformers. Polygamy was a menace to everything which puritanic Americans held sacred. Plural wifehood was an attack upon monogamy, the home and fireside, upon children, and—above all—upon the rising status of women. It was, therefore, the moral duty of all good Christians to help uproot this evil."

The effect of the national encircling of Utah by indignation, ridicule, obscene stories and a desire to do violence had two corollary effects: the first was to solidify almost the entire American people against the Mormons. The second was to solidify the Mormons against the rest of America.

CHAPTER VII

... With Presses Ready at the Drop of a Frontier

THE ANTECEDENTS OF THE CIVIL WAR in Colorado were a curious parallel to the Broderick-Terry duel in California. On March 5, 1860 at a banquet given at the Pacific House, L. W. Bliss, secretary of the stillborn Territory of Jefferson, proposed a toast to the anti-slavery forces which proved personally offensive to Dr. J.S. Stone, a judge of the miners' court in the Mountain City district. Bliss threw a glass of wine in Dr. Stone's face, Stone challenged Bliss to a duel, and two days later the antagonists faced each other at thirty paces with shotguns. Dr. Stone, the southerner, was killed by the first blast.

The tensions created by the killing were held under control during 1860, in part because of the isolation of the mountain area. The Pony Express which brought fast mail through Salt Lake did not touch Denver; newspapers came across the plains by mule team. Also, by mid-February, before the snows had begun to melt, the hardier prospectors were out again. Three new strikes had been made at the headwaters of the Arkansas River and another, the Kelly strike, at a spot called Kellyville. California Gulch would produce $1,000,000 in gold within the next two years. By summer twenty thousand prospectors were swarming over the Clear Creek district while thousands of new arrivals coming across the Kansas Territory struck west through Colorado City and Canon City over Ute Pass into South Park where new discoveries had thrown up such camp towns as Buckskin Joe and Hamilton. A hundred sixty stamp mills had been packed into wagons at the Missouri River and drawn by oxen across the Kansas plains, as many as six mills arriving in a single day.

Some hardy souls had tackled farming by irrigation methods;

over six hundred acres were in cultivation on the branches of the Arkansas River, raising the first crop of vegetables, grain and melons. The South Platte above and below Denver was lined with ranches, herds of cattle and hogs being driven in from Kansas. Down in the southerly San Luis Valley wagons were being laden with sacks of flour for the mining towns.

So much wealth was rolling down from the Rockies in pack saddles, which the freighters charged the same five per cent to haul to the Missouri River that Alexander Todd had charged the merchants of Stockton to carry their gold down to San Francisco in a butter tub, that bankers were at last attracted from the East. A private mint was established in Denver in July by two bankers who began issuing $5.00, $10 and $20 gold pieces and $5.00 greenbacks which circulated at face value.

The business of freighting the mine equipment and merchandise needed to build the towns and take care of the population soon transformed the Kansas prairies into a continuous caravan of five thousand men and eight thousand wagons, an army of forty thousand mules and oxen passing each other day and night in an industry which, as on the Comstock, grew to be second in volume only to that of mining itself.

Now the land seemed permanently opened.

The housewives of Denver formed a Ladies' Union Aid Society, a Pioneer Club and a Literary and Historical Society, as a direct result of which a new merchant opening a stationery and cigar shop, installed the first stock of books available to the new country. As a further contribution to culture the ladies waged a campaign against the hogs that were allowed to run loose in the streets to fatten off the public refuse.

A group of twenty physicians and surgeons met in Denver to form a medical society, working out a code of ethics and uniform fees.

But the prospectors were wary of lawyers. In the Sugar Loaf camp the miners plaintively laid down the rule, "No technicalities will be allowed to defeat the ends of justice." In some of the mining districts lawyers were prohibited from appearing in cases except where one of the contestants was an attorney in his own right. Throughout the mines, where jokes frequently concealed a criticism in laughter, ran the story about the lawyer who charged his client $5.00 for waking up in the night and thinking about him.

The contest to control Denver's journalism was as heated and close as the prospectors' drive to find the best sites in Gregory

Gulch. The first to arrive with the idea of setting up a newspaper was John L. Merrick, who came in with a press he had bought in St. Joseph, Missouri, one that had been used by the Mormons to print their *Evening and Morning Star* in Independence, and which had been battered and thrown into the Missouri River in 1837 when an anti-Mormon mob destroyed the printing plant.

Like the magnetism of gold, new areas and new settlements attracted men who dealt with words, with news, with ideas and human stories. They seemed to sit poised on the edges of the established lands, watchful, eager to catch the first whisperings of new excitements, the first sign of smoke from new chimneys, of men newly gathered around campfires or crude cabins. And beside them, also ready to travel at the drop of a frontier, rested their type cases and presses, as vital and symbolic a part of any pioneering movement as the pick and shovel and frying pan of the goldrusher.

Another few days' westerly ride in Merrick's wagon and the old Mormon press would have returned home to Zion!

Immediately upon his arrival in April 1859 John Merrick began the layout of the first Colorado newspaper, the *Cherry Creek Pioneer*. Hot on his trail was William N. Byers, twenty-eight-year-old Ohioan who had acquired his press in Bellevue and brought it across the plains from Omaha. Byers set up to publish the *Rocky Mountain News*. The combined populations of Auraria and Denver watched the exciting race to see which paper would come out first. Byers was more energetic than Merrick, or perhaps his press was in better condition for never having been thrown in a river, but on April 23 Byers had his *Rocky Mountain News* on the street exactly twenty minutes ahead of Merrick's *Cherry Creek Pioneer*. The population declared the *News* the winner of the race, and hence the official newspaper. The *Cherry Creek Pioneer* opened and closed with one issue.

There were no hard feelings: Merrick sold his press to Thomas Gibson, Byers's partner, then went prospecting. Failing to find any trace of gold, he returned to Denver flat broke and went to work as a printer for the *Rocky Mountain News*. In the meanwhile the Mormon press continued on its pilgrimage, for its new owner carted it up Clear Creek to Mountain City to start the *Rocky Mountain Gold Reporter*. With the coming of winter there were too few left in Gregory Gulch to read his paper so Gibson brought the press back to Denver, used it to start a paper in competition with the *Rocky Mountain News*, failed and sold the press to George West, who took it to Golden to start the *Western Mountaineer*. The following spring the paper was suspended, but the Mormon press moved on again to another small town. There is no rest for the weary.

Like Joe Goodman of Virginia City's *Territorial Enterprise*, William Byers edited the *Rocky Mountain News* with two revolvers within easy reach. His printers worked with rifles stacked near their type cases, for uncomplimentary comments in the *News* frequently brought a fusillade of bullets.

Competition between the newspapers of Auraria and Denver was of the no-holds-barred variety until a mass meeting was called of the citizens of both sides of Cherry Creek to put an end to the "malicious rivalry":

"Whereas, the towns at and near the mouth of Cherry Creek are, and ought to be, one; therefore, be it resolved, that from this time Auraria proper shall be known as Denver City, West Division."

News of secession and the firing on Fort Sumter reached Colorado swiftly. The repercussions were even swifter. On April 24 a Confederate flag was raised above a Denver store. A crowd formed, the flag was brought down; the next day a Unionist mass meeting was held in front of the leading hotel with a bonfire in the street, a band playing patriotic airs, the leading citizens making patriotic speeches. Unionist meetings were held in other towns of Colorado, but southern sympathy, though no further flags were unfurled, was equally perfervid.

On February 28, 1861 a war measure hastily passed by the United States Congress to insure that the high mountain sheep, Colorado, remained safely in the Union created Colorado Territory. President Lincoln appointed Colonel William Gilpin the first governor.

Colonel Gilpin, drawing up in front of Tremont House in the dust-covered Concord mail coach was given a rousing reception by the citizenry, was an inspired choice. He knew more about the Rocky Mountain area than any man since Broken Hand Fitzpatrick, having explored it in 1843 with Fremont's Second Expedition, traversed the southern area at the head of his troops in the war with Mexico, and led campaigns against the Indians. In a speech in Missouri in 1849 he had specifically pointed out the five leading gold-bearing areas.

William Gilpin was six feet tall, lean, with the eyes of a scholar, a sensitive nature and a majestic head, strong, slim nose, commanding mouth and beautifully trimmed chin beard. He was not only a soldier, geologist, man of action and intellect, but proved to be an expert at the process of installing civil government. Within a few days of his arrival he set out for a complete tour of the mining camps and settlements, taking a census which showed that while Denver, the largest town, had a little under three thousand inhabitants, Colorado Territory now had something over twenty-five thousand. Within a matter of weeks Governor Gilpin organized a Supreme Court, mapped out the election districts, provided for a general election to choose Colorado's delegate to Congress and members to the Colorado legislature.

At the August 19 election a Republican judge was chosen as delegate to Congress, and over ten thousand votes were cast for the members of the legislative assembly, a goodly ratio considering the fact that many of the mining regions were remote. Three weeks later the first territorial legislature met in Denver and promptly immersed itself in a hurricane of activity:

"Dividing the territory into seventeen counties, providing for the selection of county officers, enacting criminal and civil codes, recognizing the records, decisions and practices of miners' courts, Claim Clubs, the charters of the city of Denver and other cities, and passing private acts incorporating wagon roads, ditches and mining companies."

Colorado had gotten itself a government in a hurry.

Governor Gilpin had reached Colorado with neither instructions nor funds. Instructions he did not need, but the lack of funds proved a serious embarrassment. Parallel with his activities of setting up a civil government he was also organizing a Unionist army, appointing a military staff, scouring the area for firearms. Though nearly every man who came into Colorado carried arms, Governor Gilpin found the pickings lean, only a little over one hundred guns. He became convinced that southern sympathizers had organized as quickly and efficiently as he.

Fearing a swift attack which could seize control of the gold mines for the southern cause, Gilpin issued drafts with which to buy all available guns, commissioned officers to open recruiting stations, helped finance a lead smelting foundry at Boulder to provide ammunition. By the end of September 1861 he had Colorado's First Regiment filled and shortly thereafter barracked in Camp Wells, which he constructed just south of Denver.

To arm and house his soldiers and to provision them, Governor Gilpin issued $400,000 worth of drafts on the federal Government; Colorado merchants accepted them as readily as though they were gold or greenbacks. Then at the end of 1861, when he had a well-trained and -provisioned army ready to put into the field, Congress announced that Governor Gilpin had acted outside the limits of his authorization. His drafts were declared null and void.

To Denver this was a crushing blow; many of the smaller firms would be bankrupt, the stronger ones seriously embarrassed. Congress recalled Gilpin to Washington to explain his conduct. After Governor Gilpin made his report, Congress decided that all Colorado merchants who could submit itemized accounts of merchandise provided to the army would be paid in full.

Having approved Gilpin's actions, Congress promptly cashiered him as governor of Colorado Territory. The army he raised, equipped and trained was instrumental in stopping the Confederate army under General Shipley, which had been raised in Texas and was moving victoriously northward.

Judge J.S. Stone, the Confederate flag atop the Denver store, and Governor William Gilpin were the only Civil War casualties in Colorado Territory.

The Colorado territorial legislature decided to hold its second meeting in Colorado City because Mother Maggert ran a hotel there and everyone agreed she was a good cook. The delegates from the mining camps, dressed in blue flannel shirts and trousers patched with buckskin, walked one hundred forty miles over a snowy range and across South Park, sleeping in blankets by the trail when night fell, reaching Colorado City half starved, their faces blackened from the smoke of campfires, their feet blistered. George Crocker arrived in one old boot and one brogan, a slouch hat with its brim partly gone, his hair tangled and his beard yellow with dust. But handsome is as handsome does, for he was elected Speaker of the House even before his blisters had a chance to heal.

The legislature remained in Colorado City only a few days before adjourning to Denver; Mother Maggert's cuisine apparently was not able to stand up to so large a crowd.

CHAPTER VIII

"They built the Great Wall of China, didn't they?"

THE WESTERN HALF OF the first transcontinental railroad was built by New Englanders and easterners. Theodore Judah and Collis P. Huntington were from Connecticut, Charles Crocker, Leland Stanford and Mark Hopkins were from New York, Samuel S. Montague, the engineer who replaced Judah, was from New Hampshire, James H. Strobridge, the straw boss, was from Vermont.

The physical act of ground breaking took place in Sacramento on January 8, 1863, with a newly elected Governor Leland Stanford making a speech from a flag-covered platform, then turning a shovelful of earth. Charles Crocker cried out impulsively to the enthusasitic crowd:

"It is going right on, gentlemen, I assure you."

Crocker had already built a levee above the American River to support a roadbed which would not be washed out by the recurrent spring floods. Three miles beyond Sacramento he would construct the longest bridge of the proposed line, a seven-hundred-foot span over the American River, and this by a man who had never built anything bigger than a forge. When he later bragged, "I built the Central Pacific," he was telling a truth.

The cheers given Governor Stanford's speech were about the only ones heard in California, for the Big Four were known as shrewd speculators. Most people did not believe they were going to build a railroad at all, but felt that their real intent was to build a toll wagon road to the Comstock and grow rich off the freightage. William Tecumseh Sherman said:

"A railroad to the Pacific? I would hate to buy a ticket on it for my grandchildren!"

There was need for a railroad. The trip around Cape Horn was nineteen thousand miles. Across Panama the arduous journey took four weeks. The Overland Stage needed only seventeen days from Missouri to San Francisco, but could carry little freight. The heroic Pony Express riders made it in eight days, but they could carry only two saddlebags of mail. San Francisco, Virginia City, Salt Lake, Denver were split off from the rest of the nation by a geographic chasm. The rails, if Charlie Crocker could make good his boast, would not only serve as iron links connecting the East and West but would quicken the settling of the wastelands between. The transcontinental railroad would be considerably more than a war measure. Senator Henry Wilson of Massachusetts told the United States Senate:

"I would sink $100,000,000 to build the road and think I had done a great thing for my country. What are $100,000,000 in opening a railroad across the central region of this continent that shall connect the people of the Atlantic and Pacific, and bind us together?"

Could it be built? The central core of the Sierra Nevada was granite. A railroad would have to pierce that granite many times. The lowest summit at which a pass was forceable was seven thousand feet, where fifty feet of snow fell in winter. There was not merely one range, but two that had to be cut through to tame the upward grade to a rise of one hundred forty feet to the mile so that a locomotive could pull its cars. There were precipices of solid rock; gorges that would have to be bridged or filled with a million tons of dirt. Beyond, in Nevada and Utah, lay hundreds of miles of parched desert with no water for the men or animals; here it would be a matter of supply. And in Colorado there were the Rockies.

Theodore Judah had found the route, engineered the survey, made the detail maps. Collis P. Huntington raised the money, Mark Hopkins kept the books, Leland Stanford wangled the political privileges and licenses. Charlie Crocker actually, physically, corporeally, built the railroad, built it in the face of shattering obstacles, hardships, defeats and delays that stagger the stoutest heart and mind.

Giant, two-hundred-fifty-pound, forty-year-old Charles Crocker, with heavy features, a heavy voice and heavy fists, described by his contemporaries as "boastful, vain, stubborn, tactless, bull-like," said:

"I had always been the one to swim a river and carry a rope across."

There would be rivers aplenty to cross and ropes to carry. After having failed to make his pile as a gold miner, and having succeeded in the improbable career of dry goods merchant, he now had on his burly shoulders the task of materializing a dream that had been debated by visionaries for half a century.

He could sense the inner qualities of men by the smell of them; he picked as his engineer Samuel S. Montague, who had worked in the Midwest on the Rock Island and Rockford Railroad, and had gone into the mountains with Judah to help him make his definitive survey. Unlike Judah, Montague did not attempt to set company policy: he was a highly skilled and ingenious engineer who contented himself with the mechanical aspects of surveys, cuts, fills, tunnels, grades. Even Crocker's superintendent and near twin, James H. Strobridge, who like Crocker took a dim view of engineers, admitted grudgingly:

"Montague was a smart man."

Engineer Montague, as well as Crocker, had to learn as he went along, being short in experience. Strobridge did not. Big, burly, rough and tough, his job was handling men; he did it with his fists, his vocal cords, his inexhaustible vocabulary of curses, the same lionhearted courage that moved Crocker, first his boss, then his friend, then his confidant.

Crocker's first eighteen miles eastward from Sacramento to Junction, California, even though he had to build a levee and a bridge, was over flat country; he could learn as he went. He made costly mistakes in the process, but the Crocker construction company (which included Huntington, Hopkins and Stanford) profited from them, receiving $425,000.

Crocker had to content himself with those eighteen miles of track in 1863. He was reduced to a mere twelve miles in 1864.

Although a locomotive sent out from the East and assembled in Sacramento was hauling freight and a few passengers over the thirty miles of completed railroad, the Central Pacific ran out of money with which to award contracts to Crocker and Company because the federal government would not pay the subsidies until forty miles of track had been laid. Crocker roared:

"I'd be glad to take a clean shirt, and get out."

Congress kept him in a dust- and sweat-encrusted shirt for the next five years by amending Judah's Railroad Act of 1862. Miraculously, the federal government agreed with the Central Pacific geologists that the Sierra Nevada foothills began in the totally level valley seven miles east of Sacramento, instead of where they actually began, twenty-five miles east thus giving Crocker and Company $32,000 a mile instead of the allotted $16,000, netting the company an additional $500,000 in profit for the thirty miles built. This incredible feat of legerdemain earned the company the title of:

"The strongest corporation in the world, because they could move a mountain range twenty-five miles."

President Lincoln signed the new bill on July 2, 1864 with a wry joke about his being "taken"; but the Central Pacific was hopelessly bogged down, and the Union Pacific, an organization formed by eastern men at the time of the Railroad Act of 1862 to build westward from Omaha to wherever the two lines met, had not even attempted to match Crocker's thirty miles.

Nothing would stop Crocker again, not until he had laid nearly a thousand miles of rail.

With two rehearsal years behind him and Senator Wilson's promised $100,000,000 ahead of him, Charlie Crocker opened 1865 with construction in earnest. By March he had cleared forest, blasted rock and dumped fill for the eleven miles to Illinoistown; by the end of May he had fifty-six miles of railroad built into the Sierra Nevada foothills, and was earning $1000 a day by hauling passengers for ten cents a mile, freight for fifteen cents per ton per mile.

Now, with the mountains looming ahead, he ran out of labor. His agents were constantly scouring San Francisco, San Jose, Sonoma, Sacramento, but of every ten men who agreed to work for the railroad six used the free ride to get closer to the Comstock, the other four went over the hill to Nevada as soon as they had saved stage fare. Crocker was reduced to employing twelve-year-old boys to lead the horses hauling dump carts.

Then Governor Stanford and a brother of Crocker made a radical suggestion. Why not try the Chinese? There were several thousands of them in California. Aside from working over the gold gravel pits that no one else would touch, they had been allowed to work only as laundry men, houseboys and truck gardeners. When Superintendent Strobridge heard that he might be saddled with pigtailed Chinamen who weighed not much over a hundred pounds, with which to conquer the granite wall of the Sierra Nevada, he exploded profanely with a combination of contempt and rage.

His boss was smarter. Crocker in his gold-mining days had observed that the seemingly delicate Chinese were out working the gravel pits at dawn while the white men were sleeping, and were still at work at nightfall when the whites had long since quit. To "Stro's" demand of how these rice-eating weaklings were going to build a railroad, Crocker replied:

"They built the Great Wall of China, didn't they? That was almost as tough a job as this railroad, wasn't it?"

At that precise moment the remnants of Crocker's white workers threatened to strike. Crocker hired fifty Chinese in Sacramento, at $26 a month, jammed them into flatcars and took them to the railhead. Dumped out in the midst of primeval forest, the fatalistic Chinese did not even bother to look at their strange, fearsome surroundings, but pitched camp, cooked a light supper of dried cuttlefish and rice, calmly went to sleep, and at dawn were wielding the heavy picks, shovels and wheelbarrows: odd-looking little fellows in their basket hats, pigtails down their backs, blue blouses, pantaloons, soft slippers, and high birdlike talk. Stro stood around waiting for them to collapse from exhaustion, but Charlie Crocker had a knowing smile on his face; at sundown, twelve hours later, after a brutal day's labor that might have floored the huskiest white man, the calm Chinese were still going at a good clip.

A hundred more Chinese were hired within the next two days. Two thousand were working on the railroad by the summer of 1865. Their white colleagues who had been prepared to resent them found that they respected the Chinese, and were grateful at being relieved of the pick and shovel work. Crocker now contracted to have thousands more brought in by ship from China. They became known as "Crocker's Pets," called him Cholly Clocker, climbed over the hills and gorges like a swarm of blue-jacketed ants, were paid by Crocker himself on payday as he rode his sweat-covered sorrel mare into camp, calling each name off a list, dipping into his saddlebags, gold on one side, silver on the other, to put the actual coins in the hands of every man who worked for him; for that really made him the boss.

While engineer Montague ran his survey lines for the fifty miles to the summit, trying to but not succeeding in bettering Judah's blueprint, six thousand of Crocker's Pets opened 1866 by mounting the canyons, picks in hand, clinging to the sides of granite cliffs with their fingernails while cutting gaps wide enough to pass a train, crawling away from the cuts pushing dirt-filled wheelbarrows to dump down a canyon, making their way up the side of the mountain with a seventy-pound bag of black powder balanced at either end of a bamboo pole, hand-drilling in the granite, placing the black powder blasts, and frequently being blown up themselves.

Behind the Chinese came the specialists: tracklayers, bending the rails by hand, spikers, bolters, men planting telegraph poles and stringing wires so that there was always communication between Crocker at the railhead and the supply bases at the rear which sent up the ties, rails, tools, powder, food, hay. Crocker tore up and down the line, his heavy face covered with sweat and alkali dust, his sorrel mare covered with lather, bellowing, cursing, finding fault.

"Everyone was afraid of me. I was just looking for someone to find fault with all the time. My faculty of leadership grew more and more."

He needed it more and more, not only because he now faced the impregnable heart of the mountain, but because the competing Union Pacific had also begun to roll and was making rapid progress west. Unless Crocker cleared the summit of the Sierra Nevada and got down the east slope fast, the Union Pacific would usurp all those hundreds of desert miles where tracklaying was so cheap, and the return so high.

But first they had to pass Cape Horn, described as "a sheer granite buttress," over a thousand feet of vertical cliff which Crocker *could neither go through nor over*. It was solved by lowering the fearless, unquestioning and unquenchable Chinese over the side of the cliff on ropes where, with nothing between them and their ancestors but faith, they worked a twelve-hour day with hammer and chisel to carve out a hairline ledge on which their brothers could then stand to widen the cut in the side of the cliff sufficiently to notch a rim and lay a track.

The men matched the mountains.

With Cape Horn passed by May 1866, and the Sacramento *Union* declaring that the Central Pacific was a greater engineering feat than the Suez Canal, Crocker continued to drive his construction gangs up the west slope of the Sierra Nevada, passing little mining towns like Gold Run, You Bet, Red Dog and Little York, reaching Dutch Flat, where five years before Theodore Judah had first drawn the plans for the railroad on his druggist friend's counter. By November he had completed another twenty-eight miles of track at an outlay of $8,000,000, employing, feeding, housing and keeping content fifteen thousand Chinese laborers freshly out of the warm green rice paddies of Canton. Altogether he had laid ninety-four miles, and was running two trains a day. He moved up and down the line continuously, sleeping at the end of a work car, able to tell when awakened precisely where he was by the bounce, jolt or sway of the instant. He occasionally went down to Sacramento for a day, where he had installed his wife in a mansion that was a monument of bad taste.

Strobridge kept his wife with him, living always at the railhead, the only white woman on the railroad. In charge of the actual grading and tracklaying, he accomplished the miracle of keeping that triumvirate of camp followers, the saloon, gambler and prostitute, away from his crews. When a liquor merchant opened a tent Strobridge unceremoniously sent a crew to burn it down. However the Chinese refreshed themselves during the day on warm tea dipped from empty whiskey barrels, so one assumes that the tracklayers were not kept teetotalers by Stro's heroic moral efforts.

There were ever new hardships ahead: now fifteen tunnels had to be driven through granite so hard that the edge of picks and chisels melted against the stone like chocolate candy. The black blasting powder, ignited in drill holes, did little more than discolor the rock. In desperation Crocker called in a Swedish chemist who studied the granite and improvised a chemical formula called nitroglycerin to cope with it. It did, rather more successfully than the men could cope with its effects: Strobridge lost an eye in one explosion, and in another a crew of Chinese were blown so high that Crocker could not collect sufficient pieces to send back to China for burial, as provided in their contracts. No one commented; new men slipped in to take their places, numbers were crossed off a list.

Summit Tunnel was the peak of everything. Only a quarter of a mile in length, but composed of the ultimate marble spine of the mountain, it took a solid year to cut through it, thousands of Chinese working twelve-hour shifts around the clock, not only from both ends but in both directions from a shaft which had been sunk straight down the middle. The four contingents, hacking, picking, dynamiting, chiseling, could cut out only *eight inches* a day. If Collis P. Huntington juggled $500,000 from Congress by moving the Sierra Nevada twenty-five miles into the flat valley, Charlie Crocker gave it back with usurer's interest on that most expensive quarter mile in railroad history.

It need not have been so expensive, for Crocker was offered the first experimental steam drill to use on Summit Tunnel. He categorically closed his ears to his partners' agonized wails that he should at least try the drill, and expended $2,000,000 hauling goods around the Summit to work on the downslope. It was his one obtuseness in building the railroad, costing $5,000,000. It also allowed the Union Pacific time to push several more hundreds of miles west.

CHAPTER IX

The Saturnalia of Virginia City

WHILE CHARLIE CROCKER WAS conquering the Sierra Nevada, which had defied man to domesticate her to travel, Philip Diedesheimer and Adolph Sutro were daring to face the equally formidable task of subjugating the Comstock Lode: for the earth gives up her riches reluctantly.

When the Comstock miners had run into their first trouble, Philip Diedesheimer's system of square-set propping had enabled them to go safely through the soft crumbling ore, hundreds of feet into Mount Davidson. Because Diedesheimer, as superintendent of the Ophir mine, had insisted in the spring of 1862 that the mine must have a forty-five-horsepower engine, an eight-inch pump and strong hoisting machinery, the mines were rescued a second time by being pumped dry of the winter floods. As soon as the Sierra Nevada Trail was opened, a steady stream of mules and ox teams filed across the steep chest of Mount Davidson bringing in machinery ordered from San Francisco foundries. The Comstock was once again mining at full blast, with eighty stamp mills operating to extract the precious metals from the rock.

With spring there came a second mighty wave of prospectors over the Sierra Nevada, emptying out several of California's mountain counties and building Mount Davidson's population to ten thousand. There were six stage lines running into the Comstock from California, arriving each day with a motley list of passengers described as "capitalists, miners, sports, thieves, robbers and adventurers of all kinds." "Gold Canyon, from Carson River to Dayton, up through Gold Hill to C Street, was one continuous line of sawmills, quartz mills, tunnels, dumps, sluices, waterwheels, shanties. The whole canyon had swelled into metropolitan proportions and was practically a continuation of Virginia City."

Unlike the fertile, heavily timbered, rolling California land, where the California goldrushers who struck it rich could invest their findings in farmlands, cattle ranches, town properties or businesses, Nevada was dry, inhospitable to man, with boundless deserts and barren mountains. There was nothing for the freshly minted millionaires to buy with their money except additional mining claims. An important part of the $7,000,000 of gold and silver extracted in Mount Davidson's first wild disgorging of wealth was spent by Nevada's newly rich to replace the flooded-out board houses with ones of brick and stone. They tried to spend their millions in Virginia City, achieving a saturnalia of living and building not to be duplicated until Colorado's "Silver Dollar" Tabor went on a rampage.

Jerry Lynch, owner of the Lady Bryant, had his horses shod with silver, and in his mansion had a fourteen-foot walnut headboard carved to cover his bedroom wall from floor to ceiling. Another owner, Parks, imported a fresco painter from Europe to paint the dark stair landings of his $500,000 home so that the walls became sunlit gardens with lilacs and aspens. The foremen of the Ophir, Mexican, Gould and Curry, who were earning the unheard-of salaries of $40,000 a year, went on a spree, with silver harnesses on their coaches and fours, whips and carriage lamps encrusted with gold. On his wedding night one of them filled his water tank with champagne, the guests drawing their Mumm's and Veuve Cliquot from the faucet.

Sandy Bowers, married to the twice-divorced Mormon Eilley Orrum, Queen of the Comstock, took $1,000,000 out of his mine in 1863 alone. Eilley Orrum was a Scotch girl who enjoyed visions compounded of mystical combinations of numbers, snakes, goldfish, Indians and the initials of her future husband. At fifteen she was converted by a Mormon missionary and went to Utah, there marrying a bishop with the proper initials. Ten years brought her no children, but brought her husband three new wives in the form of young nieces whom Eilley had brought over from Scotland. Eilley got herself a divorce, moved to the Carson Valley where she worked in a general store and bought a crystal ball which she called a peeping stone. In the vapor of this ball she saw greater visions than ever: this new land of Nevada possessed fabulous riches in gold. She would become a millionaire, make herself a princess of the Washoe, and have a palace.

With a second Mormon husband Eilley Orrum moved over to Gold Hill in 1858, where she staked out a dozen claims. She also opened a boardinghouse, cooked for the prospectors and washed their clothes. One boarder, unable to pay his bill, deeded her his claim on the Comstock. When Brigham Young called all Saints back to Utah, Eilley remained, judged her husband's desertion a divorce, and married Sandy Bowers, teamster and muleskinner who had staked out claims next to hers.

Sandy wanted to sell his claims, urging Eilley to sell hers too, for the $3500 offered. But Eilley's peeping stone told her they would take greater riches out of the ground, that a big city would grow where their cabin stood, and that this desert would one day become a state. Oddly enough, Sandy believed her. Two years later, in a speech at the banquet he gave at International House in Virginia City, Sandy told his friends:

"I've had powerful good luck and I've money to throw to the birds. There ain't no chance for a gentleman to spend his coin in this country, and there ain't nothing much to see. So me and Mrs. Bowers is going to Europe to see the Queen of England and the other great men of them countries."

The Queen of the Comstock was not received by the Queen of England. Eilley drowned her disappointment by spending as much as $20,000 a day in London and Paris for diamond earrings and bracelets, for elaborate bedroom furniture, Algerian marbles, French glass windows, mantelpieces from Italy, silver doorknobs and hall rails made from bullion out of their own mine . . . all for the mansion back in Nevada which would be completed by the time she returned. To maintain her position as social queen of the Comstock, Eilley had Sandy bring a whole brass band from Scotland to entertain their guests. *Noblesse oblige.*

Money for the birds! In 1863 alone the Comstock mines sent $20,000,000 in bullion over the Sierra Nevada to San Francisco. In 1863 stock in the Gould and Curry mine was selling for $6000 a foot, the Ophir for $4000; the Kentuck was selling at $22,000 a share, Empire for $20,000 a share! The Gould and Curry produced $6,000,000 in metal in 1863 and again in 1864; the stockholders joyously split $3,000,000 among them. This staggering production of pure wealth so amazed the world that Emperor Louis Napoleon sent a committee from Paris to investigate the Comstock.

The orgy of spending developed Virginia City, six narrow parallel streets like tiers across the face of the mountain, into a teeming metropolis with twenty-five thousand inhabitants, four-story hotels, porters in purple livery, shops with plate-glass windows and marble fronts, terrapin, frogs' legs and champagne. The saloons had long mahogany bars, murals, marble statuary, pictures of Lola Montez, "Benicia Boy" Heenan in his fighting trunks, and Adah Isaacs Menken, not overly burdened with clothes, lashed to the back of a black stallion. Every particle of what Virginia City ate, drank, wore, lived in and used as machinery came from California, over two hundred miles of road, via Placerville, Donner Lake or Lake Tahoe, five thousand freight wagons moving over the passes in one year, with two thousand teamsters employed to handle the draught animals. Freighting became big business and totaled $12,000,000 in 1863, while the Concord coaches of the Pioneer Stage Line brought into Virginia City, and took out again, a hundred new faces every day of the year.

Mining camps are inclined to be anti-intellectual; as a Nevada hotelkeeper explained it, "This ain't no place for liberaries en such things. Men come here to make money en they ain't got time to spare loafin' around readin'." Yet in the Sierra Nevada camps the lonely prospectors had paid any price for reading matter, and in the Washoe over three hundred men subscribed to *Harper's Monthly*, more than a hundred to the *Atlantic Monthly*, while sets of Shakespeare, Dickens, Froude's *History of England* were gobbled up as soon as they appeared. Fifty copies of *Snowbound* were sold the first week it was offered for sale.

Virginia City's first attempts at public education were cut short by recalcitrant pupils shooting the teachers. Now a new teacher was hired out of the "Rowdy Fund," set up by a pair of penitent drunks who, in front of a full audience, had ripped to shreds with their knives the Comstock's first theatrical curtain. No one gave pale, slight Harry Flotz, a discouraged prospector going back to his first love, schoolteaching, more than one day; but Professor Flotz arrived in class with three navy revolvers and a bowie knife. During geography Flotz heard a whisper; like lightning one of his revolvers was trained on the offender.

"Don't do that again," he said quietly. "I never give a second warning."

Churches had as hard a time getting started as did the schools; few of the miners believed they would remain for any length of time on the side of their barren mountain, overlooking an even more barren desert. By 1864 the Catholics had built a church, hospital and separate schools for boys and girls. A Passionist church was built at Gold Hill. The Presbyterian committee was made up of shrewd businessmen who first made a profit for their church of $4700 on mining stock, then bought four lots close by on C Street and put up stores for rent so the church they built would have an income.

Only in its journalism did the Comstock create an indigenous art form. The *Territorial Enterprise* became famous all over the country for its brand of hard factual reporting—editor Joe Goodman was perfectly willing to shoot it out with anyone who felt he had been misrepresented, and did so on several occasions—combined with the telling of some of the tallest tales in the history of American journalism.

The leader of these journalistic hoaxes was William Wright, who signed himself Dan De Quille. He was "what you might call a striking figure. Skinny as a lamppost and pretty near as tall; wore a long cape and big wide black hat. Wrote a book and started peddling it all over the country from a buckboard. Whenever a fellow bought a book Dan bought him a drink. Pretty soon he'd get feeling generous and start passing books out free. Wasn't long before they was gone and he owed the company $600. Every kid in town knew Dandy Quille: his long black cape kept getting greener and seedier-looking every year."

Dan De Quille's *The Travelling Stone of Pahrangat Valley* was a progenitor of science fiction. The story described how some mysterious natural force drew all the stones to a magnetic center of the valley, only to be blown apart, and then reassembled. This "quaint," as De Quille called his fables, was so convincingly told that German scientists wrote to Virginia City asking for further information.

Into this milieu, from a mining camp where he was trying to strike it rich, walked a chap by the name of Samuel Clemens to go to work for the paper. Clemens wanted to create fiction which would distill the essence of the miners' lot but would make them see the humor in their often grim life, in which every day a comrade was blown up, crushed in a slide, or fell to his death in one of the hundreds of abandoned shafts on Mount Davidson.

Clemens began signing himself Mark Twain and, following in the brilliant footsteps of Dan De Quille, whose *The Big Bonanza* remains a classic of the Comstock, began to invent tall tales, ludicrous yarns, fantastic adventures . . . all arising out of the daily life of the hard-rock miner. The competition was tough, for De Quille's invention of "quaints" was resourceful: a high windmill on top of Mount Davidson which kept all the mines pumped dry; an ammonia tank hat for wearing across the forty-mile desert, which kept a man's head refrigerated . . .

Under this tutelage and in the hearty companionship of the *Territorial Enterprise* staff, drinking beer in the cellar composing room until dawn, Mark Twain began creating his own fantastic tales: fossilized snails which, when blasted out of hard rock, blithely crawled away; a petrified man who moved his stoneman's hands directly in front of each other, fingers spread out with the nearest thumb to its nose. The miners howled; and soon the rest of the country was laughing with them.

Territorial government had brought little law and order to the Comstock. Masked men who operated on both slopes of the Sierra Nevada held up the stages, leveling double-barreled shotguns on the passengers lined up along the road, taking the Wells Fargo box and the bars of bullion being shipped to San Francisco. Virginia City was no safer; anyone coming over the divide at night from Gold Hill or walking up the dark street toward his house had an excellent chance of being robbed. One highwayman, finding his victim had only three $20 gold pieces on him, brandished his revolver and cried:

"If you ever come along here again without any money, I'll take you a lick under the butt of the ear!"

Gun fights were nightly occurrences in the saloons. One bully called "Big Chief" killed a man having a drink at a bar, then lay down on a table and slept. No one disturbed him. The next day a friend of the slain man followed Big Chief across the desert and shot him dead. No one bothered the avenger. The few courts were involved in settling suits over the ownership of mine properties, ownership decided on the basis of where a witness might remember having seen a pile-of-stones marker a year or two before.

Who owned the gold and silver? The man who found the deep-bedded vein, or the man under whose surface claim the gold and silver veins slanted? There were no mining codes to settle this vexing problem. The federal judges of Nevada Territory appointed by Washington were sadly underpaid, $1500 a year in inflated greenbacks, a sum which would have supported them in good style for one month out of the twelve. When a judge's decision determined which contestant owned a $1,000,000 mine, bribery and corruption became an integral part of the court proceedings. Conditions in the courts grew so scandalous that:

"Judges were considered reprehensible only if they sold out to *both* sides."

Mining companies, ready to invest large amounts of capital to develop the mines, hesitated because of the corrupt lawlessness of the courts; men who wanted to bring in their wives and children hesitated because of the lawlessness of the population.

Finally the whole of the Comstock rose in mass indignation, led by William M. Stewart, dominating personality of Virginia City, described as "a red-headed, light-bearded, foaming hot politician," six feet two inches, with the bearing of a lion. "He towered above his fellow-citizens like the Colossus of Rhodes and contained as much brass in his make-up as that statue."

Earning the reputation of "the great leader of the Washoe bar," he was soon averaging $200,000 a year from his fees, one of a small group of lawyers in litigious Nevada who took out $9,000,000 in suits between 1860 and 1865, a fifth of the total value of all the gold and silver extracted from the Comstock!

Stewart was born in Galen, New York, on August 9, 1827, spent almost two years studying at Yale, but left when struck with gold fever. He was placer mining in the Sierra Nevada by 1850, became chairman of a committee that drew up the earliest mining laws in Nevada County, California, was district attorney of the county, a mining law expert and a successful mining attorney. Like so many of the California goldrushers of the decade before, Stewart joined the Comstock rush not to mine but to get in on the desert floor of law and politics.

Everyone knew "Bill" Stewart from the hour he arrived; since his mining-law reputation had preceded him, he was given the first Comstock cases involving conflict of ownership. A flamboyant, colorful personality who knew how to dramatize himself and sail smoothly with the wind:

"He placed himself on the level of the juries, spoke to their crude sense of justice and strove to convey the idea that his clients were entitled to a verdict in equity even more than by law. His opponents protested that he was endowed with a faculty of imposing the sublimest absurdities upon juries as pure and spotless truth."

With only one group did Stewart not fare so well: during a temporary crisis in 1864 he organized the mine owners to depress, uniformly, the miner's wage from $4.00 to $3.50 a day. Down the main street of Virginia City came two thousand uniformly irate miners, searching for Stewart for the purpose of a hanging. Stewart met them with an expression on his big amiable face which read:

"Look, fellers, I didn't know you'd feel this way about it."

The Comstock miners were organized. Though their first strike had failed because so many men were coming over the Sierra Nevada looking for work, the Miner's Union had achieved the first eight-hour day known in American mines. It took precisely two hours to get Stewart to persuade his mine owners' organization to restore the $4.00 a day wage. They never again tried to reduce it.

Four thousand names were signed to a petition demanding the

resignation of the three federal judges. Stewart reportedly hauled them down to the telegraph office by the scruff of the neck and stood over them while they wrote out their resignations.

For Nevada, statehood was the only solution; then it could elect its own officials and hold them responsible for their acts.

For the Union, statehood for Nevada was also a solution: Nevada's gold and silver were important in financing the war. The only road open to California was through Nevada, a road which sorely needed military policing.

President Lincoln needed Nevada's three votes to help pass the Thirteenth Amendment, which would make permanent the freeing of the slaves. He said:

"Here is the alternative: that we carry this vote, or be compelled to raise another million and fight no one knows how long. It is a question of three votes or new armies."

Bill Stewart became the dominating figure at Nevada's constitutional convention which convened at Carson City on July 4, 1864, where he set up a sound judicial structure for the incipient state. More of the delegates were originally from New York State than any other in the Union; all but four had made their way over the Sierra Nevada from California, to which they had come during the early years of the gold rush.

The proposed constitution was sent to Washington on the telegraph wires.

The $3500 telegram, longest on record at the time, paid off. President Lincoln named Nevada a state of the Union on October 31, 1864, in time for Nevada to vote in the national election.

Stewart got himself elected Nevada's first United States senator on a charming but meaningless phrase, "The Honest Miner." The *Territorial Enterprise* "quaintly" named his sumptuous mansion in Washington, where he remained for thirty years as Nevada's senator:

"The Honest Miner's Camp."

But the Comstock's problems were far from over.

CHAPTER X

Billy Ralston's "crackling, pleasure-loving town"

FRONT AND CENTER UNDER the proscenium of San Francisco stepped a new leading man who had struck color in California: William C. Ralston, who announced in the *Alta* of July 4, 1864, that his Bank of California would open the next day. "Billy" Ralston was also Nevada's Comstock Lode star. To everyone who had come to him for counsel while he was cashier and manager of an earlier bank he advised:

"Buy Comstock!"

They had, forcing the price of Gould and Curry up to $6300 a square foot, Savage to $2600 a share, Ophir to $1580, in the process putting millions of dollars of profit into the hands of San Francisco investors. San Francisco's Stock and Exchange, founded two years before by sixty prominent San Franciscans, became one of the wildest in the world. A gambling mania seized bay society that made the gold-rush gambling saloons look like charity bazaars. The pale-faced, dark-haired mysterious gamblers of the El Dorado tents of 1849, with the black sashes tied around their ruffled lace shirts, were replaced by silk-hatted brokers, while the occasional woman faro dealer multiplied into a swarm of women curb brokers:

"Beautiful ladies with well-turned ankles, tightly-laced ladies in rustling black silk, perfumed women with sparkling eyes, flashing teeth and diamond-studded ears. Weaned from homes, schoolrooms and the city's bright lights, they flitted about the Exchange picking up tips."

With the profits tumbling down from the Washoe in a gold and silver stream, Ralston invested the Bank's millions in San Francisco's mills, foundries, forges, factories to turn out the machinery needed in the Comstock, which brought San Francisco more profits to invest in more Comstock mines.

San Francisco thanked Billy Ralston for its prodigal prosperity. He was acclaimed a financial genius. Ralston loved San Francisco with the paternal passion that Captain John Sutter had for the Sacramento Valley, Colonel Mariano Vallejo for the Valley of the Moon, and Brigham Young for the valley of the Great Salt Lake.

William Chapman Ralston, son of an impoverished millwright, was born in Plymouth, Ohio, in 1826. His grandfather had run a ferry on the Ohio River; his father sank the family savings when his keelboat, loaded with goods, hit a snag. After a grade school education, Billy worked the boats of the Ohio and Mississippi rivers as a clerk, and set out for California in 1849. In Panama he met old riverboat friends who needed help in managing their shipping business to San Francisco. Billy remained for five years, ran the company profitably, became a partner at twenty-six, and journeyed to San Francisco in 1854 to direct the firm's activities. He moved quickly into partnership in a bank, displaying such sound judgment and courage in the financial crisis of 1857 that he saved a considerable portion of San Francisco's business and emerged as the idolized leader of the community at thirty-one years of age. At thirty-seven he became controller of an industrial empire, the only man produced by the Far West who might have been, in organizing talent and vision of empire, the equal of Brigham Young.

He looked considerably like Brigham Young: medium-sized, stockily built, open-faced, with clear, penetrating eyes, an enormous rounded dome of Gibraltar forehead, a kindly, almost gentle mouth out of which came some of the shrewdest and sometimes harshest words to be heard in San Francisco:

"Nevada is just a hole in the ground with silver and gold in it."

Like Brigham Young, Billy Ralston kept the door of his office at the front of the bank open to everyone. San Francisco was his empire. It was his dream to make it as successful and colorful a city as New Orleans, with which he had fallen in love at sixteen when he came down the Mississippi on the floating palace *Constitution*.

San Francisco must become the great maritime center of the Pacific coast, controlling all the shipping to the Orient; to this end he helped found lines to Hawaii and China via Japan. It must become the railroad terminus of the West; to this end he loaned Leland Stanford $300,000 of the bank's money for the Central Pacific, against the anguished protests of his directors. It must become the financial center of the Far West, industrially self-sufficient; to this end he invested a fortune in iron and cotton mills. He helped build an opera house, public parks, boulevards, libraries, schools, the handsome hotels and theatres that characterize a city of international flavor.

The hills and valleys were covered with substantial homes, but San Franciscans were not a stay-at-home people. They were importing opera companies so they might hear Verdi and Mozart, keeping the Metropolitan and California theatres filled with Shakespearean and comedy troupes, Lotta Crabtree, drawing $15,000 in one night, riding out Mission Road in gaily painted barouches to Tony Oake's Tavern, or over the Point Lobos road to the Cliff House in spite of the wind:

"Strong enough and sharp enough to blow a man baldheaded in five minutes."

The German group had their beer halls, the French their *cafés chantants*, the Italians their masquerades and restaurants for spaghetti and red wine, the big Irish contingent their St. Patrick's Day, the Latins their King Carnival, the Chinese, in a special section of the city called Chinatown, their firecracker New Year's Day. There were Spanish fiestas at Russ Gardens, bear pits and sea lions at the Willows, agricultural and mechanical exhibitions at the Mechanics' Fair.

San Francisco had standards of excellence that were the pioneer equivalent of Boston's Brahmin tradition. It was a climate that nurtured creative writers, giving them a voice in vigorous, original journals. Franklin Walker in *San Francisco's Literary Frontier* says:

"As early as 1850 there were fifty working printers. San Francisco boasted that it published more newspapers than London and that in its first decade it published more books than did all the rest of the United States west of the Mississippi. Whatever voice the western frontier might develop was sure of expression in its many literary organs, among which the *Pioneer,* the *Golden Era*, the *Hesperian*, the *Californian* and the *Overland Monthly* would compare with the best eastern journals. Wealth to produce and education and leisure to read such journals alone made them possible.

The Central Pacific, cutting through the granite of the Sierra Nevada to bind the East and West, was creating the physical ties. Western writers now sent forth on intellectual rails of words and ideas the human story of the opening of this new land, the color, the flavor and the meaning of this farthest west in the continental spread of the American people.

Joseph E. Lawrence of Long Island bought the *Golden Rea*, a weekly magazine, and turned it into San Francisco's literary club.

Lawrence, who had mined lead type in San Francisco journals since 1849, was described as having "personal beauty, geniality, honest, gentlemanly ways." He hired Bret Harte as a printer but was soon publishing his tales, as well as the early efforts of Mark Twain from Nevada, Charles Warren Stoddard, Joaquin Miller, Ina Coolbrith and a hundred other homegrown poets.

Bret Harte was the first to arrive, in 1854. Born in Albany, New York, he had worked as a teacher and in a mountain mining supply store until 1860 when he went to work for Lawrence. At twenty-four he was delicate, having "dainty aloofness and cordiality without warmth." Jessie Benton Fremont invited him to her home at Black Point overlooking the bay and strait, gave him sorely needed friendship, and got him a job in the mint where he would have more time to write. Harte, said to be the first to sense the possibilities of the scene around him, wrote and published *M'Liss, The Luck of Roaring Camp,* and went on to world fame. Mark Twain contributed humorous pieces and burlesques on San Francisco's high society, though his celebrated *Jumping Frog of Calaveras County*, which started him on his way, was first published in the East.

The gold fever days seemed far behind, though a rich new quartz area was discovered near Yuba with "ledges composed of black rock, so filled with gold as to appear bronze"; John C. Fremont's Mariposa mine was still taking out $75,000 in gold a month; and a single lump of gold worth $20,000 was discovered in Nevada County. These finds no longer precipitated rushes: northern Californians were too busy growing wheat in the fertile Sacramento and San Joaquin valleys, opening factories in San Francisco to produce shirts, neckties, hoop skirts, umbrellas, gloves, soap and perfume, boots and shoes.

The labor unions were growing stronger, the Women's Cooperative Printing Union as well as the Shoemakers' Cooperative Union, strong enough to hold an eight-hour-day convention, and in a comparatively short time push the eight-hour-day act through the legislature.

People were arriving from all over the world: three hundred thousand, four hundred thousand, then over half a million, absorbed by the end of a decade by a city that had been a group of adobe huts around a lonely, wind-swept, abandoned mud cove only twenty years before.

It was a crackling, pleasure-loving, light-stepping and high-spending city, heterogeneous, yet companionable, with its latchstring on the outside of its home, heart and purse, living at a high tempo of gaiety and excitement. Too much so, said its critics within the gates. Though there were forty churches and one hundred schools, these figures were humiliatingly dwarfed by the two hundred thirty dealers in whiskey: for San Francisco was also a hard-drinking town, guilty of "extravagances of dress, craving for excitement."

The Temperance Union fought not only the drinking and gambling—the mad goings-on at the Stock and Exchange were exempted—but the dance cellars under the city saloons. Other reform groups had laws passed forbidding the "breeding of animals within public gaze," and caused the arrest of the directors of the Anatomical Museum for putting on what they charged to be "a dirty show." Since the activities of the Vigilance Committee of 1856 San Francisco had been a law-abiding town, though the Chinese community governed itself by Old Country law: when the Wong family opened a laundry within a prohibited distance of an established washhouse, the Chinese assembled in a hall and resolved:

"We men, one heart, put forth exertion mutually to aid, must clean him out, avoid after trouble. In our companies number of friend who has ability to kill Wong San Chee, thankfully give him 2000 round dollars."

Above this perpetual Mardi Gras sat William C. Ralston, his office "looking like the waiting room of a successful physician, thronged with men, women and children." They went away with money for baseball suits, with transportation to New York to join their wives, with checks to start hospitals or any one of a hundred businesses.

Ralston and his Bank, says Dana in *The Men Who Built San Francisco,* "symbolized to the public mind the wise and beneficent use of its resources . . . the farmer, the mechanic, the miner and the capitalist found in the Bank of California a friend in need."

Ralston was making his own millions en route; a modest man, he never allowed his charitable contributions to be made public knowledge, insisted that credit for his industrial triumphs go to his associates. Yet when he bought an estate on the warm, oak-studded peninsula at Belmont he spent a staggering sum to make it the greatest baronial mansion in America, ending with a hundred twenty guest rooms, a crystal-chandeliered ballroom, separate buildings for a Turkish bath and gymnasium, stables of carved mahogany with inlaid mother-of-pearl, twenty gardeners to cultivate the grounds, a dozen Chinese boys to care for the rugs from Persia, draperies from Paris, chairs from London, porcelain from China, silver, glass, laces from Antwerp, Venice, Cairo, sculpture, ivories, rare bindings from all over the world.

With Mount Davidson properties now selling up to $7600 a square foot, Billy Ralston was not alone in his extravagance. "Bartenders, hostlers and watch peddlers had become plutocrats and had built incredible gingerbread houses on the ramparts of the city."

Two of these San Francisco bartenders, James C. Flood and William S. O'Brien, would join with two Nevada miners, John W. Mackay and James G. Fair, to become another Big Four, described by Oscar Lewis in *Silver Kings* as:

"The four men who, by their discovery and control of the richest strike of precious metals in America's mining history, amassed very large fortunes and for many years made themselves potent factors in the affairs of the entire Pacific coast."

William C. Ralston and a highly improbable partner, a real estate broker by the name of William Sharon, would be the absolute masters of the Comstock until they came into mortal combat with these Silver Kings.

William Sharon was the antithesis of genial, bland, openhanded Ralston: a small man, wearing a jet-black mustache to match his black beady eyes, with a closed-in, shut-down face that gave little to the passing public; a man who chewed tobacco and squirted it to interspersed lines of Shakespeare, dressed in a long frock coat and gambler's-style big hat. His only gambling up to the summer of 1864 was at poker, the greatest of all the Far West's gambling arts; he rarely lost, but when he did he paid with good grace.

William Sharon was an Ohioan of Quaker parentage who spent three years at Athens College, studied law in Edwin M. Stanton's office, practiced briefly in Mississippi and in 1849 came out to California searching not for gold (he and his friend John D. Fry, subsequently father-in-law to William Ralston, walked right past Gold Hill without washing out a single pan of dust) but for health. Their store in Sacramento failed, so Sharon came down to San Francisco. For a decade he dealt in San Francisco real estate, accumulating $150,000.

Now in the summer of 1864, nettled by the "chambermaids and ex-sheriffs soaring to dizzy heights in the financial firmament," he studied the Comstock situation, decided he would plunge his $150,000 to gain control of North American, of which he already owned a thousand shares, because he believed that pending lawsuits would be settled in North American's favor: the Overman mine was in bonanza; the vein should run slantwise through North American; he would make millions.

Instead, a group of unscrupulous brokers dealt him from the bottom of the deck, something no poker shark had been able to do, reselling him his own stock at a considerably increased price. He lost his $150,000, his beautiful home on Stockton Street, the last of his resources, and was obliged to ask his friend, Colonel John D. Fry, to take him to Ralston's office in the Bank of California and plead for a job. Sharon did not take the loss with good grace. Being the laughingstock of San Francisco made him a cold, embittered man... looking for an opportunity to wreak vengeance.

It was the worst possible moment to ask Billy Ralston for anything: reliable miners had just reported to him that the Comstock was flooded, finished, that it was impossible to go below the five-hundred-foot depth at which all mining had stopped. Though a last few of Diedesheimer's pumps were groaning valiantly, the mining shafts were sumps of scalding hot water that came rushing into the mines from underground volcanic rivers.

Comstock stocks on the San Francisco Stock and Exchange went crashing. Gould and Curry, which had been paying a dividend of $125 a share, fell from $6300 to $2400 to $900 a share; Ophir dropped from $1580 to $300. Most of the newly made San Francisco fortunes ran out the same hole they had come in.

Not only did Ralston have $3,000,000 of the Bank of California money invested in the Comstock mines, and more millions in the San Francisco forges, factories and foundries supplying the Comstock, but the Bank of California correspondents in Virginia City, acting as a collecting and lending agency, overdrew their account and vanished.

The job that William Sharon wanted was manager of the Bank's accounts in Virginia City. Ralston was convinced that the Mount Davidson mines were not through, but he was by no means convinced that the cold, bitter, defeated man standing before him was the right one to bring the Comstock back. To oblige Colonel Fry, his father-in-law, he gave Sharon a try, persuading his reluctant board by bringing evidence to bear that Sharon had been an incomparable poker player, and that a good poker player was precisely what was needed in the Washoe.

William Sharon had a first-rate brain, an iron courage; if the humiliating defeat on the Stock and Exchange had killed his soul, the Comstock would pay for the fatality.

CHAPTER XI

Manana Land Gets Itself Subdivided

SOUTHERN CALIFORNIA WAS AN unbroken cattle range.

Los Angeles was having a hard time getting started. Its population of forty-four hundred stood still; San Diego and Santa Barbara, only a thousand behind, had a good chance of replacing it as the metropolis. It was a village of mud huts and dirt streets with yellow adobes a block long and one story high, their flat roofs covered each year with pitch from the La Brea tar pits. Hundreds of mongrel dogs ran the plaza barking at the hoofs of horses until a rider became sufficiently annoyed, shot the dog and left him lying in the street.

In November of 1861 telegraph lines were strung from Los Angeles to San Pedro, but by January, as Newmark observed in *Sixty Years in California*, "There were so many complaints that both poles and wires had fallen to the ground, blocking the thoroughfares and entangling animals... there was soon a public demand either to repair the telegraph or to remove it altogether and throw the equipment away."

When the winter's flash floods kept all mail from the new post office building for nearly a month, the news-starved residents found their fate a little more palatable when a town wag hung a sign: TO LET.

Businessmen stood in water up to their waists, trying to save the goods on high shelves. Much of it floated out into the plaza. Some of the adobe stores melted and tumbled in, burying all the merchandise and sometimes the storekeeper as well.

Soon after "a phenomenal wind storm unroofed houses, demolished barns, prostrating trees in orchards." Adventuresome souls planting vineyards in outlying districts had their grapes eaten by bears and coyotes.

The City of the Angels seemed to be controlled by the forces of the Devil.

No government was able to function. Disputants so regularly shot out their arguments in public and wounded bystanders that the Council passed an ordinance "prohibiting everybody, except officers and travelers, from carrying a pistol, dirk, sling shot or sword." Angelenos stopped carrying swords.

Three fifths of the children had no schooling whatever; the few public schools were so poorly regarded that half of the remaining youngsters were privately educated. Though the Council figured the assessed valuation of the city at $2,000,000 it was not able to collect one penny in taxes. The city offered some lowlands for twenty-five cents an acre but there were no buyers; when two well-located business lots of a hundred twenty by a hundred sixty-five feet were offered for their delinquent taxes of $1.26 each, only one bidder showed up!

Southern California had no foundry or forge. To bore artesian wells, one had to send to San Francisco for equipment. Since Angelenos were hard pressed for drinking and washing water, ex-Mayor Marchessault set up a distributing system made out of bored pine logs fitted end to end. The wooden pipes so continually burst and flooded the streets that the mortified ex-mayor committed suicide in the council chamber, an instance of civic rectitude not soon to be surpassed.

The only good news the hard-pressed citizens had all year was an announcement that a former San Francisco dentist was offering to come to patients' homes to extract troublesome teeth.

There was no valid reason for a migration to southern California. The land was held in its original county-seized Spanish grants, with little acreage available to pioneering families. In addition the original land titles were so clouded that few would dare to invest their money or break it to the plow when they could be dispossessed. A favorite saying in the region was:

"I don't want to buy a lawsuit."

The *Southern News* said, "No one who has resided in Los Angeles County for a twelve-month is surprised at the continued repulses given to visitors who come to this section for the purpose of settling. All are told that the country is 'played out', and that there are no chances. The majority of ranches in this country have been stripped of their former herds of stock at high prices . . . and large tracts of land are daily becoming more and more valueless. If no change is permitted, ruin must be the ultimate result."

El Monte, now ten years old, located in one of the most fertile sections of the state, was still called a "lick-skillet" town. One traveler reported, "California is not now a good home for small men. It is a theatre for pioneer operations in the large, and is no place for patches." A state official maintained:

"The state should use every exertion to promote immigration of the industrious classes of Europe. We want workers; we have non-producers enough already; we have doctors, lawyers, clerks and politicians in abundance; we now want farmers, mechanics, artisans and wine-growers."

Though the settlement was eighty years old the first shade trees were only now planted by John Temple in front of his newly built Temple Building. The onlookers watched Temple's inexplicable activity with openmouthed amazement, but as the trees began to grow and cast shade the odd idea caught on and within five years pepper trees were planted on the main streets.

There were other men of energy in the community, chief among them exuberant man-of-action Phineas T. Banning, who was laughed at for trying to create a harbor and a town at Wilmington and San Pedro, twenty-two miles away from Los Angeles. Banning was born in Delaware in September 1831, the ninth of eleven children, descended from the English Phineas Banning who came to Delaware in colonial days. At the age of twelve he left home for Philadelphia with fifty cents in his pocket, and at the age of twenty came across Panama to southern California.

Banning said, "We cannot become a great city without a harbor to bring us ships and cargoes from all over the world. It's too bad San Pedro is so far away, but it's the best we've got and we'll have to make do."

The best he was able to do for a start was dredge the Wilmington estuary and run a fleet of lighters out to the anchored ships, taking off passengers and freight. In addition to his lighters he opened a stage line to San Pedro, with wagon trains to transport goods. He also envisaged a railroad from Los Angeles to San Pedro, another dream which Angelenos declared to be comical.

Rare, hopeful spot in the dismal southern California landscape was Anaheim, halfway between Los Angeles and San Bernardino, its only antecedent as a co-operative-capitalist planned community. The idea had been conceived in 1857 in San Francisco by a group of German-born carpenters, blacksmiths, watchmakers and merchants, with a brewer, miller, shoemaker, hostler, poet and musician thrown in for good measure. They were fifty families bound together in a strange land by ties of common origin and language, and the tie of being dissatisfied with the life they had found in San Francisco. They wanted to move to a warmer, drier climate where, despite the fact that not one of them was a farmer, they could pioneer on virgin soil.

Each man subscribed $750; under the leadership of George Hansen a committee was sent south to search out the best land. Hansen bought eleven hundred sixty-five acres of rich sandy loam, blessed with an equable climate and plenty of water from the Santa Ana River which ran across the property. Hansen engaged a hundred men and women with a supply of tools and work animals to subdivide the property into twenty-acre plots, to build an irrigation canal from the river and ditches to each portion of land, then to plant vines on each man's acreage, lay out a town site of forty acres in the center, fence the entire community with live willows, and each tract as well, and build closable gates across the four entrance streets to the community. The "Los Angeles Vineyard Company" was going to have its privacy!

After the vines had begun to bear, the entire colony moved from San Francisco to southern California. The shareholders had been assessed another $450 over the three-year waiting period, but each now owned twenty acres of bearing vineyard, and a homesite in the town. A committee assessed the valuation of each twenty-acre tract, running from $600 to $1400, depending on soil and location; families then drew numbers to determine which piece was to be theirs. If the plot they drew was worth $1400 the drawer paid the company an extra $200; if his plot had been evaluated at $600 the company returned $600 in cash.

The entire community, named Anaheim from a wedding of the Spanish Ana and the German word *heim* for home, pitched in to build each other's houses, buying their lumber co-operatively at wholesale. When the cost of hauling materials from the port of San Pedro proved expensive, they co-operatively built Anaheim Landing, only thirteen miles away, bought lighters from the common funds and freighted their own materials. They built a schoolhouse and a city hall and then, their co-operative job done, dissolved the company and made the transition to an individualist capitalist community, their future prosperity dependent upon their individual efforts, even as Mormon San Bernardino, purchased and developed cooperatively, had become a capitalist community.

Anaheim was a brilliant success, the town growing rapidly, the vineyards becoming the best wine-producing area in California.

The years of the Civil War brought southern California only

more bad luck. The cattle market became glutted, the rancheros could not raise enough money to meet their bills. One ranchero in Santa Barbara wrote:

"Everybody in this Town is Broke not a dollar to be seen.... Cattle can be bought at any price, Real Estate is not worth anything ... the 'Chapules' (grasshoppers) have taken possession of the Town, they have eat all the Barley, Wheat &c, there is not a thing left by them. I expect if I don't move out of this Town soon, they will eat me also."

Smallpox struck, paralyzing not only the outlying ranches, which were without doctors or vaccines, but Los Angeles, where the epidemic became so virulent around the plaza that all business was closed. People remained locked in their homes.

A series of droughts began in 1862 and lasted until 1865, killing off the burr clover and dry alfilaria on the ranges, drying up the last of the water holes. Seventy per cent of the cattle died, their carcasses piled around dry creeks and streams.

"Forbidding heaps of bones and skeletons, everywhere bleaching in the sun, symbolized the ruin of the universal industry of southern California. The days of unfenced ranchos, of enormous herds of half-wild cattle, of manorial estates and pleasure-loving paisanos came to its inevitable close."

By 1865 pasture lands were valued at ten cents an acre, range cattle at a dollar a head. Five thousand cattle were sold in Santa Barbara for thirty-seven cents each. The Californios who had made fortunes driving their cattle to the mines, only to see those fortunes dissipated in their attempt to make their Spanish and Mexican land grants stand up legally before federal land commissions and courts, now were fortunate if they could keep their ranch houses and a few surrounding acres. Five sixths of the holdings became delinquent through want of money to pay taxes.

But the tragedy of the drought and the close of the Civil War opened a new era for southern California, sun-baked *manana* land during the sixteen years since the gold rush. The country was freed for small holders. For a few dollars a man could buy five or ten or twenty acres for a farm, vineyard, orchard.

Because of the similarity of climate and the millions of acres of cheap land available, the unformed frontier society which wanted and needed them, southern California became the favorite area of escape for hundreds of families from the South who had been ruined by war and embittered by defeat. They put their remaining household effects, farm implements and tools in their wagons and wound their way westward through Texas and New Mexico.

There were emigrant trains with as many as a hundred wagons and five hundred people. They started coming because of the economic prostration of the South and continued to pour in because of the harsh untenable rule of the northern Reconstructionists. Clelland speaks of "a company of fifty Mississippi families from 'among the best families of the state' who proposed to purchase ten thousand acres in southern California and restore their broken fortunes." Very shortly the foremen and superintendents of the new southern California ranches were former Confederate officers saving up money to buy land of their own.

By 1866 the population of Los Angeles had increased so sharply that city lots were in demand for the first time in the town's history. The community experienced its first building boom, wooden houses replacing the traditional adobes. Hundreds of emigrant families were excitedly "running over the ranchos" for the best agricultural lands being subdivided.

By the following year one organization was offering a hundred thousand acres for sale. Subdividing had become big business.

The first of an army of "real estate boomers" arrived on the scene in the form of attractive Robert M. Widney, thirty years old, a big man physically, strong as an ox but literate and a natural student as well as a dynamic personality. Widney was born on an Ohio farm in 1838, hunted in the Rockies, came in a wagon train to a California mining camp in 1853, worked as a woodchopper, graduated from the new College of the Pacific, taught there without salary, studied law, learned how to draw his pistol in court to defend his honor, and arrived in Los Angeles in 1868 with $100 in cash and a small trunkful of possessions.

Widney fell madly in love with southern California, rode horseback over its hills, valleys and fields to learn intimately the nature of the terrain, opened a real estate office in an adobe on Main Street and began selling his own enthusiasm by lithographing maps and circulars describing the various kinds of land available. He drove new arrivals over the countryside in his wagon with "furious energy," and by dint of giving free legal advice and guaranteed titles was soon selling thousands of acres of precisely the right kind of land for the crops his clients intended to plant. By publishing the *Real Estate Advertiser*, in which he analyzed the area's resources and charms, he became a national authority on southern California lands. People in northern California and then the East sent sums of money to this total stranger with which to buy them acreage. Local land purchases rose from $40,000 a month to $200,000 a month.

It was only the beginning.

Co-operative and mutual groups bought land together, starting towns whole. A group of thirty Methodist families from around Stockton came south in their covered wagons, bought a portion of the San Pedro rancho at $5.00 an acre and built Compton as a temperance town, with no saloon allowed, a true innovation for the hard-drinking wild West.

Southern California took the advice of the state official who had urged the wooing of Europe's artisans. By 1867 the Danish consul in San Francisco had bought five thousand acres for a group of Danes. English representatives began negotiations for a hundred-thousand-acre tract for eager British settlers. French and Swiss groups were dickering for what had been the Azusa and Santa Anita ranchos. German emigrants were looking for a second Anaheim.

Southern California was world news.

Manana land had become the land of today.

Two banks opened, a gas plant and ice factory were started, irrigation canals dug to carry the water to long-parched fields, dams constructed to conserve the winter's water and to provide power for new mills. The rich surrounding soil brought up abundant crops of corn, wheat and barley, tobacco, flax, cotton and alfalfa, while the newly planted orchards of oranges, lemons, figs and other tropical fruits brought enviable profits. Phineas Banning's wild-eyed dream of a railroad to the port of San Pedro became a reality, with manager Banning offering all residents a free round trip on opening day and a ball that evening in the company's freight warehouse, which also served as a passenger station.

In the flush of its rose-colored dawn Los Angeles organized its first Board of Education, a Social Club, opened the Pico House, the first hotel that provided such niceties as gas and hot baths. Water and gas were piped into the city's homes. The first fire company was founded in Buffum's Saloon, but it remained a fluid organization until the end of 1868 when a fire burned down an appreciable portion of the business section and the members of the fire company could do little but stand around and enjoy the spectacle. Lynching was stopped, the Vigilance Committee disappeared.

There were a few sour notes in the sweet cacophony of growth: the City Council had raised real estate assessments as much as one hundred per cent:

"Beneath the fair exterior are seen the agonized faces and heard the fearful groans of the tax payers. The taxation is appalling."

An omnipresent complaint was against the "wandering, gypsy-like poor whites commonly known as Pikes" who had also heard of the clement weather and opulent charms of Los Angeles County. "The true Pike often lives with his family in a wagon; he is frequently a squatter on other people's lands; he carries a rifle, a lot of children and dogs, a wife and if he can read, a law book. He moves from place to place, as the humor seizes him, and is generally an injury to his neighbors. He will not work regularly, but he has a great tenacity of life, and is always ready for a lawsuit."

Los Angeles thought of itself as an up-and-coming town; but there were dissenters. Mayo says in *Los Angeles*: "Here is a sleepy little Spanish-American town of six thousand population, dozing in the sun on the farthest frontier of America. It is not a seaport; neither does it have any natural resources."

Robert M. Widney knew better. Land which had sold for seventy-five cents an acre before the migration was bringing up to $10 an acre by 1868. The Rancho Tujunga, close to Los Angeles, sold for $3300 and four months later for $6000; the Marengo ranch which brought $10,000 was resold only a year later for $25,000.

As soon as the Big Four's Central Pacific had joined the Union Pacific, probably in Utah, work would be begun on a branch line from San Francisco to Los Angeles, linking southern California with the rest of the United States. When that great day arrived, said the Los Angeles boosters, nothing could hold back southern California!

CHAPTER XII

The Sweatbox of Ralston's Ring

BY THE TIME TIGHTLIPPED William Sharon reached Virginia City in the late summer of 1864 the Wells Fargo Bank had appropriated what was left of William Ralston's best customers. Sharon went down into the mines which the Bank of California had helped finance: the Yellow Jacket, Belcher, Chollar, Gould and Curry. He found that the reports of the flooding out of the mines had been authentic; the foul air was so full of poisonous gases that the few miners trying to work the veins were constantly nauseated. To the ordinary dangers of mining in the bowels of the earth were added the terrors of Dante's Inferno; no man knew when the next movement with his pick might not release a steaming geyser of hot water, scalding him, boiling his group to death in an underground river. In the Ophir a single thrust of a pick into an innocent-looking clay seam at four hundred feet brought such a stream of hot water that two days later, when the miners descended the shaft, they found a stygian, steaming, vile-smelling lake a hundred feet long, thirty feet wide, a hundred twenty deep! Overman was totally drowned out; Yellow Jacket had to be abandoned at three hundred seventeen feet.

William Sharon was one of the few formally educated men to enter the Comstock; he put his training to work for him. He studied the reports from the mines, the records of the lawsuits. From his interviews with miners, foremen and superintendents he became convinced that the Comstock consisted of fissure veins which ran far below the present five hundred feet. Having had his nephew trained as an assayer so that he would have someone he could trust, he learned that the farther down the ore went the richer it became. Sharon studied the processes and costs of production, and came to the conclusion that in their haste and greed the mine managers had discarded valuable ores. The same story of prodigal waste held true for the mills.

His report to Ralston was clear and simple: the mines still held countless millions. Once the water was cleared and controlled the veins would be rich; the profits could be vastly higher with new efficiencies of production. The Bank of California must control, if not own, every mine and mill on the Comstock! Sharon would show them how this could be done. The only thing he was not able to demonstrate, in spite of the fact that he had spent hundreds of hours discussing it with experts, was just how they were going to keep the torrential waters out of the mines.

The one expert to whom Sharon did not bother to address himself on this critical question was a small mill operator by the name of Adolph Sutro. Why should Sharon have bothered with a man who was known on the lode as "Crazy" Sutro because of his preoccupation with a harebrained idea of driving a four-mile tunnel through the bottom of Mount Davidson, from the Carson River side to the Virginia City point of the clustered shafts, to drain off the water and the gases and provide an easy method of transporting men, material and ores? Was this not as fantastic as the "quaint" proposed by the *Territorial Enterprise* of punching a hole through the top of Mount Davidson so that Virginia City, on the east side of the mountain, could have the late afternoon sunlight?

On October 4, 1865, William Sharon reopened the Virginia City branch of the Bank of California and began lending money to distressed mills at two per cent a month, considerably under the rate charged by Wells Fargo. A few of the mines had managed to remain open by making assessments on their stockholders. When the San Francisco owners could no longer come up with funds, Sharon amiably urged the mines to avail themselves of the Bank of California funds. Ralston's associates in San Francisco said this was throwing good money after bad, but Ralston had to bring back the Comstock or go broke himself.

William Sharon's plan had been conceived whole: very quickly the smaller mills failed to meet their notes. Sharon foreclosed, took over the mills and began running them himself. Those mines still working, most of which the Bank of California now controlled, were obliged to send their ore to the mills owned by the Bank of California. This forced the bigger, independent mills into bankruptcy. Sharon took them over. When there was not enough ore to keep the mills running, the superintendents of the Bank-controlled mines were instructed to mix waste rock with the ore. While the stockholders of the mines were being bled for fresh money to get the ore out at no profit whatever, the Bank of California mills were working to capacity, earning large profits, part of which were now used to buy up newly faltering mines. What was becoming known as "Ralston's Ring" formed the Union Mill and Mining Company, a stratagem analagous to the Crocker construction company of the Central Pacific Railroad.

"Sharon fed the mills belonging to the Ring to their utmost capacity, while the few remaining independent ones were utterly starved. Their owners offered to reduce ore at half the price charged by the combine, but to no avail. Not a mine on the Lode dared to help the independents."

Within a year the Bank of California had seized all the important mills and frozen the others out of business.

William Sharon, "dandyish and calculating," had attacked his job like a man possessed, determined to earn back his competence. His office at the Bank of California became known as "Sharon's

Sweatbox"; by means of his expanding control over all surrounding lumber, water, fuel and machinery he became dictator of the Comstock.

Within two years the whole of Mount Davidson was controlled by Ralston's Ring.

The Ring was hated and called foul names by those who were being squeezed to death; but Ralston and Sharon managed to console themselves with the knowledge that each of them had already cleared $4,000,000 from the Union Mill and Mining Company.

Sharon's revenge on the Comstock had been one of the quickest and juiciest in the Far West.

Few mines on Mount Davidson were now operating profitably above the water level. The miners of Virginia City began to move away, stores closed and the Bank of California loaned another $2,000,000 of its assets to mines which were operating on a fragmentary basis. The Union Mill and Mining Company was in bonanza, and what did it matter to the bank where the profits came from? The bank was mining the mills instead of the mines. Yet even this legerdemain must end if they could not get the water out of the mines and follow the ore to lower levels.

Ralston placed an order for the largest pump ever conceived in the West. It took ten months to build in San Francisco's Vulcan Iron Works, and constituted a mammoth job of hauling over the seven-thousand-foot Sierra Nevada. The engine was so big that a forty-two by forty-foot rock chamber had to be hollowed out of the mine for it, and a twenty-two-foot-long, sixteen-foot-deep stone foundation laid to hold the bed plates.

To celebrate the installation Ralston brought up a group of Bank officials from San Francisco who were lowered down the shaft in their silk hats and broadcloth coats. The pump was turned on. "Slowly, the huge iron machine, like a great antediluvian sloth coming to life, began to move and hiss, then the friction wheels of the hoisting gear, ten feet in diameter, began to revolve. Gradually the water in the sump seemed to recede."

Ralston and Sharon joined the cheers, serving champagne and caviar to celebrate their victory over the waters of the lode. In the next eight months the Gould and Curry drove down past seven hundred feet, taking out a great quantity of ore. Then a tremendous subterranean stream of water hit the huge fifty-horsepower Vulcan motor and tossed it aside as though it were a child's toy. A hundred feet of water quickly gathered in the sump. All work was discontinued.

Billy Ralston ordered another, larger machine: one-hundred-twenty horsepower, with bigger boilers and pumps. But it would take a full year to build and install, and the water was rising.

The Comstock was in *borrasca*, a Spanish work meaning barren rock.

But not to Adolph Heinrich Joseph Sutro, born on April 29, 1830 at Aix-la-Chapelle in Prussia, one of seven sons and four daughters. Adolph attended a polytechnic school which gave him a basic training in mechanics; by the time he was sixteen he was superintendent of the family cloth factory. Two years later, after his father's death, he was sent to establish and manage a branch factory in East Prussia.

The Revolution of 1848 having ruined the Sutro business, Mrs. Sutro brought her large brood to the United States. The family settled in Baltimore, but Adolph contracted gold fever. He reached San Francisco in 1851, a few months before his twenty-first birthday: tall, massive, with a strong face, big but handsomely sculptured nose, dark hair brushed thick and wavy behind his ears, with the mind of a scholar and the temperament of a warrior.

Sutro had no intention of going to the mines, rather he was attracted by the chance for success in a new booming country. For six years, while learning the language, he made a modest living in petty trade; in 1856 he married, and opened a cigar and tobacco store on Montgomery Street in San Francisco's financial district, where fast-rising William Chapman Ralston was a near neighbor. The store was a success, there might have been a branch or two but when the Comstock's silver bullion bars were paraded through the streets of San Francisco in 1859 Sutro gave up his business and joined the rush, his second.

Early in 1860 he opened a small quartz-reducing mill at East Dayton. He did not attempt to secure quartz from the mines, but studied the tailings of other mills and evolved a process which enabled him to take over their waste ore and to extract the balance of the precious metals. It was his first step into technical industry.

Now thirty years old, a practical businessman with rudimentary scientific training, Sutro spent his spare hours going down the shafts of the mines and watching the technological methods by which the ores were extracted. What he saw of inefficiency, waste and human danger appalled him. He transferred his focus of study to the back slope of Mount Davidson where it rolled downward to meet the Carson River. After a month, on April 20, 1860, he sent a letter to the San Francisco *Alta* which opened a gargantuan twenty-year struggle:

"The working of the mines is done without any system as yet. Instead of running a tunnel from low down on the hill, and then sinking a shaft to meet it, which at once insures drainage, ventilation, and facilitates the work by going upwards, the claims (the string of about twenty separate mines) are mostly entered from above and large openings made, which requires considerable timbering, and exposes the mine to all sorts of difficulty."

During the next four years while his stamp mill earned a substantial profit, Sutro studied the geological structure of the lode and the engineering aspects of his projected tunnel, as well as the best journalistic methods of convincing the public, government, mine owners and bank officials that his tunnel was the only feasible means of letting fresh air and light into the increasingly wet, black, foul-smelling mines. He brought up from San Francisco a visiting German geologist, Baron von Richthofen, who substantiated the engineering feasibility of the tunnel and endorsed the tremendous boon it would be to the health and safety of the miners, as well as to the profits of the owners.

But the boom was on, the ores were close to the surface; if there was unbelievable waste, there was an even more incredible profit. All that Adolph Sutro earned for his efforts was the title "Crazy" Sutro, even as Theodore Judah, with dreams of a transcontinental railroad, was being called "Crazy" Judah in the Sacramento Valley.

Now late in 1864 the mines were flooded, filled with poisonous gases, the miners were falling victim not only to daily accidents but to tuberculosis; the downward progression of the mines was stopped entirely.

Adolph Sutro's first step was to go to the newly formed Nevada legislature with a petition for a right of way to tunnel through Mount Davidson. Many of the legislators "thought Sutro hopelessly insane" but they were new at the business of governing a state, and since it was clear that they would have the determined Mr. Sutro in their vestibule forevermore they agreed to pass his bill; obviously he could not possibly use the franchise, so what harm could there be in getting rid of him?

Armed with what he thought to be the first public acknowledgment of the feasibility of his plan, Sutro used the proceeds of his stamp mill to hire geologists to report on the mineral character of Mount Davidson, civil engineers to plot the best line for the tunnel to take, and journalists to popularize the advantages of a tunnel to a public from which he needed to raise $3,000,000. He formed a company, the presidency of which he gave to Nevada's first United States senator, William Stewart, then took himself down to the Bank of California, to the open-door office of William C. Ralston.

Ralston was enthralled. He said, "It would be one of the country's outstanding pieces of engineering" and would end "the paralyzing heat that kept the miners from working, the noxious gases, the ever present waters, the accidents, cave-ins, stoppages. Deep mining would become practical, safe and highly profitable." He would not only endorse the Sutro Tunnel, he would urge every mining company on the Comstock to sign Sutro's agreement. He gave Sutro a letter to this effect; he gave him no money.

It took Sutro eight long months, months he wanted to use in digging the tunnel, to get the names of the twenty-three major mines on Mount Davidson on his master contract. They were not obliged to help him finance his tunnel, but once it was completed and he had drained and ventilated their mines, they must pay him $2.00 for every ton of ore mined and carried out in cars through it, plus stipulated charges for transporting the mine workers and materials.

Ralston was delighted with Sutro's progress; if Sutro could succeed where a hundred-twenty-horsepower pump had failed, the worth of the Bank of California's investment in the Comstock would increase a hundredfold. In the spring of 1866 he gave Sutro letters of recommendation on Bank of California stationery to the important banks of New York and London:

This letter will be presented to you by Mr. Sutro of this city, who visits you with the view of laying before capitalists there a very important enterprise, known as the "Sutro Tunnel" in the State of Nevada. Too much cannot be said of the great importance of this work. The scheme has been carefully examined by scientific men, and they unhesitatingly pronounced in its favor on all points— practicability, profit and great public utility.

Like Judah before him, Adolph Sutro went first to Washington, where he was able to persuade the Congress by means of his concise, irrefutable studies that they should pass a bill giving him a right of way through federal land. But he could raise no money in the East because he lacked "home endorsement," cash subscribed in California and Nevada.

Back in Virginia City in August 1866, Sutro once again prodded the Nevada legislature into passing a resolution, this time urging Congress to give him federal funds to build his tunnel. This accomplished, he went down to San Francisco; a number of Ralston's subsidiary companies and private individuals pledged $600,000. Now Sutro could get the balance from the eastern and English banks, and probably a federal government subsidy as well. He had worked dedicatedly for six years and poured out every dollar of his earnings. Now the tunnel would become a reality.

Or would it? William Sharon came down from Virginia City for a confidential meeting with Ralston's Ring. Did the gentlemen realize the full import of what would happen if Sutro pushed his tunnel through? If every ton of ore taken out of Mount Davidson brought Mr. Sutro $2.00 forevermore? He would not only become the richest operator on the Comstock but he could control the output of very mine, since he alone could determine how fast whose ore was to be moved. He could become the virtual dictator of the Comstock, take control of the mines away from the Bank of California and supplant their Union Mill and Mining Company by opening his own mills on the Carson River where the Mount Davidson ores came out the back door of his tunnel.

And what did they really need him for? Had not Sharon, with the help of Ralston's ever larger pumps, already driven three mines below the water level? Since they were solving the water problem, what reason had they to surrender their power and their millions to this outsider whom they could not control?

Quickly and lethally the word went out: Ralston did not want Sutro to build his tunnel! The $600,000 worth of pledges were canceled. After Nevada's senators Stewart and Nye received telegrams from Ralston, they began to oppose federal aid to Sutro. Senator Stewart resigned as president of Sutro Tunnel. Virginia City merchants withdrew their support. Ralston reached every bank in the East and England to whom he had recommended Sutro, urging them to bar him.

They did.

Sutro stood deserted, even by old associates, not only in Virginia City but in San Francisco, where friends or clients of the all-powerful Ralston crossed the street when Sutro came near for fear the meeting would be reported to Ralston and their credit cut off at the Bank. George D. Lyman, who knew most of the men involved, wrote in *Ralston's Ring:*

"Sutro understood. He was a financial outlaw. For the first time he realized the immense, the overwhelming power which the Bank of California exerted. Men knew, as if by magic, that Ralston and his Ring had proscribed him. He must be crushed physically and mentally. He must be driven out of the Comstock."

They misgauged their man; but they helped to educate him. Perceiving the extent of the Ring's dynastic power and the helplessness of any individual against their might, Adolph Sutro's interest turned from the engineering and financing aspects of his tunnel to the plight of the Comstock miners, who "could work but a few minutes at a time and sweat filled their loose shoes until it ran over the tops. In some parts of the mines the heat was insupportable and men frequently fell dead in consequence." At the bottom of Crown Point the temperature read 150°, "a place for salamanders rather than men."

The next two years of frustration might have broken a less stouthearted man. In New York banking circles he found himself preceded by telegrams from Comstock mine owners declaring their contracts with him "utterly null and void." He was summoned to Washington by an investigating commission set in motion by the Bank of California lobby, which questioned him on the propriety of the federal concessions granted him. George Wharton James in *Heroes of California* reports:

"Sutro acted as his own lawyer, examining and cross-examining witnesses, and more than holding his own against the clever and skillful lawyers sent by the Bank of California to harass and defeat him."

He had to demonstrate to the commission his competence as an engineer, physicist, geologist, topographer, metallurgist, and as an expert on ventilation and drainage, in all of which he had become self-trained during the past seven years.

Congress did not rescind his right-of-way grant.

But he was destitute now, obliged to sell a lot he owned in a small California town for $200, on which he eked out a winter in Washington waiting for Congress to convene and to consider the bill granting him federal aid.

That winter could not have been dull for him, for Ralston's Ring, spearheaded by William Sharon, spent a fortune in the newspapers and magazines to defame Adolph Sutro in the minds of the American people, picturing him not merely as a visionary but as a confidence man. Sharon publicly called him "an Assyrian carpetbagger," an oblique insult to his religion.

Yet when Congress met and Sutro submitted his report, the House Committee on Mines and Mining brought him into their sessions for long expositions from his charts and diagrams. They were convinced, and recommended to the House that Adolph Sutro be loaned $5,000,000 to dig his tunnel.

It was a superb victory of a lone but dedicated individual against a combine which had millions at its command. The Ring publicly accused Sutro of bribing the committee. It was Sutro's first laugh of a hard year.

"With what?" he asked. "My two hundred dollars?"

It was a stillborn victory. At that moment, in February 1868, the United States Senate began its impeachment proceedings against President Andrew Johnson. Sutro's bill for $5,000,000, with a clear majority indicated in both Houses, failed to reach the floor.

Sutro returned to San Francisco to find himself an object of ridicule. One newspaper quipped:

"Sutro has just returned from boring Congress with his bore."

The Ring-controlled press refused to run Sutro's own statements, even at advertising rates. But the hardest of all for him to bear was the jeering of children as he walked down the street.

It took the intense fire of tragedy to sear through the influence of Ralston's Ring.

On April 7, 1869 the night shift of the Yellow Jacket, Kentuck and Crown Point mines, connected by horizontal tunnels, came up out of their shafts complaining of the smell of smoke. No sooner had the hundred miners of the day shift descended the shafts than flames, chips of burning wood and bellowing fumes spewed out of the openings as though shot out of a gun.

The whistles of the Yellow Jacket shrieked through the early morning air. Fire engines from Virginia City and Gold Hill came pounding up the road. The miners' families, the women and children and old men, came running.

The first cage ascended the Yellow Jacket shaft eight hundred feet in twenty-four seconds, saving the men who had clambered on. They had tales to tell of the furnace of flames below, of men asphyxiated, falling off platforms into the fire. The cage came up again carrying the three Bechel brothers, the eldest lying on the floor, dead, the middle brother clinging by one hand to the upright of the cage, holding in his other hand the torso of his youngest brother, whose head and arms had been decapitated by the upward plunge of the cage.

By nine in the morning the smoke had cleared sufficiently in the Kentuck shaft to allow a rescue crew to descend. They returned with two bodies. By noon firemen were able to enter the Yellow Jacket to the eight-hundred-foot level; they could recover only four more bodies. At the Crown Point the cage was sent down with a lantern hung above a message written on a large piece of pasteboard reading:

"It is death to attempt to come up from where you are. The gas in the shaft is terrible. . . . Write a word to us and send it up on the cage, and let us know where you are."

The cage came back up. No word.

Kentuck and Crown Point continued to throw off stifling columns of smoke. Firemen again entered the Yellow Jacket, carrying hose. Three inches of boiling water stood on the floor of the drifts. The bodies of men who had thrown themselves into the shaft to escape burning alive were brought to the surface. By two o'clock the next morning thirteen had been recovered. Fifty-one men, in varying states of burn and consciousness, had been saved. There were still thirty-six missing. Rescue crews volunteered. Though the fire was increasing in intensity, they found ten more bodies.

By April 10 all hope was abandoned for the twenty-six men still trapped below. The shaft openings were covered with planks, wet blankets and earth, and steam was turned into the Yellow Jacket for two days in an attempt to put out the fires.

The fires burned on, for days, for weeks. Toward the end of May one gallery was sealed.

Forty-nine men had perished.

What was unmistakably clear was that Sutro's tunnel, directly under the three mines, would have provided a quick, safe escape for the forty-nine dead miners. The mining community of the Comstock believed in its bitterness that Ralston and Sharon were responsible for the deaths.

Ralston contributed $5000 to the widows and orphans. Sharon cleared the debris, ordered work to be resumed. There would be no changes.

Except for Adolph Sutro. For days, for weeks he had not left the mines, helping in the rescue work, going below to study the nature of the damage. He saw more surely than ever that, ventilated from below, the fire could never have combined with the gases to cause the holocaust. With men and materials able to reach it, the fire could have been controlled from below. In the deepest recesses of his Old Testament soul he felt morally responsible: he had let Ralston's Ring defeat him.

But they would never stop him again. He wrote, printed and then distributed handbills through the streets of Virginia City and every mining community for miles around. He plastered huge posters to the sides of buildings, picturing in vivid colors the horror of the men trapped in the fires. For two months he worked like one possessed to acquaint the miners with a meeting he would address at Maguire's Opera House; and for two months he worked passionately on his brief, so that he could tell them the full story of his nine-year struggle against the combined wealth and power of the Ring.

On August 19, 1869, the miners of Nevada jammed Maguire's Opera House. The man who stood before them on the stage, alone, unbefriended, had grown immeasurably since he had left his cigar business a decade before to join the Comstock rush. He was a Jeremiah now, his long black hair shot with gray, his eyes flashing fire. He reviewed the stock manipulations of the Bank; the freezing out of the individual mill owners, the corrupt use of the mines for the profits of the Union Mill and Mining Company. He reviewed his own unequal contest.

"It became evident to me that the Ring entertained the opinion that their combined efforts must soon crush me out and use me up financially, physically and mentally in such an unequal contest. But...I was determined that this base, unscrupulous and mercenary combination should not carry out its purpose, and made a sacred vow that I would finish this work if I had to devote the whole balance of my life to it."

The miners, too, had nowhere to turn. Their union had been able to help only in maintaining wage scales. Adolph Sutro would be their only voice...the only one with the strength and fortitude to continue battling the Ring.

The applause was a deafening roar. When at last it quieted, Sutro had the Opera House darkened and showed magic lantern slides he had prepared of the horrors, the asphyxiation, the tortured death in the fires of the Yellow Jacket. When he had shown his last slide to a now hushed, weeping audience, he said quietly:

"Rouse up, then, fellow-citizens. You have no Andrew Jackson among you to crush out the Bank which has taken your liberties, but you have the power within yourselves. I do not mean to incite you to any violence; I do not mean to have you assert your rights by riot, force and threats...but I do mean to say that you can destroy your enemy by simple concert of action. Let all of you join in together to build the tunnel; that is the way to reach them. They do already tremble lest you will act."

Miners sitting before Adolph Sutro said they recognized his voice: it was their voice, the voice of the people. Out of their pockets, out of their savings, out of the slim coffers of the Miners' Union they assembled $50,000 in cash, the first actual hard money to be put into Sutro's hand.

It was a small, golden key that would unlock Mount Davidson.

CHAPTER XIII

The Saints War with the Gentile Merchants

IF THE OUTSIDE WORLD was chiefly caught up in the battle against polygamy, within Utah there were other problems demanding Brigham Young's attention.

The Morrisite affair was the major western religious defection from the ranks of the Mormons and, because it ended in violence, became the most widely publicized outside Utah. Joseph Morris was an uneducated Welshman converted to Mormonism in 1849, immigrating to Utah in 1853. He had been farming in the isolated community of Weber County for six years when he began to have visions and to hear revelations of himself as "the seventh angel spoken of in the Revelation of Saint John." As the new Prophet he wrote to Brigham Young, asking for an interview. Brigham Young ignored him. Morris then sent a barrage of letters to Salt Lake outlining Brigham Young's failures and the reforms needed in the Church of the Latter-day Saints.

In his own community Joseph Morris was more convincing: about a hundred of his neighbors believed that he was indeed the new Prophet. When the bishop of the ward, Richard Cook, became a convert, Brigham Young took Joseph Morris seriously for the first time, sending two of the Church's Council of Twelve, Wilford Woodruff and John Taylor, to the mouth of Weber Canyon to investigate. At a public meeting held in February 1861 Bishop Cook announced his allegiance to Prophet Morris. He was excommunicated, along with Morris and a number of others.

Weber County flamed into revolt. Morris became Prophet of a new church, with Richard Cook and John Banks as his Council. Within a year the sect, which believed in the imminent second coming of Christ, and held all their goods in common against the coming of the Day, had enrolled some six hundred former Mormons. Then an argument broke out as to whether dissident members had the right to withdraw their original chattels in toto from the commune.

Affidavits were presented to Chief Justice Kinney in Salt Lake, charging that Prophet Morris was holding four dissident members prisoner at his stronghold, Kingston Fort. Writs were served on Prophet Morris. He ignored them. The marshal reported back to Salt Lake that Morris had been protected by "at least one hundred armed men." The court now issued writs for the arrest of Prophet Morris and Councilors Cook and Banks. Robert T. Burton, described by *A Comprehensive History of the Church* as a prominent member of the Latter-day Saints, took command of the two hundred fifty troops of Mormon Militia, camped on the heights above Fort Kingston, and sent a message to the Morrisites that they had thirty minutes to surrender or they would be taken by force.

Inside the fort Prophet Morris withdrew to his quarters for a revelation. It came, but a trifle late: the thirty minutes elapsed just as he returned to his people, who were assembled in the open yard of the fort. Commanding Officer Burton gave the signal to fire. A cannon ball exploded inside the fort, killing two women and blowing the jaw off a young girl. A second cannon ball killed two more women. The militia was then ordered to close in on the fort, whereupon the Morrisites began firing. They killed a militiaman.

The siege lasted for three days. A Morrisite came out with a white flag. Commanding Officer Burton entered the fort to arrest those named in the writs. Morris is said to have cried:

"All who are for me and my God, in life and death, follow me!"

The militia fired again. Morris, Cook and Banks were killed. Two more women were shot dead. The insurrection was over.

Seventeen years later Commanding Officer Burton would be arraigned for murder; but now he was complimented by the chief justice "for the able manner in which he had discharged his duty, and with so little loss of life," in putting down what the *Deseret News* called:

"The first armed resistance to the laws that has been made in the Territory."

Ninety-six Morrisites were indicted for resisting arrest, ten of them for the murder of a militiaman. Sixty Morrisites were tried, convicted and fined $100. Seven of the ten indicted were found guilty of second degree murder and given long prison sentences.

The new federal governor, Stephen S. Harding, pardoned all the

Morrisites. The Church declared him to be:

"An officer dangerous to the peace and prosperity of the Territory, the crowning triumph of his inglorious career the turning loose upon the community a large number of criminals."

General Connor offered refuge at Camp Douglas to the Morrisites. Some of them eventually left the territory, others returned to their original Church.

A second religious dissident was W. S. Godbe, a prosperous merchant of Utah and founder of an unsuccessful literary publication in Salt Lake City, *The Utah Magazine*. In the summer of 1868 he went to New York to buy goods for his store and took with him the editor of his magazine, E.L.T. Harrison. On the long coach trip East they studied the Book of Mormon and came up with some heretical ideas. As *A Comprehensive History of the Church* says:

"The contents of the Book of Mormon, critically viewed, was a terrible test of credulity, and many of the revelations of 'the Lord' savored too much of Joseph Smith, and abounded with contradictions.... As for Brigham, many of his measures were utterly devoid of even commercial sense, and far less were they clothed with divine wisdom."

In New York City, while Godbe bought supplies for his store, his editor wrote a series of challenging questions about the Book of Mormon. During the evenings in their hotel room the two men went on their knees to pray for guidance, asking for answers to their questions. The answers came, and laid the foundation for a revised form of Mormonism which Godbe and Harrison launched as soon as they got back to Salt Lake, founding a new magazine and then a newspaper to carry the voice into the wilderness.

In the fall of 1869 the High Council in Salt Lake charged Godbe and Harrison with apostasy and excommunicated them from the Church. As inevitably happens with opposition, Godbe's rival church now gained a number of members, called Godbeites, and began to hold public meetings on Sunday. Godbe's Church of Zion was similar to Mormonism except that there was no priesthood, and the ten per cent tithe was reduced in proportion to people's ability to pay.

All of the followers of Godbe were now excommunicated. Harrison wrote:

"We inquired whether it was not possible for us to honestly differ from the presiding priesthood, and were answered that such a thing was impossible."

In his struggle with Brigham Young, Godbe lost his prosperous business and very soon his church and followers as well. Godbe himself went to England to organize a mining company which would subsequently prove successful in Utah.

When Brigham Young settled his Saints in the Great Basin, many hundred miles from his nearest neighbor, he hoped and had every right to expect several decades of isolation in which to build Zion. Instead the discovery of gold had brought thousands of rushers across Utah. With California permanently opened as a new and rich frontier, Salt Lake found itself on one of the main transcontinental thoroughfares. Merchants who came into Salt Lake, which had become known as "The Half Way House" between the Missouri River and the Pacific coast, were made welcome and enjoyed cordial relations with the Church, Christians and Jews alike, it being a source of amusement to the latter to be living in the one place in the world where they were known as gentiles, their own term, coined almost two thousand years before, to describe all peoples outside their fold. Brigham Young and his Council asked only that the gentile merchants be sympathetic to Zion and steer clear of the opponents of Mormonism. Although the profits of the gentile merchants could not be tithed as were those of the Saints, the outside capital, goods and skills were important in helping Salt Lake grow.

Goods had always been high in Salt Lake because of their scarcity and the difficulty of bringing them in. In 1961 it was claimed that:

"Gentile merchants made a hundred and twenty to six hundred percent profit on their invested capital."

Samuel Bowles, who was in Salt Lake in 1864, wrote, "Several firms did a business of a million or more dollars a year, and one firm made seventy-five percent profit that year."

It was an integral part of Brigham Young's economic philosophy to discourage his people from buying anything but imperatives, women being urged not to spend money on clothes, but to wear the austere Deseret uniform all year round. He preached against the use of tea, coffee and tobacco not only on the moral grounds that they were artificial stimulants but also because they had to be imported and would drain the sorely needed cash from the community. To the women clamoring for new styles he said in a Sunday sermon in September 1861:

"Give us a little Gentilism, the women say, let us wear hoops, because the whores wear them. I believe if they were to come with a cob stuck in their behind, you would want to do the same. There is not a day I go out but I see the women's legs, and if the wind blows you see them up to their bodies. Who cares about these Gentiles? ... I know I ought to be ashamed, but when you show your t'other end I have a right to talk about t'other end."

The men fared little better. Trying to preserve the barn-door pants for men, which folded over and buttoned on the side, and were being displaced by the convenient gentile button-down-the-front pants, Heber Kimball, Brigham Young's faithful voice, thundered:

"I am opposed to your nasty fashions and everything you wear for the sake of fashion. Did you ever see me with hermaphrodite pantaloons on? (Voice from the congregation: 'Fornication pantaloons.') Our boys are weakening their backs and their kidneys by girting themselves up as they do; they are destroying the strength of their loins and taking a course to injure their posterity."

Brigham Young added, "I consider them uncomely and indecent. If it were the fashion to go with them unbuttoned I expect you would see plenty of our Elders wearing them unbuttoned."

Brigham Young's efforts to achieve economy on the part of women's dress, perhaps accentuated by the fact that he himself had to dress twenty-seven wives and thirty-one daughters, were of heroic proportions, but did him no good, neither the thundering nor the jibes. The subject of dress was the one field in which the Mormon women, including Brigham Young's wives, rendered considerably less than total obedience.

The first conflict of mercantile interests came from inside the Church; the dissenters were the four Walker brothers, described by Morgan in *The Great Salt Lake* as:

"Central figures in the economic warfare which shook the Utah village during the last half of the 1860's."

When General Johnston's army was recalled by Congress after the Mountain Meadows massacre, it left behind large quantities of surplus material and equipment which could not be secured anywhere else in Utah, and which were sold to the Mormon merchants for a fraction of their value. The merchants flourished also on the free-spending soldiers of General Connor's troops stationed in Utah during the Civil War.

The four Walkers were English, having come to Utah in 1852 when their widowed mother was converted. They were young when they arrived, and sports-loving. To the Mormons, in their death grip with nature to wrest a living from her, sports were a foolish waste of time; but the Walker boys built and launched the first sailboat used on the Great Salt Lake. They joined the Church, paid their tithes, and were obedient—up to a point: the point at which they had achieved economic independence through their large stores.

In 1863 they refused to pay ten per cent of their income as a tithe. Their motivation appears to have been a chafing at the disciplines of the Church rather than miserliness, for they offered to pay the same ten per cent directly to the poor. To the Church this was an insufferable affront. The Walkers were so informed. One of the brothers riposted by sending a check for $500 to the bishop of his ward, the money to be used for charity. The check was taken to Brigham Young. He refused to accept it. The Walker brothers tore it up.

His power challenged, Brigham Young ordered the Mormons to stay out of the Walker stores. Their business fell from $60,000 a month to $5000. They were able to survive only because some of the Mormons, wanting or needing their goods, bought secretly. Brigham Young excommunicated the Walkers. They replied by donating $1000 to the Perpetual Emigration Fund to bring over poor converts from England.

In the October Conference of 1865 Brigham Young proposed to his congregation that they do their own merchandising and "cease to give the wealth which the Lord has given us to those who would destroy the kingdom of God and scatter us to the four winds, if they had the power. Let every one of the Latter-day Saints, male and female, decree in their hearts that they will buy of nobody else but their own faithful brethren, who will do good with the money they will thus obtain."

Then in March of 1866 S. Newton Brassfield, a gentile who had come to Salt Lake to open a business, met and courted Mrs. Mary Emma Hill, one of the plural wives of a Mormon Elder who was on a mission to England. Brassfield, who believed Mary Hill legally unmarried as a plural wife, proposed and was accepted. Mary, wanting to retrieve some household goods, went with her new husband to her former home . . . only to be stopped at the door by police. Brassfield drew a revolver, was arrested on a charge of "assault with intent to kill." The new Mrs. Brassfield went to court to secure custody of her children by Elder Hill, but the case was terminated by a shot from an alleyway while Brassfield was entering his boardinghouse in the company of a United States marshal.

Mormons who believed Mrs. Hill to have been legally married to Mr. Hill thought that Brassfield got what was coming to him. Non-Mormons inside Utah were frightened lest this be the start of a reign of terror against all gentiles. The rest of the country was appalled at the killing, refusing to believe that it had been personal vengeance at the hands of a relative of the injured Elder Hill. The federal volunteers at Camp Douglas, about to be dismissed, were retained by orders from Washington until regular troops could supplant them. Major General William Tecumseh Sherman sent Brigham Young a scorching telegram, telling Young of:

"Experienced soldiers who would be pleased at a fair opportunity to avenge any wrongs you may commit against any of our citizens."

The murderer of Newton Brassfield was never apprehended.

Six months later a second killing, that of Dr. J. King Robinson, a native of Maine who had come to Utah in 1864 as a surgeon to the troops at Camp Douglas, further alarmed the gentile community because it too was tied into a Church conflict, this time over Mormon land grants. Rumors that all public lands held by Salt Lake City were not legally theirs because the Utah Territory had failed to set up a legal municipal government, had the Mormons in a state of anxiety lest the lands be thrown into the public domain and squatters flock in to settle them. So many lawyers had already invaded Salt Lake to undertake litigation for new squatters that Brigham Young wrote to a son in England:

"Armies have not been found to operate well in breaking us up, but it is now hoped that vexatious lawsuits may do it."

Dr. Robinson was married to the daughter of a Mormon Elder, and was superintendent of a gentile Sunday school; although charged with being a head of an anti-Mormon clique, he enjoyed an excellent personal reputation. Dr. Robinson claimed title to a tract of eighty acres of land on the northern edge of the city, called Warm Springs, which the city had been using as a public bathing resort. The doctor built a shanty on the land which the City Council ordered destroyed, and a bowling alley as well. The case was being tried in the Salt Lake courts when it was terminated in the same abrupt fashion as the Brassfield case: the doctor was called out of his house one midnight on the grounds that his medical services were required, and a block from his home was set upon by a mob, including one police officer, and beaten to death.

Ex-Governor of California John B. Weller, retained by the gentiles of Utah to prosecute the case, charged the brutal crime against Church officials in his speech before the coroner's court. Brigham Young denounced the crime with vehemence in the Tabernacle, likening it, for its senselessness and brutality, to the Mountain Meadows massacre almost a decade before. The community, now split wide open by a roaring river of suspicion and fear, raised $9000 in rewards for the capture of the seven who murdered.

No one was arrested.

Late in December of 1866 twenty-three of the leading non-Mormon firms in Salt Lake came together in a meeting and decided that they had had enough, that under the proper circumstances they would get out of Zion. Their petition was submitted to the leaders of the Mormon Church, and appears to have beeen a sincere effort to settle their accounts:

"Gentlemen: As you are instructing the people of Utah, through your Bishops and missionaries, not to trade or do any business with the Gentile merchants, thereby intimidating and coercing the community to purchase only of such merchants as belong to your faith and persuasion ... believing it to be your earnest desire for all to leave the country who do not belong to your faith and creed, the undersigned Gentile merchants of Salt Lake City respectfully desire to make you the following proposition...."

As prerequisite for their "freely leaving the territory" the gentile community asked that the Church collect all accounts owed them by members in good standing; secondly, that the Church take at cash valuation, minus twenty-five per cent, all their goods, merchandise, chattels, houses and improvements.

Brigham Young could have collected most of the accounts owed by the Church members, and could have bargained on the cash value of the goods and improvements of those wanting to get out. But he knew by now that the transcontinental railroad would be completed within a few years, that the trains would run through Utah bringing a constant stream of people from both East and West. He could not keep out gentile businessmen forever; all that he could hope to do was to divert Mormon trade into Mormon channels. He also perceived that any such exorcising of the entire gentile business population from a United States territory might result in another wave of anti-Mormonism.

Brigham Young refused the petition:

"We will not obligate ourselves to collect your outstanding accounts, nor buy your goods, merchandise and other articles that you express your willingness to sell.... Your withdrawal from the territory is not a matter about which we feel any anxiety; so far as we are concerned, you are at liberty to stay or go, as you please.

"To be adverse to Gentiles because they are Gentiles, or Jews because they are Jews, is in direct opposition to the genius of our religion.... We have not the least objection to doing business with him if, in his dealings, he act in accordance with the principles of right and deport himself as a good, law-abiding citizen should."

The gentiles remained.

Having started the boycott, Brigham Young in 1867 extended it to certain other firms which he now charged with being hostile to Mormonism or collaborating with anti-Mormon agitators.

By the October 1868 Conference, in reply to his self-imposed question, "How tight are you going to draw the reins?" Brigham Young answered:

"I want to tell my brethren, my friends, and my enemies that we are going to draw the reins so tight as not to let a Latter-day Saint trade with an outsider."

The question of establishing a central wholesale and retail store in Salt Lake, to be owned by members of the Church and governed by them, was brought into focus. An organization was created, elected Brigham Young president, set up a board of directors, then drafted a constitution. Its purpose was to supply the wants of the Mormons; all profits from merchandising to remain in the hands of the Mormons. Stock in Zion's Cooperative Mercantile Institution would be offered to everyone "who shall be of good moral character and have paid their tithing according to the rules of the Church of Jesus Christ of Latter-day Saints.

"The inhabitants of Utah, convinced of the impolicy of leaving the trade and commerce of their territory to be conducted by strangers, have resolved, in public meeting assembled, to unite in a system of cooperation for the transaction of their own business.... The Directors shall tithe its net profits prior to any declaration of dividends."

The co-operative enterprise did not start from scratch; rather the directors purchased seven existing mercantile enterprises, six of which were owned by Mormons, and one by Nicholas S. Ransohoff, a Jewish gentile who had long been a friend of Brigham Young. The Z.C.M.I. slowly proceeded to open branch stores in other cities, usually absorbing an existing business. Within five years those who had invested in the Z.C.M.I. stock, or turned in their businesses for the stock, made a two hundred per cent profit on their original investment.

Now with its own official stores, the campaign to discourage Church members from buying from gentile merchants was stepped up in intensity, being preached at the Tabernacle in Salt Lake and at ward meetinghouses. It was also charged by the gentiles that the police, all of whom were Mormons, intimidated Church members who would have liked to trade elsewhere.

The results for the gentile merchants were disastrous, their businesses falling off to a tenth of what they had done before. Though a few of the larger stores were able to continue, the smaller ones either moved their stock to the new gentile community that had been established in Utah or left the territory.

There was no peace in Zion.

By 1869 the near decade of isolation due to the Civil War and the difficult years of the Reconstruction was ended. Congress began its determined concentration on Utah, polygamy and certain other aspects of Church and state control which were unacceptable to the rest of the nation. In 1869 the Cullom Bill passed the House by a three-to-one majority, and then the Senate, to become what was called:

"The first effective anti-polygamist legislation."

But the Cullom Bill, which caused an acrimonious debate on Mormonism in every town in America, was rejected by the moderate newspapers because it took away from the Mormons the right of trial by jury, and almost every vestige of self-government. No attempt was ever made to enforce it.

However it was the forerunner of legislation which would be constitutional, and which the federal government would spend a number of years enforcing. The Edmunds Bill would finally bring the federal government and Utah to grips over plural marriage. One or the other would have to succumb.

CHAPTER XIV

It Is Hard for a Land to Be Born

IT IS NEVER EASY for a land to be born.

Colorado settled hard. By autumn of 1863 Denver had only a third as many people as it had had six years before, while the formerly vigorous towns of Boulder, Colorado City and Golden, gateways to the gold fields, were in a similarly sad predicament. It had taken the same three years for the easily obtainable surface gold to run out in Colorado that it had in California and Nevada. Colorado's miners were convinced that the richest ores remained to be mined, if the proper extraction process could be found. Heavy reducing machinery hauled by ox teams across the plains and then high into the Rockies proved worthless and had to be abandoned.

Colorado's case was compounded by the trouble of the times; several thousand young men returned to their homes to enlist in the Union or Confederate armies. The total population fell to twenty thousand. All migration into the area stopped. The mines produced less money all the time, the hundred-odd mills retained merely skeleton crews. Eastern capitalists were unhappy because they had invested large sums in highly touted Colorado mines only to find that the local jokers had "salted" them and gone south with the money. All investment capital stopped coming in. Colorado, with the cleanest, freshest, most intoxicating air in the Far West, had gotten itself into bad odor.

Agriculture was booming; by 1863 it was producing $3,500,000 worth of food a year, $500,000 less than was produced in bullion. Coal was being mined in small amounts along Clear Creek, some oil was taken out near Canon City, which was used for lighting and lubrication, small flour and lumber mills were working, brickyards and stone quarries, breweries and a pottery plant at Golden, a salt works in South Park. But if the mines ran dry, if no new color was discovered, what precious metal could be used to prime the pump? How could the land grow rich, the territory become a state, the people prosper and multiply? It is not possible for a newly opened land to stand still; to do so is to wither and die; the forces of nature see to that.

Fire struck first, on April 19, 1863, at about three in the morning. As in San Francisco and Virginia City, both of which burned down at frequent intervals, there was a combination of highly available wind and no available water. The City Council had provided for a hook and ladder company and two bucket brigades, but nothing had been done about them. A number of small buildings were torn down as a potential firebreak but the winds carried the flames over them, burning the entire center of the city.

A second destroying force struck the following spring; this time there was too much water instead of too little. Cherry Creek was described by the people who built their stores, shops and homes on its banks as "an inoffensive little stream, sometimes almost invisible with its broad sandy bed, hot and dry." Heavy rains in the mountains caused the creek to rise slowly; then one midnight, while most of the town slept, the somnolent creek became a roaring torrent, taking with it the city hall and its records, the *Rocky Mountain News*, whose press and type were spread for miles below, Trinity Church and every building near its banks. Houses not swept away were taken off their foundations and moved across the street. Eight men lost their lives. On Plum Creek four thousand sheep were drowned; $25,000 in property was destroyed.

As though fire and flood were not enough, a war now developed. Colorado's plains Indians, the tall, swift-moving Arapahos, Cheyennes and Sioux, were unhappy: when the Pike's Peak gold rush started, the federal government treatied them out of eastern Colorado for what they considered a negligible $30,000 a year. When the Civil War broke out the plains Indians believed that their Great Spirit had set the white men to fighting each other so that the Indians could take back Colorado, "the land of their fathers and their buffalo."

The plains Indians, under Cheyenne Chief Black Kettle and Arapaho Chief Left Hand, started by buying horses and firearms and attacking the overland mail. When Governor Evans's emissary explained to the tribes that the government wanted them to settle on their reservation and live like white men, the chiefs replied:

"Tell the governor we are not reduced quite that low yet!"

The immediate start of the warfare was provided by an encounter between the First Colorado Cavalry and the equally well-mounted Cheyennes, followed by the murder and scalping of a settler named Hungate, his wife and two children on their ranch thirty miles south of Denver. When the four mutilated bodies were brought to Denver and put on public view, panic seized the town. Many wives and children were brought for safekeeping to the second story of the United States Mint building. Business houses were closed at dusk by order of the governor, the few guns left in Colorado were gathered, all able-bodied men drilled in the streets.

But the plains Indians did not aspire to become city fighters. They made swift attacks on stages, mail coaches, freight trains, outlying ranches, killing occupants and running off cattle, paralyzing passenger and food supply lines, earning Colorado the reputation as the most dangerous area in the United States to settle.

Emigrants for Colorado, waiting at the Missouri River, refused to travel overland. Mail was rerouted by way of Panama and California. All freighting of merchandise and equipment ceased. Prices soared out of buying sight, a few entrepreneurs taking advantage of Colorado's plight to corner the market on flour and other foodstuffs. Little meat was available, for:

"Dead cattle, full of arrows, are lying in all directions."

Washington authorized Governor Evans to enlist a militia regiment of one-hundred-day men. The governor issued a proclamation "appealing to the citizens to be good patriots and kill all hostile Indians," at the same time urging friendly tribes to gather at Fort Lyon where they would be fed and given protection. Since the *Rocky Mountain News* had recently proclaimed:

"A few months of active extermination against the red devils will bring quiet," the Indians somewhat understandably did not rush to the protection of Fort Lyon. Instead they continued their marauding, fighting through a summer of skirmishes with Colorado's militia and federal troops.

But with the harsh winter of the plains coming on, the Arapahos and Cheyennes decided that it was time to smoke the pipe of peace. They offered to exchange prisoners and call off hostilities. General S.R. Curtis of the United States Army, commanding the Department of Kansas, did not want to conciliate the Indians, maintaining that "it would be better to whip them before giving them anything more than some tobacco to smoke."

By the middle of October, Chief Left Hand brought his Arapahos to Fort Lyon, returning some of the fruits of the summer's raids. The commander of the fort, Major Scott J. Anthony, was friendly, issued them provisions and sent the Arapahos with their squaws and children to Sand Creek, on the border of their reservation. Here they were joined by the Cheyennes under Black Kettle, also with their squaws, children and a winter's provision from Fort Lyon. Together, the tribes made up a village of about eight hundred. They flew an American flag over the chief's lodge as a sign that the pipe of peace had been satisfactorily smoked. The Sioux did not come in.

At the end of November, Colonel John M. Chivington, a six-footer who had been a combination blacksmith and preacher in Kansas during the Border War over slavery, acting on his own initiative, without orders from Washington or Fort Leavenworth, decided to put an end to the bothersome Indian problem. A colonel during the Civil War, at the head of the Colorado Regiment, and now a federal officer in command of Colorado, he set forth from The Bijou, a hundred miles southeast of Fort Lyon, with the Third Regiment (the hundred-day-men) reinforced by the First Colorado Cavalry, marched to Fort Lyon, picked up two cannons and another hundred twenty-five men under Major Anthony, and covered the additional forty miles to Sand Creek without revealing his intent to anyone. He surrounded the Indian village, cut off their horses, ordered a surprise daylight attack and directed that no prisoners be taken, that all be killed.

Sand Creek was a natural trap; few of the Indians could escape. Left Hand was shot down as he walked toward the troops with his hands raised in a traditional peace gesture. Five hundred of the Indians were slaughtered, their women and children scalped. The barbarity of the American troops was equal to the worst savagery charged against the Indians during the plains wars.

By his action the intrepid Colonel Chivington united all Indians in Colorado, not only the remaining plains tribes but the Sioux, Comanche, Apaches, Kiowas and short, heavy-set mountain Utes, who traditionally hated the plains Indians more than they did the newly arrived whites, and who had been held in check by their great Chief Ouray, friend of the white settlers and highly respected by them. The winter of 1864-1865 was for Colorado an unrelenting reign of terror, the Indians destroying everything they could lay their hands on: telegraph lines, ranches, warehouses, devastating every mile of the stage route from Julesburg to Denver, firing Julesburg, attacking and killing soldiers at isolated forts. All roads to Denver were closed. The city lay under siege. Flour went up to $50 a barrel, newspapers were printed on wrapping paper. Those families remaining in the mountain areas suffered acutely.

It is hard for a land to be born. Yet, once born, it is even harder to destroy.

After the fire which burned down most of Denver, money was found for brick and stone buildings. After the flood, Denver united to help rebuild a unified city. People who lost their homes, their property, their businesses remained to rebuild, to dig in deeper.

And they never gave up searching for the Mother Lode which they were convinced lived in the heart of the Rockies.

The Colorado story resembles the California and Nevada stories in its gold and silver frame; the portrait of its people and its happenings is uniquely its own.

Take a gulch, for instance, in the Arkansas Valley at the headwaters of the Arkansas where the river is born of the fast-descending snow waters. To the west is the Saguache Range with twenty peaks standing with their bare white shoulders to the sky, eternally covered by snow. The lower ranges of hills and the valleys are covered with thick virgin forest of spruce and pine. Only a few Indians and possibly one or two white hunters had ever gazed upon this mountain paradise over which stood two of the highest peaks in America: Mount Elbert, which went up to 14,431 feet, and Mount

Massive, 14,404 feet. Above lay the Continental Divide.

Into this mountain fastness stumbled a character called Abe Lee, said to be a Virginian related to Robert E. Lee. Lee had gone out to California in 1849 and spent a whole decade mining for beans. He was at the head of one of two groups who had found a promising gulch at the headwaters of the Arkansas. Lee chose the southern end of the gulch, started panning.

"What have you got, Abe?" asked one of his comrades.

"I got the hull state of Californy in this goddam pan, that's what I got," cried Lee.

He sat down at the site of his strike, took a long swig out of his whiskey bottle, gazed at the pan of color held between his knees, then took a handful of the dirt and tossed it in the air, baptizing both himself and the land above him with gold, naming it "California Gulch." He took out a pouch of gold, lost it to the gamblers in Denver and promptly disappeared.

Or take Daniel Pound, of the breed of hunter-nomad who pretend to search for gold but do not really want to find it. He traveled with a pick, rifle, shovel and blanket roll, shot game which he roasted over a fire. In South Park he went to the trouble of building a couple of sluice boxes to wash down the dirt he was mining. A prospector came by, looked into Pound's pan and exclaimed:

"You've got gold there!"

"The hell you say," Pound replied, whereupon he picked up his pick, shovel, gun and blanket roll and fled deeper into the mountains.

Or meet Joe Higginbotham, wandering gold digger who prospected in California Gulch and also at Daniel Pound's site in South Park. One night he went to sleep beside a huge rock which he used as a windbreak; in the morning he began prospecting where he had slept. There had been gold lying beneath him all night; and there was gold in the stream at the bottom of the little valley. Joe promptly got drunk, told the news of his discovery to the first prospector who came along. The site was named Buckskin Joe because Joe Higginbotham never wore anything but buckskins; that toothsome honor was all Higginbotham got out of the great find for, like Abe Lee and Daniel Pound, he vanished without any trace of the gold he had discovered.

Or take three perennial prospectors: Dave Fulton, John Thompson and Joe Watson. Fulton was attracted to Colorado by the Pike's Peak fever, leaving a family and a farm back in Ohio. He intended to return home in a few months with enough gold to build a beautiful house and buy a carriage with matched horses to take his wife and children to church on Sunday. He stayed in the gold areas for ten years, accumulating only enough to replace his clothes and feed himself. Unlike the miners who returned to Denver when the snows fell, Fulton locked himself into a cabin with some supplies and read Thomas Paine straight through the winter.

John Thompson had come into California with Abe Lee, no one knew from where; a tall, lean man with long whiskers. He lived alone, improved and rebuilt his cabin so often that folks thought it looked like a fort. He never found any gold. People said this was because he had brought along a fiddle and preferred to play "Devil's Dream" and "The White Cockade" rather than look for the color.

Joe Watson was so well educated that everyone thought him to be a university graduate and schoolteacher. He spent his years wandering over the Rockies searching for gold . . . but not very hard. He never found any. There was always a question of whether he was not afraid of what the discovery of gold might do to him.

Take "Aunt" Clara Brown, who proved to Colorado that gold is where you find it: born into slavery in Virginia in 1800, her family was "sold apart." When she earned her freedom in 1859 she traveled directly to Central City where she opened a laundry, saved $10,000 by 1866 and returned to the South to locate her three daughters and thirty-one other relatives, bringing them all back to Colorado with her.

"After she gave everything she possessed to charity, in her last years she was cared for by the Pioneer Society, of which she was a member."

Conversely, take George Pullman, who earned a quick $150,000 not by mining but by lending money at twenty per cent interest a month. Colorado thinks Pullman also earned his idea for the Pullman car from the early cabins in which he slept, each of which had a large number of miners sleeping in tiers of bunks along the wall.

Best of all, take Augusta Tabor, sedate young New England wife of a former Vermont stonecutter with the portentous name of Horace Austin Warner Tabor. H.A.W., as he was called from his three first names, had been brought into Augusta's home by her father because he needed a stonecutter. Augusta attempted to reform Tabor of his migratory habits and drinking, and married him. Tabor dragged her out to Kansas in April 1856, where they settled in the midst of one hundred sixty acres at Manhattan, and in the midst of the John Brown free state versus slavery warfare.

At the first cry of gold in Colorado, Tabor walked off his farm, worked as a stonecutter to accumulate some cash and moved his wife and infant son to Denver. One of the earliest families to arrive, in June of 1859, they were welcomed into a stranger's cabin on condition that Augusta cook for him. While excitable H.A.W. Tabor prepared to invade the mountains he told his wife high tales of the fortune of gold he was going to find, the city he would found, the fabulous gold jewelry he was going to hang on her. Augusta, who was by now operating her first of a series of boardinghouses, wanted nothing more than a pump installed outside the cabin door so that she would not have to lug pails of water from the creek.

"Oh, Horace, riches would only make us unhappy," she replied. "This wedding band is all the gold I want on my hands. Rings would get in the way of my needle, and jewels on my throat would make other women envious and deprive me of friends."

They did worse than that: they cost Augusta her husband, whom she lost to the beauteous Baby Doe in Colorado's most bizarre love story.

"Augusta, almost alone among her contemporaries, looked upon the antelope, the buffalo, and the prairie chicken as something more than meat for the pot. No one else in later years recalled gathering wild flowers on fresh spring mornings under a bright yellow sun. And never did she come to look upon the mountains merely as heaps of rock perversely piled up by the gods to hide gold and silver treasure."

Tabor now loaded his wife and son Maxcy into an oxcart, the first prospector to take his family into the gold fields of the Rockies. They made their way slowly to Golden and camped on Clear Creek at the base of the mountains, at which point Tabor went off prospecting, leaving Augusta alone with the boy in the tent, with not another human being for miles. When night fell she used rocks to "hold down the flaps of the tent, sleeping with her son on slats from packing cases." By September they were at Idaho Springs near Gregory's diggings, but were frightened back to Denver by stories of snowslides.

The following spring the Tabor oxcart carried the family to California Gulch, now become Oro City, country to which not even the Indians had brought their squaws. The miners were so glad to see Augusta that they built her a log cabin, elected her camp cook, nurse, surgeon, and made her blouse the town safe deposit vault. Tabor opened a store and became postmaster, Augusta attending to both jobs while Tabor went hunting for the color. He did fairly well, finding $15,000 worth, but when word came of the strike at Buckskin Joe, Augusta and Maxcy were again loaded into the oxcart. Tabor and his miner friends went ahead with picks and shovels to widen the trail so the cart could pass, and on the downslope tied a thick tree to the rear axle as a brake.

The Tabors remained in the little village of Buckskin Joe for seven years, Augusta tending store, taking care of the post office while Tabor led the local politics and dreamed of great wealth. There was little to do in their snow-trapped winters when "conversation was built around the Warm Stove Mine in the back of a store, where Solid Gold was taken out by the ton and treated by the Hot-Air-Smelter." But the inactivity gave the nearly all-male camps a chance to plan their summer picnic programs, such as serving the guests rich-looking pies filled with finely ground quartz.

One day a man by the name of William Van Brooklyn came into the cabin store and, Tabor being out, offered to swap Augusta his claim in return for his board while he started a mountain express with his two mules. Augusta regretfully declined; Van Brooklyn sold his claim for $100 to two prospectors who, over the summer, took $80,000 out of the site. Tabor determined that he would always grubstake any man with a claim.

Out of that decision H.A.W. Tabor realized $20,000,000 for one day two German shoemakers, owners of a claim but no food, would come hat in hand to the Tabors to offer a third of their find for a grubstake. Tabor would give it to them, acquiring a third interest in the Little Pittsburgh silver mine at Leadville, one of the richest the world would ever know.

In 1865 the Civil War ended. The federal government investigated the Sand Creek attack, labeled it a monstrous massacre. Colonel Chivington was accorded almost sole credit for the assault; it ended his military career. The government paid the Indians $40,000 in indemnities, gave them a new reservation and a guaranteed annual income of $40 per capita for forty years. Far from mollified, the tribes took their indemnity and supplies and moved from their ancestral homes to the new reservation in Indian Territory.

With the end of the Indian dangers and the releasing of soldiers by the North and South alike, emigrants once again began moving westward to the frontier. Eastern capital, pyramided by war profits and seeking higher returns, came to Colorado to finance the deeper workings of old mines or new mill and smelting processes that would profitably reduce Colorado's refractory ones. James E. Lyon built an elaborate smelting works at Black Hawk; an enormous fifty-stamp mill was assembled in Grinnell, Iowa, and hauled for four months behind ox teams to be set up at the Minot Mining Company at Ward.

A new vitality swept Colorado. One hundred twenty-five million pounds of freight crossed the plains, seven thousand men and seven thousand wagons bringing the necessities of life from the Mississippi River. The luxuries as well; for one eighty-train wagon carted sixteen hundred barrels of liquor and twenty-seven hundred cases of champagne! The pioneer women could now buy cloaks, French-style beaver, cashmere, two-story bonnets and a new perfume alliteratively if not romantically called "Balm of a Thousand Bayonets."

An irrigation ditch was built, and for the first time there was sufficient water for Denver to plant trees, shrubs, flowers, lawns; sorely needed if one judged by Dr. Arnold Stedman's description of the town as he first saw it coming in by stage from the East:

"Ugly buildings, ungraded streets covered with dust that almost suffocated the passengers...the rude homes untouched by the hand of taste, the yards without grass or trees."

Now, suddenly, Colorado developed a new industry, the first of the Far West areas to become famous as a tourist haven: for many of those who had gone home to enlist in the war remembered the magnificent snowcapped mountain ranges and rich green valleys, and returned to stay. Back in their home communities they had reported that it was one of the most breathtakingly beautiful and dramatic sections of all America. Those searching for health came to its clear, crisp, pine-scented mountain air for the miracle of a cure.

Colorado made a heroic effort to become self-sustaining. By the end of 1866 a hundred thousand acres were under cultivation. The *Rocky Mountain News* triumphantly announced:

"Our turnips are as big as pumpkins, and the beets are beating all creation."

Jacob Donning, who owned the Green Mountain ranch near Golden, was ribbed by his neighbors when he imported alfalfa seed from California, but he planted four hundred acres in it and the rich earth brought it forth profusely.

In 1864 Congress passed an Enabling Act so Colorado could become a state. It also passed a Mining or Patent Law which for the first time gave legal ownership status to the people who worked the mines, approved the local mining codes that had been functioning by rule of thumb since the first impromptu gathering in Gregory Gulch in 1859, confirmed the farming and ranching titles for families who had developed the land with only squatters' rights, and declared all of Colorado public domain.

But it took a former professor of chemistry at Brown University in Providence, Rhode Island, to put Colorado into big-scale mining production. Nathaniel P. Hill was a trained researcher; he had made a trip out to Colorado in 1864 when the mines were unworked and the mills almost silent, to see if he could unlock through science the riddle of reducing Colorado's potential millions in gold and silver ore.

He sought the answer in books and in laboratories, then went to Europe to study the latest chemical theories and formulas for the reduction of refractory ores. His search for a process took him three years. After returning from Europe he organized the Boston and Colorado Smelting Company; investors quickly subscribed $275,000 to enable him to construct an experimental mill at Black Hawk near Central City, where James E. Lyon had tried and failed the year before.

The new smelter succeeded brilliantly where a hundred brave but insufficiently informed attempts had failed over the past five years. By Hill's method the ores were first crushed, then roasted, then "fused in a reverberatory furnace, about ten tons of mixed ores producing about one ton of matte." Costs were high, hand-chopped wood being the only source of fuel, but the returns were higher, the average assay of silver ores being $118. George Willison in *Here They Dug the Gold* writes:

"Through the new methods of Hill a period of renaissance came to enliven these torturous towns high in Gilpin County. Shafts were reopened, and mills began to clang again."

Like Diedesheimer's system of propping in the Comstock, the process was copied by dozens of new mills all over Colorado, which were soon pouring several millions of fresh gold into the bloodstream of Colorado's development. Nathaniel Hill made a fortune and ended up a United States senator, the ultimate ambition and haven for all bonanza kings.

The country attracted its first professional artist, "Mountain Charlie," Charles S. Stobie. A Zion Negro Baptist Church was established. Perhaps it was the staggering height of one's daily life, so close to heaven, but Colorado became, along with Utah, the most religious of the western areas, building more than fifty churches. The days when the pastor had to work in a grocery during the week were past.

A territorial hook and ladder company was outfitted in firemen's hats, red shirts and black pants which gave Denver a gay splash of color on parade days. The population shot up to twenty-eight thousand; the government had to build its first penitentiary.

There were obstacles and frustrations along the way. Grasshoppers, as they had in Utah, ate a season's crops. Colorado had a difficult time achieving government. Though Coloradans had voted for statehood in 1865, President Andrew Johnson acted less than totally enchanted with the idea of a Colorado, and vetoed statehood on the grounds that the territory had not legally fulfilled the Enabling Act. He replaced Governor Evans and the territorial judges with as unqualified a set of carpetbaggers as any that were plaguing the deep South. Several federal officials were caught squatting to milk the government purse.

Congress again passed an act providing for statehood in 1867. President Johnson vetoed it, this time on the basis that Colorado had insufficient population. Congress tried to override the veto but failed, and in 1868 tried again but could not muster the vote. After that they gave up for a number of years while Coloradans, fiercely independent in the Far West I-want-space-around-me tradition, stumbled along without the right to govern themselves, referring to events outside Colorado as happening "in the States."

The lack of a self-government resulted in a failure to build schools; education at the secondary level had to be provided by various religious denominations. But the theatre follows gold. San Francisco, Sacramento, Virginia City had enjoyed fine acting companies, and now at the Denver and People's theatres in Denver and the National in Central City, Coloradans saw such productions as the equestrian farce *Jeff Davis on His Last Legs*, the popular *The Ticket-of-Leave Man*, and *Othello*. Colorado's own contribution to the entertainment field also flourished in the ornately furnished saloon-gambling halls. Along with the long black mahogany bar, oil paintings, velvet hangings and imported glassware there was a stage on which as many as twenty acts now appeared in a night: singers, dancers, magicians, acrobats, comedians, minstrels and a chorus of pretty girls who mingled with the male audience and helped the lonely men buy $1.00 bottles of beer and $5.00 bottles of champagne. Upstairs, above the racket of the variety house, shielded against disturbing noise by heavy carpets, were the expensively furnished gambling rooms with their roulette wheels and card games.

A Colorado town without its own newspaper felt naked, without a voice with which to clothe itself. When Mr. Scouten, using the old Mormon press to publish the Valmont *Bulletin*, visited neighboring Boulder, the Boulderites got him drunk, then hitched up a wagon team and drove to Valmont, put Mr. Scouten's press and two stands of type cases on the wagon and drove them back to Boulder. When the publisher awakened and found his press already installed in a shop, he graciously took the hint, becoming the printer of the *Boulder Valley News*. By September 1867 Colorado was proudly boasting of its "five daily papers, eight weeklies, and two monthlies." The *Rocky Mountain News* claimed:

"We believe the people of Colorado sustain more newspapers and support them better than does any other western state or territory of the same size. The fact is highly credible to the intelligence and industry of our people."

Colorado eagerly awaited the transcontinental railroad which would pass through Denver, largest city between Omaha and Salt Lake. Daily train service, with San Francisco and Omaha only two days away, would quicken immigration, the tourist and health trades. Merchandise brought in by the railroad freights instead of ox freights would not only come days sooner but at half the cost. It would also open a daily flow of news from the East and West which would make Colorado at long last an integrated part of the United States.

But the engineers of the Union Pacific could do no better at finding a Colorado pass than had John Charles Fremont before them. Reluctantly, for the Union Pacific sorely wanted Denver's business, the prospective line through Colorado was abandoned. The Union Pacific decided in November of 1866 to lay its track due west through unsettled Wyoming and the fledgling village of Laramie, from there following the Overland Trail to Utah, avoiding Colorado even as the emigrant trains had. The Colorado Rockies, staggeringly majestic and commanding at their 14,000-foot heights, were too formidable.

Many Denverites, convinced that Denver was going to become a ghost town, sold their possessions and moved to Cheyenne, which they believed would become the great metropolis of the Rockies. Hafen in his *History of Colorado* observes:

"It was almost the last straw on the backs of the pioneers to have the railroad pass them by. These years were probably the gloomiest in Colorado's history."

Even loyal Denverites knew that the pessimists were right: to be left com₁letely off the transcontinental railroad was to wither on the high-altitude vine. Yet it took a full year for the fact to penetrate their fortress that if the mountain were keeping the iron Mahomet from coming to them, they had best grade track to Mahomet.

In November 1867, after a Board of Commerce and Trade had been organized, a meeting was called in the Denver Theatre. Out onto the stage stepped George Francis Train, fiery representative of the Chicago and Northwestern Railroad, who delivered an impassioned speech on the need for Colorado to build its own spur the one hundred seven miles north to Cheyenne and the Union Pacific. An effective slogan was coined:

PAY OR PERISH

House-to-house solicitations that began the next day among the four thousand Denverites raised $200,000 in stock subscriptions. So complete was the conviction that the railroad must be built that people without money pledged themselves to cut a quantity of railroad ties, or to do manual labor needed to grade the roadbed.

The Denver Pacific Railroad and Telegraph Company was organized and a special election called for January of 1868, at which the voters of Denver and Arapahoe counties approved a $500,000 bond issue for the railroad.

Three days before Christmas of 1869 Colorado went into bonanza again with the discovery of the Caribou silver lode, the first such strike in five years. With the Caribou find the silver lid was off the pot and Colorado would begin thirty years of mining some $140,000,000 in silver in places like Leadville, Telluride and Aspen, lodes that would make the character and drama of Colorado's next era as incredible as anything the congenitally melodramatic Far West had yet conjured up.

Colorado's railroad missed by only half a year its connection with the first transcontinental train to roll across the nation. Late in June 1870 a train came into Denver from Cheyenne, carrying passengers and freight from the main line. Without the help of congressional grants of millions of acres and dollars, the Denver Pacific had laid its roadbed to connect with the main flow of America's transcontinental traffic, and bound itself to its three sister areas.

For the Far West the era of the covered wagon, the ox team, the overland stage coach had closed.

CHAPTER XV

A Polished Laurel Tie, and a Solid Gold Spike

SEVEN THOUSAND FEET UP in the white hell of the Sierra Nevada, Charlie Crocker was meeting the snows and blizzards which Fremont and the Donners had encountered.

It was a severe winter, the winter of 1866.

The ground froze. Fifteen feet of snow and ice covered the construction line. Of the nine thousand men in the labor force, half had to work to keep the line uncovered. Crews of Chinese working the side of a cliff would hear a rumbling; in seconds an avalanche would sweep them to the bottom of a canyon. They would not be found until the spring thaw.

For the twenty-four miles from Cisco to Donner Lake all supplies had to be hauled to the summit by ox team and sled; on the downslope they had to be transferred to mud skid and log roller. The freezing Chinese, whom no previous hardship had fazed, had to be shipped back to Sacramento to keep them alive. It was impossible to keep a road open between the railroad line and the workers' camp; communication tunnels were dug under forty-foot snowdrifts. For months the three thousand remaining workmen lived underground. Engineer Montague and his crew were loaded on ox sleds and sent ahead to clear a line through the Truckee River Canyon. All work on the mountain stopped. Crocker was defeated by the snows.

But only temporarily. With spring he carted back six thousand Chinese to use their picks and chisels on the platform of ice covering the roadbed. They carried on their labors on a diet of oysters, dried cuttlefish, sweet rice crackers, dried bamboo sprouts and seaweed, with perhaps a little pork on holidays. They were thousands of miles from their green farms, with never a Chinese woman to see or

347

speak to, yet uncomplaining. Never a letter or journal or bare note in either English or Chinese has come down to tell us what they were thinking and feeling in this strange land, surrounded by a strange people and a strange tongue, on this monstrously strange job of conquering a mountain.

By now Charlie Crocker was bossing the largest labor crew yet assembled on the American continent; up to fifteen thousand Chinese alone worked from whistle to whistle. He lay awake all night in his car at the railhead planning ways to speed up the job. He lived in the construction camp, ate, slept and drank no better than his men. The laboring men saw that nobody worked harder than the boss. Like Brigham Young, he maintained a rigid military discipline, moved his men and camps like an army.

"I used to go up and down that road like a mad bull, stopping along wherever there was anything amiss, and raising Old Nick with the boys that were not up to line."

James H. Strobridge, his straw boss, who had reached San Francisco in July 1849, who had been unsuccessful as a miner, teamster and hotel manager, was foreman of a hydraulic mine when Crocker found him. Stro was very like Crocker; he had initiative, willingness to take responsibility, determination to press forward under adverse circumstances. Also like Crocker he was:

"A hard-driving taskmaster, ruthless in his treatment of the men, particularly the Chinese; forceful, profane, with a violent temper and biting tongue."

They encountered no labor trouble, for there was an underlay of challenge, of spirit, the knowledge that they were working together on one of the world's great projects, that their efforts had meaning. Crocker received millions for his work, the laborers and mechanics from $1.75 to $5.00 a day plus food. But they also earned glory; and man does not live by cuttlefish alone.

The railroad remained popular during all the years it was building, firing the minds of westerners with its daring and its great promise for the future. It was only after the completion of the line that the Far West would learn, at the price of its own blood, that it had not been set free but taken prisoner.

They made progress, but it was slow, heavy work building strong trestles across chasms and streams, making a solid roadbed that would carry the locomotives. In the spring thaws of 1867 and 1868 the ground melted under the rails like sugar under water, and all of the work had to be done over again. Yet historian Hittell maintains:

"There were no troubles encountered except what had been fully seen, appreciated and set forth by Theodore Judah in his original surveys. There were no harder rocks to be drilled than he had stated; no steeper grades to overcome than he had measured; no more extensive or difficult cuts, fills or tunnels than he had described."

Theorore D. Judah's route is in fact the almost precise route used today by the Southern Pacific Railroad, and still judged to be the best possible pass across the mountains.

The second winter on the crest of the Sierra Nevada, 1868, was as severe as the one before. The gap above Donner Lake still could not be laid with rails. Neither could the supply lines be kept open. Crocker's Pets had to retreat a second time to keep from freezing; but this time Crocker, Montague and Strobridge were not to be stopped. Erecting sawmills in the country below to turn out sixty-five million board feet of lumber and bringing up two hundred skilled carpenters to direct twenty-five hundred laborers, they built along the face of the sheer granite mountain above Donner Lake tight, snug, cliff-hanging snowsheds that covered thirty-seven of the forty miles of the wicked summit crossing: sheds that kept out the winter snows, enabling the men to work and lay track, and later enabling the trains to run in spite of the worst that winter storms could throw at them. Trainmen described them as:

"Railroading in a barn."

The sheds remain a fantastic sight even today.

It was Crocker's culminating accomplishment. Now, in June of 1868, he was able to join his rails to those already laid down the eastern slope to the Nevada line, twenty-eight miles away. The California section of the Central Pacific had cost $23,000,000 to build. Strobridge estimated that seventy per cent of this sum could have been saved had they not been in such a desperate hurry to get out into the Nevada and Utah deserts where tracklaying would be inexpensive; where they could make big profits from their government contract.

They were out on the desert now. Crocker cried to his associates, Huntington in New York, Stanford and Hopkins in San Francisco:

"Give me the materials I need, and I can build a mile a day of complete railroad."

Huntington, Hopkins and Stanford moved heaven and earth and as many as thirty-nine ships on the seas at one time to give Crocker what he wanted, for:

"Every mile built meant a profit of twice its cost."

A railhead had to be established in Nevada. The purest example of a town being born in one piece is that of Reno, called Lake's Crossing when the railroad spilled down out of the mountains. Crocker made a fast deal with Lake, the original settler who owned the land: in return for eighty acres on the north side of the Truckee River, on which Crocker agreed to build a Central Pacific station, Lake was given every alternate lot in the proposed town of Reno. Charlie Crocker could afford to be liberal in giving lots to Lake: the Central Pacific had received from the Congress five million acres of Nevada's public lands.

So powerful is the magnet of a railroad (stagecoaches were already waiting for passengers, to take them the thirty-odd miles to the Comstock) that hundreds of people rode to the location the night before the lots were to be sold, sleeping in the open spaces of the sagebrush in order to be on hand when the auction opened. One night Reno was a series of stakes in the sand; the next day it was a town with two hundred lots sold, the first bringing $600. A business block, saloons, residences sprang up. Three months later, in August 1868, the town could sit for its first portrait:

"People rush into Reno. There is no such thing as rest: Paiute squaws with their juvenile encumbrances packed neatly in small packages on their broad backs, to the gambler and rough element and the most refined mingle on the street. The tavern keepers are bent on business, provide no rest and Reno cares nothing. All day the hammer and saw is heard, and all night the fiddles scrape and the glasses clink."

Advance survey crews worked far ahead on the desert, setting out the longest possible snake-like route, avoiding terrain that would involve any construction other than the actual laying of track. After half freezing to death, the construction crews now baked under a broiling sun in 120°, with no shade. Water had to be hauled for forty miles; at night, in their boxcar homes on the freshly laid sidings, in "sizzling heat and clouds of alkali-laden dust," the men sweltered. But Crocker made good his promise by laying three hundred sixty-two miles of track by the end of 1868.

Wages for the Chinese on the Nevada and Utah deserts were raised from $26 a month to $35; they were further Americanized to the extent of wearing blue denims and shirts. But it was their Chinese coolie hats which kept them alive in the inferno of the summer sand. They never faltered ... except on the one occasion when a practical joker spread the word that deep in the Nevada desert were gigantic snakes that could swallow a Chinese quite easily in one gulp. Thousands of them started streaming westward across the desert in an effort to walk back to San Francisco.

Both the Central and the Union Pacific lines had driven hard to reach Utah and corner the Mormon transportation, a field thought to be so lucrative that Leland Stanford had spent a good part of the previous winter in Salt Lake being chummy with Brigham Young, and giving him highly profitable contracts to use his Mormons for grading and laying track.

The transcontinental railroad which had been advancing upon Brigham Young, Utah and Mormonism all during the sixties was of major concern to the Latter-day Saints. Those forces fighting Mormonism were convinced that the railroad would put an end to it. The few hundred gentiles in Utah had already nominated a candidate for territorial representative to Congress to run against the Mormon delegate; although they had had small success, accumulating only a hundred five votes, they were now trying to organize an opposition party. The influx of strangers would strengthen their hand.

Though Brigham Young said, "I wouldn't give much for a religion which could not withstand the coming of a railroad," he was nonetheless aware that, once the rails were joined in Utah, gentiles would be coming in every day. Whenever the Saints and the gentiles had had to live side by side there inevitably had been trouble. It had been his strongest hope to secure statehood before the railroad was completed, for then Utah would be free from control by Washington. He had failed to achieve this ambition.

However he co-operated with the railroads, signed contracts with both companies for the use of his manpower, taking his pay in shares of stock, an enormously shrewd investment.

Now in the beginning of 1869 the Central Pacific and the Union Pacific were ready to meet. While Congress, lobbied half out of its wits by Collis P. Huntington of the Central Pacific and General Dodge of the Union Pacific, debated just where the official joining point should be set, the Irish of the Union Pacific and the Chinese of the Central Pacific laid parallel track, each going in the opposite direction. The Chinese and the Irish were inclined to look down their differently shaped noses at each other's tracklaying talents, playing a few practical jokes: Cholly Clocker's Pets accidentally rolled boulders down on the Irish; the Irish "laid blasts rather far to the right of their own line, and a thousand graders looked on in innocent wonderment as the earth parted and the Chinese, scrapers, horses, wheelbarrows and picks fountained upward."

Charlie Crocker had the last word, as usual. On the day before the two railroad systems were to join their rails at Promontory, Utah, fifty-three miles from Ogden, Crocker bet that his Chinese could lay ten miles of track in one day. They did it, in an amazing performance of team play which proved the loyalty and skill and integration of the force that Crocker had built over a period of seven years and a thousand miles of railroad.

Promontory consisted of five saloons, quickly erected to take care of the crowd of five hundred which assembled on May 10, 1869 to watch the joining of the roads. The rain poured down and the single street was a mud bog.

At eleven in the morning a Central Pacific train from the Pacific coast and a Union Pacific train from the East, both with highly decorated engines, their whistles greeting each other ceremoniously, came nose to nose, a short unbridged gap between them. A handsomely polished piece of California laurel was produced, to serve as the connecting tie, and a solid gold California spike. In an icy wind, with a regimental band bound for San Francisco's Presidio playing music, and the Twenty-first Infantry holding back the crowd so the photographers could take pictures, a crew of Chinese in blue jackets and pantaloons brought forward the last ties, spikes and rail.

The entire nation awaited the historic moment.

Leland Stanford drove the last spike, started a speech. A telegraph dispatcher sent out the long-awaited word. In Washington, a magnetic ball above the Capitol dropped as a signal. In San Francisco, cannons were fired. By nightfall the first transcontinental trains had moved across the wedding rail in the Utah desert, just a little more than fifty miles from Ogden's Hole where the first white man had built a settlement thirty years before.

In the beginning they were one. Now again, California, Nevada, Utah and Colorado were joined.

And the Far West had become a part of the whole United States.

Book Five

GIANTS STALK THE LAND

CHAPTER I

The Tiger and the Octopus

THE FIRST RAILROAD PASSENGERS entered the Far West in May of 1869 close to the pass through the Wasatch Mountains used by the Mormons' Pioneer Party twenty-two years before, and about one hundred miles south of the California Trail which had brought in most of the emigrant trains. They traveled at a rate of nineteen miles an hour; there being little ballast on the road, the cars bumped and swayed considerably. "A good rain made the roadbed run like wet soap."

A few hours later the passengers changed to Central Pacific cars at Ogden. Excitement ran high, for they were about to begin the wildest, roughest and most romantic part of their journey, four days and nights across the deserts and mountains of Utah and Nevada, then the great climb through the Sierra Nevada and the drop down into Sacramento.

The Central Pacific was the conversation piece of the Far West. Crossing the continent by railroad became the supreme adventure for world travelers. Atlantic liners were largely empty during the months following the opening of the railroad while former Grand Tour enthusiasts made the journey across America in George Pullman's palace cars, furnished with velvet upholstery, thick carpets with intricate flower designs to be studied during the long hours while the train crossed the dust-encrusted desert. At every cry of "Deer ahead!" the men took out their pistols and a volley of shots was fired the length of the train at the fleeing animals. If buffalo were sighted men ran to the outside platform with their rifles. They could have used the fresh meat: there was no food on the train, which stopped whenever there was a station, and the stations were sometimes eight to twelve hours apart. Then the passengers dashed into the restaurant to pacify their hunger in the twenty minutes allowed.

At night the kerosene lamps were lighted and the passengers gathered around a small organ to sing western songs while the porters made up the berths. There was so much discussion in the East about the moral turpitude of women sleeping in the same car with men that the ladies retired to their berths fully dressed, armed with lethal hatpins. The most astounding experience was going through the snow tunnels which hugged the cliffs above Donner Lake, where the passengers at the window could see beneath them a thousand feet to the canyon below.

Pictures of the locomotives were cut out of journals and pinned up in homes. The speed records of the trains from junction to junction were published daily, and were more widely discussed than the scores of the newly starting baseball teams. Henry George, a young San Francisco newspaperman, wrote of the railroad:

"It will be the means of converting a wilderness into a populous empire in less time than many of the cathedrals of Europe were building."

Much of the adoration of the railroad rubbed off on the Big Four. For the scattered peoples of the Far West, isolated from friends, families, news and many kinds of merchandise, the Central Pacific Railroad became the eighth wonder of the world. Sacramento, which only a decade before had refused to talk to "Crazy" Judah or invest a dollar in his wild scheme, perceived that Huntington, Crocker, Stanford and Hopkins had become heroes to the nation. Belatedly the town, terminus of the transcontinental tracks, gave the railroad builders a testimonial banquet. Had they waited a year or two, it would have been unceremoniously canceled.

As a romantic accomplishment the Central Pacific was a great success. Economically, by the fall of 1870, it was a failure.

Theodore Judah had assumed that the passenger and freight trade from Europe would use the transcontinental railroad, foreshortening the journey to the Orient. This was nullified by the opening of the Suez Canal only a few weeks after the joining of the Central and Union Pacific tracks. Most of the Orient trade was lost. After the first months of many cars and complete sellouts to the wealthy and adventure-seeking, the daily trains sometimes carried only half a dozen passengers. After the first rush of emigrants who had wanted to move to California but could not face the ordeal of the covered wagon, settlers riding in with their families were scarce. California, and particularly San Francisco, which had looked forward to a wave of prosperity, of rising real estate values and demands for their agricultural and manufactured products, found that the eastern factories were flooding the California market and sharply underpricing California goods.

For the Big Four this economic failure was equally true.

Collis P. Huntington, Mark Hopkins, Leland Stanford and Charles Crocker were all good men with an account book, and now they could read the retrogressing figures all too clearly. They had made millions in cash from the government subsidies to build their railroad. They also owned tens of millions of acres of land containing forests, mines and good soil. In the years to come these lands would be worth more tens of millions. But what happened to them if they had to pour the fortunes they had made from constructing the railroad back into the operation of it? Mark Hopkins, the bookkeeper of the Big Four, spoke for them all when he wrote of:

"The uncertainty of continued years of anxious toil, and the uncertainty of how we may work out the problems of final success."

The four ex-Sacramento merchants had put in a decade of Herculean labor, often standing on the brink of failure. They had looked forward to the completion of the railroad as a time when they could retire and live the glamorous lives of millionaires. They asked themselves, What do we know about running a railroad? Stuart Daggett in *Chapters on the History of the Southern Pacific* says:

"Eighty per cent of the stock of the Central Pacific was offered to D. O. Mills as late as 1873 for a price of $20,000,000, and this was probably the last of several offers to different parties."

There were no buyers: partly because the price was steep, partly because there were no experienced railroad operators in the Far West. There were also a number of competing lines planned, some of them already under construction. If built northward and then east to join the Union Pacific, or through southern California to join the proposed Atlantic and Pacific Railroad to come out of Missouri, they would cause added insufficiency of business. The partners knew the Far West was not supporting one transcontinental line; it certainly could not support three.

The Big Four had a tiger by the tail. They could not run their railroad at a profit, neither could they sell it at what they considered a good price. They reasoned that the only way they could survive would be to establish a monopoly over all railroading inside the Far West.

Collis P. Huntington set out to create that monopoly.

He was described by his admirers as "a hard and cheery old man, with no more soul than a shark," as being "scrupulously dishonest," and by the San Francisco *Examiner* as "ruthless as a crocodile."

Before a mile of track was laid, Leland Stanford had contested with Collis P. Huntington for the leadership and control of management. Stanford was slow-thinking, slower talking, and not particularly shrewd; in a short time Huntington had relegated him to a secondary position. Fortunately for Stanford's outsized ego no one in the Far West knew this; for Huntington went to New York as the purchasing agent for the railroad, leaving Stanford as president, and the ostensible head of the railroad in the Far West.

But Collis P. Huntington ran the railroad. He was the chairman, the boss, the master, the king. He took a deliberate pleasure in creating a national reputation for himself as a miser.

"I'll never be remembered for the money I've given away," he told one reporter. To another he said, "Young man, you can't follow me through life by the quarters I have dropped."

Only fools and weaklings gave money to charity, or to community causes for the bettering of anything or anybody.

Fond as he was of saving money, he did his best to prevent any other human being from saving one single dollar! His enormous skill and cunning were exerted to make sure that the Central Pacific drained off all monies produced in the area where the railroad ran, leaving only a subsistence for those who produced.

When Hubert Howe Bancroft sent a writer to extract Huntington's life story, all Huntington could think to set down for posterity were the stories of how he had got the better of an adversary in a business deal. This was the salt of life to him, as well as its ripe fruit. Everything else was weakness and foolishness. There were no chinks or cracks in his armor. He did not even like the other three of the Big Four.

There was much good in the other three: Stanford, though pompous and a social climber, was of a charitable nature; Mark Hopkins was a gentle man who wanted little for himself and was the best liked; Crocker was a bully, but he liked to take care of his friends, to experiment in the mining and industrial growth of the Far West.

They were all as children in Huntington's hands; he outthought them, outmaneuvered them, outplanned them. Stanford he called a "damned old fool who did not know how to bargain"; Crocker was a burly track-laying foreman; Hopkins a glorified bookkeeper. He reduced his three partners to little more than carrier boys for the policies he determined.

Collis P. Huntington despised all men who sought public office as exhibitionists, easily and cheaply bought. He deliberately sought obscurity in order to protect his schemes to keep the federal government, the state government, the county and city governments on his payroll. He was the only instance in the history of the Far West of a man sitting three thousand miles away, in a twelve-by-twelve office in New York City, and controlling the economic and political life of California.

In May 1869 when Leland Stanford drove the golden spike that symbolically completed the transcontinental railroad, there were two independently owned short lines operating out of Sacramento to San Francisco. The California Pacific, which had been built from Sacramento to Vallejo on the east shore of San Francisco Bay, and ran ferries from there direct to San Francisco, had a hundred sixty-three miles of road and was plotting lines northward. Theirs was the quickest route to San Francisco, three and a half hours. The competing line, the Western Pacific, went from Stockton to San Jose, at which point it connected with the San Francisco and San Jose, a forty-mile railroad running along the peninsula into San Francisco. This trip took five hours.

First, the Central Pacific bought the Western Pacific and routed its passengers from Sacramento through Stockton and San Jose. But most passengers abandoned the last section of their Central Pacific tickets, paying extra fare to go on the California Pacific by way of Vallejo, the shorter route. The Big Four also lost three quarters of their freight to the California Pacific. Huntington threatened to build a parallel, competing road.

To keep all further railroad competition away from San Francisco Bay, he entered a political deal with Oakland officials which gave the Central Pacific nine miles of the Oakland and Alameda waterfront, almost the entirety of the east bay tidewater land. The Central Pacific now had a fence around half the harbor.

To complete their bay circle on the western shore, the Big Four absorbed the San Francisco and Alameda Railroad of some sixteen miles, which gave them another connection with Sacramento. They also bought the California Steam Navigation Company, which ran palatial river boats between San Francisco, Sacramento and Stockton, capturing control of passenger and freight movements to the interior of the state. By the end of 1870, working swiftly to complete their monopoly, they had also bought up the forty-mile San Francisco and San Jose Railroad, and had absorbed the proposed Southern Pacific and the Santa Clara and Pajaro Valley railroads, both of which had been projected to connect San Francisco with Los Angeles. The California Pacific also succumbed.

One obstacle remained in the way of their complete control over everything moving into California: the Pacific Mail Steamship Company, which had been set up with a government subsidy before the gold rush of 1849. The Pacific Mail was offering freightage around the Horn at such low rates that shippers preferred the slower ships to the more expensive railroad. When efforts of the Big Four to coerce the Pacific Mail into raising its rates or to sell were unavailing, they started their own Oriental and Occidental Steamship Company to compete on the same route, with lower rates. Nearly all traffic, passenger and freight, shifted to the new line. The Pacific Mail held out until the Oriental and Occidental threatened to put competing ships on the Mail's Panama run as well, then it was forced to negotiate. It agreed to charge the same rate for shipping merchandise by sea as the Central Pacific was charging by rail.

The Central Pacific, now calling itself the Southern Pacific in California, and soon to use that name for all of its lines, set out to establish its route southward. Since rails bend in any direction, a representative of the Big Four would go to a small community and say:

"If you wish us to bring our railroad through your town and help you develop, you must pay us so many thousands of dollars and so much acreage of land. If you don't undertake these obligations we will route our railroad elsewhere, and leave you here to die on the vine."

Few towns could withstand the pressure; they paid for a considerable part of the construction of the Southern Pacific through their area. When they refused to pay, the Southern Pacific bent the rails and went a few miles east or west, through another valley. If there was no competing town nearby to which the railroad could take its offer, it created a town of its own by offering homestead land.

Los Angeles, which still had only six thousand population, was so apprehensive lest the Southern Pacific by-pass it in favor of San Diego or San Bernardino that the city sought out the Big Four and acceded to all the demands: five percent of the evaluation of Los Angeles County; $150,000 in stock in Phineas Banning's Los Angeles and San Pedro Railroad; sixty-three acres for depot ground; or over $600,000 in a grant from Los Angeles to the Big Four, a per capita charge of $100.

As a justification for this practice, Daggett, the authority in the field, says that as a construction enterprise the whole Southern Pacific line was speculative. There were few customers between San Francisco and Los Angeles to use the railroad, and fewer settlers ready to take up the railroad land. The Southern Pacific would have to run for a number of years without profit.

In San Francisco the Big Four were thwarted; for San Franciscans had distrusted these men from the inception of the Central Pacific. In addition they had watched the Big Four set out unabashedly to buy an election a few years before in order to get the city's approval of a $600,000 bond loan to the Central Pacific. Of the many eyewitness documents available, William Kayser's is typical; on election morning Kayser was at one of the voting booths when he saw Philip Stanford, the governor's brother, drive up.

"He came there in a buggy and had a large crowd of men around him, and was handing money to them liberally; he held out money to all who offered to take. He said to the person standing by, 'Now go to work for the railroad; do all you can.'"

The Big Four, like Isaac Graham, presented honest faces to the world: they were rascals, and they would make no attempt to hide the fact by subtle means of concealment. The Big Four had won the election, but they had lost San Francisco. The people refused to pay the money, dragging the Central Pacific into the courts.

In 1870 Huntington wanted a fence around San Francisco which would include all of the docking areas of the entire bay front. Since these tidelands belonged to the state rather than to the city, he went to work on the California legislature in Sacramento, over which he had comprehensive coverage. The bill that was drawn would have given the Big Four control of six thousand acres and eight miles of San Francisco's bay frontage.

The city became a seething mass of protest meetings and denunciations. Handbills were distributed and newspaper attacks raised such a monumental cry that Huntington decided he had better withdraw the bill. Next he attempted to get control of Goat Island, in the bay between San Francisco and Oakland, from the federal government. San Franciscans signed petitions and sent influential delegates to Washington to fight the railroad's lobbyists there. The Southern Pacific withdrew its claim to Goat Island as a terminus.

In the end, because San Francisco did need a terminus, the city granted to the Southern Pacific thirty acres of land for warehouses, depot and roadbed to come into the city from San Jose.

The battle of the freight rates started early in the 1870s. The railroad followed the pricing methods used by Huntington when he had been a shopkeeper in Sacramento: charge all the market will bear. If you can corner the market and create a monopoly, then charge every last cent you can get.

The Southern Pacific demanded the right to inspect the books of the companies using the line, then fixed the freight rate at the point which would absorb all the profit. If a number of companies went bankrupt the Southern Pacific lowered the rates; when a company showed an increased profit, the rate was raised at once. The Southern Pacific knew intimately the details of every business.

The farmers were charged a rate which allowed them enough money to buy their seed for the coming season and to feed their families and workers; nothing more. Manufacturers were allowed enough margin to keep their plants open. When farmers or merchants in the interior of California ordered goods from the East, they were charged the full rate of shipment to San Francisco and then almost half again as much to bring the goods back to their small town, even though the train had passed through that very town on its way to San Francisco. When a gold mine was developed in the northern town of Shasta, and the owners asked the Southern Pacific to fix a rate for shipping quartz to the San Francisco mill, the rate was set at $50 a car. The mine owners began shipping three cars a day, whereupon the Southern Pacific increased the rate to $73 a car and then to $100. When the owners protested, the Southern Pacific replied that they must produce their account books, then they would be told how much profit they might make. The balance would have to go into the freight rate.

The orange growers of southern California were charged ninety cents a box to ship their fruit to the Atlantic coast, a freight charge which left them a profit of thirteen cents a box, just enough to keep their orchards on the ragged edge of poverty. When the lemon growers grew prosperous, the railroad raised the rates fifteen cents per box of lemons. This fifteen cents was several pennies over the profit made by the growers; they were forced to tear out their trees and plant other crops. In Southern California where the Big Four now owned Phineas Banning's original railroad from the port of San Pedro to Los Angeles, the Southern Pacific charged half as much for this one-hour haul as it had cost to bring the same ton of merchandise all the way from the Orient!

The shippers were not always supine. When the sheep growers of northern California found that the Southern Pacific was taking every cent of profit to ship the wool east, they rented teams of wagons and drove their wool three hundred miles down to San

Francisco Bay to waiting ships. One group of eastern merchants shipped their goods from New York to Liverpool and then from Liverpool around the Horn to San Francisco, the merchandise arriving at half the rate charged by the railroad to bring it from New York to San Francisco. Some San Francisco merchants founded the Atlantic and Pacific Steamship Company to carry goods around the Horn and across Panama; they also formed the Traffic Association of California, which almost all San Francisco shippers joined. They forced the railroad to reduce its rates, because of the long lines of idle freight cars standing in the yards; but on such perishables as fruit there was no reduction.

The policy was "all the traffic will bear." The shipper paid the railroad rates or went out of business.

The Southern Pacific had woven an almost perfect 360° monopoly, with control over legislation and legislators, the courts and most of the newspapers. The population was powerless to free itself from the death hug of the Octopus.

How could the Big Four accomplish this miracle when so many citizens were well aware of their bloodsucking propensities?

Collis P. Huntington, sitting at an austere desk in an austere room, with a black skullcap over his bald head, provided the answers in a series of indiscreet letters written to David Colton, one of his associates in California, and made public during litigation after Colton's death. Huntington told in these "Friend Colton" letters precisely how much money it cost the Southern Pacific to have each act passed by the Congress. He instructed Colton which congressman being elected from California should be given what Huntington euphoniously called "Solid reasons why he should help his friends." Huntington bought not only state legislators, congressmen and senators, but also judges as calmly as he bought locomotives and rails; every man had his price, and the price of buying a government was merely another cost of production, similar to maintaining depots or warehouses or track crews.

Any representative who would not take orders from the railroad Huntington called "a wild hog." The amount of cash that it cost to defeat anyone running for office who refused to take the railroad's orders was stated bluntly in these letters. For the first time there was laid out in the press of the nation the reason why California could not break the Southern Pacific's death grip, even when it created a Railroad Commission to set fair rates. The Big Four either got their own men elected to the commission; or, failing in this, bought the commission after it was elected.

All of this took money. That was why the freight rates had to be so high.

This was Huntington's economic and political philosophy; nothing to the end of his very long life ever changed him one iota. The names he was called in the press merely made the offending newspapers "wild hogs." He wrote to Friend Colton:

"Is it not possible to control the agent for the Associated Press in San Francisco? The matters that hurt the Southern Pacific most here are dispatches that come from San Francisco."

Or: "The Sacramento *Union* hurts us very much. If I owned the paper I would control it or burn it."

Wherever possible the Big Four bought the newspaper and used it to praise everything the railroad was doing.

One of his letters to Friend Colton which most charmed the public and was given the widest circulation ran:

"This Congress is the worst body of men ever gotten together in this country. It is the worst set of men that have ever been collected together since man was created. I think in all the world's history never before was such a wild set of demagogues honored by the name of Congress. We have been hurt some but some of the worst bills have been defeated but we cannot stand many such congressmen."

It was Collis P. Huntington's view that what was good for the Southern Pacific was good for the nation. Any public official who attempted to thwart any action of the railroad was a public enemy who would bring harm and destruction upon the United States.

The Big Four now set about to attract settlers to the lands near their lines, alternate sections of which they owned as grants from the federal government. The days when John Sutter took possession of an entire Sacramento Valley, when Mariano Vallejo owned a whole Valley of the Moon, when an Abel Stearns and a Hugo Reid in southern California could buy a Spanish land grant of a hundred thousand acres, when the members of a Bidwell or Stevens party could simply scatter over California and take by squatter's rights a large piece of fertile land, these days were irretrievably gone.

As the Southern Pacific pushed its way southward at the rate of a hundred miles a year, the railroad issued pamphlets and broadsides, and bought advertisements in the newspapers throughout America. There was written assurance that the land the settlers homesteaded would be sold to them later for $2.50 to $5.00 an acre, and that the improvements the settlers made would not become part of the evaluation.

Slowly, the families began to come in, many of them traveling in old day coaches, carrying their own bedding and tools and seed-wheat. Some families took a whole car in which they brought their children and grandparents, their furniture and farm implements, even young trees to plant. The emigrant trains were sometimes as long as the covered wagon trains of a decade before.

The brochures that had lured them west had described the country as a Garden of Eden. Now they were given no choice of where they were to settle, nor the privilege of searching out the land they would like to farm. Their railroad cars drew up by sidings somewhere in California's Long Valley, south of Fresno; the emigrants found themselves in the parched Tulare Basin, without water or trees, in a country that looked almost as desolate as had the Great Basin to the Mormons. There were no materials available with which to build homes; each family put up a shack. In summer they baked and choked in the dust storms; winds burned their young crops and freshly planted fruit trees. The winter floods washed them out of home and field, the spring frost nipped the green plants. The settlers named the place Starvation Valley.

The railroad lent no helping hand.

But the emigrants were of rugged American stock. Without money and without proper tools, with nothing to eat but crude ground corn and whatever jack rabbits they could shoot while working, the men organized themselves into a co-operative like that of the Mormons in their new, dry land, and set out to bring water down from the mountains. There were no engineers among them, they made mistakes, twice the irrigation system which they built all the way from the foothills had to be abandoned. But it was succeed or die, and they brought in a supply of water from the mountains with hundreds of ditches and canals to irrigate their fields.

On this aspect the railroad literature had not lied: the land was incredibly rich. With an amplitude of water the parched fields sprang to life in a variety of vegetables, fruits, wheat, alfalfa, anything that was planted.

Now the settlers of the Tulare Valley had something to sell. They had money with which to buy materials to build their homes, and to plant shade trees, to buy livestock and to build barns and windmills.

But they did not yet own the fields and houses they had brought to life. The land still belonged to the Southern Pacific.

CHAPTER II

Four Miles to the Mineral Belt

ADOLPH SUTRO SAT upright in a carriage, wearing a white beaver hat and Prince Albert coat, his chin high in the air, his black eyes glowing with excitement. Behind him were a number of carriages hired by his miner friends, all coming to watch him turn the first shovelful of earth for Sutro's Tunnel at the base of Mount Davidson.

Behind the doors of the Bank of California stood William Sharon, delighted that a cold drizzle had begun, certain that this was a bad omen.

Sutro gave a signal. Down the canyon they started, past Gold Hill where they picked up a band of Paiutes, down to Silver City and then to Dayton where the brass band of the Miners' Union stepped in to lead the procession the three miles through the sagebrush to a speakers' stand that Sutro had built alongside the spot where he was going to start his tunnel.

On spits, a bullock and a hog were roasting for the celebration. The band played "The Star-Spangled Banner." Sutro made a short speech, took off his white beaver and Prince Albert, rolled up his sleeves and with all the force of his tremendous will drove a pick into the base of Mount Davidson. As the first earth rolled away a cheer echoed across the floor of the Nevada desert. At that moment a rainbow appeared, its west end coming down to the mouth of the incipient tunnel. Sutro and his miners considered this a good omen.

A camera was fired. To warm their hearts and replenish their strength, Sutro, the miners and the Paiutes fell to drinking beer from kegs and to eating the roasted meat.

They could use this cheer and strength; for two thousand feet above them on the opposite crest of Mount Davidson stood the chimneys of the Washoe mines. There were four miles to go through the base of this solid mountain, through unknown rock, volcanic clay, boiling underground rivers and pockets of poisonous gas, before they could reach the shafts of the working mines. To make this long journey Sutro had $50,000 which the Miners' Union had loaned him, a few more dollars from miners who had bought individual shares at $10 each, and an expert crew which had agreed to work for $3.00 a day plus $1.00 a day in stock, worthless until the tunnel was completed.

Sharon and the Bank of California had been prepared for the blow of Sutro's pick. Even as the cheers of the miners were rolling along the Carson River, the Bank's newspapers called Sutro a wildcat swindler, a played-out carpetbagger, "a pygmy trying to bore a hole through Mount Olympus." On October 14, 1869 the Gold Hill *News* cried:

"His first pick has been heretofore, is now, and ever will be, a pick at the pockets of all honest workingmen and others whom he can 'bamboozle' into supporting him like a gentleman at other people's expense."

To begin his gentleman's life of ease and idleness Adolph Sutro, stripped to the waist, went to dig with pick and shovel at the mouth of the tunnel, working shoulder to shoulder with the group of miners who had thrown in their lot with him. It was eight years since he had published his first article in the *Alta* telling of the need for the tunnel, five years since he had begun the task of raising money for the project. During this time his ore-reducing mill had burned down, he and his wife and six children had suffered genuine privation. For Mrs. Leah Harris Sutro the long separations had been harder to endure than the sometime poverty; but worst of all had been the revilement of Sutro in the press. Leah Sutro was of the breed of Tamsen Donner and Juliet Brier:

"But for her," said Adolph Sutro, "I should have lost heart altogether. My wife never repined, never reproached me for the poverty with which we struggled, never wavered in devotion."

With the opening of the 1870s the Bank of California came into almost total possession of the Comstock Lode. To make sure that Sutro did not get any more miners to help him, William Sharon, who never lacked courage, went to the shaft of the Yellow Jacket and said to his miners:

"That famous tunnel, which was started on a barrel of champagne and 'four-bits', even if it were finished would not drain the Comstock Lode. How many men would the mining of that tunnel employ at $4.00 a day, and how good is the security for your pay? I think you would rather have the Bank of California paper than his. We oppose him and his project; therefore he makes his fight by spitefully slandering us and trying to incite you against your employers. Let no such nonsense induce you to contend against your own interests and those who are of real benefit to you."

The Bank did not content itself with such humanitarian appeals. When Ralston and his directors saw that Sutro had tunneled a hundred sixty feet into Mount Davidson in his first month of digging they put their opposition on a more simple business basis. In January 1870, after he had been excavating for only a little over two months, Sutro received a telegram from a friend in Washington urging him to take the transcontinental train east immediately: the Bank had introduced a bill into Congress to repeal his right of way.

Sutro turned the job over to a master carpenter who had worked for years in the California mines, hastened to Reno and caught the Central Pacific train east. He was delayed by snowstorms in the Rocky Mountains; when he reached Washington on March 1 he learned that Nevada's congressman, Thomas Fitch, was submitting a bill to Congress which would repeal the charge of $2.00 a ton on ore brought out through his tunnel. Without this guaranteed royalty as security, Sutro could never raise the funds he needed.

William Ralston had dispatched from San Francisco a lawyer named Hillyer to help Congressman Fitch lobby the bill through Congress. The Bank's congressman had inserted one handwritten copy of the bill in a file of papers on the Speaker's desk. On the scheduled date it would be read once, then passed by those congressmen who had been well lobbied; the others would have had no chance to study it.

Sutro had the bill printed and distributed at his own expense; this forced the measure into the open. Congress referred it to its Committee on Mines and Mining. Several of the committeemen had visited the Comstock mines; they resolutely stood by Sutro's Tunnel. Congressman Austin of Michigan reported to the committee that William Sharon had told him:

"Sir, the Bank has waved its hand over the Comstock Lode and ordered Sutro away."

Congressman William D. Kelley of Pennsylvania said to the committee:

"I propose to speak for the miners, forty-five per cent of whom die in the vigor of their young manhood, prostrated by the heat and poisoned by the atmosphere in these mines. These industrious men...swarm behind Mr. Sutro, and beg Congress to vest all the rights in him that will enable him to reduce for them the terrible doom to which the Bank of California would condemn them."

The House of Representatives defeated the Fitch Bill; yet Adolph Sutro did not dare to leave Washington for fear Hillyer and Fitch would try to pass another bill. He sat out the session even though he had prepared to go to France where the Parisian bankers, Erlanger and Company, had agreed to lend him fifteen million francs. Five days before he could sail, the Franco-Prussian War broke out. Sutro's loan was canceled.

Defeated, Sutro returned to the Comstock, to his pick and shovel. He was now a thousand feet into the mountain; but the tunnel was $50,000 into him. There was no more money with which to buy materials or pay wages. Progress slowed to a crawl.

In December 1870 Sutro again went to Washington to try to persuade Congress to grant him a loan. The Bank was there ahead of him, informing congressmen that there was not the slightest need for Sutro's Tunnel, that the Comstock was played out. Thwarted at every turn, Sutro asked the Senate and House to send an investigating committee to the Comstock. Congress agreed.

The following summer two elderly West Point army engineers and a mining engineer arrived in Virginia City. Sutro attempted to brief them on the history of Ralston, Sharon and the Bank. The commissioners said they wished to see things for themselves. They did; in the protective custody of the superintendents of the Bank-owned Ophir, Gould and Curry and Chollar-Potosi. The commissioners were taken to the dry parts of the mines, and into the coolest drifts. When they visited Sutro Tunnel they brought with them the Bank of California representative.

In the midst of Sutro's frustration a group of men arrived in Virginia City unannounced, sent for Sutro and explained that they had come from England at the request of McCalmont's Bank to examine the Comstock Lode. They did not know Mr. William Ralston nor Mr. William Sharon, nor did they want to. They had come to see Mr. Sutro. Would he show them the Comstock?

Sutro took the group through the biggest mines, showed them the sumps of water, let them feel the killing heat, smell the poisonous gases . . . as well as follow the fissure veins of gold and silver that ran ever deeper into Mount Davidson. Then he took them down Gold Canyon to the base of the mountain, showed them the beginnings of his tunnel, his engineering charts for its completion. The Englishmen looked, listened and departed, thanking him for his kindness.

A month later Sutro received a cablegram: could he come to England to discuss a loan? In two weeks he was en route. The directors of McCalmont's Bank, convinced of the lode's wealth by the Crown Point and Belcher, had accepted their investigators' advice to lend him $650,000 for his tunnel!

Sutro's head spun. Enough money to buy those new steam drills, employ hundreds of men, bring in mules and track and cars from California, penetrate at least two miles into Mount Davidson.

Sutro dashed back to the Comstock, built a town around the mouth of his tunnel, with forges, a machine shop, hotel, barrooms, a newspaper, dance hall, church, hospital, and a white Victorian house for himself, Leah, his two sons and four daughters, lashed to the side of Mount Davidson by cables to keep a Washoe zephyr from blowing it into the Carson River. Four hundred miners worked in day and night shifts, and a thousand people lived in Sutro.

In January he hastened back to Washington to be on hand when the government commissioners submitted their report. When he reached there he found that the report, already submitted to Congress, declared that Sutro's Tunnel was feasible but not necessary for safety, drainage or ventilation on Mount Davidson.

Sutro was infuriated. He demanded of the Congressional Committee on Mines, and then the Secretary of War, that the retired army engineers be summoned to Washington to testify. William Ralston sent his ablest attorney to defend the commissioners and their report. For twenty-five consecutive nights before the committee, Adolph Sutro, serving as his own attorney, questioned the commissioners, battling the Bank's attorney and superintendents sent to Washington to confound him. Published by Congress as an eight-hundred-page book called *Sutro Tunnel*, it remains a devastating expose' of monopolistic methods, and justifies George D. Lyman in writing in *Ralston's Ring:*

"Sutro demonstrated his familiarity with geology, orology, topography, metallurgy, hydrostatics, mechanics, and engineering. He was more than a match for all the brains the Bank of California could muster against him. The hearing developed into an individual's fight against corporate graft and greed and corruption. Sutro's was the voice of common humanity raised against the man who would ride upon its shoulders and exploit it for his own financial advancement."

Sutro made so strong an impression on the Committee on Mines and Mining that it threw out the report and drew up a bill which recommended that Congress lend him $2,000,000 to finish his tunnel. McCalmont's Bank, when they heard of this, loaned him another $800,000.

The easier part of the tunnel had been dug. At the stone heart of the bastion a man with a pick was impotent. Dynamite had to take its place. When the rock had stopped falling and the smoke cleared, the men came to the head of the cut to shovel the rock into cars to be hauled over track and dumped by the Carson River. Now a mile into the mountain, the air was so fouled with smoke and carbon dioxide that even the strongest men could work no longer than a twenty-minute stretch before, half fainting, they staggered back to cooler air. Yet no miner abandoned Sutro or the job: how do you walk out on a man who is working alongside you, dressed only in a breechclout and heavy boots, perspiration pouring down his powerful body while he shovels rock into dump cars?

In July 1873 Sutro sank his first air shaft, straight down the mountain, to let in fresh air. It reached the header almost five thousand feet from the entrance of the tunnel, and enabled him to hollow out another half mile of tunnel. Then a miner's pick opened a hot volcanic river, and the new air shaft filled to its brim. Now there was not enough air to keep a candle burning. The miners worked in the sickly light of a kerosene lamp which consumed what little oxygen was left; the men retched as they shoveled.

The white Victorian house lashed to the side of Mount Davidson saw little of Adolph Sutro during these months, for like Charlie Crocker he was always at the railhead; almost no hour of the day or night passed without his working with dynamite or a sharp knife to cut the oozing clay from under his feet. He brought huge blowers and air compressors over the Sierra Nevada from California, put ice helmets on his men to bring to reality Dan De Quille's "quaint" of a decade before, buried eight of his men in the miners' cemetery after explosions and cave-ins.

With every foot deeper that he penetrated into the mountain, the harder became the rock, the more demoniacal the floods of ill-smelling, boiling water. Again and again all work had to stop until the flowing river had exhausted itself out the tunnel's mouth, and Sutro could lead a work crew into the fetid darkness to feel out the extent of the damage.

It was no longer Ralston, Sharon and the Bank of California who were his chief opponents. Time too had become an enemy, even as it had with the Donner Party. William Sharon had done his job well; he had wasted the precious years. Overhead they were taking out the valuable ores which could have been coming out through his tunnel faster and cheaper, and with infinitely better working conditions for the miners. What mountain could give such wealth endlessly?

While Adolf Sutro was tunneling several hundred feet a month into the base of Ralston's kingdom, another man, Alvinza Hayward, began to bore inside the Ring itself.

The Crown Point mine, which extended more than five hundred feet across the face of the lode, had been in barren rock for years and had assessed its shareholders so heavily that the stock was down to $2.00 a share. Ralston believed that there was ore below its worked-out level; he had to believe this of all his mines in order to keep his superstructure intact. Hayward, a minority participant in Ralston's Ring, recommended that his brother-in-law, John P. Jones, who was said on the Comstock to have "a nose for ore," be given the job of boring deeper into Crown Point. Hayward was one of Ralston's closest friends, and had carried out many a secret mission for him. When he suggested "jovial, ruddy-cheeked, powerfully built Welshman" Jones as the new superintendent for Crown Point, Ralston readily agreed.

For nearly two years Jones prospected vigorously in all directions of Crown Point, using up a $250,000 assessment Ralston had put on the stock. Then the Ring abandoned hope.

No longer on salary, Jones continued to spend his days and nights below, searching, investing his savings in all the Crown Point stock he could find at $2.00. At last the hard barren rock in which he had been working grew softer, there was an occasional streak of quartz, then "the porphyry became more decomposed and friable, lighter in color, and seen with straggling red lines of iron rust." Jones pierced a clay seam and came to a fine streak of whitish quartz in which were valuable pockets of ore.

He confided in no one but Alvinza Hayward. Together they decided to steal the mine from Ralston's Ring. They secretly invested the balance of their savings in Crown Point stock, borrowing from friends wherever they could. Crown Point stock began to rise. Using a new stratagem, Jones went into the San Francisco Stock and Exchange, where he had been asking friends to carry Crown Point stock on his account, and told them he would have to get out of the stock because his son had been taken ill in the East. The market interpreted this to mean that Jones had "struck a horse," that is, had decided the mine was worthless. Investors got the tip on *Jones's sick child* (the mine, not the boy) and promptly sold their Crown Point for whatever they could get. Jones and Hayward accumulated their majority.

Now that they had control they took their crews into the mine where "nothing less than an earthquake or a volcano could have sired such a bonanza," and took out $30,000,000 in gold and silver! They would not even pay conscience money to Ralston's Ring by sending their ore to the Union Mill and Mining Company to be refined; instead they organized their own milling company.

The monopoly of Ralston's Ring had been breached.

CHAPTER III

Four Irishmen Become Silver Kings

A NEW COMBINATION MADE itself known on Mount Davidson, locking horns with the Ring, digging itself a bonanza right under William Sharon's sharp cold nose. It was another magic combination of four, forming as unlikely a plural marriage as the Big Four of the Central Pacific, yet it worked superbly, each man to his talent.

They were all Irishmen, three of them born in or near Dublin: John W. Mackay and James G. Fair, two rough pick-and-shovel miners born in the same year, 1831, as well as the same town; and William S. O'Brien, the San Francisco saloonkeeper, five years older, previously content to preside over the Auction's free lunch counter, cutting generous slabs of ham, corned beef and conversation for his customers. James C. Flood, the fourth man of the quartet, was born the same year as his San Francisco saloon partner, 1826, in New York, his impoverished emigrant parents having crossed the Atlantic just in time to make one of the Silver Kings American-born.

Three were Forty-Niners: O'Brien, who arrived first, in July; Flood, who came around the Horn; and Fair, who belied his name by being "black Irish," with curly black hair, dark skin and eyes; a quartz miner and manager of a stamp mill. Mackay was the late arrival, coming in 1851, spending eight years in the Sierra Nevada camps mining for beans and loving every moment of the rough, male mountain life. O'Brien, the generous free lunch wielder, and Mackay, the powerful pick wielder, started out wanting little from life, O'Brien desiring only enough to live on, Mackay saying that when he had put together a $25,000 poke he would quit. O'Brien, known in San Francisco as "the genial millionaire," ended obscurely with $12,000,000; Mackay died world famous with assets of perhaps $100,000,000.

Flood, O'Brien, Mackay and Fair were distinct personalities, each with his own flair and flavor. James Clair Flood was a short man with a shorter neck, bull-like shoulders, a massive face of heavy features lighted by a healthy, glowing red skin. He looked dull, but he was a clever, brainy man. He had had some New York public school education, spent eight years as an apprentice to a carriage maker, and come to California with an overpowering passion to rise in the world, to become not only wealthy but a member of the frontier's high society... and to ride in a beautiful carriage.

Ambitious Flood, wanting money fast, went to the mines in 1850 as a carpenter at $16 a day, but quickly started placering on the Feather River and accumulated $3000 in gold dust. Here, in the mining camp of Poor Man's Gulch, he met plump, round-faced, mild-mannered William S. O'Brien, who also found several thousand dollars worth of gold that winter. The two men became friends, returned to San Francisco together in 1851 and settled down as neighbors, Flood opening a livery and carriage shop, O'Brien a marine supply store. They were both wiped out in the depression of 1855.

The two friends decided to go into partnership. Simple William O'Brien, who was the best liked of the Silver Four, had more intuitive wisdom than his partner. He suggested that since San Francisco's thirst was the only appetite that did not decrease in a depression, why not open a saloon? Garbed in a high silk hat and good broadcloth suit, he stood outside the saloon using a genial conversational hook to pull customers in. Flood, who was not altogether enchanted with the implications of being a bartender, refused to work in shirt sleeves and white apron; he wore instead a fashionably cut gray business suit to protect his bourgeois social position.

Their Auction Lunch was a "bit house," two drinks for a

quarter. Bachelor O'Brien spent the happiest years of his life as host to San Francisco's businessmen. His irrepressible good nature, combined with Flood's astute bookkeeping, made the Auction Lunch thrive. When the new Stock and Exchange opened close by, Flood and O'Brien cultivated the stockbrokers and Comstock insiders who came into the saloon, sifted tips and information, bought stocks studiously and made money from the beginning. By 1868 they had put away a fair fortune, so they sold their Auction Lunch and opened a stockbrokerage office around the corner on Montgomery Street. It was in this capacity, as prudent and reliable brokers, that their partnership met the new partnership of Mackay and Fair of Virginia City; met, liked each other, and merged.

At the close of the 1860s John W. Mackay and James G. Fair stepped boldly forth into the arena of the Washoe Mountains to challenge William Sharon for the championship of the Comstock. Sharon's continuing drive to own a voting majority of stock in every mine on Mount Davidson had plunged the Bank heavily into Hale and Norcross stock, for which they paid as high as $7000 a share. It was a costly victory; the Hale and Norcross ore veins ran out, and Sharon had to unload the Bank's expensive stock for as little as $41.50 a share.

John Mackay and James Fair had little respect for Sharon, and even less fear. Sharon was basically a money and stock manipulator; Mackay and Fair were deep-fissure experts. They were convinced there were still valuable bodies of ore in the Hale and Norcross. They were also sure they could outsmart Sharon. Not the least abashed that they were taking on the Bank of California, and that they had between them only the modest amount of money Mackay had earned from a small mine, the Kentuck, they decided secretly to corner the Hale and Norcross stock and, when they had control, kick Sharon, Ralston and the Bank of California off its board of directors.

Unwilling to expose their purpose by buying the stock themselves, Mackay and Fair went "down below" to San Francisco for a conference with the two saloonkeepers turned stockbrokers, whom they had known and liked for many years. Flood and O'Brien approved of the plan, agreed to put in some money of their own, and quietly to buy up all the Hale and Norcross stock they could find. The new partnership was formed on the spot, Mackay taking three eighths, Fair two eighths, Flood and O'Brien the remaining three eighths between them.

James Flood was such a shrewd operator that he managed to

buy Hale and Norcross at low prices for a month without the exchange knowing what he was about. When the board of Hale and Norcross met, the Mackay-Fair-Flood-O'Brien partnership had a majority of stock. Sharon, taken completely by surprise, was outraged at having been outmaneuvered; but being put off the board was more a matter of prestige than profit, for what was the use fighting over a mine that had been exhausted?

Mackay and Fair, who was the newly elected superintendent of Hale and Norcross, took crews into the mine, struck in new directions, and in 1870 paid $500,000 to its stockholders. With part of their profits the new combination bought two mills with which to crush their ore, and purchased Sharon's Virginia and Gold Hill Water Company when Sharon decided there was little more water to be had.

The battle for Hale and Norcross was the merest prologue. By 1871 the mine was again played out. Mackay lost most of his gain in buying the barren Savage mine, Fair lost his in the equally barren Bullion. But in 1871 they formulated a daring plan: to buy up the thirteen hundred feet lying between two of the most productive of the original mines, the Ophir and the Gould and Curry. This area, which Sharon and other Comstock experts had declared worthless, was known as the Consolidated Virginia; its stock had depreciated to $1.00 a share after $1,000,000 had been sunk in fruitless exploration.

Mackay and Fair felt sure there were as rich veins at buried depths as had ever been found in the Ophir or Gould and Curry. In order to secure the property they set their San Francisco partners to buying stock in the six separate mines which made up the thirteen hundred feet. Flood and O'Brien bought cautiously, but this time Sharon discovered their game and was able to force the control price of the Consolidated Virginia up to $100,000. Sharon reported in high glee to Ralston that Mackay and Fair had been taken:

"The entire thirteen feet was a bankrupt piece of property worth in the market less than $40,000."

Mackay, Fair, Flood and O'Brien secured control of the Consolidated Virginia in February of 1872. They levied an assessment of $212,000 on the outstanding stock because they knew they had to go deep to have a chance. They also knew that they could not gather enough money to work through the abandoned Consolidated Virginia shaft. They needed a short cut. They appear to have taken the suggestion of the superintendent of Sharon's Gould and Curry:

"Why don't you go to the bottom of the Gould and Curry and drift northward? The shaft is twelve hundred feet deep; a tunnel would be below the workings of the Best and Belcher, the Consolidated Virginia and the California; it would be virgin ground and if there are any deep ore bodies on the fissure . . . you ought to strike them."

To the amazement of everyone on the lode, Sharon not only gave Fair and Mackay permission to use his Gould and Curry mine for their explorations, but made the whole thing easy by charging them a reasonable rate to haul their waste rock up the Gould and Curry shaft. To Ralston in San Francisco he reported triumphantly that he was now transferring the last of the Hale and Norcross dollars to the Bank of California's capacious pockets; that the Bank would soon have back its Virginia and Gold Hill Water Company as well.

From May to August William Sharon proved to be a prophet. Down at the twelve-hundred-foot level, for all their valiant effort in cutting a drift a thousand yards long under the heart of their Consolidated Virginia, nothing was hoisted up the Gould and Curry shaft but barren rock.

But Mount Davidson had not come to the end of its prodigality. One day a delicately thin vein of ore stood across the drift. Fair and Mackay began digging to follow this slight thread, losing it, then finding it, seeing it begin to widen. After three weeks of pursuit it widened to a seven-foot layer; a week later the vein was twelve feet thick. Certain they had a rich strike, the Silver Four began two simultaneous movements: Mackay and Fair, in Virginia City, sank a vertical shaft straight down the mountain to their find; Flood and O'Brien, in San Francisco, bought up the outstanding twenty-five per cent of Consolidated Virginia stock.

The true nature of their find they kept fastidiously concealed; visitors were not permitted into the ore-bearing chambers on the ground that the area was too hot. The Consolidated Virginia vein had widened to fifty feet; the side drifts cut from the main shaft showed almost solid ore.

Toward the end of October Fair and Mackay invited Dan De Quille down into the Consolidated Virginia for a scoop. Fair said to this best of all mining reporters:

"Go in and climb around. Measure it up, make up your own mind. I won't tell you a thing. People will say I posted you."

De Quille spent a half day in making a wide-eyed check, taking out with him five random selections of the Consolidated Virginia ore which an assay told him averaged $380 a ton in both gold and silver, almost ten times as rich as the average assay of Comstock ore. He broke the news to the world in a bold headline in the *Territorial Enterprise:*

HEART OF THE COMSTOCK

He declared that at a conservative estimate the gold and silver on the level he had explored must be worth $230,000,000! Diedesheimer, still the most respected of the Comstock engineers, spent several days below and then announced that the Consolidated Virginia stock should now be valued at $5000 a share. A government geologist sent out from Washington by the Director General of the Mint studied the Consolidated Virginia and gave as his opinion that the ultimate yield would be $300,000,000:

"But to guard against a chance of overestimation, I take the assays at one half, which will place the production at not less than $150,000,000."

By the first winter snow Consolidated Virginia was shipping $250,000 worth of pure bullion a month. Fair and Mackay penetrated deeper to fourteen and then fifteen hundred feet. Lord in *Comstock Mining* reported:

"When, finally, the fifteen hundred foot level was reached and richer ore than any before met with was disclosed, the fancy of the coolest brains ran wild. No discovery which matches it has been made on this earth from the day when the first miner struck a ledge with his crude pick...."

The ore was so rich that waste rock had to be added to it in order to put it through the mill.

John W. Mackay, James G. Fair, James C. Flood and William S. O'Brien became multimillionaires. Once again they had bested William Sharon and made him look the fool. Sharon now knew it would be a fight to the finish with these four Irishmen who were already being called the Silver Kings. If they were the new kings, what happened to him, the former King of the Comstock?

In San Francisco Ralston decided that the Belcher, next-door neighbor to the Crown Point, stolen by Hayward and Jones from the Ring, should logically have a continuation of the bonanza buried in its bowels. He and Sharon bought up all ten thousand shares at $1.00 each, sent in crews to dig deep... and came up with a $35,000,000 haul.

The Belcher discovery made William Sharon one of the three wealthiest men in the Far West, along with William D. Ralston and

D.O. Mills of the Bank of California. It was nine years since he had arrived on Mount Davidson, bankrupted by a stock fraud. Everyone agreed that he had enjoyed his revenge in full measure; for he had taken out no one knew quite how many tens of millions.

This was the point at which William Sharon decided that he had outgrown the Comstock, that he would be elected to the United States Senate. This would give him added prestige in the social world. He could also instigate legislation which would stop Sutro and his tunnel, and wield political power over the new Silver Kings. The Nevada legislators, who chose the state's two senators, were selected, financed and elected by the Bank of California. Sharon's decision to become a senator was as good as the election itself.

Not to Joseph Goodman, two-fisted editor of the *Territorial Enterprise*.

On the morning that William Sharon returned from San Francisco to open his campaign for the Senate, Goodman wrote a blistering editorial:

"You are probably aware that you have returned to a community where you are feared, hated and despised. Your career in Nevada for the past nine years had been one of merciless rapacity. You fostered yourself upon the vitals of the state like a hyena, and woe to him who disputed with you a single coveted morsel of your prey. You cast honor, honesty, and the commonest civilities aside...."

The miners on the Comstock agreed with this portrait; but the word that did the real damage was "hyena," which was repeated in every mine shaft in Nevada within twenty-four hours. The Comstock was not going to let Sharon have the office uncontested. Up stepped the hard-hitting Welshman, John P. Jones, hero of the Yellow Jacket fire, and a second-time hero for having stolen the Crown Point mine and its $30,000,000 fortune from under the Ring's grip. Nevada wanted Jones for its senator.

Sharon struck back. He threw an enormous block of Comstock stock onto the market, causing a furious selling wave, and the loss of almost $50,000,000 in paper value. Jones and Alvinza Hayward lost $3,000,000 between them, but they had the resources of the Crown Point to draw on. Sharon's device to ruin Jones backfired against San Francisco. A large part of the city was crippled. The name William Sharon became a dirty word, hurled as an imprecation by the thousands who had lost their funds through his depressing of the market.

Sharon next set out to ruin Jones's reputation, bringing to San Francisco Isaac Hubbell, who had been underground foreman of

Crown Point on the night of the fire disaster. Sharon offered Hubbell $50,000 if he would sign a statement charging that John P. Jones had deliberately set the fire himself.

The Nevada miners were outraged. Joe Goodman once again spoke for Nevada and central California when he wrote in the *Territorial Enterprise:*

"In this act, malice has reached the very acme of baseness and cowardice. Malevolence has never suggested a means of vengeance more monstrous."

Even Sharon's business associates in San Francisco felt that he had gone too far. A grand jury indicted Sharon for conspiracy, whereupon Billy Ralston demanded that Sharon resign from the senatorial race.

Poker player Sharon simply shrugged; he had been dealt a poor hand. Next time around he would revenge himself, even as he had on the Comstock Lode. This time his revenge would include his partner, William Ralston, who had forced him to bow out of the senatorial race.

CHAPTER IV

A Run on the Bank

OF ALL THE GAMBLERS on the San Francisco Stock and Exchange, none was more deeply involved than William Chapman Ralston, the city's financial wizard. He did not wear the gambler's red sash of two decades before; he was immaculately groomed, his only idiosyncrasy being that he studded the bosom of his white linen shirt with black cameos. He was gambling on a hundred fronts, all of them heroic in proportion, most of them constructive in character. He could afford his multimillion-dollar plunges because of Nevada, "that hole in the ground with gold and silver in it."

But to keep his empire of steamship lines, dry docks, woolen and iron mills, vineyards, tobacco fields, granaries and dozens of other producing enterprises afloat he needed singlehanded ownership of the mines and mills on the Comstock. It was not that he was greedy, he told himself, but that he wanted to build San Francisco into a great world metropolis. That was why he had used any method, fair or foul, to stop Adolph Sutro's tunnel. Sutro had been the first to challenge his domination over Mount Davidson; the man was a fanatic, and fanatics were costly to stop.

Several times Ralston had found himself with his manifold millions frozen; but on each occasion he had pulled himself out by some buccaneer maneuver. Only the year before he had desperately needed gold coin to meet a run on the Bank of California. Newly inaugurated President Ulysses S. Grant had forbidden the San Francisco Mint to hand out gold coins in exchange for gold bullion bars. Deep in the night Ralston and two friends, aided by the federal director of the Mint, opened the federal vaults and took out almost four tons of gold coins, replacing them with bullion. The next morning when the Bank of California opened its bronze doors to the waiting crowds, Ralston had $1,000,000 in gold piled up on the counters, desks and tables in full view. The combination of brigandage and showmanship turned away the pressure on his bank.

He then hastened to a nearby bank which was similarly threatened, mounted a dry-goods box on the sidewalk and cried to its milling depositors:

"Bring your books to the Bank of California. We'll accommodate you with cash!"

The run was averted.

The federal government accepted Ralston's rebuke by ruling that bullion could be exchanged freely at the Mint for gold coin. San Francisco worshiped Billy Ralston more than ever. His fame spread to London, Paris, Berlin, Rome, Stockholm: the symbolic figure of the robust, daring Far West pioneer.

At fifty-five Billy Ralston was a rugged giant of a man, who challenged the powerful tides of Golden Gate Strait and swam halfway out to Alcatraz Island on every weatherable day. His clients coming into the Bank could see his "well-shaped head, alert eyes, high-colored intelligent face" behind the glass screen of his office; they said they liked to see their captain always on duty on the bridge. The thousands of San Franciscans dependent upon his judgment and his bank for their economic security as well as their growth told each other that Billy Ralston's "dash, energy and success" gave them a sense of security. Even in his most troubled hours he presented a calm, smiling, debonair face to San Francisco. His intimates could tell when he was disturbed because of his habit, while they discussed a problem, of tearing up sheets of paper into tiny fragments and throwing them into the wastebasket. When he was troubled his aim was bad, and the floor around him would be littered with white scraps an inch deep.

As befitted the leader of the community, he was a man of boundless charity. When President Daniel Coit Gilman of the newly opened University of California, on Berkeley's golden poppy-covered hills, came to ask Billy for money to build a men's dormitory, Ralston gave him the funds for six dormitories. When the dying James Lick, known as California's shabby millionaire, came to Ralston to ask what he should do with the $5,000,000 he could not carry into the next world, Ralston replied:

"Leave them to San Francisco so that we can use your money to improve and beautify the city. Found a technical school for young boys and an old people's home for the indigent; leave your money for parks and statuary and free public baths so that San Francisco can become another immortal Rome!"

It was all done by Lick, just as Ralston had advised.

Billy Ralston's friends in the financial world of San Francisco said that Ralston caught the hares and then his friends picked out the fat ones. People named their sons after him, subdividers their streets; when the Southern Pacific Railroad wanted to name a town after him in the San Joaquin Valley, and he was too modest to accept, the town was called Modesto, Spanish for modesty. San Francisco said of him:

"He was humble; he was simple in his everyday life. It was as easy to approach him on business or on a mission of charity, as the most humble hod carrier in the city. He was known as a friend of the poor, a patron of art, a commercial tycoon, a great banker and philanthropist."

He was not always generous, nor was he always modest; his character could not help but tear into shreds whole reams of the white paper of personal conduct. Once when he was racing his powerful matched horses down the road from San Francisco to Belmont, a small boy going along the road on a nondescript horse accepted the tremendous speed as a challenge. The boy and his horse outdistanced Ralston; this humiliated him before his companions. Ralston turned back to the boy's farm and forced the boy's father to sell the horse by the bludgeoning weight of a heavy check.

Nor was he a hero to his wife. She saw little of him and could find no area of rapprochement with this overpowering wizard who was up and gone at five in the morning to survey his many projects. When she stayed at their mansion on Pine Street in town, Billy gave what became known as Lucullan feasts at Belmont. There were stories of orgies with women; after one banquet "in the course of the entertainment, befuddled guests would wander into the wrong sleeping rooms, causing much embarrassment." When the beautiful English actress Adelaide Neilson came to Ralston's California Theatre for several weeks of Shakespearean repertoire, Billy Ralston gave her a $100,000 string of diamonds, because, it was said, Miss Neilson was offended at San Francisco for not giving her a gift as it had given a $10,000 diamond solitaire to Ellie Wilton when she had played there. Naughtier minds put a somewhat different interpretation upon the $100,000 gift.

Now in 1872 William Chapman Ralston began the most ambitious building project of his life, one that he saw as a culminating stroke for the city of San Francisco: a hotel so magnificent in its structure and appointments that it would draw the wealthiest, the most famous and influential people from all over the world. When a friend asked him what he was going to call the hotel, Ralston replied with a sweet smile:

"Well, it's going to be a palace, one of the greatest palaces of the world, so why don't we just call it the Palace Hotel."

Nothing less would have satisfied him. It was a reply as indigenous to San Francisco as to Ralston. Oscar Lewis says in *Bonanza Inn*:

"Visitors from conservative eastern centers found at least half the population suffering from delusions of grandeur. Few could compete with the San Franciscans in the matter of civic pride. Newcomers were often puzzled to know what the boasting was about. To unprejudiced eyes the town was crude, noisy, unkempt, its streets lined with buildings reflecting the worst features of the debased architectural taste of the period. The town had been in existence less than three decades. It had grown far too rapidly."

It was Ralston's concept that the Palace Hotel would end this pioneer age in California, start it on an age of elegance which would make it a rival of New York, London and Paris.

His first step in the construction of the Palace Hotel was to buy an area of sand dunes south of Market Street, on which there were a couple of cottages, sand where Mariano Vallejo had shot a grizzly bear in the 1830s. The square block of land cost him $400,000. He engaged the city's leading architect, John P. Gaynor, to go east and study the Palmer House and Grand Pacific hotels in Chicago, the

Sturtevant House and New Windsor in New York. He hired Henry L. King, who had built the California Theatre, the Grand Hotel and many of his biggest factories. A high wooden wall was thrown up around the block; artesian wells were dug, and into the foundations which were to house basements and subbasements Ralston poured $1,000,000 of concrete.

The hotel was to be rectangular in shape, with three large courts to supply air and sunshine, and a vast central court with a circular driveway. Around this great court there were to be seven stories of galleries and rooms, the whole domed by glass. The hotel would overlook the city, and every room have a big bay window. The walls were double thick and reinforced with iron to prevent damage by earthquake or fire; five miles of pipe were built through the structure and a hundred twenty-five miles of electric wire, bringing such innovations as pushbuttons in each room, telegraphic communications between the hotel services, electrically operated clocks, pneumatic tubes for messages and parcels, and as the crowning touch of good taste, over seven hundred "Water closets boasting an arrangement by which the water is carried off without producing the horrid noise one usually hears."

It was Ralston's ambition to build and furnish the entire Palace Hotel with California products. Where he already had the factory going, such as the Mission Woolen Mill, he set it to making the blankets for the hotel. When he did not have the proper factory he either imported one, bought one or built one. When he needed oak planking for his floors he bought a wooded ranch in the Sierra Nevada foothills, only to discover that it grew the wrong kind of oak. When he wanted forged nails and tools, he bought a foundry. He built a key and lock factory to make the hardware, acquired the West Coast Furniture Company to manufacture the hundreds of heavy beds, dressers, tables and chairs, all out of native California laurel, that would be needed. William Sharon, whom Ralston had obliged to participate in the grandiose venture, watched these operations with a clammy eye. He protested to Ralston:

"If you are going to buy a foundry for a nail, a ranch for a plank and a manufactory to build furniture, where is this going to end?"

There were some products Ralston could neither buy nor have made in California, so he sent out orders to have rugs woven in France, plates and dishes made specially by Havilland in France. The Belfast, Ireland, warehouses were said to have been stripped of linen; rare inlaid woods were brought in from India, art works from all over the world. The Palace Hotel would cost $6,000,000 in cash out of Ralston's and Sharon's pockets, yet for a decade or two there could be no chance of filling more than half of its rooms.

By February 1873, when only two or three floors of the Palace had been constructed, the directors of the Bank of California grew uneasy about their "liquidity." The bank was supposed to have a capital of $5,000,000, but at this time $3,500,000 was loaned out to Ralston for his various enterprises: $2,000,000 in the New Montgomery Street South real estate company, through which Ralston was buying land south of Market Street to create a new business section; not too much short of $1,000,000 in the Pacific Woolen Mills, and close to $600,000 in the Kimball Carriage Company. Cash was short, the directors were frightened; they demanded that Ralston take personal responsibility for these industrial debts. Billy Ralston, tearing up sheets of paper and throwing them into his wastebasket, said wistfully to his brother:

"If you make money for these people you won't get any thanks, but if you lose money, you will be cursed for it."

D.O. Mills, the president whom Ralston had brought in to front for the Bank of California, and who had become one of the three richest men west of Chicago through Ralston's management of the bank, decided that now was the time to get out with his funds intact. He obliged Ralston to buy all his bank stock for cash, cash Ralston badly needed. Now Ralston was president of the Bank of California in name as well as fact.

Emperor Ralston was in need of another Comstock bonanza. He needed his new millions to run the incredible Belmont, where fifty to a hundred guests were invited at a time, where his elaborate stables housed the most expensive race horses to be purchased. As *paterfamilias* of San Francisco he needed also to keep all of the factories and foundries and forges open and running so that every workingman had employment and the city remained prosperous.

He had sent endless prospecting crews into the played-out mines owned by the Bank of California, searching for new veins. But the find went to his opponents, the new Silver Kings.

Having lost the Consolidated Virginia because of Sharon's advice that the property was worthless, he was now urged by Sharon to rebuy the stock of the Ophir mine, which was in *borrasca*, but which Sharon said unquestionably had the same bonanza ore at lower levels that the Silver Four were taking out of the Consolidated Virginia. Though he was growing short on capital, Ralston began pouring his funds into Ophir stock, buying it up at any price, including "Lucky" Baldwin's stock in the mine, giving Baldwin his note for $3,600,000.

Now another blow fell which indicated that his fabulous luck might not be unending. From the day that Ralston had opened the door of the California Bank in 1864 until this spring of 1875, the Bank of California was never seriously challenged as the financial leader of northern California and Nevada. But the Silver Four decided that they needed a bank of their own. They opened one in San Francisco, called it the Bank of Nevada, with a $5,000,000 capital in solid gold bullion taken out of their Consolidated Virginia. Up to this time the Silver Four had banked with Ralston; now they withdrew $1,000,000 they had on cash deposit, and $400,000 in bullion.

Billy Ralston grimly showed an untroubled face to San Francisco; but he had to borrow $2,000,000 in cash from William Sharon, in return signing over all of his rights to his beloved Palace Hotel.

Beady-eyed, pale-faced, black-mustached William Sharon was a thoroughgoing scoundrel. So unified was his one-dimensional character that all of his years in the Far West did nothing to influence, change, mollify or shape him. Sharon had vowed that he would have a seat in the United States Senate. To insure himself the votes of the Nevada legislators he had given them confidential advice to buy Ophir stock and to hold it up to a $300 price. Most of the legislators sank their life savings in Ophir, and started a speculative frenzy on the San Francisco Exchange which observers called maniacal.

With the Ophir stock only a few dollars below $300 a share, the Nevada legislature elected William Sharon to the United States Senate. When his election had been certified to the federal government, Sharon secretly sold all of his own Ophir stock; he also sold it short. The sale of his large block on the San Francisco Exchange plummeted the Ophir shares to their real value, which was almost nothing. Ralston, needing money to cover the stock he had bought on margin, began stripping himself of his individual possessions: a $16,000 ranch in Kern County, which his father-in-law, Colonel Fry, took for a fraction of its land value; his remunerative holdings in the Virginia and Truckee Railroad, which he turned over to D. O. Mills for a $750,000 loan...Sharon's manipulations cost Ralston $3,000,000 in cash; for the Ophir collapse threw the exchange into panic, the total value of all mining stocks on the Comstock declining $100,000,000.

The Nevada legislature was wiped out...which some people said was little more than it deserved. The $500,000 Sharon had spent to get himself elected he earned back on his short sales. No one got the better of William Sharon. No one, that is, until the beauteous Sarah Althea Hill, known as the "Rose of Sharon," made him the laughingstock of the country.

The stock market crash in the summer of 1875 was the most disastrous San Francisco had known. Business was paralyzed, shops and factories closed, or more properly were foreclosed. Thousands of San Franciscans who had mortgaged their homes, their savings, their jewelry were bankrupted.

Few knew that the tragedy had been engineered by United States Senator-elect William Sharon. They had idolized William Ralston, they had trusted him implicitly; and now he had led them to pauperism. The members of his Ring abandoned him, bringing in their Bank of California stock and demanding that Ralston buy it or turn over real estate to them. Ralston looked haunted now, he tore paper in great quantities and scattered it like a white rug on the floor of his office as he denuded himself one after another of his properties, all except Belmont and the Pine Street mansion.

But he had one giant manipulation in hand which could redeem him, and the Bank. That for the first time in his twenty years of service to San Francisco this deal was leveled against rather than for the interests of the city could not matter to him now that he was in desperate straits. The Spring Valley Water Company was an engineering project which was designed to bring needed water to the rapidly growing city of San Francisco. Ralston borrowed $3,000,000 on the last of his possessions to buy enough shares of the Spring Valley Water stock to own the company. With the control in his pocket he proposed to sell the water company to San Francisco for $14,500,000.

This high price was his first error; the William Ralston of a year or two before would have developed the company and presented it to San Francisco with a gesture of largess. Next he made a more serious error. Knowing that his offer had to be approved by the city government, he set out to buy the vote of the councilors and the mayor. The local press turned against their idol, called him a masked highwayman, a vicious swindler. An Associated Press reporter in San Francisco wrote the story of Ralston's attempt to corner the water market, and then corrupt the city government, and sent it out to the papers of the whole country. It was printed in the New York *Commerical Advertiser*, hurting not only Ralston's reputation but his credit in the eastern banks and his international position.

In mid-August the Silver Four determined to rid themselves of

Ralston and his competition. They further depressed the Comstock Lode stocks; those which had remained in Ralston's control became worthless.

On August 26, 1875 the rumor flashed through San Francisco that the Bank of California was in trouble. Almost immediately $1,500,000 was drawn out of the bank by depositors in large- and small-sized checks; all of the available coin and bullion was used to meet the run. By two-thirty in the afternoon the crowds had turned into a mob, frantic with fear and anxiety over its savings. They pushed and crushed and screamed and cursed trying to get into the bank. Slowly the great bronze doors, which had symbolized the prosperity and solidity and the phenomenal growth of San Francisco, were pushed shut from inside.

The Bank of California had failed.

The next morning was blazing hot even at dawn. Ralston rose early, tried to reassure his wife, then went to the bank and surrendered Belmont to his partner, William Sharon. He divested himself of his Pine Street mansion, his race horses, his vast if miscellaneous collection of art. Every last possession he had in the world he conveyed to William Sharon in trust for his creditors.

That afternoon there was a meeting of the bank directors. William Chapman Ralston gave them a complete report; he owed $9,500,000. He claimed that if he were given a chance he could muster assets of $4,500,000, and that if the directors would keep their confidence in him and approve the reorganization scheme he had worked out, he would have the Bank of California on its feet within a reasonable time, and all depositors would be paid in full.

The board, composed of members whom Ralston had made millionaires, asked him to leave the room so that they might discuss his proposal. The moment the door was shut, William Sharon jumped to his feet and moved that Ralston be forced to resign.

D.O. Mills came into Ralston's office and told him that his resignation was demanded immediately. Ralston signed the paper.

Overheated, overwrought, he made his way to Neptune Beach on the Golden Gate Strait. There he undressed in the bathhouse, dove into the cold water from an abandoned wharf and started swimming with strong strokes through the Golden Gate tides toward a stern-wheeler lying a few hundred yards off shore, and beyond that toward Alcatraz Island, the favorite goal of his swimming years.

An hour later his body was washed back onto the beach.

San Francisco went into mourning. Part of the genius of the city was dead.

CHAPTER V

Nevada Cycle of Life and Death

EIGHTEEN SEVENTY-FIVE PROVED to be the climactic year for Virginia City. John W. Mackay and James G. Fair raised the Consolidated Virginia monthly dividend from $324,000 to $1,040,000, and there were rumors that the dividends would be doubled. And why not, when the figures proved that the Consolidated Virginia and the adjoining California mine, which the partners now opened (for every share of Consolidated Virginia a man might be so fortunate as to own, the Silver Kings gave him seven twelfths of a share in the California mine), were the richest producing mines in the history of the world?

With the Consolidated Virginia and California paying over $1,000,000 a month in dividends, a speculative mania again seized San Francisco. Staggering fortunes were made in a matter of days. E. S. "Lucky" Baldwin instructed his broker, just before leaving for a vacation in Hawaii, to sell out his shares, but forgot to endorse the certificates, without which the stock could not be sold. When Baldwin returned to San Francisco he found his stock worth a hundred times the figure at which he had been willing to sell.

Even more staggering were the stories passed about as authentic news: charwomen scrubbing floors with three-carat rings on their fingers; chambermaids buying the rooming houses in which they had been working; hack drivers giving away their carriages to the first passer-by. Fever ran so high in Virginia City that in the Chinese quarter, whose residents were the Far West's most passionate gamblers, there were almost no fantan games to be found because the Chinese were gambling on stocks instead. The necessary monies needed to maintain the normal business of central California again made their way into the Stock and Exchange.

389

To get out this wealth the mines became omnivorous consumers of supplies. Each month in 1875 the Consolidated Virginia alone used a half million feet of timber, five hundred fifty cords of wood to heat the boilers, a hundred gallons of coal oil, three hundred fifty boxes of candles, twenty thousand feet of fuse, tons of steel, iron, coal.

In order to keep this supply pouring down their mine shafts, John W. Mackay and James G. Fair, who had found their color by sound mining judgment, called on the inventive genius of the area. They set up an industrial empire which rivaled that of the recently buried William C. Ralston.

Their two primary requisites were wood and water. A million feet of lumber was needed underground each month, and forty thousand cords of wood above ground to supply power for the hoists and mill machinery. The eastern slope of the Sierra Nevada had already been denuded; now the lumber had to be cut on the California side, rafted across Lake Tahoe and dragged over rough roads by teams. Since the roads were washed out each winter, the Silver Kings turned to the V-shaped flume recently invented by J.S. Haines of Genor, Nevada. The Pacific Wood Lumber and Flume Company was formed to build a flume from a pine forest northwest of Washoe Lake, fifteen miles from Reno.

The flume turned out to be one of the engineering feats of the Far West. It was a meticulously built trestle of two-inch planks nailed together, two and a half feet in width, its main supports firmly anchored, each unit-box sixteen feet long and so braced that no break could be carried beyond the one section. The hundreds of sections were smoothly fitted so that the speeding logs would not jam. Water which served as the lubricant was brought from Hunter's Creek, twenty miles away. Where the timber was cut the flume was two thousand feet higher than its destination. The heavy logs came flying over canyons, rivers, foothills and around mountains at rates of speed up to sixty miles an hour, at some points seventy feet in the air. There was a telegraph along the entire line and crews to watch the movements of the lumber until it reached the Virginia and Truckee railhead.

Virginia City had been subsisting on what water it could secure from springs at the foot of Mount Davidson, and from wells. The Silver Four, who had bought the Virginia and Gold Hill Water Company from William Sharon three years before, sent for the West's top water engineer, H. Schussler, who had created the Spring Valley Water Works for San Francisco. The only supply of water adequate to Virginia City's needs had to come from the Sierra Nevada, twenty-five miles away, separated from Mount Davidson by the Washoe Valley with its depression of seventeen hundred feet. How to bring the Sierra's waters from a mile high, across a low-lying valley, and up a mile again to Virginia City?

Engineer Schussler examined his terrain as closely as had Theodore Judah while searching in this same vicinity for a railroad pass. To the Silver Kings' question of whether it could be done, Schussler replied:

"Yes, though with great difficulty."

The nature of the difficulty became plain when Schussler went to work: he had to make a model of every yard of his seven-mile line, showing every curve and joint where it crossed narrow ravines or avoided rock formations.

It took a full year for the twelve-inch pipe to be manufactured in the San Francisco foundries. The completed project cost $2,000,000 but it was a great success. On the day the first water reached Virginia City bands played music up and down the length of C Street, the now venerable Fremont cannon, abandoned in the snow area from which this water came, was fired in celebration, and rockets were jubilantly gotten off the chest of Mount Davidson.

The pipe supplied Virginia City with over two million gallons of water every twenty-four hours. When the supply proved insufficient for the frenzied working of the mines, a second ten-inch pipeway was laid alongside the first, the supply flumes were pushed deeper into the heart of the Sierra Nevada, giant reservoirs were built for storage, and a three-thousand-foot tunnel drilled through a ridge to connect with the melted snow waters of Lake Tahoe.

Virginia City was a celebrity among cities, tales of its wealth having spread to the remotest corners of the earth. The market value on all its stock soared to $300,000,000; in its fifteen short years of life it had grown larger than century-old Los Angeles. The famous of the world made special trips to this largely subterranean community, for Virginia City was little more than a roof over the mine house below, perforated seventeen levels deep into the mountain. Former President Grant came to see what all the talk was about, as well as President Rutherford B. Hayes, Emperor Dom Pedro of Brazil, the Duke of Sutherland, whom Mackay and Fair entertained with five hundred bottles of champagne, the famous singer Adelina Patti, the infamous agnostic Robert G. Ingersoll. All were dressed in miners' hats and boots and heavy woolen coats and hurtled downward in cages to areas of such intense heat and boiling, bubbling clay that Ulysses Grant muttered, "This is as close as I want to come to hell," and agnostic Robert Ingersoll said quizzically:

"Maybe I was wrong, maybe there is a hell after all?"

The Comstock miners would have agreed with him. The three shifts, working eight hours each around the clock so that no pick handle was ever allowed to cool, stepped out of their cages at the fifteen-hundred-foot level where the richest ores were found, stripped themselves down to breechclouts, metal hats to protect their heads from cascading stones, and thick-soled boots to shield their feet from the boiling earth. In this heat of 134° no man could work more than fifteen minutes before stumbling back to a cooling station. While they worked, other men kept a spray of cold water over them, or threw towels dipped in ice water over their backs. In this year alone Consolidated Virginia consumed two million pounds of ice; every man's daily allotment was ninety-five pounds.

When a new vein was struck and the owners wanted to manipulate the stock, the miners were sometimes kept below for two weeks so word could not leak out. The rarest of viands were hauled down for them: *caviar, pâté de fois gras*, duck and lobster and steaks cooked by the town's best chefs, cases of the best French wine for their off hours, and soft mattresses to sleep on.

The miners did not complain. They amused themselves by naming the separate ledges Wake-up-Jake, Gouge-Eye, Let-er-Rip, Leviticus, and Deuteronomy. In spite of the hardships, the ever present danger of sudden death and the more lingering one from consumption, they liked their life. Virginia City was their town. After they came up in their cages and had a hot scrub in the mine shaft building, they were off to prove that they were the highest-paid miners in the world. Every other building was a richly ornamented saloon and gambling house for their entertainment; there were expensive clothing stores, theatres for plays, prize fights, music; and down the hill below C Street a red light district which, Virginia City bragged, was superior to any in the West in size, variety and amiability of its residents:

"Visitors of note, having been shown through the mines and mills and having been entertained at the Washoe Club, the C Street bars or Piper's Opera House, turned by common consent toward 'the line,' down the steep grade to the double row of white cottages that line D Street for two crowded blocks."

Virginia City was still bachelor by nature, most of the men living in the center of the town in comfortable lodging houses. The few families had homes on the bare but respectable slope above C

Street, the mine owners in their Washoe overdressed mansions, while the superintendents, foremen, doctors, lawyers, bank clerks and office help had comfortable white cottages with small, prim gardens. For the miners' families, the lower slope of town, below C Street, was a mile-long jungle of "shacks built wall to wall, huddled close to the mills or the immense dumps, their rough unpainted wooden sides bleached a uniform grey by the dry dusty summer." One could walk for blocks without seeing a bush or a blade of grass; when a Washoe zephyr blew, a tin roof or an outhouse would be picked up and deposited a block away.

The town was as naked of law as it was of paint. For the hundred killings allegedly caused by claim jumping or alcoholic quarrelings, there were thirteen culprits hanged by a hastily formed Vigilance Committee, and eight by county sheriffs. David Belasco, a young actor in Virginia City, who became one of the country's leading theatrical producers, said:

"I was one of the first to bring naturalness in death scenes, and my Virginia City experience did much to help me toward this."

One man wrote home to San Francisco, "California in '49 was a kind of vestibule of hell, but Nevada may be considered the throne room of Pluto himself. I have seen more rascality in my forty-day sojourn in this wilderness of sagebrush, sharpers and prostitutes than in a thirteen year experience in our not squeamishly moral state of California."

In this saturnalia a drunk one night tried to light his pipe with a kerosene lamp. The sun-dried walls of his lodging house caught fire. The usual Washoe zephyr was blowing. The flames swept from house to house with a speed swifter than the fastest man of the Virginia Engine Company. Houses dried out by a decade of desert sun did not so much burn down as explode into flames.

A thousand homes vanished within an hour. Dynamite was used to protect the mine buildings and mills, but everything went up in a red sheet of fire that drove the inhabitants high onto the crest of the hill clutching sentimental possessions in their arms.

The whole town burned down: businesses, hotels, schools, churches. Several of the mines caught fire. "The loss was around $10,000,000; but to Virginia City, producing this much bullion from its mines each month, the fire was shrugged off as more of an inconvenience than a serious loss." The psychology of the town was accurately reflected by stocky, tactless James G. Fair:

"The receipts and expenditures of our company total more than that of half the states in the Union."

And so, like its sister cities of the Far West that burned down periodically, Virginia City dug into the debris, and in two months had rebuilt itself into a beautiful metropolis on the side of a barren hill in the middle of a barren desert: a new Piper's Opera House that cost $150,000, the International Hotel, six stories high. The Washoe millionaires built more elaborately rococo mansions above C Street, their women imported gowns from Paris. The men dressed in Prince Alberts, brought chefs from New York and pianos from Boston. There were exclusive Washoe social clubs, weekly waltzes and quadrilles at the Entre Nous, and a social stratification depending on the amount of one's freshly mined money.

And underneath all this, the greatest of all Nevada's engineering feats had been going on night and day for six years now.

By 1875 the Sutro Tunnel had come over eight thousand feet through the bowels of the mountain, with still another twelve thousand to go before it could reach the Comstock mineral belt. While Sutro was doggedly blasting his way forward at the rate of two hundred fifty feet a month, sinking shafts down through the side of Mount Davidson for fresh air, Mackay and Fair were hauling millions of tons of rock and ore up through their shafts. For every ton that went up Sutro lost a potential $2.00 with which to pay back his more than $2,000,000 debt to the banks.

All during the month of October when Virginia City was burning over their heads, while the Consolidated Virginia and Ophir caught fire and hundreds of miles of their inner timbering burned, Sutro, stripped bare to a breechclout, worked at the head of his bore, redoubling his own and his men's efforts in the hope of pushing through before the mines could be totally retimbered and put back into work.

But it was slow going, agonizingly slow. The deeper they dug, the more impossible became the working conditions. Though crack teams were working the bore, the best of them could stand only two to three hours a day in the heat and foul air, made nauseating by the stench of the perspiring mules. Sutro installed powerful Root blowers, and when these did little more than nibble around the edges of the heavy rancid heat, imported double compressors from Kalk, Germany. Still the air remained so stagnant that the men staggered back from their drills. The boiling, viscous clay bubbled up around their feet, sucking in and cracking the stoutest timbers. Sutro dared plant only the smallest amounts of powder for fear of blowing them all into oblivion.

Yet no man faltered. They swore by Sutro and the tunnel. Back they came into the poisonous gases, the foul, unbreathable heat, the omnipresent danger. The months passed, the years, while they pushed ahead, ten thousand, twelve thousand feet from the entrance, seventeen thousand, eighteen... Now no powder could be used at all, the rock had to be dug out with stout hearts and stout picks. And finally, when at twenty thousand feet they entered the mineral belt, the sulphuric springs gave off such unendurable heat that it seemed no human could work this last, agonized hundred feet at all.

They worked it, Sutro at the head nearly every inch of the way. On July 8, 1878, eighteen years after the inception of his idea, Sutro heard the workmen of the Savage mine blasting on the other side of a thin syenite partition. Joy flooded over him: he had come like an arrow twenty thousand feet through a volcanic mountain to his target! He sent a message out his tunnel, around the mountain and up Gold Canyon to the superintendent of the Savage:

"Should your men succeed in knocking a drill hole through, let them stop and not enlarge it until I am fully notified. There should be ample time given for your men and ours to retire, for I am afraid a column, several thousand feet in length, of hot, foul air, suddenly set in motion might prove fatal to the men."

Superintendent Gillette of the Savage replied that he was ready to blast the opening. He pounded on the partition with his sledge hammer to notify Sutro that the blast was about to be set off. Sutro hammered on the rock as a reply that they were ready. The Savage miners bored eight holes in the thin wall, shoved in eight Rigorret powder cartridges while Sutro, on his side, sealed up the bottom of the drill holes with earth.

The powder cartridges were lighted from a fuse. A tremendous roar shook Mount Davidson, filling its hollow shafts and tunnels with reverberating echoes. There was a rush of smoke, and then up from Sutro's Tunnel, through the Savage, came such a blast of hot air that the miners were knocked flat, their lights put out.

The Savage miners picked themselves up and shoveled to clear away the blasted dirt and rock until they finally came to the jagged hole which had been blown open.

From this point they could look straight down ten feet onto the floor of Sutro's Tunnel. A ladder was handed down. When it reached the floor Adolph Sutro, his torso and hair covered with rock and earth from the explosion, climbed up and, in the words of one of the miners, stood in the opening of the Savage like Mephistopheles. Suddenly a rush of clean, cool air came up the more than twenty thousand feet from the Carson River through his tunnel, picked up Adolph Sutro as though he were a child and dashed him against the opposite wall of the Savage mine. Sutro stumbled to his feet, bruised and bleeding, but his face transfused with happiness.

An American flag was hoisted in the shaft of the Savage. At the mouth of the tunnel cannons were booming. The dream, the heartbreak, the brutal labor, and now at last the fulfillment.

The men had matched the mountain.

But not a moment too soon. The Crown had stopped paying dividends in 1875, at the height of Virginia City's prosperity. Belcher payed its last dividend the following year in 1876. By midsummer 1877 even Mackay and Fair began to reach strata of inferior ore. They told no one except their Stock Exchange partners in San Francisco. Quietly, discreetly, Flood and O'Brien began unloading the Consolidated Virginia and California stock.

There were still millions of tons of ore to be carried out on Sutro's causeway through his tunnel, and each ton of it returned him, his miner partners, and investor banks $2.00. Most months the tunnel took in $200,000. But the big bonanza was finished. The mines were winking out.

Adolph Sutro worked his tunnel for a year, paid all the costs of building it, then sold his interest for a sum in excess of $2,000,000, going "down below" to San Francisco to continue his heroic story as the reform mayor of San Francisco, to build upon and beautify the cliffs overlooking the Pacific Ocean.

San Francisco received the news in January of 1877 that the Consolidated Virginia had passed its monthly dividend. The reaction on the Stock and Exchange was disastrous. Glasscock says in *The Big Bonanza*:

"Literally thousands of the residents of San Francisco and other California and Nevada towns who had been substantial, progressive, productive citizens were reduced to beggary in the streets."

Each large business that closed its doors threw hundreds of employees out of work. Charitable organizations fed twenty thousand people a day. In San Francisco there began a mass movement toward Pauper Alley, a row of disreputable shacks in a poverty-stricken part of town now occupied by a whole class of San Franciscans who had, only a few days before, been prosperous and respectable, maintained spacious homes and servants. When the San Francisco city government offered $1.00 a day for manual labor on public projects, the thousands who applied included some of the city's former business executives and professional men. Charles H. Shinn says in *Story of the Mine:*

"In Pauper Alley one can walk any time in business hours and see creatures that once were millionaires. Now they live by free lunches in bar cellars and on stray dimes tossed to them for luck. Women, too, form a part of the wretched crowds that haunt the alley."

The Consolidated Virginia was still operating on a restricted scale in 1880, but the signs were evident that it would close down the next year, as would most of Virginia City's mines. And when the mines closed, what would there be to support the town? There was no industry, little agriculture or ranching. There was almost nothing by which a man could earn a dollar.

As the mines closed the miners and mill hands drifted away. The expensive shops closed, then Piper's Opera House, then the International Hotel. The mansions above C Street were abandoned, as were the rows of shanties from D Street down the hill. The more expensive saloons and gambling houses shut their doors, then the medium-priced ones and then slowly the cheapest, for there were fewer and fewer people to patronize them. The Washoe zephyr swept clouds of dust over the town in summer, and blew away whole groups of buildings in the storms of winter. Others just sank through the earth into the mine shafts below them. Shacks were taken apart and used for firewood. The *Territorial Enterprise* struggled on for a number of years, but there were few loyal souls left to read it.

Virginia City's life cycle was a short two decades, from 1859 to 1880.

What had happened to the $380,000,000 that the Comstock had poured into the bloodstream of the Far West? What had happened to the big bonanza of more than $108,000,000 that the Silver Kings alone had taken out of Mount Davidson? Who had it all?

John W. Mackay, James G. Fair, James C. Flood and William S. O'Brien had a major portion of it. Amiable, tubby, red-faced "jolly millionaire" O'Brien did very little with his, beyond supporting his brothers and sisters, nephews and nieces; he was the first of the four to die, leaving his fortune to close relations.

James Flood used his millions to buy more and more San Francisco real estate, until the day came when he owned most of downtown San Francisco, and his rents amounted to $500,000 a month. All of his leases stipulated that the tenants must keep up the improvements.

John W. Mackay left California for richer fields, acting out in the East the drama of the Commercial Cable and Postal Telegraph Company by means of which he broke the Western Union monopoly. His wife, the divorced seamstress whom he had met and married in Fair's parlor in Virginia City, left her husband for the international set of Europe where she reigned as queen for twenty years, seeing her husband for only those rare hours when he came across the Atlantic.

James G. Fair bought a seat in the United States Senate where he distinguished himself mostly by his absence. He had replaced William Sharon, but if there were any choice between these two, no one in Washington was able to discern it. Fair was sued by his wife on the grounds of "habitual adultery," the first time a United States senator had been so charged. Mrs. Fair was awarded the family mansion and almost $5,000,000 in cash.

William Sharon had a large block of the Comstock millions, as did John P. Jones, Lucky Baldwin and perhaps fifty other shrewd manipulators and mine owners.

Virginia City and everyone else had been stripped bare.

Nevada had its Carson Valley farms, with its capital at Carson City, a few hundred miles of the Central Pacific railroad track and a couple of railroad towns like Reno and Wadsworth. Here too the rapacious giants had stripped the wealth of the land. Here the Big Four of the railroad reigned.

The Carson *Morning Appeal* protested, "The Southern Pacific has never made the slightest attempt to build up Nevada and it declines to pay taxes on its lands in this state."

Another historian complained:

"Nevada was retarded for four decades by the Southern Pacific. From the first it made passenger and freight rates low enough to kill competition from stages and wagons. Once competition was good and dead it raised its rates. It enforced the vicious long and short haul system to make huge profits at the state's expense. In 1877, for example, the railroad's charge was $300 to take a carload of coal oil from New York to San Francisco. From New York to Reno, a trip three hundred six miles shorter, the charge was $536. Goods destined for Nevada towns were shipped to San Francisco and reshipped back. This system of rates prevented any Nevada towns from rising to occupy the place of Salt Lake City in Utah or Denver in Colorado."

An anti-railroad congressman from Nevada, Rollin Daggett, cried in Congress:

"Their object seems to be to crush, not to develop the industries of Nevada, and to this end the competition of special rates from California is employed when there is danger of an industry growing into importance."

Critics charged that the Southern Pacific bought the entire

Nevada legislature of 1879; that it shut down an opposing newspaper, the Eureka *Daily Leader*, and ran one opponent, F. E. Fiske, out of the state because he fought the discriminatory freight rates. Lillard comments in *Desert Challenge:*

"From 1870 on the railroad vampires sucked Nevada like an orange, gave nothing much in return, and kept the state needlessly a desert in order to keep other railroads from coming west to gobble at the rich spoils of California."

Nevada was in serious trouble.

Its land was in *borrasca.*

It would remain in barren rock until 1900 when gold would once again be discovered some two hundred miles southeast of Virginia City, and the roaring gold camps of Tonopah, Goldfield, Rhyolite and Rawhide would bring forth from the alkali flats another $250,000,000 of the royal metal.

CHAPTER VI

"Only force can settle the Mormon problem"

THE BEGINNING OF THE 1870s found just a few short of eighty-seven thousand Saints living in Utah. Mormon missionaries traveled steadily: to nearby Arizona and then to Mexico, to England, to Europe, to Palestine. No matter how difficult the times there were always Church funds available to bring in fresh converts. The long-established policy of searching for skilled artisans to build up their home community enabled them, on their twenty-second anniversary, to parade in Salt Lake every category of craftsman from horticulturist to stonecutter, from architect to carpenter, from plasterer, painter and glazer to blacksmith, sheet ironworker and tanner; from dentist, printer and engraver to butcher, baker and matchmaker.

The Church and its Saints were active and successful on many fronts. They built a gasworks to light the streets of Salt Lake, then street cars to transport the population. Though the Utah coal veins were too narrow to mine economically, less than five thousand tons having been taken out by the beginning of the 1870s, Brigham Young encouraged his Saints to search for new veins and supplied the capital with which to mine them, so that by the middle of the 1870s there was sufficient coal to meet the more urgent Mormon industrial needs.

In a picture of Logan, located in the Cache Valley some eighty miles north of Salt Lake City, Robinson in *Sinners and Saints* gives a clear view of what the Latter-day Saints meant by an ideal community:

"The Gentile does not take very kindly to Logan. There are no saloons there and no public animosities to give it what they call 'Spirit'; everybody knows his neighbour, and the sightseeing fiend is unknown. The one and only newspaper hums... on like some self-satisfied bumble bee; the opposition preacher, with a congregation of eight women and five men, does not think it worthwhile... to appeal to Heaven every week for vengeance on those who don't agree with him and his baker's dozen. There is no pomp and circumstance of war to remind the Saints of Federal surveillance, no brass cannon pointing at the town [as in Salt Lake City], no ragged uniforms at street corners. Everything is Mormon. The biggest shop is the Cooperative Store; the biggest place of worship the Tabernacle, the biggest man the President of the Stake. Everybody that meets 'Brothers' and 'Sisters' each other in the streets, and after nightfall the only man in the streets is the policeman, who as a rule retires early himself. It is a well-fed, neighbourly, primitive life among orchards and cornfields... with every bee bumbling along its own busy way, but all taking their honey back to the same hive."

Few houses had locks on their front doors.

Many of the smaller communities were so solidly Mormon that the inhabitants never laid eyes on a gentile.

In the fast-growing center of Ogden, where the Union Pacific and Central Pacific met and discharged passengers from East and West alike, there was a constant flow of outsiders into the Mormon milieu. Brigham Young said:

"If you should have visitors from those professing to be 'Christians' and they intimate a desire to preach to you, by all means invite them to do so. Of course you have the power to correct whatever false teachings or impressions your children may hear."

He made a personal contribution to the building of the first

Catholic cathedral in Utah. Roberts, a church historian, says:

"Brigham Young knew that Mormonism had nothing to fear from contact with the Christian sectarianism of the time."

During the first two Protestant sermons to Mormons in Ogden, a couple of fractious Saints started heckling the preacher. They were hushed down by the rest of the Mormon audience and later rebuked by the Church. One Protestant missionary to the Mormons commented:

"All I have got to show for twenty to thirty years of work in Utah is the conviction that I got the Saints to talk more about Jesus than they used to, and a little less proportionately about Joseph Smith."

But in their capital in Salt Lake the Mormons were never able to achieve that peace in Zion for which they had made the long trek into the wilderness. Here in Salt Lake there were not only the Temple and Tabernacle, but also the main business and political offices of the Church. By the same token here gathered the governor, the judges, marshals and other federal officers, the attorneys who were fighting the Mormons in the law courts, the editors who were attacking them in the newspapers, businessmen who were attempting to penetrate Utah's economic fabric.

The decade of the seventies opened for the Mormons with a national contest in their Tabernacle. The debate resulted from a defense of polygamy made by the Utah delegate, William H. Hooper, on the floor of Congress, and the retort of the Reverend Mr. John P. Newman, chaplain of the United States Senate, in a forceful sermon in Washington.

Believing from a report in the Salt Lake *Daily Telegraph* that Brigham Young had offered to debate this subject with him, the Reverend Mr. Newman took the train to Utah. In Salt Lake he found that Brigham Young had not issued the challenge, and so he was obliged to enter the contest against the Mormon second-string theologian, Orson Pratt.

The subject, "Does the Bible Sanction Polygamy?" brought eleven thousand spectators to the Tabernacle. The Mormons felt that if Apostle Pratt could win this debate the federal government would be obliged to accept the Principle.

The Mormons were successful in their extension of polygamy, particularly among the young people who had grown up in happy multiple-marriage households. On January 13, 1870, three thousand women had gathered at the Tabernacle in Salt Lake to pass a resolution which approved "The right of husbands to obey the highest behest of heaven: to marry as many wives as they chose;" When the federal threat to imprison all polygamist men was read in the Tabernacle, Phoebe Woodruff rose and cried to the assemblage:

"Let them grant us this last request, to make their prisons large enough to hold us, for where our husbands go, we will go too."

This evidence of good judgment so impressed Brigham Young that the following month the Mormon women were given the right to vote, one of the two earliest such franchises in the United States. As another evidence of respect, the Mormons licensed C. Georgie Snow, daughter of Judge Snow, as the first woman to practice before the Salt Lake Bar.

What now became clear to the Mormons listening to the Newman-Pratt debate in their Tabernacle, and to thousands of readers without, was that although the Old Testament did not sanction polygamy it described a good deal of it as having been practiced. Orson Pratt began quoting Deuteronomy, Chapter 21, verses 15-17, "If a man have two wives..." and Exodus 21:10, "If he take him another wife..." detailing the fact that Jacob had four wives and Lamech had two. The Reverend Mr. Newman countered by showing that the polygamists in the Bible were guilty of other crimes as well: Lamech was a polygamist, but he was a murderer and an outlaw; David was a polygamist, but he was a seducer, and a murderer of the seduced woman's husband.

The New York *Herald* reported the debates verbatim, while most other newspapers of the country gave colorful day-by-day accounts.

At the end of the third day the Reverend Mr. Newman continued his transcontinental railroad trip to California, convinced that he had demolished the biblical justification for polygamy. The Mormons were even more delighted at the opportunity that had been afforded to present their case to the American people.

When the Reverend Mr. Newman returned to Washington he learned to his chagrin that his judgment in rushing into such a contest was seriously questioned. He never forgave the Saints, who quoted him as saying, "Only force can settle the Mormon problem." As a close friend and spiritual adviser to President Ulysses S. Grant, he proved to be one of the foundation stones of an intense anti-Mormon administration.

The second pillar of President Grant's antagonism was Vice-President Schuyler Colfax, who was considered inside Utah "a great Mormon-hater." It did not always matter whether these charges of Mormon-hating were true; once they were spread among the Latter-day Saints the damage was done. Colfax had made two trips to Utah, one in 1865 and another in 1869, to persuade the

Mormons that they should abandon polygamy and conform to the laws of the United States. The Mormons had not taken Colfax's advice; he had been hurt at having his well-meant counsel rejected. Now in 1870 he was further incensed against the Mormons because he believed that Brigham Young, in a sermon in Salt Lake, had called the President and Vice-President of the United States "drunkards and gamblers." Again, it did not matter whether Brigham Young had made this charge; Vice-President Colfax was convinced that he had, and so the damage was done.

President Grant launched a two-pronged attack by appointing a governor and a secretary of the territory on the one hand, and a chief justice and two other justices for the federal courts in Utah, all of them avowedly anti-Mormon.

Governal of Utah Territory J. Wilson Shaffer, from Illinois, reportedly dying of consumption, was described as a "man of iron will, forceful, energetic, patriotic." Upon his arrival in Utah to take over his office, the Latter-day Saints were informed that he had announced:

"Never after me, by God, shall it be said the Brigham Young is Governor of Utah."

Chief Justice James B. McKean, Judges Cyrus M. Hawley and Obed F. Strickland the Mormons promptly named "the Missionary Trio." All three were charged with being "professed pious Methodists" owing their appointments to the Reverend Mr. Newman. The Mormons cried:

"Judge McKean is certainly the most dangerous of all public functionaries: a judge with a mission to execute, a judge with a policy to carry out."

Chief Justice McKean, who in his person represented the central battleground in Utah for the next five years, was born in Vermont in 1821 but had practiced law in New York. Just short of fifty years of age when he reached Utah in the summer of 1870, he carried himself erectly, had been known as an accomplished scholar, an able writer, was possessed of a genial manner; a man who had enjoyed many warm friends.

With the completion of the transcontinental railroad there came into being for the first time in Utah a well-organized "Utah Ring," composed of every opposition element from William Godbe, the Mormon who wanted the privilege of criticizing Brigham Young's acts, through the most violent Mormon-haters who wanted the Mormons wiped out completely. The Ring consisted of editors of the opposition newspapers, which were just getting started, the lawyers who had come in to file real estate claims against the

GIANTS STALK THE LAND

Mormons' possession of the Great Basin, gentile businessmen who felt they had been unjustly treated, officers of the California Volunteers who had remained in Utah to settle, and political adventurers who enjoyed fishing in troubled waters.

The Ring sent lobbyists to Washington to convince President Grant that more federal troops were needed in Utah, one of their charges being that General de Trobriand, in charge of the United States troops at Camp Douglas, was a "Jack Mormon," that is, a Mormon-lover. President Grant sent in more troops under General Phil H. Sheridan, who established a new military base, Camp Rawlins, three miles northwest of Provo.

Governor Shaffer removed as the lieutenant general commanding the Utah militia Daniel H. Wells, Brigham Young's second in the hierarchy of advisers, and in his place appointed General Patrick E. Connor, who had commanded Camp Douglas during the Civil War. Then on September 15, 1870, he issued an order which obliged all Utah militiamen to deliver up their arms. Next he prohibited musters and drills. This meant the end of the Nauvoo Legion, the strong arm on which the Mormons relied for their defense. With new federal troops arriving daily at Camp Rawlins, the Mormons gulped, delivered up a few guns as token payment and hid the rest.

Governor Shaffer thereupon died. The Saints buried him with full honors if not full grief. A dispatch from Washington on November 1, 1870, named as new governor Vernon H. Vaughan, former secretary of the territory.

Three weeks later there occurred the "Wooden Gun Rebellion." The band of the Utah Militia Third Regiment, having received some new musical instruments, decided to celebrate. Church historian Whitney observes that the Mormons also "wanted to test the attitude of the new Governor on the 'No Arms, No Drill' law." About two hundred militiamen assembled on the Twentieth Ward Square and drilled behind the music of the regimental band. They also drilled with arms. But Governor Vaughan was away. Secretary of the territory George A. Black arrested the eight officers in command, charged them with a "rebellion or insurrection against the United States." Judge Hawley had them confined in charge of the military authorities at Camp Douglas.

Church historian Roberts disputes Whitney, maintaining that there were no militiamen involved at all, only a group of young boys carrying wooden guns.

The militiamen were released from Camp Douglas.

As the fresh federal troops reached Camp Rawlins, everybody

was friendly. Merchants came in from Provo to sell "the boys in blue," the soldiers strolled through the town trying to catch the eye of the well-lectured Mormon girls. However when a group of soldiers tried to rent a hall large enough for a thirty-plate dinner party, to be followed by dancing, the Mormons turned them down; all they could get was one small table for dinner in the Cunningham Hotel.

On the night of the party some fifteen to twenty of the soldiers hired Alma Brown to take them into Provo in his wagon. Another group went in on foot. A few carried weapons. At eleven o'clock shots were heard in the street, and into the hotel dining room dashed one of the soldiers crying that his shoulder had been broken by an assailant. The officer in command of the soldiers is alleged to have ordered:

"Get your guns, we'll clean out the Mormon sons-of-bitches."

Alderman William Miller was taken prisoner and marched through the streets with soldiers prodding him in the rear with their bayonets. Councilor McDonald charged that the first floor of his house was sacked. No one was seriously hurt, though the women were frightened and many of them hid out in the cornfields all night.

The affair became celebrated as the "Provo Riot" or the "Provo Raid." The Mormons were indignant because they thought that the military authorities at the camp had ordered the raid; the rest of the country believed that the Mormons had been unfriendly in refusing a hall to the boys, and had brought the altercation on themselves.

The tensions were building.

Chief Justice McKean kept up a steady fire on the judicial front. In an equally effective pincer movement he disqualified all members of the Latter-day Saints from the grand jury. The United States marshal had summoned seven Mormons among other prospective jurors, but when George Q. Cannon, editor of the *Deseret News*, was put in the witness box, prosecuting attorney Baskin, appointed by Justice McKean, asked:

"Do you belong to the Church of the Latter-day Saints?"

"Yes."

"Isn't polygamy one of the fundamental doctrines of the Church?"

"Yes."

"You do not believe that this is adultery?"

When Mr. Cannon answered no, he was excused from jury duty. So were the other six Mormons.

In order to be naturalized, all foreign converts had to appear before Chief Justice McKean. He asked:

"Do you believe in polygamy?"

When the convert replied that multiple marriage was a part of his religion, he was refused his citizenship papers. The Mormons cried in anguish:

"In the matter of naturalizing aliens, 'NO MORMON NEED APPLY' might as well be posted over the Court entrance unless he was willing to deny his religious faith."

In the trying and sentencing of Mormon offenders before non-Mormon juries, the Englebrecht case served as a road marker in the journey toward civil war. Englebrecht, a non-Mormon, owned a large wholesale liquor store in Salt Lake. He had been arrested by the Mormons several times for selling at retail, and also for selling without a license. City Marshal J. D. T. McAllister took nineteen Mormon policemen with him to the Englebrecht store where, in the words of the Mormon historians, they "quietly but sternly" destroyed $22,000 worth of liquor, a euphemism for breaking all the bottles and kegs. Englebrecht brought suit against the marshal and the police for recovery of the property destroyed.

Chief Justice McKean impaneled a jury of non-Mormons who brought in a verdict of guilty against the Mormon marshal. McKean assessed the largest possible fine: triple damages. The Mormons appealed the case to the United States Supreme Court, protesting that all of Justice McKean's decisions were illegal because he was denying the Mormons a trial by a jury of their peers.

The gentiles inside Utah were now as militant as the Mormons. Considering Governor Vaughan to be a "Jack Mormon," they sent a lobby to Washington to exert pressure on President Grant to have him removed. So strong was their influence that Vaughan was replaced in January 1871 by George L. Woods, former governor of the Oregon Territory. The Springfield *Republican* announced jubilantly that Woods was "a pronounced anti-Mormon."

A contest began for the Utah penitentiary, which had been run by Utah for many years and was now by an act of Congress put into the hands of federal officers. The Mormon city marshal was holding as a prisoner in a Salt Lake jail a gentile by the name of Kilfoyle, who was serving a sentence for manslaughter. The federal authorities demanded that he be turned over to them because Washington had given them control of the penitentiary. The city authorities refused. Prosecuting attorney Baskin was charged by the Mormons as saying, "My way of taking possession of the prisoner Kilfoyle would have been to put the guns of Fort Douglas on the city, blow open the City Hall and jail, and force the possession of the prisoner with bayonets."

At the same time a full-scale row began between the police of Salt Lake and the commanding officers of Camp Douglas over the custody of soldiers who broke the law in Salt Lake. The Church claimed the Mormon police had a right to pick them up; federal officers maintained that the only power to arrest or charge a United States soldier with a crime was the military.

Governor Woods next proclaimed that he was taking over the appointment of superintendent of schools.

Though the disturbances were mere skirmishes, the Mormons were not sleeping calmly in their beds these nights.

Thin, fine lines like the tricklings of little rivers were beginning to appear on the solid map of Mormonism.

The anti-Mormon Ring had developed a vested interest in opposing Mormonism. The temper of the Ring was reflected by a statement of its leader, Judge McKean, who wrote to United States Attorney General Williams:

"If, in any age, there was ever a part of Christian land so utterly abandoned to the leadership of impostors, criminals and traitors, as in this territory, I have never heard of it."

On the political front, General Patrick E. Connor, federal head of the Utah militia, who in 1863 had attempted to start full-scale mining in Utah in order to create a gentile majority, earned himself the title of "The Father of the Liberal Party," a legally constituted political opposition party which could appear on the ballot. For the first time since the founding of Deseret in 1847 there were two political parties in Utah.

The party's birthplace and the capital of the subsequent violent anti-Mormon press was a gentile town northwest of Ogden called Corinne, which had been started as a railway construction camp and was now the favorite community of the gentiles of Utah. Corinne hoped to take the play away from rapidly developing Ogden, which was almost solidly Mormon, and grown to about a thousand in population. A member of the Utah *Reporter*, J.H. Beadle, describes Corinne as having "nineteen saloons, two dance halls, eighty *nymphs du pave*, popularly known in mountain English as soiled doves."

Both parties put candidates in the field for the election of the Congressional delegate. At the same time William Godbe, who was still trying to constitute the loyal opposition, started a paper of which he said:

"The *Daily Tribune* will have no sectarian bias and will be the organ of no religious party whatever."

The *Daily Tribune* under Godbe and Harrison, his co-editor, representing the "New Movement," was a moderate effort to reform and for democratic procedures inside Mormonism. Church historians agree that it was a decent, conservative paper. However it soon passed out of the hands of Godbe to become the organ of the Liberal party, and then all bars were down. It became coarse and abusive in its attitudes and in its language, classing the Mormon women with prostitutes, calling them "conks" for concubines, and the men "polygs" for polygamists.

In 1870 the Liberal party ran General George R. Maxwell, a wounded Civil War veteran who had come to Utah in 1869 as a federal land registrar, as their first candidate against the incumbent Mormon Hooper. Of the twenty thousand votes cast, Hooper got eighteen thousand five hundred and General Maxwell fifteen hundred, a surprisingly large total for the opposition when one considers that a year before not more than a few hundred gentiles would have been willing to cast an anti-Mormon ballot. General Maxwell contested the election, and sent a petition to Congress which charged Mormon Hooper with being disloyal to the federal government.

Still another force had been formed in the Gentile League of Utah, with its headquarters in Salt Lake. In the Gentile League were a number of serious and honest men who were striving for what they called a separation of Church and State; the balance of them were accused by the San Francisco *Examiner* of being a conspiracy of "small fry, poppinjay politicians and would-be statesmen."

Brigham Young had hastened the coming of the new age by building his own railroad to connect Salt Lake with Ogden and the transcontinental railroad. The Utah Central was completed in January 1870. It was built by the Mormons for their Church, which financed it; the people who did the actual work took stock in lieu of wages. When he drove the last spike Brigham Young said proudly:

"Our cities and counties are without any debt. The Utah Central Railroad is in debt, but to whom? To our own people."

The single greatest change caused by the coming of the railroad to Utah was the opening of the territory to mining, a pursuit which Brigham Young had forbidden to the Saints. There had been the one attempt producing less than $200,000 worth, at the location where General Patrick Connor had accidentally stumbled on a gold ledge, but the difficulties of getting the ore out in wagons had made it unprofitable.

In 1870 there began the fourth and final gold rush of the Far

West. The Saints had always known that the gold and silver were there; they had avoided the deposits as religiously as they had sin.

The precious metals of Utah lay in a rectangle, even as they had in California and Colorado; a rectangle cutting across the territory just south of the Great Salt Lake in Rush Valley and extending on a long line eastward through Parley Park, almost ten thousand feet up, and still farther eastward to the end of the Uintah Mountains. Southward, on the short, east side of the rectangle, the color extended to the American Fork district, then moved on a long line westward, cutting the territory in the middle, until it reached the West Mountains, and then made a right-angle turn north to Tooele. Later the color would be found in the extreme southwest corner of the territory, at Silver Reef, near St. George, exactly as the strikes were made in the San Juans in the southwest end of Colorado.

The Utah gold rush of 1870 was as unlike the rushes in California in 1849 and in Nevada and Colorado in 1859, as life in those three areas was different from the Mormon way of life. The gold and then the silver found in California's Sierra Nevada, Nevada's Washoes and Colorado's Rockies was entirely in wild, uninhabited and previously unknown, unsettled country, without government, laws, town, roads, military, police. These golden rectangles were truly the pioneer's frontier. In Utah, though many of the mines would be in as high and rugged a terrain as in California or Colorado, the prospectors would never be far away from the Mormon Church, the Mormon government, the Mormon Militia, the rigidly disciplined Saints.

"This is the most unfavorable looking country for mines that I have ever seen. The Mormons have a hard time serving the Lord in this desolate god forsaken country, and it is about time for something to turn up and take the place of sorghum and wine as a circulating medium."

The incoming miners could not form their own government; the government was there. They could not rampage over the countryside, for the Mormons controlled the four per cent of arable land, all of the water and the supplies. Nor could the miners absorb or corrupt the established residents; the Saints were beyond absorption or corruption. In California, Nevada and Colorado the miners had created cities; San Francisco, Sacramento, Virginia City, Denver, by pouring in manpower and wealth. In Utah the incoming miners had little effect on Salt Lake City, Provo or St. George, beyond bringing them extra prosperity by buying their produce. The Mormons forbade their people to have intercourse with the neighboring miners' towns.

Down in southern Utah, near St. George, Bonanza City developed into a good-sized town called Silver Reef, but when the mines played out there was nothing left to sustain it.

Mining began on a large scale in Utah, but it was a gold rush of capital rather than of individual prospectors. As in Nevada, there was almost no placer mining because there was so little water. The few hundred prospectors who came to Utah, a considerable portion of them from California, found good color and staked out claims. But in almost every case they sold out quickly to the larger mining companies and moved on.

Parley Park, east of Salt Lake City, had one of the few mines discovered by an independent prospector, Judge William T. Barbee, who had lived in Utah. The area turned out to be one of the best silver districts in the United States, but it took several years to build roads into the mountain fortress.

There was no great flood of miners with their picks and shovels and frying pans. There were no long lines of emigrant wagons crossing the plains and the Rockies, no wild excitement in the press of the nation proclaiming a "NEW ELDORADO!"

The pioneer gold seekers who had thronged into California, Nevada and Colorado had plunged into the unknown; they were not a whit frightened by this, probably because they had no conception of how rugged and rigorous that unknown could prove to be. Utah was a known quantity. It had suffered a voluminously bad press for two decades. The Mormon people were represented as unfriendly, clannish and downright antagonistic to gentile entrepreneurs. The Utah Seventier never materialized, as had his earlier cousins, the Forty-Niner and Fifty-Niner. Even when it came to seeking hard-rock miners, timbermen and the hundreds of mechanics needed to run the mines and mills, the gentile owners of Utah's gold and silver did not attempt to attract men from the close, experienced fields of Colorado to the east or Nevada and California to the west. Instead they imported their miners by shiploads from Ireland and Wales.

Compared to the wild-west sagas of California, Nevada and Colorado, Utah's development remained comparatively well behaved, though some of the new mining towns had as many as fifteen saloons, billiard parlors and maisons.

The old mines, such as the one that had been started by General Connor, were reopened and worked first. New mines were quickly opened in such places as the Uintah and Blue Ledge district near the tributaries of the Weber and Provo rivers, but they appear to have been prospected by employed mining engineers rather than bearded individuals in red shirts with a pack of bacon and sourdough on their backs. There was a saying in Utah:

"It takes a mine to develop a mine."

There were thirty-two organized mining districts, twenty individual mining corporations capitalized at sums ranging from $100,000 to $2,400,000 and eighteen reducing works. When Brigham Young laid out a branch line to Provo and tracks into the mining areas, the output of the mines rose to $3,000,000. Some of the mines were so rich that the Emma in the Wasatch Mountains was sold to British capitalists for close to $5,000,000. The Flagstaff mine owned by Nicolas Groesbeck was also sold to a British combine for $1,500,000, while a group of mines called the Last Chance, the Hiawatha, the Montezuma and the Savage was bought by a group of New York and Detroit capitalists for $1,500,000.

The gold and particularly the silver ores found in Utah were as highly assayed as those in Colorado, Nevada or California. At the Emma the run of the ore was worth from $80 to $150 a ton, while the richest deposits were worth up to $250 a ton. At the Silveropolis mine in Rush Valley, the first forty tons of ore produced $24,000 worth of silver. The famous Ontario mine, discovered the following year in the Blue Ledge district, produced $17,000,000 worth of silver, $6,250,000 being distributed in dividends to its stockholders.

Successful mills and furnaces were built by the Woodhull brothers at Murray, ten miles south of Salt Lake City; a large smelting works called the Badger State was built on South Street in Salt Lake, and Jones and Raymond built one in East Canyon... all financed and owned by gentiles. Brigham Young would not allow the church to build them or take profit from them, though he hauled the ore in his railroads which he kept expanding into the mountains and the mining areas.

To Brigham Young this gold and silver ore was contaminated; he would not allow his people to be corrupted by contact with it. William Godbe and the Walker brothers built large smelters and made fortunes from them, but they were already considered renegade Mormons. Brigham Young did not expressly forbid his young men to work in the mining towns, neither did he encourage them as he had in the sixties when he said, "Work for these capitalists, haul their ores, build their furnaces, and take your pay for it, build houses, improve your farms and make yourself better off."

In the impoverished Dixie colony it was difficult to keep the young men in control.

"The biggest price they (the Mormons) had to pay this year was the young manpower that drifted to the mines in spite of the Young Men's Mutual Improvement. All a man could do was caution the boys not to visit saloons or gambling halls, to attend to prayers...."

The temptation was strong.

"To a boy from a quiet village, the brightly lit saloons and stores and the ceaseless activity was a never-ending delight. These men, Americans, Cornishmen, Irishmen, fine specimens of manhood, after ten hours of toil, emerged from their cabins dressed in the best money can buy and walked the streets with the air of Kings."

Now there developed a new conflict; where the gentiles came into established communities and were obliged to pay taxes they found that they could get no representation either on the city assemblies or in the state legislature. These posts had always been and continued to be filled by Latter-day Saints. The old Mormon custom of having the Saints favor each other in buying and employing also backfired, for the gentiles began to discriminate by putting the Mormon out of work as soon as there was a gentile to take his place, and by refusing to buy in the Mormon stores where there was a gentile store they could patronize.

CHAPTER VII

For Brigham Young, Time Runs Out

THE CRITICAL ISSUE HAD yet to be joined: could the United States Government, under law, force the Mormons to give up polygamy?

The Mormons believed they were in a strong position not only because they maintained that any interference with their multiple marriage was an interference with their freedom to practice their religion, but because all marriages after the first public marriage were conducted in secret in the Mormon Church. There were no documents which the federal government could seize, no witnesses among the Mormons who would testify against their coreligionists. No gentile ever got close enough to a multiple marriage to give valid testimony.

Since there was no adequate federal law under which Chief Justice McKean felt he could prosecute polygamy, he decided he would try several key cases under the "lewd and licentious association" clause of the territorial law which stated that "if any man or woman not being married to each other, lewdly and lasciviously cohabitate together," they can be indicted and tried in the federal court.

However the territorial law also stipulated that "no prosecution for adultery can be commenced but on the complaint of the husband or wife."

It was rare that a Mormon wife entered a complaint against her husband's plural marriage. Now came one of those rare times. Thomas Hawkins's first wife, outraged at her husband for taking a second wife, entered a complaint against Hawkins on the grounds of adultery, giving the federal officials their first clear-cut chance to prosecute.

After Mrs. Hawkins had testified to the existence of a second Mrs. Hawkins, the non-Mormon jury found Thomas Hawkins guilty of adultery, that is, of having several wives through the sanction of the Church. He was fined $500 and sentenced to three years in prison. Hawkins appealed his case, the bond was set at $20,000 which he could not provide. The Church did not see fit to post his bond. Instead the Mormons made a joke: they said that the pompous lecture given to Hawkins by the judge was greater punishment that the imprisonment and fine.

The Mormons were not really amused; they realized that a dangerous precedent had been established which could be used against all multiple marriage. And so it was. In a matter of days Brigham Young was indicted, along with half a dozen other of the highest dignitaries of the Church. Judge McKean announced that the title of the case should be:

"Federal Authority versus Polygamic Theocracy."

A prominent gentile attorney who was offered the post of United States attorney to prosecute Brigham Young turned it down saying, "The responsibility for the United States Attorney for Utah, just at this time, is much greater than any other territory or state. The sympathy of the great mass of the people here is with the parties to be prosecuted. Ninety thousand ignorant and fanatical people have been moulded into a Theocracy, in direct conflict with the government and laws of the United States and Christian civilization."

One cartoonist showed Brigham Young, with his many wives and children beside him, asking President Grant:

"What shall I do with all these?"

"Do as I do," President Grant replied, "give them offices."

The Mormon population was incensed. They idolized Brigham Young as their great leader who spoke directly to God. Brigham Young was calm, his manner in court quiet and courteous; virtues which could not always be ascribed to Judge McKean.

Brigham Young's arrest, along with that of Daniel H. Wells, mayor of Salt Lake, and George Q. Cannon, editor of the *Deseret News*, was a sensation in every hamlet in the land. Many of the newspapers announced:

MORMONS ARMING!

The Mormons were not arming, but their arms were always within reach.

Brigham Young was admitted to bail. On October 24, 1871, he started on his annual trip to the "Dixie Mission," to St. George and other colonies, assured that the case would be set sufficiently ahead for him to have time to return to Salt Lake. Suddenly the Court decreed that he had only one week in which to return. It was impossible for him to cover the miles. Prosecuting attorney Baskin demanded that the bail be forfeited. Judge McKean refused, and set the date ahead. Brigham Young, now seventy-one years of age, hurried over three hundred fifty miles of bad winter roads in order to keep the new trial date.

The Saints were in a state of high agitation.

The trial opened on January 2, 1872, but it had not gone very far before there came startling news from Washington: the Supreme Court had unanimously agreed in the Englebrecht case that the jury had been unlawfully drawn because Mormons had been excluded. All criminal proceedings in Utah during the past eighteen months were now void; the one hundred thirty-eight prisoners held in the Utah jails and penitentiary had to be discharged immediately; in all civil cases the decisions of the court had to be thrown out. The New York *Tribune* said:

"The decision is very damaging to the National Administration."

The San Francisco *News Letter*, speaking for the majority of the country's newspapers, said:

"The decision is a virtual declaration by the highest authority in the land that no portion of the people of the United States—

however abhorrent their religious faith—can be deprived of their liberties except by due process of law."

The case against Brigham Young was summarily dropped. Thomas Hawkins was released from jail and never tried again. The first serious effort of a federal court to come to grips with polygamy had fallen afoul of its own illegal methods.

At the Annual Conference of the Latter-day Saints on February 28 Brigham Young asked his congregation:

"How much power, ability or opportunity would I have to possess to disgrace them as they have disgraced themselves?"

The Saints were certain that Chief Justice McKean and Governor Woods would be removed. They misjudged President Grant. He was not seriously taken aback by the Supreme Court decision.

At their February convention the Saints again attempted to secure statehood for Utah. Thomas Fitch, former congressman from Nevada who had opposed Sutro, delivered a speech in which he said that it was his greatest desire to see law and order restored in Utah, but that at the same time he was unalterably opposed to polygamy.

"There is no safety without a state government, but there can be no state government without concessions."

He told the Mormons that polygamy had to go, not because it was amoral or criminal, that question belonged to another sphere, he said; but because it was a political necessity.

Partly because of Brigham Young's indictment and the danger in which he and other officials of the Church had stood; partly because they recognized Fitch's speech as an ultimate truth, the convention passed Article Five which read:

"Such terms, if any, as may be prescribed by the Congress as a condition of the admission of said State into the Union, shall, if ratified by the majority vote of the people thereof, at such time and under such regulations as may be prescribed by this convention, thereupon be embraced within and constitute a part of this ordinance."

Although Orson Pratt and other Mormon leaders opposed it, George Q. Cannon and the *Deseret News*, official voice for Brigham Young and the Church, wrote that Article Five should be retained.

For the first time since their arrival in Utah, Brigham Young and the Church intimated they might be willing to give up polygamy for statehood.

And the people had been prepared! Two months before the

convention, Brigham Young had Daniel Wells tell the congregation that it was not impossible, nor would it even be strange, for God to take back the Principle of polygamy to Himself for a season, through the wickedness of His people.

The Saints might have to give up polygamy, but instead of admitting that this would be a result of compromise with the federal government, the groundwork had been laid for the belief that they were being deprived of the Principle of God because they had failed to be worthy of it.

The Saints were confidentially informed by Frank Fuller, a former secretary of Utah Territory, that their chances of being admitted as a state were good. The Mormons were also convinced that the Republican party was eager to admit new states.

In Washington Congressman James G. Blair of Missouri proposed to the Congress that a law be passed by which all existing plural marriages in Utah would be made legal, and all the children of these marriages legalized; that all pending court action against Mormons on the charge of polygamy be dismissed. No compromise could be possible which penalized Mormon women and children. From this point forward polygamy should be abandoned by the Mormon Church.

Most of the American people agreed that it would be wise to admit the Saints in return for their abolishing polygamy, thus putting an end to the vexatious question.

But Congressman Blair could find few to stand with him in this sensible solution. The Utah Ring, which did not want to see an amiable compromise effected, put pressure on President Grant and the administration to reject the Mormon offer.

Church historian Whitney says plaintively:

"The result of that outcry of the gentiles was that Congress took adverse action upon Utah's petition for Statehood, failing to even intimate, as invited to, upon what terms of compromise it would favorably consider and act upon her application for admission into the Union."

With President Grant opposed to the admission of Utah as a state, Elder Taylor now repudiated Article Five, and the idea that the Mormons had had any intention of surrendering the practice of plural marriage.

"The entire proceedings," they maintained, "were intended merely to give Congress a chance to admit us or to show why we were not admitted."

The Mormons never again made an offer. President Grant announced to Congress that, unless they gave him strong anti-polygamy measures by means of which plural marriage could be eradicated by law, the government might have to use force instead.

The lack of a real "cease and desist" law arose from a lack of knowledge of how to deal with the peculiar problem of Utah. The government had made it clear that the Mormons' political allegiance to the Union must take precedence over their religious allegiance to their Church. The Mormons maintained that they must obey the laws of God and His disciples before the laws of the Constitution or the Congress. The federal government replied in effect, "If every religion took the stand that their religious laws had precedence over the national laws, we could never become a unified nation."

Each year the Mormons made a more widely organized effort to be admitted as a state. Each year President Grant said through a thicker cloud of cigar smoke:

"I am unalterably opposed to the entrance of Utah to the Union."

The culmination of the Ring's efforts came on June 23, 1874, when Congress passed the Poland law. It was the first time that both Houses had been able to agree on serious anti-Mormon legislation. Under the Poland law a number of the most important Mormon offices, such as territorial marshal and territorial attorney general, were abolished; the jury lists had to be drawn up by the federal district courts; the names from the jury lists were to be drawn by the United States marshal; and for the first time the federal officials in Utah would have the power to sentence to the penitentiary those Mormons found guilty of the practice of polygamy, though the federal government failed to provide either the manpower or the funds for bringing into court any polygamous Mormons who did not wish to be tried.

The first election held under the Poland law came to be known by the Mormons as "bayonet rule election day." The United States marshal deputized large numbers of non-Mormon marshals and sent them out as watchers at the polls. The local Mormon officers refused to leave their posts. Officer Phillips, a Mormon, was arrested by the federal deputies; the United States deputy marshal was then arrested by the Mormon police. Daniel H. Wells, mayor of Salt Lake, was manhandled by a federal deputy; the mayor then ordered the Mormon chief of police to break up the mob in front of the City Hall. Federal officers arrested Mayor Wells for having given a "by force" order.

In September 1874, a month following the riotous election day, the first polygamy indictments were brought into court.

Ever since the Englebrecht Supreme Court decision two years before, the Mormons had been eager for a test case before the United States Supreme Court. They were convinced that the Supreme Court would declare all anti-polygamy legislation illegal because the law had to differentiate between bigamy, which was illegal, and polygamy, which was a religious tenet. The administration was equally eager for a test case; once the Supreme Court had declared Mormon polygamy unconstitutional, the last argument would be removed against forcing the Mormons to give up the practice.

In September 1874 two prominent Mormons in Salt Lake City were indicted: George Reynolds, private secretary to Brigham Young, and George Q. Cannon. Reynolds and Cannon were co-operating in this plan to test the law; they appeared before a lower court where Reynolds was tried, convicted, fined $500 and sentenced to one year's imprisonment. The case was then taken before the Supreme Court of the Utah Territory where presiding Judge McKean learned that the grand jury had been composed of an illegal number of jurymen. He threw the case out.

The following year Reynolds was indicted for a second time, but he was no longer desirous of co-operating, and had to be forced into a trial. He was again convicted; this time the court sentenced him to two years of imprisonment at hard labor, and the territorial Supreme Court upheld the verdict. The country awaited the decision of the United States Supreme Court.

President Ulysses S. Grant, in 1875, had reached the middle of his second term and he had grown fatigued with the Mormon problem. Yet the din from Utah was growing ever louder; in the election for a congressional delegate the Liberal party was able to assemble some forty-five hundred votes against the Mormons' twenty-two thousand, indicating that the proportion of non-Mormons was growing.

In the Tooele area to the south of Salt Lake, both parties padded the election rolls so heavily that a scandal ensued. The Mormon candidate was finally conceded the election, although two hundred thirty-seven of his votes were illegal. It was proved that nine hundred forty-five of the Liberal party's votes were illegal. Yet the Liberal party, by charging treason, managed to keep the elected Mormon delegate off the floor of the House for a congressional session.

When Governor Woods retired after a four-year regime, President Grant decided to earn a respite in Utah by appointing mild-mannered, genial Samuel B. Axtell, a Californian, to the governorship. Axtell gave the Mormons what the Church gratefully called "impartial, just government, religious freedom in obedience to the written law, and local self-government." The Ring's representatives got to President Grant and by exerting steady pressure managed to have Axtell removed.

President Grant's next choice for the governorship was the best governor Utah ever had. The President urged George Emery, born in Maine, graduate of Dartmouth, and a Boston lawyer, "not to take the Ringites for his advisors in Utah, but to deal justly between man and man, avoiding the extremes."

Governor Emery did better than that. Starting in June 1875, he gave Utah a brilliant regime in which he suggested important improvements in the agricultural methods, helped extend the educational system, worked out a new code of civil and penal laws based on those of California.

Having made himself liked and respected by the Mormons, Governor George Emery went before the Utah legislature to suggest that the territorial legislators pass an anti-polygamy law:

"That will prevent its extension, and will adopt such measures as look to a fair and impartial settlement of this subject as it affects the post."

In short, protect all plural marriages and children of plural marriages, but put an end to further multiple marriage. Governor Emery assured the legislators that if they would pass such a bill it would remove the last obstacle to statehood; but that the Mormons themselves would have to take this forward-looking step.

The Mormon legislature, a good portion of whom were participants in multiple marriages, refused to take the advice.

And now with the admission of Colorado into the Union in August 1876, Utah remained the only one of the Far West areas not yet an independent state.

Brigham Young had watched the opposition to the Saints grow stronger inside Utah, and more vocal throughout the nation. He was seventy-four now; his vision of a unified Church inside a unified Zion, which he had carried across the plains from Winter Quarters, held close to his heart during all the years of privation and conflict, was unfulfilled. The Saints were still in danger from within and from without. Somewhere he had failed to bind his people so tightly together that no human force could create a wedge. This unshatterable unity he must achieve before he died. He did not have much time left; the saving plan would be the child of his old age; but he must make this supreme effort before he took his departure from the Saints.

He announced his revolutionary new plan called "The United Order," a form of religious communism with which he wanted to replace the Mormon co-operative capitalist society. He had made a first effort in this direction when he formed the Zion's Cooperative Mercantile Institution which was largely Church-owned.

The Z.C.M.I. had been an over-all failure. Outside of Salt Lake and a few surrounding towns the whole concept had vanished. Not all Mormon merchants had been willing to surrender their shops; in many towns the Mormons had refused to confine their shopping to the Z.C.M.I. store. The Church complained that, next to the reluctance of their people to give the idea wholehearted support, the major reason for the failure was, as Elder Lorenzo Snow said: "The difficulty in finding men of ability, wisdom and devotedness to manage in a proper manner."

Despite the fact that the password of what the Mormons called their second period of history, from the opening of the railroad in January 1870, was "co-operation," the Mormons had failed in others of their more hopeful ventures. Ranchers had imported sheep into Utah in large quantities and when they thrived the Church, with a combination of private enterprise, had built woolen mills in Salt Lake, Bingham, Provo and Beaver. Machinery was installed at the cost of $70,000; by 1873 the mill at Provo was turning out its first cloth. But the woolen mills were not able to run profitably, for the sheep men, most of them Mormons in good standing, preferred to sell their wool outside of Utah Territory for cash instead of inside the territory where they could get only half cash and the other half in products.

The cotton being raised by the Dixie Mission in the extreme south of Utah, around St. George, although it had been profitable during the Civil War years, now proved unable to compete in the free market with southern cotton.

Brigham Young, apparently still nettled at the fact that he had been unable to control the Mormon women's dress, had seven of his daughters form the Young Ladies' Mutual Improvement Association to "promote the surrender of extravagance in dress and speech, the cultivation of habits of order, thrift, industry and charity." The organization published its own magazine, which carried instruction and the picture of the Mormon's concept of the ideal life . . . undoubtedly unread by at least two of his own wives:

Amelia, ". . . with her queenly figure, her watered silks, rings on both fore-fingers, pearl beads wound high around her throat and a locket pendant, and a little sun parasol, she affected when riding in an open carriage; Amelia with her real side-saddle, with her bright-blue brass-button habit whose skirts just missed the ground; Amelia who introduced the new corset, boned and curved to fit the fashionable figure with its full bust, narrow waist, curved hips and arched stomacher, and the steel back boards to train women in the correct carriage necessary for the Grecian bend."

Though they liked the second wife whom Brigham Young installed in the Dixie Mission, the Mormon women were not beyond taking a few friendly digs:

"Lucy Bigelow, bold-breasted woman, with blond hair the envy of other women, just as stylish as Amelia, also every bit as much a lady. When she bought a pig from Lon Tuckett she insisted on it being a lady pig."

The primary stipulations of the United Order were that every man must have a job that he liked to do; every man was entitled to a decent, dignified living from his work; no man who did not work was entitled to eat; every man was expected to work for his community as well as for himself; and no man should have more than any other in material goods.

Membership in the United Order was to be voluntary, but once a man entered it he was obliged to turn over to the Church his land, his home, his furniture, his foodstuffs, his clothing, his personal and private possessions, his tools, his farm implements, his animals, his seed. Having deeded all his property to the United Order, he would then receive back from the United Order a stewardship over as much of this property as the United Order felt he needed and should have.

This stewardship might include the very list of properties he had turned in; if his list was short and the United Order felt he needed more, he would be given a greater stewardship. Everything produced and earned beyond the standard set by the United Order would be turned over to it, to be held in the general storehouse. No member would be able to accumulate a surplus; by the same token when a member was sick, or came to old age, or drought struck, he would be taken care of.

Brigham Young was asking his people to give up their total freedom for total security. One purpose was to eliminate all competition between Mormons, and all variances in their scale of living. He also made the program a militant religious campaign in which every man, woman and child coming into the Order had to be rebaptized and rededicated to the Church of Latter-day Saints.

Elder Erastus Snow, in the Dixie Mission, said, "The great

principle involved in the United Order was 'Each for the whole and God for all.'"

When Brigham Young introduced the subject at the Forty-fourth Annual Conference of the Church he said:

"And when the question is asked, 'Whose is this?', the earnings and savings of the community, organized to sustain and promote the kingdom of God on earth, the answer will be, 'It is ours, and we are the Lord's, and all that we have belong to Him.'"

Brigham Young set out on his annual winter pilgrimage to St. George, in the south of Utah. A town called Orderville was founded where the United Order proved to be a success. The little community of Richfield came in whole, with its eight hundred head of cattle, two hundred horses, seventeen hundred sheep, a tannery, a gristmill worth $10,000, a steam saw, a lathe, and a shingle mill. Individuals came in too, in the southern settlements, a few furniture makers, half a dozen shoemakers, some twenty carpenters and masons, perhaps forty-five farmers who were working some eleven hundred acres.

But beyond these focal towns which caught fire from Brigham Young's preaching, the United Order never gained a foothold. The Saints did not want a religious communism, they wanted to be capitalists.

Brigham Young had always insisted upon complete unity among the Mormons; now he saw them being broken into classes, those who joined the United Order and those who did not. He realized that he himself had created a schism which could do serious damage to the Church. Had he instituted the United Order the moment the Mormons reached the Great Basin, when he was young and dynamic, and before there were any outsiders in the area, he might have had a chance to succeed; now he no longer had the overpowering energy and personal magnetism to bring the United Order to fruition.

"The United Order movement first languished and then quietly subsided into desuetude."

By 1875 Brigham Young was also working to extend the educational and cultural opportunities of his people. In most Mormon schools, tuition was charged. At Spanish Fork forty young people seeking an education had to cut down trees, trim the logs, haul them to town, build a schoolhouse and then make desks and benches before they could open the Young Men's Academy. Brigham Young founded the Brigham Young Academy. He also brought in Professor Careless to give Handel's *Messiah* in the Tabernacle, with its magnificent organ and incredibly fine acoustics. It was received with such tremendous enthusiasm by the Mormons that $1200 in cash poured into the box office on the first night of the production.

On March 23, 1877, the entire nation approved an act of retribution: the execution of John D. Lee at Mountain Meadows, on the very spot where the Fancher Party had been massacred in 1857, twenty years before. Lee's first trial had miscarried because the federal government was attempting to convict Brigham Young and the Church of Latter-day Saints of the massacre. In the second trial Lee was brought up for his own culpability; and his guilt was great. It was he who offered the Fancher Party the false truce, he who commanded the Utah militia that went into Mountain Meadows, he who gave the order to fire, he who had commanded the Indians who butchered the rest of the party. The two men responsible for originating the plan, Stake President Isaac C. Haight and William H. Dame, the Mormon military commander of the area, were indicted but, perhaps because they were not present at the actual massacre, were never brought to trial.

Neither Brigham Young nor any other Church official made any attempt to defend Lee. The Church was having enough trouble defending itself from allegations of complicity. Lee was bitter; he felt that he was being offered up by his Church on the sacrificial block. Yet at no time during the trial, before an all-Mormon jury, did he make any effort to involve the Church in the massacre itself.

On July 11, 1877, feeling death close at hand, Brigham Young issued his last "Circular of the First Presidency" in which he reorganized the twenty stakes in Zion so that they would be more closely knit. He also ordered free education for all Mormon children, stipulating that textbooks should be written and printed in Utah, and that:

"The teachers should be Latter-day Saints so that the children might learn only what they ought to know."

On August 29, 1877, at the age of seventy-six, he died ... "with Joseph Smith's name on his lips, surrounded by friends and family."

Twenty-five thousand of the faithful poured into Salt Lake to walk past the bier of their leader, who thirty years before had declared of the Great Basin, "This is the right place," and had brought the Saints home to the Promised Land.

"The procession was long, elaborate and organized according to the strict system so characteristic of a beehive society. It began with the Tenth Ward Band and the Glee Club. In the middle was the body borne by clerks and workmen of the deceased, with nine of the

twelve apostles and the presiding bishop as pallbearers. All the way
to Brigham Young's private cemetery the streets were filled with
spectators, many of them crying."

The eulogies in the press of the nation were friendly. They
praised Brigham Young as one of the world's great colonizers.

The sourest note came from inside Salt Lake itself, where the
anti-Mormon *Tribune* unforgivingly cried:

"Joseph Smith's prediction has been fulfilled: Brigham Young
having obtained the head of the Church has led it to Hell. . . ."

The outside world believed that with its leader gone the Church
of Latter-day Saints would fall apart.

CHAPTER VIII

Colorado Is a Character

IN MARCH 1870 a colonizing era opened in Colorado which was
as peculiar to the country as its indigenous miners and its narrow-
gauge gulch railroads; as different from the colonies of Utah,
Nevada and California as were the Rocky Mountains from the
Wasatch, the Washoe and the Sierra Nevada.

The first to arrive were three hundred Germans, a co-operative
formed by Carl Wulsten and promoted by his newspaper, the *Staats
Zeitung*, from what was described as "the nauseous back alleys and
cellars of over-crowded Chicago." They had taken the train to the
railhead at Fort Wallace, Kansas, and been transported in United
States government wagons, their household goods piled high, to
their new home. The members had mutually contracted to remain
with the colony for five years, after which the assets would be
distributed among the members and the community would become
individualist-capitalist, as had Salt Lake and Anaheim.

The hundred families chose a lovely but isolated Swiss-like
upland valley south of Canon City, between the formidable Wet

Mountains and the Sangre de Cristos. They named their colony Colfax, and broke ground the very day they arrived. They planted thirty acres of crops, co-operatively built cabins, roads, bridges, a mill, a shingle factory. In the group there were "twenty fair-haired, clear-skinned German girls, all young and goodlooking." There were also a doctor, clergyman and schoolmaster, though they pointedly refused to allow any lawyers to join. Wulsten wrote that he had been prompted to help this poorer class of German-born "who were condemned to work in greasy, ill-ventilated nerve destroying factories." The new arrivals, breathing the glorious air at the seventy-five-hundred-foot altitude, thought they were in paradise.

Each of the hundred family heads had contributed $250. Each man was paid $2.00 a day for his work in planting and building the town, and for cutting shingles for the Denver market.

But paradise was not enough. By July the colony could have used a clear-headed lawyer. First there was a revolt against Wulsten on the grounds that he was dictatorial. Then one member complained, "There is too much Kommunismus," while another cried, "Ve have been schwintle out of ebietings." When the upland valley suffered a crop failure due to an early frost (it did not help that there were no farmers in the group) there was not enough co-operative spirit left for the colonists to suffer their way through to the following spring. Many families left. The remainder had to ask for supplies from the federal government to help them over the winter.

When the community store caught fire, destroying the company's records, it also burned down the last of the group spirit. The remaining members moved to Pueblo, Colorado City and Denver. Wulsten wrote:

"Collectively a failure, it has individually become a great success, for every family is today in perfectly independent circumstances."

A second colony was founded in May, just a couple of months after Colfax, and was settled by New Yorkers. The originator was Nathan C. Meeker. As the Colfax group had been backed and publicized by Wulsten and his *Staats Zeitung* in Chicago, the new colony was promoted by Horace Greeley and his New York *Tribune* because he believed in co-operative colonies. Named the Union Colony during the first meeting in New York, its constitution said that "temperance men of good character might become members by paying a fee of $150.00." The money was used to buy good land in the Cache la Poudre Valley, north of Denver and Boulder, on the main wagon and rail road leading to Cheyenne and the Union Pacific, thus avoiding the economically dangerous isolation of Colfax.

The tract was acquired from the Denver Pacific Railroad, a building was bought in Cheyenne, moved to the open townsite and named the Hotel de Comfort. Here the colonists lived while they surveyed the town, laid out streets, planted trees, built a community hall, school and library, irrigation ditches, bridges and a high wall to close in their co-operative community. No liquor was allowed; as with the Latter-Day Saints, dancing and theatricals were encouraged to keep up the spirits.

Some members, after making the long journey, found they had no stomach for pioneering. Pabor, one of the founders, says, "The chosen ground was unbroken for miles; the wind of centuries had blown off the light soil, leaving gravel. Fifty to a hundred persons arrived daily, without enough blankets or provisions, and in the whole town there was but one well. Some seemed to forget that it was the work of a colony to create a city; they expected to see one already built. They remained to curse only so long as the next train east delayed its going."

The hard core of colonists survived the first lean winter. In Nathan Meeker they had a combination of idealist and sound business manager. By the second year the colony was selling its farm products at good prices to the adjoining mines, and building small factories. "The community was idealistic, high moral, largely religious," therefore cohesive and capable of self-discipline, even as the Mormon communities had been.

Once it was firmly on its feet, the colony changed its name to Greeley and ceased to be commonly owned; but its local government remained homogeneous, banning a billiard hall but encouraging glee clubs and strawberry festivals.

The success of Greeley started a rush of born-on-the-spot towns. A duplicate of Greeley was founded by Colonel C.N. Pratt, a land office promoter for the Denver Pacific and Kansas Pacific railroads, composed of four hundred people from Chicago who contributed $150 each. They founded Longmont, between Greeley and Denver. From March to June 1871 they put up fifty buildings, a town hall and a library. Grasshoppers ate much of their first crop, they were hard pushed for cash to pay off their land and secure title, their ditches were found inadequate in the face of floods; but the land and management were good, the people hard-working. At the end of their first year they had built two hundred houses, stores, a brickyard, a post office, and were doing well.

Colonies at Evans and Green City failed; their people moved to Greeley or to other established towns. The land had proved to be not as good, the management not as able, the spirit of co-operation not as enduring. But the example of the co-operatives gave the railroads and other large landowners the idea: the Denver and Rio Grande Railroad opened Fountain Colony, which became the successful Colorado Springs.

The Platte River Land Company subdivided an area they called Platteville, thirty-five miles north of Denver, advertising its rich land, wine-like air and health propensities. One hundred fifty portable houses were brought out from Chicago and set about the town, saving the usual first-winter suffering. By January 1872, in a little over a year, the colony could boast of eight hundred residents, business houses, a newspaper, two churches, a free reading room, two public parks, nineteen miles of canals, seven miles of shade trees, and land set aside for schools and colleges.

When the War Department decided to abandon Fort Collins, north of Greeley, General Robert A. Cameron of Greeley founded a town company, selling land memberships to homeseekers for $50 to $250. By 1873 the town had grown large enough to support its first newspaper and bank.

Colorado's territorial government, watching the success of these colonies, set up a Board of Immigration to tell the world about Colorado. Caravans came in from the eastern states, from Ohio, Michigan and Kentucky to buy land together, and then to split it up according to the ability to pay. William Green Russell, who had led the first gold prospecting party into Colorado in 1858 brought still another party from Georgia to buy land and settle around the town of Badito on the Huerfano River, south of Pueblo.

Another group of communities was about to be pioneered in Colorado's southern Rockies, this time by an individualism as rugged as the staggering fourteen-thousand-foot-high San Juan Mountains. The hero of the San Juans was one of the most unlikely characters ever to be silhouetted against Colorado's craggy backdrop, Otto Mears:

"Colorless, undersized, scraggly-bearded; orphaned by the time he was four, life had honed him down until he was as sharp and resilient as the stub end of a piece of baling wire."

When color was discovered in the country, the miners were mildly embarrassed by the fact that the land belonged to the Utes. To rescue the prospectors from this awkward situation, for the Utes were good fighters, the federal government sent Commissioner

Felix Brunot to offer bounty to the Utes to move on. The Utes decided to be difficult; soldiers were rushed into the mountains to avoid a full-scale war. Commissioner Brunot turned in despair to Otto Mears, thirty-year-old son of a Russian Jewish mother and an English father, who spoke Ute, as he did English, with a Russian accent.

Otto Mears went to his friend, the great Ute Chief Ouray and his war council; David Lavender says in *The Big Divide*, Mears was "able to squat down in a filthy, lice-infested tepee and chatter to its occupants without the least show of repugnance or superiority." Chief Ouray listened to Otto, and ended by taking himself and his chief warriors to Washington to sign a treaty granting the Utes $25,000 a year, while their pint-sized guide and host, Otto Mears, shook hands with President Grant and the Indians visited with the Grant family.

Otto Mears had done his early pioneering in California, where he was abandoned in 1851 at the age of eleven by the last of a line of unenchanted uncles. He became a tinsmith, lived in the Sierra Nevada gold fields, joined the First California Volunteers, saw service in New Mexico, and after the Civil War returned as far west as Saguache Creek, halfway between Pueblo and the western Colorado line. Here he homesteaded, raised wheat, built a gristmill, ground his flour, loaded it in a train of borrowed wagons and headed up the Arkansas River to sell it to the miners of California Gulch.

The fact that there was no road over the nine-thousand-foot mountain bothered Otto not at all: he hacked one out over Poncha Pass with an ax and shovel. While he was involved in this incidental job of road building, ex-Governor William Gilpin came riding behind him, took a good look at the widened trail and said:

"Why don't you get a permit from the territorial government to make a toll road out of this? And while you're at it, why don't you make the grade sufficiently gradual for a railway?"

Otto did. He also built a road over the trail that Fremont had hoped to traverse on his Fourth Expedition, Cochetopa Pass. Otto Mears ended by building fifteen separate passes over the Rockies, a total of almost five hundred miles of road, financed by himself and largely hand-cut by himself, up some of the steepest grades in North America. He sold several of his roads, as ex-Governor Gilpin had told him he could, to the railroad engineers.

Colorado was now discovering new silver and gold rectangles in its wildest and most inaccessible region, the southwest area. The first mining camp of Summitville was founded at 11,300 feet, one of the highest settlements in the civilized world. Lavender quotes a disgruntled but eloquent prospector:

"The San Juan is the best and worst mining country ever struck. It has more and better minerals but you see, it's no good. You can't get at it except over ranges like that (sticking his arm up at an angle of eighty degrees) and when you're in, you see you're corralled by the mountains, so you can't get your ore out."

The mines were frequently a mile straight up the side of the mountain from the town, and so Colorado had a "horse express," a horse being provided to each miner, for a fee, to carry him up to his shaft. The horse then returned by himself to the stable. All efforts of the miners to catch free rides downhill on the unoccupied horses met with total defeat.

This dismal view discouraged no one: when color is at stake there is no force that can dissuade men from pursuing it. As far back as John Baker's 1860 expedition into this rugged country the Navajos had claimed that "the royal metal" was in these mountains. The Navajos were telling the truth; in 1870 an exploring party uncovered the Little Giant gold lode, with an assay of $900 to $4000 a ton of precious metal, a higher figure than any found in the Sierra Nevada or Mount Davidson. A run was started, and the Las Animas mining district was founded.

Prospectors began coming in from as far away as California, for the past twenty years the mother lode of miners. John Moss brought in a party, found gold on the La Plata River, and set up Parrott City, after Parrott and Company of San Francisco, the firm that was shipping in their supplies. The town of Del Norte, almost twelve thousand feet high, was founded in 1872 as an outfitting center for prospectors and for freighters carrying goods over the pass to the Summitville mines. A crude stamp mill was built, a cabin erected at the new Silverton to house a post office and supply store. Soon a smelter was built, and a wagon road hewed over Stony Pass, a road lined as solidly with pack trains and wagons as had been the California Trail into Virginia City in 1860.

The rectangle was bursting with gold; when Enos Hotchkiss built a toll road from Saguache to the San Juan country his pick and shovel unearthed a tremendous lode. Lake City rose on Lake San Cristobal; Otto Mears started the *Silver World*, the first newspaper in the San Juans, in a log cabin built on a sandbed, adroitly publicizing the area. In three years it had a population of twenty-five hundred and was one of Colorado's thriving towns.

A prospector named Sam Conger, observing how the silver ore veins lay on Nevada's Comstock, remembered seeing similar terrain and rock structures while hunting elk west of Boulder, in the northern part of Colorado. Like John Bidwell, who studied the terrain around Coloma and then went north to find similar color on the Feather River, Sam Conger returned to his former hunting ground and turned up the rich Caribou lode.

Sometimes the mountains struck back at the men looting them. One winter, when Billy Maher and his Italian partner were mining in the San Juans, the snow rose to the top of their cabin. It was so cold inside that the partners had to take their potatoes to bed to keep them from freezing. Billy Maher tried to thaw out his dynamite by heating it in the stove, but it blew up, blinding and mutilating him. His partner went down the mountain for help, but the relief party of four were killed by an avalanche on their way up the mountain. Billy also died.

Transportation was a craggy problem; as the early surveying parties had learned, the Colorado Rockies had not been intended to serve as a railroad roundhouse. Colorado's early lines wound their way up narrow-gauge canyons too steep for any self-respecting mountain goat. But wherever a rich mine was brought in, no matter at what inaccessible height, a railroad was quickly built. Like its miners and its colonizers, the railroads of Colorado were peculiarly its own. The canyons were so steep and narrow that men had trouble walking up them, let alone laying ties and track. Yet laid they were, looking like Jacob's Ladder, and at tremendous expense. Nobody cared; one builder, warned that the railroad he was constructing would ruin him, paid its entire cost out of the operating profits of the first year by hauling sulphur into the mines and mills, ore and bullion out. Each new, narrow-gauge railroad, like the Colorado Central to Black Hawk in 1872, opened a new area to settlement.

The Denver and South Park Railroad had a little trouble during the financial crisis of 1873, and was able to stay alive only by hauling Sunday school excursions into the beautiful countryside. Its rivals joshed it about being the "Sunday School Line" but the Denver and South Park continued to lay track up the South Platte River, discovering a substantial substitute for ore. The river was rich with the shimmering gold and silver of trout; every morning the train pulled out loaded with anglers, dropping each of them at his favorite spot along the river, picking him up with his catch at the end of the day. On weekends the railroad had to run three sections of cars to accommodate the fishermen. The line made money and became dear to the heart of Denver.

Denver first met Richens Lacy Wootton, "Uncle Dick," on

Christmas Eve, 1858, when he arrived with a wagonload of groceries and Taos Lightning. He was an educated Virginian who had come to Bent's Fort when he was twenty looking for adventure, and found it galore as a hunter with Kit Carson. Uncle Dick, "two hundred pounds of hard muscle, with a wild shock of bristling hair to match," set out to build a twenty-seven-mile road over the Raton Pass from the southern border of Colorado to New Mexico. Finished it, too, and was soon taking in considerable sums by charging a toll of $1.50 for a wagon, twenty-five cents for a rider, five cents for cattle or sheep. That he frequently had to collect at the point of his gun seemed only normal to Uncle Dick, but he never failed to collect . . . except from the Indians, whose ancestors had been using the pass for centuries.

Where his toll road came to an end in Colorado, Wootton built a combination barn and hotel in which he housed and fed everyone coming over his pass. Like Otto Mears, he later sold his rights to a railroad, helping the Santa Fe build its grade over this same Raton Pass.

General William J. Palmer, a red-haired Philadelphian who had learned his trade in England, and set construction records for the Kansas Pacific which recently had been laid across the plains from Kansas City to Denver, planned one railroad to cross the Rockies to California, a second to go south to Mexico City. However he sold $1,000,000 worth of stock to his friends in Philadelphia and England for the more modest plan of a narrow-gauge railroad from Denver to Colorado Springs, constructing his engines and cars of such lightweight materials that they weighed only half as much as regular rolling stock. His road was a success even though, high on Palmer Lake, a windstorm might occasionally blow his engine and train off the tracks. He continued the line south to Pueblo and then up the Arkansas valley.

Palmer made enough money from his railroad to conjure up a "quaint" that would have caused both Dan De Quille and Mark Twain to drool. On the side of the mountain above Colorado Springs, the town he founded, General Palmer built himself a replica of the Duke of Marlborough's castle, importing old English church tiles to make his castle appear antique. In order not to smudge up the castle with black soot from the chimney, Palmer bored a tunnel through the mountain behind his house to carry off the smoke!

When W. A. H. Loveland built the Colorado Central and could not get his rails across the Big Divide on a direct line to California, he planned to transfer his passengers and freight to buckets and haul them over the ridge by cable, another "quaint."

Government in these remote mountains also seemed "quaint." Irving Howbert, though he had no experience in government, was nominated for county clerk by the Republicans, endorsed by the Democrats and elected. On the morning he took office in the rear of the unplastered courthouse, he saw that the ink had frozen overnight in the bottles. He quickly rented a cabin, moved the county records. In the early 1870s homesteaders and prospectors came in a steady stream; in order to enter their claims Howbert had to make the first official maps of his county. Since veterans of the Civil War wanted their pensions, Howbert had to secure a license to practice from the Pension Bureau. No one knew how to operate the telegraph line, so the manager set up instruments in Howbert's county cabin, teaching him how to send and receive messages. Miners brought in geological specimens to their government seat, so Howbert set up a Geological Institute. Because the county commissioners lived on distant ranches and mines, Howbert took care of their county duties. He was too inexperienced to know that one man could not do all this, so the whole thing worked just fine.

William A. Hamill took a fortune out of the mines, organized Clear Creek for the Republicans and boasted that "he carried the county in his vest pocket." In one election he decreed that no Democratic candidate would be allowed to run for office in Clear Creek County. The *Courier*, published by Hamill himself, turned on its owner and publically denounced him. Clear Creek County, which had been giving the Republican candidates a seven-hundred-vote majority, filled every county office with Democrats. Hamill cried wistfully:

"Do you know, they even fired cannon at me?"

Anything could happen in the rugged San Juans. In 1873 a party of twenty-one men came in from Salt Lake, guided by Alfred Packer, "a tall man, with long, dark curling hair, dark mustache and goatee, deep set, dark grey eyes." Packer knew Colorado. When the men reached Chief Ouray's camp on the Uncompahgre, near the Los Pinos Indian Agency, the chief advised them against tackling the heavy snows. Ten of the men took the chief's advice, the other ten started out in two separate parties.

Weeks later Packer returned to the Los Pinos Agency, claiming to have been abandoned by his five companions when he became snow-blind and footsore. Suspicion was aroused when he was found to have a Wells Fargo draft belonging to one of his companions, as well as another comrade's skinning knife and gun.

He was also spending money freely at the bar. Chief Ouray took one look at him and grunted:

"You too damn fat."

At that moment General Charles Adams, the Indian agent, came through Saguache. He adroitly hired Packer to guide him on a search party for the missing men. Before they could leave, Adams caught Packer in a lie about his large fund of money. Packer broke down, admitted that his companions were dead. Pressed for details, he said that Israel Swan, sixty, had died first, of starvation, and that the others had eaten him to remain alive. Five days later Humphrey had died of exhaustion, and the remaining four ate him. Frank Miller, a German butcher, was slowed by rheumatism, so the remaining three agreed to kill him. A few days later Shannon Bell shot sixteen-year-old George Noon, and the two of them ate George. Then Bell tried to kill Packer, so Packer killed Bell, carving off strips of his flesh which kept him alive until he returned to the agency.

General Adams ordered Packer to lead him to the bodies. Packer said he was lost and could not find the camp spot. But others found it, and photographed the skeletons. Four of the skulls had been crushed, apparently while the men slept; a fifth man had been shot after a struggle. Four of the skeletons had been stripped bare of flesh.

Alfred Packer was sentenced to forty years at hard labor. It is part of Colorado's apocrypha that the presiding judge leaned down from the bench and cried:

"Packer, you depraved Republican son of a such-and-such, there were only five democrats in Hinsdale County, and you ate them all!"

Colorado was at peace with itself politically, even though former President Andrew Johnson had spurned its advances toward statehood. Factions quarreled about the swift succession of governors appointed from Washington, but there were no serious differences between Colorado and the federal government. When President Grant came for a visit in 1873, Colorado stunned him by paving the sidewalk over which he walked to the Teller House in Central City with solid bars of silver bullion from the Caribou Lode. With this uncontrovertible evidence underfoot, Grant recommended to Congress that Colorado be admitted on the grounds that:

"It possesses all the elements of a prosperous state."

Jerome B. Chaffee, Colorado territorial representative, had his bill for Colorado statehood passed by the House in June 1874, but the Senate adjourned before passing the bill. The following February the Senate concurred, and President Grant signed the measure March 3, 1875.

On December 20, 1875, delegates to a constitutional convention met in the Odd Fellows Hall, on the third floor of the First National Bank Building, where they wrote the longest constitution in America, longer than the United States Constitution! The Woman's Suffrage Society cried, "Let Colorado be the first state to come into the Union with an unsullied record. Let not her fair escutcheon be stained with injustice to women." Lucy Stone wrote to the delegates:

"No part of the new constitution of Colorado will have more credit a hundred years hence, than that part which shall secure to women the right to a voice."

The delegates remained immune to the suffragettes' blandishments; however they did grant women the right to vote in school elections.

Colorado was to take its place among the states officially on August 1, 1876, eighteen years after the first Russell and Lawrence parties of gold seekers had come into her mountains and settled on Cherry Creek. But her palpitant people did not wait until then to celebrate; on July Fourth they staged a gala parade, with Professor O. J. Goldrick, who had brought education to Denver in a high silk hat, cutaway coat and yellow gloves, making a speech, and old-timers getting together to talk of "ox trains and Indian scares, of vigilance committees and first cabins, floods and grasshoppers... and dreams of great wealth."

Colorado had come of age. But it had yet to live through its most staggering strikes.

CHAPTER IX

"Come provided with a pair of navy revolvers"

DENVER HOUSEWIVES NO LONGER had to have their water delivered in barrels. The city had completed a waterworks that supplied two and a half million gallons daily. Denver, like Virginia City, had become *comme il faut* among world travelers; the Grand Duke Alexis of Russia came for a buffalo hunt with Buffalo Bill, then stunned Denver with his gold-encrusted entourage. Between 1860 and 1870 the streets were crowded and busy, yet the city had showed an actual permanent population gain of only ten human souls.

It was different now, in the thriving silver seventies, with the millions pouring down from her mountain mines. Between 1870 and 1880 Colorado's population leaped from forty thousand to almost two hundred thousand, an increase of four hundred per cent. The co-operative colonies contributed their groups, as did the railroad and privately promoted subdivisions. The large smelters were adding to the employment lists. Because of the bountiful, cheap land, Colorado was attracting its share of the emigrants from the southern states still writhing under Reconstruction.

Denver had grown so rich that it could afford to build a poorhouse. The funds were raised by the Young Ladies' Relief Society. Charity also extended its sweet face to the building of a County Hospital. Up to 1870 Colorado had no school system, as only $1.50 a year in taxes had been available per pupil. By 1876, with the growing population and wealth, public schools were built in three hundred forty districts, with high schools in Denver, Pueblo and other towns. The University of Colorado was opened at Boulder in 1877.

Colorado had grown so prosperous on its gold and silver that the 1875 panic which had serious consequences for the East had little effect on the area. Colorado was far more seriously hurt the following year when the grasshoppers, which had plagued the Far West from Salt Lake to Santa Barbara, ate three quarters of the northern Colorado crop. Nathan Meeker, editor of the Greeley *Tribune*, estimated the crop loss at $4,000,000; only a special "grasshopper appropriation" from Congress kept northern Colorado's fledgling farmers from becoming destitute.

Life was rough but colorful in the mountain mining towns, generally plastered to the side of an incredibly steep hill, with a dark, narrow gulch below. Central City, west of Denver, was the second town in size in the territory, and "perhaps the leading town in wealth and culture in the early seventies." When the Teller House opened, it had seventy rooms, filled with $20,000 worth of fine furnishings. The *Register Call* assured the world:

"All sleeping rooms are tastefully fitted with all essential conveniences. The majority are without transoms, guests may therefore lie down to peaceful slumbers undisturbed by apprehensions of getting their heads blown off."

For Far West towns baptism was by fire rather than water. Central City joined the phoenixiana in 1874 by being burned to the ground. So rich were the metals pouring out of its mines that the *Register Call* announced with a touch of the Far West's congenital modesty:

"The narrow, pent-up streets and low frame buildings were swept away. Foundations of magnificent brick buildings were laid; stately business blocks, magnificent churches, substantial school houses, with a hotel and opera house second to none in the West."

After 1875 dozens of mines were opened by prospectors swarming over the San Juans: Blossom Rock, Mineral Farm, Trout and Fisherman's Lode, mines high above the timber line on Mount Sneffels; and where there was a mine there was a town. To honor Chief Ouray the town of Ouray was founded and built in the center of the ring of silver mines. The Wet Mountain Valley was the next to reveal its true color. The town of Rosita started, quickly growing to fifteen hundred population. When a prospector uncovered the Golden Chimney mine a little farther north, the town of Querida was hatched.

Just six miles west of Boulder a peculiar mixture of gold, silver and tellurium was discovered, the single richest ore body found in Colorado. The town of Sunshine sprang up overnight, grew to twelve hundred inhabitants, spawned neighboring mushroom towns like Magnolia. But the volcanic upheaval which had put together this tellurium had been sparing in its mixture of those chemicals which, when cooled, men called gold and silver. The color faded. Sunshine went out, Magnolia ceased to bloom. The mines, and the towns, became ghosts.

Each county, as its mines were opened, became the territory's great wealth producer: Gilpin County, with its color from the Central City mines, had produced in 1871 and 1872 half of the mineral wealth of the territory. Then the Georgetown mines were brought in, and by 1874 Clear Creek County was surpassing all production. When Leadville's silver mines were discovered, Lake County surpassed Gilpin and Clear Creek.

Leadville formed the western apex of an equilateral triangle of which Denver and Colorado Springs served as the base. It was close to the Continental Divide, a neighbor of half a dozen peaks which went beyond fourteen thousand feet in height. Into this region of the highest mountain peaks on the North American continent came a prospector in 1874 by the name of William H. Stevens, a former iron miner from Minnesota who had been part of the rush to Gregory Gulch in 1859, and then to California Gulch and Buckskin Joe. "Uncle Billy" had not struck color in any of these early Colorado camps; he had made a living by rewashing abandoned placer claims. He prospected the Leadville area for two years without finding any gold; but he did acquire a valuable partner, Alvinus B. Wood, who was a trained metallurgist.

Stevens and Wood were looking for gold. Men of substance, they set up a hydraulic operation, digging a long ditch to carry the water and investing considerable money in a placer mining camp. They found that their operation could not be made profitable because they were washing down heavy sands which made it difficult to separate the gold from the gravel. Other miners in the neighborhood gave this bothersome sand a thorough cursing; but Uncle Billy Stevens and Alvinus Wood, like Allen and Hosea Grosh in Nevada, were of a scientific turn of mind. They studied the mixtures being washed down, made some mineralogical and chemical tests. They found that the unwanted heavy sand was actually a carbonate of lead, the best possible composition for carrying silver.

Stevens and Wood confided in no one, but went prospecting higher on the mountain to see if they could discover the mother lode. They found it, and quickly: a body of ore about ten feet thick; found it at the one point on the entire mountain where the ore came to the surface.

William Stevens, the business head of the partnership, hired a group of unsuccessful prospectors to mine for them. When the miners realized they were not digging up gold, but some worthless composition, they told each other they were working for crazy men. The mutterings grew to a point where Stevens realized that he and his partner were going to be driven out of the area as undesirable citizens; he confided the truth about their find to an old man named Walls. Walls promptly decided that Stevens and Wood were sane, but he quit their employ anyway, dashed up the mountainside and staked out a claim. All the other Stevens and Wood employees were close on his heels.

Word of the new strike spread through the mountains faster than Indian smoke signals. During the spring and summer of 1876 the rush was confined to miners and prospectors in the immediate neighborhood; by the following spring, when the snows began to melt, the rush was on from all areas of Colorado.

There was no shelter for the thousands of men who flooded in. Prospectors who could buy or borrow sleeping space on the floor of a tent were lucky. A sawmill was opened, and men stood in line to grab the green boards with which to throw up shanties, boardinghouses, stores, saloons and gambling halls.

One successful prospector bought the Robert E. Lee mine for $16,000, hired a crew and sank a shaft more than a hundred feet deep without finding any ore. When a syndicate offered him $30,000 for his mine he sent word down the shaft for his crew to pick up its tools and quit. The men down below were in the process of drilling a hole and putting the dynamite in; they asked the boss if they couldn't shoot just this once more.

"No, come up!" replied Dexter. "I won't put another damn cent into this hole."

The new owners "shot" Dexter's last hole. When the smoke cleared they found they had exposed a vein of silver so pure that in twenty-four hours they had mined ninety-five tons of ore worth $118,500. The cost of bringing this fortune to the surface was exactly $60.

Leadville and violence were born identical twins.

A guidebook published to direct the rush gave as its primary piece of advice, "Come provided with a good pair of navy revolvers." With the prizes worth millions of dollars, mine jumping grew to a point hitherto unknown in the history of the Far West. The smaller prospectors formed a miners' guard of "what is known as low capital men, or those whose means of defense against mine jumpers lies wholly in bullets." When a predatory gang headed by a rough customer called Williams broke into the Iron Silver mine and attempted to take it over, there was a gun battle underground in which a number of men were killed and wounded. Some of the larger mines installed guards of thirty men armed with Winchester rifles. All early disputes were settled with navy revolvers, the latter ones in the courts. William Stevens, the discoverer of all this silver, said:

"Lawsuits claimed $7,000,000 of the $11,000,000 taken from the Iron Silver Mine."

Even the clergy had their church properties jumped. The Reverend Mr. T. A. Uzell arrived in town, bought a lot and started the first church in the area. A few days later he saw that a group of strange men had unloaded lumber on his lot and were about to put up their own building. The minister explained that he was building a church there. When the strangers told him to fold his church and fade away, the Reverend Mr. Uzzell took off his coat, rolled up his sleeves and waded into those who were trying to dispossess him. The church was built.

The town that had sprung up had neither name nor government. On January 14, 1878, eighteen men, including H.A.W. Tabor, who had come in from Oro City in 1877 with just enough savings from his ten years there to open a grocery store, met in a wagon shop to set up law and order because the newspaper was running a column under the heading of "Breakfast Bullets," with a murder to be read over breakfast nearly every day. The name Carbonateville was suggested, but Leadville was decided upon because the high percentage of lead in the ores, acting as a flux in the smelting, was what was making it possible to take out the pure silver.

At this first meeting H.A.W. Tabor was chosen mayor of Leadville because of his activities in the politics of Oro City. He also became the city treasurer and postmaster. H.A.W. was still enjoying his illusions of grandeur, talking of the large fortune he was going to make even though his two decades of pioneering in Colorado had brought him but a modest living. Sociable, gregarious, generous, Tabor was still the most popular man of any community he lived in, and he seemed to grow younger in his ebullience and confidence over the years. Augusta was still the mainstay of the family; she tended the grocery store, took care of the mail in the post office, balanced the family accounts and kept it solvent.

By the summer of 1878 the story of Leadville had flashed around the world. Trails leading into Leadville from Colorado Springs by way of the Ute Pass and South Pass, from Denver by way of Turkey Creek, and from Canon City up the Arkansas River were as jammed with men and frieght haulers as had been the trail over the Sierra Nevada into Virginia City nineteen years before. The coming of the tremendous winter snows and the freezing cold at this altitude of over ten thousand feet deterred no one.

Carlyle Channing, who came into Leadville to start the *Chronicle* in January 1879, spoke of "The very tedious forty hours' journey from Denver, the mercury far below zero." When he reached Leadville he was lucky to share a small bed with a stranger.

"The main thoroughfare was pretty closely and compactly lined with houses on either side, for a distance of two miles following the contour of the gulch, all of log or rough hewn slab construction. Every other door was a saloon, dance hall or gambling den. There were no street lights, but the thousands of coal oil lamps indoors cast fitful flashes of baneful light across the way."

The eighteen-man government elected a sheriff and built a small jail, but Leadville society was slightly on the informal side. "Broken Nose Scotty," who was in jail for drunkenness, sold one of his claims to a stranger who handed him $30,000 in cash. Broken Nose paid the fines of everybody in the jail, took the party to the Tontine, known as the fashionable restaurant of Leadville, and bought them so much liquor that by midnight the entire party was drunk and back in the hoosegow.

The sporting houses were the most elaborately furnished in town. The Red Light Hall prided itself on being the most respectably kept and best-managed house. "To be sure it is a sporting house and all that term implies. The girls are rounder, rosier and more beautiful then elsewhere and will take you through the mazy waltz in refreshing movements that will make you feel that you don't care a cent whether school keeps or not so the girls are all there."

Two lady barbers came in from Chicago and a "doctor," like Marsh, Meeks and de Sandels in California, carted in an electric chair equipped with a "Galvanic Faradic Battery" which guaranteed to shake out all ailments. Another "doctor," Charles Broadbent, a phrenologist, offered to read the bumps on one's head for $2.00 and then advise one whom to marry.

Nor were the arts neglected; a tattoo specialist came to Leadville and sold the ladies tattoo monograms in two colors for $50.

Sunday was as riotous in Leadville as it had been in the Forty-Niner mining camps of the Sierra Nevada because, as the *Chronicle* acidly commented:

"There are here Materialists, the Positivists, the Buddhists, the Annihilists, the Infidels and a few believers in what is termed

Christianity. All these have but one religion and one God in common: it is the Crucified Carbonate."

The competing but equally excoriating *Democrat* commented:
"Sunday is always an occasion for fast women and rapid men to air themselves on the beautiful drive. We regret to announce that no one was killed."

Leadville never duplicated the luxurious living of Virginia City. Most of the restaurants were saloons, "where everything tasted and smelled of rancid grease." The unchanging menu was mutton, lamb, hog and steak, dinner costing ten cents including potatoes and bread, an extra nickel being charged for a cup of weak coffee.

As in Virginia City, the quotient of book readers was high. Thackeray and Disraeli were unsalable, Dickens did not get much play and Ouida fell off, but the miners enjoyed the French translations of Alphonse Daudet, Alexandre Dumas and Emile Gaboriau, with his interesting detective, Monsieur Lecoq. The newly formed Leadville Literary Society was reading Jules Verne and Wilkie Collins, while the Bel Esprit Society, of which H.A.W. Tabor was a prominent member, had evenings when poetry such as Gray's *Elegy* was read. In opera the taste was rather more elemental, the audience expressing its disappointment with *Fra Diavolo* because "only two shots were fired and only one man killed, when everybody fully expected forty flashes of fire and at least half that number of elegant corpses laid out."

The town was full of indigenous Colorado characters. George H. Fryer found a rich ore deposit which he called New Discovery. The hill was named in his honor, and hundreds of men began pouring over it, setting up claims to some of the richest mines in Colorado: the Little Chief, the Carboniferous, Hibernia, Matchless. But not George Fryer. He got drunk to celebrate his great wealth, wandered off somewhere into the night and was never seen again.

In April 1878 two German shoemakers, August Rische and George Hook, came into H.A.W. Tabor's store to ask for a grubstake. They had been prospecting up on Fryer Hill and had laid out a claim but, having gone down a number of feet, had found only barren rock. They had run out of provisions. H.A.W. was still observing the resolution he had made in Oro City that he would grubstake all miners. In return for a supply of food, August Rische and George Hook gave Tabor a one-third ownership of any mine they discovered.

On May 1, at a depth of twenty-six feet, Rische and Hook struck a silver lode. They named it the Little Pittsburgh. By July it was producing $8000 a week in ore, one third of which went to H.A.W. Tabor. At last it looked as though his twenty-year dream might come true.

George Hook had never really wanted to find great wealth. The flood of silver unnerved him. People heard him mumbling to himself, saw him acting queerly. He told his neighbors that he could not stand it any more, that all this money was making him lose his mind. In September he sold out his interest in the Little Pittsburgh to H.A.W. Tabor and Rische for $98,000, bought a good farm and died wealthy.

August Rische, the second of the poor German shoemakers, could not stand the flood of money either, and by November he was eager to get out of his bonanza. He sold his share to David H. Moffatt, who had opened the first book and stationery store in Denver, and was now a wealthy banker and roadbuilder. Moffatt paid Rische $262,000 in $1000 notes. Rische moved to Denver, became a saloon owner and went broke.

H.A.W. Tabor was now half owner of one of the richest mines in the world.

CHAPTER X

Baby Doe Finds H.A.W. Tabor

HORACE A. W. TABOR took to his sudden and voluminous wealth as naturally as he did to talking. In November 1878 after Rische left, H.A.W. and his partner David Moffatt joined in the syndicate of the Little Pittsburgh and surrounding properties to form the Little Pittsburgh Consolidated Company which the following spring was capitalized in New York at $20,000,000.

By this time H.A.W. was netting $100,000 a month! He put his money into every mine and prospect around him. He bought a third interest in the Vulture for $11,500, the next day paid $18,000 for another third, and when offered the remaining third for $25,000 refused to go higher than $20,000. A few months later he paid $250,000 for the remaining third and was delighted to get it. He bought a half interest in the Maid of Erin for $43,000, then in the New Discovery for $162,000. By the end of 1878 he had money invested in the Scooper, Dunkin, Union Emma, Denver City, Tam O'Shanter, Henrietta, Empire, Hibernia, May Queen, Elk, Little Willie, Climax and the Wheel of Fortune.

Everything he touched turned to silver. One day a man called Chicken Bill, who had been working a claim on Fryer Hill without finding anything but very dull rock, took a wagon of a dark night, went over to H.A.W.'s Little Pittsburgh and borrowed a load of Tabor's carbonate lying outside the mine shaft. He salted his mine with the carbonate, then went into town the next day, stood next to H.A.W. at a bar, pretended to be drunk and bragged about his rich find. H.A.W. bought the mine for $1000, Chicken Bill ran, and H.A.W. put a crew of miners into his new possession. He very quickly found out that he had been taken, but he only laughed and, as long as they were already on the spot, kept his men working. By the time they reached thirty feet the miners uncovered a silver vein far richer than those in the Little Pittsburgh. Tabor called his mine the Crysolite, and after a short while sold a half interest for $500,000.

Everything that Horace had promised Augusta, and that she had so desperately not wanted, had come true. He was a multimillionaire, each day making progress at becoming the richest man in the world. He managed to remain modest about it, spending much of his day in the grocery store, weighing out sugar and rice, sorting part of the day's mail. However another part of his nature determined to make Leadville one of the world's most dazzling cities, even as Billy Ralston had envisaged for San Francisco. He built the first brick building in Leadville, and when the day came to move in, brought a brass band to head a city-wide parade. He bought the most expensive fire-hose cart in San Francisco and had it hauled out to Leadville, then donated a firehouse and organized volunteer firemen whom he outfitted in red shirts with the name TABOR embossed in white flannel letters across their bosoms. He bought a valuable site on Chestnut Street below the O.K. Saloon, hired every carpenter in the county and in a month had constructed the town's first public hall which he named the Wigwam, where five thousand spectators came to hear the contestants speak for a seat in Congress.

He gave champagne dinners for everybody who came to town,

particularly politicians; for he was determined to have the capital of
Colorado transferred from Denver to Leadville. Toward this end he
would contribute a whole mountainside and pay the entire expense
of moving the capitol. He established the Tabor Light Cavalry,
which was to be a police force for the county, supported by himself.
He bought a large parcel of ground on Harrison Avenue, the main
street of the town, and built Tabor's Opera House on it, a $60,000
public gesture, arriving for the formal opening in a luxurious
carriage drawn by two matched black mares, even though he lived
just next door in a magnificent suite in the new Clarendon Hotel.
To furnish this suite he had hired six stagecoaches to bring up from
Denver onyx-topped tables, bronze statues, a solid walnut bed with
a pink lace canopy, rugs from Chicago and New York, solid
mahogany writing tables with inlaid mother-of-pearl.

When the fighting Parson Uzzell asked H.A.W. for $200 with
which to buy two chandeliers for his new church, Tabor took out
his wallet and replied:

"Sure, Parson, sure. Will two be enough?"

The clergyman assured him that they would.

"Well, I dunno," replied Tabor. "The church has gotta make a
lot of noise to be heard at all in this town." He gave the Reverend
Mr. Uzzell $500, then asked, "By the way, Tom, who's gonna play
them chandeliers?"

As H.A.W. became increasingly richer the newspapers of
Chicago and New York began running his picture almost daily,
with long stories about his character and extravagances. Augusta,
who had declared that rings would get in the way of her needle, grew
increasingly silent and unhappy. She did not like to be rich; thrift
had been instilled into her by generations of New England
ancestors. She was still wearing plain dresses, having her shoes
patched, devoting her evenings to mending tears in the family's
clothing, sewing on buttons, measuring out flour by the cup in their
grocery store. She had no confidence whatever in her husband; she
thought all this wealth undeserved. She did not feel that his
flamboyant giveaway gesture made him a good mayor, and she
knew that as city treasurer he was making no effort whatever to
keep the books.

There were quarrels when H.A.W. demanded why the wife of a
millionaire was not dressed in silks and satins, particularly when
her husband could afford to buy the whole silk industry of Japan.
And why couldn't he buy costly and beautiful jewelry for her to
wear? She was not even sure she liked her husband any more, now
that he was growing fat from too much rich food, and often came

home early in the morning drunk on champagne. When in 1879 H.A.W. managed to get himself nominated for lieutenant governor, he paid the cost of stringing a telegraph wire up the mountains into Leadville to get the news of the election. When he was elected he cried to his wife:

"I'm the governor!"

"No, Horace," Augusta replied with a wan smile, "you are only the lieutenant governor."

H.A.W. did not like to have anyone qualify his successes in this niggardly fashion. He spent less and less time with Augusta, more and more with his millionaire pals. Maxcy was like his father, exuberant, extravagant, loving the soft pleasures; he too pulled away from his mother. Augusta was left very much alone in the rococo suite at the Clarendon Hotel. She withdrew, grew increasingly lonely, increasingly distant and hostile.

She was the only one in Leadville, perhaps in all Colorado, who did not think that Horace A.W. Tabor was a great man. H.A.W. did not mind, he bought the Matchless mine on Fryer Hill for $117,000, and the mine immediately began paying him $80,000 a month.

Having outgrown the social milieu of Leadville, H.A.W. went into Denver and bought a $40,000 mansion, spending another $20,000 to decorate and furnish it. Augusta, in a flash of wisdom, said:

"Horace, I will never go up those steps if you think I will have to go down them again."

She never had to go down the steps; but H.A.W. did.

When General Palmer's Denver and Rio Grande made its triumphant entrance into Leadville to tap the rich mines, Ulysses S. Grant came out to be the guest of honor. Leadville's leading citizen, Horace A.W. Tabor, was his host, slapping the former President on the back and setting up sumptuous banquets in which the city was awash with champagne. The two men became friends.

One day when Lieutenant Governor Tabor was sitting at his customary table in a Leadville restaurant, he saw a beautiful young girl with cornsilk hair, big blue eyes and a creamy white complexion gazing fixedly at him from across the room. He invited her to his table and met Baby Doe, the daughter of an Oshkosh, Wisconsin, tailor who had married the mayor's son because she was ambitious and wanted to go places in the world. The son had failed in Oshkosh, had come out to Colorado during the gold rush to make his fortune, but had ended as a $4.00-a-day miner.

Baby Doe had not yet gone very far. She was in her twenties, gay, laughter- and fun-loving, fond of expensive clothes and surroundings and determined to get the most excitement and luxury out of life. She had heard about H.A.W. Tabor and his millions, and had invested her last few dollars in a smart traveling outfit and the fare to Leadville, to see if she could land the richest man in Colorado.

Tabor could not have fallen harder had he stumbled into the open shaft of the Little Pittsburgh. He set Baby Doe up as his mistress in an elegant suite in the Clarendon Hotel, carrying on a secret liaison. He could not see as much of her as he wanted to in Leadville, so he moved her into Denver, where he installed the soft and lovable blonde in an expensive suite at the new Windsor Hotel, showering on her all those gifts of expensive clothing, diamonds and gold that Augusta would not accept.

H.A.W. Tabor set up his office at the bar of the Broadwell House, making it the headquarters of the state Senate. It was said in Denver, as Karsner reports in *Silver Dollar*, that "He always knew whether a quorum was present by the number of corks and glasses on the bar."

He was earning prodigally and spending even more prodigally. He bought up the Broadwell in Denver for $38,000 and built what became the famous Tabor Block of stores and offices. He spent $1,000,000 for an entire square block and to build the Tabor Grand Opera House, sending two architects to Europe to pick up modern ideas, a third man to Belgium for carpets, a fourth to France for brocades and tapestries, and still a fifth to Japan for cherry logs for the interior woodwork. An obscure German painter who did the curtain in the opera house was paid $15,000. Only Billy Ralston, in the history of the Far West, had been able to spend money as prodigally as Tabor.

When the five-story building with its high tower was finished, H.A.W. walked into the theatre one day, saw an oil painting gracing the center of the proscenium.

"Hey, who is that fellow up there?"

When he was told that it was Shakespeare, he cried:

"What the hell did he ever do for Denver? Paint him out and put me up there."

A financial wizard, he could do no wrong. When he bought a controlling interest in the Chicago and Calumet Canal and Dry Dock Company for $1,200,000 people told him he was going to lose his money: instead he netted another $1,000,000 in profit. He showered money on people as though the mint were his private enterprise. He bought everything he liked and everything he saw, frequently things he did not like and had no use for. He had no idea how much money he was worth; some people said $8,000,000, some $12,000,000 to $15,000,000; but what was the difference when he would never be obliged to count it? As for Leadville and its mines, nothing could be that rich: nothing, that is, until cowboy-geologist Bob Womack brought in Colorado's Cripple Creek in 1891.

H.A.W. Tabor had only two consuming ambitions left. He wanted to marry Baby Doe, and he wanted to become a United States senator. Why should he not? he asked himself. Had not all the senators from the Far West been gold and silver magnates?

On the day that he decided to divorce Augusta he simply packed his trunk and left the house. Augusta reported that she could neither cry nor reproach him; all she could feel was a hollow ache at being abandoned by her husband after all their years together. As H.A.W. was about to close the huge front door behind him, she rushed to the balustrade and cried:

"Oh, Horace, don't leave me. You know it will be your ruin!"

It was; but Horace could not hear the voice of the oracle for the slamming of the door. He gave Augusta $250,000 in cash, the enormous mansion which she had never wanted or liked, and several valuable pieces of property. He then took Baby Doe to St. Louis, where some friends arranged a secret marriage. He had secured a divorce, also secretly, in Durango.

It was the turning point for H.A.W., though he was too blissful with his beautiful young wife to notice. The people of Denver with whom he had been popular because of his openhanded prodigality resented his divorce from Augusta in a sense that they had never resented his keeping Baby Doe in a suite at the elegant Windsor Hotel. A whole class of Denver society which had been amused by his charming ostentations and vulgarities turned against him.

Then came labor trouble, the first serious strike in the silver fields. The mines of the area were producing better than $15,000,000 a year, but when so many laborers flocked in that there were more miners than jobs, the owners in joint action decided to cut wages to $2.75 a day. The miners went out, almost to the last man. Tabor ordered his Light Cavalry into Leadville in an effort to force the men back to work. When this failed he made a fast trip to Denver and, in the absence of Governor Pitkin, ordered the state militia to Leadville to break the strike.

It did; but that was the end of Tabor's popularity among the working people of Leadville, who had thought of him as a friend, and to whom he had been simple and unpretentious and warmly generous. Now he was a capitalist, one who would use the state militia against the workingman. They turned away when he came down the street, refused to drink at the same bar with him.

Little by little the investments that had always turned out so very right began to turn out wrong. Having been elected a director of the proposed Overland Broadgauge Railway Company, he wrote a check for $1,000,000 over the railroad blueprints. No ties were laid and no dollars returned to H.A.W. He invested another $1,000,000 in the mahogany forests of Honduras, and still a third $1,000,000 in the fleet of steamers to Honduras, and railroads for that country. This $2,000,000 vanished in the jungles. He sank $1,500,000 in purported gold and silver mines in Mexico from which he extracted no metal; he bought vast quantities of alleged mineral land in Arizona and in northern Colorado. They remained barren.

He was also investing several hundred thousand dollars to win a post in the United States Senate. The Republican Committee which controlled the legislature did not dare send gauche and politically inept H.A.W. Tabor to Washington for a six-year term, but fortunately there was a thirty-day interim period coming up so that they could give him the honor for which he hungered.

Senator Horace A.W. Tabor took his beauteous Baby Doe to Washington in a $5000 private train, loading twenty-two trunks and bags on it, and traveling to Washington in a $1000 silk and lace nightshirt with solid gold buttons.

It is a matter of record that he spent $300,000 during his month in the capital. He is charged with interfering with the work of the Senate by forever inviting its members out for a drink. Since his marriage to Baby Doe had been a secret one, he wanted it made respectable. He decided to have a second ceremony and persuaded a Catholic priest to perform it. H.A.W. asked President Chester A. Arthur if he would be guest of honor at the wedding. The President, remembering that Tabor had been a friend of Grant's, and also remembering his manifold millions, agreed to do so. On the strength of President Arthur's acceptance, H.A.W. succeeded in snaring most of official and diplomatic Washington for the wedding. Their more socially astute wives stayed home, missing one of the most sumptuous feasts ever staged in the nation's capital.

Baby Doe was married with a $90,000 diamond necklace around her neck.

Within a few days the news leaked out that both H.A.W. and Baby Doe were divorced persons. The priest who had been deceived, and the Catholic Church, were profoundly shocked at this deception. President Arthur was furious.

H.A.W. didn't care. He laughed, said the joke was on them,

engaged a special train to take Baby Doe back to Denver in regal splendor. There the Republican State Committee named a new senator and elected H.A.W. their chairman: he supported most of Colorado's political machine.

A considerable portion of Leadville's $17,000,000 production of silver went into H.A.W.'s capacious pocket. Like Sandy Bowers in Virginia City, he had money to throw at the birds.

H.A.W. and Baby Doe were riding one of Colorado's short-line railroads when she informed him that he was going to become a father. H.A.W. broke out champagne for everyone on the train, the crew as well as the passengers. Their first daughter, Elizabeth Pearl, was born in what has been described as the most pretentious building in Denver: for H.A.W. had bought an even bigger mansion than Augusta was living in. He had gold medals struck off labeled *Baby Tabor*, sending them to his idea of Colorado's hundred most prominent citizens. He had a second daughter whom he named Silver Dollar because William Jennings Bryan, visiting in Denver, told H.A.W. that "the baby's laughter has the ring of a silver dollar."

Though actual cash on hand seemed to be growing shorter all the time, H.A.W. estimated his wealth at about $100,000,000. He ordered a hundred peacocks to walk around the fenced lawn of his home to amuse his two daughters, and imagined that he had so little need for additional money that he passed up the opportunity to buy the Minnie and AY mines.

The Guggenheims picked them up. Within a short time they were netting $100,000 a month from them. It was the beginning of the great Guggenheim dynasty. It was the beginning of the end for H.A.W. Tabor.

CHAPTER XI

The Climate Is Perfection...

SOUTHERN CALIFORNIA WAS HAVING its difficulties. It had managed to grow only in minor spurts. Its strongest immigration of settlers had been a consequence of the Civil War. Some two thousand newcomers had been successfully absorbed; then emigration had slowed to a trickle.

Perhaps it was the fact that southern California was still experimenting widely and failing frequently. The citrus industry, with groves of several thousand trees, said to be the largest in the world, had found that if the fruit was picked early it could be shipped east without spoiling, but the oranges were:

"Thick-skinned, sour, pithy and dry; it was an insult to the noblest of fruit to call the California product by that name. The lemons, great overgrown things, with skin half an inch thick over a dry and spongy interior, were more worthy of pity than contempt."

The wine industry was producing over a million gallons a year; it was of poor quality and sold at a low price. Olive orchards were planted, but the olives were not right for the making of oil. Some apricots, peaches and prunes were dried; the market for them was negligible.

Six acres of cotton were planted south of the business district of Los Angeles, close to where Robert M. Widney, southern California's original boomer, would soon build the University of Southern California. The cotton was of good quality, but there were no buyers.

Millions of acres of fertile land surrounding Los Angeles were without water. No one wanted them at any price.

Then in 1874 southern California began to move appreciably ahead. Silver was discovered at Cerro Gordo, high in the mountains above the Mojave Desert, some two hundred miles through almost trackless waste. Eighty teams, each with fourteen mules and three wagons, carried $2,000,000 in silver lead ingots down from the Owens River to Los Angeles, the Cerro Gordo Freight Company leaving $1000 a day in the city for mule-team provender. Considerably more was being spent for merchandise and machines for the mining community. Sending the ore out of San Pedro increased southern California's shipping. Los Angeles showed a substantial increase in miners, mechanics, suppliers of commodities. The *Express* wrote:

"It is the rich trade of the mining regions about us ... that has encouraged the building of our elegant brick blocks, and furnished tenants for our numerous stores and buildings."

The population jumped from eleven thousand in 1874 to sixteen thousand in 1875, the largest concentrated increase in the history of the sleepy town.

The Southern Pacific, working its way southward down the center of the state with large construction crews, added to the prosperity. Its Chinese laborers finally managed to conquer Tehachapi Pass by means of eighteen tunnels through the mountains, and a track which looped around itself like a basketful of horseshoes. A second Chinese crew working north from Los Angeles hacked a seven-thousand-foot tunnel out of the San Fernando Mountains. On December 6, 1876, in a miniature replica of the meeting at Promontory, Utah, the two tracks met at a spot some forty miles north of Los Angeles. Charlie Crocker made a speech. Three hundred fifty Angelenos who had come north in flag-covered trains cheered while two Chinese teams covered seven hundred fifty feet from either side in eight and a half minutes of record track laying time, after which Crocker drove a golden spike with a silver hammer.

That night there was a boisterous celebration in Buffum's, the most elegant of Los Angeles's hundred saloons, where the volunteer fire department still had its social headquarters. The celebration was triumphantly echoed by the *Express*:

"This happy consummation will be celebrated in a much more signal manner ... by the filling up of the ample domain of Los Angeles County with prosperous homes."

It just did not happen. Despite the assurance of the Southern Pacific that "There are no dangers to travelers on the beaten track in California; there are no inconveniences which a child or a tenderly reared woman would not laugh at," tourists who were supposed to flock in on the railroad to enjoy the beneficent sun never showed up. Emigrants coming westward through the Sacramento and San Joaquin valleys were so delighted with the beauty of those landscapes, the fertility of the soil, the comparative cheapness of the land, that they settled there, never getting as far as southern California.

The mines played out; the furnace at Cerro Gordo shut down for lack of ore, the springs supplying the community with water dried up, and Cerro Gordo Freight Company found need to run only one team every other day.

Smallpox once again hit Los Angeles. A severe drought wiped out the sheep industry, even as it had the cattle industry a decade before. Business began to dry up. The brick blocks and stores became vacant.

The Southern Pacific strangled trade and travel, charging $2.50 each way for the ride of twenty miles to San Pedro, with a similar prohibitive tariff on freight. Two opposition lines sprang up, a freight steamer between Los Angeles and San Francisco, and a railroad line from Los Angeles to Santa Monica, with a freight pier. They were quickly bought up by the Southern Pacific.

Los Angeles drifted slowly and steadily backwards; several thousand people packed their belongings and moved to another part of the state, or returned to their original homes. By 1880 the population had fallen to a little over eleven thousand, the number of inhabitants in 1874.

The failure to popularize southern California had not come from want of trying, for no part of the Far West had ever been temperate in talking about itself. It took a powerful force to move a man, his family and his future two to three thousand miles across strange prairie, mountain and desert. Without the impetus of a gold rush, southern California's tub thumpers knew they could bridge the geographical gap only by extravagant praise of the climate, fertility and beauty; by assurances that southern California was a frontier where a man could get in on the ground floor, where living was the cheapest in America by a full third; and where no man ever died from the fatal illness that had caused his doctor to send him west.

The Southern Pacific publicized southern California throughout the world, employing a roster of lecturers who gave glowing accounts of the country, continually advertising in the newspapers and magazines, hiring such able journalists as Charles Nordhoff and Benjamin Truman to write pamphlets and books, subsidizing newspapers which cleverly disguised the railroad's hope of land sales under the guise of news releases. The rest of the country was assured that:

"Southern California was the finest part of the state, and the best region in the whole United States for farmers."

The Los Angeles Chamber of Commerce and boards of trade spent every available dollar to promote the area. Dedicated amateurs wrote fervent letters home to relatives and friends, urging them to come. The California Immigrant Union distributed three large editions of a brochure called *All About California and the Inducements to Settle There*. The Department of Agriculture in Washington, D.C., sent out navel orange seedlings to Mrs. L.C. Tibbetts in an effort to improve the quality of the oranges. New communities like Riverside, laid out on the site of the failing Silk Center Association, a few miles from the original Mormon settlement at San Bernardino, brought in water by a well-engineered irrigation canal, and offered good land for $20 an acre ... with few takers.

The Chaffey brothers, engineers as well as businessmen, founded a Mutual Water Company in the same valley, shares of which went with every acre of land bought in their "Model Colony." They brought water down in V-shaped flumes like those perfected in Nevada during the Comstock boom, and when this water flow proved erratic constructed a three-thousand-foot tunnel to bring the water to the plains. The Chaffeys, offering fertile land halfway between Los Angeles and Riverside, with the San Gabriel Railroad connection close by, found few lookers and fewer buyers.

San Diego, near the Mexican border a hundred twenty miles to the south, with one of the world's best landlocked harbors, slept in the sun. No amount of importuning could persuade anyone to build a railroad spur to open up the land. Santa Barbara, almost as far north along the coast line as San Diego was south, and boasting some of the finest climate, brilliant sunshine and intoxicating air west of Denver, remained a somnolent village.

William E. Willmore took an option on four thousand acres along the Pacific Ocean twenty miles from Los Angeles. He named his townsite American Colony, planted trees, set out parks, paved boulevards and surveyed farm plots of twenty to thirty acres. He then bought space in over a hundred newspapers and thirty-five magazines, as well as distributing literature through the California Immigrant Union, and sent out a capable agent to recruit excursions to the American Colony. His agent managed to put together a party of sixty colonists who came in tourist cars. Every promise that Willmore had made was fulfilled, yet at the end of a year the American Colony had only a dozen houses and one store. Willmore's horsecar line, connecting with the Southern Pacific, was washed out by floodwaters. Willmore had to give up his four thousand acres.

Strenuous efforts of the Santa Fe Railroad over a period of a decade to reach the Pacific coast had been thwarted. Having with the help of Dick Wootton pushed its rail over Colorado's Raton Pass into New Mexico, and then west through Arizona right up to the pass to California at Needles, the Santa Fe was stopped because it had no license and no roadbed with which to reach the coast. The Southern Pacific had not wanted to lay track across the barren and profitless Mojave Desert, but when it saw the Santa Fe coming up to Needles, it rushed out its crews and, with a license secured by buying half of the stock of the now defunct St. Louis and San Francisco (the Frisco), built its line to Needles. The engine of the Southern Pacific, on the west bank of the Colorado River, and the engine of the Santa Fe, on the east bank, stood gazing at each other across the water, neither of them going anywhere.

The Far West was rooting for the Santa Fe to reach a terminus in Los Angeles, thus cracking the Southern Pacific's monopoly. The Santa Fe tried valiantly, even running a line down into Guaymas on Mexico's Gulf of California, and planning to continue their tracks across Mexico to the California border. They built, largely with San Diego's money and enthusiasm, a line from San Diego to San Bernardino, a distance of one hundred forty miles; however their transcontinental route through Mexico would be long and time-consuming. Even if they could move their freight from San Diego to San Bernardino, they would have no connection over the Cajon Pass and across the Mojave Desert to Needles.

The Southern Pacific held all the cards: the only existing government license to build a line east through California to Needles; control of Cajon Pass, the only route by which a line could get out of the San Bernardino Mountains; a complete set of tracks running east and west across California which could stop the Santa Fe from traveling northward through the state because it would have to secure the Southern Pacific's permission to make the crossing. The line which the Santa Fe had built up the dry stream bed of the Temecula Canyon en route to San Bernardino from San Diego was wiped out by a flash flood and their one piece of operating railroad in California was put out of commission. No terminal in Los Angeles was possible.

There seemed to be a curse on Los Angeles, even as there had been on the village of Yerba Buena, back in the 1840s.

CHAPTER XII

They suffered; they wept; sometimes they died...

NOTHING DETERRED COLLIS P. HUNTINGTON from his relentless development of his railroad empire.

He ran the entire states of California and Nevada.

It was absentee landlordship at its worst. He made short trips to California only when a crisis arose. By the decisions made in his New York office he determined how much food each family in California should eat in the course of the year, what quality of clothes they could wear, what kind of house they might live in, how much education would be available to their children.

Under his philosophy of "Everything for use, nothing for appearance," Huntington built railroad stations and warehouses up and down the length of California and across Nevada and Utah that were little more than rectangular shacks painted a dirty mustard yellow, scarring the landscape of the Far West for thirty years.

He ran the railroad, and his three partners.

That Leland Stanford was neither an original nor a profound thinker is indicated by some of the epigrams he spread among the newspaper reporters:

"If it rained $20 gold pieces until noon every day, at night there would be some men begging for their suppers."

Some people found him dull-witted and stupid, yet he succeeded in concealing his thoughts from the public by never saying anything which had not been carefully thought out many days in advance. An offhand question as to how he felt might be answered several days later by a full report.

One reason Huntington called him "a damned old fool" was that Leland Stanford put on a magnificent performance as the political leader of the state, as a railroad baron, as a multimillionaire. When the Southern Pacific offices were built at the corner of Third and Townsend streets in San Francisco, Leland Stanford had the architect draw up plans for a magnificent dining room which would have made it the equivalent of the wealthiest club in the country. Huntington dashed out in time to draw red crosses through the plan, in effect telling Stanford to bring his lunch. When Stanford moved down to San Francisco from Sacramento in 1874 he took the royal suite at the new Palace Hotel, then threw up a thirty-foot wall around two acres of the crest of Nob Hill overlooking San Francisco, the bay and Golden Gate Strait, setting the fashion for the balance of the century by building a castle which threw San Francisco's journalists into a frenzy of adjectives. There were marble steps, a vast circular entrance hall with an inlaid black marble floor depicting the signs of the zodiac, lighted by a glass dome seventy feet high. There was an East Indian reception room, a billiard room, a downstairs sitting room with huge bay windows.

When after a few years he grew tired of being confined to his Nob Hill mansion, he bought a nine-thousand-acre ranch at Palo Alto down the peninsula not far from where William Ralston had built his baronial Belmont. Stanford created another baronial mansion, with hundreds of blooded horses, two race tracks, a sixty-acre trotting park, luxurious stables, one hundred fifty employees, sixty acres of carrots for his horses alone. He also paid $1,000,000 for fifty-five thousand acres of land at the northern end of the Sacramento Valley, not far from where John Sutter had originally built his fort, on which he planted almost three million grapevines.

When he traveled on the road all construction crews and station officials were notified in advance so that they would come to attention as Governor Stanford's private car, called the Leland, rolled by. Wherever the car stopped at a crossroads or a town, all railroad employees had to come in their Sunday-go-to-meeting clothes and pay homage.

As president of the railroad he was the figurehead that is carved on the front of a ship. Huntington would not even allow him to purchase the California congressmen or judges. To Friend Colton, Huntington wrote in regard to a California congressman whom he wanted in his pocket:

"I do not think it safe for Stanford to talk with him on our matters, as it would be just like him to get up in Congress and lie about what Stanford said to him."

Yet later, through the tragic death of his only and idolized son, Leland Stanford would achieve a true immortality by the founding of Stanford University at Palo Alto; an immortality later to be thrust upon Collis P. Huntington by his nephew, Henry E. Huntington, in a philanthropic gesture involving his inherited untold millions which created the Huntington Art Gallery and Library at San Marino, California; an act, and an immortality, which doubtless has had Collis P. Huntington writhing in his grave these many years.

No greater contrast to Huntington or to Stanford can be imagined than Mark Hopkins. Known affectionately as Uncle Mark, he was the only quiet, simple and abstemious man of the quartet. He was thrifty not only in his personal life but in the business of the railroad: he would rescue from the wastebasket in the office material thrown there by clerks. When he occasionally went out on the line he would rescue a piece of scrap metal tossed aside by a work crew. He did not drink or smoke or swear, and was unimpressed by the millions that were rolling up in his private account book. It can almost be said that he was not even happy about them. Unlike Stanford, who had moved down from Sacramento with pomp and ceremony, Mark Hopkins took the Sacramento night boat down the river, in the morning walked to the Southern Pacific office in San Francisco and worked all day. After supper, which he had by himself, he walked up Sutter Street looking for a house to rent. He found a small cottage near Leavenworth, checked the roof and heating problems, learned that the rent was $35 a month, took the place, then walked back to the railroad office for a couple of hours more of work.

Uncle Mark never bought a horse or a carriage. On good days he walked to the office, on rainy days he took the horsecar. For recreation he tried to raise vegetables in the back garden of his cottage, even as he had in Sacramento. A lean man, he would drink a cup of tea at noon while his three partners, weighing two hundred ten to two hundred sixty pounds each, put away an enormous meal. He rarely entertained, rarely took his wife out. He retained all his friends from the days when he was a beginning merchant. He put on no airs and claimed no special privileges because he now had some $3,000,000 to $4,000,000 in the bank.

He had little to do with the setting of the railroad policy, nothing to do with the purchasing and corrupting of the country's politicians and courts; nevertheless he paid the bills and entered them in the account books, and never protested Huntington's actions. Yet on occasion he could put his foot down. The combined seven hundred pounds of the Big Three could not move him a fraction of an inch, for as Charlie Crocker said:

"When Hopkins wanted to, he could be the stubbornest man alive. He was hell on wheels."

The childless Hopkinses lived in the $35-a-month cottage for five years, during which time Uncle Mark took no vacations. Then his wife, Mary Hopkins, who was a distant cousin and had married Hopkins when he had come home to New York for a visit from the gold fields, revolted for the first time in her twenty years of uneventful married life. If the other partners were living in high style, why couldn't they? Mary Hopkins had spent her time reading the novels of Ouida, Mrs. Southworth and Bulwer-Lytton; she wanted a mansion castle of the type that she had been reading about in those romantic tales. Uncle Mark compromised by looking for property in North Beach near the Golden Gate Strait, but when Leland Stanford confided that he had just bought two lots up on top of tree-naked, wind-swept Nob Hill for $60,000, and offered to sell him half of it for $30,000, Hopkins went up to survey the hill, investigated the cable car just being perfected, and decided that Nob Hill was going to be the most important residential area in San Francisco. He paid Stanford the $30,000 and then turned over to his wife the building of what he thought would be a large yet simple home.

Mary Hopkins hired architects, changed her husband's beginning plans, added to them and expanded them until, when San Francisco got a first look at the Hopkins home, they found that quiet mouselike Mary Hopkins had outdone the Leland Stanfords, building a mansion that was considerably larger, more pretentious and more ornate. There was a drawing room which reproduced one of the largest chambers in the palace of the doges in Venice, a dining room seating sixty for a family which had previously entertained one couple for dinner once a month, and a bedroom which was done in semiprecious stones, the walls finished in shiny ebony inlaid with ivory.

What Uncle Mark thought about this gabled, turreted pastiche, now the largest house in the Far West, rising on the hill above his $35-a-month cottage, he kept to himself. Only once did he comment; when the newspaper reporters came to ask him what he thought of his new mansion, they found him cultivating vegetables in the back garden. He leaned on his hoe, looked up at the towers and assorted clutter above him and asked with a quizzical smile:

"Do you think the Hotel de Hopkins will ever pay dividends?"

He never got to find out. He died quietly in his sleep one night before the building was completed. This left Mary Hopkins, as the papers were quick to comment, the richest widow in America. She shortly after married an interior decorator some twenty-five years her junior, whose great pleasure was rearranging furniture. When the San Francisco papers castigated her for this marriage, she moved away in a huff and spent the rest of her life in the East. The Hotel de Hopkins dominated the city from the top of Nob Hill until the end of the century. Architectural critic Willis Poke said of the railroad barons' monstrosities:

"They cost a great deal of money, and whatever harsh criticism may fall upon them they cannot be robbed of that prestige."

Only the Silver Kings were as much despised in California as were the Railroad Kings. Many former stock investors blamed Mackay, Fair, Flood and O'Brien for their personal tragedies. California and its inhabitants, bogged down in a depression, drew cold comfort from the fact that the multimillionaires were living like lords of the manor.

The scarcity of jobs in San Francisco was aggravated by the presence of thousands of Chinese, living on a low-income scale and willing to work at low wages. When the Southern Pacific announced a wage cut in all departments, its employees threatened to strike. A mass meeting of sympathizers was held in a sand lot in front of the City Hall. It was the beginning of California's militant labor "Sand Lot" movement.

The meeting was peaceable. It might have passed unnoticed had there not been workers' riots some time before in Pittsburgh, with trains and roundhouses burned. The Southern Pacific and the San Francisco Chamber of Commerce organized a Committee of Public Safety, subscribing $100,000 in addition to guns and ammunition. When they called in William T. Coleman of vigilante fame to lead the committee he told them to put away their guns, and armed the group with pick handles. A few vocal blows were exchanged as the rival forces roamed the streets, but after a couple of days Coleman disbanded what had been named the "Pick Handle Brigade."

Peace had prevailed, and so it might have continued except for one of the pick-handle men, Denis Kearney, born in County Cork, Ireland, thirty years before, a former sailor and now a dray owner, who had been educating himself at the Lyceum of Self-Culture, particularly in the art of public speaking. Kearney was a short, heavy-set men, with short black hair, dark eyes and an enormous voice to match his ambition. The several days of activity in an organized movement had awakened his latent powers. He switched sides and became secretary of the Workingmen's Trade and Labor Union, stepping forth as the leader of a movement whose purpose he enunciated in his first neat slogan:

"Bread or blood!"

Kearney had a ready audience during that summer of 1877: the thousands of unemployed who were begging for work at a dollar a day, and none to be had. With fall, and the completion of the harvest, the migratory farm laborers flocked into town to swell his audiences in the ubiquitous sand lots left over from the sand dunes of Yerba Buena. Kearney gave them what they longed to hear: deeply emotional harangues on the political corruption of the city and state government; on the right of men to work; on the injustice of the million-dollar homes of the rich towering above them on Nob Hill while thousands of unemployed were without food for their families. Kearney's language and imagery were keyed to the intense partisanship of San Francisco's working people, who had just seen a "Pick Handle Brigade" formed to handle them.

Henry George, a California economist-journalist who was completing the final chapters of a book to be called *Progress and Poverty*, quotes Kearney at this first meeting as reading a description of the burning of Moscow as a suggestion of what might be in store for San Francisco. Kearney's next move was to convert his followers from a labor union group to a political party: the following year there was to be an election of delegates to a convention to rewrite the California constitution. He formed the Workingmen's party and set out to capture enough delegates to control the convention.

Kearney celebrated Thanksgiving Day by leading his several thousand followers up to Nob Hill to pull down the "spite fence" which Charlie Crocker had built around the home of an undertaker named Jung when the latter had declined to sell his property to Crocker so that the railroad magnate might occupy a full square block.

Kearney was arrested for inciting to riot. The San Francisco Council passed ordinances forbidding sand-lot assemblages. A Nast cartoon showed Kearney armed with a revolver and a sword, wearing a badge which read "Communist," with the torch of anarchy held aloft in one hand, and a scroll in the other inscribed: MOB RULE.

The judge released Kearney on the ground that he had not incited anyone to action. During the following weeks Kearney was arrested nearly every day, whenever he spoke, and held in jail for as long as two weeks; but no judge or jury could be found to convict him. He gathered enthusiasts with every arrest: at one point it appeared that his followers would descend upon the jail and free him by force. The California Senate passed a law, known contemptuously in San Francisco as the "Gag Law," which was aimed at preventing Kearney from speaking in public. These restrictive measures were not fashioned to soothe either San Francisco's working people or Kearney. To his next sand-lot assemblage he cried:

"If the members of the legislature overstep the limits of decency, then I say 'Hemp! Hemp! Hemp!' This is the battle cry of freedom."

The battle of the classes was taken up by the newspapers, the *Chronicle* favoring Kearney, giving him much space in order to capture what had formerly been the *Call's* working-class audience; and the *Call* correspondingly condemning his every word. Somewhere in the heat of battle the two papers changed sides. The clear result of the attempts to throttle and imprison Kearney was the enormous growth of his movement, until it included much of San Francisco's middle class.

Kearney moved from political club to political club, using them as open forums, putting down all opposition by his loud, penetrating voice, his agility with parliamentary proceedings, and the fact that he was rehearsing truthfully, albeit in incendiary stump language, the economic and political abuses of the decade. Henry George said:

"Kearney has already made what will be regarded by thousands of men as a dazzlingly brilliant success. An unknown drayman, destitute of advantages, without following or influence, he has, simply by appealing to popular discontent and arousing the uneasy timidity which is its correlative, risen to the rank of a great leader, and drunk the sweets of power and fame."

Kearney had not had himself nominated for the constitutional convention, but his Workingmen's party slate, calling for "an eight hour day, direct election of United States senators, compulsory free education, state regulation of railroads, more equitable taxation, and exclusion of Chinese laborers," was gaining so much favor that the Republicans and Democrats combined on a so-called Non-Partisan ticket in an effort to defeat him and his "alarmingly radical" demands. Though they managed to elect a number of their fusion candidates from other parts of the state, the Workingmen's party carried San Francisco by a wide margin and sent a robust delegation of its members to the convention.

Kearney's delegates had been chosen from the untrained and inexperienced ranks of San Francisco's labor. They were no match for the Southern Pacific's lawyers. Since he had not run for office, Kearney could not appear in the debates, nor lead his forces. The Workingmen's party joined with the farm block to win a few reforms, but the convention bogged down in debate designed to obscure rather than clarify the state's problems.

Kearney's following in San Francisco and central California was bitterly disappointed in the thin result of their campaign enthusiasm. Kearney, trying to consolidate his movement in a fiery public speech, was fined $1000 and given a stiff jail sentence. This time the opposition made the sentence stick; and this time Kearney's followers did not rise in wrath to descend upon the jail. Chagrined, let down, tired of the agitation, they turned aside. What had been California's first militant labor-political movement went out in a whimper. As Denis Kearney later wrote to Lord Bryce, who had spoken poorly of Kearney and his movement in *The American Commonwealth:*

"I was poor, with a helpless family, and I went to work to provide for their comfort. I am opposed to strikes in a Republic, where the ballot of a millionaire's gardener or coachman cancels that of their master."

Denis Kearney had started the Far West's militant labor and social reform movement. He had languished in jail. But the Southern Pacific could not relax. Elsewhere it was running into a more immediate resistance.

In 1877, after the settlers of Tulare Valley had developed their arid lands into a fruitful valley, the Southern Pacific took possession of its land grants from the federal government.

The settlers, who had been promised that the land they broke would be theirs at rates of $2.50 to $5.00 an acre, now learned that it was being offered on the open market for $25 to $40 an acre. Their farms would be sold to whoever was willing to pay the highest price. All the improvements they had put in: the irrigation system, the canals and ditches, the roads, the plowed fields, the orchards, houses and barns belonged to the Southern Pacific and would have to be bought at the Southern Pacific's prices!

Accustomed to co-operate in order to survive, the settlers formed a Settlers' League, sent a statement of their case, along with the original Southern Pacific contract, to their representatives in Congress. Unfortunately the Southern Pacific owned these congressmen. The settlers hired lawyers and took their case to the federal court; the Southern Pacific owned the court, which upheld the railroad.

The Southern Pacific was advertising its land all over the country. Purchasers, not knowing the history of the Tulare Basin, came in to buy. Houses were built, the new occupants tapped the settlers' irrigation canals. One night the Settlers' League moved in a body to one of the new houses, removed the owner and his possessions and set fire to the oil-soaked house. The newcomers moved away. No one could be persuaded to buy in the Tulare Basin.

Shortly after word of the burning reached the offices of the Southern Pacific, two strangers, Hartt and Crow, got off the Southern Pacific train at Hanford. Each had been offered a farm belonging to a Tulare Basin settler if he could hold the farm against the Settlers' League. Hartt and Crow had brought with them an arsenal of shotguns, revolvers and bullets.

On the morning of May 10, 1880, the marshal of the district, having been given writs of eviction by the court against the settlers, moved in to eject. While the League, headed by Major Thomas A. McQuiddy, was meeting in another part of the valley, the marshal in one buggy, and Hartt and Crow in another, rode up to a house belonging to a settler named Branden, removed all of Branden's possessions and declared Hartt the new owner. The sheriff, with Hartt and Crow still behind him, then moved on to a farm owned by Brewer.

The meeting of the Settlers' League was informed of the happenings at the Branden house. The settlers came across country to the Brewer house. The marshal explained that he had a writ to dispossess Brewer. The Settlers' League members said they could not allow this until the Supreme Court had passed on their case, suggesting that the sheriff go peaceably with them to the railroad station and leave the district. The sheriff agreed.

As four of the settlers started to go off with the sheriff, Hartt took a shotgun from where it had been hidden on the floor of his buggy and cried:

"Let's shoot!"

A settler named Harris walked toward the buggy, ordering Hartt and Crow to give up their weapons. Crow put his shotgun to his shoulder and fired full into Harris's face.

Another settler, Henderson, drew his revolver. Hartt grabbed up a rifle and jumped to the ground. Henderson caught him with a shot in the stomach. A second blast came from Crow's shotgun, killing Henderson. Crow then jumped out of the buggy and began shooting into the group of farmers. Every bullet found a mark: Daniel Kelly received three slugs, Iver Kneutson was killed as he tried to draw his revolver, Edward Haymaker was shot in the head,

Archibald MacGregor was shot twice in the chest, started running across the field to safety and was shot in the back. Crow started to make for the protection of a nearby barn. Major McQuiddy cried:

"Don't let that man escape!"

Crow was followed to the neighboring farm. He had just drawn a bead on two of his pursuers when a settler across the wheat fields caught him in his sights and pulled the trigger. Crow fell dead in a ditch.

Back at the Brewer farm the three men already dead, Kneutson, Harris and Henderson, were laid out on the porch. The wounded men, Kelly, MacGregor and Haymaker, and Hartt was well, were taken inside the house. Doctors were summoned. Haymaker survived. The rest died that night.

The Southern Pacific took control of the situation. Since the only telegraph dispatchers were in the railroad stations, they were instructed to allow no messages to go over the wires except official company business. Then the country was informed of "an armed insurrection which had closed down the wires." In San Francisco, Crocker headed a delegation which went from newspaper to newspaper informing the press that their two agents sent into the Tulare Basin had been murdered by a gang of guerrillas and hoodlums.

That was the version the country's papers printed. The five dead members of the Settlers' League were buried on May 12. Every man, woman and child in the Tulare Basin marched in the funeral procession.

The Southern Pacific did not send flowers.

A few days later the families of the dead men were evicted.

But the truth came out, as it always will. In a matter of days, reporters were in the Tulare Basin interviewing eyewitnesses, getting the truth about Hartt and Crow, and the telegraph lines. Accurate stories of the battle of Mussel Slough were spread over the papers of the nation.

This did not help the settlers of the Tulare Valley. Unable to buy their own homes and farms, they were dispossessed and had to move away.

Some years later, in a different part of the state, another Settlers' League came to grips with the Octopus. Faced with the identical tactic by the Southern Pacific, they managed to retain possession of their farms until a decision came down from the Supreme Court. The Supreme Court ruled in their favor. The settlers bought their land at the prices originally provided by the railroad, the same $2.50

and $5.00 price guaranteed by the Southern Pacific to the settlers of the Tulare Basin.

By his lies, his ruthlessness, his trickery, Collis P. Huntington helped open the land. By promising that the land was good and that it was cheap, and that they would prosper, he brought people to break the prairie, the desert, the sandy loam, the arid areas. He offered transportation to people who could not move otherwise. They suffered; they wept; sometimes they died; but their families remained to develop the country.

Yet no tenable civilization could rise until after he was dead and the vast powers of his empire were smashed; until the people he brought in, held serfs for several decades, could once again be free: for only free men create an authentic civilization.

Giants had stalked the land. They had opened it, developed it, ravished it. They had destroyed each other, and frequently themselves.

But the land survived.

Book Six

AN ERA ENDS,
A NEW STORY BEGINS

CHAPTER I

Southern California Has Its Eighty-Seveners

FOR TWENTY YEARS SOUTHERN California had poured energy, money, talent and millions of printed words into a publicizing campaign with which it was determined to sell itself to the world. Southern California was for sale; millions of acres were available at small cost. The nation was wooed with a lover's ardency. Now in 1887 much of it was seduced.

What royal metal caused the boom? Neither gold nor silver, but iron in the form of rails.

The Santa Fe Railroad, which the year before had completed its line from Kansas City to Chicago, its eastern terminus, was determined to have a southern California terminus. It waited only long enough to make sure that it had a workable roadbed from San Bernardino to Los Angeles, which it accomplished by buying the Los Angeles and San Gabriel, to make a sharp cut in the freight rates, as it had been threatening to do these many years while struggling against the Southern Pacific's strangle hold. Then the Santa Fe cut the passenger fare from Kansas City to Los Angeles from $100 to $95. The Southern Pacific dropped its fare to $85, the Santa Fe came back with $80, the Southern Pacific slashed to $60, the Santa Fe to $50, the Southern Pacific to $40, the Santa Fe to $25.

The great day for passengers came on March 6, 1887 when early in the morning the Southern Pacific cut its rate to $12 to meet the Santa Fe rate. The Santa Fe dropped to $10, the Southern Pacific matched this reduction, but within a matter of minutes the Santa Fe had cut to $8.00.

Passengers in the eastern cities were running frantically between railroad stations, with ticket sellers promising that they would meet any reduced rate offered by the opposing line. The buyers were also assured that if the fare was cut at any time while they were en route they would be given a refund.

Then, just before noon, somebody got confused. The Santa Fe refused to go below the $8.00 rate for the ride from Kansas City to Los Angeles, but the Southern Pacific, thinking its opponent had again cut the fare, came down to $6.00 and then, again informed erroneously that the Santa Fe had met the drop, to $4.00.

At noon the nation was electrified to find that the Southern Pacific was offering a transcontinental railroad journey to California for $1.00!

Suddenly all of the thousands of people who had been interested or intrigued by the idea of cheap land in the Far West, who had dreamed that they one day might make the long voyage to the Pacific coast, who had for years been inundated with southern California's picture of itself as the garden spot of the nation, decided that now was the time to go as the guests of the Southern Pacific or the Santa Fe. And when within a few days the rate rose to $10 and finally settled at $25 it did not discourage those who had made up their minds.

Groups of families and friends, business or farming associates made up traveling communities. Those who could afford to came by Pullman; the rest took over what became known as Emigrant or Zulu cars, with folding slats that flattened down into beds. Sometimes one member of the party traveled in a freight car to watch over the livestock. The women cooked steaks and made coffee over an oil burner, and washed their husbands' and childrens' clothes.

Excursion trains in three to five sections came into Los Angeles every day of the week, with hundreds on board. The Southern Pacific claimed it alone brought in a hundred twenty thousand people in 1887. People found themselves sleeping three in a bed, most of them housed under the tents which ringed the settlement like a bivouacked army.

A decade before the Los Angeles Chamber of Commerce could bring itself to boast of only nine thousand inhabitants, now it had at least two thousand fast-talking, mesmeric real estate salesmen. The avalanche of land boomers that flooded into southern California was the equivalent of the gold rush of the Forty-Niners into the Sierra Nevada.

The opening of a new town, anywhere from five to forty miles out from Los Angeles, was advertised for days in advance. Though no one in the city knew anything about the land being offered:

"Men stood excitedly in line for days at a time in order to get first choice of lots in a new subdivision."

The carnival aspect of the boom was intensified when a circus went broke and the land promoters engaged the entire show, freaks as well as the lions and tigers, the elephants and the giraffes, to march in parades announcing the opening of new subdivisions.

Prospective buyers, promised free transportation, free lunch, free music and free entertainment, thronged to the railroad station on the day of the auction, were helped onto flatcars that were decorated with flags and bunting. With a brass band playing at its loudest, they were taken over the railroad lines to the new tracts, sometimes little more than desert areas that had been worth perhaps $1.00 an acre the week before, and where twenty-five-foot lots were now sold for hundreds of dollars, changing hands as many as three times in a single day. Few kept any record of the buying or selling.

Pasadena promoter John McDonald put together moonlight train excursions, with a band playing romantic music and folks buying land in the dark so fast that, as one eyewitness testified, McDonald needed two assistants to help him take in the money under lantern light.

The activity resembled nothing so much as the speculation on the San Francisco Stock and Exchange during the height of the Comstock bonanzas. In the hot dusty summer months of June, July and August the trading was so frenzied that $38,000,000 worth of real estate changed hands in Los Angeles County. Each day saw five new towns platted, mapped and recorded. Eighty thousand dollars worth of property was sold within two hours after the opening of a new Santa Ana subdivision. Fullerton passed this figure by selling $92,000 worth in half a day. At Whittier, founded by Quakers from Illinois, Indiana and Iowa, $400,000 worth of lots were sold in the first three days of the subdivision. By the end of 1887, $100,000,000 in paper profits had been made, or as much as was taken out of the Sierra Nevada gold fields in the years of 1849 and 1852.

"Los Angeles was a crowded, seething city of promoters, amateur and professional; hotels bulged with occupants, prices soared to astronomic levels, and everywhere—on the streets, in print, in homes and clubs—the incessant topic was land."

Almost no one escaped the mounting fever. Policemen were observed selling lots to strangers while walking their beats, dentists as well as mechanics and teamsters were promoting subdivisions. Some of the brokers were unable to sign their own names. Ten-by-twelve fruit stands were rented as real estate offices for $100 a month, a thousand offices were conducted on desks in stores and homes. Promoters without the dignity of a desk roamed the streets with their subdivisions in their hats.

As in the wildest speculative days in San Francisco, scrubwomen, ditch diggers, cooks bought a lot at ten per cent down, sold it immediately for a profit, then bought more lots on the installment plan. In a new subdivision called Monrovia prospectors could buy lots for $30 down, the balance to be paid over a period of months. With a small investment, men and women ran up profits of thousands of dollars. The saloons in Los Angeles became twenty-four-hour real estate brokerages. Investors became so excited at the news of an impending subdivision that they pursued the owners through the streets, and even sought them out in church to buy their properties in advance.

As the mines had been salted to catch the tenderfoot, so was Los Angeles inundated by hundreds of what became known as "Escrow Indians," sharks who had had their training in the wildest days of the Kansas land boom. There were few tricks they did not know: they tied oranges onto Joshua trees the night before an auction, then sold the land as citrus-bearing orchards. They had imaginative lithographs printed showing their town with a health sanitarium on one corner, a fashionable hotel on the other, palm-lined streets and groves or orange trees just beyond the buildings.

A town plat called Chicago Park laid out in the sandy bed of the San Gabriel River was advertised with lithographs showing the river full of water and steamers wending their way up to the docks of the town. The fact that the San Gabriel was dry for four years out of five, and at its fullest had only a few inches of water along its bottom, did not faze the promoters.

Promoters promised that the land they were selling would grow everything known in the tropics and the subtropics, that it contained oil, iron, gold and silver. Land advertised as having water privileges was found by the buyers to be under water; villa sites sold as having great scenic attractions would be located by their buyers after exhausting climbs up the mountainsides, on top of a precipice. Acreage in paper towns, seven out of ten of which never materialized, was sold for $500 on the promise that every acre would yield $1000 of profits in oranges.

To sell lots in new Long Beach, the former ill-fated American Colony of William E. Willmore, the promoters advertised not only sprinkled streets, a bathhouse, hot and cold running water, but as a clinching argument a billiard room for ladies in the hotel.

Everything that had failed to work for the American Colony was now a tremendous success for Long Beach.

Described by the Los Angeles *Times* as "dudes, loafers, paupers, those who expect to astonish the natives, those who are afraid to pull off their coats, cheap politicians, business scrubs and impecunious clerks," the Escrow Indians were able to turn intelligent people into gulls.

And why not, when the lands immediately resold, and then sold still once again before the original buyers were out of earshot?

Legitimate realtors of Los Angeles were piqued into running competing advertisements:

"What do you prefer? In the new city of *Multcraze* thirty miles from Los Angeles, three miles from the nearest residence, amidst beautiful desert sand, sagebrush and large stones, a lot forty-five by one hundred thirty for $350; or one mile from Los Angeles city limits, surrounded by magnificent improvements, rich, level, loamy land at $350 an acre?"

Even the honest promoters went in for unabashed exaggeration. For the subdivision of Rowena the promoters advertised:

"You need not till the soil, you can look on while the earth sends forth her plenty."

Another promised, "Half an acre in lemons is sufficient for the support of a family"; while a third publicist cried:

"If you want to pick a melon in this country you have to get on horseback!"

One town's boomers claimed, "No fog, no frost, no alkali, no adobe."

A few months later a wit added, "No town."

Most of the new settlements opened in the hot, fertile valleys east of Los Angeles, where years before El Monte and San Bernardino had been started, met with instant acceptance. Such a one was Azusa, north of El Monte, where so tremendous a promotional campaign was waged that, just as during the opening of Reno, men stood in line all night before the morning of the sale, with the one who had the second place reported as refusing to accept $1000 for his advantageous spot, and the fifth one in line turning down $500. "Not one in a hundred had seen the townsite," yet $280,000 worth of lots were sold on the first day of the auction. At the end of the summer the promoters of Azusa showed profits of $1,175,000.

The speculative newcomers had plenty of capital to invest, capital which they doubled and trebled within a week of their arrival. They poked fun at reluctant long-time residents of Los

Angeles for being timid and refusing to participate in the land rush.

The population skyrocketed to more than a hundred thousand. The city government was galvanized into action. It cleaned up the plaza with a pick and shovel crew, created Eastlake Park out of a bog, converted Main, Spring, Broadway and Hill streets from dusty roads to paved thoroughfares on which they ran bright new streetcars. When a whirlwind named "Billy" Workman was elected mayor, and property owners refused to cooperate, Mayor Workman sent in crews in the dark of night, particularly after a rain, to put up signs which read:

"Fares for Ferrying Across, Twenty-Five Cents," or, "No Duck Hunting Allowed in This Pond!"

As they had in the silver rush of Leadville and the San Juans, builders stood in line at the mills to grab the unseasoned planks to put up new houses, business blocks, hotels. Wells Fargo freightage jumped from three hundred thousand pounds to seven million. All business boomed; and the boom had such generative power that it rolled one hundred twenty miles southward to San Diego near the Mexican border; moved on its own momentum a hundred miles northward through Santa Barbara on the coast; through the hot central valley to Bakersfield and still farther northward into the Tulare Valley of Mussel Slough memory. It moved eastward through the San Gabriel, Santa Ana and San Bernardino valleys all the way to San Bernardino; it rolled westward to the ocean, forming towns at every possible lagoon and small bay. Yet Philip D. Armour, the meat packer, said at the height of the influx:

"This is merely preliminary to a boom that will outclass the present activity as thunder to the crack of a hickory nut."

Northern California, which had enjoyed its rush thirty-eight years before, was miffed at being neglected. The public prints editorialized acidly:

"The average Eastern mind conceives of California as a small tract of country situated in and about Los Angeles. The result shows the pecuniary value of cheek."

Angelenos gleefully said it was about time.

The southern California boom of 1887, one of the most "colorful and uproarious" of the Far Wast, was confined to that particular year. By spring of 1888 the party was over, a speculative orgy like William Sharon's manipulation of the Ophir.

About three out of every ten new towns were promoted by developers who intended to make them permanent and to share in their growth: Glendale, Burbank, Azusa, Monrovia, Arcadia,

Claremont, Cucamonga, Colton, the last founded by a small group of Germans on a three-hundred-acre plat where the Southern Pacific set up a station, railway yards and warehouses to make it a railroad center.

These developers chose their land and their locations wisely, spent months and thousands of dollars building irrigation canals to bring in water from the hills, paved the streets, built schools, churches, city halls, homes and business shops. At Inglewood, between Los Angeles and the sea, the promoters put in eleven miles of water pipe and offered free lumber to buyers who would improve their property. They also built a hotel and sold lots as the conservative price of from $200 to $750, attracting a population of some three hundred. The promoters of Redondo Beach, who thought of it as a potential harbor for Los Angeles, built a $100,000 iron pier. Pasadena, co-operatively founded in 1874 by a group of Indians who had frozen through an appalling winter, was growing at a rate equal to that of Los Angeles. The Chaffey brothers' "Model Colony" became Ontario, and prospered. Riverside, with its irrigation system and fertile soil, unwanted for years, blossomed.

Those towns which had consisted of nothing more than a survey and a map vanished even from memory. The last individuals to hold the property lost their investments.

The victims of the Escrow Indians were frequently the natives, who had withstood all appeals to invest their money in the new subdivisions, only to be overcome at the last minute, plunge their life savings . . . then find themselves the last man on the line, with their plot of land in a field or desert highly overpriced or completely without value. In larger measure the victims included the prosperous tourists, well-to-do businessmen out to investigate this new center of wealth, "invalids and prospective middle class settlers chiefly from farms in the north central states. The outstanding characteristic of these people was their prosperity."

Though the agricultural richness of the land had been one of the chief advertised virtues, the farmers had been too busy buying and selling real estate to harvest their crops. A number of merchants who had been sucked into the vortex found themselves broke and out of business. One newspaper regretted editorially:

"The lively times of the past few years have spoiled many a good mechanic, many a farmer and many of our best tradesmen."

Many of the middle-aged and middle class who had come to retire in southern California years before, and had been unable to resist the hysteria, discovered that their little competence was gone.

The large sums of money that had been spent for surveys and

newspaper advertising slowed to a trickle, then vanished; hundreds of newly formed chambers of commerce, boards of trade and realty syndicates blew away like tumbleweed. Eighteen hundred tract maps sat gathering dust in the Los Angeles County Courthouse. Boom buyers were heard to lament that it was hard to live on climate alone.

Southern California was dazed, unable to return to its painfully slow process of growth.

It was said that the boom did not burst, it gradually shriveled up. By April 1, 1888 a few harsh facts began to emerge: tourists simply had not settled in anything like the numbers expected. The banks, nervous about the paper boom, had cut down on credit involved in real estate. Many who had made large profits buying and selling land realized that their gains amounted to soft signatures by people who had been speculating precisely as they had. Those who had property left to sell saw that they had to sell their land quickly and get out some cash, or they would be left empty-handed.

The buyer became extinct. Those who decided that they would sell quickly, decided they would sell cheaply; land selling for $80 an acre was thrown onto the market at $20. Those new towns in which money, integrity and brains had been invested, where people had gone to live, retained a considerable portion of their population as well as their land value. The alkali lands, the desert areas, the rocky plains were in a matter of days almost worthless.

The banks, having served as a break to runaway inflation, now carried from week to week and month to month those settlers who had bought land to develop on a permanent basis; and so many were saved from bankruptcy. But a myriad of ghost towns, a dozen each in the San Gabriel and Santa Ana valleys, some eighteen in the San Bernardino Valley and another twenty between Los Angeles and the seacoast, dried up and disappeared.

The boom, in spite of its extravaganza nature, its Escrow Indians who made their way eastward over the Rockies with their loot, brought southern California many permanent benefits: some thirty-two thousand new inhabitants were going to stick it out, multiplying Los Angeles's population by several hundred per cent. It was an increase which would need housing and industry. One hundred houses a month had been built, an over-all investment of about $5,000,000 in capital. Many miles of local railroad track had been laid, eastward through the San Gabriel Valley, northward through the San Fernando Valley, westward to Santa Monica, Long Beach and other ocean points, the Santa Fe stopping at at least twenty small towns on its route through the San Gabriel Valley to San Bernardino.

Many new schools had been built. Four colleges were started. A dozen new business blocks had been opened in Los Angeles. The city limits had been extended in all four directions; it had become a cosmopolitan center.

Dumke comments in *The Boom of the Eighties in Southern California*, "The boom was significant . . . it wiped out forever the last traces of Spanish-Mexican pastoral economy. The gold rush made northern California a real part of the United States; the boom of the eighties did precisely that for the South."

The "sleepy little town dozing in the sun" had been broken wide open by American get-rich-quick methods. The manana influence was banished. Los Angeles was on its way to becoming a San Francisco, Salt Lake City or Denver.

CHAPTER II

The Southern Pacific Loses Its Fence

THE ROBUSTIOUS COMPETITION OF the Santa Fe had brought the Southern Pacific to heel in southern California. The first substantial victory against the monopoly of the Southern Pacific on its home ground was won on the Oakland waterfront in the war waged by John L. Davie, cowpuncher, miner and opera singer. An improbable character, Davie kept a store in Oakland in which he sold coal and books, a highly improbable combination of products.

In 1894, having been persuaded by a salesman that a third logical contender for his efforts was salt, Davie decided that he would build a warehouse on the Oakland waterfront to house his merchandise. He selected an available building site on the estuary where seagoing vessels could bring him supplies, and then took his plans to the Oakland city officials who supervised the area. Since the Southern Pacific still controlled the Oakland city government, a politician named Tom Carrothers refused to grant Davie the right to build his warehouse: Davie would have to build on land owned by the Southern Pacific so that the railroad could control the traffic in and out of the warehouse, and be able to set the freight rates.

Instead, Davie leased two acres of a small parcel owned by the Morgan Oyster Company, under control of the state rather than the city of Oakland. He filled in the marshland and built a warehouse; but when he went to San Francisco to order three thousand tons of coal, the dealer told him:

"We can't send ships to Oakland, the railroad has a fence around the city."

Davie went back to Oakland and had a conference with a group of young oyster pirates, one of them named Jack London, whom he had permitted to keep their headquarters on the land he leased. The oyster pirates had suffered at the hands of the Southern Pacific guards and hated the railroad as much as the farmers or merchants. Davie bought up the guns and ammunition he could find in Oakland, handed them over to the young scrappers and then ordered the three thousand tons of coal to be delivered to his estuary warehouse.

Davie landed his coal, as well as a supply of salt, storing them in the warehouse. The following Monday morning when he came down to the waterfront he found that a fence had been thrown up around his two acres, and a crew of wreckers were taking apart his warehouse plank by plank, throwing the lumber into the estuary. This subtle method of dissuasion had been used by the railroad for many years.

Davie started to use his fists on the wreckers but was laid out by a plank. When he had regained consciousness, had had a drink in a nearby saloon and washed out his wound, he returned with a rifle in his hand and two pistols strapped around his waist.

The Southern Pacific wreckers knew he was not fooling. They backed away from his guns, and from the crowd of interested, sympathetic Oaklanders who had followed Davie to the estuary. Five of the wreckers were backed into the water. The crowd roared its approval, then helped Davie tear down the Southern Pacific fence.

By now the San Francisco reporters had come across the bay to get their stories. The next day Davie found himself celebrated as the leader of Oakland's "waterfront war," the first man to slug it out with the Southern Pacific since the Mussel Slough settlers had taken on Hartt and Crow.

Political boss Carrothers called out the Oakland police to arrest Davie. The local residents, antagonized by this open use of their police force to serve the Southern Pacific's monopoly, gathered five hundred strong to support Davie. His loyal and armed oyster pirates took the first assault of police clubs, and struck back, Davie's supporters right behind them. The police were routed.

It was a second victory for Davie, leaving him in possession of his property, and with the public so solidly behind him that the Southern Pacific hesitated, momentarily, to use violence for a third time.

In the next drive to unseat Davie the railroad loaded a grain barge with a gang of its guards on the Hartt and Crow order. The barge was to be floated in to Davie's leased land with the high tide, at which point the armed Southern Pacific personnel would swarm ashore, drive Davie and his followers off the waterfront, and retain permanent possession. Two locomotives came down the tracks alongside the estuary with long chains that were attached to the barge so that it could be pulled in to shore more quickly.

Oakland gathered to watch the battle. Davie and several of his best men put out in a rowboat, sawed the chains in two. The oyster pirates laid down a pontoon bridge of rowboats and skiffs, reached the barge and gave the Southern Pacific guards a thorough pummeling, many of them landing in the water.

For a third time Davie had beat the Southern Pacific.

The Far West cheered.

John L. Davie was a hero. He took the applause with modesty, joining a committee of Oaklanders, who were tired of the expensive and slow service given by the Southern Pacific's ferries across the bay, to install the fast vessel *Rosalie* as a competing nickel ferry. The Southern Pacific had its members on the State Harbor Commission refuse the *Rosalie* dock space in San Francisco. When the *Rosalie* found a spot down from the regular docks, its passengers were blackened with coal dumped on them from above. When they tried to debark at another dock hundreds of horses and drays pulled up in a solid wall to block their exit. Davie organized a crew of tough longshoremen to drive the drays away and keep the San Francisco exit clear.

On the Oakland-Alameda side there was only the one docking space. The Southern Pacific adjusted its schedules so that one of its slow boats was always ahead of the *Rosalie*, holding it back.

Davie, under the informal guidance of President Cleveland's Secretary of the Navy, Thomas Lamont, who was visiting Oakland, checked the structure of the *Rosalie's* bow. The next day as the Southern Pacific's *Alameda* crawled up the estuary, ignoring the *Rosalie's* whistle to move over and let her pass, the *Rosalie* put on full steam and crashed into the rear end of the *Alameda*. The captain of the *Alameda* was forced to beach his boat in the mud flats, while her passengers had to get off and wade through mud up to their knees.

Though the Southern Pacific's boats now quickly pulled out of the way when the *Rosalie* tooted her horn, this did not terminate the "War of the *Rosalie*." The railroad next refused to open its drawbridge between Oakland and Alameda to allow the *Rosalie* to reach its terminus. The tender of the drawbridge was importuned by the captain of the *Rosalie*; his duties as a public servant were explained to him by lawyers. But he had his orders from the Southern Pacific, and nothing could persuade him to open.

One day a seeming idler walked onto the drawbridge and stood gazing down into the estuary. When the *Rosalie* came up to the bridge, a sailor quickly threw a rope to the stranger, who pulled up a hawser and attached it to one of the stout posts of the bridge. The *Rosalie* backed down the estuary, taking the bridge with it.

John L. Davie was arrested for this deed, but he was never brought to trial. His spunk proved to the captive people of Oakland and San Francisco that the Southern Pacific could be whipped. It would take a few more years, until the master-minding Collis P. Huntington died in 1900, and an anti-railroad governor, Hiram Johnson, could be elected in 1910 on a "throw the Southern Pacific out of politics" campaign. But what the Santa Fe and its fight for a Los Angeles terminus had accomplished for southern California, John L. Davie had achieved in central California.

They had broken the back of the steel Octopus.

CHAPTER III

"This sure is some Cripple Creek!"

COLORADO'S LAST GREAT GOLD field in the Sierra Nevada, Comstock Lode and Pike's Peak tradition, the last of the open gold camps before mining fell to giant corporations, was Cripple Creek. The process of discovering Cripple Creek took cowboy Bob Womack thirteen years. During that time he became part of a Far West triumvirate: "Crazy" Judah, "Crazy" Sutro and "Crazy" Womack. In the rich symphony of Cripple Creek Bob Womack was the arranger and conductor; the others, though they took the wealth and Bob profited no more from his discovery than had James W. Marshall at Coloma or the Grosh brothers at Mount Davidson, remain piccolo players.

Cripple Creek was ten thousand feet high. Fifty miles to the south were the snow-covered Sangre de Cristos, where Fremont's men had faltered; to the west was the Continental Divide. There were groves of spruce and aspen on the hills and rolling down the gulches.

Bob Womack, born in Kentucky in 1844, was brought to Colorado in 1861 by his father; at seventeen he was already a six-footer, strong and clumsy as a bear. He worked the gold and silver mines around Idaho Springs, in six years developing into an intuitive geologist. His only other talent was his horsemanship; it was alleged that, in the tradition of the 1840 Californios, he could lean from the saddle while going at full speed and pick up a bottle of bourbon with his teeth.

Womack senior bought a ranch a few miles from Colorado Springs, settled his family there and ran cattle. Bob's efficient sister Lida ran the house. She tried to make a cowboy out of Bob. He remained out with his horse all day, but instead of watching the calves he spent his time panning for gold on Little Fountain Creek.

In 1871 the Levi Weltys from Ohio, friends of the Womacks who had come to Colorado to find gold but were now cattle ranching near Colorado Springs instead, grew dissatisfied because General Palmer's railroad and town were attracting too many new settlers. Welty and his three sons rode up Ute Pass and thirty-five miles over the hills to a remote Ute Trading post called Florissant. From here they rode nine miles south, and below Mount Pisgah found a beautiful valley with a stream winding down its center and mountainsides steep enough to hold their cattle.

While the Weltys were putting a covering over a spring a log got away from the grip of one brother, hurting another. The father's gun went off accidentally, injuring his hand. One of the calves, frightened by the noise, broke a leg trying to jump the stream. Levi Welty exclaimed in exasperation:

"Well, boys, this sure is some cripple creek!"

Bob Womack's brother William had gone home to Kentucky and returned with a wife, Ida. Miss Lida could not abide Miss Ida, so William and his wife, taking Bob with them, went to settle near the Weltys at Cripple Creek. Bob homesteaded a hundred sixty acres, built himself a log cabin at a spot he named Poverty Gulch, and seemingly settled down to the life of a cowboy. Actually he was riding around Cripple Creek searching for quartz outcroppings that would indicate veins of precious metal, pocking the landscape with his diggings. Some three years before, a United States Geological and Geographical Survey mapping the county west of Pike's Peak had said that the Cripple Creek area was a volcanic formation. Near-illiterate Bob Womack was the only one who put two and two together: volcanic formations were the ones which held gold and silver.

On a morning in May 1878, while Bob was giving his horse a drink at the spring where the name Cripple Creek had been born, he picked up a piece of rock about nine inches long which was not much heavier than wood. He knew that he held in his hand the first clue to the gold field: for this piece of rock was a "float," or a fragment of stone that had broken off from a now buried rock outcropping. If the float had gold in it, so would the buried stratum of rock from which it had broken off.

Bob mailed the float to a friend for an assay. The assayer wanted to know why anyone would spend thirty-five cents to assay a rotting piece of rock. Bob's friend insisted, then rushed up to Cripple Creek to tell Bob that his float was gold-bearing ore assaying at $200 a ton.

Bob tried to interest Colorado Springs people in investing their time and money to help him find the gold. No one took bourbon-toting Bob seriously. Horace W. Bennett, who with Julius A. Myers, his real estate partner, had bought the Broken Box ranch and four Cripple Creek homesteads on Myers's insistence, took some of Bob's newly found float into Denver just to stop Bob from pestering him. E.E. Burlingame, a famous assayer, took a quick look at the rocks and threw them in the wastebasket.

Then came the "Mount Pisgah hoax," above Cripple Creek: two prospectors salted a mine, and five thousand eager gold seekers flooded in from all over Colorado.

Bob Womack did not give up. He staked his first gold claim in October 1886, after eight years of searching at Cripple Creek. He worked his "Grand View," located at the end of a float trail, but found no gold.

In 1889 he made friends with a Colorado Springs dentist named John P. Grannis, and took him to the basement of Palmer Hall at Colorado College where a map on the wall showed the Cripple Creek area in yellow, the color used to indicate the heart of a volcanic eruption. Dr. Grannis had no money, but he borrowed $500 from the bank and grubstaked Bob in return for half of the gold Bob found. Bob quit his sister's employ and went to work in earnest near the Grand View claim. In September 1890 he began to find pieces of float in the gravel he was shoveling. He dug a hole ten feet deep, pushed out shafts east, west and north, struck his first real outcrop, rock two feet wide. The center of the shaft had some color.

It was gold.

Bob called his mine the El Paso. He blasted for a week. Then he and Dr. Grannis engaged mining professor Henry Lamb to come to Cripple Creek to examine their find. Lamb took out his own specimens, and reported that they carried $250 of gold to the ton.

Colorado Springs cried "Hoax!" and refused to invest a dollar. Bob put the specimens in Seldomridge's grain store window. Nobody looked at them. Dr. Grannis begged his friend Hiram Rogers, owner of the *Gazette*, to study the ore and run a story on it. Rogers declined.

Bob was stymied. He had no money to work his gold mine.

Forty-four-year-old Edward De La Vergne of Colorado Springs was taking an assaying course from Professor Henry Lamb. Lamb recommended that De La Vergne study the terrain at Cripple Creek. Passing Seldomridge's store window, Ed saw Bob's ore specimens, sought him out and pumped him dry of information. He then went up to Cripple Creek, surveyed the volcanic area and laid out mining claims.

Still Colorado Springs was uninterested.

Bob Womack got drunk once more, shot out a few street lights in exasperation and landed in jail. When he awoke in his basement jail on Sunday morning he pounded on the ceiling for the volunteer fireman above to come and let him out, as was his custom.

This Sunday he was released by James Doyle and James F. Burns, two carpenters. Bob indignantly told them that he would soon be a rich man from his Cripple Creek mines, and then no one would be able to arrest him.

Loquacious and well-liked Doyle and Burns spread the word around Colorado Springs that Bob's gold mine was authentic. For the first time in fourteen years Bob was questioned seriously about Cripple Creek, by the county clerk, the city treasurer, a commissioner and a judge, a real estate man, a lawyer. But in order to secure more money for Bob to work their mine Dr. Grannis had to borrow from the bank again, this time being obliged to put up his dental tools as security.

Prospectors began moving into Cripple Creek. On April 5, 1891 a meeting was held at Bennett's and Myers's Broken Box ranch, the mining laws of the Sierra Nevada were adopted, a six-mile-square mining district was established. Bob Womack lost his chance at immortality by having the name Womack Mining District lose out to Cripple Creek Mining District by a few votes.

News of the miners' meeting spread quickly. A rush of prospectors from Aspen and South Park began, accompanied by a flock of tenderfeet from the towns, whom the old-timers tried to teach "not to treat dynamite like stick candy." After a couple of them had blown themselves up, a grizzled prospector snorted: "Folks claim they got sense enough to keep their pants buttoned in a blizzard. I'm mean enough to doubt that statement."

Bob was not mining, he was too busy showing other prospectors where the best claims lay. When Winfield Scott Stratton, a veteran prospector who had been working as a $3.00-a-day carpenter in Colorado Springs, told Bob that Cripple Creek showed less promise than any gold camp he had ever seen, Bob took Stratton on a tour of the area. Stratton located several claims, decided they were worthless, packed his tools and returned to Colorado Springs. But he would be back...to sell his Independence mine for $10,000,000 in cash.

In May there were a hundred prospectors, in June two hundred, in August four hundred. The town of Cripple Creek was founded by D. C. Williams, who opened a boardinghouse in a tent; a saloon, consisting of a plank over two beer barrels, was inaugurated. One of the Welty boys started a stage line to Florissant, the old Ute trading post on the road to Colorado Springs.

Cripple Creek was one vast gold mine. A man named Jones, not knowing where to stake his claim, threw his hat high in the air, sank his pick where it fell . . . and uncovered a vein which assayed at $600 a ton.

Yet very little gold was taken out during that summer of 1891; the color was hard to get at, manpower and machinery were not available, capital still wanted no part of this Bob Womack rush. The miners used up their cash and supplies while summer turned to fall.

Help came at the last moment, from Count James Pourtales, described as "A Bismarck imperialist," who had come to Colorado in pursuit of his beautiful French cousin Berthe. Pourtales married her in Colorado Springs, after which they took command of the international society centering in General Palmer's sophisticated summer resort.

Count Pourtales was an able businessman; he took over a near-bankrupt dairy farm called Broadmoor and turned it into a financial success. He then subdivided the Broadmoor farm, building and opening an international casino in June 1891. But General Palmer did not want a roulette casino changing the high moral tone of Colorado Springs.

Needing money, Count Pourtales went to Cripple Creek and met Ed De La Vergne, who was sitting on top of one of Cripple Creek's many gold veins without a dollar to develop it. The count informed the Colorado newspapers that he and a friend were buying the Buena Vista claim on Bull Hill for $80,000; that he was able to see with his naked eye $1,000,000 of gold in the mine; and that there were at least another hundred sites in Cripple Creek equally valuable.

Colorado Springs, the closest town, was convinced. There was a rush of capital into Cripple Creek. Marshall Sprague relates in *Money Mountain*:

"The Count's sense of timing, the social prestige and the glamour of his name made the announcement immensely effective. It changed the entire attitude toward Cripple Creek, removed the memory of the Mt. Pisgah hoax, and broke the dreary stalemate."

Bob Womack, who did not really want to mine, sold his half interest in the El Paso to Dr. Grannis for $300, and Dr. Grannis sold four fifths of the El Paso for $8000 in order to clear his dental instruments. Judge Colburn of Colorado Springs, who had questioned Bob Womack only a few months before, paid $10,000 for a one tenth interest in the El Paso. Winfield Scott Stratton, who had been peddling his Washington mine for $500, now sold it to one of Pourtales's partners for $80,000 in cash. James J. Hagerman, one of the richest men in Colorado Springs, put up $225,000 to back the working of the Buena Vista, and to buy up twenty-one surrounding claims on Bull Hill to create the Isabella Gold Mining Company.

The upland pasture with its hundred pock holes dug by Bob Womack over thirteen years was converted into a roaring mining camp, with a thousand men coming in a month, frequently followed by their wives and families. Horace Bennett, who had been outraged when his partner Myers insisted that they buy the Broken Box ranch, now found that they owned practially all of the land on which the town had to be built. The new town began at the shack that Bob Womack had built at Poverty Gulch, and was named in honor of Fremont. As a reward for believing this land would always be worthless Bennett took the name of the main street for himself; Myers had to be content with the secondary cross street.

Lots on Bennett Avenue sold quickly at $25 in the main blocks, and $50 for corners. The early purchases were made by those first entrepreneurs of the mining camp, the gamblers, the dance hall men, the saloonkeepers and the madams. Ed De La Vergne laid out a competing townsite of some thirteen hundred acres, most of them straight up and down the mountain. This townsite became known as Cripple Creek. He made an earnest effort to attract high society:

"All the best people are building homes out of the saloon and gambling area."

Like all other mining camps of the Far West, Fremont and Cripple Creek had no government, no law, no light, no water and no paved streets. Bennett Avenue was on such a steep slope that its north side was fifteen feet lower than its south side, giving birth to the Cripple Creek joke:

"A man broke his neck last night falling off Bennett Avenue."

The two towns shared a marshal. His sole duty consisted in relieving the prospectors, in particular the tenderfeet, of their guns as they came into camp, and then selling them in aid of a school fund. After a year the settlements merged, became the town of Cripple Creek, elected a mayor and installed a rudimentary government, with a water system and arc lights. Colorado had another community.

The town now had a five thousand population. The beautiful groves of aspen and spruce had been cut down and sawed at the mills, the streets were solid rows of unpainted two-room board shacks, with attics for sleeping. By 1893 lots on Bennett Avenue were selling for $3000 to $5000. Cripple Creek thrived, with eight lumber yards, twenty-six saloons, ten meat markets, nine hotels, forty-four lawyers' offices and thirty-six real estate offices. The firm of Horace Bennett and Julius Myers took more than $1,000,000 out of their town of Fremont before it joined Cripple Creek.

Bob Womack was now a completely happy man. When he walked down the street or entered a saloon people would exclaim to the newcomers:

"There's Bob Womack, the fellow who discovered Cripple Creek."

Bob spent his time in three-day poker sessions, drinking in the saloons, dancing in the Bon Ton, Red Light and Casino. Cripple Creek was his town. The production of gold rose from $50,000 a month to $200,000 during 1893, and the population to more than twelve thousand by New Year's Day of 1894. Bob's former cow pasture was alive with men crying, "Fire!" dynamite blasts going off so often that the housewives had their laundry showered with flying dirt and gravel. Bob kept possession of the Womack Placer, but he did not work it. When Stratton sold his Independence mine Bob commented:

"Poor old man Stratton, all that money to worry about. I don't envy him one bit."

Cripple Creek developed a cosmopolitan air. The tent boardinghouse had grown into the Anheuser-Busch Hotel, with separate bedrooms instead of one long room divided by canvas partitions. The next year the Continental bragged that it could sleep two hundred if you counted those sleeping on the dining-room tables at night. The crowd in the Continental dining room was so heavy that the silverware never was washed between customers.

As had happened in Denver, the first Sunday school meeting was held at the back of a saloon, the Buckhorn. The owner, a famous faro dealer and manager of a Cripple Creek bordello, sensitively covered her bar and the gambling equipment with canvas, then ordered all her girls to dress in their sedate traveling outfits and sat them in a row on top of the bar to listen to the Sunday school lesson.

Just before Christmas of 1893 Bob Womack sold the Womack Placer for $500, changed his money into one-dollar bills at Nolan's Saloon, got higher than the surrounding Sangre de Cristos on breakfast bourbon, then stood on the corner of Third and Bennett streets handing a one-dollar bill to every child who came by.

It was a charming gesture; but he was now destitute.

For Bob Womack the town had grown too big; it would reach

fifty thousand inhabitants by the end of the decade. And too busy, its payroll rising from $50 a month in 1891 to $1,000,000 a month, its yearly output of gold estimated at $20,000,000. People no longer cared about Bob. They no longer pointed him out as the discoverer of Cripple Creek. More and more of them saw him only as a middle-aged, usually drunken bum wandering from saloon to saloon.

The principal character of Cripple Creek now became Winfield Scott Stratton, known as "Old Man" Stratton, though he had been only forty-two years old when Bob showed him over Cripple Creek in 1891. Stratton was a "slightly built, thin-faced, serious man with white hair, solitary by nature, a man who had spent seventeen years prospecting over the gold fields of the Far West with only his burro for company." In earlier years he had erected a huge silver dollar over H.A.W. Tabor's Bank of Leadville.

Old Man Stratton invited in with him the two volunteer firemen, Burns and Doyle, who owned claims next to his, so that they could assemble enough cash to fight the hundreds of claims filed against them. Stratton also hired the brightest young lawyer he could find and cleared every last claim for something over $1,000,000.

By spring of 1894 Stratton and his Irish partners owned practically the whole of Battle Mountain, with its tens of millions of gold. Though the capacity of his plant was six hundred tons a day, Stratton refused to dig out more than $2000 worth a month, maintaining that Cripple Creek must not be exploited ruthlessly and then left a ghost town. When Cripple Creek burned down, with the aid of a stiff wind similar to the Washoe zephyr which had wiped out Virginia City in 1875, almost the entire population was dispossessed. Stratton moved into the emergency, exclaiming:

"We've got to move and move fast! No time to get money pledges. Charge everything to me. We'll divide the bills afterward."

In 1892 Colorado elected Davis H. Waite, a sixty-seven-year-old reformer with a flowing white beard, as Populist governor of Colorado. Populism in Colorado was close to Denis Kearney's sand lot movement and Workingmen's party platform in California. It called for the direct election of senators, an eight-hour day, a secret ballot and an income tax. The movement was one of protest by the working people against the economic and political control of the Colorado millionaires.

The newly formed Western Federation of Miners sent in John Calderwood, who quickly organized two thirds of the miners in the Cripple Creek District on a standard of a $3.00, eight-hour-day wage scale. Some of the mine owners felt this to be a challenge that could not be ignored. They agreed uniformly to a nine-hour work day for the same $3.00.

In February 1894 Calderwood pulled his five hundred union miners out of the nine-hour mines. The eight-hour mines continued to work. Governor Waite was behind the miners. Calderwood was a brilliant organizer; he talked quietly but collected $1400 from the Cripple Creek businessmen, $4500 a month from the working miners, and with other contributions set up a union kitchen and fed his miners and their families.

The union had the popular side of the dispute; everyone in Colorado saw that the mines working eight hours were taking out ample profits, and felt that the nine-hour mine owners were being greedy. When Jimmy Burns said he was happy that his miners had joined the Western Federation of Miners because "Every worker has a right to improve his status by bargaining collectively," the Cripple Creek *Crusher* said with its usual mining camp *reductio ad absurdum* humor:

"Upon receipt of Mr. Burns' statement at the El Paso Club, three members collapsed on the pool table and died of apoplexy."

During the ensuing months Cripple Creek got the reputation of being a rough, tough and violent class-war town. The nine-hour mine owners secured injunctions from the court to restrain the Western Federation of Miners, announcing that they would run their mines with non-union miners.

The miners armed themselves. The mine owners hired armed deputy sheriffs to take over the mining region. Governor Waite sent in the state militia to occupy a position between the deputies and the striking miners, most of whom carried dynamite cartridges as well as guns.

There was a night battle. Two men were killed, five strikers were captured by the deputies. Sheriff Bowers of Colorado Springs organized twelve hundred volunteer deputies to move on Cripple Creek to put down the insurrection.

There was another battle in which the miners, concealed behind every rock in the area, fired on the Colorado Springs deputies. The deputies, in the confusion, shot each other. The state militia disarmed both sides.

The Cripple Creek miners emerged from their one-hundred-thirty-day strike, described as "the longest and bitterest of all American labor disputes up to that time," with a victory. All mines operated on an eight-hour day, and under a management-union contract.

Prosperity returned. Cripple Creek produced $432,000,000 of

gold, more than the total value of gold and silver taken out of the Comstock Lode, and almost a quarter of the $2,000,000,000 yielded up by the prodigal Sierra Nevada.

Bob Womack, shortly after the turn of the century, suffered a paralytic stroke. He lay in bed in a room his sister Lida built onto her home for him. The editor of the Colorado Springs *Gazette* announced a "Bob Womack Relief Fund" to raise $5000. Each week the *Gazette* ran front-page stories of what Bob had done for Colorado Springs: he had created about thirty millionaires, tripled its population and land values, turned it from a three-month summer resort into a rich, world-renowned city.

The campaign brought in a total of $812. The editor of the *Gazette* at last called it off in shame.

Cripple Creek was the "last of the great nineteenth century camps with their frenzied activities, big populations and rampant individualism." Its gold lived well into Colorado's twentieth century, building universities, hospitals, railroads, towns and tunnels, developing the cattle, sugar beet, oil, health and tourist industries. A contemporary historian writes:

"Colorado is a happy land. It is also a wealthy land. The wealth gives its people health, good education, leisure and a serene optimism about life. The wealth traces back to two great equal events: the discovery in 1878 of Leadville, the world's greatest silver camp, and the discovery in 1890 of Cripple Creek, the world's greatest gold camp."

Throw in the discovery of Jackson and Chicago gulches in 1859, Idaho Springs, California Gulch and Buckskin Joe, Central City and Georgetown, the Caribou Lode, the San Juan color around Del Norte, Silverton and Lake City and there is a forty-year record of gold and silver being fed into Colorado's blood stream, developing the country from a wilderness to a thriving civilization.

The gods were good to Colorado.

CHAPTER IV

H.A.W. Tabor Completes His Cycle

BOB WOMACK HAD NEVER ridden the wave of his golden discovery. For H.A.W. Tabor, the silver tide was running out.

When William Jennings Bryan was in Denver and provided the name of Silver Dollar for H.A.W.'s and Baby Doe's infant daughter, he also tried to warn H.A.W. that the gold men in the eastern money market were determined to demonetize silver. Economists were beginning to say that silver was as common as dirt, that the rest of the world would not accept it in exchange. There was strong pressure in Washington for Congress to repeal the 1890 Sherman Silver Act, and for the government to cease buying and minting silver. There was no other substantial market for the metal; this one act of Congress could bring the price of silver below its production cost.

Horace A.W. Tabor paid not the slightest attention to his alarmist friend. Colorado's businessmen had just elected him president of the Denver Chamber of Commerce and of the Board of Trade; in H.A.W.'s reasoning these tributes made him the outstanding business talent in Colorado. He continued to keep up the Tabor Grand Opera House in Denver and Tabor's Opera House in Leadville, both of them enormously expensive, as well as the Tabor Block, which did not return its cost.

He went on his merry, riotous way, losing as much as $3500 in a single poker pot, giving away hundreds of thousands of dollars to every friend, moocher or confidence man who made a touch. He ran his mansion in princely style; he and Baby Doe bought furs, jewelry, carriages, furniture, art objects.

Tabor did not bother to pay the bills. The tradesmen rarely pressed him. After all, wasn't he a multimillionaire?

In the general panic and depression of 1893 caused by the fall of gold reserves, business failures and the suspension of six hundred banks, mostly in the South and West, with men out of work and standing in breadlines, with violent strikes such as the American Railway Union's protest against the Pullman Company convulsing the land, H.A.W. Tabor bought three-year-old Silver Dollar a $900 rose point lace dress and handmade shoes, in addition to a diamond locket and diamond pin to celebrate her birthday. He also made up an album of the child's pictures, with "Silver Dollar Tabor" spun across the cover in solid gold letters. The albums, costing $400 each, were distributed by H.A.W. and Baby Doe to their friends.

In August 1893 President Cleveland called a special session of Congress, and urged that the 1890 Sherman Silver Act be repealed, that the country be put on a gold standard. In October Congress repealed the act, taking silver out of the realm of precious metal.

For the first time since the two German shoemakers Hook and Rische had made their strike at the Little Pittsburgh, Tabor was scared. He gathered up his voluminous papers, unread over the years, and took them to a Denver lawyer.

It did not take the lawyer long to learn that the bulk of H.A.W.'s millions of dollars' worth of investments was totally worthless. From the discovery of the Matchless in 1879 until this moment the account books showed that H.A.W. had spent $12,000,000 in cash, over and beyond his investments in the Tabor Block, the two theatres and his mansion.

With the demonetization of silver, he was forced to close down the Matchless, which had been his real source of income. Now there was no money to live on. And now that he was in trouble there descended upon him merchants from all over Colorado with their bills. The bills were authentic, even though H.A.W., looking at them through dazed eyes, could not remember a tenth of the purchases. The unpaid bills added up to $1,000,000. Next came his gambling companions, many of them professionals, holding his I.O.U.s for hundreds of thousands of dollars.

First went the Tabor Block, sold to meet the merchants' bills. Then he was obliged to sell the Tabor Opera House in Leadville to pay his debts in the mining area. The Tabor Grand Opera in Denver went next, to satisfy the gamblers' I.O.U.'s.

Now there began a long line of vans, pulling up to the door of the mansion on Capitol Hill. Out went the expensive furniture, the rugs and draperies and art objects gathered from all over the world at staggering prices. Everything was carted away except the actual beds and chairs and tables being used by H.A.W., Baby Doe and their two daughters. Then the house itself was sold.

H.A.W. Tabor was broke. He had only one asset left, Baby Doe's jewels. He would not, he could not ask her to give up her last possessions, for without them the Tabor family would be destitute. Besides, a terrible fear had been gnawing at H.A.W. He knew that Baby Doe had sought him out because he was the richest man in Colorado, had become his mistress because he could set her up in a luxurious hotel suite, give her beautiful clothing, carriages and jewelry. Countless times during their marriage she had thanked him for rescuing her from grimy poverty. He knew what all of Denver was saying, and part of it with satisfaction: one morning he would wake up to find that Baby Doe had fled with her jewels and private possessions, enough to keep her comfortable for the rest of her life. What did she want with a sixty-five-year old man, his eyes watery, his pride crushed, who had nothing to live on?

Baby Doe Tabor fooled them. Only thirty-three years old, a beautiful blonde with soft skin and dazzling eyes, a woman who could find a new place for herself, she instead gathered together all of her jewelry and other valuables and gave them to H.A.W., insisting that he sell them to meet the remaining obligations which an honorable man must discharge.

Soon they had all gone down the hopper.

The Tabors found a cottage on a side street which they rented for $30 a month. With stunning suddenness they had made the transition from millionaire almost to pauper.

Frequently the main meal of the day consisted of soup bones. Baby Doe counted out her pennies for bread, boiled the same tea leaves over and over until they were too bitter to be used, cut up her luxurious silk gowns and converted them into dresses for her daughters. She never complained or reproached H.A.W. She was in the full flush of her own maturity and strength, a tower of resolution alongside the crumbling wall of H.A.W.'s anxieties and desperation. She was not dismayed by this seemingly cruel twist of fate. She had confidence in H.A.W. She kept telling him that he was the greatest man in Colorado, that nothing could keep him down, that any day now he would make his recovery and there would be fresh millions with which to move back into a mansion.

H.A.W. could not bear to be about the cottage or face his own failure. In the morning he would leave early, go to the outskirts of town and spend the whole day sitting dejectedly on a rock staring into space. At dark he would shuffle home.

Augusta might have helped him. She was a wealthy woman, having invested her money wisely, and counting it in the millions.

But Augusta was bitter. She sold the mansion that H.A.W. had bought for them so many years before, moved out to Pasadena, California, and died shortly thereafter. Her entire estate went to her son Maxcy. Maxcy apparently tried to help his father a little in the beginning, but he soon walked out of the scene and did not talk to him again.

No man in Colorado who owed H.A.W. money, who had borrowed $100 or $10,000, or who had lived off his largess during the prosperous years came forward to pay any part of that debt. H.A.W was too proud to ask; perhaps he knew it would be useless. All around Denver were the wealthy men who had been his friends for thirteen or more years, a number of them millionaires. Some of the richest had worked for H.A.W., had been given their start by him. But they did not volunteer help.

When the Tabors reached the point where there was not a nickel left to buy food, Baby Doe found a couple of Silver Dollar's birthday albums, tore off the child's gold-lettered name, twisted the letters out of shape so that they could not be recognized and gave them to H.A.W. to take to a dealer in old gold.

Only once did H.A.W. rouse himself from his lethargy. He remembered that he owned a gold claim north of Denver, at Boulder. No gold had been found in that area, but H.A.W. gathered some mining tools, went to Boulder, stripped off his coat and began work with a pick, shovel and placer pan.

He dug for two months, dug his heart out. There was no gold. Wearily, his last chance gone, H.A.W. threw aside his tools and trudged back to Denver. Baby Doe was still there, cooking and scrubbing and sewing for her daughters.

They were at rock bottom. H.A.W.'s pride released its grip on him. He walked to the Brown Palace Hotel where a dozen of his wealthy friends hung out. He moved quickly through the lobby for fear of being stopped and ejected as a tramp.

He saw a group of mining men sitting in a circle in the foyer. He knew all of them. They had been his pals for years. The man he picked out for the touch was Winfield Scott Stratton, a generous man. Hope flared in H.A.W.'s heart; old man Stratton would never turn him down. He whispered over Stratton's shoulder:

"Can you lend me $100?"

Stratton waved a dismissing hand in the direction of the face at his shoulder, said coldly:

"Go away."

H.A.W. rushed out of the hotel and half ran, half stumbled

along the street, tears flooding down his face. Stratton asked who the fellow was who had just tried to make a touch.

"That was Senator Tabor," replied Stratton's friend.

"What?" cried Stratton. "Tabor wanted a hundred?"

He picked himself up, ran down the street to overtake H.A.W. He apologized, said he had not recognized him, reached in his pocket and pulled out a roll of bills, about $500, which he pressed upon H.A.W. Then he asked:

"Tabor, wouldn't you like to be postmaster of Denver? I can have Senator Wolcott get you the appointment from President McKinley."

H.A.W. said ruefully, "I donated the land that post office now stands on."

"I know, I know," said Stratton, "but would you like to be postmaster?"

H.A.W. received his appointment as postmaster of Denver on January 13, 1898. He moved Baby Doe and the two girls out of the cottage and into the Windsor Hotel. His salary was $3500 a year. He resolved to make a good postmaster, better than he had been in Oro City when Augusta had been there to do the work. He was on the job at nine in the morning and was still working when the last of the clerks went home at night. He brought his lunch, which he ate at his desk, and when he had a drink it was a beer. He was considerate of the employees under him, but saw that the post office was run on an efficient basis; it was, ironically, the first time H.A.W. Tabor ever achieved efficiency. Baby Doe complained only once: she loved the theatre and she commented how hard it was they could no longer afford tickets to the Tabor Grand Opera House.

H.A.W lived to the end of the century. In April 1899, while taking a stroll, he went into the Tabor Grand Opera House and stood gazing at the oil portrait of himself, which the new owners had allowed to remain hanging.

Suddenly a sharp pain cut through his innards. He made his way home. His appendix had burst. As he was dying, he said to Baby Doe:

"Whatever happens, hold on to the Matchless. It will give you back all that I have lost."

There is nothing like death to repatriate a man. All of Colorado turned out for the funeral. The body was put on view in the governor's room in the Capitol, guarded by the state militia, while thousands streamed past to take a last look. Flags were hung at half-mast, telegrams and letters of condolence were received by

Baby Doe from people in high places. Leadville sent a six-foot floral design of roses in the shape of a cornucopia, a perfect tribute: for H.A.W. had been the Horn of Plenty to Leadville.

The funeral was converted into a parade, with four bands playing, militia, police and firemen marching, and a good part of Denver walking in its wake. At the cemetery Baby Doe buried her face in the mass of flowers covering the coffin, and wept.

It was the last time she did. After eking out a living in Denver for three years, she took herself and her two daughters to Leadville to the Matchless mine. They moved into the abandoned tool house, one room and a lean-to, its timbers rotting, its broken windows boarded up, freezing cold in winter.

When their money ran out Baby Doe dressed herself and the girls in discarded miners' clothing. She herself wore an old shirt, a drab and aged black dress, and a man's overcoat which also served as her blanket at night. For years she tried to protect the Matchless, to keep the water out, to keep the machinery and timbers from further decay. She guarded the property with a shotgun, warning off anyone who tried to intrude.

Baby Doe lived deep into the twentieth century. She never left Leadville, whose silver mines were abandoned, except for an occasional trip into Denver in an attempt to raise money to develop the Matchless. In her half man's, half woman's clothing, coarse black stockings hanging in folds above her heavy work shoes, her feet wrapped in burlap to keep out the cold, a motoring hat pulled down low over her head, she became a ghost wandering about a ghost town.

She died at the Matchless, where she had remained for nearly thirty years, faithful to Horace Tabor and to his parting instructions:

"Hold on to the Matchless. It will give you back all that I have lost."

The one and only thing he never lost was Baby Doe's love.

Leadville and Baby Doe Tabor had become an inherent part of Colorado's colorful, errant youth.

CHAPTER V

The Saints Come to Judgment Day

ON JANUARY 6, 1879 the United States Supreme Court handed down its decision in the Reynolds case, which the Saints had been so eager to bring before the high tribunal in Washington, D.C. It was a unanimous decision that the Anti-Polygamy Law of 1862 was constitutional. Eliza Snow, official Mormon poet, made no attempt at rhyme when she cried:

"Yea, let us cause thousands of honorable, loving wives to be stigmatized as prostitutes, and their offspring as bastards..."

Three months later, in the Miles polygamy case, the Saints won a victory which appeared to invalidate the Supreme Court decision. John Miles's first wife, Carrie Owens, claimed that she had been decoyed from her home in England, brought to Utah, "rushed through an unnatural ceremony with two other women," forcibly dragged back to August M. Cannon's house, "and there cruelly outraged in the name of religion."

Mayor Daniel Wells, called to the stand to testify on the marriage of Miles to his plural wife, Emily Spencer, refused to give evidence concerning this marriage, or any of the secret ceremonies performed in the Temple. Threatened with a contempt charge, Mayor Wells cried:

"It is a principle of my life never to betray a friend, my religion, or my God!"

Wells was sentenced to two days in the penitentiary. When he was released the Saints staged a celebration, with Wells sitting alongside President of the Quorum John Taylor in a barouche drawn by four white horses.

Miles was convicted of polygamy by the non-Mormon jury, and sentenced to five years in prison. But the United States Supreme

497

Court overruled the verdict on the grounds that Miles's marriage to Carrie Owens was the only one proved, and that Carrie Owens, as a wife, could not testify against her husband.

It was a heady victory: the law could not force a Mormon to reveal the secrets of his religion.

Stymied on the polygamy front, the federal officers in Utah tried to convict the Church of murder by bringing to trial Dr. Peter Clinton and Utah militia commander Robert T. Burton, who had been responsible for the killings in the Morrisite affair fifteen years before. The juries, composed of Mormons and non-Mormons, acquitted both men; the prosecution succeeded only in keeping the newspapers filled with accusations of violence and murder against the Church itself.

For thirty years the country had been amazed at the unanimity of the Mormon vote in elections. The gentiles inside Utah now revealed what they termed the "spy-ballot system": a number was put on every ballot, with each voter's name and number registered, so that a Mormon's voting record over the years was always available to the Church authorities. What had formerly been called Church discipline was now interpreted as Church terror: no Mormon dared go against the Church's instructions for fear of reprisal.

A considerable portion of the country accepted the "spy ballot" as proof of the charges that the Mormons represented a Church and State combination. The all-Mormon territorial legislature quickly repealed the numbered ballot. At the same time it stiffened the residence requirements for voters, thus cutting down on the number of gentile miners who could vote, which brought screams of anguish from the Liberal party.

Secretary of State William M. Evarts, in President Rutherford B. Hayes's Cabinet, in an effort to keep out the English, German and Scandinavian converts who were making their way to Utah, asked these foreign countries to prohibit the converts from coming to America on the grounds that after they reached Utah they would enter into polygamy, which was unlawful in the United States. The London *Times* asked:

"How are we to curtail the freedom of action of men and women who have contravened no law?"

Now in 1880 the Mormons elected a new president to succeed Brigham Young: John Taylor, seventy-two-year-old native-born Englishman who had been converted by Parley Pratt in Canada. He had become an Apostle in 1838, organized the Mormon Battalion at Winter Quarters, and done missionary work in England, France and Germany where he published newspapers for the Church. Taylor was over six feet, well-proportioned, with a massive head and deep-set gray eyes.

With the solidity and permanence of a new president of the Church of Latter-day Saints, polygamy and the Church-state became the burning American issues of the day.

Utah's new governor was Eli H. Murray, a lawyer who rose to the rank of brigadier general in the Civil War and had been for the past few years a United States marshal in Kentucky. In his Fourth of July speech to a gentile audience he was reported to the Saints as saying:

"The tree of liberty is rich enough in timber to construct scaffolds and coffins for all those who may treasonably conspire to break down our constitution and violate its written laws."

The Utah Ring and the Salt Lake *Tribune* printed its daily vial of accusation for the nation's press to copy. Livid books were published by writers who had never been inside Utah; incendiary pamphlets were distributed free by the tens of thousands. Women's groups were formed throughout the country to oppose polygamy. The Episcopal, Presbyterian and Methodist churches, in their national meetings and in bulletins, issued strong blasts:

"Mormonism includes Diabolism, Animalism, Mohammedanism..."

The Saints elected as their congressional representative George Q. Cannon, who was reputed to have four wives. Governor Murray refused to certify Cannon to the Congress on the grounds that he was not a citizen, and sent the defeated Liberal party candidate instead. Cannon went to Washington and eloquently pled his case before the House; but the image of a man who had four wives, all at the same time, proved too much for the congressmen to swallow. Cannon was barred from Congress.

The nation was bone-weary of the unending quarrels. It was interested now in only two stark realities: how was polygamy to be crushed? How was Utah to earn its statehood?

The Edmunds Bill was passed on March 13, 1882. It was drastic, but it made an effort to protect the innocent. Children of polygamous marriages born before January 1, 1883, that is, conceived before the passage of the bill, were legitimatized. Mormons who had entered into polygamous marriages prior to the bill could, by coming into the federal court and making public the record of their marriages, be granted amnesty. But future plural marriages and the continued practice of existing plural marriage were defined as crimes, punishable by five years imprisonment. For the first time funds were made available to hire federal marshals to track down multiple marriages, gather evidence of cohabitation, and bring the unrepentant into court. Mormons who believed in polygamy were barred from jury duty.

Though the provision was not contained in the Edmunds Bill, the Saints were assured on all sides that if they would accept the bill, and abandon polygamy, statehood would be forthcoming speedily.

The Church was not convinced that the federal government had either the means or the mechanism to crush polygamy. President John Taylor said calmly to his congregation in April:

"Let us treat this storm as we did the snowstorm through which we came this morning: put up our coat collars and wait till the storm subsides."

It took time for the federal marshals to get their machinery of detection into operation, for the task was a formidable one. Records of plural marriage were entombed in the Temple. Witnesses to the marriages were bound to secrecy. The marshals had only a few sources of evidence: hostile gentiles, apostate Mormons or Mormons who had quarreled with the men being investigated; and the marshal's day-by-day tracking and following of each subject until he had evidence of who the suspect's wives were, who his children were, and what homes he maintained.

Not for a full year, until 1883, were the first prosecutions begun. Since the Mormons believed that the federal government had to establish sexual relations in order to prove unlawful cohabitation, pregnant plural wives brought into court either had to betray their husbands to the authorities, publicly deny knowing who the father of their child was, a moral hardship, or refuse to answer and stand in contempt of court. The federal judges did not enjoy sending pregnant women to jail, but the law was followed in an attempt to convince the Mormons that all children now being born to plural marriages would be stigmatized as illegitimate. One woman, sentenced for contempt, had her baby in jail two days later.

As the difficulty of gathering evidence became apparent, the Department of Justice in Washington increased the amount of available funds and the number of deputies working in Utah. The courts decreed that it was no longer necessary to prove sexual relations in order to prove the crime, that the evidence was complete "when a man to all outward appearances is living or associating with more than one woman as his wife." The federal judges informed the juries that in order to convict they did not need testimony that the man had associated "continuously" with a plural wife; he could be convicted if he had associated with a plural wife for as little as one week.

Now the marshals could provide evidence, and make it stand up in court. Now the gentile juries could and did convict. Now in 1884 the polygamous Mormons began entering the penitentiary for five-year terms. Now the plural wives were left alone, without means of support for themselves or their children. The prisoners' farms began to run down, their businesses to fall off; even the first wives and their children, left in legal possession of the husband's property, began to suffer.

Now for the first time the Mormons became frightened as they saw an increasing number of their neighbors convicted. The feeling began to spread through Utah that at last the federal government had found a way to outlaw polygamy. Roberts cried that:

"The victims were hunted down like criminals and unnecessary harshness was employed at their arrests."

The Church was indignant that "hunting cohabs" had become, in their opinion, the most lucrative employment in Utah, with the marshals being paid twenty dollars for every polygamist they arrested. The Mormons were also indignant with each other, claiming that the Saints were doing the Church great damage by gossiping, by dropping names and evidence into the laps of the deputies.

The Mormons protested against what they called "a hateful system of espionage" in which the marshals pretended they were peddlers or tourists or even tramps, working their way through guile into the Mormon home, extracting information from the families by starting gossip. They charged the marshals with plying small children on the way from school with questions about their mothers and fathers; of peering into windows of bedrooms at night, of breaking into houses with axes, of rousing pregnant women in the middle of the night and obliging them to drive to neighboring towns where they could be brought up on charges. To the Mormons it seemed as though there were an army of marshals marching across Utah.

The marshals retaliated by claiming that no innocent person was ever convicted of polygamy. The Mormons granted that this was true, but made the countercharge that in the terrorizing of whole communities the innocent were obliged to suffer along with the guilty.

What became increasingly obvious in 1884 was that there was no escape from the marshals: they were in every city, town and hamlet;

they had lists of every man suspected of having plural wives or plural habitations; they had lists of children born to plural wives; they knew not only every house in which a plural wife lived, but in which bedroom.

Nellie White, a music teacher in Salt Lake City, who lived in the home of Bishop Jared Roundy apparently as a boarder, was arrested as Bishop Roundy's plural wife. When she refused to give evidence as to her marriage to the bishop, she was sent to the penitentiary. Marshals took up a day and night vigil outside the house of Mrs. Susan Smith because they were after Lydia Spencer, who was rooming there, and against whom they had evidence of being a plural wife. Lydia Spencer vanished for a number of days; the moment she returned to her lodgings she was arrested. Rodger Clawson was arrested as her husband. He openly admitted that Lydia was his plural wife, yet refused to plead guilty. He was fined $800 on two counts and sent to the penitentiary for four years.

In Beaver, a woman named Jane, who was a fourth wife, was caught in her mother's home where she had gone to bear her first child. A marshal and his deputy walked into the house at eleven o'clock at night, turning a flashlight on the faces of the sleeping Saints until they found Jane. Jane and her husband, who was asleep in the barn, were brought into court.

Occasionally, the marshals were outwitted; a squad of them rode up to the door of Bishop Clawson to subpoena Mrs. Clawson but the bishop refused to let them in the house. Mrs. Clawson's brother, dressed in his sister's clothing, escaped conspicuously out the back door, drawing off the marshals in a wild and bootless chase.

In February 1885 President Taylor fled to a hiding place. A large number of apostles, bishops, presidents of stakes and other influential higher-ups left their homes and began living in secrecy. The Church was now without a head in Salt Lake, except as papers and instructions were brought in from President Taylor and the councilors in hiding.

The nation took this flight with high scorn, the press excoriating the men in hiding as "fleeing shepherds." The Saints justified the conduct of their leaders by claiming they had not fled but had retired. They said, "Moses fled from the face of the Pharaoh, Samuel the Prophet hid himself, David, the Lord's anointed, fled, even Jesus avoided persecution."

A reward of $500 was offered for information leading to the arrest of George Q. Cannon. On his way to San Francisco, Cannon was detained by a Nevada sheriff. A marshal from Utah went to Nevada and placed Cannon under arrest, putting him on a train to return to Salt Lake City and stand trial. Early in the morning, as the train reached Promontory, Cannon left the sleeping car, went out to the platform and, say the Mormons, "lost his balance and fell from the train that went at the speed of twelve miles an hour. Of course the absurd notion that he wanted to escape was prevalent."

Cannon continued the trip into Salt Lake guarded by soldiers with loaded muskets. Immediately upon arrival he was taken as a prisoner into the Third District Court. His bail was placed at $45,000, which he paid, and then forfeited in another flight. Two years later he was caught and sent to the penitentiary.

In the first test case of "segregation," a new principle under which polygamous offenders could be convicted for each offense, Lorenzo Snow was assessed triple damages for the same multiple marriage and given three times the maximum penalty in the penitentiary. This was one more shattering blow to the morale of the Mormons.

Some sympathy for the hunted was expressed, but as the hunt grew warmer the violence of feeling grew stronger on both sides. In Salt Lake City what were known as "filth pots," quart glass jars filled with human excrement, were thrown into the homes of the United States Commissioner William McKay. On July 4, 1885, instead of celebrating Independence Day, the Mormon officials of Salt Lake lowered the flags to half mast because "it was a time of mourning for the Latter-day Saints."

Joseph W. McMurrin, a night watchman in the Church tithing office, was shot in the abdomen by United States Marshal Henry F. Collin, who had been working on a cohab case against McMurrin's father. Collin claimed McMurrin shot at him first. A petition sent to President Grover Cleveland by the gentiles brought a battery of artillery from Omaha, additional United States troops and the establishing of a provost guard to keep the peace in Salt Lake City.

By the end of 1885 there were several hundred Mormons in the penitentiary. The efforts of polygamous husbands to remain in their homes, to farm their lands, to run their businesses or to hold their jobs were becoming increasingly impossible.

The Saints had come to judgment day.

CHAPTER VI

Utah, Forty-fifth State

WITH THE MARSHALS combing every community, the Mormons created an Underground which they likened to the one used by emancipationists. A code system was set up whereby outlying farms and remote hamlets were designated in terms of letters or secret symbols. Runners were kept moving between the hide-outs and the Church in Salt Lake, passing on instructions and news. The Saints knew the valley hide-outs which could be approached from only one direction; day and night guards were posted, every deputy was observed and followed throughout his investigations; word was sent ahead that the "deps" were on their way. Railroad personnel was so highly organized that if a marshal or deputy got on a train, the polygamists in the next town were already gone by the time the train pulled into the station.

In 1885 Marshal Edwin Ireland complained to the Attorney General's office in Washington that "the county sheriffs and deputies and entire police of the towns [Mormon] are employed to watch the movements of [federal] officers and secretly to aid the criminal witnesses to escape." He reported that "his deputies were dogged by spies, refused room and board by Mormons, and had to go in pairs in order to be safe from molestation."

Through 1885 and 1886 some Mormons were able to move their plural wives and children from hide-out to hide-out, keeping in advance of the deputies. Other men sent their wives into small Mormon communities where they would be safe unless "individuals in such a place were at outs with the Church or had some grievance against a given plural family, then they might turn informer." George McKay settled one wife with her children on each of his several ranches, all of them except the first wife living under assumed names. Many plural wives had to leave their husband and children behind, go into a strange town, find jobs and live in isolation.

At first barns, attics and haystacks were used by the polygamists trying to remain in hiding, but the deputies captured so many of them that more effective concealment had to be evolved. The Temple at St. George, which allowed no gentile to enter its doors, hid a number of polygamists. The fugitive third wife of Adam Winthrop cooked for them. When deputies were seen coming toward the town, church bells were tolled and the polygamous community fled to its shelters. Runners would cover an entire countryside, warning every house and farm for miles around that the "deps" were coming. Mormon men cut off their beards and mustaches, dyed their hair, took to wandering from neighborhood to neighborhood, peddling books and supplies under assumed names.

Life in the Underground was hard on the women and the children. Alice, the second wife of George Yates, whose second baby was born while she was hiding, said, "I never had a place to lay my head that I could call my own." Emory Fairchild lost five children because his wives had to remain in hiding, without the assistance of a doctor or a midwife. Samuel Spaulding's second wife tells:

"When my children came, the first wife was the only one I had. She was no midwife, but she was my only doctor for fear people would fine out. When my baby cried, I had to feed it and try to cover its head. At night I had to lie in that little bedroom and stifle my baby's cries."

A daughter of Stanley Winters writes, "We moved from place to place; as soon as people learned who we were mother moved on. We went to school and church, but we weren't allowed to associate with other children for fear we would give ourselves away. Mother took in washings."

A daughter of polygamist Edward Gilbert testifies, "The officers sometimes came at three in the morning to search the house. . . . We never knew where father was so if the officers asked us, we couldn't tell them."

In the beginning the plural wives said they would stand firm on their legal and religious rights, yet one mother cried, "What I shall do when assailed by these persecutors will be just what the other poor Mormon women do: snatch up my baby and run to the fields, the hills, sleep on the ground, under the bushes, anywhere and forget all about my braggadocio."

The children of polygamous marriages had no permanent home. They were not allowed to talk to anyone, to divulge their true names or where they came from. They were not allowed to play with other children for fear some secret might escape them; and they never knew when they would be forced to flee to still another strange town, house or barn. They saw their fathers for only a fleeting hour in the dark of night every few months. They lived in poverty, for it was up to the mothers to support the children by any means they could. No funds of the Church were made available to them. The children slowly began to realize that they were guilty of some crime. Probably their greatest burden was the attitude of the non-polygamous Mormons, as more and more of the polygamists were captured and arrested, that these children were unlike other Mormon children, that they were illegitimate and would be so branded for the rest of their lives. In many communities the plural children became pariahs.

A daughter of John Vance's second wife said that all children of plural marriages had been treated "exactly as any other children...until the raids began." Now they were frequently treated badly by the first wife and her children since these were the only ones legitimately entitled to their father's name. Children of plural marriages began to resent their fathers for having brought this condition upon them. Nor did it help them when the father was arrested and sent to prison.

A number of the polygamists higher up in the economic scale went on long missions to Europe to escape arrest. The wealthier ones sent their wives to Mexico or Hawaii or to neighboring states. Life in hiding was not always bitter; stories from the H.O. ranch, where President John Taylor stayed, tell of the men passing the hours pitching quoits, and of Saturday night hoedowns.

But time was working for the deputies. Each day saw the evidence grow tighter around each polygamist's wives, and the trails over which he moved them. Little by little the hiding places were found and rendered useless. There was no town without its constant raids.

The Mormon families of monogamous marriages grew fatigued and finally outraged at what was happening to them because there were polygamists in their midst; for business was disrupted, the peace shattered. Many now began to admit that although polygamy had in the earlier years been followed because of the Principle, in later years some polygamists had married again because they had fallen in love with younger or more attractive women. They began to say that polygamy had to go. If the Principle had been sent to them by God they would not now be so relentlessly persecuted for obeying God's edict. Polygamy was defeated; the sooner it was over, the better for everyone concerned.

John Weber's third wife told how someone in an apparently loyal community informed the deputies that her husband "always came home at daylight to water his mules." First wives who had never outgrown their chagrin or unhappiness over their husbands having taken other wives now reported the whereabouts of the polygamous families. Joseph M. Carey's first wife gave information about her husband which forced Carey to escape to Mexico. However there were still first wives who remained fanatically loyal and would ride all night through the countryside to warn their husband, living in hiding with a second or third wife, that the deputies had learned of his whereabouts.

While there were martyrs among the men, like the one who had been in prison three times, and when asked if he would abandon polygamy replied, "No, sir, they are the women God gave me. They are my wives and children," there were far more who began to say, like Jonathan Baker:

"I visited my home by stealth in the night not daring to be seen in daylight. It don't feel very good to be hunted like a beast or a criminal."

Richard Field, who had been hiding in the Underground for four years, whose farm had deteriorated and whose home, which was his pride and joy, had badly run down, said that he "couldn't go on like this." Field went to Ogden with his first wife and gave himself up. He was fined but not sent to the penitentiary; he returned to his home and his farm, where he was watched only to make sure that he had no further relations with his second and third wives. Other men, grown weary and seeing that Field was not molested, also gave themselves up, were fined, and returned to their first families.

The United States Government was by no means satisfied with the results of the Utah war. The governor and judges insisted that the Church was still performing plural marriages, that children were still being born in plural marriages, and that many polygamists, probably several times the number that had actually been convicted, were still free in Utah. Nor had Congress' effort to break up the Church-state been successful. The Utah Commission, consisting of five able and conscientious men, had been unable to loosen the Church's control over the territorial legislature or town councils. The Church was rich, having over $1,000,000 in tangible assets, and a large sum in the Emigration Fund with which to bring new Saints to Utah.

In February 1887 Congress passed the Edmunds-Tucker Bill which amended and strengthened the Edmunds Act. The new law made convictions easier for unlawful cohabitation, abolished women's suffrage in Utah, abolished the Nauvoo Legion, set up an oath which residents had to take, forswearing polygamy before they could vote. But what was most important, the Edmunds-Tucker Act dissolved the Mormon Church as a corporation, abolished the Emigration Fund Company and escheated all Mormon property except its Church buildings and cemeteries: that is, took away from the Mormon Church all of its assets: its bank accounts, its stocks and bonds and real estate and every other form of wealth, putting them under the control of the federal government.

Up to the passage of the Edmunds-Tucker Act the Mormon Church was still advising its people to hold fast to the Principle and keep out of the way of the deputies. The high officials of the Church were sure that in the long run they would defeat the federal government. On April 5, 1886 President John Taylor issued a statement from hiding:

"The trials of the Saints in the courts are not trials of vulgar criminals, but this is a religious persecution. . . . While polygamy was the battle cry, the object was to take away all forms of political power."

Now the Church was struck a death blow.

The Mormons moved in many directions to forestall the Edmunds-Tucker Act. The Church corporation was dissolved and reorganized in the form of a group of smaller corporations, each holding its own assets, and held in the name of a trustworthy Mormon official. For the first time the Saints failed to put up a solid People's party slate, and fused with the Liberal party, putting on their ticket one alderman and three councilors who were gentile, electing the fusion ticket by a more than two-to-one majority.

But the device to save their property and funds was declared unconstitutional by the Utah Supreme Court, a decision that was upheld by the United States Supreme Court, which also declared the Edmunds-Tucker Act constitutional in its entirety. The federal government decreed that since the Mormon Church corporation was dissolved, and there was no Mormon organization which was legally entitled to its properties, these properties would be dispersed by the United States Government for charitable and educational purposes.

Without funds emigration stopped dead in its tracks. Those in the Church hierarchy who had been able to remain in Canada, Hawaii, England or Europe found their money cut off and had to return home. Those who had maintained successful hide-outs in Utah soon found that they were running through their personal assets.

With the loyalty oath declared legal by the United States Supreme Court, so many Mormons were disenfranchised because they would not repudiate polygamy that in the next election the Liberal party defeated the Mormons for the first time in the history of Utah. George M. Scott, a gentile hardware merchant, became mayor of Salt Lake City.

In 1887 President John Taylor died in hiding. The Church got along for eighteen months on what they called an "apostolic interim," being governed by its twelve Apostles. In April 1889 it elected as president Wilfred Woodruff, in whose wagon Brigham Young had raised up on an elbow, gazed at the Great Basin and said, "It is enough. This is the right place." Woodruff came into leadership in a time of total defeat.

The federal government continued to send funds into Utah. More deputies were hired. Arrests took place daily. It became almost impossible for a polygamist to escape. Hundreds of the Church's leading Elders were in prison; some of its ablest men, needed to run Utah and the Church affairs, managed to remain in exile with their waning resources, but were useless for the Church's purposes. Thirteen hundred Mormons either were in the penitentiary or had already served long terms, their farms and businesses having suffered severely.

And now in 1890 there was a third bill pending before Congress, the Cullom-Struble Bill which, if passed, would disenfranchise every Mormon in Utah, thus turning the entire city, county and territorial government over to the gentiles, as well as deprive the Mormons of their American citizenship.

The monogamous Mormon population was shocked.

This was the end of the road. Most Saints decided that they would give up their Church before they would give up their American citizenship. Mass defections were set in motion. This was clearly evident to the Church Elders, who no longer had the money, the political power or the influence to control their members. By 1890 the Apostles realized that they faced the destruction and the end of the Church of Jesus Christ of Latter-day Saints.

Rather than see the Mormon Church annihilated, President Wilfred Woodruff, with the approval of the Twelve Apostles and a great majority of the Mormon members, issued the Woodruff Manifesto.

First, President Woodruff denied that the Church was teaching polygamy; secondly, he denied that the Church was performing, or would in the future perform, polygamous marriages; thirdly, he articulated a decree which the Mormon Church was committed to obey:

"Inasmuch as laws have been enacted by Congress forbidding plural marriage, which laws have been pronounced constitutional by the court of last resort, I hereby declare my intention to submit to those laws, and to use my influence with the members of the Church over which I preside to have them do likewise."

George Q. Cannon spoke for the Church when it was criticized for not having abandoned polygamy years before, sparing the Saints the chaos and anguish:

"We have waited for the Lord to move in the matter."

To make certain that the Church was not merely going to give lip service to the Woodruff Manifesto, the federal government put the Elders under oath and subjected them to rigid cross-examination. The Elders unequivocally told the rest of the country that the Manifesto was a result of the inspiration of God upon the mind of their president; it was the word of God to the Church prohibiting the practice of polygamy; polygamous living was in violation of the law, as was the contracting of plural marriage; the practice of polygamy was definitely abandoned. Any Mormon violating the laws against polygamy was liable to excommunication from the Mormon Church.

The Latter-day Saints were responsible neither for the introduction nor for the discontinuance of polygamy; the Lord had ordered it and the Lord had discontinued it. The Saints ended their forty-year controversy by telling the American public that in surrendering the Principle the Mormon Church was obeying God, not man.

Though a petition was sent to President Harrison in 1891 for amnesty for all those polygamous Mormons still held in the penitentiary, President Harrison waited a considerable time to make sure that the Woodruff Manifesto would be carried out. Then, in 1893, after the People's party had been dissolved in Utah, and the Republican and Democratic parties had taken over, President Harrison signed the bill which put an end to all Mormon imprisonment for polygamy.

The movement for statehood was started immediately after the Woodruff Manifesto. It was delayed because of fear in Utah and in

Washington that, as Roberts says, "The Church authorities would dominate the political action of its members, and thus control to its liking and purpose the State."

In 1892 a Home Rule Bill was introduced into Congress by the Democrats which returned almost full self-government to the Mormons. It passed the House but was never brought to the floor of the Senate because full statehood was now in view. By 1894 an enabling act for Utah to become a state had passed the House and the Senate. On October 25, 1894, it was approved by President Cleveland.

The funds, assets and properties of the Mormons, some small part of which had been used for education within Utah, were not returned to the Church by the federal government. The following year, under its first election, the Mormons issued a "political manifesto" which in effect declared that the officials of the Church should not and could not run for public office because they would not have the time to do full justice to the duties and the responsibilities of both jobs.

On January 4, 1896, eighteen months short of a half century after the Pioneer Party had first come down into the Great Basin, President Cleveland concluded his admission message by welcoming Utah into the Union:

"On an equal footing with the original states."

When news of President Cleveland's proclamation reached Utah there was great joy and enthusiasm. Salt Lake City bells were rung, guns were fired, whistles blew and the joyous Saints thronged the streets.

The wars were over. Peace had come to Zion.

Utah had become a state, rejoining Colorado, Nevada and California. The Far West was whole again.

CHAPTER VII

The Rose of Sharon

FORMER UNITED STATES SENATOR William Sharon was the lord of Belmont and the owner of the Palace Hotel, having absorbed everything that had formerly been William Ralston's. As far as San Francisco could tell, sixty-four-year-old Sharon's chief pleasure was still his poker playing. He managed to keep "constitutionally unobstrusive," until he ran afoul of Sarah Althea Hill.

The trouble for Sharon began on September 8, 1883 when a woman named Gertie Deitz went into Superior Court in San Francisco to charge William Sharon with adultery. Sharon was arrested, booked in the police court and released on bail. The magistrate was puzzled: how could Sharon, a widower, have committed adultery with Miss Gertie Deitz?

A newspaperman named William N. Neilson, who had filed the complaint for Gertie Deitz, informed the court that adultery had been committed by William Sharon because he, Neilson, had in his possession a secret marriage contract entered into by Sharon and a second woman.

The judge in the police court dismissed the case. William Sharon then sent his lawyer into the Federal Circuit Court in San Francisco to have the alleged marriage contract declared fraudulent.

Miss Sarah Althea Hill now made her entrance into the state Superior Court. She was a strikingly beautiful and wellborn woman of thirty, from Cape Girardeau in Missouri. Miss Hill declared that she had been married to William Sharon since August 25, 1880 and that she had in her possession the secret marriage document referred to by William N. Neilson.

As Mrs. William Sharon she asked the state Superior Court to grant her a divorce from Sharon, appropriate alimony and counsel fees, and a division of the community property.

William Sharon loudly swore that the marriage contract was a forgery and a fraud. He was being dealt from the bottom of the deck!

Sarah Althea Hill testified that she had been making a little money in mining stocks; and that when she met Sharon in the Bank of California, having first been introduced to him at Redwood City in the spring of 1880, he commented on the modest nature of her profits, told her that he was going to build up a certain stock and suggested that she call on him in his rooms at the Palace Hotel. Sarah declined the honor. The next time she bumped into Sharon he said that he was disappointed that she had not called on him. Sarah replied that it would be more fitting if he called on her instead.

"That evening he called ... at my room in the Baldwin. He made himself agreeable for an old gentleman, recited some poetry and sang 'Auld Lang Syne.' He began telling me how he liked the girls and how the girls liked him, and couldn't I learn to like an old man like him?"

The picture of cold, beady-eyed, remorseless Sharon sentimentally pleading to be liked rocked San Francisco with raucous laughter.

Sharon offered Sarah the position of his inamorata, in return for which he guaranteed her $1000 a month in cash, his daughter Flora's white horse and, as Sarah said, "lots of other things."

A sense of revenge swept over Far Westerners who had been betrayed and impoverished by William Sharon, as they re-created the scene in which Sharon tried to get his hands on an attractive young woman in an outright purchase of her favors, and as they began to suspect that Sarah Althea Hill, articulate, charmingly groomed, very much the lady, was going to make her story stick. They named her the "Rose of Sharon."

"I told him he had made a mistake in the lady," she recounted, "that I was an honest girl and had my own affairs to look after. He said that he only said that to tease me; that he inquired about me and learned that I was a respectable girl of good family and he wanted to marry me. I said that was a different matter. He said that if we should be married it would have to be done secretly. I said I would not consent to that, and he said it was necessary as he had sent a girl to Philadelphia with her mother who would create a scandal about him if he got married."

To prove that he was telling the truth about the girl whom he had sent to Philadelphia, Sharon took a letter out of his pocket, tore off part of it, enough to prove his point, and gave it to Sarah.

Convinced, Sarah agreed to become his secret wife. Sharon then dictated to her:

"In the City and County of San Francisco, State of California, on the 25th day of August, A.D. 1880, I, Senator William Sharon, of the State of Nevada, age 60 years, do here, in the presence of Almighty God, take Sarah Althea Hill, of the City of San Francisco, Cal., to be my lawful and wedded wife, and do here acknowledge myself to be the husband of Sarah Althea Hill.

"W.M. Sharon

"August 25, 1880"

Sharon set Sarah up in a suite of rooms at the Grand Hotel, which he owned. They lived together as husband and wife, Sharon making so little pretense of concealing his relationship that he took Sarah with him to the reception for his daughter's marriage.

When Sharon fell ill for a second time during their fourteen months of living together, he decided he was going to die and that he had best get back the secret marriage document. He asked Sarah for it. She told him that she had mislaid it. They quarreled. Sharon grabbed her by the throat and choked her until she fell unconscious to the floor. He dragged her to the closet of the bedroom, believing her dead. Shortly after, she was told by the manager of the Grand Hotel to get out of her suite. Sarah went to the Palace to see Sharon, but was refused admission to his room.

"That afternoon I went out to see my grandmother, and when I returned to my home I found every door of my rooms taken off, the bells out and the carpets ripped up. I had only my furniture and the bare floor. My maid had fled in fright and I was left alone."

Sarah further testified, "He said I should sign a paper or he would turn me out of the hotel and disgrace me. I refused ... it was some kind of agreement by which I was to get $100,000 and $500 per month. I was also to give up the contract and acknowledge that I had no claim on him...."

When William Sharon first took the stand to refute this testimony, the jammed courtroom was disappointed; they could not hear what he had to say for, as he apologized to the Court, "He did not have his false teeth with him." However he spoke loud enough for the court clerk to record that he had not offered Sarah $1000 a month to live with him, but only $500; that he had not signed any secret marriage agreement; that the "Dear Wife" letters

Sarah had produced were equally fraudulent and forged; that he had never offered her any $100,000 to give up her marriage contract and put an end to the relationship.

Who was telling the truth? Sharon's reputation was all too well known in San Francisco. But what of Sarah Althea Hill? Was she, as Sharon said to a group of newspapermen, just a loose woman?

From Judge John L. Wilson of Cape Girardeau, Missouri, and published in the San Francisco *Bulletin* came a letter telling of Sarah's background. Her father had been a lawyer of high repute, a member of the Missouri legislature who had left his children a solid estate. A second judge in Cape Girardeau in whose household Sarah had lived after the death of her parents said, "She is possessed of a fine mind and a handsome presence, and I was surprised to hear of her engagement with Senator Sharon. His millions would hardly compensate a handsome and accomplished young woman for his age and reputation."

Sarah had come to California ten years before with an uncle and her brother. She had lived with her grandmother for a time, and later with her brother. She had never married. Sharon set private detectives on her trail to dig up every shred of evidence they could find about her past. They came up with a young man by the name of Burchard who testified in court that he had met Sarah in Sharon's company at the Palace Hotel, and again at Belmont, that they had become engaged, and that he had had intimate relations with her.

Sarah was outraged, and rightly so: for upon cross-examination Burchard began to contradict himself so patently that he was indicted for perjury. San Francisco believed that Burchard had been hired by Sharon.

At this point the trial took on an added fillip. Though Sarah already had six attorneys, David S. Terry, who had shot and killed David C. Broderick in a duel on the sand dunes in San Francisco twenty-five years before, now became Sarah's seventh lawyer. Terry, a widower, was some sixty years old, a handsome man full of an enormous outgoing vitality. He came into court with a knife hidden in a scabbard under his left armpit, a knife which he would not hesitate to draw before the case was over. In June 1884 the San Francisco *Alta* reported:

"Their seats are invariably side by side . . . all her confidences are made to him. More often than not he escorts her to and from lunch, or at the theatre . . . each as oblivious to criticizing spectators as a pair of freshly-betrothed lovers."

Sarah Althea Hill's case hinged on the validity of the marriage contract, which Sarah now produced in court. It proved to be a worn and much-handled sheet of ruled note paper, with Sharon's signature up toward the top on one side of the page, with only four lines of writing above it, the contract having been begun on the reverse side of the page. The defense claimed that this proved the paper to be a forgery; it was an autograph Sharon had given at the top of a piece of paper to protect himself from just such frauds. Sharon claimed that even the signature was a forgery.

The Rose of Sharon case kept William Sharon in a sweatbox for a year and two months, with sixty-one days of evidence and counterevidence which the presiding judge described as "a mass of perjury." There was criticism of Sarah for entering so informally into a marriage relationship; the public did not approve her outbursts of temper in court. Nonetheless William Sharon's reputation had preceded him; it was the consensus that Sharon had signed the marriage contract believing that it was extralegal, that it would not hold up in a court, and would probably never be presented because it would put Sarah in an equivocal position: a typical William Sharon minipulation in a process of inflating and deflating the sex market.

On December 24, 1884 Judge Sullivan came into court and read his voluminous decision for something close to three hours, then decreed to a hushed courtroom:

"I have reached the conclusion that William Sharon . . . by virtue of his secret contract of marriage, or written consent thereto . . . has become and now is the husband of Sarah Althea Sharon. In violation of his marriage vow, he has been guilty of willfully abandoning his wife. Under the laws of this state, Sarah Althea Sharon . . . is entitled to a decree of this court dissolving the bond of marriage . . . the plaintiff is, in my judgment, entitled to a decree of divorce . . . and a division of the common property."

It was a magnificent victory for Sarah, entitling her to a considerable portion of Sharon's fortune, $20,000,000 of which were out in open view and could be lassoed for dividing. Sharon was also ordered to pay Sarah $2500 a month as alimony, and to pay her counsel fees of $60,000. Nevadans and Californians chuckled with delight, even those who did not give full credence to the marriage contract. William Sharon had got his comeuppance.

Sharon was apoplectic with rage. He declared that he would drop every last dollar of his millions into San Francisco Bay rather than see Sarah get one of them. He went back into the Federal Circuit Court, where he previously had attempted to have the marriage contract declared null and void; for almost another year he and his attorneys fought to have a judgment returned in his favor.

He died on November 13, 1885, at the age of sixty-four, believing that he had been licked, and emitting as his last act before facing his Maker a vituperative blast against Sarah Althea Hill.

No one mourned. In a wave of nostalgia for William Chapman Ralston, San Franciscans felt they had been avenged.

Six weeks after Sharon's death, Judge Deady of the United States Circuit Court handed down a decision declaring the marriage contract forged and fraudulent.

Two weeks later, on January 7, 1886, David Terry married Sarah at his home in Stockton.

For two years Terry worked indefatigably in the California State Supreme Court, where the Sharon estate was suing for a reversal, and on January 31, 1888 the Supreme Court upheld the Superior Court, declaring the marriage contract legal and valid.

In this contest, which had now lasted over five years, the Terrys were leading by two victories in the state court over one defeat in the federal court. Sharon's heirs now went back into the Federal Circuit Court asking that, with Sharon's death, the original verdict of fraud be revived.

Assigned to sit with two federal judges on the Circuit Court to rehear the evidence was United States Supreme Court Justice Stephen J. Field, traveling circuit while the Supreme Court was adjourned in Washington. Justice Field was a Forty-Niner who had been born in Connecticut, the son of a Congregational minister. He had been educated by his father, traveled widely in Europe and had come to California to dig not the gold of the mines but the gold of the law. He had been a close personal friend of David C. Broderick, as well as his protege, and had never forgiven David Terry for challenging Broderick and for killing him. The two men had been political opponents and personal enemies for close to thirty years.

On September 3, 1888 Justice Field came into the court with his two fellow judges, put on his spectacles and began to read his review of the case. Before long it was obvious that he was going to sustain the judgment of the Federal Circuit Court and declare the contract a forgery. Sarah jumped to her feet crying:

"You have been paid to render this decision."

Justice Field said quietly, "Remove that woman from the courtroom."

When a marshal approached Sarah, Terry shouted, "Don't touch my wife, get a written order."

The marshal took Sarah by the arm. Terry screamed, "No goddamn man shall touch my wife," and hit the marshal in the mouth with his fist. The other deputies subdued him. Court attaches took Sarah to the marshal's office. When Terry came to the door and Marshal Frank tried to prevent his entering, Terry drew from his underarm holster the same kind of bowie knife with which he had stabbed the deputy of the Vigilance Committee back in 1856.

Justice Field sentenced David S. Terry to six months in the Alameda County prison for contempt of court, and Sarah Terry for three months. They spent much of their time in prison plotting revenge on Justice Field.

In the summer of the following year, 1889, the California State Supreme Court reversed itself by ruling that "the contract itself, assuming it to be genuine, followed only by *secret cohabitation*, did not constitute a marriage under the laws of the state."

This was a final blow to the Terrys. In their inflamed minds Justice Field became the author of their humiliation and defeat.

The people of San Francisco became uneasy when it was learned that Justice Field was once again coming to California to ride the Circuit Court. Marshal Frank insisted that he must have a deputy marshal along to guard him.

On August 13, 1889 Justice Field, after sitting in a case in Los Angeles, boarded the Southern Pacific train for San Francisco accompanied by the deputy marshal assigned to him, David Neagle. That night David Terry and Sarah boarded the train at Fresno. Justice Field, informed by the deputy that the Terrys were on board, said quietly, "I hope they will have a good sleep."

The next morning the train stopped at Lathrop in order that the passengers might have their breakfast at the station restaurant. Deputy Marshal Neagle urged Justice Field to have his breakfast on board. Stephen Field had been something of a brawler himself in the early 1850s in Marysville, which town he had helped found. He declined to show fear.

The Terrys and Justice Field with his deputy sat at tables about twenty-five feet apart. Breakfast had hardly begun before Sarah turned to whisper something to her husband, then hurriedly left the room. David Terry rose, walked over to Justice Field's table and quickly struck the seated man two blows in the face and head with his fists. Deputy Marshal Neagle cried, "Stop that!" and made his way between them.

David Terry moved his right arm over his left breast toward the knife in its sheath under his armpit. Neagle raised his pistol and shot twice. Terry fell to the floor, lay with his face up to the horrified spectators, and died. At that moment Sarah reappeared at the entrance door of the restaurant. The proprietor took from her a bag containing a loaded pistol. Sarah rushed to her husband, threw herself upon him, sobbing in wild grief.

Deputy Neagle was placed under arrest. At Sarah's demand a warrant was also written out for Justice Field. Charges against both men were dismissed on the grounds of self-defense.

Thus David S. Terry, who had lived by the sword, died in violence. The ghost of David C. Broderick was avenged.

With the death of Sharon and Terry, central California's half-century-long era of the pioneer closed. The new age would not come into clear view until after the earthquake and fire of 1906 burned William Ralston's San Francisco to the ground and the city was entirely rebuilt.

But the larger-than-life-size founding fathers were gone.

CHAPTER VIII

The Far West Sits for Its Portrait

LIFE HAD BEEN LIVED at a swift pace in the Far West, with the pioneers immersed in each new day. They had not had the time to pause in the midst of plowing a field, discovering a mine, building a railroad or a city to cry:

"Wait! Don't let this get lost! Set it down on paper, preserve the records, establish the facts, write the biographies before the cast has been scattered, capture the color of the new land before its riches have been dissipated and it is too late to document the story."

Yet without the word there cannot be the book. Without the book the story of man vanishes.

Hubert Howe Bancroft was of the stature of Theodore Judah and Adolph Sutro. He stalked history in order to re-create it. He understood the value of all that had gone into the making of the

West, cherishing every act and deed of it, good or evil. He dedicated himself to accumulating the record and preserving it.

Bancroft was the prototype of the westerly migration.

He was six feet two and powerfully built, with a large, open, flat face, enormous, serious eyes, a small compact mouth dwarfed between a big chin below and a quite ample nose above, a thatch of dark hair which he parted almost down at the right ear and combed in a great swath across his big head. He was born in Granville, Ohio, in May 1832, just two hundred years after the first Bancroft had reached New England from London. His parents had been born in New England but met on neighboring farms in Ohio. His mother was a schoolmarm for a number of years before her marriage, and the son, although he had been taken out of grammar school because of a quarrel with a teacher over methods, never got the love of teaching or books out of his blood.

At sixteen Bancroft made his way to Buffalo where he went to work in the printing shop of his brother-in-law George H. Derby, stitching and binding reports. At the end of six months the foreman let him go; since he had been working without wages, his brother-in-law loaned him fare back home. He also gave him a supply of books on consignment which Bancroft peddled through Ohio from a wagon. Soon he had to send to Buffalo for a new shipment. Derby invited him back to Buffalo at a salary of $100 a year; here Bancroft spent five years learning about the printing, binding and selling of books.

In February 1852 he set sail for California at his brother-in-law's request to take care of a shipment of $5000 worth of books which Derby was sending to the Pacific coast. Two earlier shipments had been lost, one through fire, the other through fraud. California was a new and potentially profitable book market providing the right man could be found to handle the business.

Because of the gold-rush fever Bancroft decided that Sacramento was a better prospect than San Francisco, and wrote Derby to send a shipment of books to him there. During the eight months of waiting he joined his father and one of his brothers who were working in the diggings at Long Bar. Here he cut trees and hauled wood and quartz until his shipment of books could arrive.

In November 1852 he received news that George Derby had died. Bancroft was on his own. Sacramento, which recently had burned down, and then been flooded by the American and Sacramento rivers, no longer appeared to him to have the prospects of San Francisco. He sold the shipment of books outright to a San Francisco firm in order that his sister might derive the benefits of a quick transaction, then moved to Crescent City with a small supply of books and stationery where he kept the accounts of a store in return for space in which to sell his merchandise.

In 1856 he went home to Ohio to visit with his family. When he was ready to return to California his sister, Mrs. Derby, urged him to collect the $5500 that was outstanding in her estate and invest it for her by launching himself in the book business in San Francisco. Bancroft, now twenty-four, went to New York to persuade the publishers to ship him books on credit. They had lost so regularly on California shipments that at first they refused; then, because he was the only bookseller who had actually been in the Far West, they decided to send him $10,000 worth of merchandise around Cape Horn.

In December 1856 the firm of Hubert Howe Bancroft and Company opened a small store, with Bancroft sleeping on a cot behind the counter. He had as a partner young George Kenny, who had come out with him from Ohio in 1852; Kenny was a jovial Irishman and a good salesman.

Bancroft was a highly capable businessman. The firm flourished. The following year he returned to New York where he was able to persuade the publishers to send him $70,000 worth of books on consignment. He enlarged his quarters, took over a three-story building on Merchant Street, increased his staff, brought out his young brothers to help him. He was able to bind people to him in terms of loyalty and friendship, and shrewd enough to pick and train capable men. He was soon able to travel to Europe on purchasing trips, and to remain away for six months at a time.

In 1868, only a decade after he had swept out his own store at six in the morning, he bought a large piece of property in the 700 block on Market Street, which was considered a ridiculous distance into the country, and built himself a solid five-story establishment. He installed printing presses, book binderies, facilities for engraving and lithographing, a complete music department, printed schoolbooks, stationery, legal forms and texts. He also began to do some original publishing, putting out more than three hundred books on religion, history, travel and exploration within the next seven years.

Books proved to be his Mormon's Bar. He was acknowledged to have the largest, most diverse and prosperous book and stationery house in the Far West.

One day he asked an assistant to gather together all of the books about California that were in the house. When the titles were brought to him there proved to be as many as seventy-five. Bancroft said, "That is doing very well; I did not imagine there were so many." From this modest beginning he decided it might be interesting and perhaps even valuable to put together a library of all publications pertaining to the area.

In the beginning it was a part-time pursuit; he found a book here, a pamphlet there, sometimes a whole box of volumes. Since he had a comfortable income from his business he bought everything he came across. He also began scanning the shops in other cities, watching bookstore catalogues that came in the mail. When he visited London and asked the booksellers if they had any western Americana, they asked:

"What's that? No, we have none."

Bancroft spent days ransacking their shelves and storage rooms and came up with dozens of titles, many of which he had never heard about. When he brought back several hundred volumes to San Francisco and saw that his collection had grown to a thousand items, he began to realize something of the dimension of the task he had set for himself.

As his collection grew to ten thousand volumes his perspective widened. He had started only with Californiana; now he saw that one could not understand California without including all the land west of the Missouri. Soon he was forced to the realization that no one could know the West without delving back into the several hundred years that the country had been owned by Spain, as well as the time of the pastoral paradise during its haphazard ownership by Mexico.

When he returned from London he received a catalogue from Leipzig, Germany, telling of the coming sale of the Andrade Library of seven thousand works of Mexicana, a library which Andrade had turned over to the Emperor Maximilian. Bancroft saw that the Andrade catalogue contained hundreds of items that were imperative to complete the historical background of the West; and so he authorized a book agent in London to go to the sale for him and spend up to $5000.

Out of this collection Bancroft acquired another three thousand items. From that time forward he had his agents attend auctions all over England and Europe, buying everything that pertained to western Americana: newspapers, pamphlets, manuscripts, records. In 1880 he bought a large part of another Mexican collection for $30,000, his chief competitor being the British Museum.

By 1870 Bancroft had assembled sixteen thousand volumes of a library which would ultimately go up to sixty thousand, in addition to some five thousand volumes of western newspapers. Since the building which housed his business was not fireproof, he bought a lot at the corner of Mission and Valencia streets and built a two-story brick structure to house the library alone . . . the first library of western Americana.

His work appeared to be completed.

Yet Bancroft was by no means satisfied. During the years of acquisition he had come to realize that the mere gathering of these materials under one roof was not enough. A second ambition, which had been growing in him, was to organize the voluminous material so that scholars and historians all over the world could know what was there, that writers might come to this new land, this new civilization, study its parts, and ask, "What does it all mean?"

At the beginning he fumbled and experimented, spending months of his time and that of half a dozen assistants, and $30,000 in cash, attempting unsuccessfully to put together an encyclopedia of western history. He then assayed a method of compiling a complete index of his thousands of volumes.

Like Charlie Crocker, who had never worked with anything larger than a village forge before he tackled and built a railroad, Bancroft had had no training as a historian, he had never been to high school or college, he had never done any research, and he had never written anything more than a letter. He knew nothing about library science. Nor were trained librarians available to him. For his index Bancroft had to train several dozen men, and spend $35,000 on the task. He believed his time and money well invested, for as John W. Caughey quotes him in *Hubert Howe Bancroft:*

"A man may seat himself at a bare table and say to a boy, bring me all that is known about . . . the mines of Nevada, . . . and straightway, as at the call of a magician, such knowledge is spread before him with the volumes opened at the page."

Having assembled his material and completed its indexing, Bancroft now went forward to an ultimate ambition:

"I would strike at once for the highest, brightest mark before me . . . history writing I conceive to be among the highest of human occupations, and this should be my choice."

Bancroft set up his *Literary Industries*, as he would later title his autobiography. He intended to publish a volume on every phase of western Americana beginning with the aboriginal Indians. Indefatigable physically, he wrote standing at a big circular desk built on a revolving dais covered with his many reference books, so that he could turn the table and bring before him the volume he wanted; stood there writing for eleven or twelve hours a day.

Each step of the way he had to break ground, just as surely as John Bidwell, Elisha Stevens or Brigham Young. With each new book he found himself out on the high seas in a howling storm, without compass or chart. When he wrote his five-volume *Native Races* there were no anthropologists in the West from whom he could learn, and no established method of writing anthropology. Into the two-volume *Popular Tribunals* he put a whole study of how law and government came to a frontier.

To help extract the facts from his library of books Bancroft hired good students, former newspapermen, teachers, world travelers, linguists, installing them on the fifth floor of the Bancroft business house, training from beginning to end over six hundred men and women in the double task of research and writing. His standards were high, he required intelligence and devotion to the task at hand. No one of his assistants began as a historian or a biographer; not one, with the single exception of a Mrs. Victor, was a published author prior to working with Bancroft. When he came to blank spots, found that his material was scant because so few of the people who had participated in the opening and settling of the land had written their personal memoirs, he hired another staff of men and sent them out over the West and into the homes of the pioneers to extract their reminiscences. They also copied letters, records, diaries: invaluable documentation.

And to sell his volumes as they were completed, Bancroft created a vigorous sales campaign that was a half century ahead of itself: he printed brochures, used clever sales approaches, quotations and recommendations, trained salesmen. He sent his representatives all over the West and into Mexico to sell not merely one volume of the *Works*, but the entire series of thirty-nine volumes, the subscribers to receive two or three volumes a year, and to pay for them as they were published.

His organization for the sale of his work was as effective as his collecting, indexing and writing. In the long run, as a professional bookseller, he was able to distribute over a quarter of a million volumes and take in $1,000,000 . . . almost enough money to pay back the cost of the vast project.

When summing up his work in the concluding, thirty-ninth volume, Bancroft wrote:

"What was this task? It was first of all to save to the world a mass of valuable human experiences, which otherwise, in the hurry and scramble attending the securing of wealth, power, or place in this new field of enterprise, would have dropped out of existence. These experiences were all the more valuable from the fact that they were new; the conditions attending their origin and evolution never had before existed in the history of mankind, and never could occur again."

In the process of accomplishing the heroic task he had set for himself, Hubert Howe Bancroft lived as courageous a Far West drama as any of the characters he portrayed in his *Works*: for he too had had to plunge into an unmapped land, break trail over mountains and across white salt deserts.

When Hubert Howe Bancroft said, "No state or nation...has had its early annals so (thoroughly) gathered and preserved," he was telling only a simple truth: he had created the greatest of all source histories of the West. Yet feeling against him was intense. During the last two decades of his life he was vilified by academic historians as inaccurate in his methods, one not to be relied upon or trusted; a man of intemperate nature and bad judgment who had criticized the actions of certain Far West pioneers.

The Society of California Pioneers, which had previously voted him an honorary member, deprived him of that membership, charging:

"That upon the principle of 'false in one thing false in all' Bancroft's 'History of California,' so-called, is, in the opinion of this society, unworthy of credence as authority, or as a source of correct information for present or future generations, and merits the just condemnation of every fair-minded man."

When he wanted to sell his library to the University of California in Berkeley at a modest appraisal of its value so that it could have a permanent home and be available to students forevermore, he met with the same opposition. It would take the university many years of hard and devoted work, led by a brilliant new young president, Benjamin I. Wheeler, to bring the thousands of columns so arduously collected to the university...sometime after the turn of the century.

It was a symbolic moment when Mariano Vallejo came to Bancroft, saw the significance of what he was doing, and gave to the library his priceless collection of papers, in addition writing his own story for Bancroft's records.

Thus the man who in his own person had served as a bridge between the pastoral Far West and the American Far West joined hands with the man who was fashioning a bridge between the nineteenth century and the twentieth, a bridge over which generations of people could make their way back into one of the most colorful, dramatic, tumultuous and heroic sagas of man's movement across the face of the earth.

CHAPTER IX

The Time, the Place, the Cast

THIS HAS BEEN the story of the opening of a land and the building of a civilization.

It has been told in terms of the people who opened that land and built that civilization, each life story an integral part of the mosaic. The Far West was the hero.

The land had a common cast of characters. What happened in any one region was of tremendous consequence to the others. Their biographies, their resources and destinies were so closely bound together that each was ineradicably woven into the fabric of the whole. For in the beginning they were one.

Now in 1900 an era had ended. A settled society would build itself in a twentieth-century image upon the rugged pilings of the past.

Again, as in 1840, there would be trouble in the land. But there would be those who would claim that the Far West had become the West Pole, another Valley of the Nile, cradle of a culture richer and freer than any the world had known.

Acknowledgments, Bibliography and Sources

A narrative of this nature, which attempts to cover a wide area in both time and space, would be almost impossible to write were it not for the tremendous body of work already existing in the field. In this respect I have been doubly fortunate, for my predecessors as well as my contemporaries in the Far West area have frequently been as dedicated researchers as they were talented writers.

In my California bibliography and research I was aided by Eleanor Bancroft of the Bancroft Library, Berkeley; John W. Caughey of the University of California at Los Angeles; Joseph Henry Jackson; Oscar Lewis; Mary Helen Peterson of the Los Angeles Public Library; George R. Stewart of the University of California. The libraries that helped me in California were the Library of the University of California at Los Angeles; the Bancroft and the University of California libraries at Berkeley; the California State Library at Sacramento; the Huntington Library at San Marino; the Los Angeles, Beverly Hills, Anaheim and Compton Public Libraries.

In Colorado I was helped by Fred Rosenstock of the Bargain Bookstore, who kept supplying me with rare and valuable books of Colorado source materials; by the librarians of the Western History Department of the Denver Public Library, in particular Mrs. Alys Freeze, who also read galleys; and by Fred M. Mazulla, who loaned me books out of his private collection.

In Nevada I was guided, as well as furnished important books of Nevada history, by Mrs. Clara Beatty, director of the Nevada State Historical Society; and by Ruth Hadley of the University of Nevada Library, who helped me to assemble a Nevada bibliography.

In Utah I am indebted to Leonard H. Kirkpatrick, librarian of the University of Utah, who provided me with needed books from the University of Utah Library and, when these could not be circulated, sent me his personal copies; he also read galleys, as did William Mulder, editor of the *Western Humanities Review*. I am grateful to Levi Edgar Young, of the Church of Latter-day Saints, for the privilege of studying the official Church Library in Salt Lake City.

I have listed only those books and publications which provided specific material used in the writing of this book. In an effort to make the bibliography as useful as possible to further researchers, I have divided the titles under the headings of California, Colorado, Nevada and Utah, and under these geographic headings I have further broken down the source material into specific and easily identified subjects or headings. Many of the volumes, of course, contain material applying to the other areas; they were classified according to their predominant material. The first two categories of "Mountain Men" and "Transportation" applied so generally to the entire Far West that I thought it better to list them separately.

The quatrain on the title page is from "The Coming American," by Sam Walter Foss, stanza one.

GENERAL

MOUNTAIN MEN: Hiram W. Chittenden, *A History of the American Fur Trade of the Far West* (2 vols.); Robert G. Cleland, *This Reckless Breed of Men*; Harrison C. Dale, *The Ashley-Smith Explorations*; Bernard De Voto, *Across the Wide Missouri*; T.C. Elliott, *Peter Skene Ogden*; Alpheus H. Favour, *Old Bill Williams*; LeRoy R. Hafen and W.S. Ghent, *Broken Hand* (Fitzpatrick); Washington Irving, *The Adventures of Captain Bonneville*; James O. Pattie, *The Personal Narrative of James Ohio Pattie of Kentucky;* De Witt C. Peters, *Kit Carson's Life and Adventures;* Ruxton (autobiography), *Ruxton of the Rockies*; Edwin L. Sabin, *Kit Carson Days* (2 vols.); Maurice S. Sullivan, *The Travels of Jedediah Smith*; Stanley Vestal, *Jim Bridger*.

TRANSPORTATION: William Banning and George H. Banning, *Six Horses*; Carl I. Wheat, "A Sketch of the Life of Theodore D. Judah," *California Historical Society Quarterly*, Vol. IV; Arthur Chapman, *The Pony Express*; Stuart Daggett, *Chapters on the History of the Southern Pacific*; Howard R. Driggs, *The Pony Express Goes Through*; Seymour Dunbar, *A History of Travel in America* (Vol. IV); John D. Galloway, *The First Transcontinental Railroad;* LeRoy R. Hafen, *The Overland Mail*; Steward H. Holbrook, *The Story of American Railroads;* Edward Hungerford, *Wells Fargo*; W. Turrentine Jackson, *Wagon Roads West*; Lewis B. Lesley (editor), *Uncle Sam's Camels*; Oscar Lewis, *Sea Routes* to the Gold Fields; James Marshall, *Santa Fe*; John Moody, *The Railroad Builders*; Charles E. Russell, *Stories of the Great Railroads*; Edwin L. Sabin, *Building the Pacific Railway*; Neill C. Wilson and Frank J. Taylor, *Southern Pacific*.

CALIFORNIA

BIBLIOGRAPHY: Robert E. Cowan, *A Bibliography of the History of California: 1510-1930* (2 vols. and Index); Owen C. Coy, *A Guide to California History*.

BIOGRAPHY: *Lucky Baldwin* by C. B. Glasscock; *Hubert Howe Bancroft* by John W. Caughey; Sam Brannan (*The First Forty-Niner*), by James A. B. Scherer; *Sam Brannan* by Louis J. Stellman; *Thomas Hart Benton* by William M. Meigs; *Thomas Hart Benton* by Theodore Roosevelt; *The Life of David C. Broderick* by Jeremiah Lynch; William T. Coleman (*The Lion of the Vigilantes*), By James A. B. Scherer; Gen. Patrick E. Connor (*Soldiers of the Overland*), by Fred B. Rogers; Lotta Crabtree (*Troupers of the Gold Coast*), by Constance Rourke; *Sir James Douglas* by Walter N. Sage; *Stephen J. Field* by Carl B. Swisher; *Forgotten Pioneers* by Thomas F. Prendergast; *Fremont and '49* by Frederic S. Dellenbaugh; *Fremont* by Allan Nevins; *Henry George* by Charles A. Barker; *The Lives of William Hartnell* by Susanna Bryant Dakin; *Heroes of California* by George W. James; *Controversial Mark Hopkins* by Estelle Latta; *Collis P. Huntington* by Orinda W. Evans; *William B. Ide* by George Kirov; *William B. Ide* by Simeon Ide; "The Kearney Agitation in California" (*Popular Science Monthly*, August 1880), by Henry George; *Thomas Starr King* by Charles W. Wendte; *Thomas Oliver Larkin (Chapters in the Early Life of)*, by Robert J. Parker; Thomas O. Larkin (*From Cowhides to Golden Fleece*), by Reuben L. Underhill; *Love Stories of Old California* by Mrs. Fremont Older; *John Marsh* by George D. Lyman; *James W. Marshall* by George F. Parsons; *The Truth about Murieta* by J.C. Cunningham; *Emperor Norton* by Allen S. Lane; *Polk, the Diary of a President* by Allan Nevins (editor); William C. Ralston (*The Man Who Built San Francisco*), by Julian Dana; *Ralston's Ring* by George D. Lyman; Hugo Reid (*A Scotch Paisano*), by Susanna B. Dakin; *Representatives and Leading Men of the Pacific* by Oscar T. Shuck; *Sir George Simpson* by Arthur S. Morton; *Adolph Sutro* by Eugenia K. Holmes; *Sutter* by James P. Zollinger; *Sutter of California* by Julian Dana; *The Big Four* by Oscar Lewis; *Vallejo* by Myrtle McKittrick; *Vallejo* by Harry D. Hubard; Charles Wilkes (*The Hidden Coasts*), by Daniel Henderson.

HISTORY: Gerturde Atherton, *California*; H. H. Bancroft, *Chronicles of the Builders of the Commonwealth; History of California* (7 vols.); *Literary Industries; Popular Tribunals* (2 vols.); Charles A. and Mary R. Beard,

The Rise of American Civilization; James Bryce, *The American Commonwealth* (2 vols.); John Caughey, *California; History of the Pacific Coast*; Charles E. Chapman, *A History of California: The Spanish Period*; Robert G. Cleland, *From Wilderness to Empire; Pathfinders;* Bernard De Voto, *The Year of Decision: 1846; Across the Wide Missouri;* Joseph S. Eldredge, *History of California* (5 vols.); William H. Ellison, *A Self-Governing Dominion;* Myrtle Garrison, *Romance and History of California Ranchos;* Robert V. Hine, *California's Utopian Colonies*; John S. Hittel, *The Resources of California;* Theodore H. Hittell, *History of California* (4 vols.); Rockwell D. Hunt and Nellie Van De Grift Sanchez, *A Short History of California*; Elijah R. Kennedy, *The Contest for California;* Oscar Lewis, *California Heritage; High Sierra Country;* Alexander McLeod, *Pigtails and Gold Dust*; Frederick L. Paxson, *History of The American Frontier*; Irving B. Richman, *California Under Spain and Mexico*; W. W. Robinson, *Land in California*; Josiah Royce, *California*; James A. B. Scherer, *Thirty-First Star*; D.A. Shaw, *Eldorado*; Lee Shippey, *It's an Old California Custom*; *The Mother Lode Country* (California Division of Mines); Frederick J. Turner, *The Frontier in American History;* Stewart Edward White, *Old California.*

ORIGINAL SOURCES: James J. Ayers, *Reminiscences of Early California*; General John Bidwell, *In California Before the Gold Rush; A Journey to California*; Edwin Bryant, *What I Saw in California*; Walter Colton, *Three Years in California*; Richard H. Dana, *Two Years Before the Mast*; William Heath Davis, *Seventy-Five Years in California*; T. J. Farnham, *Life, Adventures, and Travels*; John C. Fremont, *Memories of My Life; Fremont's Expeditions;* Jessie Benton Fremont, *Far West Sketches*; Abraham P. Nasatir, *French Activities in California*; Erwin G. Gudde, *Sutter's Own Story* (diary); Lansford W. Hastings, *The Emigrant's Guide to Oregon and California*; Overton Johnson and William H. Winter, *Route Across the Rocky Mountains*; Frank A. Leach, *Recollections of a Newspaper Man*; *The Larkin Papers* (Vols. I-IV); Duflot De Mofras, *Travels on the Pacific Coast* (2 vols.); Joseph W. Revere, *A Tour of Duty in California*; Alfred Robinson, *Life in California Before the Conquest;* Sir George Simpson, *Narrative of a Journey Round the World* (Vols. I-II); Charles Wilkes, *Narrative of the United States Exploring Expedition* (5 vols.).

THE GOLD RUSH: J. Goldsborough Bruff, *Gold Rush;* Franklin A. Buck, *A Yankee Trader in the Gold Rush*; John W. Caughey, *Gold Is the Cornerstone; Rushing for Gold* (editor); Alonzo Delano, *Across the Plains and Among the Diggings;* C.B. Glasscock, *A Golden Highway*; Archer B. Hulbert, *Forty-Niners*; Joseph H. Jackson, *Anybody's Gold; Bad Company*; T. F. Jones, *Leaves from an Argonaut's Notebook*; Frank Marryat, *Mountains and Molehills*; Robert O'Brien, *California Called Them*; Edwin L. Sabin, *Gold Seekers of '49*; D. A. Shaw, *El*

Acknowledgments and Bibliography 531

Dorado; Dame Shirley, *The Shirley Letters from the California Mines*; Bayard Taylor, *Eldorado*; Stewart E. White, *The Forty-Niners*.

SAN FRANCISCO: Anonymous, *San Francisco: Past and Present* (Vol. I); Herbert Asbury, *The Barbary Coast;* Gertrude Atherton, *My San Francisco*; Stanton A. Coblentz, *Villains and Vigilantes*; Charles C. Dobie, *San Francisco, A Pageant*; Zoeth S. Eldredge, *The Beginnings of San Francisco* (2 vols.); John S. Hittel, *A History of the City of San Francisco*; Pauline Jacobson, *City of the Golden 'Fifties*; Oscar Lewis and Carroll D. Hall, *Bonanza Inn*; Felix Riesenberg, Jr., *Golden Gate*; Frank Soule, *The Annals of San Francisco*; Franklin Walker, *San Francisco's Literary Frontier*; Evelyn Wells, *Champagne Days of San Francisco*; Mary F. Williams, *History of the San Francisco Committee of Vigilance of 1851*.

LOS ANGELES AND SOUTHERN CALIFORNIA: Sarah Bixby-Smith, *Adobe Days*; Robert G. Cleland, *The Cattle on a Thousand Hills*; Glenn S. Dumke, *The Boom of the Eighties in Southern California*; Morrow Mayo, *Los Angeles*; Remi A. Nadeau, *City Makers* (Los Angeles); Harris Newmark, *Sixty Years in Southern California*; William B. Rice, *The Los Angeles Star;* William A. Spaulding, *History of Los Angeles* (Vol. I); Theodore S. Van Dyke, *Millionaires of a Day*; Franklin Walker, *A Literary History of Southern California*; Charles D. Willard, *History of Los Angeles*.

THE EMIGRANT TRAINS: Julia C. Altrocchi, *The Old California Trail*; John Bidwell, *Echoes of the Past*; Irene D. Paden, *The Wake of the Prairie Schooner*; George R. Stewart, *The Opening of the California Trail* (The Stevens Party).

DONNER PARTY: Homer Croy, *Wheels West*; C. F. McGlaskan, *History of the Donner Party*; George R. Stewart, *Ordeal by Hunger*.

DEATH VALLEY PARTY: W. A. Chalfant, *Death Valley*; Margaret Long, *The Shadow of the Arrow*; William L. Manly, *Death Valley in '49*.

INDIANS: H. H. Bancroft, *The Native Races* (5 vols.); Edward W. Gifford and Gwendoline H. Block, *California Indian Nights Entertainments*; A. L. Kroeber, *Handbook of the Indians of California*.

PLACES: Julian Dana, *The Sacramento*; Hoover, Rensch and Rensch, *Historic Spots in California*; A. C. Jochmus, *The City of Monterey*; R. A. Thompson, *The Russian Settlement in California*; W. P.A. American Guide Series, *California*.

GENERAL RERERENCES: *Album of American History, Atlas of American History*, James Truslow Adams (editor); *Dictionary of American*

Biography; Dictionary of American History; Harper's Encyclopaedia of United States History; Narrative and Critical History of America.

THESES: *Dr. John Marsh*, by Emily J. Ulsh (M.A., U. of Cal.); *John A. Sutter*, by Clarence J. Du Four (Ph.D., U. of Cal.); *The North Bay Shore During the Spanish and Mexican Regime,* by Alice M. Cleaveland (M.A., U. of Cal.).

COLORADO

BIBLIOGRAPHY: Virginia Lee Wilcox, *Colorado* (a selected bibliography of its literature, 1858-1952).

HISTORY: Hubert H. Bancroft, *Nevada, Colorado and Wyoming*; O.L. Baskin (publishers), *History of Arkansas Valley, Colorado; History of Clear Creek and Boulder Valleys;* William Brandon, *The Men and the Mountain* (Fremont's Fourth Expedition); Arthur H. Carhart, *Colorado*; Bernard De Voto, *Across the Wide Missouri;* Percy Fritz, *Colorado, the Centennial State*; LeRoy R. Hafen, *Colorado and Its People* (4 vols.); *Colorado: The Story of a Western Commonwealth*; LeRoy R. and Ann W. Hafen, *Colorado*; Frank Hall, *History of the State of Colorado* (4 vols.); A.A. Hayes, *New Colorado and the Santa Fe Trail*; G.H. Heap, *Central Route to the Pacific*; Henderson, Renaud, etc., *Colorado*; David Lavender, *Bent's Fort*; *The Big Divide*; A.B. Legard, *Colorado*; Forbes Parkhill, *The Wildest of the West*; Richards & Co. (bookstore), *Summering in Colorado;* Melvin Schoberlin, *From Candles to Footlights* (the theatre); George F. Ruxton, *Life in the Far West;* Jerome C. Smiley and Frank C. Goudy, *Semi-Centennial History of Colorado* (2 vols.); Justin H. Smith, *The War with Mexico*; Ansel Watrous, *History of Larimer County, Colorado;* William C. Whitford, *Colorado Volunteers in the Civil War.*

BIOGRAPHY: *Memories of a Lifetime in the Pikes Peak Region* by Irving Howbert; *Midas of the Rockies* (Winfield Scott Stratton), by Frank Waters; *The Case of Alfred Packer* by Paul H. Gantt; H.A.W. Tabor *(Silver Dollar)*, by David Karsner; *Silver Queen* (Baby Doe Tabor), by Caroline Bancroft; *Some Pioneers of Colorado* by Luella Shaw; *Tales of the Colorado Pioneers* by Alice P. Hill; *Reminiscences of William Larimer.*

MINING: GOLD AND SILVER: Frank Fossett, *Colorado: Historical, Descriptive and Statistical Work on the Rocky Mountain Gold and Silver Mining Region; Colorado: Its Gold and Silver Mines, and Farm and Stock Ranges, and Health and Pleasure Resorts*; Don L. and Jean Harvey Griswold, *The Carbonate Camp Called Leadville*; LeRoy R. Hafen, *Colorado Gold Rush:* 1858-1859; Ovando J. Hollister, *Mines of Colorado*; John W. Horner, *Silver Town* (Georgetown); Marshall

Sprague, *Money Mountain* (Cripple Creek); Emma Langdon, *The Cripple Creek Strike*; Henry Villard, *The Past and Present of the Pike's Peak Gold Regions*; George F. Willison, *Here They Dug the Gold* (Pike's Peak gold rush); Muriel S. Wolle, *Stampede to Timberline*.

COLONIZATION: James F. Willard, *The Union Colony at Greeley, Colorado;* James F. Willard and Colin B. Goodykoontz, *Experiments in Colorado Colonization.*

DENVER: O.L. Baskin, *History of the City of Denver;* Jerome C. Smiley, *History of Denver*; J.E. Wharton, *History of the City of Denver.*

GUIDES: W.P.A. American Guide Series, *Colorado; Ghost Towns of Colorado.*

NEVADA

BIBLIOGRAPHY: Russell R. Elliott, *Bibliography of Nevada History.*

HISTORY: Sam P. Davis (editor), *History of Nevada* (2 vols.); Effie M. Mack, *Nevada*; James G. Scrugham (editor), *Nevada: A Narrative of the Conquest of a Frontier Land* (3 vols.); Thomas Wren (editor), *A History of the State of Nevada.*

THE COMSTOCK LODE: Lucius Beebe and Charles Clegg, *Legends of the Comstock Lode; Sutro Tunnel*, Congressional Report, 1872; Wells Drury, *An Editor on the Comstock Lode*; John D. Galloway, *Early Engineering Works Contributory to the Comstock*; C.B. Glasscock, *The Big Bonanza*; Eliot Lord, *Comstock Mining and Miners; The Drama of Virginia City*; George D. Lyman, *The Saga of the Comstock Lode*; Charles H. Shinn, *The Story of the Mine.*

BIOGRAPHY: *Eilley Orrum* by Swift Paine; *Ralston's Ring* by George D. Lyman; *Silver Kings* by Oscar Lewis; *Reminiscences of William M. Stewart; Adolph Sutro* by Eugenia K. Holmes.

GUIDE, PLACES, DESCRIPTIONS: Charles Kelly, *Salt Desert Trails*; Richard G. Lillard, *Desert Challenge*; Max Miller, *Reno*; Dale L. Morgan, *The Humboldt*; W.P.A. American Guide Series, *Nevada.*

GENERAL: Lucius Beebe, *Comstock Commotion*; Lucius Beebe and Charles Clegg, *Virginia and Truckee*; C.B. Glasscock, *Gold in Them Hills;* Katherine Hillyer and Katherine Best, *The Amazing Story of Piper's Opera House* (pamphlet); Maestretti, Hicks and Smith, *The Constitution of the State of Nevada;* Nevada Historical Society Papers, 1907-1924; Harolds Club, Reno (publisher), *Pioneer Nevada.*

UTAH

BIBLIOGRAPHY: L.H. Kirkpatrick, *Holdings of the University of Utah on Utah and the Church of Jesus Christ of Latter-Day Saints.*

ORIGINAL SOURCES: Joseph Smith, *The Book of Mormon*; Brigham Young, *Journal of Discourses* (19 vols.).

HISTORY: Hubert H. Bancroft, *History of Utah*; Juanita Brooks, *The Mountain Meadows Massacre*; John Evans, *The Story of Utah*; Frank A. Golder, *The March of the Mormon Battalion*; William Linn, *The Story of the Mormons*; Andrew L. Neff, *History of Utah*; B.H. Roberts, *A Comprehensive History of the Church of Jesus Christ of Latter-day Saints* (6 vols.); Orson F. Whitney, *History of Utah* (4 vols.).

GUIDES, PLACES AND DESCRIPTIONS: Richard F. Burton, *The City of the Saints*; H.L.A. Culmer, *Resources and Attractions of Utah*; Henry Inman and William F. Cody, *The Great Salt Lake Trail*; Dale L. Morgan, *The Great Salt Lake*; Jules Remy, *A Journey to Great Salt Lake City* (Vol. I); Phil Robinson, *Sinners and Saints*; Wallace Stegner, *Mormon Country*; Maurine Whipple, *This Is the Place: Utah*; W.P.A. American Guide Series, *Utah.*

POLYGAMY: Emily M. Austin, *Mormonism, or Life Among the Mormons*; Hartford Publishing Co., *The Mormon Wife*; Helen K. Whitney, *Why We Practice Plural Marriage*; Kimball Young, *Isn't One Wife Enough?*

BIOGRAPHY: *Sam Brannan and the California Mormons* by Paul Bailey; Parley P. Pratt (*The Archer of Paradise*), by Reva Stanley; Joseph Smith (*No Man Knows My History*), by Fawn M. Brodie; *Brigham Young* by M.R. Werner.

COLONIZING: Samuel Bowles, *Across the Continent*; Leland H. Creer, *The Founding of an Empire*; Milton R. Hunter, *Brigham Young the Colonizer.*

LIFE OF THE GENTILES: Robert J. Dwyer, *The Gentile Comes to Utah* (Ph.D. thesis); Leon L. Watters, *The Pioneer Jews of Utah.*

AUTOBIOGRAPHIES: R.N. Baskin, *Reminiscences of Early Utah*; William Clayton, *William Clayton's Journal*; Parley P. Pratt, *Autobiography of Parley Parker Pratt.*

GROUP LIFE: Ephraim Ericksen, *The Psychological and Ethical Aspects of Mormon Group Life*; Lowry Nelson, *The Mormon Village.*

ANTI-MORMON: J. H. Beadle, *Life in Utah*; Frank J. Cannon and Harvey J.

O'Higgins, *Under the Prophet in Utah*; Charles Kelly and Hoffman Birney, *Holy Murder*; Ann Eliza Young, *Wife No. 19*.

GENERAL: Charles Ellis, *Utah, 1847-1870*; John D. Fitzgerald, *Papa Married a Mormon*; Charles Kelly, *Salt Desert Trails*; George D. Pyper, *The Romance of an Old Playhouse; Reed Smoot Case* (4 vols.), U. S. Senate Proceedings.

MAGAZINES AND NEWSPAPERS: *The Latter Day Saints Millennial Star* (Vol. X); *Utah Historical Quarterly* (Vol. XIX); *The Utah University Quarterly*.

Some Source Notes on Quotations

BOOK ONE

Page

4 "commanded over by Colonel Vallejo," Zollinger, *Sutter*, 55-56.

5 "Well, my god," Ibid., 57.

5 "I noticed the hat must," Ibid.

7 "A large number of deer," Ibid., 66.

9 "I was insulted," Bancroft, *History of Cal.*, IV, 3.

9 "a Puritanic strength," McKittrick, *Vallejo*, 4.

10 "Kept guard over," Ibid., 20-21.

15 "Graham was the worst," Bancroft, IV, 7.

15 "noted for being a bummer," Ibid.

16 "about three o'clock," Ibid., 18.

BOOK TWO

26 "California is a country," Bancroft, IV, 212.

26 "We have also," Dakin, *Lives of William Hartnell*, 251.

28 "It is too late now," Zollinger, 101.

29 "The presidio of Monterey," De Mofras, *Travels*, 211-12.

Page

30 "The state of Society," Wilkes, *U.S. Exploring Exped.*, V, 198.

30 "compared the climate," Ibid., 154.

31 The country has," Ibid., 151-152.

31 "I was surprised," Ibid., 152.

31 "In his brilliant uniform," Zollinger, 112.

32 "The difficulty of coming," *St. Louis (Mo.) Daily Argus,* Oct. 31, 1840, 2.

33 "This is beyond all comparison," Ibid.

33 "a genius for invention," Hunt, *John Bidwell*, 22.

33 "Robidoux's description," Ibid., 35-36.

33 "purchase a suitable," Ibid., 36.

34 "Our committee fell to pieces," Ibid., 37.

35 "Compared to the trials," Ibid., 46.

35 "Started early," Ibid., 60.

35 "valleys between peaks," Ibid., 67.

36 "If I ever get back," Ibid., 66.

37 "they arrived here," Lyman, *John Marsh*, 249.

37 "The company has already," Hunt, 92.

Page

38   "I was marched," Bidwell, *Echoes of the Past*, 72, 73.

40   "Streams were out," Hunt, 96.

41   "As long as he had anything," Zollinger, 113.

41   "He was one of those," Ibid., 114.

46   "Carson and Truth," Nevins, *Fremont*, 101.

46   "There is no man," Ibid.

49   "The unsettled state," Bancroft, IV, 301.

50   "This change in the aspect," Ibid., 310.

50   "I may forfeit," Ibid., 306-7.

51   "Myself again having been honored," Hastings, *Emigrant's Guide*.

55   "scenery very wild," Fremont, *Memoirs*, 189-90.

56   "To explore unknown regions," Cleland, *This Reckless Breed*, 283.

57   "We continued down the valley," Fremont, 309.

58   "This mighty range," Ibid., 152.

58   "Rock upon rock," Ibid., 155.

58   "Far below us," Ibid., 333.

58   "There is the little mountain," Ibid.

65   "He was born," Stewart, *Opening of the Cal. Trail*, 40.

67   "The poor footsore oxen," Ibid., 67.

70   "a tilted cap," Dana, *Sutter*, 162.

71   "In case I should be killed," Zollinger, 143.

76   "It will no doubt," Larkin Papers, IV, 4.

76   "The route I wished," Fremont, 432.

76   "It had never before," Carson, *Own Story*.

Page

76   "Nearly upon the line," Fremont, 432-33.

77   "a sandy, barren plain," Nevins, 213.

78   "The Mexican troops," Larkin Papers, III, 266.

78   "The future destiny," Ibid., IV, 44-45.

79   "Why is an American," Ibid., 185.

80   "In the afternoon," Fremont, 459.

80   "moved up the mountain," Ibid.

80   "If we are attacked," Nevins, 228.

81   "a band of robbers," Ibid., 229.

82   "I held a confidential," Nevins, *Polk*, 22.

82-83   "In addition to your Consular," Larkin Papers, IV, 4-6.

83   "Has not enjoyed," Ibid., 302.

83   "I have seen his name," Zollinger, 193.

84   "Being absolved from any duty," Nevins, *Fremont*, 247.

84   "I saw the way," Fremont, 490.

86   "Almost the whole party," Bancroft, V, 111-12.

86   "Gentlemen, what is it," McKittrick, 261.

89   "I am also informed," Fremont, 519.

91   "Captain Fremont," Nevins, *Fremont*, 277.

92   "I have determined," Hittell, *Hist. of Cal.*, VII, 463.

95   "wearing a buckskin," Colton, *Three Years in Cal.*, 32.

95   "Our bay is full," Ibid., 85.

95   "The custom had been,"

Page

Ibid," Ibid., 41.
95-96 "as chaste," Ibid., 43.
96 "Law which fails," Ibid., 66.
96 "If there is," Ibid., 48.
102 "A more ragged," Nevins, *Fremont*, 300.
103 "I feel myself," Bancroft, V, 426.
106 "Put spurs to your mules," DeVoto, *Year of Decision*, 302.
106 "The Californians were," Ibid., 307.
106 "It is barely possible," Ibid., 180.
107 "There is a nigher route," Ibid.
109 "Two days and two nights," Stewart, *Ordeal by Hunger*, 42.
111 "The trap which closed," Ibid., 87.
112 "they stripped the flesh," Ibid., 133.
115 "in sight," ibid., 248.
116 "The Mormons believed," Neff, *Hist. of Utah*, 72.
117 "fixing a set," Werner, *Brigham Young*, 226.
117 "I saw them get religion," Ibid., 10-11.
118 "I am getting them away," Ibid., 206.
118 "The business of the Saints," Neff, 79.
118 "Without Brigham Young," Werner, v.
118 "I will recognize the site," Ibid., 230.
119 "had frosts, cold climate," Whitney, *Hist. of Utah*, VI, 319.
119 "imprudent to bring," Roberts, *Comprehensive Hist. of the Church*, III, 201.
120 "The brethren will play

Page

cards," Werner, 222-23.
121 "My impressions are," Ibid., 231.
121 "For three or four miles," Whitney, VI, 330.
122 "The Spirit of light," Roberts, III, 223.
122 "It is enough," Werner, 231.
122 "no man will be suffered," Ibid., 234.
123 "Thirty-five acres of land," Neff, 97.
126 "an old school gentleman," Zollinger, 218.
127 "It is hard to conceive," Ibid., 227.
129 "The river here flowed," Parsons, *Marshall*, 53-54.
129 "Having strolled," Ibid., 56-57.
130 "Boys, by God," Zollinger, 236.
130 "There! Didn't I tell you," Ibid., 234.

BOOK THREE

134 "I have made a discovery," Bancroft, VI, 43.
134 "We have found gold," Zollinger, 243.
136 "The instrument of discovery," Caughey, *Gold Is the Cornerstone*, 16.
136 "Gold!" Bancroft, VI, 56.
137 "A general of the United States Army," Colton, 248.
137 "A frenzy seized my soul," Caughey, 22-23.
137 "everyone has gold... fever," Underhill, *From Cowhides to Golden Fleece*, 168.
137 "My sons," Bancroft, VI, 65.
140 "The miners needed," Shinn,

Page

Mining Camps, 112.

140 "no man shall grumble," Ibid., 107.

141 "Cursing the country," Bancroft, VI, 96.

142 "Confer on them," Ibid., V, 611.

142 "People are running," Ibid., VI, 114-15.

142-43 "The accounts of the abundance," Caughey, 42.

144 "Well authenticated accounts," Soule, *Annals of San Fran.*, 210.

144 "We pay at the rate," Colton, 279.

145 "We cannot imagine," Underhill, 168.

146 "Indians, Negroes, Kanakas," Zollinger, 263-64.

149 "a beautiful green," Pratt, *Autobiography*, 404.

150 "If we were to go," Neff, 132.

154 "The winds were caught," Brandon, *Men and the Mountain*, 157.

155 "By now they were skeletal," Ibid., 210.

156 "We passed and repassed," Ibid., 238-39.

156-57 "I can go no further," Ibid., 242.

159 "Just arrived," Caughey, 91.

159-60 "a valley rich," Ibid., 115.

160 "Scribbling asses," Ibid., 116.

160 "The Humboldt," Hulbert, *Forty-Niners*, 214.

161 "editors, ministers," Caughey, 45.

161 "mine for beans," Ibid., 174.

162 "Have two shirts," Ibid., 183.

163 "This street is impassable," Asbury, *Barbary Coast*, 13.

164 "a marching laboratory," Caughey, 107.

Page

164 "a grim old fellow," Bancroft, VI, 275.

166 "Territorial Government," Bancroft, *Hist. of Utah*, 444.

169 "Gentlemen, this is the happiest," Ellison, *Self-Governing Dominion*, 44.

171 "If you all wish to go," Manly, *Death Valley in '49*, 107.

172 "The region of mirage," Bancroft, *Hist. of Cal.*, VI, 152.

172 "I was left," Long, *Shadow of the Arrow*, 198.

173 "Don't you think," Ibid., 199.

173 "I have never kept the company," Ibid., 199-200.

173 "She was the one," Manly, 464.

173 "Twenty miles across naked dunes," Long, 200.

174 "Give up?" Ibid., 228.

174 "Water!" Ibid., 204.

174 "I have a presentiment," Ibid., 205.

175 "If those boys," Manly, 205.

176 "The boys have come!" Chalfant, *Death Valley*, 33.

177 "When one of these great," Soule, 616.

177 "I grew up," Lewis, *Big Four*, 55.

177 "I built the Central Pacific!" Ibid., 49.

178 "One man works hard," Ibid., 53.

178 "This figure," Asbury, 33-34.

180 "There is no water," Lyman, *Saga of the Comstock Lode*, 10.

182 "The true use of gold," Werner, 256.

183 "Mounting his box," Bancroft, *Hist. of Cal.*, VI, 348.

Page

183 "a settlement in the vicinity," Neff, 219.

183-84 "The Williams Ranch," Ibid., 218-19.

184 "I was sick," Ibid., 220.

187 "A group of responsbile," Williams, *Hist. of San Fran. Com. of Vig. of 1851*, 204.

187 "Gentlemen, as I understand it," Coblentz, *Villains and Vigilantes*, 70.

187-88 "The backwash of the gold rush," Mayo, *Los Angeles*, 35.

188 "Their condition lasted," Willard, *Hist. of Los Angeles*, 283.

190 "I know Zachary Taylor," Werner, 379.

190 "vain and ambitious," Bancroft, *Hist. of Utah*, 456.

190 "If I had but crooked," Werner, 379.

190 "Had been compelled," Bancroft, *Hist. of Utah*, 460.

191 "Not only for time," Neff, 559.

191 "Multiplication of the species," Ibid.

192 "I think there is only," Ibid.

192 "There is not a single," Ibid.

192 "If you tell them," Werner, 299.

192 "I would rather," Ibid., 301.

193 "The cat is out," Ibid., 296.

193 "The cat has many," Ibid.

193 "For a man of God," Linn, *Story of the Mormons*, 587.

193 "Church doctrine," *Utah*, W.P.A. Amer. Guide Series, 65-66.

194 "Imagine a company," Shirley, *Shirley Letters*, 102-3.

194 "... if a person works," Ibid., 36.

195 "sleek and fat," Ibid., 143.

195 "In the space," Ibid., 161.

196 "The famous bandit," Jackson, *Bad Company*, 11.

199 "forward packages," Hungerford, *Wells Fargo*, 7.

201 "I don't know who," Lyman, *John Marsh*, 286.

201 "He is the very man," Ibid.

203 "all the heads and remains," Cleland, *Pathfinders*, 78.

205 "Honest, brave," Scherer, *Lion of the Vigilantes*, 142.

206 "Let the law," Ibid., 159.

206 "The members of the Vigilance Committee," Ibid., 164.

209 "long frock coats," Coblentz, 235.

209 "Who made the laws," Scherer, 192.

210 "I never saw such things," Mack, *Hist. of Nevada*, 150.

211 "Citizens of Carson Valley," Morgan, *Humboldt*, 203.

212 "On the result," Lyman, *Saga*, 17.

213 "I have my doubts," Morgan, 204.

213 "The Mormon girls," Ibid., 203.

214 "found a perfect monster," Lyman, *Saga*, 17.

216 "You have struck it," Ibid., 34.

217 "I am and will be governor," Bancroft, *Hist. of Utah*, 481.

218 "mild-mannered," Neff, 181.

218 "The Mormons look up," Ibid., 448.

219 "gambler and bully," Bancroft, *Hist. of Utah*, 490.

219 "civil laws of the territory,"

Page

Neff, 442.

219 "My power will not be," Werner, 397.

219 "The Mormons believing," Neff, 455.

221 "There are sins," Werner, 402.

221 "Send twenty-five hundred troops," Ibid., 387.

221 "The United States," Brooks, *Mountain Meadows Massacre*, 27.

223 "Halt!" Ibid., 52.

223 "Leaped from the brush," Ibid., 53.

224 "There is no excuse," Neff, 429-30.

229 "Two forlorn groups," Smiley, *Hist. of Denver*.

229 "sandy-haired . . . cracker," Lavender, *Big Divide*, 63.

230 "Built a big fire," Willison, *Here They Dug the Gold*, 50.

231 "Gold Hunters," Fossett, *Colorado*, 125.

BOOK FOUR

235 "Gold in Kansas," Hafen, *Hist. of Colo.*, I, 147.

235 "The two little words," Ibid., 170.

236 "light hearts," Ibid., 172.

237 "Men from all parts," Ibid., 152.

237 "We never hanged," Smiley, 349.

238 "refused to have," Hafen, II, 557-64.

238 "his pockets," *Colorado*, W.P.A. Amer. Guide Series, 39-40.

238 "We've got a school!" Ibid., 40.

239 "Stake me off," Hill, *Tales of the Colo. Pioneers*, 103.

239 "Ho, everyone," Ibid., 65.

Page

239 "the Astor House," Willison, 81.

240 "Wanted: a girl," Hill, 92-94.

240 "Know all men," Ibid., 62.

240 "Gone to burry," Hafen, I, 272.

240 "Barber-ous," Ibid.

241 "Died," Schoberlin, *From Candles to Footlights*, 13.

241 "painted women," Ibid., 20.

242 "No one indulging," Willison, 23.

243 "Here lies the body," Bancroft, *Nev., Colo. and Wyo.*, 374.

243 "You always have," Lewis, 32.

244 "Be home tonight," Ibid., 5.

244 "He had always," *Cal. Hist. Soc. Quart.*, Sept. 1925, 211n.

245 "Here comes Crazy Judah!" Ibid., 227n.

245 "No day passed," Lewis, 17.

246 "passed from hand," *Cal. Hist. Soc. Quart.*, 242-43.

246 "Anna, remember," Ibid., 244n.

247 "If you want to see," Lewis, 27.

248 "We have drawn," Ibid., 35.

250 "I say that a dissolution," Kennedy, *Contest for Cal.*, 64.

250 "Broderick's professed," Ibid., 50.

251 "He was put forward," Lynch, *Life of David C. Broderick*, 208-9

251 "So light and delicate," Ibid., 218.

251 "Gentlemen," Ibid., 227.

251 "They have killed me," Kennedy, 56.

251 "California had always," Ibid., 69.

252 "If this Union is," Ibid., 72.

252 "Far to the east," Hittell, IV,

Page

V, 40.

325 "at least one hundred," Ibid., 44.

325 "All who are," Ibid., 47.

325 "for the able manner," Ibid., 48.

325 "The first armed resistance," Ibid.

326 "An officer dangerous," Ibid., 50-51.

326 "The contents of the Book," Ibid., 260.

326 "We inquired whether," Ibid., 265-66.

327 "Several firms," Neff, 782.

327-28 "Give us a little," Werner, 314.

328 "I am opposed," Ibid., 319.

328 "I consider them uncomely," Ibid., 318-19.

328 "Central figures," Morgan, *Great Salt Lake*, 287-88.

329 "cease to give," Roberts, V, 211.

330 "Experienced soldiers," Ibid., 189.

330 "Armies have not been found," Ibid., 200.

331 "Gentlemen: As you are," Neff, 816-17.

331 "We will not obligate," Ibid., 819.

331-32 "To be adverse," Roberts, V, 213.

332 "who shall be of good," Neff, 826.

332 "The inhabitants of Utah," Roberts, V, 220.

334 "an inoffensive," Smiley, 371.

335 "Tell the governor," Hafen, I, 310.

336 "Dead cattle," Ibid., 311.

336 "A few months," Ibid., 168.

338 "What have you got," Karsner, *Silver Dollar*, 46.

338 "You've got gold," Ibid., 61.

Page

339 "After she gave," Hafen, II, 565.

340 "Oh, Horace," Karsner, 34.

340 "hold down the flaps," Ibid., 457.

341 "conversation was built," Lavender, 71.

342 "Balm of a Thousand," Hafen, I, 243.

342 "Ugly buildings," Ibid., II, 392.

342 "Our turnips," Ibid., I, 291.

343 "Through the new methods," Willison, 67.

345 "We believe," Hafen, II, 253.

345 "It was almost," Ibid., 180.

346 "Pay or Perish," Ibid., 183.

348 "I used to go up," Bancroft, *Hist. of Cal.*, VII, 568.

348-49 "There were no troubles," Hittel, 484.

349 "Give me the," Lewis, *Big Four*, 90.

349 "Every mile built," Ibid.

351 "last blasts rather," Ibid., 92.

BOOK FIVE

356 "It will be the means," Lewis, *Big Four*, 321-22.

357 "The uncertainty," Ibid., 104-5.

357 "Eighty per cent," Daggett, *Chapters on the Hist. of the S.P.*, 105

357-58 "a hard and cheery," Lewis, *Big Four*, 211.

358 "I'll never be remembered," Ibid., 213.

358 "damned old fool," Ibid., 252.

361 "He came there in a buggy," Ibid., 316.

364 "It is not possible," Ibid.

364 "The Sacramento *Union*," Ibid.

Page

364   "This Congress is the worst," Ibid., 317.
367   "a pygmy," Lyman, *Ralston's Ring*, 154.
367   "His first pick," Ibid., 155.
367   "But for her," Holmes, *Adolph Sutro*, 22.
367   "That famous tunnel," Lyman, *Ralston's Ring*, 156.
368   "Sir, the Bank," Ibid., 169.
368   "I propose to speak," Ibid., 169-70.
370   "Sutro demonstrated," Ibid., 188.
372   "jovial, ruddy-cheeked," Ibid., 172.
372   "the porphyry," Ibid., 174.
376   "The entire thirteen," Shinn, *Story of the Mine*, 179.
377   "Why don't you go," Lewis, *Silver Kings*, 135.
377   "Go in and climb," Ibid., 139.
378   "But to guard," Ibid., 143.
379   "You are probably aware," Lyman, *Ralston's Ring*, 213.
380   "In this act," *Enterprise*, May 10, 1872.
380   "that hole in the ground," Dana, *Man who Built San Fran.*, 201.
381   "Bring your books," Lyman, *Ralston's Ring*, 162.
382   "Leave them," Ibid., 204.
383   "Visitors," Lewis, *Bonanza Inn*, 5-6.
384   "water closets," Ibid., 26.
384   "If you are," Ibid., 28.
392   "This is as close," Lewis, *Silver Kings*, 23.
392   "Maybe I was," Ibid., 22.
392   "Visitors of note," Ibid., 22.
393   "shacks built," Ibid., 25.
393   "I was one of," Lillard, 217-18.
393   "California in '49," Ibid., 224.

Page

395   "Should your men," Lyman, *Ralston's Ring*, 265.
396   "Literally thousands," Glasscock, 293.
396-97   "In Pauper Alley," Shinn, *Story of the Mine*, 153.
398   "The Southern Pacific," Lillard, 29.
398   "Nevada was retarded," Ibid., 26.
398   "Their object seems," Ibid., 28.
399   "From 1870 on," Ibid., 29.
400   "The Gentile does not," Robinson, *Sinners and Saints*, 130-31.
400   "If you should have," Roberts, V, 495-96.
401   "Brigham Young," Ibid.
401   "The right of husbands," Whitney, II, 395-420.
402   "Let them grant," Ibid., 397-400.
402   "If a man have," Ibid., 440-86.
402   "If he take him another," Ibid.
402   "Only force can settle," Ibid.
402   "a great Mormon-hater," Ibid., 320-26.
403   "drunkards and gamblers," Ibid.
403   "man of iron," Ibid., 488-90.
403   "Never after me," Ibid.
403   "The Missionary Trio," Ibid., 545-46.
403   "professed pious," Ibid.
403   "Judge McKean," Ibid., 553.
404   "wanted to test," Ibid., 532-33.
404   "rebellion," Ibid.
405   "the boys in blue," Ibid., 507-12.
405   "Get your guns," Ibid.
405   "Do you belong," Ibid., 585-88.
406   "Do you believe," Roberts, V, 382-86.

Page

487 "Poor old man," Ibid., 107.
488 "We've got to move," Ibid., 194.
488 "Every worker," Ibid., 138.
488 "Upon receipt," Ibid.
490 "Colorado is a happy," Ibid., 292.
494 "Can you lend me," Karsner, 272-73.
495 "Whatever happens," Ibid., 283.
497 "Yea, let us," Dwyer, 115-17.
497 "rushed," Roberts, V, 541-44.
497 "It is a principle," Ibid., 546.
498 "How are we to," Ibid., 550-55.
499 "The tree," Ibid., 616.
499 "Mormonism," Ibid., VI, 21-23.
500 "Let us treat," Whitney, IV, 274.
500 "when a man," Roberts, VI, 114.
501 "The victims," Ibid., 115.
502 "Moses fled," Ibid., 125.
503 "lost his balance," Ibid., 128-29.
503 "it was a time," Ibid., 159.
504 "the county," Young, 400.
504 "individuals," Ibid., 387.
505 "I never had," Ibid, 380.
505 "When my children," Ibid., 390.
505 "We moved," Ibid., 402.

Page

505 "The officers," Ibid.
505 "What I shall," Ibid., 383.
506 "No, sir," Ibid., 406.
506 "I visited my home," Ibid., 383.
508 "The trials," Ibid., 380.
510 "Inasmuch," Roberts, VI, 215-23.
510 "We have waited," Ibid.
511 "The Church authorities," Ibid., 302-3.
511 "On an equal," Ibid., VI, 337.
513 "That evening he called," Lewis, *Bonanza Inn*, 123.
513 "I told him," Ibid., 124.
514 "In the City," Ibid., 125.
514 "That afternoon," Ibid., 136.
514 "He said," Ibid., 140.
515 "She is possessed," Ibid., 122.
516 "I have reached," Ibid., 175-76.
517 "You have been paid," Ibid., 189-90.
517 "Don't touch," Ibid., 190.
518 "Stop that!" Ibid., 194.
523 "A man may seat," Caughey, *Bancroft*, 97.
523 "I would strike," Bancroft, *Literary Industries*, 228-29.
524 "What was this task?" Ibid., 2.
525 "That upon the principle," Caughey, *Bancroft*, 342-43.

Index